A CIRCLE OF QUIET

Also by Madeleine L'Engle

The Summer of the Great-grandmother
The Irrational Season
Ladder of Angels
The Sphinx at Dawn

The Crosswicks Journal
BOOK 1

A Circle of Quiet

Madeleine L'Engle

HarperSanFrancisco

A Division of HarperCollins*Publishers*

Hardcover edition published in 1972 by Farrar, Straus & Giroux.
Reprinted by arrangement with Farrar, Straus & Giroux.

A CIRCLE OF QUIET. Copyright © 1972 by Madeleine L'Engle Franklin.
All rights reserved. Printed in the United States of America. No part of
this book may be used or reproduced in any manner whatsoever without written permission except in the case of brief quotations embodied
in critical articles and reviews. For information address HarperCollins
Publishers, 10 East 53rd Street, New York, NY 10022.

LC 79-65524
ISBN 0-06-254503-5

   92   93   94   95   CWI   20   19   18   17   16

This book is for Charlotte Rebecca Jones

ONE

We are four generations under one roof this summer, from infant Charlotte to almost-ninety Great-grandmother. This is a situation which is getting rarer and rarer in this day and age when families are divided by large distances and small dwellings. Josephine and Alan and the babies come from England; Great-grandmother from the Deep South; Hugh and I and our younger children from New York; and our assorted "adopted" children from as far afield as Mexico and as close as across the road; all to be together in Crosswicks, our big, old-fashioned New England farmhouse. It's an ancient house by American standards—well over two hundred years old. It still seems old to me, although Josephine and Alan, in Lincoln, live close by the oldest inhabited house in Europe, built in the eleven-hundreds.

When our children were little and we lived in Crosswicks year round, they liked to count things. They started to count the books, but stopped after they got to three thousand. They also counted beds, and figured that as long as all the double beds held two people, we could sleep twenty-one; that, of course, included the attic. We are using the attic this summer, though we haven't yet slept twenty-one. A lot of the time it is twelve, and even more to feed. Cooking is the only part of housekeeping I manage with any grace; it's something like writing a book: you look in the refrigerator and see what's there, choose all the ingredients you need, and a few your husband

3

thinks you don't need, and put them all together to concoct a dish. Vacuum cleaners are simply something more for me to trip over; and a kitchen floor, no matter how grubby, looks better before I wax it. The sight of a meal's worth of dirty dishes, pots, and pans makes me want to run in the other direction. Every so often I need out; something will throw me into total disproportion, and I have to get away from everybody—away from all these people I love most in the world—in order to regain a sense of proportion.

I like hanging sheets on lines strung under the apple trees—the birds like it, too. I enjoy going out to the incinerator after dark and watching the flames; my bad feelings burn away with the trash. But the house is still visible, and I can hear the sounds from within; often I need to get away completely, if only for a few minutes. My special place is a small brook in a green glade, a circle of quiet from which there is no visible sign of human beings. There's a natural stone bridge over the brook, and I sit there, dangling my legs and looking through the foliage at the sky reflected in the water, and things slowly come back into perspective. If the insects are biting me—and they usually are; no place is quite perfect—I use the pliable branch of a shadblow tree as a fan. The brook wanders through a tunnel of foliage, and the birds sing more sweetly there than anywhere else; or perhaps it is just that when I am at the brook I have time to be aware of them, and I move slowly into a kind of peace that is marvelous, "annihilating all that's made to a green thought in a green shade." If I sit for a while, then my impatience, crossness, frustration, are indeed annihilated, and my sense of humor returns.

It's a ten-minute walk to the brook. I cross the lawn and go through the willow tree which splashes its fountain of green down onto the grass so that it's almost impossible to mow

4

around it. If it's raining and I really need the brook badly, I go in my grandfather's old leather hunting coat and a strange yellow knitted hat from Ireland (one of my children, seeing me set off, asked, "Who do you think you are, Mother? Mrs Whatsit?"); it's amazing what passing the half-century mark does to free one to be eccentric. When my hair gets wet I look like a drowned ostrich, and I much prefer resembling an amiable, myopic giraffe as I wade through the wet clover of the large pasture. It's already been hayed twice this summer: does the neighboring farmer, who uses our pastures in addition to his own, hay clover? I was born in the middle of the asphalt island of Manhattan, and even nearly a decade of living in Crosswicks all year round has not made me conversant with bucolic terms. When Hugh and I bought the house the spring after we were married (we walked into a run-down place that hadn't been loved for years, and it opened its arms to us) and I saw cows in the pasture, they didn't look like cows to me. My idea of cows was from illustrations in children's books.

After the pasture is traversed, I walk through a smaller pasture which has been let go to seed because of all the rocks, and is now filled with thistles. Then there is a stone wall to be climbed; the only poison ivy around here grows on and by the stones of this wall, and I'm trying to kill it by smothering it with wet Sunday *Times*es; my children have made me very aware of the danger of using chemical sprays. Perhaps I've discovered a new use for *The New York Times*? (We also use it for the cats.) I think the poison ivy is less flourishing than it was; at any rate *The New York Times* is not going to unbalance the ecology. I love the *ology* words; *ology*: the word about. *Eco*, man's dwelling place. The word about where man lives.

Once I'm over the stone wall, the terrain changes. I step into a large field full of rocks left from glacial deposits; there are many ancient apple trees which, this summer, are laden with fruit. From the stone wall to the brook takes two balls of twine. Unreliable eyes make my vision variable, and there are days when my string path is extremely helpful, although, as my husband remarks, "All anybody who wants to find your secret hideout needs to do is climb the stone wall and follow the string."

That's all right. All secret places need to be shared occasionally. So the string guides me across a high ridge where there are large outcroppings of glacial stone, including our special star-watching rock. Then the path becomes full of tussocks and hummocks; my legs are etched by the thorns of blackberry brambles and wild roses. Earlier this summer the laurel burst from snow into fire, and a few weeks later we found a field of sweet wild strawberries. And then there are blueberry bushes, not very many, but a few, taller than I am and, to me, infinitely beautiful.

The burning bush: somehow I visualize it as much like one of these blueberry bushes. The bush burned, was alive with flame and was not consumed. Why? Isn't it because, as a bush, it was perfect? It was exactly as a bush is meant to be. A bush certainly doesn't have the opportunity for prideful and selfish choices, for self-destruction, that we human beings do. It *is*. It is a pure example of ontology. Ecology—ontology—the words fascinate me. Ontology is one of my son-in-law's favorite words, and I'm apt to get drunk on words, to go on jags; ontology is my jag for this summer, and I'm grateful to Alan for it—as for so much else. Ontology: the word about the essence of things; the word about being.

I go to the brook because I get out of being, out of the essential. So I'm not like the bush, then. I put all my prickliness, selfishness, in-turnedness, onto my *is*ness; we all tend to, and when we burn, this part of us is consumed. When I go past the tallest blueberry bush, where my twine is tied to one of the branches, I think that the part of us that has to be burned away is something like the deadwood on the bush; it has to go, to be burned in the terrible fire of reality, until there is nothing left but our ontological selves; what we are meant to be.

I go to the brook and my tensions and frustrations are lost as I spend a happy hour sitting right in the water and trying to clear it of the clogging debris left by a fallen tree.

. . 2 . .

Still damp, with fingernails broken and dirty, and a few extra scratches on my legs, I return to the house and go up to my Private Workroom. When Hugh and I bought Crosswicks, this room, which is over the garage, was used for chickens. The garage is even older than the house, having originally been the first trading post on the old Indian Trail. It was turned into a garage about ten years before we came. There were still strips of wallpaper downstairs with the car and upstairs with the chicken coops. When we moved in, the chickens were gone but the floor was covered with hay and chicken droppings—marvelous for Hugh's garden, and we shoveled this organic fertilizer out the window.

It was almost fifteen years before we were able to turn it into my study, and it was supposed to be Absolutely Private. Nobody was allowed up without special invitation. The children called it the Ivory Tower, and it is still called the Tower, though it is neither ivory nor private nor, in fact, tower.

This summer Alan has taken it over for his doctoral thesis. I am privileged to have him read me the first draft, and to offer occasional suggestions as to syntax and construction. I tell him about the blueberry bush and my thoughts about the burning bush, and he turns to his thesis where he reads me a quotation from Sartre about the *isness* of an oak tree; but Sartre felt depressed and threatened by this; the idea that the oak tree simply *is* seemed to diminish him. I suppose the perfect *isness* of anything would be frightening without the hope of God. An oak tree is, and it doesn't matter to it—at least Sartre thinks it doesn't; it is not a thinking oak. Man is; it matters to him; this is terrifying unless it matters to God, too, because this is the only possible reason we can matter to ourselves: not because we are sufficient unto ourselves—I am not: my husband, my family, my friends give me my meaning and, in a sense, my being, so that I know that I, like the burning bush, or the oak tree, am ontological: essential: real.

. . 3 . .

For the last two weeks of July this summer I abandoned the family, the kitchen stove, the brook, and flew out to Ohio State University to be Writer in Residence for a special program of Reading Fellows. It was a completely different world from the community of Crosswicks, and yet it too was community, and there were many aspects of each which overlapped and intertwined.

I learned, a good many years ago, that it is impossible for me to have a seminar in writing practices without coming to care deeply about my students. I may, and do, remain objective about their writing, but I am committed to them as persons. And I learn from them probably more than they learn from me. During those two tight-packed weeks at O.S.U. I lived, worked, ate with about twenty-five young men and women from all over the United States, who had already had teaching experience and who had been together for a full year of intensive reading and study. I was with them for their final two weeks. The first night, Dr. Charlotte Huck and Dr. Martha King took me out to dinner. They had never had a Writer in Residence before. I had never been a Writer in Residence before. We sat in an elegant roof-top restaurant which looked out over all of Columbus, and I, hoping to be able to relax and enjoy my dinner, asked, "Just exactly what do you want me to do, these two weeks?"

Martha took a calm sip of her Old-fashioned. "I was hoping it would emerge."

It did. I had brought a lot of notes, and the morning session was a general lecture and discussion, while the afternoon session was a sort of crash course in writing practices, with specific daily writing assignments. I had expected, during the question periods after both morning and afternoon sessions, that I would get questions about writing, and teaching children something about the arts; mostly I got questions about the nature of the universe. Perhaps the questions weren't as direct as those I get from high-school or grade-school students, because these men and women were experienced and sophisticated; but their queries were aimed in the same direction.

In the beginning we were all a little tentative with each other, as though we were going into a cold lake, and testing the water first. I knew that these students, most with master's degrees, and many on their way to Ph.D.'s—or, as Alan rather casually says, Phids—knew far more about theories of education than I do, and yet I had been asked to talk to them about creativity, and teaching creativity to children. The first morning I decided that we'd never get anywhere if I worried about getting my feet wet.

They were a varied group, as varied as our Crosswicks community. Their age ranged from early twenties to late forties. They were black, white, yellow; there were Roman Catholic nuns, a lay preacher from the Christian Church, Southern Baptists, agnostics, atheists. Therefore, there was a certain difference in our vocabulary; I wanted to be very careful that when we used a word everybody would understand it in the same way, and this meant that we did a lot of stopping to define. Often I would use a word which I hoped did not already have a preconditioned meaning for them. Ontology, for instance. It was a legitimate excuse to use my word-for-the-summer, and it's a word that has a lot to do with creativity and teaching.

It was the first time that I'd been forced to think consciously about creativity in connection with little children, rather than the older ones for whom I often write. I was trying to think out loud about the concentration essential for all artists, and in the very little child I found the perfect example. The concentration of a small child at play is analogous to the concentration of the artist of any discipline. In real play, which is real concentration, the child is not only outside time, he is outside *himself*. He has thrown himself completely into whatever it is that he is doing. A child playing a game, building a sand castle, painting a picture, is completely *in* what he is doing. His *self*-consciousness is gone; his consciousness is wholly focused outside himself.

I had just witnessed this in Crosswicks, observing an eighteen-month-old lying on her stomach on the grass watching a colony of ants, watching with total, spontaneous concentration. And I had played ring-around-a-rosy with her; we skipped around in a circle, grandparents, parents, assorted teenagers, wholly outside ourselves, holding hands, falling in abandon onto the lawn, joining in the child's shrieks of delighted laughter.

And with her we were outside self and outside time.

When we are *self*-conscious, we cannot be wholly aware; we must throw ourselves out first. This throwing ourselves away is the act of creativity. So, when we wholly concentrate, like a child in play, or an artist at work, then we share in the act of creating. We not only escape time, we also escape our self-conscious selves.

The Greeks had a word for ultimate self-consciousness which I find illuminating: *hubris*: pride: pride in the sense of putting oneself in the center of the universe. The strange and terrible thing is that this kind of total self-consciousness invariably ends in self-annihilation. The great tragedians have always understood this, from Sophocles to Shakespeare. We witness it in history in such people as Tiberius, Eva Perón, Hitler.

I was timid about putting forth most of these thoughts, but this kind of timidity is itself a form of pride. The moment that humility becomes self-conscious, it becomes hubris. One cannot be humble and aware of oneself at the same time. Therefore, the act of creating—painting a picture, singing a song, writing a story—is a humble act? This was a new thought to me. Humility is throwing oneself away in complete concentration on something or someone else.

I remember learning to skip rope. It's not too difficult when you hold the rope yourself. But then there's learning to jump into a rope swung by two other children, learning to jump in without breaking the rhythm and tripping over the rope. It can't be done unless you have that special kind of creative courage which is unself-conscious: the moment you wonder whether or not you can do it, you can't.

So, talking to that diverse group of students in July, I jumped in, as I had finally learned to jump into the rhythm of the curving rope.

Creativity is an act of discovering. The very small child, the baby, is still unself-conscious enough to take joy in discovering himself: he discovers his fingers; he gives them his complete, unself-conscious concentration. Self-conscious adults have done great damage by their misunderstanding—for instance, their attitude towards the child discovering his genitals. Unless the child has been taught corruption incredibly early, this is an unself-conscious discovery of himself, a humble joy of discovery, bearing no resemblance whatsoever to self-conscious auto-eroticism. We, as adults, often fall into perversity in other areas of discovery: i.e., some modern (and not so modern) art in all forms, where the artist is concentrating more on himself than on his painting or music or story. I would venture a guess that an artist concentrating wholly unself-consciously, wholly thrown into his work, is incapable of producing pornography. All perversion is self-gratification. In true love, the lover's pleasure comes in giving himself wholly to the loved one. When we try to give ourselves to ourselves, that is not only perversion, it is ultimately suicide.

A writer may be self-conscious about his work before and after but not during the writing. If I am self-conscious during the actual writing of a scene, then it ends up in the round file. All those rejected chapters, those reams of paper: am I helping to unbalance the ecology?

The kind of unself-consciousness I'm thinking about becomes clearer to me when I turn to a different discipline: for instance, that of playing a Bach fugue at the piano, precisely because I will never be a good enough pianist to play a Bach fugue as it should be played. But when I am actually sitting at the piano, all there is for me is the music. I am wholly in it, unless I fumble so badly that I perforce become self-conscious. Mostly, no matter how inadequate my playing, the music is all that matters: I am outside time, outside self, in play, in joy. When we can play with the unself-conscious concentration of a child, this is: art: prayer: love.

When I talk to any kind of a group, it works only if I throw myself wholly outside of myself and into the job. I may—and do—go through pride, anxiety, inadequacy beforehand, and perhaps after, but not during. The work itself knocks me out of the way. When, as sometimes happens, I am given an overdose of praise, my conscious mind is at first startled, jolted, and then it simply swats the words away, like a fly, a biting fly: it knows such words are dangerous.

And yet—I remember these honey-sweet words, and this remembering itself is vain. Ah, surely it is vain to think about words of praise. It is permissible for us to be pleased that a job has been well done, but we can't take any personal credit for it. We can only be grateful that the work itself knocks self-consciousness out of the way, for it is only thus that the work can be done.

. . 4 . .

The first thing I tried to do was to learn their names. To be known by name is terribly important, though I tend, as usual, to carry my feeling for the name to disproportionate lengths. There is nothing more frightening, for instance, than being a patient in a hospital where you are a number and a case first, and a person second, if at all.

And then there's Emily Brontë . . .

One day, a summer ago, I paid our grocery bill for the month. Our new checkbook was with my husband in the city, but I had a rather elderly checkbook which did not have the mandatory

13

cybernetic salad in the bottom left-hand corner. However, I had the money in the bank, and I had my right and proper signature on the check. I was brought up to believe that, if I need to, I can use a piece of birch bark, write in the name of the bank, the person to whom the money is to go, the sum, the signature, and this constitutes a valid check.

But my check bounced. When it was explained to me that this was because it was missing some magnetic gibberish, I was furious. I was furious at the dinner table, furious so loudly that my husband was forced to bang on the table and shout at me to shut up.

I shut up. But I didn't forget it. Everything I feel about names, about ontology, really, had been violated. Then, at Christmastime, a friend bought something for me, and I reached for a check to repay him the ten dollars and fifty cents. Because I have both French Huguenot and Scots blood I am stubborn and frugal: I saw no reason why my old checks weren't still valid, and I wasn't about to waste them.

My friend said, "Oh, come off it, Madeleine, you know that check won't go through."

His job is to handle vast sums of money daily; he knows what he's talking about. I asked, "Do you really and truly mean that my signature, my *name*, means nothing, absolutely nothing at all?"

"That's what I mean."

It was a wet and windy day. I looked at the rain slashing against the windows, pulled out a check with cybernetic salad in the bottom left-hand corner, said, "All right, then, I feel like Emily Brontë today," and signed it *Emily Brontë*.

My friend was not amused. "Madeleine, what are you doing?"

"You just told me that my name means nothing, absolutely nothing at all. Okay, so I feel like Emily Brontë and I don't see why I shouldn't sign it Emily Brontë. Take it—just for fun—and let's see what happens."

"I know perfectly well what's going to happen. I won't get my money."

But after lunch he came in, looking rather sheepish. He had his ten dollars and fifty cents, and no questions asked at the bank about the signature. "But it won't go through with your monthly statement. It'll bounce."

"All right. If it bounces I'll write you another check."

It did not bounce. I now have cancelled checks signed Emily Brontë, Jane Austen, and Elizabeth Barrett Browning.

In the battle between Madeleine and the machine, at this point the machine is winning.

. . 5 . .

A signature; a name; the very being of the person you talk to, the child you teach, is at stake.

One day during the morning session at Ohio State, Yetta said, "We have to give the child a self-image."

Yetta (it means "The given," and surely Yetta is a gift) is from Alabama. She is black, and gentle, with a core of steel; she has much to be bitter about, and angry; but she also knows how to love. When she said that about the self-image, I stopped her. "Hold everything, Yetta. All my little red warning flags are out. I sniff danger here. Do we want to give the child an *image* of himself—mirror vision? Or do we want what is real?"

That stopped us all. Nobody had thought very much before

about the repercussions in the words: self-image: it's part of the jargon. But I was concerned that we use such words and phrases carefully, knowing precisely what we meant.

What is a self-image? Who started talking about one? I rather fancy it was Madison Avenue. Picture Satan in a business suit, with well-groomed horns and a superbly switching tail, sitting at his huge executive's desk, thinking, "Aha! If I can substitute images for reality I can get a lot more people under my domination."

Do I exaggerate? Possibly. Nevertheless, I am honestly unhappy about Madison Avenue. The advertiser is in business to sell his product to as many people as possible. We forget that most successful high-pressure advertising campaigns deal subtly with our weaknesses, our insecure longing for status (I've never quite overcome my yearning to earn a Merit Badge as a housewife), so that we are being manipulated. A pitch to make us buy a new car or a new stove when our old one is perfectly good, so that we'll have a better "image" of ourselves, doesn't make sense, but it's what the advertiser's in business for. And the powers of darkness know exactly where to infiltrate.

Give the public the "image" of what it thinks it ought to be, or what television commercials or glossy magazine ads have convinced us we ought to be, and we will buy more of the product, become closer to the image, and further from reality.

But what is a true image? *Imagination* comes from "image." An image is not in itself intrinsically wrong. What is true real? Can an image be ontological? The medieval mystics say that the true image and the true real met once and for all on the cross: once and for all: and yet they still meet daily.

And what does all this mean in an un-air-conditioned classroom in Columbus, Ohio, on a hot morning in late July?

It's not a question to be settled either by saints or by Satan. It is something absolutely essential to a writer. Imagery is one of the writer's chief tools. Where would we be without the images given in metaphor and simile?

Metaphor: *She speaks poniards, and every word stabs.* Simile: *My love is like a red, red rose.* "Like" is our simile word. Madison Avenue is by no means the first to misuse "like," but I was told that the man who wrote the famous "Winston tastes good like a cigarette should" did it with contempt for those at whom the commercial was aimed. Over and over again we hear "like" misused this way: *I feel like I'm going to throw up; well, you know, Mother, like I really do need it because . . . ; tell it like it is.* Every time "like" is misused, it is weakened as a simile word.

I'm not against changes in the language. I love new words, and not only the ologies. I've just discovered "widdershins": against the direction of the sun. In Crosswicks the bath water runs out clockwise; in Australia, widdershins. I love anything that is going to make language richer and stronger. But when words are used in a way that is going to weaken language, it has nothing to do with the beautiful way that they can wriggle and wiggle and develop and enrich our speech, but instead it is impoverishing, diminishing. If our language is watered down, then mankind becomes less human, and less free—though we may buy more of the product.

So. An image is something that helps us catch a glimpse of reality. A poet, a storyteller, could not work without images. Nevertheless, an image is only an image, a reflection not unlike the reflections of the shadows of reality in Plato's cave.

If an image is not easy to define, an icon is even more difficult. We usually think of icons as corrupt images which ought to be broken. But it is only the icon misused (like *"like"* misused) which needs breaking. A true icon is not a reflection; it is like a metaphor, a different, *unlike* look at something, and carries within it something of that at which it looks. In Russia or Greece, when a painter begins to learn about icons, he is taught that the icon must never look *like* the person it portrays, it must never be an attempt at a photographic likeness, otherwise it becomes only an image. An icon, if it "works," is more than itself; it bears a fragment of reality.

Red flags of danger again: it is precisely because an icon touches on reality that it far too often becomes an idol. All of us who need icons—and I am convinced that all artists do—also need an iconoclast close by. I'm lucky: my husband is an iconoclast par excellence.

The idea that an icon must not look like the person it portrays used to bother me. But my husband is an actor; there are many times when he has to be away, on an out-of-town tryout of a play, for instance. And I have found that the longer we have been married, and the more deeply I love him, the less I "see" him visually. "Close your eyes," I'm in the habit of telling my students of all ages, "and think about the person you love most in the world. Do you really see him visually? Or don't you see on a much deeper level? It's lots easier to visualize people we don't know very well."

I've noticed in many of my favorite novels that the minor characters are more minutely described, much more physical detail is given about them, than about the hero. A protagonist should be an icon for the reader. A photograph can be a simile, an image; it can seldom be a metaphor, an icon. And though I love snapshots of family and friends, there are times when the camera's reproduction pushes me further away rather than bringing me closer to the people I love most.

But I do have icons. I think we all do, whether we want to admit it or not. I had a very special one for years without realizing that this is what it was. During the almost-decade that we lived in Crosswicks year round, all kinds of things happened to knock my sense of humor out of joint. There were two years when illness or accident kept someone in the hospital so constantly that it became a joke: "Oh, not *you* again!" Friends would telephone, laughing, and ask, "What's happened now?"

Sometime, during those years, I read *The Man in the Grey Flannel Suit*. What I remember from it is the reference to "the tired thirties." I was always tired. So was Hugh. During the decade between thirty and forty, most couples are raising small children, and we were no exception. Hugh was struggling to support his growing family in the strange world outside the theatre. And there was I, absolutely stuck in bucology, with the washing machine freezing at least once a week, the kitchen never above 55° when the wind blew from the northwest, not able to write until after my little ones were in bed, by which time I was so tired that I often quite literally fell asleep with my head on the typewriter.

The various pressures of twentieth-century living have made it almost impossible for the young mother with pre-school children to have any solitude. During the long drag of years before our youngest child went to school, my love for my family and my need to write were in acute conflict. The problem was really that I put two things first. My husband and children came first. So did my writing. Bump.

Crosswicks is isolated, which is one of the things we love about it, but it meant that if the children were to have playmates outside their own siblings, I had to drive them somewhere, or pick up some other children and bring them here. The house was usually full of kids, and that's the way we wanted it, but there were times when for at least a full minute I thought of following Gauguin: I needed a desert island, and time to write.

Well, somehow or other, like a lot of other women who have quite deliberately and happily chosen to be mothers, and work at another vocation as well, I did manage to get a lot of writing done. But during that decade when I was in my thirties, I couldn't sell anything. If a writer says he doesn't care whether he is published or not, I don't believe him. I care. Undoubtedly I care too much. But we do not write for ourselves alone. I write about what concerns me, and I want to share my concerns. I want what I write to be read. Every rejection slip—and you could paper walls with my rejection slips—was like the rejection of me, myself, and certainly of my *amour-propre*. I learned all kinds of essential lessons during those years of rejection, and I'm glad to have had them, but I wouldn't want to have to go through them again. (I'm getting to icons: wait.)

I was, perhaps, out of joint with time. Two of my books for children were rejected for reasons which would be considered absurd today. Publisher after publisher turned down *Meet the Austins* because it begins with a death. Publisher after publisher turned down *A Wrinkle in Time* because it deals overtly with the problem of evil, and it was too difficult for children, and was it a children's or an adults' book, anyhow? My adult novels were rejected, too. *A Winter's Love* was *too* moral: the married protagonist refuses an affair because of the strength of her responsibility towards marriage. Then, shortly before my fortieth birthday, both *Meet the Austins* and an adult novel, *The Lost Innocent*, had been in publishing houses long enough to get my hopes up. I knew that *The Lost Innocent* was being considered very seriously; one editor was strong for it; another was almost equally enthusiastic; a third hated it; and they were waiting for the opinion of a fourth editor who had just come back from Europe. I tried not to think about it, but this was not quite possible. And there was that fortieth birthday coming up.

I didn't dread being forty; I looked forward to it. My thirties had been such a rough decade in so many ways that I was eager for change. Surely, with the new decade, luck would turn.

On my birthday I was, as usual, out in the Tower working on a book. The children were in school. My husband was at work and would be getting the mail. He called, saying, "I'm sorry to have to tell you this on your birthday, but you'd never trust me again if I kept it from you. ———has rejected *The Lost Innocent.*"

This seemed an obvious sign from heaven. I should stop trying to write. All during the decade of my thirties (the world's fifties) I went through spasms of guilt because I spent so much time writing, because I wasn't like a good New England housewife and mother. When I scrubbed the kitchen floor, the family cheered. I couldn't make decent pie crust. I always managed to get something red in with the white laundry in the washing machine, so that everybody wore streaky pink underwear. And with all the hours I spent writing, I was still not pulling my own weight financially.

So the rejection on the fortieth birthday seemed an unmistakable command: Stop this foolishness and learn to make cherry pie.

I covered the typewriter in a great gesture of renunciation. Then I walked around and around the room, bawling my head off. I was totally, unutterably miserable.

Suddenly I stopped, because I realized what my subconscious mind was doing while I was sobbing: my subconscious mind was busy working out a novel about failure.

I uncovered the typewriter. In my journal I recorded this moment of decision, for that's what it was. I had to write. I had no choice in the matter. It was not up to me to say I would stop, because I could not. It didn't matter how small or inadequate my talent. If I never had another book published, and it was very clear to me that this was a real possibility, I still had to go on writing.

I'm glad I made this decision in the moment of failure. It's easy to say you're a writer when things are going well. When the decision is made in the abyss, then it is quite clear that it is not one's own decision at all.

In the moment of failure I knew that the idea of Madeleine, who had to write in order to be, was not image.

And what about that icon?

During those difficult years I was very much aware that if I lost my ability to laugh, I wouldn't be able to write, either. If I started taking myself and my failure too seriously, then the writing would become something that was *mine*, that I could manipulate, that I could take personal credit—or discredit—for. When a book was rejected, I would allow myself twenty-four hours of private unhappiness. I'm sure I wasn't as successful in keeping my misery from the family as I tried to be, but I did try. Our house fronts on a dirt road—we didn't have the land with the brook, then—and I would go down the lane to do my weeping. I found that I could play games with the children during dinner (Buzz and Botticelli were our favorites), but I couldn't listen to Bach. But perhaps what was most helpful—and still is—is a white china laughing Buddha which sits on my desk in the Tower. He laughs at me, never with ridicule, but lovingly, tolerantly: you *are* taking yourself seriously, aren't you, Madeleine? What matters is the book itself. If it is as good a book as you can write at this moment in time, that is what counts. Success is pleasant; of course you want it; but it isn't what makes you write.

No, it's not. I found that out on the morning of my fortieth birthday.

My white china Buddha is an icon. He has never become an idol.

. . 6 . .

My fiftieth birthday was quite unlike my fortieth, but equally memorable, and lots funnier. I always remind people about my birthdays; nobody is ever able to say, "But why didn't you tell me?" I start telling weeks ahead. A birthday, mine, my family's, my friends', is an opportunity for a feast day, a party, for getting together. When it came time for my fiftieth birthday I thought to myself: Half a century! This time I don't need to remind anybody. They'll surely do something splendid.

So I was silent.

The twenty-ninth of November that year was the day after Thanksgiving. Josephine and Alan had gone to England at the end of the summer. Maria was home, and had brought her current beau. Hugh was in previews for a play which was to open the following week, so he was legitimately preoccupied. Tom Tallis was coming for my birthday dinner, and he had also procured, through an Iranian friend, a real, right, and proper hookah for Bion, who is one of his innumerable godchildren—only he knows how many: I think he said that our granddaughter Charlotte is the twenty-ninth.

On that fiftieth, half-century, birthday, it was obvious that, under all the circumstances, I would have to cook dinner, rather than be taken out. So I cooked it, an excellent dinner, roast beef, red and juicy; broccoli with hollandaise sauce; Yorkshire pudding; all the assorted accompanying goodies. Tallis had brought some splendid champagne. We had barely finished dinner when Hugh had to rush off to the theatre. Maria and

23

her friend had a party to go to; Bion and Tallis played with the hookah and drank up all my champagne; and I did the dishes. While I was getting things organized in the kitchen, the two dogs, Oliver and Tyrrell, stole the rest of the roast beef from the sideboard and ate it.

Alan wrote me from England, "Madeleine, you were so good about not reminding people about your birthday this year."

I wrote back, "Never again. My birthday is the twenty-ninth of November and next year I will be fifty-one and I want people to DO something about it."

The fortieth. The fiftieth. And the sixtieth? It's still almost a decade off. It's not up to me to think about it. Or where I may be.

. . 7 . .

The title of a book is as important as one's right and proper signature on a check. A book may have a Library of Congress number, as a check may have that cybernetic salad, but a book, like Emily Brontë, like you, like me, must have its own name. Some books get born with names: *The Arm of the Starfish. The Young Unicorns.* We had to search for the proper name for *A Wrinkle in Time,* and it was my mother who came up with it, during a night of insomnia. I went into her room with a cup of coffee in the morning, and she said, "I think I have a title for your book, and it's right out of the text: A Wrinkle in Time." Of course! It's perfect.

But what to call this book? It's gone through a number of names, some proposed by me, some by friends. The final title was brought up by Bob Giroux, right out of the text. But before he came on it, there were several other names which we considered. *The Burning Bush*. Not bad. In a sense it's what the book is about. But it sounds too philosophical, and as though I were about to come up with answers to unanswerable questions. No; it's out.

The full first draft of the book was written during a Crosswicks summer. Crosswicks means *where the two roads meet*. What about that as a title? Hugh and I rather liked it. F S & G didn't.

Then Hugh suggested, also out of the text, *On the One Hand*. That, too, was vetoed.

Tallis, sitting in the Crosswicks living room, resplendent in his kilt, proposed *Word, Words, and the Word*. Yes, that's a fine title, but it seems too big, too grand, for this book which is essentially small and personal: a letter.

My *Letter from Crosswicks*. (That's how I think of it.)

A letter to the world? In a sense, yes. But that's still too big, too general. And this, like all letters, is particular.

To whom, then, is it addressed?

It is first and foremost a letter to Hugh, my husband who has put up with me for almost twenty-five years. And then it's a letter to all the librarians, teachers, students, who have been so warm and generous and giving with me during these past few years as I've traveled about the country on speaking and teaching jaunts. And it's to Clare Costello and Liz Nichols and Martha King, who asked me to write it, Clare and Liz several years ago; Martha, just this past July at O.S.U. To them all I replied, brushing it off, "It's a lovely idea, but not for me. I'm a storyteller. I have a hard enough time writing a twenty-minute lecture, much less a whole book of non-fiction."

But I hadn't been home from O.S.U. for more than a few days when the book woke me up in the middle of the night, clamoring to be written. As usual, I had no choice.

And it is also a letter of love to my mother and my children and the friends of my right hand, like Tallis, those who have made me know who I am, who have taught me the meaning of ontology, who, like my husband, bear with me, pick me up when I fall down, literally and figuratively, for I frequently do both; who shove me back into a sense of proportion and a sense of humor.

My dears: here: to you.

.. 8 ..

Once, when I was very unhappy, Hugh and I had to go to a large cocktail party. There was nothing I wanted to do less than get dressed up and have to radiate charm to swarms of people. But we went, and I tried. There was a woman at the party who very quickly had too much to drink because she was lost; she had been widowed; she had not been able to find a new life which was valuable, or in which she felt she had any value. She talked to me and cried into her drink and suddenly she said, "You're a very happy person, aren't you?"

I had, at that point, legitimate reason to be miserable. But her question stopped me in my tracks. I looked at her in surprise and gratitude and said, "Yes. I am."

This was ten years ago. But the answer is still the same. The better word, of course, is joy, because it doesn't have anything to do with pain, physical or spiritual. I have been wholly in joy when I have been in pain—childbirth is the obvious example. Joy is what has made the pain bearable and, in the end, creative rather than destructive.

To be fifty-one in the world of today and to be able to say, "I am a happy person," may seem irresponsible. But it is not. It is what keeps me capable of making a response. I do not understand it, or need to.

Meanwhile, I am grateful.

And the unknown woman who gave me the revelation is one of the people to whom I am writing this letter.

. . 9 . .

Like all love letters, it is personal; there isn't any other way for me to write it. Just as I realized, that first morning at O.S.U. that I was standing in front of a group of people all of whom were experts in the field in which I was supposed to lecture to them, and my only hope was not to try to be an expert but to offer them myself and all that writing has taught me in the past half century, so my only hope in this book is to do the same thing.

In thinking about my reservations I fall over a kind of false humility which is really only pride. My job is to write the book. That is all. Nothing else.

But pride comes in. Tallis asked me, about a book I had just finished, "How is it?" "I don't know. I never know." I never do know. He pushed me, "But what do you really think of it?" "I think it's good." And this was true, too. If something deep within even the most tentative and minor of artists didn't think his work was good, he would stop, forever.

H. A. Williams (and what an extraordinary world this is: we met and became friends long after I had copied down these words which he wrote while he was at Trinity College in Cambridge) says: "Because the Holy Spirit is within us, because He can be known only subjectively, only, that is, by means of what I am, we shall never feel absolutely certain that it is in fact the

27

Spirit who is working. This is the price that has to be paid for inspiration of every kind. Is it all nonsense after all? I suppose that's why an artist or writer is so sensitive about the reception of his work. If the critics tear it to pieces, they echo his own inevitable doubts of his validity." Yes.

My husband is my most ruthless critic. Tallis runs him a close second. Sometimes he will say, "It's been said better before." Of course. It's all been said better before. If I thought I had to say it better than anybody else, I'd never start. Better or worse is immaterial. The thing is that it has to be said; by me; ontologically. We each have to say it, to say it our own way. Not of our own *will*, but as it comes out through us. Good or bad, great or little: that isn't what human creation is about. It is that we have to try; to put it down in pigment, or words, or musical notations, or we die.

While I was at Smith, Mary Ellen Chase gave a morning talk to the entire college in John M. Greene Hall. What I remember of this particular talk is that she said that literature could be divided into three categories: "Majah, minah, and mediocah." Majah, minah, and mediocah became passwords on campus. I'm sure that all of us who were young and arrogant could not bear the idea that we would ever be either minah or mediocah. When I am thinking straight I know that it is not important. I don't always think straight. There is still in me the childish child who wants to "show" all the teachers, editors, good house-wives, or the socially graceful, that I can—as the jargon goes—compete.

Yesterday while I was down by the brook I read the following lines from the fourth chapter of Ecclesiasticus, or the Book of Wisdom, and it could not have been better timed, because I had been feeling deprecatory about my words; I had, in a sense, already been protecting myself against any rejection later on, protecting myself by that destructive false humility. These words took me by the scruff of the neck and threw me back into better perspective:

> . . . do not be over-modest in your own cause,
> for there is a modesty that leads to sin,
> as well as a modesty that brings honour and favour.
> Do not be untrue to yourself in deference to another,
> or so diffident that you fail in your duty . . .
> for wisdom shows itself by speech
> and a man's education must find expression in words. . . .
> Do not let yourself be a doormat to a fool
> or curry favour with the powerful.
> Fight to the death for truth,
> and the Lord God will fight on your side.

Majah, minah, mediocah: it is not my problem.

.. 10 ..

But what about that self-image?

We talked, this July in Columbus, about how you can be walking down the street and you will catch a glimpse of yourself reflected in a store window and think: who is that? Oh, no, it's not!

But it is.

We really don't know what we look like. We are moderately careful to spend a certain amount of time in front of the mirror; we choose the mirror before which we comb our hair, shave, or put on lipstick or eyeshadow, with a good deal of attention. We don't use a distorted mirror, or ones like those in the fun houses at fairs and carnivals. The bathroom mirror tells us a certain amount about our outside selves.

But the inner, essential self?

I don't know what I'm like. I get glimpses of myself in other people's eyes. I try to be careful whom I use as a mirror: my husband; my children; my mother; the friends of my right hand. If I do something which disappoints them I can easily read it in their response. They mirror their pleasure or approval, too.

But we aren't always careful of our mirrors. I'm not. I made the mistake of thinking that I "ought" not to write because I wasn't making money, and therefore in the eyes of many people around me I had no business to spend hours every day at the typewriter. I felt a failure not only because my books weren't being published but because I couldn't emulate our neighboring New England housewives. I was looking in the wrong mirrors. I still do, and far too often. I catch myself at it, but usually afterwards. If I have not consciously thought, "What will the neighbors think?" I've acted as though I had.

I've looked for an image in someone else's mirror, and so have avoided seeing myself.

We did manage, that morning in Columbus, to delete the word *image*. "All right," Yetta said, "I think I understand. But I still think we need to give the child a self."

But when I was getting ready for bed that night it occurred to me that no teacher can hope to give the child a self unless the teacher knows what a self is, unless the teacher *is* a self. Here we are, living in a world of "identity crises," and most of us have no idea what an identity is.

Half the problem is that an identity is something which must be understood intuitively, rather than in terms of provable fact. An infinite question is often destroyed by finite answers. To define everything is to annihilate much that gives us laughter and joy. I found that I could think about this strange thing, the self, only in terms of the characters in the novel I was writing, or in terms of other people, never of myself. If I try self-consciously to become a person, I will never be one. The most real people, those who are able to forget their selfish selves, who have true compassion, are usually the most distinct individuals. But that comes second. Personhood comes first, and our civilization tempts, if not teaches, us to reverse the process.

As usual, we bump into paradox and contradiction.

The people I know who are the most concerned about their individuality, who probe constantly into motives, who are always turned inwards towards their own reactions, usually become less and less individual, less and less spontaneous, more and more afraid of the consequences of giving themselves away. They are perhaps more consistent than the rest of us, but also less real.

When Alan first started reading his thesis to me, he was concerned that Herbert Kelly, about whom he was writing, came out as a contradictory character. But Kelly *was* contradictory, and I said, "Why shouldn't he be? The deeper and richer a personality is, the more full it is of paradox and contradiction. It's only a shallow character who offers us no problems of contrast." A perfect person would be inhuman. I like the fact that in ancient Chinese art the great painters always included a deliberate flaw in their work: human creation is never perfect.

We find the same thing in literature. The truly great books are flawed: *The Brothers Karamazov* is unwieldy in structure; a present-day editor would probably want to cut the Grand Inquisitor scene because it isn't necessary to the plot. For me, *The Brothers Karamazov* is one of the greatest novels ever written, and this is perhaps because of, rather than in spite of, its human faults. *Hamlet* is usually considered Shakespeare's finest play, and yet nobody has ever satisfactorily, once and for all, been able to analyze or pin down Hamlet's character.

When I start a new seminar I tell my students that I will undoubtedly contradict myself, and that I will mean both things. But an acceptance of contradiction is no excuse for fuzzy thinking. We do have to use our minds as far as they will take us, yet acknowledging that they cannot take us all the way.

We *can* give a child a self-image. But is this a good idea? Hitler did a devastating job at that kind of thing. So does Chairman Mao. To settle for this because we can't give a child a self is manipulation, coercion, and ultimately the coward's way out.

I haven't defined a self, nor do I want to. A self is not something static, tied up in a pretty parcel and handed to the child, finished and complete. A self is always becoming. *Being* does mean becoming, but we run so fast that it is only when we seem to stop—as sitting on the rock at the brook—that we are aware of our own *isness*, of being. But certainly this is not static, for this awareness of being is always a way of moving from the selfish self—the self-image—and towards the real.

Who am I, then? Who are you?

. . 11 . .

I first became aware of myself as self, as Pascal's reed ("Man is only a reed, the feeblest reed in nature; but he is a thinking reed"), when I was seven or eight years old. We lived in an apartment on East 82nd Street in New York. My bedroom window looked out on the court, and I could see into the apartments across the way. One evening when I was looking out I saw a woman undressing by her open window. She took off her dress, stretched, stood there in her slip, not moving, not doing anything, just standing there, being.

And that was my moment of awareness (of ontology?): that woman across the court who did not know me, and whom I did not know, was a person. She had thoughts of her own. She *was*. Our lives would never touch. I would never know her name. And yet it was she who revealed to me my first glimpse of personhood.

When I woke up in the morning the wonder of that revelation was still with me. There was a woman across the court, and she had dreams and inner conversations which were just as real as mine and which did not include me. But she was there, she was real, and so, therefore, was everybody else in the world. And so, therefore, was I.

I got out of bed and stood in front of the mirror and for the first time looked at myself consciously. I, too, was real, standing there thin and gawky in a white nightgown. I did more than exist. I *was*.

That afternoon when I went to the park I looked at everybody I passed on the street, full of the wonder of their realness.

.. 12 ..

I could share this experience with my friends in Ohio, although I still could not tell them how to give a child a self, or what a self is. And I had another experience to share with them, one which helps me to get a glimpse of the burning bush out of the corner of my eye.

We hadn't spent more than one winter at Crosswicks when I found myself the choir director in the village church. I had no

33

qualifications as choir director beyond a passionate love of music, and I knew nothing about church music; in fact, since the crisis in faith (more jargon) that so often comes during college, I had seldom darkened the doors of a church when a service was going on. Neither had my husband.

But when our children were born, two things happened simultaneously. We cleaned up our language; we had been careless about four-letter words—I'd been rather proud of those I'd picked up from stage hands; we no longer used them indiscriminately. And we discovered that we did not want our children to grow up in a world which was centered on man to the exclusion of God. We did know that bedtime prayers were not enough and that it made no sense whatsoever to send the children to Sunday School unless we went to church ourselves. The inconsistency of parents who use the church as a free baby-sitting service on Sunday mornings, while they stay home and read the Sunday papers, did not have to be pointed out to us. I found myself earnestly explaining to the young minister that I did not believe in God, "but I've discovered that I can't live as though I didn't believe in him. As long as I don't need to say any more than that I try to live as though I believe in God, I would very much like to come to church—if you'll let me."

So I became the choir director. Grandma was the organist and she had been the organist since she started playing for Sunday School when she was eleven years old, and she was, when we first knew her, up in her eighties. She had had a large family, and in all those years had missed only two Sundays. Hugh and I visualized Grandma rushing through the last hymn just in time to go have her baby so she could be back in church the following Sunday.

Grandma and I loved each other. She had been distressed

because the church had been for so long without a choir, and would bring in occasional soloists. But the standard of music was low, what I called "Blood of the lamb-y." When I was asked to get together a group of people in the village who might like to sing on a few Sundays during the year, I replied, "No, but I'll start a choir, if you like. And we'll sing every Sunday. Summer, too. God doesn't take the summer off, and if we have a choir, neither will we." I might not believe in God, but I knew that much about him.

The choir was completely volunteer, and completely ecumenical. Before ecumenism was "in," we had Episcopalian, Lutheran, Presbyterian, Dutch Reform, Methodist, and Southern Baptist choristers, and all in the Congregational Church. Musically, I was certainly Episcopalian. It was the church into which I was born, and my father loved good church music. In New York as a child I was taken to church much as I was taken to the opera.

I wanted the choir to be good. I wanted us to sing good music, and to be a success. Some of the volunteer singers had beautiful voices; one had a great one. Some of them couldn't stay in tune and pulled the whole group down into a flat, sodden mass. One woman stayed in key, all right, but at full volume at all times, and with an unpleasant, nasal whine. If the choir was to be a success, the obvious first thing to do was to ease out some of the problem voices.

I couldn't do it. I don't know why, but something told me that every single person in that choir was more important than the music. 'But the music is going to be terrible,' I wailed to this invisible voice. 'That doesn't matter. That's not the reason for this choir.' I didn't ask what was, but struggled along. The extraordinary, lovely thing was that the music got to be pretty good, far better, I am now convinced, than it would have been if I'd put the music first and the people second. I suppose, long before I'd heard the word, I was being ontological.

I did have subversive means of getting my own way about what music we sang. I'd bring out something I loved, Palestrina, for instance, and everybody would groan, so I'd put it away. A couple of weeks later I'd bring it out again, and someone would remark, "That's kind of nice." "I'm afraid it's too difficult for us," I'd say, and put it away again. Two more weeks, and out it would come, and someone would exclaim, "That's beautiful! Can we learn that?" And we did, and everybody loved it. I, in my turn, learned to love some of the music I had felt "above."

As the choir developed, choice of music became limited by only one factor: Grandma, growing older, could no longer play in sharps. I felt great sympathy with her in this. Flats are lots easier than sharps for me, too. At first she could play in three sharps, then two, and finally none. Quinn, our young minister, would select hymns which fitted well with his sermon, and I'd have to say, "Sorry, Quinn, you can't have that; it's in four sharps."

And Grandma preferred major to minor. But, because we loved each other, that was no problem. I'd put my arm about her tiny, bowed little back (her legs could barely stretch to reach the organ pedals) and say, "Grandma, will you let us sing this, please? I know it's minor, but we've done major anthems for three weeks, and I love this one." "All right, Madeleine. For you." I don't think Grandma ever liked the minor anthems, but she played them most graciously.

Grandma and the choir taught me something about persons, how to be a self myself, and how to honor the self in others.

One evening I went to choir rehearsal; in the morning's mail had been a rejection slip. The choir was singing well, and I went to the back of the church to listen to the anthem and see if the voices were balanced, and caught myself thinking bitterly, "Is this all I'm good for? to direct a second-rate choir in a village church?"

I was in that area of despair where one is incapable of being ontological. In my definition of the word, this is sin.

A winter ago I was asked by the Children's Book Council to write a story, and agreed to do so. I was telling Tallis about it, and said, "I'm really very nervous about this." He looked at me contemptuously: "You don't think *you*'re going to have anything to do with it, do you?" "No," I retorted, "but I could get in the way." Mostly, while I was directing the choir, I didn't get in the way, and I hadn't yet reached the stage of either understanding or being self-conscious about such things. But getting in the way does bother me whenever I lead a seminar. It bothered me at O.S.U., and yet I knew that the moment I started worrying about whether or not I was good enough for the job, I wouldn't be able to do it.

If I accept the fact that I, ontologically speaking, was born a writer, was named Madeleine, am an inextricable blend of writer, wife, mother, then my virtue, or talent, is quite aside from the point. When I accepted myself as Madeleine on my fortieth birthday, not a computer's punch-out, or my social-security number, or the post-office date on the latest rejection slip, it had nothing to do with the degree of my talent. I could, during the long years of failure, console myself with the fact that van Gogh sold precisely one picture while he lived, and that he was considered an impossible painter. I could try to reassure my agent when he was concerned about the damaging effect on me of so much failure; he was afraid it would kill my talent. Can this happen? I don't know, I just don't know.

I think that all artists, regardless of degree of talent, are a painful, paradoxical combination of certainty and uncertainty, of arrogance and humility, constantly in need of reassurance, and yet with a stubborn streak of faith in their validity, no matter what. When I look back on that decade of total failure—it's been a mixture, both before, and since—there was, even on the days of rejection slips, a tiny, stubborn refusal to be completely put down. And I think, too, and possibly most important, that there is a faith simply in the validity of art; when we talk about ourselves as being part of the company of such people as Mozart or van Gogh or Dostoevsky, it has nothing to do with comparisons, or pitting talent against talent; it has everything to do with a way of looking at the universe. My husband said, "But people might think you're putting yourself alongside Dostoevsky." The idea is so impossible that I can only laugh in incredulity. Dostoevsky is a giant; I look up to him; I sit at his feet; perhaps I will be able to learn something from him. But we do face the same direction, no matter how giant his stride, how small mine.

During that dreadful decade I pinned on my workroom wall a cartoon in which a writer, bearing a rejected manuscript, is dejectedly leaving a publisher's office; the caption says, "We're very sorry, Mr. Tolstoy, but we aren't in the market for a war story right now." That cartoon got me through some bad hours. It didn't mean that I was setting myself beside Tolstoy.

On the other hand I was anything but comforted when Hugh thought to console me by pointing out some published stories which "aren't nearly as good as yours. Doesn't that make you feel better?" "Of course it doesn't make me feel better!" I cried. "You're absolutely right, I write much better than that. Why should it make me feel better to have bad writing published? If it were better than mine, then I wouldn't mind, then I *would* feel better."

It was great writing which kept me going, the company of the Brontës, William Blake, Alexandre Dumas. But there's still pride to fall over, not pride in the sense of self-respect, but in that Greek sense of *hubris*: pride against the gods; do-it-yourself-ism, which the Greeks understood to mean "I can do it myself just as well as, if not better than, the gods." When my hubris gets pricked, I bleed; or at any rate my hubris bleeds. Mine is still sore from something a friend of mine, a friend of the right hand, whom we will call Will, said to me shortly before I went to Ohio: what Will said is that in group conversation I am apt to seem as though I were going to say something extremely important, and then come out with the obvious. I thought of this accusation while I was in Columbus. Certainly much of what I was fumblingly trying to say during the seminars was obvious. But the obvious needs to be said. Sometimes the obvious is so obscured by brilliant analysis that it gets lost.

Am I trying, as I so often do, to rationalize? Do Will's words still rankle—and they do—because the implication was not just that I come out with the obvious, but that my obvious is shallow? But the obvious need not be shallow. Sometimes it is profound and painful, and can be written off only by being called obvious. Not that I think that Will does this—he does not—but it can be a danger for any intellectual.

In another conversation, Will and I discussed the peril of falling into the trap of intellectual elitism. The older I grow, the more this insidious form of snobbery seems a snare and a delusion. We probably have more scientific knowledge at our fingertips today than ever before, and yet we are incapable of handling this knowledge creatively; we cannot avoid mutilating diseases, devastating wars, or control earthquake or tornado; and we are in grave danger of destroying our planet entirely because we cannot control what our intellect has unleashed, from cobalt bombs to polluting laundry detergents.

More personally, my intellect is a stumbling block to much that makes life worth living: laughter; love; a willing acceptance of being created. The rational intellect doesn't have a great deal to do with love, and it doesn't have a great deal to do with art. I am often, in my writing, great leaps ahead of where I am in my thinking, and my thinking has to work its way slowly up to what the "superconscious" has already shown me in a story or poem. Facing this does help to eradicate do-it-yourself hubris from an artist's attitude towards his painting or music or writing. My characters pull me, push me, take me further than I want to go, fling open doors to rooms I don't want to enter, throw me out into interstellar space, and all this long before my mind is ready for it.

There's a reason for that, chaps!

While Alan was in school, his science teacher was an inept young man who kept blowing things up, remarking through the stench of chemical smoke and the crashing of broken glass, "There's a reason for that, chaps."

I must be willing to accept the explosions which take place

deep down in the heart of the volcano, sending up an occasional burst of flame into the daylight of consciousness.

With my naked intellect I cannot believe in God, particularly a loving God. My intellect is convinced that any idea of the person's continuing and growing after death is absurd; logic goes no further than dust to dust. Images, in the literary sense of the word, take me much further. Without my glasses I can see nothing but a vague blur. When I put them on, I become functional. But who is doing the seeing? The lenses of the spectacles are not. I am. There is an essential, ontological me—that part of me which is not consumed in the burning—which is (to use imagery again) that which I was created to be, the imaginative Adam and Eve as they were in the pre-history days of the Garden. Some of our children talk about going back to the garden; we can't do that; but we can travel in the direction which will lead us to that place where we may find out who we really are.

.. 15 ..

Not long ago I was one of several "children's writers" on a panel. I had not been told that we were expected to begin by making a statement as to why we write for children. Because of the seating arrangements, I was "on" second. The first writer had written down his reasons, and good ones they were, too, though not mine. Sometimes when we have to speak suddenly we come closer to the truth than when we have time to think. I said, "I suppose I write for children because I'm not bright enough to understand the difference between a children's and an adults' novel."

These words seem to me to contain considerable truth, as well as considerable naïveté. There's something a little humiliating about having to accept that, at fifty-one, one is naïve. I am. I would, quite often, like to be grownup, wise, and sophisticated. But these gifts are not mine.

I was comforted, two days after the panel, when I read an article on William James, written by a brilliant novelist and essayist, a writer of my own generation, a critic taken seriously by our contemporaries. In this essay it was evident that the author agreed with those who consider James naïve in his attitude towards religion and the supernatural; James's hope for something beyond the abyss of nothingness after death is cited as evidence of his naïveté. With a shock of joy I realized in what good company I am: William James, pushing beyond the rational world to that wilder, freer place on the other side of the intellect. Gregory of Nyssa and his brilliant sister, Macrina, meeting at her deathbed and talking, unashamed and unafraid, of their love for their friends, for each other, and of the extraordinary vistas soon to open for Macrina. Socrates, drinking hemlock, and talking with calm certainty about what lies ahead for him. Many others, all more brilliant, more erudite, more sophisticated than I.

And there are, too, the high-school students who come to me to talk about the transcendent, about God, about the hope for a meaning to all life, no matter how terrible and irrational it may sometimes seem.

I look at many of the brilliant, sophisticated intellectuals of my generation, struggling through psychoanalysis, balancing sleeping pills with waking pills, teetering on the thin edge of despair, and think that perhaps they have not found the answer after all.

Well, of course, neither have I. It is not up to me to do so. I am finite; in the earthly sense, mortal; with a good mind flawed by naïveté; dependent on my friends; on hope; on joy.

.. 16 ..

It is all, as usual, paradox. I have to use what intellect I have in order to write books, but I write the kind of books I do in order that I may try to set down glimpses of things that are on the other side of the intellect. We do not go around, or discard the intellect, but we must go through and beyond it. If we are given minds we are required to use them, but not limit ourselves by them.

It's a strange thing that despite the anti-intellectualism in our country, we also set so much store by I Q's and objective testing in our schools and colleges and businesses. Is passing a course in statistics really a legitimate requirement for a Ph.D.? Does the preliminary testing by which a child is placed in school really tell us enough about him? One of the teachers at O.S.U. brought this up. How do you teach, and show your concern for the student who isn't very bright?

An I Q cannot measure artistic ability. A potential Picasso may be a flop at objective vocabulary or number tests. An I Q does not measure a capacity for love. One of the most moving and perceptive sets of letters I've ever received came from a class of retarded children who had had *A Wrinkle in Time* read aloud to them. Their teacher apologized for their handwriting and mistakes in spelling and grammar; she needn't have; she obviously loved them and had taught them to express love; maybe that's more important than social studies. Maybe that's what Yetta meant by giving the child a self.

Children have helped to give me a self in their conversations with me and in their letters. There are always the letters which are no more than a class assignment: Write an author. But far more often there are letters remarkable for their depth of understanding, and which move me to the point of tears. And, lest I begin to take personal credit, there is a letter—one of my favorites—from a girl who really poured it on: "Dear Miss L'Engle, you are one of the greatest writers of all time," and so on, fulsome phrase after fulsome phrase. She signed her name and then wrote, "P. S. I have not yet read any of your books, but I am sure they will be good when I do." This helps give me a self, too!

How do we teach a child—our own, or those in a classroom—to have compassion: to allow people to be different; to understand that like is not equal; to experiment; to laugh; to love; to accept the fact that the most important questions a human being can ask do not have—or need—answers.

Cynthia, one of our Crosswicks family this summer, is thirteen. She has wanted to be a nurse ever since she can remember, and she'll make a very fine one. She was completely firm with the babies, and they adored her. When Thomas, the amber cat, had a bladder infection, Cynthia decided it would be good practice for her to give him his medication. It isn't easy to give a large and stubborn cat unpleasant medication, but Cynthia managed, and with no help, either. We had been discussing, down by the brook, how nothing really important in life is in the realm of provable fact. Cynthia is pragmatic; she had her doubts.

"What about love?" I asked her as we were crossing the big meadow on the way home. "Can you prove anything about love?"

She held down an old strand of barbed wire for me. "I guess not."

"What *is* love?"

"A feeling."

"No," I said, "a feeling is something love is *not*." Cynthia didn't like this; neither do I, lots of the time.

"Why not?"

I asked her, "You love your parents, don't you?"

"Yes."

"Aren't there some days when all your feelings about them are bad? When you're furious with them, and all you *feel* is anger, or that they've been unfair?"

"Yes."

"But you still love them, don't you?"

"Yes."

We were silent for a while because we were picking daisies to make daisy wreaths for the babies. Cynthia was much more diligent about it than I was; I was thinking more about our conversation than about daisies, or even the babies.

Love can't be pinned down by a definition, and it certainly can't be proved, any more than anything else important in life can be proved. Love is people, is a person. A friend of ours, Hugh Bishop of Mirfield, says in one of his books: "Love is not an emotion. It is a policy." Those words have often helped me when all my feelings were unlovely. In a summer household as large as ours I often have to act on those words. I am slowly coming to understand with my heart as well as my head that love is not a feeling. It is a person.

It also has a lot to do with compassion, and with creation.

There are educationists (as jargon has it) who think that creativity itself can be taught, and who write learned, and frequently dull, treatises on methods of teaching it. It is rather as though they were trying to eat air, with the usual result. The creative impulse, like love, can be killed, but it cannot be taught. What a teacher or librarian or parent can do, in working with children, is to give the flame enough oxygen so that it can burn. As far as I'm concerned, this providing of oxygen is one of the noblest of all vocations.

But even among those who admit that talent, genius, the creative impulse (or whatever one calls it) can neither be taught nor defined, there seem to be two diametrically opposed theories as to what it is. One is expressed most clearly by a group of psychiatrists, many of whom studied with Freud, who have been successful in helping well-known writers to recover from writer's block, so we cannot afford to take them lightly.

A few years ago I came across a definition of the writer in *The New York Times*: "The writer, like the alcoholic and the homosexual, is an orally regressed psychic masochist, and artistic creation is an alibi." I looked across the Sunday paper to my husband: "Darling, did you know that I am an orally regressed psychic masochist and I write only as an alibi?"

It's perfectly possible that this is true, but it still strikes me as hilarious. (Does orally regressed mean being unable to talk? If so, I was orally regressed as a solitary, overshy only child. But ever since I learned that I *could* talk, it has been practically impossible to shut me up.)

I have been accused by several friends and acquaintances of being anti-intellectual (I can't win), and also of being "against psychiatrists." I don't really think I am. That would be as silly as being "against dentists" or "against barbers." I do think that psychiatry is still a very young science, not unlike surgery when the surgeons were barbers. If you absolutely had to have a leg amputated in the seventeenth century, you went to a barber; you didn't rush to him for a scratch. I've seen psychiatry save and redeem. I've also seen people going year after year to psychiatrists or therapists and growing steadily more self-centered.

Most of us like being the center of the universe; no wonder these people don't want to give up their bi-weekly sessions. I've also seen them regress in their work and deteriorate in personal relationships. But, my friends tell me, that means it's a bad psychiatrist. True, perhaps.

I'm still less than happy about the school of psychiatry which says that all writers—and all is meant, not just an occasional crackpot—all writers are Peeping Toms, in the clinical sense; this is not meant as a poetic image. No writer is capable of love. The impulse to write is only a neurotic symptom of disease. Any time a writer mentions a mountain it is a breast image. These doctors see phallic symbols, anal symbols, oral symbols, in everything. Once Hugh and I were invited to a large cocktail party—I'm not sure why, because all the other guests were psychiatrists. I dressed up and put on high-heeled shoes, because my 6′ 3″ husband likes me in them when we go out. When we arrived everybody was standing around, as one does at a cocktail party, and almost every man there was shorter than I am. And my feet hurt. So I took off my uncomfortable elegant shoes and put them under a chair. During the party almost every doctor there came to me and asked me confidentially, "Why did you take off your shoes?" And did not believe me when I told them. Perhaps I did have some devious sexual motive: fascinating thought.

I'm quite willing to admit that all images in all forms of art have multiple meanings, and one of the meanings is usually a sex meaning. Let's just think about mountains: one of the most beautiful mountain ranges in our country is the Grand Tetons, which means the Great Breasts. Why not? The idea of nature as mother is hardly new, and I think I've made it clear that I'm all for the pleasures of the body. When, as a very young girl, I read that Freud said that the baby at its mother's breast experi-

47

ences sexual pleasure, and so does the mother, I was naïvely shocked. When I nursed my own babies I knew what he meant; it was pure sensual delight. It was also an unmitigated act of love, an affirmation of creation.

But I think we tend to confuse the word sex, in the sense of rutting, with the enjoyment of our senses. Breasts are to be enjoyed, and to name the Grand Tetons thus is wholly appropriate. Then, when we read, "And it shall come to pass in the last days, that the mountain of the Lord's house shall be established in the top of the mountains, and shall be exalted above the hills," or, "Sometimes we see a cloud that's dragonish; / A Vapour sometime like a bear or lion, / A tower'd citadel, a pendant rock, / A forked mountain, or blue promontory / With trees upon't, that nod unto the world / And mock our eyes with air: thou hast seen these signs; / They are black vesper's pageants," the imagery expands. An image, this kind of image, like the reality it stands for, always touches on mystery.

I'm always a little doubtful about people who complain about the vast sums spent on such things as moon exploration, saying that none of this is necessary for our military defenses. Whether or no, the practical reasons aren't why we want to explore space. We must push out to the moon, the solar system, our galaxy, the galaxies beyond, because they are there, because they are mysterious. We must explore them in the same way that our great-grandparents pushed across the prairies in covered wagons, not knowing what lay beyond the mountains; in much the same way that Abraham left the comfort of home and went out into the wilderness.

As our heads reel with the enormity of the macrocosm without us, we turn and become dizzy with the microcosm within us; the world of the physicist who pursues the infinitely small things in the physical world; and the psychologists who are exploring the depths of our personalities: I am all for this as long as we remember mystery; as long as we don't ignore joy. The people who would limit art to a neurosis totally forget about joy.

I have a friend, a beautiful and talented young woman, who is afraid to have a child and who is afraid to use her talent to write. She does not yet understand the joy that follows the pain of birth. I've experienced the pain and joy of the birth of babies and the birth of books and there's nothing like it: when a child who has been conceived in love is born to a man and woman, the joy of that birth sings throughout the universe. The joy of writing or composing or painting is much the same, and the insemination comes not from the artist himself but from his relationship with those he loves, with the whole world.

All real art is, in its true sense, religious; it is a religious impulse; there is no such thing as a non-religious subject. But much bad or downright sacrilegious art depicts so-called religious subjects. I've had some glorious times visiting the Sisters and lecturing to the novices at Mundelein College. On my first visit, the Sisters, knowing that I was not Roman Catholic but Anglican, were terribly curious about me; never have I had so many questions asked, questions about ultimate things, questions that put me on my toes: I felt like a strange life-form from another planet being questioned by the natives. Early in the day, when we were all still a little tentative with each other, several of the professed nuns were taking me on a tour of the dormitories. In one of the rooms was what I thought to be an appalling picture of Jesus, wishy-washy, powerless, plain bad art. The senior nun fixed me with a stern eye and demanded, "Madeleine, what do you think of that?" I swallowed and answered, "I think it's ghastly." To which the Sisters chorused, "Oh, thank God."

That so-called sacred picture was totally secular. Conversely, much great religious art has been written or painted or composed by people who thought they were atheists. Picasso, for instance, makes me think of Dorothy Sayers's story of the Japanese gentleman who, in discussing the mysterious concept of the Trinity in Christianity, said, "Honorable Father, very good. Honorable Son, very good. Honorable Bird I do not understand at all."

Very few of us understand Honorable Bird, except to acknowledge that without his power and grace nothing would be written, painted, or composed at all. To say anything beyond this about the creative process is like pulling all the petals off a flower in order to analyze it, and ending up having destroyed the flower.

Now I don't suppose I'd react quite so sharply to those petal-pullers, the writers of psychiatric books who call writers of fiction Peeping Toms, if there weren't a grain of truth in what they say. A writer does need to have a tremendous curiosity about everything and everyone, to have a trained and insatiable awareness. But this must go along with an honest commitment to and involvement in human nature, as against the ghoulish curiosity which makes some people gorge themselves on the newspapers that concentrate on bloody accidents, murders, and sex crimes. This kind of curiosity is selfish, and is in the wrong sense detached from the scenes which it is lasciviously compelled to observe.

Detachment and involvement: the artist must have both. The link between them is compassion. It has taken me over fifty years to begin to get a glimmer of what this means.

Several years ago two of my friends in far-flung places, one in Europe, one in the Northwest, both made the mistake of writing to me—the letters arrived within a week of each other—that I was a harp string, constantly vibrating. I don't remember their exact phrasing, but the general idea was that I was sensitive, vulnerable, quivering with pain, my own and everybody else's, and that this came out in my writing, particularly in my poems, some of which I was sharing with them.

The trouble with this lovely metaphorical comparison was that it made me take myself—not my verses, but myself—far too seriously. My vulnerable vanity was definitely tickled by the comparison to the sensitive artist, delicately tuned, suffering more than duller folk . . .

I'm not sure what laughed me out of this, but something did, promptly; it might have been simply walking into the apartment and having my kids call out, "Hey, Mother, what's for dinner?" or, "Don't burn the peas again tonight."

Compassion means to suffer with, but it doesn't mean to get lost in the suffering, so that it becomes exclusively one's own. I tend to do this, to replace the person for whom I am feeling compassion with myself.

I learned this—though it's still a bit of a problem—shortly after Hugh and I were married, and I was pregnant with our first child. I answered the telephone to learn that a friend of ours had lost a child, a twelve-year-old girl who was thrown from a horse and killed. And I was lost, not in compassion but in passion. The child's mother was an old friend of Hugh's; I didn't know her very well; if I had, certainly my own suffering over the death of her child (the death of all children; the death, potentially, of my child) would have made me completely useless to her. I did realize this, dimly, even while thinking that Hugh was being far too objective about it; that he wasn't *feeling* a thing.

I am just learning to realize what Cynthia and I talked about. It is not that in compassion one cuts oneself off from feeling, only from one's own selfishness, self-centeredness.

It's an odd thing, another paradox, this balance of involvement and detachment, and perhaps one should not think about it too self-consciously. But I get asked about it, and so I try to fumble for a partial answer. We cannot afford, either as writers or as human beings, to be detached from the human predicament, because this is what we write about, and it is the predicament we ourselves are in. We are always on stage, actors in the human drama. But we are also and simultaneously members of the audience: it takes both performer and audience to "create" a drama.

This awareness came to my creative unconscious long before I understood it with my mind. One of the first assignments given by Leonard Ehrlich, who came to Smith for a year to teach writing, and who is one of the many teachers to whom I owe an eternal debt of gratitude, was to write a story in the present tense, using the first person. I wrote an oddly detached story, one that I was at that time really incapable of writing. But it wrenched itself out of me, leaving me physically drained and emotionally exhilarated. It was the story of a painter watching his wife die; he loved her; he was in an agony of grief; he hated his friends who did or who did not come to help. But all the time his wife was dying he could not stop one part of his mind from considering exactly how to paint her, how to mix the colors to show the shadow of death moving across her face.

Of course I didn't realize then that the story was teaching me the ambivalence of involvement/detachment, subjectivity/objectivity that happens to all artists. I say "happens" advisedly; we cannot make ourselves detached; this would be slightly demonic. But we can try, when we write, to be objective. Shortly after writing this story I read Chekhov's letters and copied in my journal: "When you depict sad or unhappy people, and want to touch people's hearts, try to be colder—it gives their grief a background against which it stands out in sharper relief." And he went on to say that the writer does—and must—suffer with his characters, but he "must do this so that the reader does not notice it. The more objective, the stronger will be the effect."

An English poet—I copied his uncredited words in my journal over twenty years ago—said that poetry is like ice cream; tremendous heat is needed in generating it, but during the actual "making" there must be ice, otherwise the ice cream will melt. All the scenes that move me deeply while I am writing them end up in the wastepaper basket.

Kierkegaard says, "A poet is an unhappy creature whose heart is tortured by deepest suffering but whose lips are so formed that when his sighs and cries stream out over them, their sound becomes like the sound of beautiful music. . . . And men flock about the poet saying, 'Sing for us soon again; that is to say, may new sufferings torture your soul, and may your lips continue to be formed as before.'"

All right, but I'd better not take it too seriously; at any rate, I'd better not *feel* it. If I become subjective about pain, no matter what causes it, then it becomes destructive, not creative. Colette said to a young poet who complained to her that he was unhappy, "Mais personne ne t'a demandé d'être heureux. Travaille!"

. . 17 . .

Is the impulse to write, to work out one's unhappiness in work, neurotic? I couldn't care less. In one of her books, Dr. Karen

Horney describes the neurotic personality, detailing the symptoms, and remarks: At this point probably every one of you is going to think, I have all these symptoms. The difference is that the neurotic personality is controlled *by* the symptoms, and the healthy personality is in control of them.

A young priest friend said to me one day at lunch that he is disturbed by his brethren giving so much importance to the "mental health" of themselves and their flocks. "It is a very bad thing," he said, "when we confuse mental health and sanctity."

That night during a wakeful period I thought about all the people in history, literature, art, whom I most admire: Mozart, Shakespeare, Homer, El Greco, St. John, Chekhov, Gregory of Nyssa, Dostoevsky, Emily Brontë: not one of them would qualify for a mental-health certificate. It's been a small game with me this summer to ask, "Do *you* know anybody you really admire, who has really been important to the world in a creative way, who would qualify for a mental-health certificate?" So far nobody has come up with one.

What is mental health, anyhow? If we were all what is generally thought of as mentally healthy, I have a terrible fear that we'd all be alike. Even as we're rushing towards the end of another thousand years, we are still terrified by nonconformity; our nonconforming hippies are at least as conformist as the conformists against whom they are rebelling. I can't think of one great human being in the arts, or in history generally, who conformed, who succeeded, as educational experts tell us children must succeed, with his peer group. We discussed this at Ohio State, and it worried the young teachers. If a child in their classrooms does not succeed with his peer group, then it would seem to many that both child and teacher have failed.

Have they? If we ever, God forbid, manage to make each child succeed with his peer group, we will produce a race of bland and faceless nonentities, and all poetry and mystery will vanish from the face of the earth. Somehow I am not too worried. Surely every teacher must want each child to succeed, with Yetta must hope to help him find a self, but this self may be a nonconforming self. And surely there will always be the occasional prickly child who rejects all efforts, who kicks the other children, bites teacher's hand, is unloving and unlovable, and yet who will, one day, produce—perhaps out of this very unloveliness—a work of art which sings of love.

I am encouraged as I look at some of those who have listened to their "different drum": Einstein was hopeless at school math and commented wryly on his inadequacy in human relations. Winston Churchill was an abysmal failure in his early school years. Byron, that revolutionary student, had to compensate for a club foot; Demosthenes for a stutter; and Homer was blind. Socrates couldn't manage his wife, and infuriated his countrymen. And what about Jesus, if we need an ultimate example of failure with one's peers?

Or an ultimate example of love?

. . 18 . .

I've known for a long time that we know nothing about love, that we do not have love, until we give it away. Grandma showed me this very clearly during my choir-directing days.

In a sense Grandma was the organ, and the organ was Grandma; it was, as McLuhan might say, an extension of Grandma. She lived alone with Grandpa in a tiny little house, and if Grandpa was her love, the organ was her vocation, and one cannot have a vocation without love. Grandpa was old, even older than Grandma, and not well; often she would be up with him all night. It wasn't a surprise to anybody when one morning Grandpa simply did not wake up.

Two days earlier one of Grandma's cousins and close friends had died, and she was to be buried the afternoon of the day that Grandpa died. People asked, "But who will play the organ for the funeral?"

Her daughter called me. "Madeleine, Grandma wants to play for Grandpa's funeral. What shall we do?"

My response was, "You can't take the organ away from Grandma, today of all days. Let her do whatever she wants to do."

Grandma played, of course. To keep everybody happy (she loved us all that much), she got a friend in to play an anthem. But she herself sat at the organ for the rest of the service.

I'm not sure how long after this it was that a man and his wife started some vicious and absurdly untrue gossip about Hugh and me and three other couples, all with jobs in the church: we were, between us, a trustee, a deacon, Sunday School superintendent, Sunday School teachers, choir members and director, and general scrubbers. The man and his wife were leaving town, and why they wanted to destroy those of us who had tried to be their friends we will never know. They were, I suppose, sick (the wife was what my godmother once called menopoisonous), and their lies were so fantastic that one could only be amazed, not angry. Basically, the accusation was that we were all Communist agents. It would have been funny indeed except for one thing: people were eager to believe the lies. It was during the sad reign of Senator Joseph McCarthy; witch-hunting was in the air; but we were still unprepared.

We ought not to have been so shocked and hurt. An eagerness to believe ill of others in order to feel virtuous oneself is to some extent in all of us. It is perhaps more visible in small communities. Certainly it is not unique in our village. But we *were* hurt, desperately hurt. Hugh and I knew nothing about it until Thanksgiving afternoon, when the other three couples asked if they could come over for a conference. At first it seemed so incredible that we tended not to take it seriously, to laugh, and probably that was what we ought to have done. But our laughter stopped. Someone said, "If that's the way they feel about us, if they want us out of the church, then I think we ought to get out. I think the thing to do is for all of us to resign. I don't mean that we should stop going to church, but we shouldn't hold any offices in it."

This was the consensus. I was the lone voice saying, "No!" I loved the choir; I loved my high-school Sunday free-for-all discussion group; I might be terribly unsure about God, but I was happy working in his house. I said, "If we resign, it's admitting that they're right about us." But finally I gave in, so that the resignation would be unanimous. We wrote it out—I forget exactly what we said—and sent it to the senior and junior deacons.

In a village our size, everybody knows everybody: the senior deacon was the father of two of the brightest boys in my discussion group; the junior deacon, who would become senior deacon at the first of the year, is our family doctor; his youngest daughter was—still is—one of our daughter Josephine's friends. This kind of close relationship existed for all of us.

So we waited for their response.

And went to choir rehearsal.

The story, in various versions, was, of course, all over town. When I walked into the church Grandma was there to meet me; she had to talk to me before we started rehearsal. Now, I was quite certain that Grandma would have heard the whole sorry tale from a great many people who would like to see us put down. I loved Grandma, and I thought that Grandma loved me, but I doubted her.

Grandma said to me, "Madeleine, I just want you to know that if you go, I go, too."

Grandma was offering to give up the organ. Grandma was giving me herself.

That absolute gesture of love is what remains with me.

The deacons tore up our resignation. The gossip blew over—though, after all these years, there are still a few people with whom I feel very tentative. But only a few.

. . 19 . .

Grandma gave me herself, and so helped to give me myself. Is that what Yetta was getting at? Yetta being Yetta, I think it was. But it's one thing to talk consciously about giving oneself away and another to do it, for it must be done completely unself-consciously; it is not a do-it-yourself activity. No computer can teach it; no computer can show a child compassion, or how to allow people to be different, to experiment, to love. Almost all the joyful things of life are outside the measure of I Q tests, are beyond the realm of provable fact. A person is needed. But if any teacher, no matter how qualified, no matter how loving, goes into a classroom thinking, "I am going to give a child a self," it can't possibly happen.

Zeke, one of the Fellows at O.S.U., saw this quickly. Zeke is a Ph.D. candidate, father of four, lay preacher in a Pentecostal church; we couldn't come from more different traditions, but we found that we had all the essential things in common. The morning after Yetta had started the discussion on giving the child a self, Zeke brought me this quotation from G. A. Young, an Omaha psychiatrist: "The compulsion for me to get my cotton-pickin' fingers on my fellow man is the natural result of my belief that I have the *word*. If I do have the word and feel surrounded by unmolded clay, I have no choice but to mold. When I do this, I begin playing God, and as a result usually raise the devil."

"Oh, yes," I said, "let's share this with everybody." And I had a similar quotation for Zeke, written about a hundred years earlier, by George MacDonald, Congregational parson and writer of superb fantasy for both children and adults. I had taken with me to Ohio a small collection of extracts from MacDonald, compiled by C. S. Lewis, and read the following quotation one morning before breakfast, and wrote in my journal that it was vitally important for me to remember it during the two Writer in Residence weeks: "Am I going to do a good deed? Then, of all times,—Father, into thy hands: lest the enemy should have me now."

Just as I had wanted to copy the G. A. Young, Zeke wanted to copy the MacDonald.

"There's one sort of important difference," I said, tentatively, because it was just coming into my conscious mind, and I wasn't sure I could find the right words for it. "George MacDonald implies that as long as we put ourselves into God's hands, then maybe something good *can* happen, not because of us, but because he helps. I have a feeling that if I read only G. A. Young, I'd be terrified ever to enter a classroom again, or start another book." And then I said, "I've just remembered another quotation: this one's from the Psalms. Whenever I'm going to teach a class or give a speech, I always think of it, and hold onto it: Not unto us, O Lord, not unto us, but unto thy Name give the praise; for thy loving mercy, and for thy truth's sake."

"Yes," Zeke said, and marked that down, too.

It was easy to say this to Zeke, because we work from the same premise. It wasn't easy to say it to the entire group. I'm always afraid of sounding pompous, or pious, in the pejorative sense of piosity. When I was an extremely naughty child in an English boarding school, the worst thing that we could call anybody was "pi." I still think it's an abominable characteristic.

And, I suppose, quoting MacDonald and the Psalms, and then sounding off about them myself, I was afraid of looking as though I were going to deliver a mountain and coming forth with a mouse: of being obvious.

I wonder if I will ever learn not to apologize for the obvious?

.. 20 ..

There has been much to teach me about the ontology of things this summer: the blueberry bush; Thomas, the amber cat, and Tyrrell, the large amber dog, diligently washing each other's faces in harmony and amity; the younger members of the Crosswicks family climbing up onto our big four-poster bed for hot chocolate at midnight; the babies' incredibly beautiful bare bodies as I help give them their baths before dinner: all these, and many more awarenesses, are proof of my word for this summer.

It is this kind of awareness which I demand from my students in the seminar in writing practices I give somewhere or other each year. I like the name *writing practices* better than *Creative Writing*. As I have said, nobody can teach creative writing—run like mad from anybody who thinks he can. But one can teach practices, like finger exercises on the piano; one can share the tools of the trade, and what one has gleaned from the great writers: it is the great writers themselves who do the teaching, rather than the leader of a seminar. It doesn't take long for the gifted student to realize that there are certain things the great writers always do, and certain things they never do; it is from these that we learn.

Henry James tells us: *Render, do not report.* The writing of fiction is an entirely different discipline from the writing of journalism, and I have to warn my students that I can teach them nothing about journalism; a journalist *must* report; he tells, rather than shows. The two techniques are almost diametrically opposite. The writer of fiction—and I include in this all the works of the imagination, poetry, plays, realistic novels, fantasy—may never tell; he must show, and show through the five senses. "Describe this room in which we're sitting," I say, "and make use of all five of your senses. Don't tell us. Show us." The beginning writer finds this difficult. I have to repeat and repeat: fiction is built upon the concrete. A news article is essentially transitory and may be built upon sand. The house of fiction must be built upon rock. Feel, smell, taste, hear, see: *show* it.

Dante says: "You cannot understand what I write unless you understand it in a fourfold way: on the literal level, the moral level, the allegorical level, and the anagogical level." What is this anagogical level? It's not easy to define, because it is out of the realm of provable fact. It is most easily discernible in the great works of fantasy, such as Dante's own *Inferno*. The best science fiction is anagogical; the Apocalypse is anagogical. Thinking about icons helps me to understand what Dante meant by the word "anagogical." I do not believe that it is a level that is ever used consciously even by the greatest writers. It is that level of a book which breaks the bounds of time and space and gives us a glimpse of the truth, that truth which casts the shadows into Plato's cave, the shadows which are all we mortals are able to see.

I have had to accept that one cannot talk even in the most technical way about the writing of fiction, without talking about being (the why of the blueberry bush). Even the driest rules of syntax involve, in their explication, a sharing of self. Someone asks, for instance, why we need bother with syntax at all. I reply that Herbert Read says that the only difference between man and beast is syntax; and a hot discussion is on. I would worry more about our digressions if some very fine writing didn't come out of these seminars.

All explanations involve particulars; one cannot render without being specific. Try to explain anything in generalities: it just doesn't work. There are particular rules to the baking of a cake (I can hear my family and friends asking: "How would *you* know? when did you last bake a cake?" I'll tell you about my last cake later; it's important), the cooking of a boeuf bourguignon (I do know how to do that), or the putting together of an automobile engine, or a radio, or a television set. This need for particularity is equally true in storytelling. The great writers start out by giving the reader, immediately, the ontology of the protagonist; or, to put it in the form of a literary rule, a writer should immediately tell the reader four things:

1: Who the story is about.
2: What he is doing.
3: Where he is doing it.
4: When he is doing it.

The reader must be placed in action, space, and time. In a good story we find out very quickly about the hero the things we want to know about ourselves.

One cannot discuss structure in writing without discussing

structure in all life; it is impossible to talk about why anybody writes a book or paints a picture or composes a symphony without talking about the nature of the universe. I warn my students that when I get dogmatic about such weighty matters it is usually when I am most unsure of myself. "Any time I make a categorical statement, and I'm going to make lots of them during these sessions, we had all better beware." I am learning to expect questions I cannot answer—that's easy; I just say that I can't answer them. What is far more difficult is questions I would rather not answer.

A winter ago I had an after-school seminar for high-school students and in one of the early sessions Una, a brilliant fifteen-year-old, a born writer who came to Harlem from Panama five years ago, and only then discovered the conflict between races, asked me out of the blue: "Mrs. Franklin, do you really and truly believe in God with no doubts at all?"

"Oh, Una, I really and truly believe in God with all kinds of doubts."

But I base my life on this belief.

. . 21 . .

Una kept pushing me, wanting to know (I think wanting to be reassured) if I really believed in God. One day she brought it up at the beginning of the class, and the others seemed to want to talk too, so I plunged in: "There are three ways you can live life—three again—remember that the great writers almost always do things in threes. You can live life as though it's all a cosmic accident; we're nothing but an irritating skin disease on the face of the earth. Maybe you can live your life as though everything's a bad joke. I can't."

63

They couldn't, either, though for some of the kids who sat around the table that day not much had happened to make them think that life is anything else.

"Or you can go out at night and look at the stars and think, yes, they were created by a prime mover, and so were you, but he's aloof perfection, impassible, indifferent to his creation. He doesn't care, or, if he cares, he only cares about the ultimate end of his creation, and so what happens to any part of it on the way is really a matter of indifference. You don't matter to him, I don't matter to him, except possibly as a means to an end. I can't live that way, either."

Again there was general agreement.

"Then there's a third way: to live as though you believe that the power behind the universe is a power of love, a personal power of love, a love so great that all of us really *do* matter to him. He loves us so much that every single one of our lives has meaning; he really does know about the fall of every sparrow, and the hairs of our head are really counted. That's the only way I can live."

That seemed to make a certain amount of sense to them, so I thought that it was time to get down to the business of writing practices. Such discussions are inevitable in a writing seminar, and anything that stretches the mind is a help to the potential author. But my main job is to try to share the tools of the trade, so I said, "Now let's talk about punctuation. Punctuation is one of your chief tools in writing a story. I break the rules of punctuation over and over again, but before you may break a rule you must know what it is, and exactly why you're breaking it."

So we did a small run-down on punctuation, and I told them some of the devices I've found useful. When I'm giving conversation in the present I use a double quotation mark: ". When I'm giving conversation in the past of a story, I use a single

64

quotation mark: . And when I'm using interior conversation, interior monologue, I use the French symbol for conversation: —. This saves a lot of "he thought" and "she thought."

I love semicolons and colons. And punctuation serves to indicate rhythm. A semicolon is a longer pause than a comma, and a colon means really sitting back and taking note, but doesn't indicate a conclusion, like a period mark, or, as the English call it, a full stop.

Dashes should be used with respect. I seldom use them in a novel, except in conversation. I love them in letters. Exclamations and italics are like four-letter words, best used very sparingly.

Copy editors, except the present one at F S & G, who is an artist herself, are apt to monkey around with punctuation. You have to watch them like a hawk.

When *A Wrinkle in Time* went into galleys, the copy editor —I'm glad I haven't the faintest idea who it was—had him/herself a ball. First of all, I do spell the English way; I was in an English boarding school when I was twelve, thirteen, and fourteen, and these are the years when spelling gets set. After I had been made to write h-o-n-o-u-r, for instance, a hundred times on a blackboard several hundred times, it was almost impossible for me to spell it h-o-n-o-r. The English use t-o-w-a-r-d-s and we use t-o-w-a-r-d. I like to use them both, depending on the rhythm of the sentence and the letter which begins the following word; sometimes the *s* is needed; sometimes not: this is, I realize, rather erratic, and I can't blame the copy editor who tries to talk me out of it. Then there's *grey*, which is English, and one very definite, bird-wing, ocean-wave color to me; and *gray*, which is American, and a flatter, more metallic color. Then there are the *c* and *s* words, such as practice or practise. About words like these I'm simply in a state of confusion, rather than aesthetic persuasion, as with *grey* or *towards*, and the copy editor can have his way. On the whole I tell the copy editor to go ahead and make the spelling American, but don't muck around with the punctuation.

The worst thing the copy editor did with *A Wrinkle in Time* was with the three strange Mrs Ws. Now, Mr and Mrs are usually spelled Mr and Mrs in England, and Mr. and Mrs. in America. Usually I spell them the American way, or try to remember to. But the Mrs W were extra-special as well as extra-terrestrial, and I very deliberately did not put the period after their Mrs's. With Mr. and Mrs. Murry, who, scientists or no, were solid earth folk, I did put in the period. It was important to me. It was, I should have thought, obvious that it was done with forethought, but the copy editor went through the manuscript and put a period after every Mrs Whatsit, Mrs Who, and Mrs Which.

When I got the galleys I was appalled. I called my editor and told him what had happened. He was sorry, though certainly it was not a matter of vital import to him, as it was to me. He said, "If you insist, we'll take the periods out, but it will cost a fortune." If I insisted I would be acting like an impossible and temperamental author (I am convinced that I am the most gentle, pliable, easily managed author-wife-mother who ever walked the earth), and my editors would not be pleased. And they were taking a risk on a book that almost every other publisher in the business had turned down, and I was more than grateful. So I didn't insist. But it bothered me (it still does).

When the book was done in England, at last I was able to get the punctuation the way I wanted it: joy! though (temperamental author again?) I wasn't wholly satisfied on two counts: the publishers thought the book was too long for English children, and a few cuts were made; they weren't disastrous, but I think they shouldn't have been made; everything that could be cut had already been cut before the original publication. Then, I was asked if I would mind if the setting of the story were identified as being in America. I replied that I didn't think it was very important, but if they felt it to be essential, go ahead.

The first sentence of the book is very carefully and deliberately that old war-horse:

It was a dark and stormy night.

Period. End of sentence. End of paragraph.

The English edition begins, "It was a dark and stormy night in a small village in the United States."

I was naturally delighted when Penguin Publications decided to make a Puffin Book out of it. But lo, the Puffin copy editor took the periods out after Mr. and Mrs. Murry, too.

Ah, well.

TWO

How did we come to spend almost a decade year round at Crosswicks?

We bought the house a few months after we were married, for the astounding sum—astounding even a quarter of a century ago—of sixty-three hundred dollars. *Sic.* It was where we were going to sink our roots deep into the ground; it was our piece of land. I think it meant something unique to me because I had never before lived in a *house*. I was born in New York; we lived in an apartment. In Europe we lived in hotels, or *pensions,* or some kind of rented place which was not our own. When I got out of college I shared an apartment in Greenwich Village with three other girls, then moved to my own. Hugh and I started our married life in an apartment. But Crosswicks was a house, a real house. We planted trees, trees which would take an entire lifetime to mature. The great elms in front of the house, the bridal elms, had been planted as each of the original daughters of the house was married. Our trees, too, were an affirmation. This was where we wanted to raise our family—we hoped for six children.

Hugh was doing well in the theatre, but Crosswicks was too far to commute, and he loved Crosswicks. The spring before his thirty-fifth birthday—we had spent only summers in Crosswicks for the first years—he said that if he were ever to earn a living outside the theatre it would have to be at once, before he was too old. Within a month of that pronouncement I was pregnant with our son, Bion, and this seemed to be the moment to make the decision. But, we discovered, thirty-five is already too old. Hugh had a degree in speech from Northwestern University, but he had no training or degree in engineering or business, which knocked out the possibility of a white-collar job.

So he decided he'd get a blue-collar job and applied at several of the "shops" in Clovenford, the nearest town. When he was given the routine tests he came out as a genius; he was told that he couldn't possibly be put on a machine with that kind of rating. For a while we were near despair. But suddenly we found ourselves the owners of the General Store, a run-down store in the center of the village, the only store. The post office was in it, and people used to pick up a loaf of bread when they got their mail in the morning, or a pack of cigarettes when they got the evening paper. But it had lots of potential. At first Hugh had visions of an old-fashioned general store, with a cracker barrel and jars of licorice sticks. But we aren't on the tourist route. What was needed in the village was a plain, honest-to-goodness grocery store, and if we were to make any kind of a living for ourselves and our children, that was what we had to provide.

We did. Hugh, with no background whatsoever in this area —an actor, from a family of lawyers—built up a splendid business; he wrote and mimeographed a weekly newspaper, giving town news, meetings, birthdays, anniversaries, along with the week's specials. The husband of the soprano with the most beautiful voice in the choir needed a job, and they were talking of leaving town: I couldn't bear losing that voice, so we took Chuck on part-time, very shortly full-time, and within a year he became our butcher, friend, and general uncle; we couldn't have managed without him.

While the store was a-building, Hugh was happy. It was like

a Double-Crostic for him. But a business gets to a plateau; it reaches its peak, and there is no way to go further except to start another store. A chain of stores was hardly what Hugh really wanted. He'd made a success of one store, and that was enough. Our children were out of diapers, and we couldn't have any more babies, so one night I said, "Are you really still happy with the store?" "No. Not now." "Then sell it."

He had left the theatre forever. Forever lasted nine years. We learned a lot in those nine years, and we made friends who are definitely forever.

How to tell a little about those growing years? As I tell my students, one must particularize; show, do not tell. Perhaps if I remember the particular story of the Brechsteins, it will set, a little more clearly, the scene in which Grandma offered me her life.

Whenever anybody moves into a village as small as ours, it's a big event. We all live so close together, we know each other so well, that each new family can actively affect the climate of the town.

I was one of the first to see the Brechsteins. I was at the store as usual during the noon hour, and Wilberforce Smith came in for some teat dilators for his cows and asked if I'd seen the new people who'd bought the old Taylor house. And about an hour later Mrs. Brechstein came in.

She had on tight-fitting orange slacks in a day when women wore slacks because they were convenient to work in, not for chic: it was a little immoral to wear slacks for chic; Mrs. Brechstein's slacks were anything but practical. She wore them with a chartreuse shirt and dangly bronze earrings. Her two little boys had on shabby blue jeans and one of them had a hole in his T-shirt. It wasn't the kind of shabbiness we're used to in this village, where nobody has very much money but neither is anybody destitute. It was ostentatious. It was as much a costume as Mrs. Brechstein's orange pants.

All right, let's be honest. I didn't like her right from the start. There was the way she and the children were dressed—I dress oddly enough; I have a feeling I'm referred to in the village as "Poor Hugh Franklin's wife." There was the way she made me feel a failure; I had a book making the forlorn rounds of many publishing houses, and she managed to rub the rejections in, simply by constantly asking me about something I considered my own business. There was even the way she asked me if our eggs were fresh.

She went back to the meat department that first day, and I could hear her saying that she could get a certain cut of meat cheaper at the A & P. (How can any store with the glorious name of The Great Atlantic and Pacific Tea Company call itself the A & P?) As I was checking her out and putting her purchases in a bag I asked her how they were getting on, if they were getting settled, and if there was anything we could do to help them.

She smiled at me condescendingly and said that if she decided to pick up odds and ends at the store, it might be simpler for her to have a charge account. "The name is Brechstein, you know," she drawled, "and of course we're *so* often confused with the Chosen People, but I assure you that our credit rating is impeccable."

I told her, with what I thought was creditable mildness, that so was the credit of all our Jewish customers.

"But we don't happen to be Jewish," she said, smiling at me tolerantly, as though I hadn't been able to understand her in the first place.

"I'm so sorry," I murmured absently as I rang up the cash register.

As she left, Wilberforce Smith came in again, this time for cigars for himself, and bag balm for his cows, and accompanied by the second selectman, Harry Nottingham. "Seen the Jews who bought the old Taylor house?" Harry asked him.

"Ayeh."

"Putting in two new bathrooms," Harry said. "Must be mighty full of piss."

Well, you see, that's all part of it. I don't mean the Brechsteins. When Hugh and I first took over the General Store there weren't many people around who hadn't been born within ten miles of the Center. And we, like almost all the young couples who moved in shortly after the war, had a naïve idea, as we filled our houses with furniture and furnaces and families, joined the church and the P.T.A., that after a year or so we would no longer be considered newcomers but would be accepted as belonging to the village.

But there's a story, and I doubt if it's apocryphal, of the young couple who moved into a New England village with their infant son. The baby grew up there, lived and worked there, and died in his nineties. He had no immediate family, so the villagers gave him a splendid funeral and erected a monument to him on which they had inscribed: DEARLY BELOVED THOUGH A STRANGER AMONG US.

One day Mrs. Brechstein came into the store and said accusingly, "I hear there was a Republican caucus last night."

"Yes, I believe there was."

"Why weren't we told about it?"

"I suppose for the same reason that we weren't. They didn't want us to know."

"Why on earth wouldn't they want us to know?" It was obvious that she thought newcomers were a lot better qualified than the old Yankees to handle town government. I wasn't sure of that, being an apolitical creature, but I did want the opportunity to know what was going on.

Wilberforce Smith came in then to get his paper. "Ask Mr. Smith," I said. "He used to be a state senator."

So Mrs. Brechstein bustled up to him.

"It was posted on the door of the Town Hall," he growled.

"But who goes and looks at the door of the Town Hall?"

She had a point. When people want anything spread around the village, they don't post a minuscule sign on the door of the Town Hall, hidden by the shadows of the elms. They make three signs, one for the filling station, one for the firehouse, one for the store. I'd offered time and time again to make the signs for town meetings or caucuses.

When I wasn't asked, and blustered to Hugh about the comparative cleanness of Tammany Hall, he said, "Look at it their way. They don't want newcomers butting in and telling them how to run things. You can't blame them. Everybody hates change."

"I don't."

"Sure you do. Remember looking at the baby tonight and saying you hated having him change so quickly? Same difference. And around here everything had been going on peacefully for years and years, and suddenly after the war a lot of people move in who promptly have quantities of small children, and suddenly everybody has to shell out a lot of money for a new school, and taxes go up, and naturally everybody yaps."

He was tactful enough not to mention that his clumsy, five-foot-ten-inch wife, trying unsuccessfully in the store to learn to say "to-may-to" instead of "to-mah-to," reading Schopenhauer behind the counter, or writing in a journal between customers, must have seemed a very peculiar bird to the people who came in to our store.

76

"I think it's un-American," Mrs. Brechstein was saying to Wilberforce Smith. "Positively un-American."

Wilberforce Smith chewed on his cigar and narrowed his eyes. I thought maybe I was going to enjoy a good fight between the two of them, but Wilberforce shrugged and went out.

"I don't understand it," Mrs. Brechstein said. "I don't understand it at all."

I was really on her side, though I wasn't about to admit it. I tried to explain, sounding like a record of Hugh when he talks reasonably to me—something which is necessary far too often. "Well, you can't blame them for resenting it when people like us come along and buy up the big old houses for our families and then splash on fresh coats of white paint a lot of the old people can't afford, and put in flush toilets when they've struggled with outhouses, and buy automatic washing machines and dryers and dishwashers. And now a family has put in a swimming pool. There's been a lot of talk about that swimming pool."

"I don't see why there should be," Mrs. Brechstein said coldly, and I could see she didn't like being included in the "us."

It bothered me as much as it did Mrs. Brechstein. Because we heard plenty in the store. We got it from both sides. We heard people say to us in a perfectly friendly way that everything would be all right if it weren't for the newcomers; but they hadn't forgotten we were newcomers ourselves (my actor husband was a lot better at the role of country storekeeper than I was; he refers to it now as his "longest run"). In a store, of course, the customer is always right, and it was my husband's displeasure I had to live with if I lost my temper there, and not the person whose remarks rankled.

One weekend when the Brechsteins had been in their house for a little over a month, we were invited to dinner by the people with the pool. They lived quite near the Brechsteins, and my hostess told me she'd invited them too. "Aren't they just fascinating?" she asked me. "We're so lucky to have cultured people like that move into town."

Maybe I just see Mrs. Brechstein from the wrong side of the counter.

But that was the night that Mrs. Brechstein made the first of her famous remarks. We'd all been for a swim, and in spite of the warmth of the June evening a cool night breeze had come up, and all of us women congregated in the Pools' lovely bedroom were shivering as we rubbed ourselves down and dressed. We all knew each other pretty well, having moved into town at more or less the same time, and having served together on innumerable church and school committees. I don't think any of us is particularly prudish, but there was something a little too deliberate about the way Mrs. Brechstein walked around stark staring naked and then leaned her elbows on Mrs. Pool's bureau, looking at the pictures of the little Pools, and of Mr. Pool, most handsome in his navy lieutenant's uniform.

Mrs. Brechstein remarked to Mrs. Pool, "For a man who's spent most of his life selling insurance, your husband has quite an interesting mind." But that, though not exactly the epitome of tact, was not the famous remark. I finished dressing and turned to see Mrs. Brechstein, still naked, sitting on Mrs. Pool's bed and pulling one sheer stocking up onto one gloriously tanned leg. Her leg was not the only tanned part of her, and her body did not have the usual white areas.

"Of course every intelligent woman," she was saying, "should have at least one affair after she's married. How else can she possibly continue to interest her husband?"

The words fell like stones into troubled waters.

"Well!" Mrs. Pool exclaimed brightly. "Let's all go downstairs and have some dinner, shall we?"

The next day, almost everyone who was at the party happened to drop in at the store.

"Of course she didn't mean it."

"Oh, yes, she did, she meant every word."

"She was drunk, then."

"No, she wasn't. She was stone-cold sober."

"She drank like a fish."

"She can certainly hold it, you have to say that for her."

"I'm out of luck if that's the only way I can manage to hold on to *my* husband."

I got an earful.

A few days later I got a different kind of earful.

The Brechsteins, like everybody else in the village, new and old (except the Pools) took their children swimming in the pond. Sometimes the mothers swam, too, but most of the time they sat around and kept an eye on the kids and gossiped. If it didn't seem too unfriendly, I sat on a rock a few feet out in the pond and tried to write. And we all tried to welcome the Brechsteins and their two skinny little boys. When the boys threw stones, nobody liked it, but in all honesty the Brechsteins were not the only people around who did not believe in disciplining their kids. Even so, permissive upbringing, much as I disapprove of it, and allowing the tots to express themselves at all costs, seemed to sit even less well on the Brechsteins than on anybody else. However, the thing that stuck most in the craw was their response to such well-intentioned questions as:

"How are you enjoying life in the country?"

"Isn't it much pleasanter than life in the city?"

"Isn't it wonderful for the children here?"

The answers ran something like, "No, we much prefer the city to the country. The children have no cultural opportunities here. There are so few people one can talk with."

Naturally the next thing that happened was someone leaning across the counter saying, "So-and-so is sure the Brechsteins are Communists."

I suppose the same thing happens in many communities; I know it does. But our village is where I've witnessed it happening. The minute Wilberforce Smith and any of his friends and relatives don't like anything a new resident does, out comes the Communist label. Well: Hugh and I had had our share of this kind of gratuitous slander, and it made me feel for the Brechsteins, though it couldn't make me like them.

In the autumn with the start of the school year the Brechstein boys went to the village school; there were quite a few sharp comments about the Brechsteins' actually condescending to send their children to our public school; wouldn't have thought it would be good enough for them. Mrs. Brechstein spoke loudly on all matters at P.T.A. meetings, and Mr. Brechstein joined the volunteer firemen, though he wasn't wanted, which must have been unfortunately obvious. One of the most tactless things he did was to win enormously at the regular weekly firemen's poker game.

One evening about six-thirty, as I was waiting for Hugh to come home, and the children were setting the table, we heard the sickening wail of the fire siren. It was, fortunately, only a chimney fire, but the next morning it was all over town that Mr. Brechstein had been telling the firemen how to do everything. The worst thing about it, Mr. Pool reported, was that the man had some sensible ideas. The firemen had grudgingly followed them and hated him all the more for being right. But Wilberforce Smith leaned over the counter, talking to two of the farmers who happened to be in the store, and said, "Damn' interfering fool doesn't even know what he's talking about. I wouldn't raise a finger to help if his house burned down. Serve him right. We don't want newcomers telling us to do things we can do in our sleep."

The Brechsteins were, of course, atheists, but the little boys wanted to go to Sunday School with their friends, so the parents, after too many too public conversations on the subject, decided it wouldn't contaminate them permanently, and let them go. The next thing we knew, the Brechsteins were single-handedly going from door to door trying to raise money for the fire escape.

We'd all been working in our own quiet ways on that fire escape for some time. It bothered all of us that the inadequate Sunday School facilities, particularly the kindergarten and primary rooms, were fire traps, and we'd been working very hard trying to do something about it. Most New Englanders, including my husband, who may come from Oklahoma but fits well in the New England landscape, will not do today what can be done tomorrow, but we were beginning to make progress. The fire escape was going to be brought up again at the annual church meeting in January, and we all felt that the money would be appropriated and that perhaps we might even get somewhere on building a parish house with proper Sunday School facilities.

When Mr. Brechstein came to our house, full of zeal and enthusiasm and talked about the safety of the kiddies' bodies as well as their souls, I wanted to tell him, Listen, Mr. B., you've just killed all our chances of a fire escape. Don't you, with all your pretensions to intellect and knowledge of psychology, know that if you want to get something like this done in New England (and most likely in Oklahoma and Okinawa, in Nebraska and Nepal, in Georgia, U.S.A., and Georgia, U.S.S.R.)

you have to sell it to a couple of open-minded old residents and let *them* do the canvassing? But he was somehow so pathetically eager, and he looked, with his balding head with the curly dark hair over the ears, so like a spaniel, that I dug down into my pocketbook instead.

"Fire is something you can't be too careful about," Mr. Brechstein said. "Next week we're having our whole house re-wired as a precaution." He then told me that perhaps his wife might find time to read one of my little books when she had finished the stack of important novels by her bed.

Anyhow, most people forgot the fire escape and remembered the Brechsteins.

"I won't have that damned Communist telling me what to do."

"They ought to be driven out of town."

"They better watch out."

Of course Wilberforce Smith and his gang were behind most of the talk, or at least gave it the gentle push that was all that was needed to get it going, and if anybody had asked me whom I liked least, Mr. Brechstein or Wilberforce Smith, I'd have been hard put to it to decide.

One afternoon Mrs. Brechstein dropped into the store for some odds and ends, and nobody else happened to be there.

"Why," she demanded, looking me straight in the eye, "doesn't anybody like us?" I was too embarrassed to say anything. "No, please tell me. We both know it's true. I didn't expect to find intimate friends in a place like this, of course, but—"

"Well, maybe it's because you *did*n't expect to find friends," I said tentatively.

"But it's more than that. I can do without friends, with my

independent mind, but I don't understand the feeling of dislike we get everywhere we go."

"Well," I fumbled, "you know you've talked a good deal about how you bring your children up, about how you never tell them what to do but try unobtrusively to guide their minds to the right decisions? It might be better if you treated everybody else that way, too."

"What do you mean?" she demanded.

"People around here don't like being told what to do. It isn't just the fire escape. It's everything else. You tell us all how we should run our lives, what we should read and what we should think of what we read, and what kind of wall-paper we should use and what colors we should wear, and even who we should go to bed with."

"What do you mean by that last remark?" she snapped. And then to my horror a great tear slipped out of one eye and trick-led down her cheek. "Of course I know what you mean," she said. "I'd had too much to drink and I was scared out of my wits by all of you people who knew each other so well. And I *did* expect to make friends but I didn't know how. So I said it just to bolster my self-confidence. Of course I don't go around hav-ing affairs. I just thought it would make you—make you—" And she rushed out of the store and got in her car and drove off, leaving her bread on the counter.

I was appalled. And ashamed. Surely we should have real-ized. All that brashness. All that arrogance. Just a front, and one we should have been able to see through.

Hugh and I talked it over that evening. Mr. Brechstein had come to him, too, with complaints about the unfriendliness of New Englanders, their lack of hospitality, their suspicious na-tures.

"I don't think I'll ever really like them," I said, "but I do feel terribly sorry for them now. They've managed to hit me so often on my vulnerable spots that I never stopped to look at it from their point of view. Pretty Brechsteiny of me, wasn't it?"

Just after we had first fallen into sleep, that deep, heavy sleep out of which it is almost impossible to rouse, the fire siren started. The wild screech going up and down the scale, up and down, over and over, shattering the peace of the night, pierced insistently through my subconscious, until at last I was aware that I was listening to something. I lay there and started to shiver as I always do when I hear the siren. Up and down, on and on, over and over, the high, penetrating scream probed through sleep. I raised up on one elbow and looked over at Hugh, and he was still sound asleep.

—He's so tired, I thought, —he's been working so hard lately, I can't wake him.

I turned over on my side. Still the siren screamed. —Suppose it was our house, and somebody else's wife said to herself, My husband's so tired, I don't want to get him up to go out in the cold . . .

I took Hugh's shoulder and shook it gently. "Hugh. Hugh. It's the fire siren." He groaned and rolled over. "It's the fire siren," I said again.

Suddenly and all at once he was awake, swinging his legs out of bed, going to the south windows, then the east windows, standing with his bare feet on the ice-cold floor.

"It's in the center, and it's a big fire," he said suddenly, and started to dress.

"Please dress warmly," I begged. "I know you're rushing but please don't forget your boots. You won't be any help to anybody if you freeze." Do *all* men, if their wives don't plead with them, tend to dash out of the house in midwinter as though it were July?

I got out of bed and went to the window, and the east was lit with a great glow. I thought of all the houses in the center, but the bloody smear was so general that it was impossible to tell where the fire actually was. "It looks as though it might be the church," I said.

"If it is, thank God it's at a time when there's nobody in it." Hugh pulled a ski sweater over his head.

"And Mr. Brechstein will be right as usual." I tried to make myself smile. Hugh went downstairs and out into the dark, and I could hear the cold engine of the car cough as he started it. Before he was out of the garage there was the sound of another car hurrying down the road, and then another, from the two farms above us, and then Hugh was following them. I knew that I couldn't go to bed till he got home, so I pulled on my bathrobe and stood again at the east window looking at the horrible red glare. It was so violent that I could see bursts of flame thrusting flares up into the night. The phone rang and I ran to answer it. It couldn't be that something had happened to Hugh; he'd scarcely had time to get to the center.

It was my neighbor up the road. "Madeleine, do you know where the fire is?"

"No. It's in the center. It looks as though it might be the church. Has Howard gone?"

"Ayeh. If you hear where it is, call me, will you?"

"Yes, and same to you, please." I was too nervous to sit down, to read, to try to write. I went to the kitchen and put the kettle on for tea, then went upstairs and checked the children, tucked them in, walked our little boy to the bathroom, tidied up some clothes that had fallen on the closet floor, picked up Raggedy

Ann and tucked her back in beside a small sleeping girl, went back down to the kitchen and drank a cup of tea. There was no possible hope that those flames might be from a chimney fire. I thought of the church, the beautiful church, well over two hundred years old, with the tall white spire visible for miles, with the bell that could be heard for miles too, that tolled for the hours, for births, weddings, deaths.

I looked in the refrigerator to see what I could make into a sandwich for Hugh when he got home. The phone again: my neighbor: "Madeleine, it's not the church. It's down the hill to Brechsteins'."

'I wouldn't raise a finger,' Wilberforce Smith had said, 'if his house burned down.' There had even been some wild talk about burning those Commies out.

The phone again. It would wake the children. But no, the fire alarm had not penetrated their sleep; it would take more than the phone to rouse the children. "It's the Brechsteins'," I was able to say this time.

It takes more than the scream of a fire siren, more than the insistent ring of the phone, to rouse the children. Were those little beasts the Brechstein boys all right? Little beasts or no, the thought of a child in a burning house is an unbearable one. I rushed upstairs to stand looking at our own children, lying safe and sweet in their beds. Naughty and noisy as they might be by day, at night they looked like cherubs; all children do, and I was sure the Brechstein boys were no exception.

My neighbor rang again. "It's the wing of the house. Not a chance of saving it, but they might be able to save the main house."

The wing. The wing was where the boys' bedroom was.

If it weren't for our sleeping children, how many of us would have followed our men over to the fire? We were thinking of

86

the Brechstein boys; we were thinking of our men trying to fight the flames; none of us, native or newcomer, could stop our nervous pacing, and the phone was our only relief from the tension.

"Those boys sleep in the wing."

"Yes. I know."

"Do you suppose they're all right?"

"My Johnny gave Peter Brechstein a bloody nose in school today. The kid asked for it, but now—"

"They've called the Northridge fire department, too."

"Yes, and Clovenford."

I drank another cup of tea. I checked on the children once more. I stood at the window and the glare had died down. There was no longer the bright bursting of flames, and the sky looked only murky and sick, and at last I realized that part of the light was coming from dawn.

A car came up the road, and then another, and then the kitchen door opened and I ran to meet Hugh. His face was black with soot and he looked exhausted. While I fixed him something to eat and drink he began to tell me about it. "It was the wing of the Brechsteins' house. Burned clear down. But they saved the main house. Couldn't possibly have done it if everybody hadn't got there so quickly."

"But the boys, what about the boys?" I asked.

"Wilberforce Smith went in after them," Hugh told me. "Burned his hands badly, too, but the boys weren't touched."

Relief surged through me. "No one was really hurt?"

"No. Everybody's okay. Mr. Brechstein worked like a madman. Everybody did."

"You included," I said.

"A lot of them are still there. Don't dare leave while it's still smoldering."

"How did the fire start?"

"Nobody knows for sure. Probably faulty wiring." He stretched and yawned.

"Try to get a nap," I begged, "before time to get up."

A nap, of course, was all it was, hardly even that, because we simply lay in our big bed holding each other, taking comfort in touch, the beating of the heart, the gentle motion of breath, holding each other in the manner of the human being in time of danger, sorrow, death.

Then there was the usual rush of getting the children ready for school, Hugh off for the store, and then the phone started ringing, and we were all off in a mad whirl of baking pies and cakes for the men still working in the debris of what had been the long white wing of the house, and collecting clothes for the Brechsteins, and cleaning up the main house so that there was no sign of smoke or water or broken windows, and for a few splendid days thousands of cups of coffee were swallowed and all the tensions were miraculously eased, and the church women held a kitchen shower for the Brechsteins because the kitchen had been in the wing, and Mrs. Brechstein managed not to put her foot in her mouth, and people forgot for an evening who was old and who was new and nobody called anybody else a Communist. It was at least a week before somebody came into the store and said angrily, "Did you hear what the Brechsteins did *now*?"

Perhaps New Englanders are unfriendly, and perhaps I'll never understand or like either the Brechsteins or Wilberforce Smith, and perhaps we'll never feel anything but newcomers in this tight little community.

But where, after we have made the great decision to leave the security of childhood and move on into the vastness of maturity, does anybody ever feel completely at home?

Children and grownups ask me the same questions about my stories, though children, less inhibited, ask more: How old are you? How much money do you make?

One standard question from young and old is: Do you write about real people, and about what really happened?

The answer is no. But also yes. My husband says, and I'm afraid with justification, that by the time I've finished a book I have no idea what in it is fabrication and what is actuality; and he adds that this holds true not only for novels but for most of my life. We do live, all of us, on many different levels, and for most artists the world of imagination is more real than the world of the kitchen sink.

When my mother apologizes for the many things that gave me a childhood that was rather different from the normal, happy, American ideal, I try to convince her of my immense gratitude. She at least has to admit that I've got a lot of material for a lot of books out of it, because every single one of my adolescent heroines is based on my own experience.

When someone comes in to me when I'm deep in writing, I have a moment of frightening transition when I don't know where I am, and then I have to leave the "real" world of my story for what often seems the less real world, the daily, dearly loved world of husband and children and household chores.

Perhaps the story of the Brechsteins will help sort things out. There are, in one sense, no Brechsteins. I think I made the name up. If we must be psychoanalytical about why I made up that particular name, it was, I fancy, because I was having trouble with my piano—keys stuck, strings broke—and I dreamed of a Steinway or a Bechstein grand. Their story is just one of a series of sketches I wrote one winter of inner and outer cold, and it's hardly even a story. I wrote it over a decade ago, while we were still living year round in the country, so I'm more able to be objective about it than something written more recently, and it is, in its setting, more overtly autobiographical than most of my stories.

But with this sketch, as with all my stories, the idea simply comes to me and asks to be written; all I am aware of, on the conscious level of writing, is the story, and the imaginary people in it, and if I have, in fact, written from "real life" I'm usually not aware of it for months—or years.

All right. Our house is our house. The store is our store. My husband and I are ourselves. The emotional premise of the sketch, the feeling of being a stranger and sojourner—all this is true. This is the way it is. We did have a difficult time getting a fire escape for the second floor of the church, though probably most of us have forgotten it by now; it's only this story which makes me remember it, and I haven't thought about it for years, or how desperately important it was to us then.

We also have a parish house, and notices for town meetings and caucuses are posted where everybody will see them. But there will always, I suspect, be a line, bridgeable but always there, between old and new members in every small community.

There is no Wilberforce Smith. He is totally unlike the two fine first selectmen we have known since we bought Crosswicks. If I try hard to pin him down, he might be a mixture of two or three different people who came into the store, but I'm not really sure, and from my point of view it doesn't matter, because who he is is Wilberforce Smith.

As for the Brechsteins, there was a new family in town, from Chicago, who were resented and called Communists because they tried to push World Federalism at a time when an interest in the United Nations was considered un-American. Then there was another family, in the village for one summer only, a mother, father, and barely adolescent girl. The wife had written a scholarly book on the number of times contemporary writers use eight-letter words (or something like that; she used a computer); the husband was a sociologist. We had been asked to be nice to them, to help them feel at home, and I looked forward to someone who might enjoy talking about writing and music.

They turned out to be Brechsteiny, all right. Our girls and their friends finally stopped trying to get along with the "Brechstein" girl, and I thought they were noble to try as long as they did. Mrs. Brechstein certainly made me feel obvious, to say the least. I was not, she made it clear, her intellectual equal, and when she pontificated about her book she bored me, and everybody else. Mr. Brechstein looked down on Hugh for running a grocery store. I think that Mrs. Brechstein actually did make the famous remark about the necessity for a wife to have an affair, but I'm not sure. At the end of the summer they left the village and our lives, and I wish them well.

The fire siren always sends chills of terror through me. There was a night when it blew, when I did not want to pry Hugh out of his needed sleep, when the sky to the east was lit with flame and we did not know, for a long time, where the fire was, when it might have been the church, or any of the houses in the center, when I did all the things that the me of the Brechstein sketch did. It was not a house, after all, but a barn; bad enough, for the loss of a barn is disastrous for a farmer; and not all the cows were saved.

In writing about the Brechsteins I was writing about all kinds of things which were on my mind, my conscious, sub-, and super-conscious mind. After I had finished it, and the story itself reminded me that we are all strangers and sojourners on this earth, I was far more reconciled to not knowing about a Republican caucus than I had been before—though it didn't stop me from trying to make such meetings generally known. I have my own idea of what is American.

A note about our village here, our beloved village which can always be counted on to come through in time of crisis. Maybe Wilberforce Smith is everybody who makes me angry with self-centered narrow-mindedness and then undoes me utterly by an act of selfless nobility, such as Wilberforce going into the burning house for the little boys. When Senator Joe McCarthy began making his Communist accusations on television, we thought we'd hear a lot of pro-McCarthy talk in the store: but no: the Yankee sense of fair play came to the fore. McCarthy had gone too far. For a long time after his obscenities there were no more accusations around here of Communism.

A village is very much like boarding school (I was in boarding schools for ten years, so I know whereof I talk): let any threat come from outside, and everybody, old and new, Republican and Democrat, white-collar worker or blue, will band together.

Perhaps that is what our divided world needs now: a threat from outside. Certainly, as one good American said, if we do not hang together we will hang separately.

. . 3 . .

Thinking about the Brechsteins, attempting the not-quite possible task of separating fact from fiction in this sketch, teaches me something about the nature of reality. On one level, one might say that the Brechsteins are not real. But they are. It is through the Brechsteins, through the world of the imagination which takes us beyond the restrictions of provable fact, that we touch the hem of truth. The world we live in, the world we are able to know with our intellect, is limited and bounded by our finiteness. We glimpse reality only occasionally, and for me it happens most often when I write, when I start out using all the "real" things which my senses and my mind can know, and then suddenly a world opens before me.

Reality: I can only affirm that the people in my stories have as complete and free a life of their own as do my family and friends; to the extent that they become alive for the reader, the story has succeeded. For me, this says a lot about the nature of reality.

The only inadvertent exceptions I've made to my usual unknowing where or from whom my characters spring, are Rob Austin, who simply is our youngest child, and there's nothing I can do about it; and Canon Tallis, who walked, unexpected, into J.F.K. Airport when Adam Eddington was waiting to fly to Lisbon. If I tried consciously to write about an actual person, I would be limited by that person; the character could not do anything that the person, as far as I understand him, would not do. But an imaginary character is not limited; he does and says all kinds of things I don't expect, and often don't want. When a character wants to do one thing and I want him to do another, the character is usually right.

But I don't suppose it's possible for a writer to create a wholly imaginary character. Whether we are aware of it or not, we are drawing from every human being we have ever known, have passed casually in the street, sat next to on the subway, stood behind in the check-out line at the supermarket. Perhaps one might say that we draw constantly from our subconscious minds, and undoubtedly this is true, but more important than

93

that is the super-conscious level which comes to our aid in writing—or painting or composing—or teaching, or listening to a friend.

When I was writing *The Arm of the Starfish*, I had the story thoroughly plotted, and there was no Joshua Archer in it. Nevertheless, when Adam Eddington woke up in the Ritz Hotel in Lisbon, there was a young man sitting in his room, a young man named Joshua Archer, and Joshua was as much of a surprise to me as he was to Adam, and he changed the plot radically. He made me rewrite at least half the book.

But I do have to know, with all five senses, the places in which these unpredictable people move. When I was working on the story of Mariana Alcoforado, the Portuguese nun, I realized that I couldn't possibly get really deep into it until I had been to Portugal, to Beja, where Mariana's convent was, until I had touched, tasted, smelled, heard, seen. I had been thinking of Portugal as something like the South of France, which I knew with my senses, but I was aware that this wasn't good enough. When some movie money came through, Hugh said, "All right, now we'll go to Portugal."

We left two days after Christmas, sending our children back here to stay with friends. We were in Portugal ten days, ten intensely profitable days, because I got two books out of it, *The Love Letters* and *The Arm of the Starfish*. Our plane, like Adam's, could not land in Lisbon because of the fog, and went on to Madrid; like Adam, we spent the day in the Prado. We, too, took a bumpy Caravelle back to Lisbon. We stayed in the Ritz for two nights, so I knew what that room where Joshua appeared was like. On our way back from the south of Portugal we stayed at the Avenida Palace, where Adam went after Poly had disappeared from the Caravelle; the room in which Dr. O'Keefe told him to wait was the room in which we stayed.

During those ten days I wrote over two hundred pages of journal.

"Turn out the light," Hugh would sometimes say, testily.

"I can't, I haven't got it all down yet."

"Write it tomorrow."

"I can't, I have to do it now, while it's still alive."

He is very good about understanding, and even encouraging, this.

. . 4 . .

An author is responsible for his characters in much the same way that a parent is for his children, or a teacher for his students. Sometimes this manifold responsibility weighs heavily on me; I want to retreat entirely, lest I do damage. But we have to accept the stark fact that we not only can but inevitably will do damage. It's that Omaha psychiatrist versus George Mac-Donald, perhaps?

At a meeting of the Children's Book Committee of the Authors Guild a couple of winters ago, we had a hot argument about this. The kind of responsibility I'm thinking about is both difficult and dangerous, especially where it affects children. But we're living in a difficult and dangerous world, and no amount of sticking our heads in the sand is going to make it any easier. Western man has tried for too many centuries to fool himself that he lives in a rational world. No. There's a story about a man who, while walking along the street, was almost hit on the head and killed by an enormous falling beam. This was his moment of realization that he did not live in a rational world but a world in which men's lives can be cut off by a random blow on the head, and the discovery shook him so deeply that he was impelled to leave his wife and children, who were the major part of his old, rational world. My own response to the wild unpredictability of the universe has been to write stories, to play the piano, to read, listen to music, look at paintings—not that the world may become explainable and reasonable but that I may rejoice in the freedom which unaccountability gives us.

We sat there in the Authors Guild, looking out the windows to a stricken city, paralyzed at that time by a strike of fuel-oil deliverers in the midst of a flu epidemic; people were dying because of this strike, dying for fringe benefits, mostly people in the ghetto parts of the city where landlords don't care whether the buildings are heated or not. Only a short while behind us— and ahead of us—were other strikes, garbage-collector strikes (we keep having these, and the city gets more and more attractive to rats, rodent and human); student strikes; teacher strikes; phone-company strikes; welfare-recipient strikes; transit strikes; you name it, we've had it—or we will have it. I sometimes wonder if the ancient Romans were as aware of their crumbling civilization as we New Yorkers can't help being of ours; did they, too, sometimes sit around a candlelit dinner table with friends, and wonder how many times they would be able to meet thus; did they, too, draw closer together because of the anger and dark outside?

We, of the Children's Book Committee, sat in our pleasant skyscraper room and discussed a possible program for the next meeting of the Guild. I suggested that we ask each other, "What is the responsibility of the writer today?"

Someone asked—I think it was Ann Petry or Elizabeth George Speare, two of the writers I most admire: "Do you mean as a person or as a writer?"

I tried to explain that I, for one, was not separable. I can't, as I think I've made plain, be pulled apart like a jigsaw puzzle that can be dismantled and then put back together again. I am, for better or worse, writer, wife, mother, and all these bits of me are inseparably blended to make up the human being who is—or who is not—responsible.

"But books are a story," someone else said. "That's what they have to be: entertainment. They shouldn't be anything else."

Well, of course. The story comes, and it is pure story. That's all I set out to write. But I don't believe that we can write any kind of story without including, whether we intend to or not, our response to the world around us.

The writing of a book may be a solitary business; it is done alone. The writer sits down with paper and pen, or typewriter, and, withdrawn from the world, tries to set down the story that is crying to be written. We write alone, but we do not write in isolation. No matter how fantastic a story line may be, it still comes out of our response to what is happening to us and to the world in which we live.

Last summer in England, when I was talking at the college where Alan is teaching, someone said, "But what about the mystery writers? They don't make any response to the problems of the world in their stories." And I cried, "Oh, but they do!" and cited some of my favorite writers, Josephine Tey, John Dickson Carr, Dorothy Sayers—I could go on and on—and said, "Think about them. Their mysteries may be nothing but exciting stories on the surface, but there's a definite moral response to the world in every single one of the really good ones."

It wasn't till this summer that it occurred to me that most of my favorite mystery writers are English, and use the language literately; their syntax is not an insult to the reader. Even more important, most of them write out of a belief in a universe created by a God of love.

Something odd and sad: I originally wrote that many of my

favorite mystery writers were practicing Christians, and two people whose opinion I respect told me that the word "Christian" would turn people off. This certainly says something about the state of Christianity today. I wouldn't mind if to be a Christian were accepted as being the dangerous thing which it is; I wouldn't mind if, when a group of Christians meet for bread and wine, we might well be interrupted and jailed for subversive activities; I wouldn't mind if, once again, we were being thrown to the lions. I do mind, desperately, that the word "Christian" means for so many people smugness, and piosity, and holier-than-thouness. Who, today, can recognize a Christian because of "how those Christians love one another"?

No wonder our youth is confused and in pain; they long for God, for the transcendent, and are offered, far too often, either piosity or sociology, neither of which meets their needs, and they are introduced to churches which have become buildings that are a safe place to go to escape the awful demands of God.

As for the mystery writers, I stand by what I said: no one whose life is not based on the faith that the universe is in the hands of a responsible God would dare to become so intimately involved with death, and the evil in men's hearts.

To be responsible means precisely what the word implies: to be capable of giving a response. It isn't only the Flower Children or Hell's Angels who are opting out of society. A writer who writes a story which has no response to what is going on in the world is not only copping out himself but helping others to be irresponsible, too. I mentioned that all of us on the Children's Book Committee *do* give our response to the world around us in our books, even if only by implication. I brought up several books written by the members of the committee, books which are perfect examples of the kind of responsibility I am talking about, and added, "You're my friends, and you've read *The Young Unicorns* [it had recently been published]; you know there's more than just the story. If what I have to say is right, or if it is wrong, I'm responsible for it, and I can't pretend that I'm not, just because it's difficult."

To refuse to respond is in itself a response. Those of us who write are responsible for the effect of our books. Those who teach, who suggest books to either children or adults, are responsible for their choices. Like it or not, we either add to the darkness of indifference and out-and-out evil which surround us or we light a candle to see by.

We can surely no longer pretend that our children are growing up into a peaceful, secure, and civilized world. We've come to the point where it's irresponsible to try to protect them from the irrational world they will have to live in when they grow up. The children themselves haven't yet isolated themselves by selfishness and indifference; they do not fall easily into the error of despair; they are considerably braver than most grownups. Our responsibility to them is not to pretend that if we don't look, evil will go away, but to give them weapons against it.

One of the greatest weapons of all is laughter, a gift for fun, a sense of play which is sadly missing from the grownup world. When one of our children got isolated by a fit of sulks, my husband would say very seriously, "Look at me. Now, don't laugh. Whatever you do, don't laugh." Nobody could manage to stay long-faced for very long, and communication was reestablished. When Hugh and I are out of sorts with each other, it is always laughter that breaks through the anger and withdrawal.

Paradox again: to take ourselves seriously enough to take ourselves lightly. If every hair of my head is counted, then in the very scheme of the cosmos I matter; I am created by a power who cares about the sparrow, and the rabbit in the snare, and the people on the crowded streets; who calls the stars by name. And you. And me.

When I remember this it is as though pounds were lifted from me. I can take myself lightly, and share in the laughter of the white china Buddha on my desk.

. . 5 . .

A spring ago, on the Sunday which in the calendar of the church is called Pentecost, the young people's group conducted the worship service. The church stands in the center of the village, a white colonial building with pillars, a proper fire escape, and a tall spire; someone once told me that it is the tallest spire in the state. The interior, alas, was redone during the worst excesses of Victorianism, but it is still a dignified and austere place of worship.

The young people started their service with a pop record about the need for love to conquer hate. As the record played, they danced in the chancel, improvising their steps and movements to what each one felt the record was saying. I was sitting towards the front, but the sense of shock behind me was tangible. I didn't need to turn around to realize that at least one person was getting up and walking out. When the record was over, one of the girls, a senior in high school, went to the lectern and told us that the Pilgrim Fellowship was not there to shock the congregation but to try to explain what was on their minds, to try to communicate to the grownups what they were feeling. And she talked about the importance of being an individual. She cared passionately.

I had sung with this girl's mother in choir. I had felt a helpless anguish when the oldest little girl, who should now be in college, died of cancer. What was being said from the lectern by this high-school senior came from everything her growing up had taught her. But someone else left the church.

Then one of the boys came forward. His mother, too, had been in the choir; we had carried our youngest children at the same time. I had watched him learn to walk and talk; our boys have been friends all their lives. What he had to say on this Pentecost was that he was no longer able to believe in the god who is talked about in church and Sunday School. If he was to believe in God, he had to find him in people, and he found him when he walked alone in the woods. Someone else walked out.

Then our nearest neighbor's boy, our son's close friend, came forward. He talked about war, and killing, and napalm bombs and burning babies and killing, killing, killing, and more people left.

Then the young people, still trying, came down into the congregation to pass the peace, the old tradition of the early centuries, where each person in the congregation turns to his neighbor, takes his hand, or embraces him, saying, "Peace be with you."

But by then the abyss between adolescent and adult was too great to be bridged.

On the first Pentecost, people of many races and languages were together, and each spoke in his own tongue, and everybody was able to understand everybody else. And here we were on Pentecost two thousand years later and there had been no understanding at all.

Most of the village was as much shocked by the lack in communication as by what some considered irreverence on the part of the young people. For the rest of the spring and summer Quinn held open meetings every other Sunday evening, where the generations could get together to try to communicate. This isn't always easy, and it isn't only the middle-aged who refuse to listen, who will not even try to understand another point of view. One boy would not get it through his head that for all adults God is not necessarily an old man in a white beard and nightgown sitting on a cloud. As far as this boy was concerned, this old gentleman was the adult's god, and therefore he did not believe in God. There were some parents who felt that love of country implies no freedom to criticize the country; I wonder if they also felt that to criticize or attempt to correct their children meant that they did not love them? This isn't what love means.

But at least people came to these meetings; they tried; and we got enough laughter out of the extremists—who didn't like being thought amusing—so that the laughter itself helped us knock down walls. And our varied languages were no longer quite so incomprehensible.

.. 6 ..

Last spring I conducted a seminar through the auspices of the P.E.N. and the Cathedral. The seminar was black, Wasp, Jew, Oriental, and this is the way I most like it to be, for this very diversity helps break down prejudice; if I—inevitably—become involved with the members of a seminar, so do they with each other. It wasn't long before we all knew each other by name, which meant that Una was Una first and black and militant second; that Jock was Jock first and privileged and Wasp second; that he could say, after hearing Una read a tragic story out of her own experience, "Una, I really envy you; that's awful, all that, but it makes me realize how sheltered I've been." Una, in her turn, for the first time saw some of her experiences as valuable in her understanding of herself and the world around her, saw and felt the extraordinary hope that comes from experience which comes from tribulation. We all asked, "Why is it that we learn from the things which hurt us? Why do we need pain before we can grow?" There aren't any easy answers to this one, but all artists know the truth of it, and not only artists: it was Jung who said that there is no coming to life without pain.

I learned from Una, from Jock, from all of them. One of the best things about these kids is that they don't worry about hurting any adult's feelings when they talk about the world we've made for them to live in. We've made a mess of it, there's no evading that. Nevertheless, no matter what we think of our educational system, more people today are literate than ever before. On the whole, even in desperate areas of poverty, most children have access to television sets, which—despite the mediocrity of many programs—give them a more sophisticated knowledge of what is going on in all corners of the world than any previous generation ever had. Because of our extraordinary technological advances in the last few decades, more opportunities are open to more young people than ever before.

But talk with them. What have we educated them for? Have we given them too heavy a diet materially and neglected them spiritually? They have a sense of eschatology (another of those *ology* words: the word about the end of time, the word about the last things) that my generation, even growing up into the Second World War, didn't experience. This spring our eleventh-grade son, calling home from boarding school, kept saying, "I don't have time," which is how many young people feel: if they aren't killed in a war which they don't understand, they'll die of lung cancer from the polluted environment, or radiation effects from milk containing Strontium 90, or simply rainfall or snowfall.

There was one snowfall at the Cathedral this winter which was a horrifying illustration of our ecology. I spend eight hours a day in the library of the Cathedral; I wandered in several years ago to write—there were too many disturbances at home —and became librarian by default. I have no qualifications, but I had no qualifications as choir director, either. And it is a perfect place for me, a big room full of books, including a splendid reference section; bay windows looking across the Close to the Cathedral itself; and an aura which says to me: Write.

Una, when asked to describe the library, where we held our seminar sessions, wrote, "When I walk in here I feel I can be myself." So do I. And it is run on the academic year, so I am free for our Crosswicks summers.

Back to the snowfall and ecology: I am allowed to bring my dogs to work with me. They lie quietly on a blanket by my desk; they are obedient and know that they are not allowed to jump up when someone comes in; and most people love them almost as much as I do. Just outside the library is a large fenced-in stretch of greensward, known as the Canon's Green, where all the Cathedral dogs romp. My dogs have many friends: Monarch, the bishop's corgi; Cynthia's two dachshunds; and Oliver and Tyrrell's greatest friend is Fritz, Tallis's Weimaraner, the size of a great Dane.

On the afternoon after this particular snowfall, Fritz and Tyrrell had a glorious time romping, taking great bites of snow, throwing it at each other, rolling in it. Oliver, our ancient collie, now dead of dignified old age, was feeling much too arthritic to do anything but stand and watch tolerantly. Later in the afternoon Tyrrell vomited, and so did Fritz. Tallis called our veterinary friend, who said that it was the snow; he'd had any number of calls from people complaining that their dogs had been throwing up. I told my husband when I got home that evening, and he said, "Last night when I was in Riverside Park walking the dogs, the snow looked so pure and beautiful that I held up my face and opened my mouth to it. How horrible to think that we can't do that any more."

Our children used to eat the snow when they were little, here at Crosswicks (maybe it's still all right here); we made toffee in it. Is Josephine going to have to say to her babies, "Be careful not to get the snow in your mouth, it might kill you"?

This sense of urgency has always been with my children, and those I work and talk with. They've grown up knowing that at any moment we could blow up our planet if some madman pushes the wrong button. During the Cuban crisis, when our youngest child was a second grader, we were listening to the news and when the weather report was announced he said, "Storms tomorrow. If there is a tomorrow."

Children, not without reason, blame the adults. But they want to talk about it with us, which is, in itself, an advance and a development. I know that I'm lucky when we talk, because the fact that they've read my books and responded to them means that walls between us are already down. During my happy day at Sidwell Friends School, several of the high-school students said to me, "We can't talk to our parents because they don't remember what it was like to be our age."

Memory is one of the most essential of the writer's tools, and a writer finds it easy to have total recall, just as other people find it easy to balance a checkbook—something entirely beyond my capacity. But the adolescents today are concerned over a general lack of memory in their parents and teachers, and it is this forgetfulness of what it is like to be twelve, or seventeen, or twenty-one, that is largely responsible for the famous generation gap. The young look at the amnesiac over-thirties and say, "We look at the adults around us, and if this is what it means to be grownup, then we say, No! We don't ever want to be like most of the adults we see."

So they dress as differently from us as they possibly can; they wear wild hairdos and symbolic jewelry; in a secular world they are crying out for transcendence; they try to get our attention in the most extreme ways; if we don't listen, they throw a bomb.

Una and I talked about this. She allied herself with the militants, and yet, with her open, loving face she talked to me about it. I said one day, "I can see you getting frustrated enough to throw a bomb, Una, but I can't see you throwing it in a building with anybody in it." We both did a lot of thinking about how far frustration can legitimately push us.

So the challenge I face with children is the redemption of adulthood. We must make it evident that maturity is the fulfillment of childhood and adolescence, not a diminishing; that it is an affirmation of life, not a denial; that it is entering fully into our essential selves.

I don't go along with the people who say they'd never want to live their childhoods again; I treasure every bit of mine, all the pains as well as the joy of discovery. But I also love being a grownup. To be half a century plus is wonderfully exciting, because I haven't lost any of my past, and am free to stand on the rock of all that the past has taught me as I look towards the future.

The youngsters' rejection of adults often shocks us so much that we in turn reject the rejection and are angered at the violent means by which they repudiate parents and teachers. They drop out of school and college because it just doesn't seem worthwhile. Or they want a college degree without having to work for it. Or they have trial marriages, or just share a pad, rather than entering into relationships which are intended to last for life, often following the example of parents who have separated or divorced, with the concomitant philosophy that if you try marriage and it doesn't work, you quit. They are rebelling not against our morality and discipline but against our lack of morality and our lack of discipline. They are unwilling to commit themselves with promises of fidelity in relationships because they have known too many grownups make these promises and then break them as though they didn't matter. Somehow or other, promises, as well as adulthood, must be redeemed. My seminar students asked me, "But isn't it better not to make the promises at all? Isn't it more honest?"

I shook my head. "No. I don't think so. And I think I do have a right to talk to you about this, because I've been married to the same man for almost twenty-five years, and we love each other more now than we did twenty-five years ago. When we were married we made promises, and we took them seriously. No relationship between two people which is worth anything is static. If a man and wife tell me they've never had a quarrel, I suspect that something is festering under the skin. There've been a number of times in my marriage when—if I hadn't made promises—I'd have quit. I'm sure this is equally true of Hugh; I'm not an easy person to live with."

I'm quite sure that Hugh and I would never have reached the relationship we have today if we hadn't made promises. Perhaps we made them youthfully, and blindly, not knowing all that was implied; but the very promises have been a saving grace.

It is generally accepted that youngsters, and not only those from the inner city but also those from the affluent suburbs and ex-urbs, are experimenting with sex and drugs, hard drugs. One bitter reason is that our country in general assumes that "the pursuit of happiness" really means "the pursuit of pleasure" and that therefore pleasure is the greatest good. For every discomfort there is a pill. Half the ads in our glossy magazines are for hard liquor: You're depressed? Get sloshed; feel good. Drink this, eat that, swallow the other, and your sex appeal will rise. Stay young, don't grow up, avoid contamination with death: have fun, fun, fun.

If pleasure is the greatest good, then why not seek it in drugs?

Another cause is the need of the human being for loyalty. Where home loyalties are lost, the drug subculture is an alternative. With the breakdown of close-knit family life, kids are desperately searching for new relationships. Small houses with no room for grandparents or stray aunts and uncles; fathers whose jobs keep them on the move—all this, as well as the shattering of families by divorce, has denied children the security of growing up in a close family unit, and they have to search desperately for another group to which they can be committed. There is no lack of commitment in the Black Panthers, or the Young Lords, or even Hell's Angels.

Then there's the need for adventure; we're not providing legitimate adventure for many of them: how many ghetto high-school kids can qualify for the Peace Corps or Vista? so they seek adventure illegitimately.

There have been a number of times during the past years when one of my "children" has come into the library, puttered around the bookshelves until we were alone, and then sat by my desk to talk about love: should I sleep with him? does he love me? is this girl just having me on? what do you really think about marriage? every boy you go out with expects you to make out, all the way; the girls want anything they can get out of you, but I think this one is different; how do you know if you're pregnant? my parents don't like her, they think she's a tramp, but she isn't, and I love her.

They really don't want me to answer their questions, nor should I. If I have not already answered them ontologically, nothing I say is going to make any sense. Where I can be of use is in being willing to listen while they spread their problem out between us; they can then see it themselves in better perspective.

But over the years two questions of mine have evolved which make sense to me.

I ask the boy or girl how work is going: Are you functioning at a better level than usual? Do you find that you are getting more work done in less time? If you are, then I think that you can trust this love. If you find that you can't work well, that you're functioning under par, then I think something may be wrong.

A lovely example of this is Josephine: the spring she and Alan were engaged, when she was eighteen and a sophomore at Smith, they found out that they could not possibly be apart more than two weeks at a time; either Alan would go up to Northampton, or Josephine would come down to New York.

She knew that she would be getting married ten days after the close of college. And her grades went steadily up.

The other question I ask my "children" is: what about your relations with the rest of the world? It's all right in the very beginning for you to be the only two people in the world, but after that your ability to love should become greater and greater. If you find that you love lots more people than you ever did before, then I think that you can trust this love. If you find that you need to be exclusive, that you don't like being around other people, then I think that something may be wrong.

This doesn't mean that two people who love each other don't need time alone. Two people in the first glory of new love must have great waves of time in which to discover each other. But there is a kind of exclusiveness in some loves, a kind of inturning, which augurs trouble to come.

Hugh was the wiser of the two of us when we were first married. I would have been perfectly content to go off to a desert isle with him. But he saw to it that our circle was kept wide until it became natural for me, too. There is nothing that makes me happier than sitting around the dinner table and talking until the candles are burned down.

I have been wondering this summer why our love has seemed deeper, tenderer than ever before. It's taken us twenty-five years, almost, but perhaps at last we are willing to let each other be; as we are; two diametrically opposite human beings in many ways, which has often led to storminess. But I think we are both learning not to chafe at the other's particular isness. This is the best reason I can think of why ontology is my word for the summer.

A Russian priest, Father Anthony, told me, "To say to anyone 'I love you' is tantamount to saying 'You shall live forever.' "

I am slowly beginning to learn something about immortality.

Our children are hungry for words like Father Anthony's. They have a passionate need for the dimension of transcendence, mysticism, way-outness. We're not offering it to them legitimately. The tendency of the churches to be relevant and more-secular-than-thou does not answer our need for the transcendent. As George Tyrrell wrote about a hundred years ago, "If [man's] craving for the mysterious, the wonderful, the supernatural, be not fed on true religion, it will feed itself on the garbage of any superstition that is offered to it."

Hence the interest in mind-expanding drugs, in black magic, occultism, and a kind of superficial Buddhism or Hinduism, as though these totally demanding disciplines could be mastered overnight. And everybody, it seems, is looking to the stars, towards astrology and the occult in general. A friend and I recently had a talk which clarified a few things for me. He told me about going into a Doubleday bookstore and seeing, over the section marked RELIGION, a handwritten card: OCCULT. When he next went to that bookstore, RELIGION was gone: OCCULT was in.

I started going on in high philosophical vein about what a snare and a delusion this is, and could see that he thought I wasn't being very bright.

Suddenly I said, "Hey, I think I know why astrology has such tremendous appeal. The year and month and day you are born matters. The very moment you are born matters. This gives people a sense of their own value as persons that the church hasn't been giving them."

"Now," he said, "you're cooking with gas."

To matter in the scheme of the cosmos: this is better theology than all our sociology. It is, in fact, all that God has promised to us: that we matter. That he cares. As far as I know, no great prophet has promised people that God will give them social justice, though he may have threatened doom and extinction if the people themselves don't do something about it. If God cares about us, we have to care about each other.

Sociology is rational. God is not.

God knows the very moment we are born.

<hr />

.. 9 ..

We often respond to the rejection and contempt of youth towards parents by such thoughts as: Why would my child feel or act this way? I've always given him everything he wants. I've made do with less just so he could have a good allowance and all the clothes and cars he wants. I haven't made harsh rules; he can stay out as late as he likes, and I never question who he's with. And this is the thanks I get.

Happily, more and more of us are coming to realize that such a parent is an ogre to the under-thirties. This kind of parent has given the child all the material goods of the world and not enough of the structured and disciplined love that would make the child truly free. Such a parent has earned, instead of the respect and admiration he was trying to buy, nothing but distrust and contempt. He is the "ugly adult" the child does not want to become.

What about the mothers who loathe the thought of getting old, who think it a disgrace to look or act their age, as though becoming mature were something to be ashamed of instead of rejoiced in, mothers who pride themselves on dressing like their teenage daughters, and consider it a compliment when people say they look like sisters. Perhaps the daughter doesn't want a sister; perhaps she wants a mother. Here I am grateful for my resemblance to the giraffe—this is one temptation not available to me. On the rare occasions when someone, thinking to flatter and please, has made the "more like a sister than her mother" remark, my reaction has been rejection. I'd far rather be a reasonable-looking fifty-one than a raddled thirty.

And what about the men who make a fetish of being hearty pals to their sons? What sixteen-year-old boy wants a forty-year-old man as a pal? I'm not talking about friendship; that's something else again. Maybe he'd rather have a father instead, a father who, with love, says, You may go this far and no further, a father who makes rules and sets limits, who, when he says no, means no. Friendship, regardless of chronology, is based on mutual respect.

There's enough French in my blood for me to agree with the European attitude that the very young can be charming and delightful and pretty but only a mature woman can be beautiful; and only a mature man can be strong enough to be truly tender.

Jung disagreed with Freud that the decisive period in our lives is the first years. Instead, Jung felt that the decisive period is that in which my husband and I are now, the period of our middle years, when we have passed through childhood with its dependency on our parents; when we've weathered the storms of adolescence and the first probings into the ultimate questions; when we've gone through early adulthood with its problems of career and marriage and bringing up our babies; and for the first time in our lives find ourselves alone before the crucial problem of who, after all these years, we are. All the protective covering of the first three stages is gone, and we are suddenly alone with ourselves and have to look directly at the great and unique problem of the meaning of our own particular existence in this particular universe.

The breakup of many marriages at precisely this point is another symptom of our refusal to accept this vitally important period of our lives. We have—particularly in the United States, particularly in the suburbs—allowed ourselves to live in a child-centered world; the children have become more important to the parents than the parents are to each other; and suddenly the children grow up and leave the nest and the parents find themselves alone with each other, and discover with horror that there is nobody there. Their youth is gone, and they haven't become anybody, least of all themselves, and in their terror they have to escape from themselves even further.

So we extol the virtue of chronological, rather than actual, youth. Our younger daughter amused us highly several years ago at the dinner table by looking at us and saying, "Well, really, Mother and Daddy, you're finished. I mean, it's all ahead of us, but you've had it." She could not understand what we found so hilarious.

One of our children came to us as a legacy from her parents, close friends of ours who died within a year of each other, leaving a seven-year-old daughter. These two deaths, sudden, unexpected, must have seemed to the little girl like total betrayal. "Not her Mommy!" one of her friends cried. To the small child Mommy is still god, and therefore immortal, and must not betray the child and the universe by dying.

For various legal reasons, Maria was not allowed to come to us for several months after her mother's death, and this period of being homeless, without family, was wholly destructive, adding to the loss and upheaval. Her quite natural response was to test the cosmos: if there is any structure or reason to life, prove it. She broke rules, because only thus could she have it shown to her that there are rules. It was my husband who came up with the one punishment which had any effect when she got completely out of hand: we took away all rules. You don't want to go to bed at bedtime? Stay up as late as you like. It's your turn to set the table? Forget it. You don't want to wear the dress Mother's put out for you? Wear whatever you like. You enjoy living in a pigpen? Fine, don't tidy your room.

This was the one thing she could not stand, to have us remove the security of loving discipline. It wasn't more than a short while before we would find her stealing into the dining room to set the table.

Possibly one of the reasons so many of us have relinquished our proper roles as parents is a reaction to the warning of Zeke's psychiatrist from Omaha: we are so afraid of manipulating, of taking away essential freedom and replacing it with imprisoning structures, that we withdraw. Added to this, the widespread misunderstanding of psychiatrists' warnings about the prevalent abuses of parenthood intimidates us. We read about the mother forcing her son to be dependent on her, so that, psychologically, she emasculates him; he becomes incapable of love and blunders into the grey world of narcissism. The father, we are told, forces his superego on his son, thereby diminishing his free will and his capacity to become a man in his own right. And of course there's the old bugaboo of the Oedipus complex, the boy "wanting" his mother and ending up looking for a "girl just like the girl who married dear old Dad." And the girl "falling in love" with her father at puberty and looking for a father, rather than a lover, in her husband.

We swallow half truths without understanding the very real and important truths behind these mythical analogies, and in our terror of becoming destructive mothers and fathers, we refuse to be parents at all. We abdicate parenthood and turn over our responsibilities to strangers; the Sunday School teacher will teach morality (while we brag at the dinner table of "getting around" the government on our income tax); the biology teacher will give sex guidance (it's too embarrassing); the comics and the villains on TV will take care of leisure time and keep the children out of our hair and, what is worse, teach them passivity. If the kids are opting out, we have opted out first.

Sometimes Hugh and I feel that if we have done anything right with our children it has been an accident and a miracle; often we realize, in retrospect, that the things we thought were best weren't really very good at all. Perhaps our children have taught themselves more on our mistakes than on our good will. But we still have to have the courage to make decisions, to say yes, here; no, there.

And there are compensations, lovely unexpected surprises. For instance, one night at dinner after the children's school report cards had arrived in the morning, Maria said, "Mother and Daddy, we really appreciate the way you talked about all the good things on our report cards and didn't yell at us about the bad." (She had had a D in math: so did I, during my school days, far too often.) She went on, "You've no idea how awful most of the kids' parents are; they hit them and yell at them and never even notice if they get a good grade in something." And to our amazement she repeated, "We really do appreciate you."

So, by a happy accident, we had done something right!

.. 10 ..

Something very wrong that our generation, as a whole, has done is to set one example for our children that may be more telling than we realize: we respect old age even less than they do. Our parents, as they grow old, are frequently shuffled off into homes or institutions. We persuade ourselves that they'll be happier there, they'll be better off with their "own kind" (chronological segregation seems to me one of the worst sins of all), but actually the real problem is that we have neither the time nor the space for them in this urban, technological world. I don't speak out of any righteous isolation and I know of no easy solution. My grandfather lived to be one hundred and one. For ninety-five years he was a vital, brilliant human being. At ninety-five he retired—up until his ninety-fifth birthday he went to work every day. When he stopped work, the rest of him began stopping, too. In the end he was little more than a child, and things were—to say the least—not easy. He was not put in an old people's home—our modern equivalent of Bedlam— because my mother took care of him. But, for many people, Bedlam is the only solution. My own mother is now ninety, and not well. I know how I hope to meet the problems which will inevitably arise, but I am not sure that I will be able to.

As for me, when my time comes, I'd like to be put out on an ice floe.

I heard a doctor say that the living tend to withdraw emotionally from the dying, thereby driving them deeper into isolation. Not to withdraw takes tremendous strength. To pull back is a temptation; it doesn't hurt nearly as much as remaining open. But I saw a horrendous example of a family withdrawing from a long death and this, if anything, will keep me from it.

A friend of mine, a writer, only a few years older than I, got cancer of the lungs which almost immediately spread to the brain, giving the effect of a stroke that paralyzed one side. She was put in hospital where she was given powerful radiation treatment which gave her radiation sickness; she looked like a victim of Hiroshima; her hair came out until there were only a few wisps left. She lost weight massively. She lay there in her hospital bed, able to move one hand, to mumble a few words, looking like an ancient mummy. Within this terrifying travesty

117

of a human body she was trapped; she was. I went fairly often, with two of her friends, to see her. At first when we talked to her she could mumble that she was glad to see us. Later on she could no longer speak, but she was still there; she still was. Somewhere the essential being of the bush still lived beneath the burning. If I held her hand she could respond with a pressure. For quite a long while she had strength enough to take my hand, to put it to her lips, her fearful, dried, dying lips, and cover it with little loving kisses. After a while all she could do was to let me know with her fingers against mine that she was still there, that the touch of a hand could still reach her.

Her husband and her two children, both college age, had stopped going to see her. It was too painful for them. It is dangerous to judge; but I judged. I was only a friend; she needed her family and they were abandoning her; they had completely withdrawn emotionally. She was, as far as they were concerned, already dead.

But she wasn't dead. She was there, and she needed to be touched. The essential part of her which could not be consumed needed to be recognized. It wasn't that difficult for me and the other two friends to go to her. She was not our mother, child, wife. Our lives would be basically unchanged by her death, except in the sense that our lives are changed by every death. And I think that we all, except perhaps nurses and doctors who see it all the time, have a primitive instinct to withdraw from death, even if we manage to conceal our pulling away. There is always the *memento mori*, the realization that death is contagious; it is contracted the moment we are conceived.

I always took a bath when I got home from the hospital.

It takes a tremendous maturity, a maturity I don't possess, to strike the balance of involvement/detachment which makes us creatively useful, able to be compassionate, to be involved in the other person's suffering rather than in our own response to it. False compassion, or sentimentality, always leads us to escape by withdrawing, by becoming cold and impassive and wounding.

As modern medicine keeps people alive far beyond the old threescore years and ten, the problem increases. Evading a realistic acceptance of death and old age hurts not only our parents but our children, and even when it *is* accepted responsibly, it is criticized. Friends of ours in New York are being censured because the wife's father is dying in their apartment: he should be put in a hospital, they are told; how can you let your children see death?

But this old man does not require specialized nursing; he does require love and acceptance, and he can have this in his own family in a way in which it can never be given even in the best of hospitals. Which children are being shown the true example of mature love? Those who are asked to share life and death? Or those who are "spared" all unpleasantness? Which children are being helped to become redeemed adults?

And here I come to a dichotomy in my thinking as far as my own children are concerned. I cannot bear the thought of being a burden to them, of becoming senile and silly and an exacerbation. I would be willing—I hope—to accept such a burden myself, but I never want to *be* one. There is something more than pride involved here. We've taken a wrong turning somewhere, so long ago, that we no longer know what is the right way.

I was deeply involved in the deaths of both my grandmothers. I was affected and perhaps scarred, but I think the scarring came more from misguided attempts on the part of varied adults to push me aside, keep things secret, protect me from what I already knew, than from my parents allowing me to share in both life and death.

After my maternal grandmother's death I was taken to the funeral, but not to the cemetery. I remember being in the house with my grandmother's dog, who showed his loss by retreating under the bed in which she had died, and refusing to move. I sat alone in my small bedroom and the sea wind blew and the waves rolled slowly, unremittingly, in to shore, and my own grief and incomprehension of death became too much for me to bear. So I picked up a book, a book I had already read and loved, and moved out of my own world of numb pain and into the world of the book. I do not think that this was escape or evasion. The heroine of the book had her own problems with loneliness and anxiety and death. Sharing these, being totally in this different world for an hour or so, helped me understand my own feelings.

. . 11 . .

After a day spent in the emergency room of a city hospital, a day in which I was surrounded by accidents, dying children, irritable patients, many of whom spoke no English and could not follow directions, incredible patience on the part of under-staffed doctors and nurses, I felt somewhat the same sense of irrationality in the world around me (all these people were there by accident) as did the man who was almost killed by the falling beam. Whenever this occurs I turn to the piano, to my typewriter, to a book. We turn to stories and pictures and music because they show us who and what and why we are, and what our relationship is to life and death, what is essential, and what, despite the arbitrariness of falling beams, will not burn. Paul Klee said, "Art does not reproduce the visible. Rather, it makes visible." It is not then, at its best, a mirror but an icon. It takes the chaos in which we live and shows us structure and pattern, not the structure of conformity which imprisons but the structure which liberates, sets us free to become growing, mature human beings. We are a generation which is crying loudly to tear down all structure in order to find freedom, and discovering, when order is demolished, that instead of freedom we have death.

A year ago I taught a seminar in writing practices at the General Theological Seminary in Chelsea. One evening I walked in and announced, "Tonight we are going to talk about structure," well aware that I was stirring up a hornet's nest. One cannot talk about structure in literature without talking about it in all of life, and structure, that year, was out. But I wanted to show structure not as restrictive, pharisaic law but as the means of freedom.

We started out discussing the structure of some of the great novels and plays, and went on to structure in poetry, moving from the rhythmic structure of "free" verse to the incredible obedience to structure demanded in the sonnet. The sonnet, as I discovered during the writing of *Wrinkle,* is for me the perfect analogy of the structure which liberates. Meg is to return to the evil planet, Camazotz, in a final attempt to free her little brother from the grip of the rigid structure which imprisons. Mrs Whatsit, one of the extraterrestrial beings who befriend her, says,

"I cannot pretend that we are doing anything but sending you into the gravest kind of danger. I have to acknowledge quite openly that it may be a fatal danger. I know this. But I do not believe it. And the Happy Medium doesn't believe it, either."

"Can't she see what's going to happen?" Calvin asked.

"Oh, not in this kind of thing." Mrs Whatsit sounded surprised at his question. "If we knew ahead of time what was going to happen, we'd be—we'd be like the people in Camazotz, with no lives of our own, with everything all planned and done for us. How can I explain it to you? Oh, I know. In your language you have a form of poetry called the sonnet."

"Yes, yes," Calvin said impatiently. "What's that got to do with the Happy Medium?"

"Kindly pay me the courtesy of listening to me." Mrs Whatsit's voice was stern, and for a moment Calvin stopped pawing the ground like a nervous colt. "It is a very strict form of poetry, is it not?"

"Yes."

"There are fourteen lines, I believe, all in iambic pentameter. That's a very strict rhythm or meter, yes?"

"Yes." Calvin nodded.

"And each line has to end with a precise rhyme pattern. And if the poet does not do it exactly this way, it is not a sonnet, is it?"

"No."

"But within this strict form the poet has complete freedom to say whatever he wants, doesn't he?"

"Yes." Calvin nodded again.

"So," Mrs Whatsit said.

"So what?"

"Oh, do not be stupid, boy!" Mrs Whatsit scolded. "You know perfectly well what I am driving at!"

"You mean you're comparing our lives to a sonnet? A strict form, but freedom within it?"

"Yes," Mrs Whatsit said. "You're given the form, but you have to write the sonnet yourself. What you say is completely up to you."

Well, there it is: an analogy.

To speak analogously is to admit that you can't say it directly; you really can't say it at all; it's outside the realm of provable fact. But it is not a coincidence that some of the greatest poetry in the English language is in the form of the sonnet. The haiku is one of the most popular forms of poetry today: what could be more structured?

But the students talked loudly about wanting to be free to dance, to make love, to be themselves. So do I. So we left literature and talked about the body, and I kept asking questions: what is it in you which gives you this freedom? Finally one of the young men, with great reluctance, pulled out the word: skeleton. It is our bones, our structure, which frees us to dance, to make love. Without our structure we would be an imprisoned, amorphous blob of flesh, incapable of response. The amoeba has a minimum of structure, but I doubt if it has much fun.

.. 12 ..

This time in Crosswicks is a respite, perhaps an irresponsible one. For this brief time I am more aware of a baby learning a new word, of the splashing of the brook after a rain, of the is-ness of lying in our big four-poster bed on a night when I retire with the babies and watch the green fade from the trees which surround our windows. But I am very much aware that what we are all, in our country and around the world, going to do in the next weeks and months and years is of inestimable importance. In the past few years we have seen more violence and horror than we would have thought possible, and there aren't any signs that it is going to stop without a great deal of pain and anguish.

Thomas Mann wrote that if the German writers had, through their fiction, made richer promises than Hitler, it would have been Hitler, rather than the writers, who would have had to flee the country. The idea of this kind of responsibility hit me a lot harder than the idea of being an orally regressed psychic masochist.

I am naïve again, perhaps, in thinking that the love and laughter of Crosswicks is, in its own way, the kind of responsibility Mann was talking about. I do not think that it is naïve to think that it is the tiny, particular acts of love and joy which are going to swing the balance, rather than general, impersonal charities. These acts are spontaneous, unself-conscious, realized only late if at all. They may be as quiet as pulling a blanket up over a sleeping baby. Or as noisy as the night of trumpets and stars.

One Saturday this summer was the occasion of the annual Firemen's Rally. They came down the lane in their red fire trucks, around our corner and down the lane to the fairgrounds; they came from four states, and seven counties in Connecticut, and Great-grandmother had a splendid time sitting out on the lawn watching them. In the evening after the rally there was a carnival, and Dana and Margie, two of our summer "children," went with Hugh, coming home with enormous trumpets, like the ones used to announce the arrival of kings in color movie spectaculars—except that these are plastic. But they make a glorious wild bray which sounds like the trumpeting of an elephant. Sunday evening was clear and luminous so we went to the star-watching rock and welcomed the arrival of each star with a blast of trumpet. We lay there, in an odd assortment of coats; I had on an embroidered coat a friend had bought in Dubrovnik; the two girls had on ancient fur coats; and we were covered with blankets. We needed them, even though the rock itself still held the warmth of the sun, our own star, and radiated a gentle heat to us as we lay there and watched the sky, blowing the trumpets and sharing a can of insect repellent and listening to the crickets and the katydids and trying to identify the other night singers, and then outsinging them with all the nursery rhymes and songs and hymns we could think of which had stars and alleluias in them.

And I was totally back in joy. I didn't realize I had been out of it, caught in small problems and disappointments and frustrations, until it came surging back. It was as radiant as the rock, and I lay there, listening to the girls trumpeting, and occasionally being handed one of the trumpets so that I could make a loud blast myself, and I half expected to hear a herd of elephants come thundering across the far pastures in answer to our call.

And joy is always a promise.

THREE

One day this past spring a young man who works part-time for the Cathedral came into the library to let off steam. He is not a Christian, and he hates the church in any structured form—what is sometimes called the Establishment. (I war against the Establishment, too, but I want it to be there for me to hit at.) He began judgmentally denouncing all the clergy for being hypocrites.

"Wait a minute," I said. "Just what do you mean by hypocrite?"

They did not, it seemed, live up to his standard for clergymen. I was willing to concede that not only was this undoubtedly true but they probably didn't live up to their own standards for clergymen, either. Trying not to be equally judgmental, because everything I said to him hit my own weaknesses, I said, "You talk a lot about your integrity, but you go on working here, taking every advantage the Cathedral gives you, and disapproving vocally of everything it stands for. How do you manage that? How close is the 'you' of your ideals to the 'you' of reality? When I react the way you've just been doing about someone else's behavior, it usually stops me short if I remember how far my actual self is from the self I would like to be."

One of the reasons this young man and I are friends is not so much that he is willing to stand there and let me pontificate but that he understands what I'm getting at. "You mean," he said slowly, "that what I'm really doing, underneath, is talking about myself?"

"Yes, but not only you. All of us. We all do it."

The most "whole" people I know are those in whom the gap between the "ontological" self and the daily self is the smallest. The Latin *integer* means untouched; intact. In mathematics, an integer is a whole number. The people I know who are intact don't have to worry about their integrity; they are incapable of doing anything which would break it.

It's a sad commentary on our world that "integrity" has slowly been coming to mean self-centeredness. Most people who worry about their integrity are thinking about it in terms of themselves. It's a great excuse for not doing something you really don't want to do, or are afraid to do: "I can't do that and keep my integrity." Integrity, like humility, is a quality which vanishes the moment we are conscious of it in ourselves. We see it only in others.

The gap between our "real" and "actual" selves is, to some degree, in all of us; no one is completely whole. It's part of what makes us human beings instead of gods. It's part of our heritage from our mythical forebears, from Adam and Eve. When we refuse to face this gap in ourselves, we widen it.

It is only a sacramental view of life which helps me to understand and bear this gap; it is only my "icons," which, lovingly and laughingly, point it out to me: not only the Buddha; throughout the years others have come to help me.

People like Una, as well as Buddhas, can be icons for me. Una feels, with justification, that she has been betrayed by the Establishment. One of these betrayals came when she went to church and was made to feel unwelcome because she was black. Una is for revolution. And so, I discover, am I.

What is the Establishment? What is revolution?

They are not incompatible. Each is essential to the life of the other. If they are to live at all, they must live symbiotically, each taking nourishment from the other, each giving nourishment in return. The Establishment is not, thank God, the Pentagon, or corruption in the White House or governors' palaces or small-town halls. It is not church buildings of any denomination. It is not organized groups, political parties, hierarchies, synods, councils, or whatever. It is simply the company of people who acknowledge that we cannot live in isolation, or by our own virtue, but need community and mystery, expressed in the small family, and then the larger families of village, church, city, country, globe.

Because we are human, these communities tend to become rigid. They stop evolving, revolving, which is essential to their life, as is the revolution of the earth about the sun essential to the life of our planet, our full family and basic establishment. Hence, we must constantly be in a state of revolution, or we die. But revolution does not mean that the earth flings away from the sun into structureless chaos. As I understand the beauty of the earth's dance around the sun, so also do I understand the constant revolution of the community of the Son.

But we forget, and our revolutions run down and die, like a record on an old, windup phonograph.

My own forgetfulness, the gap between the real, revolutionary me and the less alive creature who pulls me back, is usually only too apparent. But my husband and I have been encouraged by the fact that we ourselves have learned something about love and honor and loyalty as we have tried to teach these values to our children. And I have learned from the very stories I write. This is a humbling process, but also a joyful one.

So my hope, each day as I grow older, is that this will never be simply chronological aging—which is a nuisance and frequently a bore—the old 'bod' at over half a century has had hard use; it won't take what it did a few years ago—but that I will also grow into maturity, where the experience which can be acquired only through chronology will teach me how to be more aware, open, unafraid to be vulnerable, involved, committed, to accept disagreement without feeling threatened (repeat and underline this one), to understand that I cannot take myself seriously until I stop taking myself seriously—to be, in fact, a true adult.

To be.

.. 2 ..

The focus of our days is the dinner table, whether, as often happens in the winter nowadays, it is just Hugh and me or I am cooking for a dozen or more. When the children were in school I didn't care what time we ate dinner as long as we ate it together. If Hugh were going to be late, then we would all be late. If he had to be at the theatre early, we would eat early. This was the time the community (except for the very small babies) gathered together, when I saw most clearly illustrated the beautiful principle of unity in diversity: we were one, but we were certainly diverse, a living example of the fact that like and equal are not the same thing.

While Alan was teaching and finishing his master's degree, he ate a good many meals with us, for he often had to be in our neighborhood. Somehow it often happens at our table that we get into great and lovely battles (Alan and I seldom *fight*; when we do we are like two five-year-olds, and neither of us can bear it until we have made up). My usual battles with him are lovely because we are basically on the same side; they are nevertheless battles. Sometimes my husband acts as devil's advocate; he's very good at it. Sometimes the adversary is the darkness that roams the earth. During one dinner, Alan mentioned the men who feel that it is not God who is dead, as some theologians were then saying, but language that is dead. If language is to be revived or, like the phoenix, born of its own ashes, then violence must be done to it.

This seemed to me to be a distinct threat. If language is dead, so is my profession. How can one write books in a dead language? And what did he mean by "doing violence to language"? I began to argue heatedly, and in the midst of my own argument I began to see that doing violence to language means precisely the opposite of what I thought it meant. To do violence to language, in the sense in which he used the phrase, is not to use long words, or strange orders of words, or even to do anything unusual at all with the words in which we attempt to communicate. It means really speaking to each other, destroying platitudes and jargon and all the safe cushions of small talk with which we insulate ourselves; not being afraid to talk about the things we don't talk about, the ultimate things that really matter. It means turning again to the words that affirm meaning, reason, unity, that teach responsible rather than selfish love. And sometimes, doing violence to language means not using it at all, not being afraid of being silent together, of being silent alone. Then, through the thunderous silence, we may be able to hear a still, small voice, and words will be born anew.

Tallis says that the greatest music ever written is the silence between the Crucifixus and the Resurrexus est in Bach's Mass in B minor. Yes; and I would add that some of the greatest writing mankind has ever produced comes in the caesura; the pause between words.

Why are we so afraid of silence? Teenagers cannot study without their records; they walk along the street with their transistors. Grownups are as bad if not worse; we turn on the TV or the radio the minute we come into the house or start the car. The pollution of noise in our cities is as destructive as the pollution of air. We show our fear of silence in our conversation: I wonder if the orally-minded Elizabethans used "um" and "er" the way we do? And increasingly prevalent is what my husband calls an articulated pause: "You know." We interject "you know" meaninglessly into every sentence, in order that the flow of our speech should not be interrupted by such a terrifying thing as silence.

If I look to myself I find, as usual, contradiction. Ever since I've had a record player I've written to music—not all music, mostly Bach and Mozart and Scarlatti and people like that—but music: sound.

Yet when I went on my first retreat I slipped into silence as though into the cool waters of the sea. I felt totally, completely, easily at home in silence.

With the people I love most I can sit in silence indefinitely.

We need both for our full development; the joy of the sense of sound; and the equally great joy of its absence.

. . 3 . .

Our youngest child, when he first became conscious of vocabulary, often did violence to words in absurd little ways which delighted us. Hugh and I listened seriously, lest we make him self-conscious, or think we were laughing at him. We needn't have worried; he plunged into vocabulary like a sea gull into water, entirely fascinated with whatever he came up with. Even the laughter of his elder siblings did not deter him, and he is now happily malaproping in Latin, French, and German. One day, aged seven, he came home from school highly indignant because the boys' gym period had been curtailed. "We only had ten minutes of gym," he said, "and that was all anesthetics."

This was not just something to laugh at; it sent me back to my own, dreaded gym periods where anesthetics rather than calisthenics would have been more than welcome. Any team I was on lost automatically; when teams were chosen, mine was the last name to be reluctantly called out, and the team which had the bad luck to get me let out uninhibited groans. I now have this emotion at my fingertips if I need it for a story I'm writing; or if I need it to comfort some child who is going through a similar experience. It does us good to listen to things differently.

I remember "anesthetics" not only because it reminded me of my own pains over gym but because this small, delectable laugh came while I was in the middle of a very bad period, literarily speaking, and needed any reason for laughter, no matter how trivial. *A Wrinkle in Time* was on its long search for a publisher. Finally one, who had kept the manuscript for three months, turned it down on the Monday before Christmas. I remember sitting on the foot of our bed, tying up Christmas presents, and feeling cold and numb: anesthetized. I was congratulating myself on being controlled and grownup, and found out only later that I'd made a mess of the Christmas presents; I'd sent some heady perfume to a confirmed bachelor, and a sober necktie to a sixteen-year-old girl. So I called Theron, my agent: "Send the manuscript back to me. Nobody's ever going to take it, it's too peculiar, and it just isn't fair to the family." He didn't want to send it back, but I was cold and stubborn, and finally he gave in.

My mother was with us for the holidays, and shortly after Christmas I had a small party for her with some of her old friends. One of them, Hester Stover, more than ever dear to me now, said, "Madeleine, you must meet my friend, John Farrar." I made some kind of disgruntled noise, because I never wanted to see another publisher; I was back to thinking I ought to learn to bake cherry pie. But Hester, going to a good deal of trouble, insisted on setting up an appointment, and I took the subway down to John Farrar's office. I just happened to have that rather bulky manuscript under my arm.

He couldn't have been kinder or warmer. He knew some of my other work and was generous enough to say that he liked it, and he asked me what I was up to now. I explained that I had a book that I kind of liked, but nobody else did, or if they did, they were afraid of it.

I left it with him. Within two weeks I was having lunch with him and Hal Vursell, and signing a contract. "But don't be disappointed if it doesn't do well," they told me. "We're publishing it because we love it."

It is a right and proper Cinderella story. And I'm sure Cinderella appreciated her ball gown more because she'd been forced to sit by the ashes in rags for a long time before her fairy godmother arrived. There's another moral to the fairy tale, too: the golden coach can very easily turn back into a pumpkin.

And here's where I must stretch the image a little further: glass slippers went with the ball gown and the golden coach, and glass slippers are fragile things. If one's feet grow too big, the slippers break; if one stamps around instead of dancing in them, they shatter.

136

Both children and adults ask me: "What did you do when you heard that *A Wrinkle in Time* had won the Newbery Medal?"

It's an easy question to answer, because it's a moment I couldn't possibly forget. It was in the morning, just as I was hurrying the children off to school. My husband, who was in a play on Broadway, was asleep, and if there's an unbreakable rule in our household, it is that we do not wake Daddy up in the morning, and we don't speak to him until after he's had two cups of coffee, read the paper, and done his crossword puzzle.

The telephone rang. It was long distance, and an impossible connection. I couldn't hear anything. The operator told me to hang up and she'd try again. The long-distance phone ringing unexpectedly always makes me nervous: is something wrong with one of the grandparents? The phone rang again, and still the connection was full of static and roaring, so the operator told me to hang up and she'd try once more. This time I could barely hear a voice: "This is Ruth Gagliardo, of the Newbery-Caldecott committee." There was a pause, and she asked, "Can you hear me?" "Yes, I can hear you." Then she told me that *Wrinkle* had won the medal. My response was an inarticulate squawk; Ruth told me later that it was a special pleasure to her to have me *that* excited.

We hung up, and I flew through the dining room and the living room like a winged giraffe, burst open the bedroom door, flew in, gave a great leap, and landed on the bed on top of my startled husband.

Joy!

Farrar, Straus and Giroux have now published ten of my books, and I hope we will be bedfellows forever. They are generous with me in all kinds of ways, and I appreciate especially that they will let me try many different forms of writing. One of the reasons I went unhappily from publishing house to publishing house before F S & G took me on was that I would write a book, it would have a moderate success, and then the publisher would want me to do another book like it: you've done it in pink, dear, now do it in blue. But I'd write something quite different, and there I was, out in the cold again. My friends at Farrar, Straus and Giroux allow me to experiment, which is the only way a writer grows.

After the unexpected success of *Wrinkle* I was invited to quite a lot of literary bashes, and frequently was approached by publishers who had rejected *Wrinkle*. "I wish you had sent the book to us." I usually could respond, "But I did." One publisher absolutely refused to believe that his house had rejected the book, and I had to go to my journal and show him the page where I had recorded my misery on the day that his house had said no. "But *I* never saw it," he cried. "It never got to me."

There's a reason for this, chaps—though, like Alan's chemistry master, I'm not sure what it is. No senior editor could possibly read all the manuscripts that come across his desk. A manuscript by an unknown writer obviously must be read first by someone with less experience than the senior editor's, and there seems to be no solution to that problem. Editors are aware that good books are rejected because of this. Even a published writer is often read by the most junior of readers; *Wrinkle* was my seventh book. In about half the houses to which it was sent it was given the dignity of being read by one of the senior editors; in the other half it was not. And it is, I suppose, an odd book.

When Hal Vursell was asked why they had accepted it when other publishers were afraid of it, he replied, both privately and publicly in a published article from which I quote briefly: "We have all, from time to time, chosen and published obviously superior books, a book not written to prescription or formula, one

138

which we passionately believed to be far better than nine-tenths of what was currently being offered, only to have that very book still-born. Now editors have emotions, too, and when this happens, believe it or not, they bleed. All of us have a longer or shorter list of such books we still mourn. But if this happens to an editor too often, he loses his ability to judge and dare creatively; he has a strong urge to retreat permanently to the sluggish waters of 'safe' publishing. So to have refused *A Wrinkle in Time* carries no stigma of editorial cowardice; the bravest of us pause from time to time to bind up our wounds. It was our own good fortune that the manuscript reached us at a moment when we were ready to do battle again."

It was my good fortune, too.

But one must not take good fortune too seriously. A librarian told me, with anxiety on my behalf, that she had known authors who, after winning such an award, were unable to write again; it produced such self-consciousness that the result was writer's block. I was able to assure her that I was deep in the middle of another book, and that when I am writing I think of nothing but the book. Success or failure matters to me—and matters too much—*after* the book is written. I know what the book wanted to be, for each book has its own ontology; but have I managed, in revision after revision, to catch enough of the essential book that cried out to me to write it? I am never sure.

Strange: if a review is good, I am delighted, but I don't take it quite seriously. If a review is bad, I fall right into that old trap of hurt pride: hubris.

During the writing, however, there is nothing but the book itself.

During the ten years when practically nothing I wrote was published, I was as much writer qua writer as I am now; it may happen that there will come another time when I can't find anyone to publish my work. If this happens it will matter. It will hurt. But I did learn, on that fortieth birthday, that success is not my motivation.

I am grateful for that terrible birthday, which helps me to wear glass slippers lightly, very lightly. My laughing white china Buddha helps, too. He is barefooted.

. . 4 . .

One unexpected and joyful result of the Newbery Medal has been friends. I can't possibly name them all; if I mention A. I can't leave out B., and then there's C., and on down through the whole alphabet. They have come to me, these warm and generous people, through talks across the country: a few minutes' conversation, real talk, with somebody will lead to a correspondence out of which a deep friendship will grow. It just happens that several people have spoken lately about how we must learn not to *need* anybody; I know that I need my friends. All of them, even those I seldom see.

I enjoy trekking about the country to give talks: I don't do too many—my job is to write, not lecture, and it is also to stay home with my family and do the cooking. But I do love my occasional jaunts, although my hands still get cold with nervousness before I speak. It is not good to be too nervous, but I think it is essential to be a little nervous; one ought to care that much. My husband tells me that no matter how long a play has been running, he feels the same kind of nervousness every night before he goes on stage. It may be partly pride, but I think that it's mostly the desire to do a good job, not for one's own satisfaction, but for the sake of the job itself. It's part of what

Zeke and I talked about this July, and why I always say that psalm verse before starting.

I also enjoy being on panels, either with grownups or with teenagers. One day Hal Vursell called me, after having made arrangements for me to be on a radio program where six youngsters from schools all over New York talk to a writer about his book. I'd been on this particular program several times before, and always enjoyed it, even if the kids pull no punches. If they don't like something they say so. I learn, probably, more from what they don't like than from their unqualified appreciation.

Hal said, "Now I have something to tell you that I think will please you. Miss X said, 'We do like to have Miss L'Engle on this program. Lots of people become very prima donna-ish when they've had as much success as she has, but it hasn't affected her at all.'"

Hasn't it?

Of course it has. It's made me free to go out to meet people without tangling in the pride which is an inevitable part of the sense of failure. W. Somerset Maugham said, "The common idea that success spoils people by making them vain, egotistic and self-complacent is erroneous; on the contrary, it makes them, for the most part, humble, tolerant, and kind. Failure makes people bitter and cruel."

I recorded this rather bitterly in my journal during the time of failure. It's true. My very small success has had a joyfully liberating effect; so has passing the half-century mark and being happily married; I am free to reach out and touch people without being misunderstood.

5

When I talk with teachers ("in-depth" talking, I think the current jargon would have it) about teaching and the effect that teachers have on the lives of children I tell about two very different teachers I encountered in my early years in New York.

I spent three years when I was very young in a school which was, as far as I was concerned, a foretaste of hell. It was a private school with a fine reputation, academically and socially. It was one of the "proper" schools for a New York child to attend. It did not occur to me that I could tell my parents that I was unhappy. I assumed that it was something to be gone through, and that if I was unhappy I had no one but myself to blame.

In a sense, that is undoubtedly true, but it is not wholly true. At least some of it was the school's fault, and my home-room teacher's fault in particular.

A lot of emphasis was put on athletic prowess in that school. I was a poor runner not just because of innate clumsiness but because an illness when I was three had left one leg shorter than the other, and whenever I was tired I limped. Undoubtedly I was too sensitive to the groans and moans of my classmates at gym; I should have been able to shrug it off and laugh; I couldn't. So my unpopularity quickly extended beyond the gym to the rest of the school world. Our teacher, whose name I happily do not remember, accepted my classmates' assessment of me. Not only was Madeleine clumsy; she was dumb. It wasn't long before I stopped doing my homework: what was the use? The teacher always found fault with it, found something to laugh at, always held it up as an example of what not to do. When I went back to our apartment after school I read books of my own choosing, and I wrote stories and poems, painted pictures, played the piano.

Out of the varied humiliations of that school there are two which stand out particularly. One must have happened during the first year there, and it caused me to discover the perfidy of adults. My parents might be rather more Olympian than the parents of most American children—I did not see a great deal of them while I was a child; at night, for instance, they dined at eight, and always in dinner clothes, and I had my supper in the nursery—but they were models of integrity. I could not imagine an adult doing anything that was wrong.

Adults can, and do, and perhaps the earlier we discover it, the better for us. I was about eight, certainly old enough to have forgotten what it is like to wet one's pants. One day in French class I asked to be excused. The French teacher must have been having problems with children wanting to leave the room for other reasons, and using the bathroom as an excuse, because she forbade me to go. I asked her three times, and three times was told, No. When the bell for the end of class rang I bolted from my desk and ran, but I couldn't quite make it, and spent the rest of the afternoon sodden and shamed.

When my mother heard what had happened, she demanded to see the principal. I remember with awful clarity the scene in the principal's office, after the French teacher had been summoned. She said, "But Madeleine never asked to go to the bathroom. If she had only raised her hand, of course I would have excused her."

She was believed. I suppose the principal had to believe the teacher, rather than the child with wet clothes. I was reprimanded gently, told to ask the next time, and not to lie about it afterwards, it really wasn't anything dreadful to make that kind of mistake.

To have an adult lie, and to have another adult not know that it was a lie; to tell the truth myself and not be believed: the earth shook on its foundations.

I wrote about this incident in *Camilla,* and writing about it helped: to take it away from the personal and objectify it made it comprehensible; I found that I had it in me to pity the French teacher and the principal.

The second of the two incidents happened the spring of my last year there—for it made my mother change schools the following year. A poetry contest was announced for the entire lower school; the judge was to be the head of the upper-school English Department. The entries weren't screened by the home-room teachers, otherwise I wouldn't have had a chance of getting anything in.

When I won, there was great sound and fury. My teacher said that Madeleine must have copied the poem; she couldn't possibly have written it; she isn't very bright, you know.

It was an issue big enough for my parents to hear about it. My mother produced the poems and stories I had been writing while I should have been doing homework, and it was finally conceded that Madeleine could have written that poem after all.

I learned a lot about writing in this school—not directly, because I don't think anybody taught me anything academically—but simply from doing it in order to survive. At O.S.U. this July we asked each other: how much pain and rejection and failure and humiliation can a child take? Pain can be a creative teacher, but there is a point where it is totally destructive. The span of endurance varies from child to child; it is never infinite. What would have happened if my parents had not been able to remove me from that particular school where teacher and student alike had me pegged as different and therefore a failure?

I remember quite clearly coming home in the afternoon, putting my school bag down, and thinking, calmly and bitterly, "I am the cripple, the unpopular girl," leaving my book bag where it lay, and writing a story for myself where the heroine was the kind of girl I would have liked to be.

Warning, parents, teachers, friends: once a child starts to think of himself this way, it's almost impossible for the "image" —I think that's the right word here—to be changed. A few weeks ago the girlfriend of one of my ex-students called me long distance, weeping, because they were having problems. We talked for quite a long time, and I made some reference to my own youthful clumsiness in love, and she said in astonishment, "*You* were that way, too! I've always thought of you as being beautiful and wise and strong."

I was considerably more astonished than she. I still tend to think of myself in the mirror set up for me in that one school. I was given a self-image there, and not a self, and a self-image imposed on one in youth is impossible to get rid of entirely, no matter how much love and affirmation one is given later. Even after all these years, my instinctive image of myself is of someone gawky, clumsy, inadequate, stupid, unwanted, unattractive, in the way . . .

A good deal of the time I can laugh about it. Two schools later—an English one—the irritated form mistress snapped, "Madeleine, can't you come into a room without knocking over the furniture?" I couldn't then, and seldom can now. It doesn't bother me as much as it used to. I simply accept my multifarious black-and-blue spots. But there are times when I wish I believed in reincarnation. I would like to live a life as a ballerina.

6

At the school which followed that unfortunate one, I encountered a teacher whose name and face I *do* remember. I was there only a year, because the following summer we went to Europe to live; but a great deal can be accomplished in a year. My home-room teacher was one of five or six great teachers whose influence has helped shape my life. A young woman on her first job, she was the first to see any potential in a shy, gauche child. My mother tells of my bursting into our apartment, calling out joyfully, "Mother, Mother, you ought to scold me for the sin of gluttony!"

"Whatever for?"

"Miss Clapp liked my story so much that she read it out loud to the whole class, and I was so happy I just gloated and gloated."

Miss Clapp was Margaret Clapp, recently retired as president of Wellesley College.

She didn't make me over completely; I never became graceful, or good at gym, or the most popular girl in school. But I did make friends. And I wrote at least as much during that year, while doing my homework as well, as I had written before. I wrote a sequel to the *Odyssey*, with Telemachus as the hero, and painted lurid illustrations, for a class project. I also wrote my first novel. Fortunately it has been lost, but I remember the plot. It had to do with triplets, boys; one was superb at sports; one was superb academically; and the third was superb socially. So they passed themselves off as one young man and, considering their combined talents, they did very well indeed. Then one of them fell in love and wanted to marry, and he had to tell his sweetheart that he was only one-third of himself.

She walked away from him. All was over. I recall the last line, because I still remember how grownup and sophisticated I felt as I wrote it: "He said nothing. What was there to say?"

I wrote poems, too. Looking through some old journals, I came across several. There was one, notable for its arrogance, if nothing else:

We lived on 82nd Street and the Metropolitan Museum was my short cut to Central Park. I wrote:

I go into the museum
and look at all the pictures on the walls.
Instead of feeling my own insignificance
I want to go straight home and paint.

A great painting, or symphony, or play, doesn't diminish us, but enlarges us, and we, too, want to make our own cry of affirmation to the power of creation behind the universe. This surge of creativity has nothing to do with competition, or degree of talent. When I hear a superb pianist, I can't wait to get to my own piano, and I play about as well now as I did when I was ten. A great novel, rather than discouraging me, simply makes me want to write. This response on the part of any artist is the need to make incarnate the new awareness we have been granted through the genius of someone else.

I used the word "arrogant" about those verses. I take it back. I don't think it's arrogance at all. It is beauty crying out for more beauty.

Surely Miss Clapp must have taught me more than I remember. She encouraged me not only to write but to read, giving me books that would stretch my mind and my vocabulary, push me beyond my capacity. There weren't any limited-vocabulary books in those days. I learned vocabulary by coming across new words in my reading for fun (I'm not speaking about textbooks; that's a different matter and I'm not qualified either to criticize or to praise them). I didn't stop to look up the new words; I was far too interested in what I was reading. By the time I'd come across a word in two or three books, the shades of its meaning would automatically come clear, and the word would be added to my vocabulary.

I have a profound conviction that it is most dangerous to tamper with the word. I've been asked why it's wrong to provide the author of a pleasure book, a non-textbook, with a controlled-vocabularly list. First of all, to give an author a list of words and tell him to write a book for children using no word that is not on the list strikes me as blasphemy. What would have happened to Beatrix Potter if she had written in the time of controlled vocabulary? Lettuce has a *soporific* effect on Peter Rabbit. "Come come, Beatrix, that word is beyond a child's vocabulary." "But it's the right word, it's the only possible word." "Nonsense. You can't use soporific because it's outside the child's reading capacity. You can say that lettuce made Peter feel sleepy."

I shudder.

To give a writer a controlled-vocabulary list is manipulating both writer and reader. It keeps the child within his present capacity, on the bland assumption that growth is even and orderly and rational, instead of something that happens in great unexpected leaps and bounds. It ties the author down and takes away his creative freedom, and completely ignores the fact that the good writer will always limit himself. The simplest word is almost always the right word. I am convinced that Beatrix Potter used "soporific" because it was, it really and truly was, the only right word for lettuce at that moment. One of my favorite authors, Anon, wrote, centuries ago:

The written word
Should be clean as bone,
Clear as light,
Firm as stone.
Two words are not
As good as one.

I should pay more attention to those lines than I do. The writer who listens to them will do his own limiting, but it will come from inside, it will come from a creative response and not from an arbitrary restriction, which is the structure that imprisons instead of the structure that liberates.

The more limited our language is, the more limited we are; the more limited the literature we give to our children, the more limited their capacity to respond, and therefore, in their turn, to create. The more our vocabulary is controlled, the less we will be able to think for ourselves. We do think in words, and the fewer words we know, the more restricted our thoughts. As our vocabulary expands, so does our power to think. Try to comprehend an abstract idea without words: we may be able to imagine a turkey dinner. But try something more complicated; try to ask questions, to look for meaning: without words we don't get very far. If we limit and distort language, we limit and distort personality.

Madison Avenue, my old bugaboo, is one of the greatest of all limiters. The more vocabulary is limited, the less people will be able to think for themselves, the more they can be manipulated, and the more of the product they will buy: selling the product is Madison Avenue's end; limiting the public's capacity to think for itself is its means.

"What Madison Avenue wants to do," I said to the students at

O.S.U., deliberately using a violent word for shock value, "is screw the public."

In my excitement—I feel very strongly about this—I used the phrase several times. I found out later at dinner with several of the students and an elderly professor that he was the only one who had even noticed the phrase. He mentioned it at dinner, wondering why I had used it, and the others looked completely baffled.

I explained that I had used it deliberately, because I wanted to emphasize what I was saying, and therefore wanted to use a word which would have shock value. But, except to a man who had passed his seventieth birthday, it hadn't.

Alas. What have we done to our good, bawdy, Anglo-Saxon four-letter words? We have not done violence to them; we have done the opposite. We have blunted them so with overuse that they no longer have any real meaning for us.

"Screw the public," said I, at half a century plus one, and the students, all younger, took it for granted. It had no more impact than if I had said, "Madison Avenue is trying to *do* the public."

When will we be able to redeem our shock words? They have been turned to marshmallows. They need violence done to them again; they need to be wrested from banality; saved for the crucial moment. We no longer have anything to cry in time of crisis.

"Help!" we bleat. And no one hears us. "Help" is another of those four-letter words that don't mean anything any more.

. . 7 . .

It's another of those odd contradictions: we combine controlled vocabulary with totally uncontrolled vocabulary and end up with our language impoverished. It strikes me as somewhat odd that the people who use God's name most frequently, both in life and in literature, usually don't believe in him. Yet their speech and/or writing is liberally sprinkled with "God" and "Jesus" and "Chrissakes." But if I pause and think, it's quite apparent that there's a reason for that . . .

Another contemporary contradiction is that more books are being published today than ever before but educated people are reading less. Over a decade ago I was sent a questionnaire from college; the questionnaire, when collated, would give some idea of what we had done and become since graduation. One of the questions was, "How many books have you read in the past year?"

Most of the girls with whom I went to college were moderately privileged intellectually. Smith has never been an easy college to get into. I felt very ashamed when I answered that particular question, "Two or three books a week."

When the questionnaire was collated there was horror at the answer to that particular question: a high percentage had read no books at all.

All right: our children were little; this is not an age of many servants; most of us had a good deal to struggle with. But *no* books? I read while I'm stirring the white sauce, while I'm in the subway, in the bath.

I don't believe it's coincidence that there was at this same time a great deal of emphasis on controlling not only vocabulary but the content of the books children were to read: no reference to death, to evil, to sex. Not only were new books which mentioned these taboos not being published, but children were no longer given many of the books I grew up on, myths and fairy tales and nursery rhymes. But I have never forgotten the things I learned from Mother Goose, Hans Christian Andersen, and the Brothers Grimm, some of whose stories are admittedly pretty grim.

Consider the grimness of these stories. I read them unexpurgated. My children have my old copy. Some of the stories deal quite openly with evil and sin and death, and the suffering of the innocent while the wicked flourish. The princess doesn't always get the prince. The clever, wicked fellow often triumphs over innocent virtue. Is it or isn't it a good idea to let our children read this kind of story?

I'm like most mothers; my immediate instinct is protective. I tend to be very much a mother lion when it comes to my cubs. But then I remember the eagles, who also love their fledglings. In their great, beautiful nests, protected from all danger by their tremendous height, where no marauder can menace the little ones, the mother and father eagle have carefully woven thorns. These thorns are sharply turned inwards so that the fledglings won't be *too* comfortable.

My husband and I have tried never to make the nest too cozy. And we certainly did not limit our children's reading—or did we? In that paradoxical sense, I suppose yes, we did. My husband, after a hard day's work, enjoys sitting down and relaxing over a Martini before dinner; this is good, this quiet hour of talk and laughter. But we didn't ask our small children to come and share Martinis with us. There is a proper time and a proper place. It's the same with books. We didn't read Faulkner's *Sanctuary* aloud at their bedtime. Nevertheless, we were aware that we had to try to prepare them for the rough world outside the nest. Hans Christian Andersen lets the little match girl die. The Red Queen is pretty rough with Alice, and Lewis Carroll makes no bones about the fact that the sweet little oysters end up by getting eaten. In my mother's old Victorian children's novels, death was often an integral part of the story.

It has been said, and truly said, that reading the Grimms, that weeping for the death of the Selfish Giant, that having witches be bad, and trolls ferocious, leaves its mark on the children. So it does.

When I was little a group of older children terrorized me with games of witches taken from fairy tales. It may—or may not—be because of this that I take the current interest in witchcraft seriously; I do not take evil lightly, or think that it's unimportant and can be coped with easily.

An example of the permanent effect of a book is that of *Charlotte's Web* on our elder daughter. She read it, aged eight, and when she had finished she was in a mood all day, very close to tears because of Charlotte's death at the end. I tried to explain to her that according to the spider calendar Charlotte had lived to be a very old lady, and had had a fine life, lived as long as any spider does, and longer than many. But that only partially comforted her. Then we came to Wilbur the pig.

"Mother," she said, "why did Mr. Zuckerman want to kill Wilbur?"

"Well, Mr. Zuckerman was a farmer, and farmers do kill pigs and sell them for meat."

"Have *we* ever eaten pig?"

"Yes. Often."

"When?"

"Well, whenever we have ham, that's pig. Or bacon. Or pork chops. Or sausage."

"I *hate* sausage!"

Sausage had always been one of her favorite dishes. But to this day she does not care for pig. She denies that Wilbur had anything to do with this, but she has little to say when I inform her that the entire conversation above is reproduced, verbatim, from my journal.

Wilbur the pig left his mark, whether she remembers it or not. But has it blighted her life? I doubt it. She is a beautiful and fulfilled young woman, doing precisely what she ought to be doing. I am convinced that all the Wilbur the pigs of her life have helped prepare her to be the mature human being which she is; I have a vast amount to learn from the maturity of my first-born child.

There are many ways of thinking about how much we should, or should not, protect our children from the rough facts of life. It's said that the greatest single thing the Greeks contributed to civilization was giving us: "on the one hand" and "on the other hand." So what I am saying, no matter how categorically I state it, is simply "on the one hand," and a very fallible hand it is. The older I grow, the more grateful I am for the fact that there is far less overprotection of our children, at least in the book world, than there was a decade ago, even while I quite openly admit that Wilbur the pig, evil witches, ravenous foxes, *do* leave their marks on children.

But do we want unmarked children? Are they to go out into the adult world all bland and similar and unscarred? Is wrapping in cotton wool, literary or otherwise, the kind of guidance we owe them?

My mother lived a wild kind of life in her day. She may be a *grande dame* now, but in her youth she rode camels across the desert, watched ancient religious rituals from a Moslem harem, was chased by bandits down the Yangtze River. During one time of crisis, her best friend, who grew up as unscarred as it is possible to grow, came to offer help and sympathy, and instead burst into tears, crying, "I envy you! I envy you! You've had a terrible life, but you've *lived!*"

Once more: I don't mean that we should turn our children

out of the nest at the age of two to earn their own livings; no pre-school gin or *Lady Chatterley's Lover;* we do need a sense of timing; and where we seem to have been off in one direction a year ago, now we're overbalancing in the other direction. Alan showed me the outline for the Religious Knowledge course for the tenth grade at one of the more famous boys' schools in New England. The general title was: The Problem of God, from Aristotle to Sartre.

Sorry, whoever you are who went to great pains to make this outline, but I think this is sheer madness. Even a postgraduate student working for an advanced degree in theology could hardly cover the Problem of God from Aristotle to Sartre in a semester. This kind of thing is more than likely to dispose of God forever as far as a tenth grader is concerned.

I feel the same way about schools which proudly announce that they are giving inexperienced students in one year the *Canterbury Tales, Paradise Lost,* the plays of Shakespeare, *and* the Victorian novel *and* the Russian novel *and* contemporary French literature *and*. . . . The result is that the kids often don't read the books at the right time because they think they've already read them. We do owe our children intelligent guid-ance, mitigated by a sense of humor. There's a great deal of difference between guidance and censorship, though there's a thin line of demarcation and we can't always keep to it. We're going to fall off the knife's edge, one way or another. The best way to guide children without coercion is to be ourselves. Some-times we can fool adults about what we are; it's not so easy with children; they're going to see through us, no matter how elabo-rate our defenses. But this is one reason they're so exciting to work with; their vision is still clear.

Phillips Brooks said that "preaching is truth mediated by personality." Surely one can substitute teaching for preaching. It's what makes teaching and preaching and writing an activity of a human being instead of a machine.

One morning in Ohio someone brought up the separation of church and state, and the fact that hymns and prayers are now forbidden in public schools, and I agreed with those who felt that any kind of religious proselytizing in a public school is an impertinence—an independent school, obviously, is another question.

"But," I found myself saying, "you will find that you cannot help teaching children your own religion, whatever it is. If you are an atheist, that will be clear to them, even if you think you're teaching nothing but social studies. If a belief in God motivates your life, the children are going to know that, too, whether you ever mention God or not. If you are more interested in money than anything else, that's not going to escape them. You've got to accept the fact that you are basically not teaching a subject, you are teaching children. Subjects can probably be better taught by machines than by you. But if we teach our children only by machines, what will we get? Little machines. They need you, you as persons." And I quoted Emerson: "What you are speaks so loudly over your head that I cannot hear what you say."

So I know, with a sense of responsibility that hits me with a cold fist in the pit of my stomach, that what I *am* is going to make more difference to my own children and those I talk to and teach than anything I tell them.

Perhaps the fact that I do not remember the teacher who accused me of copying that poem tells something about her: I do not remember her name; I do not remember what she looked like, the color of her hair or eyes, her age, or the kind of clothes she wore. I remember exactly what Miss Clapp looked like, her hair style, makeup, little idiosyncrasies of dress and manner which were wonderfully dear to me. But that other teacher: nothing. When she decided that I was neither bright nor attractive nor worth her attention, she excluded me, and this is the most terrible thing one human being can do to another. She ended up annihilating herself.

To annihilate. That is murder.

We kill each other in small ways all the time.

At O.S.U. we discussed dividing grades into sections according to so-called ability. Every teacher there was against it. Every teacher there believed that a student in the lowest group is rendered incapable of achieving simply by being placed in that group. "So I'm in the dumb group. That's what they think of me. There's no use trying, because they know I can't do it."

Murder.

I didn't try to learn anything for the annihilating teacher for just these reasons.

I worry about this. I worry about it in myself. When I am angry or hurt, do I tend to try to exclude the person who has hurt me?

I said that a photograph could not be an icon. In one strange, austere way there are photographs of two people in my prayer book which are icons for me. I keep them there for that precise reason. They are people I would rather forget. They have brought into my life such bitterness and pain that my instinct is to wipe them out of my memory and my life.

And that is murder.

I had, through some miracle, already managed to understand this, when I came across these words of George MacDonald's:

It may be infinitely less evil to murder a man than to refuse to forgive him. The former may be a moment of passion: the latter is the heart's choice. It is spiritual murder, the worst, to hate, to brood over the feeling that excludes, that, in our microcosm, kills the image, the idea of the hated.

Thank you, Grandfather George.

He has come to my rescue many times, has said to me just what I needed to have said in a moment of doubt or confusion. When I was a little girl my grandfather used to send me books from London each Christmas. The first thing I did was smell them, open them, stick my nose in them, because English printer's ink smells quite different from American: smell, and then read. I loved the English Children's Annuals with their mixture of story, information, and comic strips; I loved Oscar Wilde's fairy tales; and I loved George MacDonald, beginning with *The Princess and the Goblin* and *The Princess and Curdie*. Like all great fantasists, he has taught me about life, life in eternity rather than chronology, life in that time in which we are real.

And he has finally made me understand what lack of forgiveness means. I cannot stay angry; this is not a virtue in me; I am physically incapable of going to bed out of sorts with anybody. But, although I have not stayed mad, have I excluded? put from my mind the person who has upset me? It is this which is the act of unforgiving.

I will remember this, I hope, each day when I come upon those two photographs of two very separate and different people. So, yes: those images have moved from image to icon. They have within them more than they are in themselves; in them I glimpse, for at least a fragment of a second, the forgiveness of God.

The Greeks, as usual, had a word for the forgiving kind of love which never excludes. They call it agapé. There are many definitions of agapé, but the best I know is in one of Edward

Nason West's books: agapé means "a profound concern for the welfare of another without any desire to control that other, to be thanked by that other, or to enjoy the process."

Not easy. But if we can follow it, it will mean that we will never exclude. Not the old, the ill, the dying. Not the people who have hurt us, who have done us wrong. Or the people to whom we have done wrong. Or our children.

I wrote out this definition of agapé on the blackboard at O.S.U. I have written it on other blackboards, quoted it in lectures. It teaches me not only about forgiveness but about how to hope to give guidance without manipulation.

.. 8 ..

A play like *The Skin of Our Teeth,* a book like *Charlotte's Web* or *Alice in Wonderland* are not defined at either end by an age limit. A book that is *only* for grownups, or *only* for six-year-olds, or adolescents, may serve a purpose, but it is a limited purpose, and is usually bounded by its place in time and culture. The most exciting books break out of this confinement and can be read at any period in time, in any country in the world, and by a reader of any age. One Crosswicks summer our sixteen-year-old alternated happily between *Anna Karenina* and C. S. Lewis's *Narnia* allegories. Our fourteen-year-old read H. G. Wells, Ray Bradbury, and Louisa May Alcott. Our eleven-year-old read farm journals, and Captain Mayne Reid's travel adventures, books which had belonged to his great-grandfather.

I think that was the summer I was writing *The Moon by Night,* a story that, as far as travel line goes, is based on the ten-week camping trip our own family took. I read the children the first draft, and they said, "No, Mother, you've stuck too close to your journals. It isn't real yet." They were right. I threw it all out, started again, and let it become considerably more real.

I think this has something to do with violence to words in the sense that Alan was talking about it. The first draft was nothing but an image, a mirror vision, with no reality of its own. Out of the image the writer tries to wrest reality. Perhaps the writer must, like Alice, go through the mirror into the country on the other side.

And we get back to: What is real?

What, Yetta, is a self?

. . 9 . .

We talk about identities and lose them; it's something like looking the Gorgon in the face and turning to stone. In American education today we too often either emphasize the sciences at the expense of the humanities or we have permissive schools where the child is allowed to express himself without restriction. It's too early to gather statistics (ugh) about how many great artists have come out of permissive schools, but I doubt if either of the educational extremes produces the right weather for art.

I learned about both art and identity in my structured, unliberal schools, probably a lot more than if I'd been allowed to indulge in unlimited self-expression. When I first went to an English boarding school, writing again provided my salvation. We were never alone. If we wanted solitude it was thought that we must have some perverse reason. We had fifteen-minute bath "hours" three times a week: we were supposed to bathe modestly in our underclothes; I love nothing better than the glorious sensuous feeling of water on my body and would bathe in the normal way, then rush into my underclothes and dip under water, always afraid of being caught and held up as an example of American depravity (If I did anything wrong it was an international incident); while we were bathing, the matron was apt to peer either over or under the partitions.

We were never allowed in our rooms alone, or in the class-rooms. The only way to solitude was through the world of note-book, a story, a play. So we learned to concentrate. I earned my right to be a bit different—a writer of tales—over the incident of the chewing gum. The mistresses assumed that all Americans chew gum. "All Americans"—absurd generality: I was *me*. And one of my particular oddities is that I was one of the one in ten who is born without the tooth on either side of the two front teeth. Usually when this happens the second teeth are simply allowed to grow together. If the dentist had let this happen with me, it would have given my face a narrow look, so he made a gold upper plate on which were fastened two small teeth; while the mouth is growing, a permanent bridge cannot be used. It was easy for me to take my tongue and loosen the gold bridge, which covered the entire roof of my mouth, and I often did so. One morning at assembly, when the roll was being taken, I was happily sucking my gold bridge, and the mistress taking the roll call saw me, assumed that I was chewing gum, and snapped at me, "Come here." Obediently I walked up in front of the entire expectant school. She held out her hand. "Spit." I spat. She looked with horror at the gold bridge with the two small teeth.

After that moment of glory I was allowed to be good at writ-ing and bad at hockey and net ball. I wrote subversively in the classroom during actual lessons, or during our so-called "free" time in the common room, with all kinds of commotion going on all about me, records, arguments, noisy games. As a result of this early discipline, I can concentrate in any amount of noise. I wrote my first novel while I was on tour with a play, in dressing rooms, waiting in railroad stations, anywhere I had a moment to pull out my notebook and pen.

I am grateful for having been taught concentration so early. I don't need to wait for the ideal situation in which to write. Or for inspiration. Inspiration does not always precede the act of writing; it often follows it. I go to my typewriter with reluctance; I check the ribbon; I check my black felt pens; I polish my collection of spectacles; finally I start to put words, almost any words, down on paper.

Usually, then, the words themselves will start to flow; they push me, rather than vice versa.

Carl Van Vechten wrote, "While dining recently in a public dining room with Christopher Isherwood, we were approached by an eager youth who proceeded to ask 'literary' questions, firing them at us with alarming earnestness. We answered them as well as we could, but when he hit upon that cliché, 'Why do you write with a pen or on the typewriter? Why don't you dictate?' I knew how to answer directly and truthfully. 'An author doesn't write with his mind, he writes with his hands.' Isherwood, immediately struck by the validity of this statement, was also amazed by it. 'Have you ever said or written that before?' he demanded. I assured him that the remark was both spontaneous and pristine."

And true. I copied it in my journal in January of 1952, and even with all the innovations of simpler tape machines, cassettes, dictaphones, it still holds.

It is out of this world that poetry comes, and music, and sculpture, the tangible world of hard work, manual labor, of practicing finger exercises every day. As a storyteller my job is to tell a good story; to learn to do this so that I can, indeed, write "with my hands," I must learn everything I can about structure and technique; I cannot neglect my practicing.

An artist of any kind is like a violin which has to be tuned regularly; it doesn't stay in tune by itself. Any musical instrument has to be played, or it dies, quite literally. In Washington, D.C., there's a magnificent collection of ancient instruments, but they'd be valueless wood and catgut if the finest musicians —the men of the Budapest String Quartet, for instance— weren't brought in to play them regularly.

Alan plays the violin about as well as I play the piano, and we have a lovely time making music together; we sound to ourselves as though we were, say, Isaac Stern and Artur Rubinstein. Our family and friends are tolerant—for a while, at any rate; though sometimes at the end of a party, when it's time for the last guests to go home, Hugh or Josephine will suggest that Alan and I play some Bartók.

Music is our relaxation, not our work. We turn to music when we "feel" like it. But I cannot write just when I feel like it, or I will have nothing to write with. Like the violin, I must be tuned and practiced on constantly. This can sometimes be hard on family and friends, but it's essential, and I'm blessed with people who put up with my absent-mindedness when I'm in the middle of a book, and my vocal enthusiasm for the subject matter of my enterprise, which I carry far beyond the dignity of wife and mother—or grownup.

One spring I was going on delightedly about something while I was cooking dinner, and Josephine startled me by saying, "Oh, Mother, you're such a child." I must have looked appalled, because she flung her arms around me and cried, "But we love you this way! We wouldn't want you to be just any old mother." So I was comforted. But opening oneself to this kind of remark, true though it be, is one of the many hazards of having writing

as profession and vocation. I really don't see how it can be anything but both, because it's the last thing any sensible person
would choose as a profession, with the possible exception of
Hugh's. We've always thought of the precariousness of our live-
lihood as being rather hard on our children, but I looked at the
whole thing with fresh eyes when Alan, the first winter we
knew him, stood at my desk in the Cathedral library and remarked, "I think you and Hugh live more existentially than
most people."

I felt we'd made it: we, like Sartre and Camus and Kierkegaard, were existential; we were really with it. It doesn't matter
that I'm still not quite sure what living existentially means,
though I have a suspicion that it's not far from living ontologically, because it's one of those words that's outside the realm of
provable fact and touches on mystery. Nothing important is
completely explicable. After twenty-five years there is much
about my husband which is still mysterious to me, one reason
why marriage remains exciting. Friendship goes on as my
friends and I make new and often painful discoveries about
each other. A great work of art never palls because there are
always new insights to be found: has anyone ever learned at
what the Mona Lisa is smiling? Or what El Greco's St. Andrew
and St. Francis are talking about across a gap of eleven hundred
years? I was in *The Cherry Orchard* for two seasons, one on
Broadway, one on the road. Chekhov had something new to
teach me every single performance.

.. 10 ..

A word written with the hands: it is tangible: I can be careless
with these hand-hewn words but not as careless as I often am

with my tongue. I should be more careful how I use the word "thing." I use it in two totally opposing ways. For a person or a group or a government to treat people as things is a mortal sin. That's one meaning.

The other is equally important. In a sense, to use "thing" in this second way is to take it away as thing, for essentially there is no such thing as a thing. Or, every single thing, every possible thing, is holy. I see proof of incarnation everywhere I turn. Here in Crosswicks I see it in the purple smoke of the mountains; the dark blue of fir trees against the green of maples and dying elms; the strong, sarxy stink of manure freshly spread on the pasture. In New York I find it in the sight of a spindly, naked, dead-looking tree in the barren island on Broadway near our apartment, the bare branches suddenly bursting forth with magnolia blossoms in the spring: what courage! I find it in snow (even deadly snow) falling past the lamps in Riverside Park when we walk the dogs at night.

And then, both in Crosswicks and in New York, there are my special things, my Lares and Penates, like the white Buddha.

The Piano:

When I am stuck in writing a book, when I am stuck in a problem in life, if I go to the piano and play Bach for an hour, the problem is usually either resolved or accepted. I find, as I grow older, that I turn less to the romantics and more to the baroque composers, though they've always been my favorites. In college I asked if I could learn something with more *feeling* in it, and my professor gave me some Chopin. What I had really been wanting, of course, was Bach.

And I did, years earlier, discover counterpoint for myself. We were visiting my grandmother in the South. What I remember most about her big old house was that there was a small conservatory, always green-smelling and warm, and that there were birds in it; and I remember her white, cluttered bedroom, off which was a screened sleeping porch entirely surrounded by trees covered with Spanish moss and filled with the singing of birds; and I remember the music room, with double doors leading to the living room. I spent a lot of time there, the doors closed, and one evening after dinner I was leafing through some old music and came across a rondeau by Rameau. I hadn't been taking piano lessons for more than a year or so, and I will never forget the shock of joy with wh.... I heard my left hand repeating what my right hand had been doing, heard both hands together, one starting the melody, the second coming in with it: the feeling of discovery, of sheer bliss, is still vivid.

Here in Crosswicks we have my mother's piano. It is older than I am, has become difficult to tune, is not always predictable. Keys stick. Notes do not always sound when struck. When we moved back to New York for the winters it was clear that the piano would not stand another transition. In any case, we did not want to empty the house completely; it still had to be Crosswicks.

For a while we lived in a lovely but almost empty apartment. My mother came up from the South to visit, and one day she said, "You do miss a piano, don't you?" Yes, I did. Desperately. We kept our eyes and ears open for a second-hand piano, and eventually found one which Mother bought for me. It was not a great piano, but neither am I a great pianist. For a good many years it was perfectly adequate. Then it got to the point where the bass sounded dead and the treble sounded tinny, and tuning didn't help it at all.

One evening we were at Tallis's for dinner. The friend who had cashed Emily Brontë's check and I were with him out in the kitchen. Hugh was coming up after rehearsal; had he been there he probably would have shut me up, but I was beefing about the piano, and said, "If one of your ritzy friends is break-ing up a big house and wants to dispose of a piano, I'm in the market."

The following Sunday after church we were again up in Tal-lis's apartment, and he staggered us by announcing, "Made-leine, I've decided to give you my piano."

Hugh's response was, "You can't! Where will you put your pictures?" For the top of the piano was covered with dozens of photographs—friends, godchildren, people from all over the world, famous and infamous, majah, minah . . .

The piano is a Steinway grand. It came to Tallis from Austin Strong, the playwright. It has been played by Paderewski and Rachmaninoff. It has also almost undoubtedly been played by my mother, though none of us knew this at the time. Austin Strong was a friend of my father's; they were of the same gen-eration, and they saw each other weekly at the Players Club. My mother was a splendid pianist, and one of my earliest mem-ories is hearing her run through an opera score while friends from the Met stood around the piano and sang.

The piano is now in our living room in New York. Tallis quite often remarks that things know where they belong. And The Piano is quite definitely an icon. I am convinced that the fact that Paderewski and Rachmaninoff have played it affects my own playing; the first night it was in our apartment I took my bath while Hugh walked the dogs, but instead of going to bed, I wrapped myself in a huge towel and, unable to resist, went to the piano. When Hugh came in he began to fumble with the dials on the radio-phonograph control, which are out in the hall by the front door. "What are you doing?" I asked him. He answered in surprise, "Are *you* playing? I thought it was WQXR." Such was the effect of The Piano.

A circle is considered the perfect form of art. In a novel or play, the resolution of the story is usually hinted at in the first sentence. One contemporary painter is so convinced that in the circle perfection is to be found that he paints only circles; circles within circles, without circles, imposed on, across, through circles. The Piano, in a sense, has come full circle: from my mother's fingers to mine, and through our dearest friend.

If it is a thing it is a holy thing: hallowed by love.

. . 11 . .

Simply the fact of The Piano has taught me something about love, love in the ancient sense of charity. Here is another word which needs to be redeemed. Charity has come to mean to many people a human response which is cold, uncaring, grudging, unwilling to share, duty-bound, untouchable. Whereas true charity is reflected in the words of a song popular among young people: "See me, feel me, touch me, heal me." Our kids are once again trying to find out what touching people means. They are aware that it doesn't mean the empty embrace on greeting by two acquaintances who don't know each other nearly well enough for something as fiery as touch. I'm not sure that the kids understand equally well that it also has nothing to do with the vast, meaningless orgies which are now commonplace on stage and screen; we're so used to seeing the nude body, female breasts, masculine torsos, faces distorted in what's purported to be orgasm, that we are even less aware of them than we are of the destructive smog which we breathe daily in our cities—but these scenes are part of the smog.

Hugh and I went the other night to one of these films, a wildly imaginative, beautifully photographed, two hours of obscenity; obscene's root meaning is *off-stage*; that which should not be seen on stage. Take the obscenity, in this meaning, out of that film, and it wouldn't have lasted five minutes. As we left the theatre, I said to Hugh, "If only there'd been some simple, healthy ——ing or ——ing on the screen, it would have been a clean relief." Later on, when I felt more reasonable, I said, "The extraordinary, awful thing about that movie was that in spite of all the sex shown, all the homosexual and nymphomaniac orgasms, nobody *touched* anybody else. Not once."

We have forgotten how to touch each other, and we try desperately to do it in wrong, impossible ways which push us further and further apart. Sometimes when Hugh and I are in a large group I need to touch him; the only way this touch can be realized is if it is tiny and unobtrusive; if I put my arms around him in the middle of a cocktail party we wouldn't touch at all. But if I stand by him and let my finger brush momentarily against his, we meet; we are together. Too many of us have forgotten that this tiny gesture, this incredibly potent flame, can be as powerful an act of love as any other. We impoverish our lives when we limit our expressions of love. Alan said once, impatiently, "Why are people so hung up on genitalia?"

I have a strong suspicion that all the emphasis on the superficialities of sex, on allurement, on catching one's man, on wowing a girl, ends up destroying what they so shrilly advocate. We all know that a marriage based solely on the pursuit of pleasure doesn't often last long; we cannot spend all our lives in bed.

What concerns me most in the present prevalent freedom— no, not freedom, license, which is a very different thing—about the act of sex, is blunting the particular. If bedding becomes a series of one-night stands, it becomes a general thing-in-itself, instead of a very particular act between two particular, unique, irreproducible, irreplaceable persons. When it becomes a thing-in-itself, it is reduced to the de-personing realm of the general, which I presume is where Madison Avenue wants it; replace that powerful four-letter word, love, with the weaker three-letter word, sex, and people will buy more of our contemporary aphrodisiacs: faster and more lethal automobiles; more anti-perspirants (my mother once met a woman whose husband was one of the biggest deodorant manufacturers in the country; she let slip that he was also an ex-undertaker, and his product was made of embalming fluid), toilet water to replace the real aphrodisiac body odor of the clean and healthy male and female; buy, buy, buy, and you will be more attractive, more seductive, more like everybody else: more general.

The Greeks in their wisdom had four words for our one, *love*: there was charity, agapé; sexual love, eros; family love, storgé; friendship, philia.

But charity, agapé, really covers them all; if the other three don't also partake of charity, they go sour.

How do we loosen the noose? How do we recover charity? Please, my friends, do not turn off, do not slam doors when I call it Christian charity. Perhaps this means the opposite of what you think, the opposite of what we are.

In a brilliant article on a recent Fellini film, Gilbert Highet remarks that we are about to enter the post-Christian world. I am no good with chronology, but it seems to me that we have been in the post-Christian world since 1054 when the Eastern and Western worlds split, or maybe even earlier when Constantine made Christianity mandatory instead of dangerous and forbidden. Many people who have rejected the church today have done so because the establishment which calls itself Christian so often behaves in an unchristian manner; because, in the name of Christ, we have so often been intolerably cruel to other human beings. Too many priests and ministers have been seduced by the post-Christian world. Within it, however, lies the tiny, almost extinguished flame of the Christian world, kept alive by the often ignored remnant. If I do not feel despair at the state of the world today it is because I have an eager hope that the Christian world is going to be born again—not a reversion to the first years, but a breaking forth into something new and living and brilliant.

Half the congregation at the Cathedral on Sunday is under thirty; lots of them are long-haired and barefooted; lots of them aren't Episcopalian or any other so-called Christian denomination. But they are looking for the rebirth of Christianity. So are the kids in communes, though many of them aren't looking in the right places—but they are looking. Perhaps our age will not produce the great prophet, like Isaiah, that we seek; but I'm not at all sure that we haven't already produced unrecognized prophets of considerable stature. Prophets are seldom popular in their own day. Perhaps the Christian world I look towards will not be called Christian; the powers of darkness may have succeeded in trampling on the Name so that we will not be able to recognize it again for a great many years. I think the name does matter, and I keep listening for it.

There is a group of young ex-drug addicts in California called the Jesus Freaks. They have turned against drugs, and the transitory values of the world around them. I have met a group of Jesus Freaks in New York. They are, in an ancient, Pentecostal sense, trying to find truth, and what love really means. I'm not sure that they're looking in the right direction—though they may be. The important thing is that groups of Jesus Freaks should exist in the nineteen-seventies at all. There weren't any around in the sixties. Something extraordinary and new is emerging, and it gives me hope.

One spring one of my students showed me her notebook, in which she had written, "The only good artist is a dead one. All artists should be shot after they have finished producing. If they are allowed to live, they will start commenting on their works, and I have never heard an artist say anything intelligent about what he had done. . . . Beethoven had the right idea: he played one of his sonatas for someone, and when he had finished, the person said, 'That's very nice, but what does it mean?' And Beethoven sat down and played the whole thing over."

She wasn't being insulting; she was being accurate. I'm incapable of saying anything intelligent about anything I've written. When anybody asks "What are you writing about now?" if I try to reply, the book-in-the-works sounds so idiotic to me that I think, 'Why am I trying to write *that* puerile junk?' So now I give up; if I could talk about it, I wouldn't have to write it.

Dmitri Mitropoulos was asked if he could explain the extraordinary effect his conducting had on orchestra and audience alike, and he answered that he wouldn't even try to explain it, for fear that he might become like the centipede who was asked by a humble little bug which of his hundred legs moved first when he walked. The centipede, responding to the admiration with immense pride, began to analyze the question, and has not walked since.

Bug or centipede, we're apt to get tangled up in legs when we begin to analyze the creative process: what is it? why do people write—or paint—or sing?

If I grope for an answer, I glimpse it only in parable. There's a story Quinn told me which says a lot to me:

While he was at Yale Divinity School, he and all the young married students were given the opportunity of spending an informal evening with a well-known child psychologist. They were free to ask him anything they wanted to about children and family life, and one of the young mothers wanted to know why it is that everything in the household seems to fall apart around dinnertime.

The doctor answered, "You yourselves know the obvious reasons: the children are tired; it's the end of the day; they're hungry; they're ready for bed, so they respond by being whiny and fractious. You're tired, too—you've been struggling with diapers and formulas and housework, and you're apt to be edgy and short-tempered. Your husbands, coming home from their day's work, are also tired and not at all interested in hearing about your domestic problems, and they respond to the five o'clock tensions by being irritable and often not as understanding as they might be otherwise. These are the obvious reasons and you all know them. The real reason—" and here he stopped and said—"you will probably want to contradict me—the real reason is that we are all afraid of the dark."

There was indeed a clamor of contradiction, and the doctor responded by saying, "The very violence of your reaction proves the truth of my words."

Not long after Quinn had left Yale and become minister of the Congregational church here in the village, he held a meeting for mothers of nursery-school-age children, and several of the mothers brought up a problem that had been bothering them: what do you do or say to your children when they're afraid to go to bed in the dark?

There was a long and troubled silence. Finally one of the mothers who was a little braver than the others stuck out her neck: "You give him a night light."

I'm afraid of the dark—not afraid to go up the stairs in the physical darkness of night, but afraid of the shadows of another kind of dark, the darkness of nothingness, of hate, of evil.

So we rush around trying to light candles. Some are real: books are candles for me; so is music; so is friendship. Others blow up in our faces, like too much alcohol and too many sleeping pills or pep pills. Or hard drugs. Or sex where there isn't any love.

I think it was Toynbee who said that we are a sick society because we have refused to accept death and infinity. Our funeral practices open themselves up to satire, but they are only a symptom. There's an insurance commercial on the radio which says, "If something should happen to you," with the implication that without some unforeseen accident of course you'll never die. I am acutely uncomfortable when people talk about "passing away" because they're afraid to say "die." When I die I will die; I won't pass away, or pass on, or pass out. I will die.

Small children do not yet have a sense of chronology and therefore live in eternity; they are far more willing to accept death than we are. When his dearly loved grandfather died, our young son shut up like a clam. It seemed to his older sisters that he didn't care. We said, Wait. That night during his prayers he reached the point in his "God bless" prayer when it was time to name his grandfather, and stopped. He started over, came to the same point, and stopped again. Started once more, and finally said, "And God, please take care of Grandfather wherever you want him to be, another star or wherever you think, and make him be all right, and we love him. Amen."

I think I was even more relieved than the girls that he had not been indifferent, or shoving death away, but had been thinking, accepting.

Red, a seventeen-year-old boy who lived in our building in

New York, often dropped into our apartment shortly before dinner. He was an only child, and our normal noisiness appealed to him. And he liked to wander into Hugh's and my room, where I had my desk, and talk. One evening he came in as I was, as usual, banging away on the typewriter. "Madeleine, are you afraid of death?"

I turned around. "Of course, Red."

"Thank God. Nobody's ever admitted it to me before."

I've had people tell me they aren't afraid of death. I don't think I believe them any more than I believe writers who tell me they don't care what anybody thinks of their work. My agnostic faith does not, at its worst, include pie in the sky. If it runs along the same lines as does William James's, it cannot evade acceptance of responsibility, judgment, and change. Whatever death involves, it will be different, a venture into the unknown, and we are all afraid of the dark. At least I am—a fear made bearable by faith and joy.

The same spring that Red asked me that question, Hugh was on tour with a play, and Bion, with a high, undiagnosed fever, had to go to the hospital. Various loving (though misguided) friends, knowing that he missed the animals at home, brought him two goldfish and two turtles. He had been home from the hospital only a few days when both goldfish were found floating on top of the water. Being of a scientifically skeptical turn of mind, he refused to accept our verdict and insisted on waiting for the doctor's afternoon visit. The doctor's properly certified pronouncement of death was accepted, and we then had an elegant burial at sea, all of us walking the length of the hall singing a lugubrious hymn and then solemnly flushing the goldfish down the toilet. Amen.

The turtles grew and flourished. I tended them while the children were at camp. When we spent a few weeks here at

Crosswicks the change of water didn't agree with the turtles, so I took a bucket and went a mile to a spring-fed pond, and the turtles survived. But the following spring James, the younger of the two, began to suffer from soft-shell. Bion got advice from the neighboring pet shop and gave both James and Elroy, the elder turtle, baths in a special anti-soft-shell solution. In spite of this, one day when he came home from school we had to tell him that James was dead. Now, a turtle can be a very important thing to a small boy. He had kissed James and Elroy when he went off to camp (have you ever tried kissing a turtle?) and greeted them joyfully on his return. And even if, because of school and his roller-skate ice-hockey team, he sometimes forgot to change their water or to feed them, they mattered to him. James's death was a real blow. He went into his room and flung himself on his bed and sobbed. By dinnertime he had recovered and was quite philosophical and cheerful. "I think it did me good to cry. I got it off my head."

But when it came to disposing of the remains he was quite definite. James could not have a burial at sea like the goldfish, who had been members of the family for so short a time, and who were, after all, fish. James, he announced, had to be taken up to Crosswicks come summer, and be buried in the apple orchard "where he belongs."

"But," we protested, "we aren't going to the country for weeks. We can't just keep James till then. He'll smell."

Bion was calm but definite. "Then we'll have to preserve him. The animals in Jo's biology set are in preservative."

Well, I ended up freezing James. I wrapped him in aluminum foil, put him in an envelope, sealed it, marked it James, and put it in the refrigerator. Every time I defrosted, there was James, and usually at dinner someone would crack, "Turtle soup tonight, Mother?" But we did take James up to Crosswicks and bury him in the orchard, ringing a dinner bell to give the procedure proper dignity.

Our old collie, Oliver, died this past winter. It had always been understood that when Oliver died he would be buried in the Canon's Yard at the Cathedral, near his old friend, Tempête, Tallis's English setter. But Oliver died in midwinter when the ground had been frozen solid for weeks. There was no possible chance that a grave could be dug for him. I asked the veterinary who had given him his final shot what was the usual procedure, and he began going on about dog cemeteries and cremation urns. I was still standing in the office with the old dog lying on the table. I had stayed with him, my hand on him, while the shot took effect, and this had surprised the vet: "Most people don't want to see it. They're afraid." And then he started talking to me about the sickening sentimentality of dog ceme-teries. I said, "Oliver needed me while he was dying. He doesn't need me now. I'm not sentimental about his body. What is the simplest thing?" "The city will pick him up and cremate him and dispose of the ashes." "All right. Please have that done." It cost ten dollars, I think. It was all quite simple and, under the circumstances, right and proper.

But I found, later on when I got around to feeling, that I did mind, I minded badly, that Oliver wasn't buried in the Canon's Yard with Tempête.

I am neither logical nor theological about this. I don't have the word about it at all.

I am afraid of the dark.

And if I ask about this fear, do not offer me pie in the sky or talk to me in the narrow world of logical proof. Answer me, please, with the *St. Matthew Passion;* with *Twelfth Night;*

with *Guernica;* with simile and metaphor, image and icon. There isn't any other way to express or to understand anything which transcends material facts.

.. 13 ..

In these strange and difficult years since man has learned to split, though not to fathom the dark and dangerous heart of the atom, the attitude towards the language of myth has altered radically. It is the scientists themselves who have shaken our faith in their omnipotence, by their open admission that they have rediscovered how little they know, how few answers they really have.

Before they discovered nuclear fission and fusion, before they discovered the terrible fallibility this power revealed to them, many scientists were atheists; we don't need God if everything is explainable—in which case we would not need the language of the imagination and there would be no poets or storytellers. But on that day in 1945 in the desert in New Mexico when a group of men exploded the first atomic bomb, on that day when a light brighter than a thousand suns touched the sands of Alamogordo and those who had made it happen watched the mushroom cloud that has hovered over us ever since, this attitude changed. It is the scientists themselves who today are telling us that they cannot tell us everything—even as we walk on the surface of the moon, even as we probe into the strange and further field of genetics. The deepest scientific truths cannot be expressed directly. We hear this from men like Pollard, who has remained a distinguished scientist and has also become a priest. Fred Hoyle is a famous astrophysicist; but when he has an idea that goes beyond present knowledge (something very different from wisdom) or that might upset some tired old pragmatic scientist, he turns to writing fantasy, where he can communicate ideas that are too big, too violent, too brilliant to be rendered directly.

The myths of man have always made it clear that it is impossible for us to look at the flame of reality directly and survive. Semele insisted on seeing her lover in his own form, as god, and was struck dead. In the Old Testament it is explicitly stated, many times, that man cannot look on the living God and live. How, then, do "myths" become part of experience?

In my church we observe, with considerable discipline, the season known as Lent. After its austerities, the brilliance of Easter will shine with greater joy. In the Jewish religion candles are lit, one each night for seven nights, for Hanukkah. The Hindus celebrate Dewali, the festival of lights, in which every house is ablaze with lights to rejoice in the victory of good over evil. In every culture there is a symbolic festival of light conquering darkness.

If we are not going to deny our children the darker side of life, we owe it to them to show them that there is also this wild brilliance, this light of the sun: although we cannot look at it directly, it is nevertheless by the light of the sun that we see. If we are to turn towards the sunlight, we must also turn away from the cult of the common man and return to the uncommon man, to the hero. We all need heroes, and here again we can learn from the child's acceptance of the fact that he needs someone beyond himself to look up to.

I feel about the cult of the common man somewhat as I do about restricted vocabulary and rapid reading. The common man lives within his capacity; he is probable as well as common; because of this he will choose the safe way. But mankind has progressed only when an uncommon man has done the improbable, and often the impossible, has had the courage to go into the darkness, and has been willing, out of the nettle, danger, to pluck the flower, safety.

Physiologically our backbones are not made for standing upright—one reason we human beings have so much back trouble. We have the backbones of four-footed animals, and had our ancestors limited themselves to their capacity, we would still be down on all fours, and therefore incapable of picking up a flower, a strange stone, a book, and holding it in front of our eyes.

But somewhere, sometime back in the far reaches of history, some uncommon man did the improbable, burst beyond the bounds of his capacity, and stood up on his hind legs so that his front paws were freed to hold something up to be looked at. And the road of evolution changed.

The uncommon man has done the impossible and there has been that much more light in the world because of it. Children respond to heroes by thinking creatively and sometimes in breaking beyond the bounds of the impossible in their turn, and so becoming heroes themselves.

But this is the Age, among other things, of the Anti-hero. This is the Age of Do-it-yourself; Do-it-yourself Oil Paintings: Just Follow the Numbers; Do-it-yourself Home Organ Lessons; Do-it-yourself Instant Culture.

But I can't do it myself. I need a hero. Sometimes I have chosen pretty shoddy ones, as I have chosen faulty mirrors in which to see myself. But a hero I must have. A hero shows me what fallible man, despite and even *with* his faults, can do: I cannot do it myself; and yet I can do anything: not as much of a paradox as it might seem.

In looking towards a hero, we are less restricted and curtailed in our own lives. A hero provides us with a point of reference.

Charlotte Napier, in *The Love Letters*, tries to explain this to João Ferreira: "Supposing you were sitting in a train standing still in a great railroad station. And supposing the train on the track next to yours began to move. It would seem to you that it was your train that was moving, and in the opposite direction. The only way you could tell about yourself, which way you were going, or even if you were going anywhere at all, would be to find a point of reference, something standing still, perhaps a person on the next platform; and in relation to this person you could judge your own direction and motion. The person standing still on the platform wouldn't be telling you where you were going or what was happening, but without him you wouldn't know. You don't need to yell out the train window and ask directions. All you need to do is see your point of reference."

Miss Clapp for me was a point of reference, not nearly as much because of what she taught me directly as because of what she was.

All teachers must face the fact that they are potential points of reference. The greatest challenge a teacher has to accept is the courage to be; if we *are,* we make mistakes; we say too much where we should have said nothing; we do not speak where a word might have made all the difference. If we are, we will make terrible errors. But we still have to have the courage to struggle on, trusting in our own points of reference to show us the way.

I once gave an assignment to a very assorted group of eleventh and twelfth graders to write a character study of someone they truly admired. They had been coming up with a strong crop of villains, and I pointed out that it's lots easier to write a villain than an admirable character, and I wanted them to try a positive, rather than a negative, character study. It didn't have to be anyone living; it could be someone from any time in history who was, to them, truly admirable; or it could be someone from fiction, a novel or a play or an epic poem; or it could be someone completely imaginary, their own ideal of what an admirable person ought to be. It was one of the least structured assignments I'd given them.

One of the boys, black and brilliant, had already admitted to me during a conference that his first reaction to almost any situation was resentment. It was obvious that his own feelings of hate and anger were disturbing to him—this was before militancy was as general and as accepted as it is today—and that he wanted to get rid of them. He was very open in discussing his problems but, even while he was asking for help, he was pessimistic about solutions. When he handed in this particular paper he had done part of a character study of someone who, I felt, turned out to be quite unadmirable. At the bottom he had written, "I'm terribly sorry about this paper. I really tried, but I can't do it. I can't think of anybody I admire."

The other kids made suggestions: John F. Kennedy; Abraham Lincoln; Martin Luther King; Marie Curie; Cesar Chavez. He listened politely but not one name drew a real spark from him.

No wonder he is unhappy and confused! To be sixteen years old and have nobody to admire means to have no point of reference. I know that he was then and undoubtedly is still running into situations where a reaction of resentment is almost inevitable. And what can one do to help? In terms of action, not very much. All I knew to do was to care about him, and to show him that I cared. When I walk through the streets of the Upper West Side of New York, my own little gestures of love in this angry world seem sadly inadequate. But they are all I have to give, and I am just falling prey to thinking that I can—or ought —to do it myself, if I underestimate them.

St. John said, "And the light shineth in the darkness; and the darkness comprehended it not." The light shines in the darkness and the darkness does not understand it, and cannot extinguish it (I need the double meaning here of the word *comprehend*). This is the great cry of affirmation that is heard over and over again in our imaginative literature, in all art. It is a light to lighten our darkness, to guide us, and we do not need to know, in the realm of provable fact, exactly where it is going to take us.

FOUR

Alexander Schmemann, the Russian Orthodox theologian, says that Pope John XXIII's greatness lay in his not being afraid to open himself up to ideas that could not be contained in neat parcels, in not having to see the end of a road in order to have the courage to take the first steps.

We tend, today, to want to have a road map of exactly where we are going. We want to know whether or not we have succeeded in everything we do. It's all right to want to know—we wouldn't be human if we didn't—but we also have to understand that a lot of the time we aren't going to know.

The young people I talk with are, themselves, taking the first steps on a road leading into the unknown. They are at that most difficult of beginnings, the beginning of their adult selves. Their increasing consciousness of this may be responsible for the fact that some of them refuse the challenge to step boldly out into the dark. Being somewhat (*somewhat!* I can hear my husband say) of an extremist myself, I tend to have more sympathy with complete opting out than with the search for security and fringe benefits. I have more hope that someone who has shouted, "Stop the world, I want to get off!" can get back on and enjoy the ride, than someone who wants more cushions. My sympathy is automatically with the rebellious student rather than with the authorities. I was told that I was denied Phi Beta Kappa on behavior. Certainly I fought, with a small group of other rebels, for all kinds of academic reform. The year after I graduated there was an article in *The New York Times* listing all the reforms we had fought for and crediting them to the member of the administration who had tried hardest to block our way. This struck me as wildly comic, though during the battles themselves I had failed to find this person amusing.

But because I have a violent temper, because I know just how devastating the results of my own violence can be when it is uncontrolled, I knew, even back in my schooldays, that trying to fight for right by violence wasn't right—for me. Is there a time when one *has* to fight with violence? My mind and emotions do not agree here. I still think violence should be the last possible weapon, used only when everything else has been tried. And even then . . . I don't know. Could Hitler have been stopped except by out-and-out war? I don't think so. On the other hand, it was Gandhi who toppled the British Empire, not the militants . . .

I listen to the news and hear of war and rumor of war, of crime and wanton destruction and loss of humanity, and think of Ionesco's brilliant play, *Rhinoceros*. It starts out in a small French village on a Sunday morning; everything is normal and ordinary; the people in the village are very much like the people we know, like us. Then a rhinoceros strolls through the village square, and this first rhinoceros is like a presage of plague, because the people of the village start, one by one, turning into rhinos; they are willing to give up being their particular selves, to give up being human beings, to become beasts. And one of the characters says, "Oh, why couldn't all this happen in some other country so we could just read about it in the papers?"

But it's happening here. There are rhinos wandering about our land, and it is the younger generation which is most apt to see them. No, that's too easy, that's not fair; we must not make any kind of chronological segregation here, any more than in old people's homes. It's not a matter of chronology. I am afraid of people of any age who are willing to be involved in distant generalities but shy away from particularities; and I suspect that most writers, artists, share my feelings, because we deal in particulars.

In *Two Cheers for Democracy* E. M. Forster says, "I hate the idea of causes, and if I had to choose between betraying my country and betraying my friend, I hope I should have the guts to betray my country."

This is a statement no good Communist should accept; a Communist will—or should—betray any friend, parent, child, for the party. When we choose a generality, an idea, a cause, instead of a person, when this becomes the accepted, the required thing to do, then it doesn't matter if villages are destroyed by bombs; traffic deaths become statistics; starving babies can be forgotten when the television is turned off; and there will no longer be anybody who will read or write a poem or a story, who will look at or paint a picture, who will listen to or compose a symphony. No young man will walk whistling up the street. No young girl will sing about the love in her heart.

. . 2 . .

Children can teach us by their instinctive particularity. They learn through the particulars of their senses, and I learn from them. My children see to it, for instance, that I am kept *au courant* with their music, and I like it, not because it is sometimes noisy and meaningless, but because it is trying to express in today's medium the hope that there is, somewhere, somehow, structure and meaning in the world.

"Listen to the words, Mother," they tell me. "Maybe you won't go for the music, but you'll like the words."

They are words which on first hearing may make little sense, but they are words which are trying to break through the restrictions of our blunted vocabulary. "See me, feel me, touch me, heal me," the song says. And another: "If you let me make love to you, then why won't you let me touch you?" The need for love, for community, for being together, for being, for *isness*, sounds loud and clear in these songs. There is a passion for peace, a hatred of violence, a trying to break through to the place where two people can reach out and hold one another.

Dangerous, I suppose. No wonder people left the Congregational church when the kids played their own music, sang their own words.

Our youngest child is perhaps more determined than the others that I like the music. On the other hand, not long ago, when he and his best friend came out to the Tower to see me, he asked what I was playing on the phonograph. "Couperin." "Cool. Can we borrow it?"

When Bion was in first grade, Hugh and I went to New York for three days to celebrate our anniversary. When we returned, the first-grade teacher came into the store and told Hugh that while we were away our son had seemed perfectly happy; there was no noticeable difference in his behavior. However, the children in first grade did a lot of painting, and Bion, while we were away, painted only in black. The day we returned there was again no noticeable difference in his behavior, but his paintings were a violent joyfulness of color.

It certainly gave us pause.

Painting, writing, acting, are for him, as for his parents, a sign of order and meaning in the universe, and in today's strange world. Whether we like this world or not, whether we consider it progress or not, whether we think it one of the most exciting and challenging times in the history of mankind or not, it is here. This is a fact we cannot change by any form of escapism, nihilism, secularity, or do-it-yourself-ism.

My mother has seen the advent of gas light to replace oil lamps, of electric light to replace gas. She has seen the advent of the telephone, wireless, cables, television, all our means of instant communication. She has seen the development of bicycles, automobiles, prop planes, jet planes, rockets to the moon. And she has seen the explosion not only of technology but of population; there are more people alive now on this planet than have died in all the time since the world began.

Can we produce a single human being like Leonardo, who could reach out into every area of the world of his day? Our children have never known a world without machines: dishwashers, washing machines, dryers, electric beaters, blenders, furnaces, electric pumps, saws, computers—there are more machines than we can possibly count; beware, beware, lest they take us over.

We can't absorb it all. We know too much, too quickly, and one of the worst effects of this avalanche of technology is the loss of compassion.

Newsprint is too small for me now; I listen to the news on WQXR. I find that I always listen carefully to the weather: this affects *me*. If there is some kind of strike going on in New York —there usually is—which will inconvenience me, I get highly indignant. I am apt to pay less attention when the daily figures for deaths on battlefields are given; it is too far away; I cannot cope emotionally. Occasionally it hits me hard when I hear the announcer say that there were *only* fifty-four deaths this week:

only? what about the mothers, wives, sweethearts, children, of the fifty-four men who were killed? But it has to happen close at home before I can truly feel compassion.

We are lost unless we can recover compassion, without which we will never understand charity. We must find, once more, community, a sense of family, of belonging to each other. No wonder our kids are struggling to start communes. No wonder they will follow insane leaders who pull them into a morass of dope or murder. If they have no heroes, if we don't provide guidance, they are open to manipulation.

Marshall McLuhan speaks of the earth as being a global village, and it is, but we have lost the sense of family which is an essential part of a village. During our Crosswicks years we had the reality of this belonging, despite divisions between old and new residents; if tragedy struck anybody in the village, everybody knew it, and everybody suffered with those who suffered: old and new, Republican and Democrat, Catholic and Protestant. Because the store was at the crossroads, across from church and firehouse and filling station, Hugh and I always knew what was going on.

"They say there was a first-grade kid hit by a car. Who was it, Madeleine?"

I knew, because someone had come, white-faced, into the store, saying, "I was on my way up from Clovenford, and there was this little kid lying all bloody on the road; she belongs to those new people who just moved into the old Williamson house." The little girl was in the same room in school with one of our children; I knew what she looked like; she was not just any child, but one, particular, little girl. I felt in body and bone, heart and spirit, the pain her mother must be feeling. I continued with my work, trying to pray on that deep, underneath level. And the whole village responded, as it always does in emergency. The husband was out of town; there were offers by other husbands to get in touch with him; the nearest neighbors wanted to spend the night with the mother so she wouldn't be alone; food, quantities of food, as always, was brought in. This was a tragedy with a happy ending; there was loss of blood but no vital injury. The child was back in school in a few weeks. But we cared. It was close enough to all of us so that we were able to have compassion in a way that most of us cannot for the babies dying of starvation, or earthquake, or war, all over the globe.

Compassion is nothing one feels with the intellect alone. Compassion is particular; it is never general.

.. 3 ..

One hot afternoon the fire siren rang and Quinn went with the firemen to the top of a steep hill where a car was burning; the flames were completely out of control, and inside the inferno was an entire family, a mother, father, and four children.

At his seminary, Quinn had been taught that God, being perfect, is impassible and cannot suffer. That evening he stormed, "If God didn't care, then I don't want him."

I cried out, "Of course he cared! He was there in that burning car. If he wasn't, then he isn't God."

General compassion is useless. An aloof, general god is useless. Unless we, too, are in that burning car, we are useless.

It is still taught in some seminaries that it is a heresy to think that God can suffer with us. But what does the incarnation show us but the ultimate act of particularity? This is what compassion is all about.

. . 4 . .

It's no coincidence that just at this point in our insight into our mysteriousness as human beings struggling towards compassion, we are also moving into an awakened interest in the language of myth and fairy tale. The language of logical argument, of proofs, is the language of the limited self we know and can manipulate. But the language of parable and poetry, of storytelling, moves from the imprisoned language of the provable into the freed language of what I must, for lack of another word, continue to call faith. For me this involves trust not in "the gods" but in God. But if the word God has understandably become offensive to many, then the language of poetry and story involves faith in the unknown potential in the human being, faith in courage and honor and nobility, faith in love, our love of each other, and our dependence on each other. And it involves for me a constantly renewed awareness of the fact that if I am a human being who writes, and who sends my stories out into the world for people to read, then I must have the courage to make a commitment to the unknown and unknowable (in the sense of intellectual proof), the world of love and particularity which gives light to the darkness.

I'm a bit worried about the present fashionableness of myth, about all the books and articles and definitions, about the fact that myth has suddenly become meaningful and relevant ("Come, ranks of devils, assemble, I have a new battlefield for you: myth: Infiltrate!"). The current brouhaha about myth is blunting our awareness of it, as our vocabulary has been blunted. But that doesn't make it any less a vehicle of truth. Overexposure may make us see, even more than usual, through a glass, darkly; but the violent truth of myth is still there for us. I begin to understand why parables are sometimes used to *conceal* truth; it is another of those illuminating paradoxes.

My white china Buddha can conceal as well as reveal truth; but somewhere in the maze in which I wander, the dead ends of selfishness, silliness, sadness, I am guided, and I do not need to know precisely how. We are finite human beings, with finite minds; the intellect, no matter how brilliant, is limited; we must go beyond it in our search for truth.

An atheistic professor at one of the great universities—Harvard, I think—told his students, "You shall know the truth, and the truth shall make you free." He also told them that he couldn't remember the source of this particular quotation, but no matter, it was terribly important.

Yes. But it isn't just enough to know the truth ourselves: it is not a secret to be hoarded. How do we dare hope to share it without blundering too deeply into falsehood?

One day we were sitting around the kitchen table drinking tea, and my husband and our ten-year-old son got into a heated argument about baseball. Bion said, "But, Daddy, you just don't understand." Hugh replied in his reasonable way, "It's not that I don't understand. I just don't agree with you." To which our son returned, "If you don't agree with me you don't understand."

Most of us feel this way. If you don't agree with me you don't understand. But it takes a child to admit it. Today there is much loose talk about communication and about truth, and little understanding of what either one of them is. The language, which is ontological rather than intellectual, has little to do with the "linguistic sciences," which tend to smother language, rather than doing Alan's kind of violence to it. The linguistic sciences' emphasis on simplifying communication produces the odd result of so complicating it that we evade it entirely. Communication is never easy, as we discovered at Babel.

The primary needs can be filled without language. We can eat, sleep, make love, build a house, bear children, without language. But we cannot ask questions. We cannot ask, "Who am I? Who are you? Why?"

One of our best writers of teenage books, someone whose work I deeply admire, wrote an article saying that he is not going to write for teenagers any more because his sons have now grown up, and teenagers have changed so that he no longer understands them.

I am horrified. He is implying that he no longer has a language in which to communicate with teenagers, because teenagers have changed; but it is not change that makes language invalid, it is refusal to change. Teenagers, like the rest of us, are always changing. Every generation is different. Teenagers during the time when the Black Plague was decimating the world were unlike young people who lived in less violent centuries. To say that you won't write for teenagers any more because they have changed makes no more sense than to say that you won't write for adults any more, because today's world is so different from the pre-bomb world. It also implies that you write differently when you write for teenagers than when you write for adults.

If you are a responsible writer, you don't. The same rules that apply to *The Brothers Karamazov* (my archetypical adult novel) apply to *Peter Rabbit* (my archetypical picture book). The same rules that apply to Dante's *Divine Comedy* apply to *The Wind in the Willows*. Mankind is always in the human predicament, and this is what people write about. A good children's book is not easier to write than a good adults' book, and it poses to the writer the identical problem of trying to communicate his vision in a language that is not obsolete. This doesn't mean using current slang, but finding a language that will still be understood when this year's catch phrases have been replaced.

One of the most helpful tools a writer has is his journals. Whenever someone asks how to become an author, I suggest keeping a journal. A journal is not a diary, where you record the weather and the engagements of the day. A journal is a notebook in which one can, hopefully, be ontological.

A little more pragmatically, a journal, at least one that is not written for publication, and mine most certainly are not, is a place where you can unload, dump, let go. It is, among other practical things, a safety valve. If I am in the slough of despond, if I am in a rage, if I am, as so often, out of proportion and perspective, then, once I have dumped it all in the journal, I am able to move from subjectivity to at least an approach to objectivity, and my family has been spared one of Madeleine's excessive moods. A journal is also a place in which joy gets recorded, because joy is too bright a flame in me not to burn if it doesn't get expressed in words. And it's where I jot down ideas for stories, descriptions of a face seen on a subway, a sunset seen over the Hudson, or our Litchfield Hills. If I need, when writing a story, to recapture a mood, there it is, ready to live again for me. On the empirical level, if we have a family argument about when or where something happened, and the others don't agree with me, if I say, "But I know I'm right this time, I'll go get my journal," they usually give up. If I've remembered not only the event but the journal it's in, I'm almost always right—at least about that. In most other arguments I'm wrong.

Sometimes, on the children's birthdays, they enjoy having me go back to an old journal and read to them about their birth, and about their early years. The journals *are* full of family snapshots—not taken by me, however. My husband says that he never even properly sees a batch of snapshots before I've pasted them in my journal. And of course a journal is inviolate; I may read sections aloud from mine, but nobody, not even Hugh, is allowed to touch them.

A journal is useful in precisely the same way for a children's book as for an adult one. At O.S.U. I kept remarking hopefully each day that possibly, before I left, I might have some kind of definition of the difference between an adult novel and a true children's book. I never did—at least nothing that satisfied me any more than my instinctive reaction on the panel: that I'm not bright enough to know the difference.

"Why do you write for children?" My immediate response to this question is, "I don't." Of course I don't. I don't suppose most children's writers do. But the kids won't let me off this easily.

If you want to raise my blood pressure, suggest that writers turn to writing children's books because it's easier than writing for grownups; so they write children's books because they can't make it in the adult field.

If it's not good enough for adults, it's not good enough for children. If a book that is going to be marketed for children does not interest me, a grownup, then I am dishonoring the children for whom the book is intended, and I am dishonoring books. And words.

Sometimes I answer that if I have something I want to say that is too difficult for adults to swallow, then I will write it in a book for children. This is usually good for a slightly startled laugh, but it's perfectly true. Children still haven't closed themselves off with fear of the unknown, fear of revolution, or the scramble for security. They are still familiar with the inborn vocabulary of myth. It was adults who thought that children would be afraid of the Dark Thing in *Wrinkle,* not children, who understand the need to see thingness, non-ness, and to fight it.

When I am feeling unsure about my writing, it is not because I am worried about the difference between adult and juvenile fiction, but because I am worrying that I am neglecting other responsibilities, and so misusing my freedom; I've gone through periods of confusion and downright stupidity. It was our eldest child, with her remarkable ability to see and accept what *is,* who said to me a good many years ago, "Mother, you've been getting cross and edgy with us, and you haven't been doing much writing. We wish you'd get back to the typewriter."

So I write whichever book is clamoring to be written, for children or adults. But which or what is the difference is still a mystery to me.

Sometimes I play around with the words "childish" and "childlike," but the difference between them has been pointed out to us so often that it has become part of that obvious to which I am prone. But don't let that stop me.

I am part of every place I have been: the path to the brook; the New York streets and my "short cut" through the Metropolitan Museum. All the places I have ever walked, talked, slept, have changed and formed me.

I am part of all the people I have known. There was a black morning when the friend who cashed the Emily Brontë check and I, both walking through separate hells, acknowledged that we would not survive were it not for our friends who, simply by being our friends, harrowed hell for us.

I am still every age that I have been. Because I was once a child, I am always a child. Because I was once a searching adolescent, given to moods and ecstasies, these are still part of me, and always will be. Because I was once a rebellious student, there is and always will be in me the student crying out for reform.

This does not mean that I ought to be trapped or enclosed in any of these ages, the perpetual student, the delayed adolescent, the childish adult, but that they are in me to be drawn on; to forget is a form of suicide; my past is part of what makes the present Madeleine and must not be denied or rejected or forgotten.

Far too many people misunderstand what *putting away childish things* means, and think that forgetting what it is like to think and feel and touch and smell and taste and see and hear like a three-year-old or a thirteen-year-old or a twenty-three-year-old means being grownup. When I'm with these people I, like the kids, feel that if this is what it means to be a grownup, then I don't ever want to be one.

Instead of which, if I can retain a child's awareness and joy, and *be* fifty-one, then I will really learn what it means to be grownup. I still have a long way to go.

So with books. A childish book, like a childish person, is limited, unspontaneous, closed in, certainly doesn't appeal to a true grownup. But the childlike book, like the childlike person, breaks out of all boundaries. Here again joy is the key. A decade ago we took the children through Monticello, and I remember the feeling we all had of the *fun* Jefferson must have had with his experiments, his preposterous perpetual clock, for instance: what sheer, childlike delight it must have given him. I fancy that Lewis Carroll was truly happy when he was with children, and especially when he was writing for them. Joy sparks the pages of *Alice,* and how much more profound it is than most of his ponderous writing for grownups. Mozart, in pain, unhappy, wrote sheer childlike joy: *The Magic Flute* is a gloriously absurd fairy tale. His piano sonatas sound deceptively childlike; they are as difficult to play as any music ever written.

Lewis Carroll may have thought that he was writing a book for a specific little girl; he was also writing for himself; mostly for himself. The children's writer clarifies things for himself, not by wrapping them up in tight and tidy packages, but in opening himself up to them. One of the greatest delights of writing is in seeing words we never expected appear on the page. But first of all we have to go through the fear that accompanies all beginnings—no, not fear, but awe: I am awed at my temerity when I sit down at the piano to play a Mozart sonata; I am awed when I sit down at the typewriter to start a new book and so step out into that wild land where the forgotten language is the native tongue. Then, and then only, when I have got my feet wet in a distant brook, as real as the one at Crosswicks, am I free to communicate to others what I have seen.

There is a lovely Talmudic story that when the Children of Israel reached the Red Sea, and Moses struck his staff on the shore, the waters of the sea did not part to let them through. The Israelites stood there at the edge of the water and nothing happened until one of the men plunged in. Then the waters rolled back.

. . 5 . .

Juvenile or adult, *War and Peace* or *Treasure Island*, *Pride and Prejudice* or *Beauty and the Beast*, a great work of the imagination is one of the highest forms of communication of truth that mankind has reached. But a great piece of literature does not try to coerce you to believe it or to agree with it. A great piece of literature simply *is*.

It is a vehicle of truth, but it is not a blueprint, and we tend to confuse the two. A vivid example of this confusion was evident in a faculty workshop I attended. The school which was the host for the day runs from nursery through twelfth grade, and there was a good deal of searching by the teachers of the little ones as to what it is safe to tell them. We all agreed that one must never lie to them, but there was considerable disagreement as to just what constitutes this "safe" truth.

I found myself, as always, trying to remind everybody that truth is not just provable fact, and that the children themselves don't have the trouble in recognizing this that we do.

A specialist, a Ph.D. who teaches college students how to teach little children, was brought in to give us a morning of lecture and discussion. She told us a great deal about helping the child to be at home in the material and sensory world, to know what is sold in supermarkets, to know how raisins feel, or a daisy petal. Everything she told us was of the utmost importance, because she was deeply concerned with the tangible world in which the children have to live and function. But she never went beyond it, and the world of the imagination was never mentioned. When I asked her if children were to be denied the world of fantasy and myth and fairy tale, she had no answer. Of course they need fairy tales: she was willing to concede this at the same time that it was apparent that these stories had, for her, no place whatsover in the so-called *real* world for which she was trying to prepare teachers to prepare children.

This delightful professor (and she was delightful, though I have a suspicion she might not be amused at being called a Phid) is not an unusual children's specialist. I have met her—as it were—all across the country. There are thousands of her ilk, all full of degrees and facts and computed information, much of which is, indeed, vitally important. In schools all over the country there is a tremendous emphasis on preparing the child for the physical, material world, in giving him sensory experience, in taking him on field trips, in putting at his disposal all the latest discoveries in the world of fact, of preparing him for the world in which Euclidean geometry is true, where a table must have a solid top and be able to stand on its four feet, and where a square, even a human one, must be square.

But what is frightening is that far too many of these authorities on child guidance go on to tell us that anything beyond this pragmatic knowledge is not necessary, that anything else is *dishonest*, as a result of which many children today are growing up losing great areas of truth. The tragically comic thing is that these specialists are unwittingly contradicting themselves: they know that according to contemporary science Euclidean geometry is not "true"; a table is neither flat nor solid; and they emphasize the truth of Einstein's geometry and the new physics and biology as well as the new math.

Nevertheless, they are preparing the children to live in the functional Euclidean world exclusively, and keeping from them the vast open reaches of the imagination that led Einstein to soar out among the galaxies and bring back to us ever widening circles of truth. Just as we are taught that our universe is constantly expanding out into space at enormous speeds, so too our imagination must expand as we search for the knowledge that will in its turn expand into wisdom, and from wisdom into truth.

But this is violent, and therefore frightening.

Children are less easily frightened than we are. They have no problem in understanding how Alice could walk through the mirror into the country on the other side; some of them have done it themselves. And they all understand princesses, of course. Haven't they all been badly bruised by peas? And then there's the princess who spat forth toads and snakes whenever she opened her mouth to speak, and her sister whose lips issued pieces of pure gold. I still have many days when everything I say seems to turn into toads. The days of gold, alas, don't come nearly as often. Children understand this immediately; *why* is it a toad day? There isn't any logical, provable reason. The gold days are just as irrational; they are pure grace; a gift.

. . 6 . .

In one of his books, Edward Nason West tells of a time in his youth when he got so furious at another young man that he hit him. The other young man's response was a calm, "I see that words fail you."

What do we do when words fail us? They frequently fail me, and often when I'm using them in the vastest quantity, struggling to push through them to what I'm trying to express. Often they fail me entirely, as when young people ask me ultimate and unanswerable questions. It has been very helpful to remember that quite a few reputable scholars, including one Socrates, made a point, when asked such a question, of saying, "I don't know."

But children want to know, and perhaps it is our desire not to let them down that has led us into the mistake of teaching them only the answerables. This *is* a mistake, and we mustn't refuse to allow them to ask the unanswerables just because we can't provide tidy little answers. In our fear of the unprovable we mustn't forget that they can learn from *The Tempest* as well as social studies; that they can learn from Aesop as well as the new math; that *The Ugly Duckling* need not be discarded in favor of driver education. There is a violent kind of truth in the most primitive myths, a truth we need today, because probably the most important thing those first storytellers did for their listeners back in the dim past in their tales of gods and giants and fabulous beasts was to affirm that the gods are not irrational, that there is structure and meaning in the universe, that God is responsible to his creation.

Truth happens in these myths. That is why they have lasted. If they weren't expressions of truth they would long have been forgotten. One of the great historical pieces of evidence is the Bible, both the Old and New Testaments. Many books which were once in the Bible have dropped out of sight through the centuries. Those that have stayed with us are those that contain truth that speaks to us in our daily living, right where we are now.

In the beginning God created the heaven and the earth. . . . The extraordinary, the marvelous thing about Genesis is not how unscientific it is but how amazingly accurate it is. How could the ancient Israelites have known the exact order of a theory of evolution that wasn't to be formulated by scientists for thousands of years? Here is a truth that cuts across barriers of time and space.

So myth, fantasy, fairy tale contain an iconic truth, and in turning to their language we are not going backwards but forwards to that language which is not obsolete. We must not take from our children—or ourselves—the truth that is in the world of the imagination.

I look at the babies; we make daisy chains and play ring-around-a-rosy and put two candles on a birthday cake, and I wonder: what can we give a child that will stay with him when there is nothing left?

All we have, I think, is the truth, the truth that will set him free, not a limited, provable truth, but the open, growing, evolving truth that is not afraid.

.. 7 ..

During a panel discussion on drugs, homosexuality, pornography—"problems" in children's books—I suggested to the young teenagers on the panel that if they wanted facts about these subjects, they turn to non-fiction, to scientific articles. One of them asked, "But can't we find truth in fiction, too?"

"Who said anything about truth? I told you to check *facts* in non-fiction articles. If you are looking for truth, the place to look for it is exactly in stories, in paintings, in music."

We may find the facts about intercourse in an article; but we learn about love in that very contemporary play, *Romeo and Juliet*. We learn about insemination and childbirth in film strips and lectures; but we learn about creation in

Tiger! Tiger! burning bright
In the forests of the night,
What immortal hand or eye
Dare frame thy fearful symmetry?

It is an extraordinary and beautiful thing that God, in creation, uses precisely the same tools and rules as the artist; he works with the beauty of matter; the reality of things; the discoveries of the senses, all five of them; so that we, in turn, may hear the grass growing; see a face springing to life in love and laughter; feel another human hand or the velvet of a puppy's ear; taste food prepared and offered in love; smell—oh, so many things: food, sewers, each other, flowers, books, new-mown grass, dirt . . .

Here, in the offerings of creation, the oblations of story and song, are our glimpses of truth.

. . 8 . .

One summer Hugh and I went, more or less by accident, to a burlesque show. We'd gone down to the Village to see an off-Broadway play in which a friend was appearing, found that he was out that night because he'd strained his back. We thought we'd rather wait to see the show when he returned to it, and directly across the street was a marquee proclaiming Ann Corio in *This Is Burlesque.*

"How about it?"

"Fine."

It was great fun. A series of pretty young girls came out on stage and danced while removing their clothing. I was filled with envy not so much for their lovely bodies as for the way they could twirl the tassels on their breasts: clockwise, counter-clockwise (widdershins!): it was superb.

Towards the end of the performance one stripper came out who was a little older than the others, possibly a little beyond her prime. But she had a diaphanous scarf in her hands, and she twirled and swirled this about her as she removed her clothes, and Hugh remarked, "She's beautiful." It was only she, of all the strippers, who gave the audience a feeling of mystery.

If we accept the mysterious as the "fairest thing in life," we must also accept the fact that there are rules to it. A rule is not necessarily rigid and unbending; it can even have a question mark at the end of it. I wish that we worried more about asking the right questions instead of being so hung up on finding answers. I don't *need* to know the difference between a children's book and an adult one; it's the questions that have come from thinking about it that are important. I wish we'd stop finding answers for everything. One of the reasons my generation has mucked up the world to such an extent is our loss of the sense of the mysterious.

One night after dinner a group of us were talking about the supernatural, and one of our dinner guests said that when the electric light was invented, people began to lose the dimension of the supernatural. In the days before we could touch a switch and flood every section of the room with light, there were always shadows in the corner, shadows which moved with candlelight, with firelight; and these shadows were an outward and visible sign that things are not always what they seem; there are things which are not visible to the mortal human being; there are things beyond our ken.

One of my favorite theologians is Albert Einstein. He writes, "The fairest thing we can experience is the mysterious. It is the fundamental emotion which stands at the cradle of true art and true science. He who knows it not, who can no longer wonder, can no longer feel amazement, is as good as dead, a snuffed-out candle."

Our younger daughter is engaged to a theoretical chemist who delights me in many ways, not the least of which is that he looks like Einstein, and, it seems to me, thinks like Einstein, too. He's finishing a post-Ph.D. grant at the University of Pennsylvania and showed me his most recent publication: "Look, Madeleine, nothing but equations! I'm getting rid of words entirely." When the world around him gets too much in his Einsteinian hair he murmurs, "All I want is to be left alone with my numbers."

He will learn, I am confident, that his numbers themselves will not allow him to stay alone with them, that they will shove him around, as words shove me (he may think he's getting rid of words, but his formulas are full of Greek letters). He is also learning the strange rules of the mysterious. Einstein writes, "What is the meaning of human life, or, for that matter, of the life of any creature? To know the answer to this question means to be religious. You ask: Does it make any sense, then, to pose this question? I answer: The man who regards his own life and that of his fellow creatures as meaningless is not merely unhappy, but hardly fit for life." He also says, "The true value of a human being is determined primarily by the measure and the sense in which he has attained liberation from self."

Science, literature, art, theology: it is all the same ridiculous, glorious, mysterious language.

It was while I was steeping myself in Einstein, Planck, and various other physicists and cosmologists during the writing of *Wrinkle* that I came across and was fascinated by the first law of thermodynamics, which is one of the rules of the mysterious. It tells us that energy and heat are mutually convertible, but if you get energy you lose heat, and if you get heat you lose energy. Or, to put it in non-scientific layman's language, you don't get something for nothing.

A science-fiction story tells of a machine that was invented that could produce everything needed for man's comfort on earth: food and furniture; refrigerators and radios; clothes and cars. There were a few wise men who warned people that one cannot continually take without putting back, or the supply will be depleted, but they were laughed at. After several centuries of the machine giving freedom from all material want, schools were teaching that the old myth that the earth was once larger than the moon was rank superstition. And at the end of the story there is one toothless old man clinging to a tiny and depleted fragment of earth.

How does the first law of thermodynamics apply to the making of books? Most of us realize that if we buy our groceries or gasoline from a place that gives trading stamps, we are paying for the trading stamps in higher prices. It may be fun, but it's not something for nothing. I trust that most of us are not like the woman who left her neighborhood market, paid thirty cents to ride a bus, went to another market, bought five pounds of sugar for which she paid one cent less than she would have in the first market, paid thirty cents to ride home, and was triumphantly convinced that she had saved money.

I'm not referring to the rising cost of books—that's another story—but to books which are afraid of the mysterious, leave nothing to our imagination, and try to break the first law of thermodynamics.

There are the four-letter-word books which have ruined our four-letter words. I was horrified recently to see the word "shit" irresponsibly used in a book for the ten to twelves, not because these children have never heard the word, but because these words, sex scenes, normal and perverse, have become big business and children's writers are joining adult (?) writers in cashing in on it. Something for nothing: there is no word, no action, which is of itself out of place if it springs from artistic necessity, if it is paid for by the fact that it is essential to the life of a story.

I am bored with the sex books which are demolishing sex—or trying to, because the intent is ultimately murder. Orville Prescott mentioned in a review, with a deep, figurative sigh, the sex scene that seems to have become *de rigueur* in the modern novel. This is a peculiar kind of perversion, this voyeurism. I'm totally against any kind of legal censorship, but I'm fed up with play-by-play descriptions of the act of intercourse. If we've made love, we don't need to be told about it; if we haven't, a description of its physiological progress isn't going to tell us anything. When the writer leaves something to the readers' imagination he is like the beautiful burlesque stripper who, with her diaphanous veil, added a sense of mystery to the human body.

The sexiest books I know, are those like *Anna Karenina* and *Phaedre*; or, if we want realism, what about that arch-realist, Flaubert? *Madame Bovary*, for instance: for sheer power in giving us the sense of uncontrollable physical passion no one can beat the scene in which Emma and her lover, Léon, get into a carriage, "a carriage with drawn shades," that is seen driving on and on through the streets, "sealed tighter than a tomb and tossing like a ship." The picture of this carriage with the drawn shades is far more sexually potent than any diagram of what was going on within it. In this climate of mystery, passion can flourish far more strongly than in the clinical glare of the laboratory.

Hemingway is not known for his reticence, and yet one of his most poignant love scenes is in *For Whom the Bell Tolls*, where Robert and Maria are together in the sleeping bag, and all Hemingway says is, "The earth shook beneath them."

Now some readers, both adolescent and supposedly mature, *are* looking for pornography. They come into bookstores and libraries hunting for substitute life, for vicarious sex. When they ask for books that pander to their desire for four-letter words, for descriptions of intercourse, for something for nothing, they're not unlike addicts looking for substitute pleasure.

Censorship is not the answer. I have intense respect for all the librarians and teachers who guide but do not manipulate. I know of at least one librarian who starts her readers on what they ask for, on what they think they want; then, when she gets to know them, when she has made friends, she offers something with a little more substance, and then, when that is accepted and swallowed, something with even a little more. And without exception, she says, when the real thing is accepted, the desire for the cheap substitute goes. Something for something is far more satisfying than something for nothing. "Take what you want, said God," runs an old Spanish saying. "Take it, and pay for it."

The taboos about death and sin which delayed some of my books' being published in the children's field have now been broken; it would seem that everything goes. But this is not quite true. When we break one taboo, we replace it with another. Alan remarked to me that just as we suffered from the sexual repression of Victorianism, so we are beginning to suffer from the spiritual repression of this century. Even in the church, the transcendent, the mysterious, the irrational in God is taboo; God is the Great Sociologist.

But: warning: there is, in art, no subject which is in itself taboo, either for children or adults. The way in which the subject is handled is what matters. The same subject can be obscene and repellent, or alive and loving, depending on the artist. And the reader. I had a troubled letter from a librarian in California who had received a number of phone calls from the parents of the high-school children who were passing *A Wrinkle in Time* around because of the sex passages. She gave me page numbers, and I rushed to the bookcase, eager to read my sex scenes. They were the descriptions of tessering. I wrote back that if one wants to, one can find sex symbols in anything, and I thought those in *A Wrinkle in Time* were probably healthier than those in some of the other books I knew high-school students were reading that year, and suggested that she relax about it.

I read lots of adult novels when I was a child; the parts about sex were mostly outside my vocabulary and definitely outside my experience; I didn't understand them and slid over them. Unless a grownup, looking horrified, tells us that we shouldn't read a book because it is "dirty," we, as children, won't even see the dirt because it is outside our field of vision; we have not yet been corrupted by repressive taboos. And children are a great deal less naïve and fragile than many adults give them credit for being.

Whatever the contemporary taboos may be, all great books are imbued with Einstein's quality of the mysterious, and keep its rules. Is this, then, going to enable us to tell, out of the large quantity of books published each year, which ones are going to join the ranks of the great and which will be forgotten? I doubt it. And I don't think this matters.

A truly great work of art breaks beyond the bounds of the period and culture in which it is created, so final judgment on a current book has to be deferred until it can be seen outside this present moment.

How, then, do publishers judge? A publisher has to use his sense of smell, and he has to be a hardheaded businessman, or he won't be a publisher for long. Not many make the mistake of the men in the television industry who wait with bated breath for the Nielsen reports, for Trendex, to tell them what the viewer wants, and then proceed to give the viewer more of what the calculating machine has ordained that the viewer wants. I don't think most people in the book business fall into the error of thinking that the machines, the public-opinion polls, the best-seller lists, know what the public wants. Then who does?

I do. You, my dears, do. Because we *are* the public. We do have to have faith in our own convictions. We are not machines, but living human beings who sign our own checks with our own names; and I have a lot more faith in us than I do in

Trendex. It is human beings who have the wisdom to spot a book that perhaps a publisher is *not* pushing, that gets ignored by reviewers, but that will still be selling long after the immediate success: examples: *Lord of the Flies. The Lord of the Rings. Narcissus and Goldmund.* Students, once they discovered these books, went wild over them, students who still had not lost sight of the particular in the forest of generalities.

Josephine's godfather is now an important man in the world of the English theatre. When he first started work in a London producer's office, hadn't been there very long, and didn't know many people, he was invited to a large and fashionable supper party. He was having a lovely time, because Toby always has a lovely time; he has complete and passionate interest in people. And he doesn't have to wait for anybody to tell him who's important at a party, whom he "ought" to be speaking to. In the midst of his pleasure he noticed a slender man sitting off by himself with nobody paying much attention to him. So Toby immediately went over to pay him some attention, to make sure that he wasn't unhappy. They got along famously, and after a while the quiet man identified himself as General Sir Frederick Browning, Comptroller and Treasurer for Their Royal Highnesses Princess Elizabeth and Prince Philip. He was also the husband of Daphne du Maurier, and one of the most "important" people at the party. He asked Toby if he'd like to go to Buckingham Palace the next day to see the Royal Art Collection and to have a guided tour of the whole palace. A few minutes later Gertrude Lawrence came up and said, "Toby, do you appreciate what an honor this is? I've known Boy for years, and he's never invited *me* to see the king's pictures." Of course Toby asked if he might bring Gertie too, but that's another story.

Toby isn't afraid to stick his neck out; he doesn't try to play it safe. He doesn't depend on Trendex rather than his own opinion. Because he is, thank God, human, he sometimes makes mistakes; but he wouldn't be where he is now if his opinion hadn't far more often been right than wrong. Or if he hadn't been willing to take risks for what he believes in.

One decade in the nineteenth century produced Hawthorne's *The Scarlet Letter* and *The House of Seven Gables*, Emerson's *English Traits* and *Representative Men*, Melville's *Moby Dick*, Thoreau's *Walden*, and Whitman's *Leaves of Grass*, and—reminds *The New York Times*, my source for this information—"none of these achieved more than a modest sale." In 1853 Thoreau was informed by his publishers that *A Week on the Concord and Merrimack Rivers* had sold 219 copies since its publication four years before, so they sent him the remainder. He wrote, "I now have a library of nearly nine hundred volumes, over seven hundred of which I wrote myself." That same year, seventy thousand copies were sold of a book called *Fern Leaves from Fannie's Portfolio*.

We never know when a book is going to be like the quiet man Toby found in a corner of the fashionable supper party, when it is going to turn out to be a Sir Frederick Browning. It's far more exciting to be enthusiastic about the real book that deals with life in all its particularity than to allow ourselves to be dazzled by the cheap substitute that tickles the palate for the moment but leaves us with a hangover. And all we have to rely on to tell the difference is ourselves, not a computer.

I'm all for realism in the book business, but I'm afraid of cynicism, and the two are often too close for comfort. Books must be sold, or there will be no more publishers, or booksellers, or librarians—or writers, majah, minah, or mediocah. We remember the reputable publisher who published a recent flaming best seller knowing that it stank—but that it would sell. We all know writers who write solely to make money, and this is a perfectly legitimate business. It is quite proper to render unto Caesar the things which are Caesar's. But there is something in us that knows that this is not enough, which reaches out for something more, which longs for Einstein's realm.

. . 9 . .

In Smith I majored in English literature, and one of the required courses was Chaucer. I loved him. It fills me with joy to know that Chaucer, with his explosive, bawdy, colorful imagination, changed the course of the English language. If it had not been for Chaucer breaking with tradition and writing in the language of the common people, instead of the more elegant Latin or French, we might be speaking a kind of bastard Norman today.

I wonder: if Chaucer hadn't come along, what would have happened to Shakespeare when he picked up his pen two hundred or so years later? There's an idea for a story, one day . . .

In the final exam in the Chaucer course we were asked why he used certain verbal devices, certain adjectives, why he had certain characters behave in certain ways. And I wrote, "I don't think Chaucer had any idea why he did any of these things. That isn't the way people write."

I believe this as strongly now as I did then. Most of what is best in writing isn't done deliberately.

Am I implying that an author should sit around like a pseudomystic in his pad, drinking endless cups of espresso and smoking pot and waiting for enlightenment?

Hardly. That isn't how things happen, either.

Hugh and I heard Rudolf Serkin play Beethoven's *Appas-*

sionata sonata in Symphony Hall in Boston many years ago. It was one of those great, unpredictable moments. When the last notes had been lost in the silence, the crowd not only applauded, cheered, stamped, we stood on our chairs: this doesn't happen often in Boston.

But if Serkin did not practice eight hours a day, every day, the moment of inspiration, when it came, would have been lost; nothing would have happened; there would have been no instrument through which the revelation could be revealed.

I try to remember this when I dump an entire draft of a novel into the wastepaper basket. It *isn't* wasted paper. It's my five-finger exercises. It's necessary practicing before the performance.

. . 10 . .

I am often asked how I came to write *A Wrinkle in Time*. Even with all the hindsight of which I am capable I can't quite explain it. It was during a time of transition. We had sold the store, were leaving the safe, small world of the village, and going back to the city and the theatre. While we were on our ten-week camping trip from the Atlantic to the Pacific and back again, we drove through a world of deserts and buttes and leafless mountains, wholly new and alien to me. And suddenly into my mind came the names, *Mrs Whatsit. Mrs Who. Mrs Which*. I turned around to the children and said, "Hey, kids, listen to these three great names that just popped into my mind; I'll have to write a book about them."

But why did those names come to me just then, and from where? I haven't the faintest idea. I suppose that my writing mind, which is always at work no matter what is happening on the surface level, took over from there. I had brought along some Eddington, some Einstein, a few other books on cosmology—I was on a cosmological jag at that time, partly, I suppose, because it satisfied my longing for God better than books of theology; and the influence of these books on *Wrinkle* is obvious. I was also quite consciously writing my own affirmation of a universe which is created by a power of love.

When the book was rejected by publisher after publisher, I cried out in my journal. I wrote, after an early rejection, "X turned down *Wrinkle,* turned it down with one hand while saying that he loved it, but didn't quite dare do it, as it isn't really classifiable. I know it isn't really classifiable, and am wondering if I'll have to go through the usual hell with this that I seem to go through with everything I write. But this book I'm sure of. If I've ever written a book that says what I feel about God and the universe, this is it. This is my psalm of praise . . ."

And again, "And yesterday morning before we left, there was a letter from Hugh saying that X has turned down *Wrinkle.* Perhaps I'm slowly becoming inured. I went through a few hours of the usual primitive despairing rage, but I could show none of it as I was with the children driving down to the city. Am I really getting so that I can stand it better? Perhaps the fury and bitterness builds up. But all there is today is a heaviness that makes all household chores wearily difficult. All work seems a little harder . . . In a book I'm reading about Fitzgerald, there is a sentence about 'second-rate writers who pass themselves off as geniuses.' But how does anybody know? A writer is far too tied up in his work, if he is really a writer, to know whether it is second-rate or a work of genius. And how many writers who have been considered second-rate, and yet have persisted in believing in themselves, have been discovered and hailed as geniuses after their deaths; or writers who have been highly acclaimed during their lives have been forgotten forever shortly after? or writers who are true geniuses have never been discovered at all? Does it really matter if we are geniuses or second-rate? If we are majah, minah, or mediocah? As for *Wrinkle*, for once I have the arrogance to know in my heart that this is something good. But if it is constantly turned down will I be able to keep the faith that I still have in it? Will I begin to doubt?"

I'm ashamed of all the wailing, but I did it. "Why do I love this Tower so when I have done so much bitter weeping in it? X has turned down *Wrinkle*, too, and this has really thrown me. I cared terribly about having them take it, and they turned it down so quickly, two days, that I know it hasn't had a fair reading. Someone lower down who just sent a form-type of rejection. This is one of the times when I think I'm yelling with complete and utter reason."

Does it sound as though I use my journals for nothing but weeping and wailing and gnashing of teeth? I don't. Much of this book is right out of the pages of my journals, those everything-books, and much from the scribbling of this summer just passing. And I don't mean to dwell on failure and bitterness and rejection. If I bring it up again here it is for two reasons: it may give a little courage to someone else who is going through a similar stretch. And I know now that the bleakness of that period of my life, bleak in many areas, was an essential part of my growing up, both as a woman and as a writer. And in the midst of the bleakness I could write—a few days after one of the *Wrinkle* rejections—"I've been writing hard on the new book, and am tired and happy." And, "Here I am in what would certainly be considered my middle years, and yet I feel as young and eager and open to development as I did when I was twenty-one."

It was a long time after these fairly close-together entries that *Wrinkle* went to Farrar, Straus and Giroux. I worked on what was eventually to become *The Love Letters*. I recorded a happy evening of singing rounds at the table. I worried about not being a good enough wife. Or mother. I was joyful. In misery. In other words, I suppose I behaved normally for a writer.

This was 1960. In 1963 when I was in Chicago to receive the Newbery Medal for *A Wrinkle in Time,* a woman who was a fine editor for me with *And Both Were Young,* but who had rejected both the *Austins* and *Wrinkle,* said to me, "I know I should have published these books. But I wonder: if I had accepted *A Wrinkle in Time,* would it have been the right moment for it? If it had been published then, maybe you wouldn't be here now."

She is a very wise woman.

The ancient Israelites, crossing the desert, missing the very imprisonment of the days in Egypt, taking too long to get to the Promised Land, wailed, "We remember the fish, which we did eat in Egypt freely; the cucumbers, and the melons, and the leeks, and the onions, and the garlick." They complained about the manna which had been sent them, and were angry and demanding. "Lust came upon them in the wilderness; and they importuned God. And he gave them their desire, and sent leanness withal into their soul," wrote the Psalmist.

Thank you, God, for not giving in to my importunate demands.

. . 11 . .

To balance the precarious triangle of wife-mother-writer: it was, is, a problem. And what did I mean by trying to "be good"?

To knock down selfishness, self-will, I suppose. And this is not a do-it-yourself job. We can no more "try" to be virtuous than we can try to be humble, or to act with integrity.

Virtue, that odd, old-fashioned word: we have all known so-called virtuous women, professional do-gooders, busybodies; they have no lives of their own, so they try to interfere with others.

How we have blunted this word which comes from the French: Cooper's *Thesaurus Linguae Romanae et Britannicae* says: "Vertue, strength, puissance, prowesse, valiantnesse, man-linesse, manhoode, power."

A description, surely, of the man every young girl seeks, the man strong enough to be gentle, powerful enough to be tender.

I am grateful to the virtuous men I have encountered in this world: my father who, in the trenches, would not send his men anywhere he would not go himself; he was known as "Bonnie Prince Charlie."

My husband, who has had the puissance and valiantnesse to put up with me for a quarter of a century.

The friends of my right hand.

.. 12 ..

They guide me with their virtue, particularly when I bumble into "I can do it myself." One day the children came home from school, bringing with them a discussion about precisely this: in an emergency one must not depend on law or on structure but on judging the situation as it arises, and then making the "lov-ing" decision. We must meet each particular situation sepa-rately, with no general preconceptions. This is very well in the-ory, and it is paradoxical of me to have reservations, but I do.

What sends up those little red flags of warning is the assumption that in a crisis we will possess the calm reason with which to make the loving decision. It presupposes that man is perfectible of his own effort—just try a little harder, chaps, and it will be all right.

Collectively and separately my generation has tried pretty hard, and it isn't all right.

In a moment of crisis we don't act out of reasoned judgment but on our conditioned reflexes. We may be able to send men to the moon, but we'd better remember we're still closely related to Pavlov's dog. Think about driving a car: only the beginning driver *thinks* as he performs each action; the seasoned driver's body works kinesthetically; steering wheel, brake, accelerator—if you have to think about using each one of these you won't dare drive on a major highway. A driver prevents an accident because of his conditioned reflexes; hands and feet respond more quickly than thought.

I'm convinced the same thing is true in all other kinds of crisis, too. We react to our conditioning built up of every single decision we've made all our lives; who we have used as our mirrors; as our points of reference. If our slow and reasoned decisions are generally wise, those which have to be made quickly are apt to be wise, too. If our reasoned decisions are foolish, so will be those of the sudden situation.

One of the girls gave this example: a group of men are in the Arctic. One is badly hurt. If the others leave him to get back to safety themselves, he will die. If they stay with him, they will all very likely die before help comes. The reasonable decision, the ethical decision in this situation, she was told, is for the others to leave so that only one man will die.

Everything in me rebels. It was the reasonable decision made once before when Caiaphas said that it is expedient that one man die for the sake of the nation.

What would E. M. Forster think? To leave your friend and save the group is not, after all, the particular. It is the general once again.

We killed one man for the sake of the nation once. Didn't we learn anything?

.. 13 ..

It leads me back to Pope John daring to make a decision without knowing what was going to happen. I hope that I, like E. M. Forster, would choose to stay with my friend, and perhaps die. But I would not need to be able to predict the outcome to make the choice. If one must predict every outcome, then the logical thing *is* to save those you can and leave your friend to die.

Something that happened when we lived in the country helps me here. During our General Store, diaper, and snowsuit years, Hugh did a good deal of lay preaching. He did not talk as a minister or priest but simply as a human being, a father, a man, sharing his thoughts with the members of the congregation. One Sunday he was asked to talk in a church in a nearby town. I could not be with him, because I could not leave the choir; we were doing a difficult anthem, and it wasn't only that I was needed to "conduct." I was needed for moral support—not only by the choir; the anthem was in three sharps at the time when Grandma would occasionally still tackle sharps.

When Hugh came home he was despondent. He had talked about family, about the relationship of parents and children. He had talked from his heart about things important to him and to every parent, and he had felt from the congregation nothing but a wall of blankness. They had sat there politely; they hadn't coughed; but he felt that there had been no response whatsoever.

The next day a car drove up to the store, and a man Hugh had never seen before got out and came in. "Mr. Franklin, I just had to come tell you. I heard you at church yesterday. I'm a contractor just starting out for myself. I work hard, and I'm doing all right, but I've been all tied up in knots. I haven't been able to eat and sleep, and when the kids have asked me questions I've snapped at them, and a couple of times I've had my wife in tears. Yesterday I came home from church and I joked with the kids at the table, and it was the first time we've laughed during a meal in I can't tell you when. Afterwards I helped my girl with her spelling. She's been having a tough time, and I managed to make it make sense to her. Then I went out and played ball with my son. The knot was gone from my stomach, and I slept all night like a baby. I had to come tell you."

But if he hadn't come to tell Hugh, the result would have been the same. If we accept the responsibility of a situation, there is a response, whether we know it or not, and whether it's the response we expect—or want. Perhaps we may be required to die with our friend?

. . 14 . .

Suppose the strange little iceberg that is the human mind (the largest part submerged, ignored, feared) is also likened to a living radio or television set. With our conscious, surface selves we are able to tune in only a very few wave lengths. But there are others, and sometimes in our dreams we will pick up a scene from a distant, unknown, seemingly non-rational channel—but is it non-rational? Or is it in another language, using metaphors and similes with which we are not yet familiar?

"Consciousness expanding" is part of the current jargon. When I was very young and even more naïve than I am now, living alone in Greenwich Village, something in my non-rational mind rejected suggestions made to me by people older and far cleverer than I, that I should sleep with them because such experience was necessary for my development as a writer. The same kind of instinctive non-rational rejection came to me when a young man offered me LSD; he was taking it, and he thought in it to find all the answers. For a moment I was tempted. But I have watched him becoming more and more confused as he uses the drug to try to move more deeply into himself; as he tries to find himself he succeeds only in losing himself. He was talking about his self-searching one day to Will and me as he prepared to take a "trip." Will asked, "But what do you really expect from it?" He answered, "Instant meditation."

We don't hurt ourselves—except aesthetically, which is not to be taken lightly—by drinking instant coffee or eating powdered eggs, but we do hurt ourselves when we try to take short cuts to find out who we are, and what our place in the universe.

Not that I am against consciousness expanding: I want as much of my little iceberg as possible out in the full light of the sun, and I want to be clearly aware of the beautiful country beneath the waters. All forms of art are consciousness expanders, and I am convinced that they will take us further, and more consciously, than drugs. For me, writing is the obvious one. But so is reading the great writers. So is going to a museum, or listening to a Schubert Quartet, or, better still, sitting at the piano and making music, no matter how fumblingly. And so are our dreams. I want to remember them, not so that I can recount them at boring length, but so that I will be less insular, less afraid to travel in foreign lands. We are very foolish if we shrug and patronizingly consider that these voyages are not real.

My husband is automatically suspicious of what is commonly called mysticism, or the supernatural. He is right to be dubious. This is dangerous territory, and to experiment foolishly can lead to death and damnation. I don't understand mysticism, but I do know that the kind of Be-a-Mystic-in-One-Easy-Lesson-in-Contemplation which is becoming fashionable has nothing whatsoever to do with the real thing. I think that one cannot be a mystic consciously any more than one can have integrity or be humble consciously. But there are, indeed, Horatio, more things in heaven and earth than our philosophies can account for. So I send out two messages from the realm where truth has nothing to do with provable fact.

The first message is not very cosmic in importance, but it is definitely outside the bounds of proof.

When I first started as librarian of the Cathedral, I, with Oliver, our old collie, took a route which led up Broadway, then turned east at 110th Street. We would then proceed up either the south or the north side of the street, depending on whether the light was red or green at that point. One morning we were walking up the north side, and Oliver gave a tremendous leap, as though he had been frightened by something, and almost threw me. I didn't pay much attention when the same thing happened the next time, but when it happened a third time, when it happened every time we passed one particular building, I began to wonder. Oliver would either fling to the end of his leash or he would make an elaborate, quivering circle around something I could not see.

I told my husband, the calm humanist, the iconoclast, the reasonable intellectual. Naturally he doubted; he laughed. The next time we were going to dinner with one of our friends at the Cathedral, he took Oliver's leash. Although I hated to see Oliver frightened (I now walked him only up the south side), I found myself wanting something to happen. It did. Oliver nearly threw him.

For over a year Hugh kept testing him; sometimes Oliver would only press, trembling, against Hugh as we walked by. But something always happened; Oliver saw, felt, feared, something that we did not, and whatever this thing was, it was evil.

When I tell this story and friends pooh-pooh, I turn to Hugh for corroboration. "Oh, it happened," he says. "I can't explain it, but it very definitely happened."

. . 15 . .

The second message moves deeper into the ocean.

When I was little we usually visited my maternal grandmother during the summer when she lived at the beach. I called my grandmother Dearma, because I thought that's what all grandmothers were called. The Saint-Gaudens children called old Madame Saint-Gaudens Dearma, and as I look at the snapshots of very small Madeleine with the formidable mother of Augustus Saint-Gaudens, and think of my own grandmother, equally austere and dignified, it seems an oddly familiar name even for a grandchild. Now that I have grandchildren of my own, I understand this total lack of awe rather better.

In any case, I called my magnificent grandmother Dearma, and I loved the house at the beach in a special way. It was there that I was first taken out at night to see stars, and where I first sensed ultimate design in the universe. I've always had a feeling of personal communication with stars, not in the sense of astrology but in the sense of feeling a consciousness which encompasses all the tiny human consciousness on earth and enlarges it.

When we returned to the United States after several years abroad, we went to spend the summer at the beach with Dearma. What I am going to tell happened at summer's end. It was Sunday night. During the day it had been hot and sunny, and friends and relations dropped by to see us and Dearma; we sat on the veranda and rocked, fanned ourselves with palm-leaf fans, and drank cool drinks. It was quiet, and typical of a Southern Sunday. We went early to bed.

While I was getting undressed I had the strange, almost asthmatic feeling of pressure that sometimes comes before a thunderstorm. Thunderstorms are frequent at the beach, but I knew that this oppression did not come from storm. It was a presage of something terrible.

It never occurred to me to tell my parents. I did tell God. My faith was still a child's faith, and still very much my own. My school was Anglican, with chapel morning and evening; I never felt the presence of God very strongly there; I did feel him at night in bed when at last I could be alone in dark and silence. So I prayed to him now: Please, don't let anything terrible happen. Please.

The answer was very clear; not in words, though I am going to have to set it down in words, but in certainty:

Not only was something terrible going to happen, but I now

knew what that something was to be: my grandmother would die that night.

Dearma was in her seventies; her heart was not very good; but there was nothing to indicate imminent death. I was too young to have heard about second sight or pre-vision. I am not at all sure what my parents would have said had I gone in to them. I did not. I prayed and prayed that the answer would be changed, but it was not.

I didn't do much sleeping. I would slide in and out of the shallows of sleep, always on the edge of wakefulness, always listening, waiting. Sometime in the very early hours of the morning I sat up, completely awake, as though I had heard a sudden noise, though I had not. I listened. Nothing. But I knew that this was the time to get my parents. I went to their room and woke them, saying, "Please go in to Dearma."

We went in and she was breathing strangely, her last breaths. She was not conscious; she went to bed and to sleep and died. The doctor came and pronounced her dead. The breathing had stopped; she was very still.

There was no wind. The ocean seemed to be holding its breath.

Coffee, as usual in times of stress, was brewed by somebody. At dawn my mother and I went swimming. I think Father stayed with Dearma.

I remember putting on my bathing suit and walking across the beach with my mother in the strange cool of dawn, totally in communion with her, walking silently into the shallow ocean, into the waves, and into a sunrise more beautiful than any I remember before or since. It was the sunrise which made everything bearable, which helped me to accept that death is a part of life.

There are more things, Horatio. We will never understand them all, not now, not here. But we are foolish to underestimate them, explain them away, pretend they do not exist.

. . 16 . .

So Einstein's calling on the necessity for mystery in the scientist's life did not surprise me. I was rather more startled to discover Freud saying that the two groups of people who defy psychological knowledge are the artists and the saints. None of the rules of psychology hold for them. Thornton Wilder also classed artists and saints together in *Our Town*. After Emily dies she is allowed to come back to earth to relive a day, and she is torn apart by her awareness of all that she has always taken for granted. She asks the stage manager, "Do any human beings ever realize life while they live it?—every, every minute?" And he answers, "No. The saints and poets, maybe—they do, some."

Tallis once told me that a great mathematician said, "Mathematics is the conscious setting aside of facts until we have found a conclusion." Einstein's own work demonstrates his words on the mysterious; he did not come to his theories by working them out consciously; rather, he took enormous leaps, like Nureyev defying gravity, and there were his conclusions waiting for him, out in the realm of the mysterious. After that he had to go back and get it all worked out mathematically.

Copernicus discovered that the earth revolves around the sun in the same mysterious way the great artist works. Mathematically, it *can* be proved that the sun, the planets, the stars, all revolve around our earth, that we *are* the center of the universe. But this was not an artistically beautiful equation, and this bothered Copernicus. He didn't have any idea that he was going to discover that we revolve around a middle-sized sun in a back-wash of our particular galaxy; what he was interested in was making a mathematically elegant equation. He did, and as a result the entire theory of the universe changed; it shook some people's belief in God—it's rather nice to think that the universe was created entirely for the benefit of mankind. For others this discovery, and all the discoveries of science, strengthens faith in God's glory and mystery.

The great astronomer, Tycho Brahe, put on his court robes before going to his telescope. The artist should have the same reverence in approaching his work. Something happens in his life, in the world around him, which is the equivalent of an ignoble mathematical equation. So he "puts on his court robes" and sometimes, as a result, we get a *House of Atreus*, or a *Dr. Faustus*, or a *Wuthering Heights*; or, I venture to say, a *Wind in the Willows*, or a *Sleeping Beauty*, or an *Alice Through the Looking Glass*.

Why do we try to cut down the forests and remove the brambles and thorny roses of this radiant land?

One of my English aunts now lives in an ancient, rheumatism-producing castle in Scotland, because it has been in her husband's family since before the Norman Conquest. But she lived for many years in Kenya, where, after her first husband's death, she managed his vast estate singlehanded. On one of her rare trips to the United States she was staying in New York, at the Hotel Plaza. And she was puzzled because she was wakened, every morning, by the roaring of the lions, exactly as though she were still in Kenya. Lions on the island of Manhattan? It seemed most unlikely, and she mentioned it to a friend. The friend became most agitated over my Aunt Alexandra's mental health, and insisted on setting up an appointment with a well-known psychiatrist who, when Alexandra's symptom was described, felt that it was urgent that she see him at once. Fortunately, before the appointment, Alexandra mentioned hearing lions at dawn to another friend, who laughed and said, "Of course. You're hearing the lions in the Central Park Zoo. It's just across from the Plaza."

I wish we didn't try to turn real lions into imaginary ones. The lions are not imaginary. They are real. I have experienced a lot of lions in my lifetime, and these encounters are what I write about, and why I write as a storyteller: it's the best way to make the lions visible. But the lions must be those of my own experience. Our projecting from the tangible present into the "what if" of the imagination must be within the boundaries of our own journeying.

. . 17 . .

When I do something wrong I tend to alibi, to make excuses, blame someone else. Until I can accept whatever it is that I have done, I am only widening the gap between my real and my ontological self, and I am thus excluding myself so that I begin to think that I am unforgivable.

We need to be forgiven:

to be forgiven in this time when fish are dying in our rivers; in this time of poison gas dumped on the ocean floor and in the less and less breathable air of our cities, of children starving; being burned to death in wars which stumble on; being attacked by rats in their cribs . . .

we need to be forgiven in this grey atmosphere which clogs the lungs so that we cannot breathe, and breathless, spiritless, can no longer discern what is right and what is wrong, what is our right hand and what is our left, what is justice and what tyranny, what is life and what is death.

I heard a man of brilliance cry out that God has withdrawn from nations when they have turned from Him, and surely we are a stiff-necked people; why should He not withdraw?

But then I remember Jonah accusing God of overlenience, of foolishness, mercy, and compassion.

We desperately need the foolishness of God.

. . 18 . .

During my last year in boarding school I had attained the elevated position of Head of School; I was editor of the yearbook and literary magazine, played leading roles in the school plays. I had finally made it. I also had all the answers, theologically speaking. I went, with all the other Episcopalians in the school, to the Episcopal church on Sunday; it bored me totally, and it was then that I picked up the habit of writing poetry during sermons. When it came to the General Confession in Morning Prayer I was, with proper humility, willing to concede that I occasionally left undone a few things which I ought to have done (I was, after all, very busy), and I occasionally did a few things which I ought not to have done (I was, after all, not "pi"); but I was not willing to say that I was a miserable offender and that there was no health in me.

It's a stage we all go through; it takes a certain amount of living to strike the strange balance between the two errors either of regarding ourselves as unforgivable or as not needing forgiveness.

During the Crosswicks years when the children were little, a

233

new hymnal was put out for the Congregational church. In the back is a section of prayers, and it includes the General Confession from the Book of Common Prayer. It is an interesting commentary on human nature in this confused century that precisely those words which I could not, would not say as an adolescent were deleted from the Congregational prayers.

By that time, in the midst of my fumbling agnosticism, it had become very clear to me that I *was* a miserable offender, and that there was very little health in me. I wasn't falling into that peculiar trap of *hubris* which tempts one into thinking that one is sinfuler than thou. If I never got through a day when I didn't do at least one thing I regretted, this was assuredly true of everybody else I knew. Perhaps my friends were not tempted, as I was, to do a Gauguin, but they had their own major temptations. Perhaps their sins of omission were less in the housewifely area than mine, but surely they had their own equivalent. I was rather upset by the mutilation of the Confession.

"It's all right to think you can be virtuous if you try just a little harder when you're an adolescent," I told Quinn, "but I don't like having the church behave like an adolescent."

When we moved back to New York a series of those non-coincidences started me back into the church in which I was born, the church of John Donne, Lancelot Andrewes, Shakespeare. A friend of Alan's, doing his Ph.D. in seventeenth-century English literature, became an Anglican, saying that one can hardly spend so much time with all these people without sharing their beliefs. When, shortly after our return, the Episcopal church put out a trial liturgy, I was unhappy with it for two major reasons: it was not worded in the best language of which we are capable; and it made the confession before receiving communion optional.

We haven't done a very good job of righting the wrongs of

our parents or our peers, my generation. We can't say to our children, here is a green and peaceful world we have prepared for you and your children: enjoy it. We can offer them only war and pollution and senility. And this is the time we decide, in our churches, that we're so virtuous we don't need to be forgiven: symbolically, iconically forgiven.

If the Lord's table is the prototype of the family table, then, if I think in terms of the family table, I know that I cannot sit down to bread and wine until I've said I'm sorry, until reparations have been made, relations restored. When one of our children had done something particularly unworthy, if it had come out into the open before dinner, if there had been an "I'm sorry," and there had been acceptance, and love, then would follow the happiest dinner possible, full of laughter and fun. If there was something still hidden; if one child, or as sometimes happens, one parent, was out of joint with the family and the world, that would destroy the atmosphere of the whole meal.

What is true of the family table is, in another sense, true of the conjugal bed. Twin beds make no sense to me. I can understand an occasional need for a separate room, but not separate beds. If a man and wife get into bed together it is very difficult to stay mad. Both Hugh and I have tried, and it hasn't worked. The touch of a hand is enough to dissolve me into tenderness; the touch of a cold foot enough to dissolve me into laughter. One way or another, reparation is made, relations restored, love returned.

Only a human being can say *I'm sorry. Forgive me.* This is part of our particularity. It is part of what makes us capable of tears, capable of laughter.

I've mentioned Dana, Dana Catherine de Ruiz, who has been a member of the Crosswicks family for so long that I cannot remember a time when she has not been a bright and beautiful part of it. We knew her first as a girl in the grade above Josephine at school. The two of them were pleasant acquaintances but became real friends one summer when they were both on the same job, were both overworked, and fled together to sit in an ancient cemetery for a small respite. If you will think about it, there are not many people with whom you can sit on a tombstone and be at peace.

One day as we were walking home down the lane, Dana said, "I don't think of you as my godmother. I think of you as my godfriend." Surely that is the right description of our relationship. Dana may be young enough to be my daughter in chronology; in eternity she is considerably older than I am. There is nothing we don't talk about, and we share a great many friends —but since our friends range in age from one year to ninety, that's not as odd as it may sound.

Dana knows that the idea of a Little Gidding, that community of people in England three and a half centuries ago, working together, suffering together, rejoicing together, never losing an awareness of their responsibility to the entire world, is immensely appealing to me. I certainly understand, in my blood and bones, the need young people today have to group together in "communes," to try to bind up in community the wounds of our present fragmentation. This is what I am groping towards myself, and what I find tangible in the summer in our Crosswicks family, and in the winter in the family of the Cathedral Close.

Walking down the lane through the shifting shadows of the trees, I mentioned longingly to Dana my desire to live, eventually, in a Little Gidding kind of community, and she said calmly, "You do."

Yes. Wherever there is unity in diversity, then we are free to be ourselves; it cannot be done in isolation; we need each other.

Before we eat dinner at night we all join hands around the table, and, for me, this circle of love is the visible symbol of all I hope for, and all that Dana meant.

. . 20 . .

One of the things I am most grateful for is my very lack of ability as a pastry cook. A decade ago when we first moved back to New York from Crosswicks, we put our children in a nearby school, St. Hilda's and St. Hugh's. We did some soul-searching over this, because we feel strongly about the value of the American public-school system and we wanted to be part of it. My husband went through the Tulsa public schools. I, growing up in New York and Europe, went only to private or independent schools. I hope it's because I was for so long in school abroad that I know so little about American geography. When Hugh and I were in a play in Chicago, the stage manager came in to the theatre with her dog, saying that they had had such a lovely walk by the lake. "Oh, did you walk around it?" I asked.

I was given a geography book for Christmas.

Hugh and I were married in Chicago during the run of another play—we met in *The Cherry Orchard* and married in *The Joyous Season*, and after the play closed we bought a very second-hand car and set off to see his family in Oklahoma, and mine in the South. I remember two things about the car: the license plates for Illinois in 1946 were made of soybeans; and there was something wrong with the gearshift; it kept slipping back into neutral. We drove through the Ozarks with one hand holding the recalcitrant gearshift in high.

I had never been west of Chicago, and I knew nothing about Oklahoma. I blush to report that I asked Hugh if the streets of Tulsa were paved. Granted, he was leading me on. It was when he told me that his mother put on shoes to go to church that I realized that I was being had.

But it isn't fair to blame independent school education. And the public school in our neighborhood when we returned to the city was one of the worst in New York. We were, and are, more than grateful for St. Hilda's and St. Hugh's—and of course, with a name like St. Hugh, it was obviously the place for us.

One day the children came home with the usual mimeographed petition for a cake for the bazaar. They were new at the school and they wanted their mother to do the right thing. "Please, Mother." So I baked a cake.

I'm as bad at cakes as I am at cherry pies. The last cherry pie I made was shortly after we were married and Hugh had some people from the Theatre Guild in for dinner, and I was determined to impress them with my wifely virtues. When it was time for dessert I didn't think the pie crust was brown enough, so I put it under the broiler. We had to get the fire extinguisher.

So I made a cake for my children's sake. It tasted delicious. But it didn't look the way it tasted. It was lopsided: a mess. I wrote the headmistress a note which ran more or less like this: "I tried. I baked a cake. Because my family loves me, they will eat it. But it is obvious that this is not the way in which I can be of use to the school. Is there anything else I could do, more in line with my talents? Is there a play we could help with, or anything like that?"

238

Within a few days Hugh and I found that we were directing the Christmas pageant, with the entire Cathedral of St. John the Divine as our stage: Mr. and Mrs. Max Reinhardt. It's quite something to see the three kings march in their glorious costumes the length of two city blocks.

If I had been able to bake that cake for the school cake sale I might still be in darkness. Father Anthony (I speak of him so casually: he is Metropolitan of Surozh and Exarch of the Russian Patriarchal in Western Europe) said last spring that it is good to have turned to God as he did, as I did, after a time of darkness, because then one truly knows what it is like to be dead, and now to be alive.

Hugh and I first ran into Canon Tallis when we were directing the pageant at the Cathedral, after my cake-baking fiasco. Ran into is right. We clashed. He did not like vast quantities of school children in the Cathedral during Advent, that austere time of eschatology, reenacting the Christmas story out of chronology. He bristled when he saw us. We bristled when we saw him. We could conceive of no reason why the pageant wasn't the most important thing in the world, why he didn't put at our disposal all the facilities of the Cathedral.

Later, when I knew him better, I explained to him, passionately, that the chronology of the pageant wasn't really what was important; Christmas is an arbitrary date anyhow; the important thing was that the children should have some idea of Christmas beyond street-corner Santa Clauses and loudspeakers braying out Christmas carols. "Don't you understand that many of them won't have any Christmas otherwise? They won't even go to church. If it's not to be a blasphemy they'll have to have it here, now, before the school vacation begins, out of chronology —but in real time."

Thus Madeleine the agnostic.

But we did, after that, have all the cooperation possible from the Cathedral staff.

Later on I went to Canon Tallis, almost by accident, when I was in trouble. I'd made an appointment with another canon at the Cathedral, and his secretary forgot to put the appointment in his book. He was full of apologies, but had to be away, so couldn't see me later, and suggested Tallis. Canon Tallis was the last person I wanted to see. Something told me that it would either work magnificently or be totally horrible.

It worked magnificently.

It wasn't that my problem was solved but that I had help in bearing it. I also told him all my intellectual doubts, my total incredulity about the incarnation; the idea that God could pitch his tent among men was absurd. Of course! It still is.

I had talked with several Congregational minister friends about my intellectual doubts. I was eager to be converted—I didn't like atheism or agnosticism; I was by then well aware that I am not self-sufficient, that I needed the dimension of transcendence. They were eager to convert me. But they explained everything. For every question I asked, they had an answer. They tried to reach me through my mind.

First of all, my mind is not that good. I'm not stupid; I did graduate from Smith with honors. But I am, basically, not an intellectual. Nevertheless, I knew that I could not throw away my mind, and it was not the discoveries of science that bothered me. On the contrary. The book I read during this period which brought me closest to God was one that never mentioned God, *The Limitations of Science,* by J. W. N. Sullivan.

My minister friends gave me all kinds of theological books to read, mostly by German theologians. The more I read, the further I was shoved away from any kind of acceptance. I would read logical explanations of the totally mysterious scandal of particularity and think: if I have to believe all this bunk, then Christianity is not for me. One line in the Book of Common Prayer made sense to me: *the mystery of the word made flesh*. If only my friends would admit that it *was* a mystery, and stop giving me explanations! I wrote in my journal: "I talk to people—oh, people I respect, people I like—and yet I never feel any sense of terrific excitement in their own lives about Jesus, in the way that the early Christians must have been excited so that they were transfigured by Jesus. In no one, no one, no matter how loudly they talk about salvation being possible only through Jesus, do I find this great thing *showing* in them, glowing in them, lighting their lives, as it must if it is to make any sense today at all." I was, I am sure, less than fair; nevertheless that was what reasonable explanations did to me.

Canon Tallis did not explain anything. He listened to my doubts in silence. I think he thought they were really very unimportant. As far as my specific, daily problems were concerned, I found that I could take them more lightly, could laugh more easily.

Then spring came. Hugh was away with the tour of *Luther*. He'd had a fine time playing Cardinal Cajetan on Broadway, and we felt that he should go on tour. But all kinds of things happened that spring. Bion, eleven, started running a high fever, for which no explanation could be found. At the hospital the doctor assured me that there was a physical cause, and they would go on testing until they found it. For forty-eight hours I lived with the knowledge that the doctor thought that Bion had cancer of the liver. He had been talking to me in abstruse medical terms, but one of my closest friends is a doctor, and I more or less went through medical school with her, and suddenly the doctor looked at me and said, "Do you know what I am talking about?"

"Yes. I'm afraid I do."

"We're re-testing, and I'll call you as soon as the results are in."

Hugh and I were trying not to phone each other too often; we called about every three days. He would be phoning the evening that we would know the results. By shortly after six, when Hugh usually called, I had not heard anything. Then the phone rang, and I dreaded telling Hugh what we feared; there was never any question of keeping it from him; he'd hear it in my voice. But it was not Hugh, it was the doctor, and it was not cancer.

Then Hugh's father died, and he had to fly from Chicago to Tulsa for the funeral. He called me from Chicago before leaving; I already knew, because I had talked to his sister that morning. While Hugh and I were talking, I could hear his voice break, and he said in astonishment, "Isn't it extraordinary, this is the first time I've felt anything about Dad, talking to you." But of course we both knew that it wasn't extraordinary at all.

Then happy news. Josephine was to be salutatorian of her class, graduating at sixteen. We were joyful and proud. But Hugh couldn't come for graduation, because he had taken time off from the play for his father's funeral. And Bion was still in the hospital.

Then something happened, something so wounding that it cannot possibly be written down. Think of two of the people you love most in the world; think of a situation in which both are agonizingly hurt and you are powerless to do anything to help. It is far easier to bear pain for ourselves than for those we love, especially when part of it is that we cannot share the pain but must stand by, unable to alleviate it.

Canon Tallis hardly knew us at all, then. But he stepped in. What he did is involved with all that I cannot write. The point right now is that this was the moment of light for me, because it was an act of love, Love made visible.

And that did it. Possibly nothing he could have done for me, myself, would have illuminated the world for me as did this act of love towards those I love. Because of this love, this particular (never general) Christian love, my intellectual reservations no longer made the least difference. I had seen love in action, and that was all the proof I needed.

.. 21 ..

There is no more beautiful witness to the mystery of the word made flesh than a baby's naked body. I remember with sensory clarity sitting with one of my babies on my lap and running my hand over the incredibly pure smoothness of the bare back and thinking that any mother, holding her child thus, must have at least an echo of what it is like to be Mary; that in touching the particular created matter, flesh, of our child, we are touching the Incarnation. Alan, holding his daughter on his lap, running his hand over her bare back with the same tactile appreciation with which I had touched my children, made a similar remark.

Once, when I was in the hospital, the smooth and beautiful white back of the woman in the bed next to mine, a young woman dying of cancer, was a stabbing and bitter reminder of the ultimate end of all matter.

But not just our human bodies: all matter: the stars in their courses: everything: the end of time.

Meanwhile we are in time, and the flesh is to be honored. At all ages. For me, this summer, this has been made clear in a threefold way: I have fed, bathed, played pat-a-cake with my grandbabies. In the night when I wake up, as I usually do, I always reach out with a foot, a hand, to touch my husband's body; I go back to sleep with my hand on his warm flesh. And my mother is almost ninety and preparing to move into a different country. I do not understand the mysteries of the flesh, but I know that we must not be afraid to reach out to each other, to hold hands, to touch.

In our bedroom there is a large old rocking chair which was in the attic of Crosswicks when we bought it. It seems to have been made especially for mothers and babies. I have sat in it and nursed my babe in the middle of the night. I have sung innumerable lullabies from it. When Hugh was in *Medea*, which was sent overseas in 1951 by the State Department, I sat in the rocking chair, carrying his child within me and holding our first-born in my arms, singing all the old lullabies, but especially *Sweet and Low* because of "over the Western sea," and "Bring him again to me."

This summer I sit in the rocking chair and rock and sing with one or other of my granddaughters. I sing the same songs I sang all those years ago. It feels utterly right. Natural. The same.

But it isn't the same. I may be holding a baby just as I used to hold a baby, but chronology has done many things in the intervening years, to the world, to our country, to my children, to me. I may feel, rocking a small, loving body, no older than I felt rocking that body's mother. But I am older bodily; my energy span is not as long as it used to be; at night my limbs ache with fatigue; my eyes are even older than the rest of me. It is going to seem very early—it is going to *be* very early—when the babies wake up: Alan, Josephine, Cynthia, and I take turns getting up and going downstairs with them, giving them breakfast, making the coffee. Is it my turn again so quickly?

Chronology: the word about the measurable passage of time, although its duration varies: how long is a toothache? how long is standing in line at the supermarket? how long is a tramp through the fields with the dogs? or dinner with friends, or a sunset, or the birth of a baby?

Chronology, the time which changes things, makes them grow older, wears them out, and manages to dispose of them, chronologically, forever.

Thank God there is kairos, too: again the Greeks were wiser than we are. They had two words for time: *chronos* and *kairos*.

Kairos is not measurable. Kairos is ontological. In kairos we *are*, we are fully in isness, not negatively, as Sartre saw the isness of the oak tree, but fully, wholly, positively. Kairos can sometimes enter, penetrate, break through chronos: the child at play, the painter at his easel, Serkin playing the *Appassionata*, are in kairos. The saint at prayer, friends around the dinner table, the mother reaching out her arms for her newborn baby, are in kairos. The bush, the burning bush, is in kairos, not any burning bush, but the very particular burning bush before which Moses removed his shoes; the bush I pass on my way to the brook. In kairos that part of us which is not consumed in the burning is wholly awake. We too often let it fall asleep, not as the baby in my arms droops into sleepiness, but dully, bluntingly.

I sit in the rocking chair with a baby in my arms, and I am in both kairos and chronos. In chronos I may be nothing more than some cybernetic salad on the bottom left-hand corner of a check; or my social-security number; or my passport number. In kairos I am known by name: Madeleine.

The baby doesn't know about chronos yet.

I'm off to the brook again. Summer is almost over; the golden rod is aflame. The bush burns with the red of autumn. The family has scattered, is scattering, to England, Mexico, Florida, California, to the big house across the lane and up the road. I've already started moving things back to New York. We are having a deep, gentle, September rain, which the land, the trees, the brook need thirstily. Yesterday I waded downstream for a long time, wet from the waters of the brook itself, from the rain, from the drops shaking from the leaves as I pushed under, over, through the overhanging trees.

The brook, the bush, the sun-warmed rock, as in the song, have seen, felt, touched, healed me.

Gregory of Nyssa points out that Moses's vision of God began with the light, with the visible burning bush, the bush which was bright with fire and was not consumed; but afterwards, God spoke to him in a cloud. After the glory which could be seen with human eyes, he began to see the glory which is beyond and after light.

The shadows are deepening all around us. Now is the time when we must begin to see our world and ourselves in a different way.

THE SUMMER OF THE GREAT-GRANDMOTHER

The Crosswicks Journal
BOOK 2

THE
SUMMER
OF THE
GREAT-GRANDMOTHER

Madeleine L'Engle

HarperSanFrancisco
A Division of HarperCollins*Publishers*

LC 79-65523
ISBN 0-06-254506-5

92 93 94 CWI 18 17 16 15 14 13

for the great-grandmother

Contents

I

Summer's Beginning

1

————

Tᴴɪs ɪs ᴛʜᴇ sᴜᴍᴍᴇʀ of the great-grandmother, more her summer than any other summer. This is the summer after her ninetieth birthday, the summer of the swift descent.

Once, when I was around twelve, we took a twenty-mile toboggan ride down a Swiss mountainside. The men guiding the toboggan were experienced mountaineers; the accelerating speed was wildly exciting. Mother and I both clutched the sides of the toboggan as we careened around sharply banked curves. The guides could keep it on the hard-packed snow of the path, but they could not stop it in its descent. My mother's plunge into senility reminds me of that toboggan ride.

When I look at the long green and gold days of this summer, the beautiful days are probably more beautiful, and the horrible days more horrible, than in actuality. But there's no denying that it's a summer of extremes.

It might be said with some justification that all our summers are summers of extremes, because when the larger family gathers together we are a group of opinionated, noisily articulate, varied and variable beings. It is fortunate for us all that Crosswicks is a largish, two-hundred-and-some-year-old farmhouse; even so, when four generations' worth of strong-willed people assemble under one roof, the joints of the house seem to creak in an effort to expand. If we all strive toward moderation, it is because we, like the ancient Greeks, are natively immoderate.

This is our fourth four-generation summer. Four Junes ago Mother's namesake and first great-grandchild, Madeleine, was born. We call her Léna, to avoid confusion in this household of Madeleines. Charlotte, the second great-granddaughter, was born fourteen months later. My mother is very proud of being the Great-grandmother.

But she is hardly the gentle little old lady who sits by the fireside and knits. My knowledge of her is limited by my own chronology; I was not around for nearly forty years of her life, and her premotherhood existence was exotic and adventurous; in the days before planes she traveled by camel and donkey; she strode casually through a world which is gone and which I will never see except through her eyes. The woman I have experienced only as loving and gentle mother has, for the past several years, been revealing new and demanding facets. When she wants something she makes her desires known in no uncertain terms, and she's not above using her cane as a weapon. She gathers puppies and kittens into her lap; she likes her bourbon before dinner; she's a witty raconteur; and the extraordinary thing about her descent into senility is that there are occasional wild, brilliant flashes which reveal more of my mother-Madeleine than I ever knew when she was simply my mother.

4

But she is my mother; there is this indisputable, biological fact which blocks my attempts at objectivity. I love her, and the change in her changes me, too.

ॐ

She was born in the Deep South, spent her married life wandering the globe, in New York and London, and now, in her old age, prefers the more clement weather of North Florida for the winters. But her presence in Crosswicks has always been part of the summers. A friend asked me, "Did you invite your mother to spend the summers with you or did she invite herself?"

I was a little taken aback. "There wasn't ever any question of inviting. We just said, 'When are you coming?'"

"Did you discuss it with Hugh?"

I don't think it ever needed discussion. My mother and my husband have always loved each other—after the very first when Mother wasn't happy about the idea of my marrying an actor. She and Hugh are much alike, in character, in temperament. A stranger would be apt to take Mother and Hugh for mother and son, and me for the in-law. We have always thought of her as part of Crosswicks. She helped make it grow from the dilapidated, unloved old building it was when we first saw it, a quarter of a century ago, to the home it is now. She helped plan my workroom out over the garage, a beautiful study which the children named the Tower. When we lived in Crosswicks year round, while our children were little, she usually spent one of the winter months with us; when we moved back

5

to New York for the school year, this was even more fun for her, because we could go to the theatre, the opera.

I have been so used to having my mother be my friend as well as my mother, to having her be Hugh's friend, that I was surprised at the idea of "inviting" her to spend the summer, and at the implication that this is not the usual way of things.

Perhaps it's not, but having Mother spend the summer in Crosswicks is part of the chronology of the house.

～

Hugh and I drive to New York, to the airport, to meet her and bring her the hundred miles to Crosswicks. I am shocked when I see her. The plane flight has been harder on her than we had anticipated; the toboggan has continued its descent at an accelerating pace since we saw her at the ninetieth-birthday celebration on April 30. She is confused during the two and a half hours' drive. I hold her hand and try to point out familiar landmarks.

"I don't remember it," she says anxiously. Only occasionally will she see a building, a turn of the road, a special view, and say, "I know this! I've been here before . . . Haven't I?"

We stop at our usual halfway place, the Red Rooster, for lunch, but Mother is too nervous to eat, and we stay only a few minutes, while Hugh and I quickly swallow hamburgers. I continue to hold her hand, to pet her. My emotions are turned off; I do not feel, any more than one feels pain after a deep cut. The body provides its own anesthesia for the first minutes after a wound, and stitches can be put in without novocaine; my feelings are equally numbed. We complete the drive, and I am anxious only to get Mother home, and to bed, in the room which has been hers for a quarter of a century. My thoughts do not project beyond this to the rest of the summer.

I feel very tired, and somehow as though somebody had kicked me.

2

Mᴜ ᴍᴏᴛʜᴇʀ does not come to Crosswicks in isolated chronology; she comes to a house which, like a
river, continuously flows with living. The summer of
the great-grandmother began several weeks before
her arrival, early in June, while she was still in the
South, and her great-granddaughters were still living in England, where their parents, Alan and Josephine, were preparing to break up their home in
Lincoln and return to New York. Our younger
daughter, Maria, and Peter, with impatience and impetuousness similar to Hugh's and mine a quarter of
a century ago, couldn't wait for them. So on the fifth
of June Crosswicks was filled with the joy and laughter of a tiny wedding.

The apple blossoms were barely over, the lawn
still white from petal-fall. There were a few lingering
daffodils in cold and shady corners which keep small
drifts of snow long after the rest of the grass has
started to turn green. The lilac, purple and white,
was in full bloom (the white lilac tree outside
Mother's window was a birthday present to her
twenty-odd years ago); early daisies and ubiquitous
dandelions brightened the big field. Hugh mowed
the lawn, trimmed around rocks and trees. Our son,

Bion, just graduated from high school, made count-less trips to the dump, fifteen miles away—there's nothing like a wedding to insure a proper house-cleaning. And I cooked as though we expected to feed an army instead of a small wedding party.

Maria and I had long, quiet talks. Like her sister Josephine before her, she was apprehensive as the moment approached. I assured her that I had been too. We grew closer in sharing experience.

Peter and I talked, too. He said, "Maria is wor-ried that you don't love me as much as you love Alan." I assured him, "I love you just as much for being Peter as I love Alan for being Alan."

Alan is English, an Anglican priest and theo-logian. Peter is Jewish, and a theoretical chemist, and that's a superb pair of sons-in-law. A few days ago Peter showed me his most recent published paper and paid me the honor of expecting me to under-stand his strings of equations, Greek letters, and an occasional English word. He leaves pads of yellow paper lying around on which he has been scrawling a long equation he is trying to think through. Oc-casionally I will glimpse, off in the corner of my mind, something of what he is driving at, and this happens just often enough to encourage me.

On the day of the wedding, our friend and fam-ily godfather, Canon Tom Tallis, drove up to Cross-wicks from St. John's Cathedral in New York to per-form the wedding ceremony.

In the same large, L-shaped living room where Peter and Maria stood to become man and wife, Hugh and I, newly married, had put on wallpaper, yellow and grey colonial wallpaper which is still on the walls, still beautiful (we are very good wall-paperers). Hugh had spent hours pulling the old bark from the ceiling beams, scrubbing them down; these were the first important acts of making Crosswicks our home. Several years later I rocked Bion in an ancient wooden cradle in front of the fireplace in the long end of the L. The Christmas tree was always in the corner of the L, in front of the heavy door, the "funeral door" which blew in during the blizzard of '88. One Christmas Eve, when our children were small, we all set off for church, leaving the wrapped presents under the tree, and a puppy in the kitchen. When we got home the puppy had got loose and had joyfully unwrapped every single package. Thank-you letters that year ran something like, "Thank you for the lovely present . . ." because nobody had any idea who had sent what.

I have wept in this room; made love in this room, in front of the fire on a cold winter's night; I have waited anxiously for my husband to make a long drive home the length of New England during a terrible wind and snow storm. The house has absorbed and contained much of my married life, of my "grownup" years. The fullness of life in this room filled my heart as we waited for Tallis to begin.

The family wedding party stood in a semicircle—Hugh and me; Peter's mother and two sisters; Bion; plus the cats and dogs, interested in the whole event and ever ready to participate. Tyrrell, Josephine and Alan's dog, half shepherd, half golden retriever, who has been with us for the three years they have been in England, retired under the sofa. The two Irish setter puppies, Faba, who belongs to Tallis, and her sister, Dulcie, who is ours, are less well behaved and I had to order them, firmly, "Sit." Then the words of the wedding ceremony took over and I found that I was close to tears in the presence of these aweful vows my daughter and Peter were taking, the same vows which Hugh and I took, the vows which have held us together through many rough patches.

When I hugged and kissed Maria after the final words were said, I whispered to her, "Now that there has been a wedding here, the house is truly blessed."

That night when everybody had left, except for Hugh and Bion and me, and Hugh and I were ensconced wearily in our four-poster bed, reading, the phone rang. It was Maria and Peter, calling from the International Motel at JFK airport, bubbling with happiness, thanking us—and everybody—for their day; sharing their joy. Josephine and Alan had called from the same place on their wedding night; our travel agent had kept reassuring us that the rooms were soundproof, and it took us a long time to realize that he was referring to the sound of planes.

Laughing, we turned off the lights.

3

AND SO THE SUMMER began with something quite
ordinary, two young people getting married. We put
the house back into its usual disorder, and I began to
concentrate on Mother's arrival. When we went
South for the ninetieth-birthday party, we all realized that if Mother was to spend the summer
months in Crosswicks as usual, she would have to
have a great deal more care than ever before. So we
began putting together a bouquet of young girls to
tend her, twenty-four hours a day, seven days a
week. These girls, friends of our children, are of
high school and college age, and this is their summer
job. I talked with them informally, trying to tell them
what we expected of them, and somehow sensing intuitively that the job was going to be more exacting
than any of us anticipated.

The week before Mother's arrival I was to spend
teaching at a writers' conference in the Midwest, and
I set off, feeling that everything was under control,
as much as is humanly possible. How to take care
of my mother's summer was my single-minded concern, and I thought I had the summer pretty well
organized.

Then, as so often happens when I think that everything is under control, the unexpected struck. My second night at the conference, Hugh phoned and during the conversation told me, trying to make light of it, that he had been feeling some numbness in his feet. He had gone to our doctor, who had made an appointment for him with a neurologist; this could not be arranged for until a week after Mother's arrival.

I hung up, hoping I had kept my voice steady. Only a short while ago a cousin had died of a brain tumor; the first symptom was numbness in the feet. I could not guess whether or not Hugh remembered this. I knew, from the timbre of his voice when we talked again the next night, that he was more concerned than he wanted me to know.

So we moved into the same kind of cold waiting we had known once before, when three-year-old Josephine, during Christmastime, showed all the symptoms of leukemia. The pediatrician, examining her, had talked in obscure medical terminology, and I finally cut him short by saying, "What you mean is that you suspect leukemia—don't you?" "It is a possibility, yes." Once the words were out, he was much more gentle, much more human with us than he had been while he was pussyfooting.

Hugh and I shared our fear mostly in silence. We will never forget the merry little girl's lethargy and pallor, or her quiet stoicism in the hospital lab. Nor will we ever forget the world opening out again when the tests indicated an infection which was already beginning to clear up.

While I was at the writers' conference our sharing had to be on that silent level which precludes words. This was certainly no time to voice my fears to Hugh, or his to me. The only way I could be a wife to him was to affirm silently a courage and endurance I was very uncertain I had.

One of the problems of being a storyteller is the cultivated ability to extrapolate; in every situation all the *what if*s come to me. Often my fears are foolish: if Hugh is ten minutes late in getting home from the theatre he has not necessarily been pushed under a subway train or been stabbed. This time I knew the fear was not the child of my overvivid imagination; it was quite possible that I might have to face my husband's death even before my mother's. My powers of extrapolation were kind enough to slam the door on themselves, at least momentarily.

Still shaken, I went to give a lecture. I talked, as I had originally planned to do, about the precariousness of all life. And I told about walking in midtown New York and having a stone from a nearby half-built skyscraper crash to the sidewalk just behind me. Had I been a fraction of a second slower I would have been killed. And I said that the artist's response to the irrationality of the world is to paint or sing or write, not to impose restrictive rules but to rejoice in pattern and meaning, for there is something in all artists which rejects coincidence and accident. And I went on to say that we must meet the precariousness of the universe without self-pity, and with dignity and courage. It was what I had prepared, several weeks before, to talk about, tying it all in with writing, and our responsibility not to make vain promises of "everything will be all right" to our children. But that day the words were swords which turned to me, to teach me. To challenge me to accept my own words.

14

Listening to the lecture was one old and close friend who knew of my fears about Hugh, and I was sustained by the necessity not to let her down. What I cannot do for myself, I can sometimes do for somebody else.

That evening in my hotel room where nobody would overhear, I called Pat in Florida. Pat is a doctor, and we have been friends ever since we were in high school. I knew that she would not fob me off with easy answers, and she did not. She did, however, explain calmly and rationally all the things other than a brain tumor which could cause the symptoms. When I hung up I was still fearful, but I knew that there were alternatives.

In any case, one cannot sustain the heights of anguish for too long; this appears to be one of the built-in safety mechanisms of the psyche, and it is a saving grace. My fears for Hugh continued to give me an occasional kick in the pit of the stomach, but mostly they stayed decently in the background, and I was able to get on with the business of daily chores; complete the series of lectures and seminars; return to Crosswicks; prepare for Mother's arrival.

At the moment it is all a chill business because I am living in the cold place of the absence of meaning. And yet I know that if there is anything radically wrong with Hugh I cannot survive it myself, or be a wife and strength and help to him, or be a daughter to my mother, or be a person for my family and friends, unless there is a promise of meaning.

My frail hope is that I was able to lecture while I was impaled on the point of anguish, and that I lec-

tured well—no need for false humility here—and I
certainly could not have done it if I truly felt that the
universe has no meaning, that there is no point to
Hugh's life; or my mother's; or mine.

4

I AM TIRED, and numb. Mother's first two nights in Crosswicks I do not get any sleep, despite my fatigue. She needs more attention during the night than we had expected. The two girls who do night duty are young and completely inexperienced in nursing; Vicki has another year in high school; she was born during the years we lived in Crosswicks year round; it is difficult for me to realize that she is now a young woman, and a very capable young woman. Janet, too, I have known all her life; her father died when she was a baby, and her mother only a summer ago, and I wonder if she does not feel a certain irony in taking care of an old woman who has lived long past normal life expectancy. And I feel that the two girls need help, not physical help, simply my being there, awake and available if they need me.

After the first two wakeful nights it is clear to me how competent they are, and that I must get some rest.

&

It's a good thing to have all the props pulled out from under us occasionally. It gives us some sense of what is rock under our feet, and what is sand. It stops us from taking anything for granted. It has also taught me a lot about living in the immediate moment. I am somehow managing to live one day, one hour at a time. I have to. Hugh is in Crosswicks for four days, and somehow or other I am able simply to be with him, without projecting into the future. When he goes back to New York he will be going to the neurologist.

Each evening after dinner I walk the dogs down the lane for a few minutes, to catch my breath and regain perspective. The girls prepare the great-grandmother for bed, and we learned the first night that this is done more easily if I am out of the house; if I am there she calls for me, and will not do anything for any of us.

This night, when I return, she has been put to bed, and the larger family—Hugh, Bion, Josephine, the girls, assorted friends and neighbors (Maria and Peter are not back from their honeymoon)—have gathered in the living room to play poker with ancient poker chips. Alan is out in the Tower writing. I'm not a poker player either, so I go in to say good night to Mother and sit with her for a while. Our quiet times together have always been in the morning, over coffee, and at night before bedtime. For a moment, a flash, she is there, is herself, and we laugh at Tyrrell lying on her back, all four legs spread out, tail wagging in this upside-down position. Thomas, the amber cat, is also on his back, lying beside the big dog, rear legs abandoned, forepaws folded prayerfully across his chest. Titus, the yellow puffball kitten, is in Mother's lap, purring.

Then the moment is gone. "Something's wrong,"

my mother says. "I don't know what it is, but something's wrong."

"It's all right, Mother. Nothing is wrong."

"It is, it is. Something's wrong. I want to go home." This has been a constant refrain since her arrival. "I want to go home. I want to go home."

"You *are* home, Mother. You're with your family, with all your children."

"I want to go home."

Yesterday Alan put his arms around me to give me comfort, and said, "Yes, she wants to go home, but she doesn't mean down South."

Her fear touches off an enormous wave of protectiveness in me, and I know no way to keep her terror at bay.

"I want to go home," she repeats.

I sit on the bed beside her, and hold her hand. She fumbles with the other hand for the bell we have rigged up for her. A summer ago she used it sparingly; this summer it seems that the raucous buzz goes off every few minutes. "Mother, you don't need to ring for the girls. I'm right here."

"Where are they?"

"In the living room."

"What are they doing?"

"Playing poker."

She reaches again for the bell.

"Don't call them, Mother. I'm right here." I am obviously a poor substitute. Why am I hurt? This is not my mother who is rejecting me, my mother who was always patient, tolerant, wise.

Then she turns toward me, reaches for me. "I'm scared. I'm scared."

I put my arms around her and hold her. I hold

her as I held my children when they were small and afraid in the night; as, this summer, I hold my grandchildren. I hold her as she, once upon a time and long ago, held me. And I say the same words, the classic, maternal, instinctive words of reassurance. "Don't be afraid. I'm here. It's all right."

"Something's wrong. I'm scared. I'm scared."

I cradle her and repeat, "It's all right."

What's all right? What am I promising her? I'm scared too. I don't know what will happen when Hugh goes to the neurologist. I don't know what's going to happen with my mother this summer. I don't know what the message may be the next time the phone rings. What's all right? How can I say it?

But I do. I hold her close, and kiss her, and murmur, "It's all right, Mother. It's all right."

I mean these words. I do not understand them, but I mean them. Perhaps one day I will find out what I mean. They are implicit in everything I write. I caught a hint of them during that lecture, even as I was cautioning against false promises. They are behind everything, the cooking of meals, walking the dogs, talking with the girls. I may never find out with my intellectual self what I mean, but if I am given enough glimpses perhaps these will add up to enough so that my heart will understand. It does not; not yet.

❧

When Mother is quiet and moving into sleep, I go up to bed. Hugh's and my room is directly over hers. If any architect of theatre or concert hall wants to study acoustics, all he needs to do is come to Crosswicks. A pin dropped at one end of the house can be heard in the other. Bion's room is up in the attic, over ours. If he plays music up there at night, a loudspeaker might as well be concealed in one of the heavy, pineappled posts of our big bed. If I can hear Bion, Mother can hear me. I tiptoe very softly, very carefully.

But it works two ways. Mother can hear any sound from our bedroom. I can also hear her.

The poker players disperse. The household settles down for the night. Cynthia brings me a mug of cocoa with whipped cream *and* a marshmallow. I thank her, saying, "This will put me to sleep."

Cynthia goes into the next room, the nursery, where she sleeps with the two little girls. Her father is one of the canons at the Cathedral in New York, and ever since Léna made my mother a great-grand-mother, Cynthia has spent at least part of the summer with us, helping with the children.

I sip the hot cocoa, but it does not put me to sleep. When the rest of the house is quiet, I am still awake, listening for every sound downstairs. I hear Mother turn over, call out. She sounds frightened. I know that I mustn't keep rushing downstairs at her least sound, but I get halfway out of bed, listening, listening. I go out into the hall and stand by the stairs. But there is no further sound. I go back to bed and turn on the light to read and wait for Hugh, who will be reading downstairs for a while in order not to disturb me.

I have found that the German philosophers with their long, cumbersome sentences (never use three words when you can use a hundred and three) are soporific. It is seldom that I can read Kant for more than half an hour without my eyelids drooping.

21

After a while I turn off the light, but I am still sleeping with one ear open as I did when the children were little, listening for Mother, for the grandbabies, waiting for Hugh.

I sit up in bed: what is that?

It is Bion, climbing up the blue spruce and in through the nursery window so as not to disturb his grandmother by coming in downstairs. He and some of the poker players have been for a midnight swim at Mohawk Pond. He stands in the doorway between nursery and bedroom to talk. I hold my fingers to my lips, not for Cynthia and the babies, who are sound asleep, but for his grandmother.

We planted the blue spruce before he was born. By the time he was a baby, it was big enough for us to use for our outdoor Christmas tree; it could be seen from the main road, a mile downhill, and we always turned it on to welcome Hugh on his way home. The last Christmas we spent at Crosswicks before moving back to New York for the school year, I had to stand on the kitchen step stool, on tiptoe, to fling the string of lights over the top branches. Now the tree is as tall as the house, and Bion can use it for his private, if prickly, stairway.

We whisper for a while, and then he says, "Go to sleep, Mother."

To sleep, perchance to dream.

I love my dreams, and the good ones are so good that they more than compensate for the occasional bad ones, when I wake up and reach out to touch my sleeping husband for comfort. In the past few years my mother has moved slowly into the realm of nightmare; her dreams are frightening; they are controlled and distorted by clogged arteries. She has never slept well, but now she is becoming afraid to sleep.

I hear Bion tramping up the stairs to his attic bedroom. From her crib Charlotte gives a dream cry. There is no sound at all from Mother's room. I must try to sleep.

5

On MONDAY, Hugh goes down to New York; to the television studio; to the neurologist. All day I am conscious of the telephone. Waiting. Of course it is one day when all kinds of people phone, and although I know that Hugh will not call before late afternoon, my heart jolts with each ring.

The day moves slowly. The children blow dandelion clocks, and their white stars seed the lawn: Hugh will be furious. The sun seems to hold still in the sky. But there are things to do, meals to cook, beds to be made, small duties which push the day along. When the phone rings and I hear Hugh's voice, the timbre strong and vibrant, I know that the news is good. The numbness in the feet is caused by diabetes, is controllable. If I had not been worried about a brain tumor I might have been horribly upset, but we have known about the mild diabetes for over a year; I have already learned how to cook without sugar; all I feel is lightness with the weight of my worst fears removed. I soar like one of the butterflies the children and the puppies love to chase across the big field.

Now that the sword of Damocles has been lifted from our heads, and there's a hope of a future together, I still must neither count on nor fear that future, but live in the present moment, the now. And I must turn my heart fully to Mother, and not let it be torn too much by her infinitely pathetic degeneration. I must not retreat when she is horrid with me, but let it roll off—almost impossible, but I will try. And I must not project into the future and worry about this descent being a long one.

It has not come all at once; there were strong intimations of it more than five years ago, at the time of Josephine and Alan's wedding; and it was definitely accelerated when Mother was given general anesthesia for an intestinal resection when she was eighty-seven. But until this year her mind has been like a summer sky with small white clouds occasionally moving across and blotting out the light of the sun. Each year the sky has become cloudier; there have been fewer periods of sunlight. This summer the sunlight in the sky of my mother's mind, when it shines at all, glimmers through cloud.

ₜₒ

Maria and Peter come back from their honeymoon. They are based in Peter's apartment in Philadelphia, where he has been doing post-doctoral work at the University of Pennsylvania, but they come frequently to Crosswicks.

The best part of these slow, long summer days, so different from the rest of the year, is early evening and dinnertime, when the family gathers together after the day's work, the noisy, extreme, diverse people who keep me going. I get dinner started, and then we all sit in the living room for an hour.

The little girls are already fed, bathed, and in their nightclothes; like the puppies and the cats they wander around looking for cuddles and cookies. Léna likes to choose what I am to wear; I enjoy, if there's time, taking a hot, soaky bath, then putting on a long dress or skirt. Léna points to the clothes in my closet: "Dis one, Gan-mad-len."

Gan-mad-len. Her attempt at Grandmadeleine. Charlotte cannot get that far. I am Madden. Neither of the little girls can get her tongue around Great-grandmother, and Léna comes up with Gracchi, which sticks. How to spell it? It sounds something halfway between Grokkie and Grakkie, and Gracchi is as close as I can get to what it sounds like to me. Sometimes Mother is aware enough to be charmed by her new title.

Josephine, too, enjoys a bath and a change of clothes before dinner. Maria wears low-waisted, bell-bottom trousers, which are most becoming to her.

As for the men, Hugh comes in from his vegetable garden wearing frayed shorts made out of an old pair of trousers, and honest sweat. He doesn't call his garden organic, or macrobiotic; he simply gardens the way the first dwellers in Crosswicks gardened, with manure and compost, and no chemical sprays or powders. He brings lettuces and tomatoes and young onions and carrots and peppers and the first small cauliflower into the kitchen and sits down, tired and contented. I make a sauce, and we take the young, raw vegetables into the living room for hors d'oeuvres.

Alan has on a purple, Russian-necked shirt, and comes in from the kitchen bearing freshly made hot clam dip. Peter looks, as usual, like Einstein, hair and all. Bion has been out painting fences all day, and wears jeans and a large quantity of white paint. This is a summer of transition for him, this time between school and college, and it is the first summer since he started high school that he hasn't been away from home for at least a month on some job or other. It is good to have him around, and he has enough painting jobs to keep him busy. He puts a record on the player and drapes six foot four inches of young man over a large chair.

Margie and Cynthia come in with the great-grandmother between them, and settle her on the small sofa. Margie's family lives up the road from us, and one of Margie's older sisters babysat for us when Margie herself was a baby. Margie and Cynthia; Vicki and Janet; Clara, our friend and neighbor from down the road; Bion's friend, Jane, who comes to take the long weekend duty to give the others a break; Polly, from across the lane: it's a multiple job for all of them. They help with the great-grandmother; help with the babies; help with the dishes and housecleaning; everybody pitches in. Cynthia bakes cakes—my cooking falls down when it comes to pastry. Margie cleans and polishes everything and keeps the house full of flowers from the garden, from fields and hedges. This used to be my mother's job; it is something else old age has taken away from her; and from us.

Clara, older, stronger, more experienced than the girls, picks the great-grandmother up nearly every morning and puts her in the bathtub; brushes her still-beautiful hair; dispenses love generously wherever it is needed. The girls bring laughter and music and life. These extraordinary helpers are all ordinary, everyday people, and I couldn't get along without them.

I realize, with a pang, how privileged we are to be able to keep my mother with us. This is how it should be, but what would I do if we lived in a tiny house and did not have the girls and Clara to help? Would I be able to keep her with us, or would I have to put her in a "home"—what an obscene misuse of a word! Homes for the aged, nursing homes, are one of the horrors of our time, but for many people there is no alternative. And even though we have room, and the girls to help us, there are still those who think that my mother should be put away. Put away. Everything in me revolts at the thought. But my belief that we are supposed to share all of life with each other, dying and decay as well as feasting and fun, is being put to the test.

This summer I look at my mother sitting on the small sofa during the hour before dinner and I do not know her; I am looking at a stranger, not because she is old and shrunken and lined, but because the light behind her face is no longer there. Up until a few years ago she was an example of a woman who has experienced life fully, and who grows yearly more beautiful with age. There is little character or loveliness in the face of someone who has avoided suffering, shunned risk, rejected life. It was only when suffering, risk, and life were taken from her by atherosclerosis that Mother's face became an unfamiliar one. (I asked Pat, "What do you call it? Arteriosclerosis? Atherosclerosis?" "Most lay people say arterio, but it's athero.")

A house, like a human being, reflects its experiences. And I do not think that a house can be a happy house if no one has cried in it, if no one has died in it. If this seems contradictory, I can't help it. I rebel against death, yet I know that it is how I respond to death's inevitability that is going to make me less or more fully alive. The house helps me here, because it is a warm and welcoming house, full of life, and yet during the past two hundred years it must have contained many deaths.

Death is the most ordinary thing in the world, and so is birth. Someone is being born at this very moment. Someone is dying. Ordinary, and yet completely extraordinary. The marvel of having my babies is something I will never forget. The feeling of staggering uniqueness I had at the death of my father, the death of several close friends, was very different, but equally acute. Death may be an ordinary, everyday affair, but it is not a statistic. It is something that happens to people.

The most ordinary of deaths is the death of a parent. In this twentieth century we are likely to outlive our mothers and fathers, and more parents are dying senile than ever before. Perhaps this is why old age is respected less. So what I am experiencing this summer (though our doctor tells us that Mother is far from dying) is something I share with a great many other people. And I feel the need to reach out and say, "This is how it is for me. How is it for you?"

6

Tallis returns from his vacation in England and phones. "How goes it?" He can tell by my voice that the going is rough, and his response is to drive himself right up in his ancient Thunderbird. His own mother died not long ago at ninety-three; he does not need to say anything, nor do I; I know that he knows.

Everybody in Great-grandmamá's retinue enjoys him; long after I have gone to bed they sit around the dining-room table, by candlelight, talking deep into the night.

Sometimes Tallis drives up with our mutual friend, whom we call Anton, because of his resemblance to Chekhov. When Mother first saw Anton with his Chekhovian beard, she announced in a loud clear voice that it was horrible. "I hate it. But you may kiss me anyhow."

Anton, like Tallis, is horrified at the changes in the great-grandmother. Only a summer ago we all sat at the dinner table and laughed while Anton refused to pass the old lady a seventh ear of fresh-picked corn—"I don't know how I ever dared try to stop her," he said. Only a year ago we all literally almost fell off our chairs with laughter when Anton complimented me on dinner and Mother commented, "It ought to be good. I've taught Madeleine everything she knows about cooking." Somehow or other, even through the Depression, Mother almost always managed to have someone in the kitchen. Now, when she is at home in the South, she has an entire retinue, so that she is cooked for and cared for seven days a week.

When Hugh and I were first married and Mother came to visit us, she would offer to help in the kitchen, and she was just about as much help as the grandbabies; and, as with the grandbabies, I had to think up things for her to do. My nanny used to laugh and tell me that when Mother was giving a dinner party, the house would be spick-and-span, and at the last minute in would come Mother with flowers to arrange, leaving leaves and petals on the newly vacuumed rug.

She has always left a trail of flowers behind her. Despite her incorrigible scattering of greenery, she had enormous talent for arranging flowers. When the rather sparse flower garden at Crosswicks had nothing to offer, she could take a collection of weeds from the hedges at the side of the lane, and create a work of art. It wasn't Japanese at all—she was much too lavish—but her arrangements were uniquely hers, and uniquely beautiful. I miss them.

7

THERE IS MUSIC I will never again be able to hear without being plunged into the atmosphere of this summer. It was a year ago that Margie discovered *The Magic Flute*. She played the glockenspiel in the school band, and the charming music of the glock in Mozart's opera delighted her so that she played our records at least daily. The music is more poignant this summer, because she puts it on whenever the great-grandmother is having a bad day. It hurts Margie's lovingness that love is not enough, that it cannot push back the slide into senility.

Bion's new find is Vaughan Williams's *Fantasia on a Theme by Tallis*. This is one of his favorites in the evening before dinner, and Mother still responds to music—it is the last thing to call her forth from the cloud. On the other side of the record are two pieces by Elgar, Introduction and Allegro for String Quartet and Serenade in E minor, which are unfamiliar to Mother (we discovered the Thomas Tallis together, while I was in college), and each evening she tells Bion how beautiful the music is, and asks him, "What is this lovely music, Bion?" "It's Elgar, Grandmother."

During the day the young people play "their"

music. It is understood that this is the time for the Beatles, for Buffalo Springfield, for the Who. Mother does not like such music, and it is good for her to respond to it, to announce loudly how horrible it is. At least it is my theory that it is good, that she should not be isolated by the narrowing of old age. A lot of the time I don't like the music either, but I do not ask to have it turned down. If it is important for Mother to be as full a part as possible of this multi-generation household, it is important for Hugh and me, too.

It is tacitly understood that the evening is reserved for Tallis, Elgar, Bach, Mozart (though not *The Magic Flute;* we've had that with the vacuum cleaner). Sometimes Alan and I will play violin and piano, which, for some reason, Mother has always enjoyed. She is still likely to notice, and remark, when I play a false note; if we are not accurate with tempo, she beats it out on the arm of the little sofa.

Music has always been part of the fabric of her life, so it is not surprising that it is the last thing to reach her. As a young girl, she studied music in Berlin and played well enough to do concert work, which she hated; she went through an agony of anxiety except when playing for friends. During my early childhood, when we lived in New York, my parents used to have an open supper party every Sunday evening, and there were anywhere from half a dozen to two dozen people there. These evenings were centered around the piano—the same piano on which I play in Crosswicks, a piano considerably older than I am, but still with a felicitous tone and a responsive keyboard. Mother used to be able to read piano music the way most of us read a novel, and when friends from the Metropolitan Opera Company were there on Sundays, which was nearly every Sunday during the opera season, Mother would sit down at the piano and read off the score of *Götterdämmerung* or *La Bohème,* while the singers (and sometimes the non-singers) sang. I used to slip out of my room on those Sunday evenings, slide behind the long, red sofa, thence under the piano, to sit hidden behind the music rack and listen. Of course some of the guests spied me and were amused enough not to tell; it was not until I myself confessed that Mother learned I was not in bed asleep during these musical evenings.

One afternoon my closest friend, a "poor little rich girl," came to play; our great joy was to dress up in Mother's old evening clothes, and we both much preferred my parents' small apartment to her parents' enormous, Italianate mansion. That day for some reason her mother came to call for her, instead of the usual nurse or governess. My mother was playing the piano, and Mrs. W. stood for a long time outside the front door, listening. When she came in she told Mother that she was a friend of George Gershwin's, and that he was looking for someone to play two piano with, and suggested that Mother was just the person. "I was too shy," Mother told me later. "It's one of the greatest regrets of my life."

How do I reconcile my mother then and my mother now?

ఌ

One evening before dinner Bion puts on Ravel's *Bolero.* We manage not to groan. How many times have we heard it? It's been a favorite of his ever since he discovered music. I look at Mother and wonder if there is a flicker of remembrance about the evening in Paris when she and Father heard *Bolero* performed for the first time ever, anywhere. We are so familiar with its repetitive, hypnotic rhythm that it is impossible for me to imagine hearing it completely freshly. Mother said that after the last long mesmerizing note died away the audience sat silent, stunned, and then burst into roars of cheering.

Another first performance at which she was present was that of César Franck's Symphony in D minor. This time the response was not applause but boos, and it was Hector Berlioz who led the audience in the heckling. A friend of Franck's went backstage and asked him how the symphony had sounded, and Franck smiled gently and said that it sounded just as he had hoped it would.

It is as difficult to imagine booing such melodious music as it is to imagine never having heard *Bolero*. But Mother was there, and her response was eternal dislike of Berlioz and a closed ear to all his music. His behavior and his composing were coupled forever in her mind. She wanted the artists she admired to be perfect in all ways, and it always upset her that her adored Wagner was "such a horrid man."

Last summer there were many evenings when the past was still available to her, and mornings when we sat together to drink our coffee and she could still tell me stories. She used to be a witty conversationalist, and I could get her out of bed by saying, "Mother, you have to help me. I've got things to do in the kitchen, and I can't leave the guests alone." Like an old race horse at the sound of the bell she would go into the living room, and from the kitchen I could hear laughter, and know that all was well. Not so this summer. She talks very little. It is all turned in, and it goes nowhere. She is trapped in a lonely, fearful present.

I want to open her memory, but I don't have the password. I want to cry out, "Open, sesame!" so that the door to this treasure cave will open, but it is permanently locked.

After dinner the girls get her ready for bed, and then I go to sit with her for a few minutes. The prevailing westerly wind has dropped, and it is unusually hot for our house on the hill. I sit there, not talking, holding Mother's hand, and remember another hot evening, in the apartment in New York, when I was a small child. Mother was sitting on the side of my bed, much as I now sit by her, stroking my head and pushing my perspiration-damp hair back from my forehead.

In the hall, between my parents' room and mine, hung an old etching of Castle Conway, in Wales. It's a charming picture, and I have always loved it because of the story my mother told me about it that night. It was probably the heat which reminded her, and my usual demand, "Tell me a story about you and Father." One hot summer evening, long before I was born, she walked through the hall and glanced at the etching of Castle Conway and said, "Oh, Charles, it's so hot. I wish we could go to Castle Conway." "Come on!" he cried, and swept her out of the house without toothbrush or change of clothes, and into a taxi, and by midnight they were on a ship sailing across the Atlantic. In those days a trip could be as spontaneous as that. My parents were not poor, but neither were they, by today's standards, affluent. Father was a playwright and journalist, and their pocketbook waned and swelled like the moon; this must have been one of the full-moon moments.

I hold my mother's hand and ask her, "Do you remember the time you and Father went to Castle Conway?"

She has forgotten, she who so short a time ago still remembered everything, and it troubles her, so I change the subject.

Her loss of memory is the loss of her self, her uniqueness, and this frightens me, for myself, as well as for her. Memory is probably my most essential tool as a storyteller, and the creative use of memory takes structure, enormous, disciplined structure, in a world where structure is unfashionable. Like the Red King, I'm apt to remember inaccurately what I don't write down in journal or notebook. "The horror of that moment," the king went on, "I shall never, *never* forget." "You will, though," the queen said, "if you don't make a memorandum of it."

Will I ever forget the intenseness of my anxiety about Hugh? Relief is already blunting the so-recent fear. I am already relaxing into the casual acceptance of a husband. Sooner or later I will get cross with him again, lose my temper, get hurt by something trivial. But I am sure that I shall never, *never* quite forget, and the setting down of the panic in my journal as well as my heart may be what will keep me from ever again taking a husband I love for granted.

And my mother's loss of memory will keep me from taking memory for granted.

ॐ

Who is this cross old woman for whom I can do nothing right? I don't know her. She is not my mother. I am not her daughter. She won't eat anything I cook, so we resort to games. I do the cooking as usual—and I'm quite a good cook; it's one of my

37

few domestic virtues, and the only part of house-keeping which I enjoy—and someone will say, "Eat Alan's soup, Grandmother. You know you like Alan's soup." Or, "Have some of Hugh's delicious salad." She won't eat the salad, when Hugh is in New York, until we tell her that Hugh made the dressing before he left.

I know that it is a classic symptom of athero-sclerosis, this turning against the person you love most, and this knowledge is secure above my eye-brows, but very shaky below. There is something atavistic in us which resents, rejects, this reversal of roles. I want my mother to be my mother.

And she is not. Not any more. Not ever again.

8

I GO SEARCHING FOR HER.

My first memories of her are early, and are memories of smell, that oft-neglected sense, which is perhaps the first sense we use fully. Mother always smelled beautiful. I remember burrowing into her neck just for the soft loveliness of scented skin.

After smell came sound, the sound of her voice, singing to me, talking. I took the beauty of her voice for granted until I was almost grown up.

Scent. Sound. Vision.

I remember going into her room just before dinner, when she was sitting at her dressing table, rubbing sweet-smelling creams and lotions into her face. She had a set of ivory rollers from Paris, which I liked to play with; and a silver-backed nail buffer. Sometimes she let me buff my own nails until they were a pearly pink. The cake of French rouge, and the buffing, makes for a much prettier nail than lacquer.

I watched her brush her hair, a dark mahogany with red glints, thick and wavy, with a deep widow's peak. On the bed her evening dress was laid out; I remember one of flowered chiffon, short in front and long in back, that short-lived style of the twenties. Her shoes were bronze kid, and as tiny as Cinderella's.

My father, too, dressed for dinner every night, even when they were not having company or going out. Mother said that Father would dress for dinner in the desert or the jungle, and that he often told her that without him she'd be on the beach in two weeks. I doubt that. Until recently, I have never seen her anything but immaculate, erect, patrician. Now she has diminished; she is tiny and slumped and we have to dress her and fix her hair, but she is aware that she still has beautiful legs and she likes to show them. She responds to men, and she likes young people, which is not unusual.

Her father, my grandfather, who died at a hundred and one, responded to women and liked young people. One of the worst things about our attitude toward old people is the assumption that they ought to be herded together with other old people. Grandfather lived past that stage; he had, as he remarked, no contemporaries. He played golf until he was ninety-five, having cut down, at ninety, from thirty-six holes to eighteen because his younger companions couldn't keep up with him. He made the great mistake of retiring at ninety-five, and from then on began the slide into senility.

My mother tended him, with considerable assistance. Nevertheless, the psychological drain was on her, and it told in other ways, too. She has never been very strong, and several times during Grandfather's last years she told me that she did not think she would live to be very old. "But I don't want to," she added. "Don't grieve for me if I die. I don't ever want to be like Papa."

"Of course I'll grieve for you. But I don't want you to be like Grandfather, either."

Grandfather was dominant, powerful, ruthless, charming, wicked, brilliant, made and spent fortunes. It was strange to see the great man becoming an ancient baby. One night when he was around a hundred, Mother was sitting with him after he'd been put to bed, sitting with her father much as I now sit with my mother. He clasped her hand tightly, looked at her like a child, and asked, "Who is going to go with me when I die?"

જ⋑

We bring nothing with us into the world, and certainly we can take nothing out. We die alone. But I wish that most deaths today did not come in nursing homes or in hospitals. Death is an act which should not happen in such brutal settings. Future generations may well regard our hospitals and "rest" homes and institutions for the mentally ill with as much horror as we regard Bedlam.

Meanwhile, at Crosswicks I blunder along, and will continue to blunder as long as I can, although I am well aware that at the end of the summer there will be decisions to be made. Several years ago I promised Mother that I would never put her in a nursing home, and I may have to break that promise, deny what I affirm, because I will have no choice.

Her first night in Crosswicks this summer I called Vicki and Janet aside. "Sometimes at night Grandmother rings her bell too late, and can't make it to the bathroom in time. If this happens, call me. You're only supposed to listen for her at night, and take her to the bathroom if she needs to go, not to clean up if she's—incontinent."

Incontinent. I hesitated over the word. And my motives in telling the girls to call me if Mother soils herself were certainly mixed—but then, I have never had a completely unmixed motive in my life.

Part of it was consideration for the girls. They are not being paid to take over the more unpleasant parts of nursing. Another reason is that I did not want anybody to witness the humiliation of my aristocratic mother.

The girls do not call me. Almost every morning when I come hurrying downstairs they are washing the great-grandmother, changing the sheets—the washing machine goes constantly, sheets, diapers, work clothes—I am very grateful, this summer, for all my mechanical kitchen and laundry helpers. The girls are patient and gentle with Mother. I think they, too, feel that this is an unfair ploy on the part of life; it is wrong that we should lose control of our most private functions.

Old age has been compared to being once again like a baby; it is called second childhood. It is not. It is something very different. Charlotte is not yet two, and not yet completely toilet trained. Her soiled diapers have the still-innocuous odor of a baby's. As we grow older we, as well as our environment, become polluted. The smell of both urine and feces becomes yearly stronger.

In hospitals, in nursing homes, when people become incontinent this weakness is used against them. We have all heard far too many tales of elderly patients ringing for the bedpan, waiting fifteen minutes, half an hour, and finally not being able to control themselves any longer; and then, when the overworked nurse eventually arrives, the patient is scolded for lack of control.

There are not enough nurses, or aides, or orderlies. A hospital is no longer a good place for a person who is ill. I have my own account. After the birth of our first child, during the postwar boom of babies in the late 1940's, the eminent gynecologist who delivered Josephine did not check the placenta, and a large amount remained inside me. Three and a half weeks later, I hemorrhaged massively and was rushed to the hospital in the middle of the night. In this enlightened twentieth century I had childbed fever, and came very close to dying. One night I rang for the bedpan and, after waiting for over an hour, I wet the bed. And was roundly berated. I was young enough to fight back.

Mother is beyond that, and the idea of having her abused over a soiled bed is one of many reasons why putting her in a hospital or nursing home is still impossible to me.

෨

One morning I dress Mother in a fresh nightgown while Vicki and Janet finish with the bed. Most mornings, Mother hardly seems to notice what has happened, or to care. She will murmur, "I'm cold. I want to go back to bed"—she who used to be so fastidious, so sweet-smelling. But this morning as I sit with my arms around her while the girls ready the bed, she leans against me and, suddenly herself, she says, "Oh, darling, I'm so ashamed about everything."

My heart weeps.

43

9

Then the clouds close over again, and it is a bad day, a bad evening. She balks at going into the dining room and, once there, refuses to eat. She picks up her empty salad plate and there is a wild gleam in her eye as she says, "I can break this plate if I want to."

I say, "But you don't want to, Mother." It would be better to keep my mouth shut. But this is my mother, my rational, courteous, Southern gentlewoman mother, behaving in this irrational manner.

After dinner I call the dogs and go down the lane and weep. I have done a lot of crying on the lane. I cried whenever a book was rejected with an impersonal printed rejection slip. I cried when Hugh and I had a misunderstanding. Now I cry because I want my mother to die.

❧

And I cry out of fear for myself. Will I ever be like that, a travesty of a person? It was the last thing she would have wanted, to live in this unliving, unloving manner. I look up at the sky and shout at the stars, "Take her, God! Take her!"

A few days ago I asked our doctor and friend, "John, is Mother dying?"

"Nature is not that kind. Your mother's blood pressure is better than yours."

Mine tends to drop when I'm tired; probably better than if it rose.

John suggested that we rent a hospital bed to make caring for her easier. How long is this going to go on? Is it fair to subject the entire family to this? What is it doing to the little girls? They have already experienced a different kind of death, in moving here from England, from Lincoln, the only home they have known. Léna said goodbye to her English great-grandmother. "We're going to America, and we'll never, ever see you again." True, but it didn't go down very well.

In the spring Josephine had a miscarriage, and this death, for the children, was not so much the death of a tiny, unformed life they had never known, as the fact that their mother, the foundation of their world, could be suddenly and without warning taken from them. Will it wound them or strengthen them to be in this house this summer?

It's one thing for me. I'm the only child. Is it fair to make the whole family suffer for what I believe? I talked awhile, earlier this summer, about wanting my mother to have a dignified death. But there is nothing dignified about incontinence and senility.

She is *my* mother. I have no brothers and sisters with whom to share responsibilities and decisions. The others, no matter how close, are at one remove at least. Have I the right to drag them through this with me? It is, in any case, not only my decision. The entire household is involved. After our discussions we come to no decisions, but I feel sustained and

supported. We have talked today, in the hot sunlight, on this lane where I am walking now in the
starlight. The strength of the family gives me
strength. The dogs know that I am upset, and I do
not mind letting go in front of them. They dash
down the lane, into the bushes, circle back, and sniff
me anxiously. Their concern makes me break into a
loud sob, and Tyrrell leaps to give my wet face a loving lick. We are too far from the house for anybody
to hear me, but it is time for me to dry my eyes and
go home.

ॐ

I learned several years ago that a four-generation
summer can be a good one only if we all have our
own survival routines. Each one of us must manage
to find a time of solitude and privacy. Hugh, when
he is in Crosswicks, goes to his garden. Alan goes out
to the Tower to read and write. I do not want to take
my pain out on the rest of the family, so every afternoon, before time to cook dinner, I go across the
fields to the brook, pushing through the tall grass
nearly ready for its first haying, with the dogs circling joyfully about me. When I am out of sight
Mother is apt to send for me. "Where's Madeleine?
Get Madeleine." At the brook I'm beyond the reach
of even a loud shout. If anybody really wants me,
somebody has to come fetch me.

I used to feel guilty about spending morning
hours working on a book; about fleeing to the brook
in the afternoon. It took several summers of being
totally frazzled by September to make me realize that
this was a false guilt. I'm much more use to family
and friends when I'm not physically and spiritually
depleted than when I spend my energies as though

46

they were unlimited. They are not. The time at the typewriter and the time at the brook refresh me and put me into a more workable perspective.

ঌ

Across the brook is a stone bridge; it is not a natural bridge; it was put there a century or more ago by skillful hands and no modern stone-moving tools. It was probably part of one of the early roads, barely wide enough for a single horse and rider. I sit on it and dangle my legs over the gentle flowing of the water, shaded by maple and beech, birch and ash trees. I need perspective, and how to find it? caught in the middle of things, never quite able to avoid subjectivity, or to get the thinking me and the feeling me to coincide.

This makes me confused, makes me lose sight of reality. I feel my lacks as wife, daughter, mother; and if I dwell too much on my lacks they become even greater, and I am further from—not just reality, but the truth of this summer. Will I ever know it?

When Josephine was just a year old, I spent most of the summer alone at Crosswicks because Hugh was off working at various summer theatres, and Mother had broken her ankle in the spring and so could not join us until August. During these solitary weeks I wrote a full first draft of a book. It was my fourth full-length novel, and I had reluctantly put the third on the shelf, after many revisions; so I felt especially precarious about the summer's work, and I knew that how I would feel about that particular summer for the rest of my life was going to depend on what happened with my manuscript.

The book was well received by the publisher and—eventually—the press, and is still, after all these years, selling. And so, I remember that summer as a "good" summer. If the book had been rejected, it would be forever in my memory a "bad" summer. That's irrational, but it's the way things are.

So what of the verisimilitude of that long-gone summer? Do I know it at all? It was a time of solitude, rather than loneliness, because I was happy with my writing, happy with my baby. But what was it *really* like? I don't know.

So I will probably never fathom the reality of this summer. What is the truth of the ninety-year-old woman waiting for me at the house, who is changed beyond recognition and yet who is still my mother?

For a human being, truth is verisimilitude, a likeness to what is real, which is as close as we can get to reality. It has taken me many years to learn that reality is far more than meets the human eye, or ear, or mind, and that the greatest minds have never attained more than fragmentary flashes of what is really real.

Below me on a flat, mossy stone in the brook sits a small green frog. What is a frog? What is the reality of a frog? I was fascinated by a scientific article which showed pictures of a frog as seen by a human eye, by a bird's eye, by a snake's eye. Each saw a very different creature. Which frog was more real?

All of us in Crosswicks this summer see a different person when we look at my mother. Vicki and Janet and Margie have known her all their lives, as Jo's and Maria's and Bion's grandmother. For my children, she has been a very special grandmother. When Josephine had mononucleosis the first winter of her marriage, she didn't get well until she was sent down to Grandmother to be petted and pampered and cosseted. Bion, each spring vacation, says,

"I have to go South for a week with Grandmother." I know a very different person from the one my children do. I know only a fragment of this old lady. She is far more than I can begin to understand. She was fifty-five when my father died; the woman he was married to for nearly thirty years is not the woman I know. I have pictures of her when she was a baby, a young girl, a bride, but this past of my mother's is beyond my comprehension. I am far from understanding her reality.

The Greeks come to my help again; they have a word for the realness of things, the essence of a frog, of the stone bridge I am sitting on, of my mother: *ousia*.

If I am to be constant in loving and honoring my mother I must not lose sight of *ousia*. It's a good word; it's my new word. Last summer my word was *ontology:* the word about being. This summer I need to go a step further, to *ousia*, the essence of being, to that which is really real.

The frog makes a small, clunking noise and hops to another stone and sits, his pale green throat pulsing. He *is:* frog: unworried by the self-consciousness with which the human animal is stuck; it is our blessing and our curse; not only do we know, we know that we know. And we are not often willing to face how little we know.

I learn slowly, and always the hard way. Trying to be what I am not, and cannot be, is not only arrogant, it is stupid. If I spend the entire day hovering around Mother, trying to be the perfect daughter, available every time she asks, "Where's Madeleine?"; if I get up early with my grandbabies and then stay up late with my actor husband and get no rest during the day; if I have no time in which to write; if I

49

make myself a martyr to appease my false guilt, then I am falling into the age-old trap of pride. I fall into it too often.

A conversation with a friend helped open my eyes. Connie is about ten years older than I am, and her mother died a year ago, and Connie is filled with guilt. Now I happen to know that Connie was more than just a dutiful daughter; she kept her mother at home until a hospital was inevitable; she visited her daily thereafter; the difficult old woman was treated with love and kindness; and I told Connie that if anybody had little cause for guilt, it was she. But the guilt was obviously there, and a sore weight. So I said that we all, all of us without exception, have cause for guilt about our parents, and that I had far more cause than she. Then I heard myself saying, "I don't think real guilt is ever much of a problem for us. It's false guilt that causes the trouble." Connie gave me a funny, surprised look, and said, "I think you're right."

And a load of guilt fell from my own shoulders.

I certainly have legitimate cause for both real and false guilt with my mother. But when I try to be the perfect daughter, to be in control of the situation, I become impaled on false guilt and become overtired and irritable.

It is only by accepting real guilt that I am able to feel free of guilt as I sit on the stone bridge and cool my feet in the dappled shade and admire the pop eyes of the frog; and it comes to me that if I am not free to accept guilt when I do wrong, then I am not free at all. If all my mistakes are excused, if there's an alibi, a rationalization for every blunder, then I am not free at all. I have become subhuman.

At best I am far from a perfect wife, or mother,

or daughter. I do all kinds of things which aren't right, which aren't sensitive or understanding. I neglect all kinds of things which I ought to do. But Connie made me realize that one reason I don't feel guilty is that I no longer feel I have to be perfect. I am not in charge of the universe, whereas a humanist has to be, and when something goes wrong, tiny, delicate Connie, like most convinced humanists I've known, becomes enclosed with self-blame because she can't cope with the situation, and this inability presents her with a picture of herself which is not the all-competent, in-control-of-everything person she wants to see.

It is a trap we all fall into on occasion, but it is particularly open to the intelligent atheist. There is no God, and if there is, he's not arranging things very well; therefore, I must be in charge. If I don't succeed, if I am not perfect, I carry the weight of the whole universe on my shoulders.

And so the false guilt which follows the refusal to admit any failure is inevitable.

10

It is only when I can shake off the load of false guilt that I can contemplate death. I do not like thinking about death. I am bad about death. Death is not—despite the Romantics—natural. Death is the enemy, and I hate it. My only weapon against death is to do my dying freely, consciously. This summer is practice in dying for me as well as for my mother.

Our lives are a series of births and deaths: we die to one period and must be born to another. We die to childhood and are born to adolescence; to our high-school selves and (if we are fortunate) to our college selves; we die to our college selves and are born into the "real" world; to our unmarried selves and into our married. To become a parent is birth to a new self for the mother and father as well as for the baby. When Hugh and I moved from the city to live year round at Crosswicks, this was death to one way of life and birth to another. Then nine years later when we took our children, aged seven, ten, and twelve, out of a big house, a quiet village, a small country school, and moved back to New York and the world of the theatre, this was another experience of death and birth.

Both life and death are present for me in the house this summer. I look at Mother, and think that if I am to reflect on the eventual death of her body, of all bodies, in a way that is not destructive, I must never lose sight of those other deaths which precede the final, physical death, the deaths over which we have some freedom; the death of self-will, self-indulgence, self-deception, all those self-devices which, instead of making us more fully alive, make us less.

The times I have been most fully me are when I have been wholly involved in someone or something else; when I am listening, rather than talking; cooking a special, festive dinner; struggling with a fugue at the piano; putting a baby to bed; writing. A long-dead philosopher said that if we practice dying enough during our lives we will hardly notice the moment of transition when the actual time comes. But I am far from a saint, and I am seldom able to practice consciously this kind of dying; it is not a do-it-yourself activity. I know about it only after it has happened, and I am only now beginning to recognize it for what it is.

It has nothing to do with long-faced self-righteousness, with pomposity or piousity. It does not preclude play or laughter. It is light, not heavy; merry, not sad; and it is realistic and never sentimental.

Our lives are given a certain dignity by their very evanescence. If there were never to be an end to my quiet moments at the brook, if I could sit on the rock forever, I would not treasure these minutes so much. If our associations with the people we love were to have no termination, we would not value them as much as we do. Human love is an extraordinary gift, but like all flesh it is corruptible. Death or distance separates all lovers. My awareness of my husband is sharpened by impermanence.

Would we really value anything we could have forever and ever? This is not the first time death has come close to my heart. I was close to the deaths of my grandparents, my father, many relatives and friends. When Hugh and I were in our early thirties, four of our closest friends died, people who were so intimate a part of our lives that their dying changed the very fabric of our days. All four of these deaths were unexpected, and only Don, a fine actor in his seventies, was not cut off *in medias res*.

Of these four deaths the one which changed our lives most irrevocably was Liz's, because it brought seven-year-old Maria into our family.

Our phone rang one quiet January evening while we were getting ready for dinner. If *The Magic Flute* will always mean Crosswicks and Margie; if the Tallis *Variations* will always mean this one particular summer; Glück's *Orpheo ed Euridice* will always remind me of Arthur, because it was on the record player when the phone rang. I answered, and Liz said, "Arthur's dead."

The next day she came up with Maria, leaving her with us for a month while she tried to get things in order. Arthur had left no will; his business, a small publishing house, had been largely in his head. Liz and Arthur had a joint bank account and at Arthur's death it was frozen; Liz had only the money in her pocket, and had to borrow from friends to get through the next few weeks.

During the summer Maria came to us again. All of Maria's few birthdays had been in Crosswicks, so we had the usual party under the apple trees, with balloons and presents tied to the branches, turning the tiny orchard into birthday trees. Before her wedding, Maria told me that the birthday trees are one of the happiest memories of her childhood, and this warms the cockles of my heart.

Liz came up to Crosswicks to get Maria, and to rest for a few days. One evening toward bedtime, we went outdoors to watch for shooting stars and to talk. There was a bite in the air, and we took blankets and wore elderly fur coats which would be rejected by any thrift shop, coats we keep in the pantry hall for dog walking and star watching.

We lay on the lawn on the north of the house, looking across a large pasture to the trees and the hills beyond. Liz told me that Arthur's estate was almost settled, thanks to a lawyer friend, and that he had also drawn up a will for her. She was preparing to start rehearsals in an excellent role in a play that had every smell of a hit, and she was beginning to look toward the future with eagerness. She had left the theatre when Maria was born; she was returning now both because acting was her joy and because it was the way she had been trained to earn her living.

A bright star fizzed across the sky and went out.

Then Liz said, "If anything should happen to me—not that I expect it to—but if anything should, would you and Hugh take care of Maria? I know you love her, and would bring her up the way I want."

I told Hugh about the conversation and we forgot about it until the following November, one morning before dawn when the phone rang. The phone is on Hugh's side of the bed, and he answered it.

A phone call at that time of day usually means something wrong, and I could tell from Hugh's shocked voice that it was not a wrong number or anything unimportant. He said, "Liz is dead."

During rehearsal the day before, she had been

stricken by a bad headache which rapidly became worse. It was finally so bad that the stage manager took her home in a cab. Her mother was minding Maria, and opened the door. The stage manager said, reassuringly, "It's a bad headache. The theatre doctor has given her some medication, and she'll feel better soon."

It was not just a bad headache; it was a cerebral hemorrhage, and Liz was dead before morning.

Liz died on the twenty-sixth of November. The funeral was on the twenty-ninth: my birthday.

We drove down to New York to the funeral home. Funeral "home"—another obscenity. Right after the service, Maria came up to me and caught hold of my hand and would not let go. When it came time to leave the cloying and fetid atmosphere of the funeral home, Maria kept repeating to anyone who came near her, "I'm staying with Aunt Madeleine. I'm going where she goes. I'm not going anywhere she doesn't go. I'm staying with her."

So Hugh and I, Maria, and Ezra, the lawyer who had been so helpful to Liz, went to a nearby restaurant for something to eat, and Ezra disappeared. We didn't know where he'd gone, or why, and just as we were beginning to wonder, he walked in, saying, "We couldn't just let your birthday go by," and handed me a corsage, and a rosebud for Maria.

Late that night, back in Goshen, I wrote, "Let me start now to write a little about the events of the past hours—and one of the strangest birthdays I ever had." I wrote about the funeral, and the lunch, and then going back to the apartment with Maria. I'd climbed up the several flights of stairs with Maria still holding tightly to my hand, and I recorded in my journal some of the things she said. "Can I come live with you? . . . Can I live with you forever and ever? . . . Can I spend next Christmas with you? and the next? and the next? and the next? I hope . . . I'd like to adopt you. Do you think you could adopt me? . . . Would Mommy want me to come live with you? . . . Will Bion and Jo be my real brother and sister, then?" She was grasping for answers, for reassurance. Her grandmother had asked her, "Do you want to come to your mother's funeral, Maria? Of course you don't have to come if you don't want to, but you can come if you like." What a responsibility to put on an already shocked seven-year-old!

I wrote the next day, "I know I've left out all kinds of important things, but it's terribly difficult to write with so many interruptions, and besides we're terribly tired still, emotionally and mentally.

"We got home around five o'clock and Hugh went right to the store and I got dinner. It was choir night, so I knew we'd have to hurry. While I was getting dinner the phone rang; one of our close friends had been rushed to Boston for emergency surgery for an intestinal stoppage. My heart began to thud: O God, not something else! Even after her husband had assured me that the operation had been successful and she was going to be all right, I still felt panic at the ruthlessness of fate, and our total inability to stop the phone ringing with a message of another tragedy. Meanwhile, I must seem as normal as possible for the children, who are very shaken by the death of the beautiful woman they called Aunt Liz."

I wrote, "We had a steak for dinner to mark my birthday, and then I dashed over to choir, and it was a good rehearsal, and as I dismissed them, Grandma [who has played the church organ for seventy plus years and is called Grandma by us all] started to play 'Happy Birthday,' and everybody sang, and Gill said I got bright pink. I said I couldn't think of a nicer way to spend my birthday than directing choir, and then Herb said, 'Look who's here,' and there was Hugh standing in the doorway and I said, 'What are you doing here!' and it was for birthday cake and tea and coffee downstairs. What a darling thing for them to do! The birthday cake had *'Happy birthday, Boss'* on it, and Ella had set the table prettily, and the whole thing gave me a warm glow and somehow made the whole day seem all right.

"Today has been cold and raw. I wrote another number for the operetta—how do people who don't have work bear things? . . . The moment I felt the loss of Liz most was Wednesday evening, walking from the parking lot on Thirteenth Street to Sixteenth Street . . . I'd left the car there so often and then walked over to Liz's, and suddenly I realized what had happened and that it was never to be again, and felt my first real rush of grief . . . I'm bone-tired but I must write to Maria. Tired and let-down and tense and sad and depressed. . . ."

There were a number of unexpected problems to be overcome before Maria could come to us, and she had an extremely upsetting several weeks, including Christmas, until I was abruptly telephoned, on the morning of January 5, to come down to New York—one hundred miles—and fetch her.

When we got back to Crosswicks late that afternoon, there was a small shape huddled in the back of our garage; it was Bella, a seventeen-year-old girl who used to babysit for us until her family moved away when she was fifteen. She sat waiting for us on an old tricycle, shivering in an inadequate coat, pregnant, and unmarried. So our family increased rapidly. It is odd how large events are indicated by small ones. The first difference I noticed was how quickly the toilet paper and toothpaste got used up.

Worrying about Maria and Bella usurped all other emotion, so that I had no time to grieve for Liz, a grieving that is still to be done. We can put off such essential acts when necessary, but not indefinitely. During the years of our friendship Liz and I talked as only friends of the right hand can talk; she took a goodly number of confidences of mine to the grave with her; I carry secrets of hers locked in my heart. When I pass her picture each day I feel a brief, almost unacknowledged stab.

ह๛

I lie back on the rock which holds the warmth of the sun and look up at the sky. The clouds are moving across the heat-hazy blue from the northwest: good weather tomorrow. A hawk breaks across the sky with a powerful swoop. He is very sure of himself. I am not a hawk, and I will never be that certain.

But I am peaceful, lying on the rock for half an hour until time to return to the house and start dinner.

11

THE LIFE OF AN ACTOR is sometimes considered to be unreal, to be a sham. But I have been close to many actors and actresses and they have made me feel that an actor in his various roles is trying on aspects of himself, is trying to find out who he is, what is the nature of humankind, much as I struggle with the same questions through the characters in my stories. If the actor plunges into this openly and vulnerably, he shares his discoveries with the audience; his insights become ours. I have learned both about Hugh and about myself from his "play acting." From a presidential candidate to a fifteenth-century cardinal to a twentieth-century con man, he moves with ease and grace, and I discover things about him in this way that I might never learn in the ordinary process of daily living. This summer we turn television on every day to watch Hugh as an urbane, ever courteous physician, Dr. Charles Tyler. The television set is in Mother's room and she would not miss this program. But one day she refuses to acknowledge that the man on the screen is Hugh. "That is not Hugh," she announces in her most authoritarian way. "That is somebody else pretending to be Hugh." Nobody can convince her. I'm glad that I am not alone in saying, "But it *is* Hugh." She is so definite that I almost find myself wondering.

How do I know that Hugh is Hugh and not anybody else? That I am me? That this stranger questioning my husband's identity is my mother? Suddenly the whole structure of human identity seems
precarious, but perhaps part of my confusion is
caused by fatigue. Last night was another of those
nights when I couldn't help staying awake almost all
night, listening. Mother was calling out, and I had to
decide each time whether or not to go downstairs.
Mostly I thought she was calling in her sleep, and
not really wanting anyone. She can still find her
buzzer, or call the girls. What I listen for is fear in
her voice, because I cannot bear the thought of having her afraid alone in the night.

But for me to stay awake all night, fearful of her
fear, is folly. Janet and Vicki are on folding cots in
the living room, by the open door. There is only the
narrow, New England front hall between living
room and Mother's open bedroom door. The two
girls are there to tend Grandmother, as they call her.
They are there so that the rest of us can sleep. For
me to spend half the night up on my elbow, listening, is sheer stupidity. I'll never last the summer this
way, and what good will that do Mother?

In the Tower there is a couch which pulls out
from under the eaves to become a double bed. The
only sensible thing for me to do from now on is to
sleep out there, the one place where I can't hear everything that is going on in the house; sensible not
only for my sake but for Mother's, for the whole
household.

But her fears concern me, and I don't know how
to assuage them. Far too often during the day, especially as she is being moved from her bed to the big
chair by the window in the kitchen, she will repeat,

like a needle stuck in one groove on a record, "I'm afraid, I'm afraid, I'm afraid." She cannot tell us what she's afraid of, except falling. We all promise her that we won't let her fall. "It's all right, Grandmother. We're with you, we'll hold you. It's all right."

It is an instinctive refrain, even in the very young girls. We are surely promising her more than that we won't let her fall; perhaps the girls aren't aware of all that they imply, but it is in their voices. It is in mine, and I have certainly learned that "Mother," no matter how much she may want to, cannot stop accidents, cannot stop war, cannot stop death, cannot control the future. I am promising something beyond all this; I am promising a reasonable and loving power behind the creation of the universe, and this is something I am going to have to think about, and to question.

Whenever possible, two of us move the great-grandmother, one on each side, holding her close and tight. I hope that the constant physical support will give her some of the spiritual support she needs, because her fears are as much of the future as they are of falling. When her mind clears at all, she is afraid of the trip back South, and I am convinced that she cannot make it; it took too much out of her to come to Crosswicks, and she has failed radically since then. All we can do is try to ease her fear, her fear of leaving us, not to take the plane down South, but leaving us to go into the unknown country of death. She used to tell me that she was not afraid of death, but "I'm afraid of the mechanics of dying." Yet *timor mortis* is in her now, unspoken, but apparent to us all.

During the day the big chair is the best place for

her, because she is part of all the household there. The windows in the dining half of the kitchen are an expanse of about fifteen feet, and from them she can watch Hugh working in the garden, watch the babies on their swings or in their little paddle pool. She can look through the open doorway into the living room, where Margie is polishing brass. She can see me at the stove, or cleaning vegetables in the long sink. Josephine or Alan will read to her, or try to talk to her. Clara brushes her hair, still thick and white and wavy and beautiful, until she relaxes under the gentleness and forgets her fear. When Maria and Peter are with us they, too, try to keep her in life. A great deal of the time she watches nothing, but nods in her chair, and doesn't even notice the usual kitchen noisiness, babies, pots and pans, the pantry door which doesn't shut unless it's slammed loudly, conversations, snatches of song . . .

This morning I said to Clara that Mother has often wished she could die like Grandfather, just turn over in bed and die, and we both agreed that if she could do just that, it would be the best possible thing. She is older at ninety than Grandfather was at a hundred. After the big one-hundredth birthday party, Grandfather decided to die, and it took him just a little over a year to wind down. Mother is fighting, fighting death, fighting us. Last night she started to throw a fork at Bion; fortunately her hand picked up her napkin instead. She makes wild accusations. "How can anybody be so cruel to anybody? My own daughter, how can anybody be so cruel?"

I am foolish enough to be hurt, even though I know that the *ousia* of my mother could never say such a thing, that she has always loved me and always will. Part of what she is doing now is an act, put on for Josephine and Alan's benefit or anybody else available to be an audience, but only part; in any case, it's an act she's not responsible for, and can't control. She is no longer able to govern what is happening in her brain. There are only the rarest, briefest flashes of a person in this huddled, frightened, frightening, ancient woman.

I begin to understand that her atypical rage is an instinctive rebellion against her total inability to control what is going on in the arteries of her brain. We have learned that when any group of people is oppressed for too long, no matter how peaceable they may be natively, powerlessness and impotence will eventually lead to violence. Surely Mother's outbursts of violence come from that part of her subconscious mind which still functions through the devouring of arteries by atherosclerosis. It is frustration which sparks the wild rage.

And my own angers startle me. My boiling point seems to get lower day by day, and it is small, unimportant things which cause the volcano to erupt.

This summer, when writing is next to impossible, walking the dogs to the brook is my outlet. Sometimes I cry out at the imperturbable green surrounding me: "How can you let something like this happen to my mother? Why can't you let her die!"

A bird gives a call and flies off. The throat of the little green frog flutters with anxiety, and I quiet down. But if I get it out of me this way, I'm not as apt to take it out on the family. Out it has to get, one way or another. I do not understand why it is not, as usual, work on a book. Most of the time I can write my way through anything; I have written some of my best poems in hospitals, waiting for X rays; in the middle of the night when pain keeps me awake.

But my creative energy is being drained. When I was pregnant with Josephine, a friend who was a successful dancer and the mother of several children told me that a woman cannot be creative in two ways simultaneously, and that I would not be able to write while I was carrying the baby. Obviously she could not do a *tour jeté* when she was five months pregnant, but I saw no reason not to go on writing, and write I did. The odd thing is that nothing I wrote during my pregnancies ever came, itself, to term. It was like practicing finger exercises, absolutely essential for the playing of the fugue, but it did not lead to the fugue till after the baby was born. I do not understand this, but I do not think it coincidence.

In a reverse way, sharing my mother's long, slow dying consumes my creative energy. I manage one angry and bitter story, and feel better for it, but most of me is involved in Mother's battle. Watching her slowly being snuffed out is the opposite of pregnancy, depleting instead of fulfilling; I am exhausted by conflict.

Periodically I check with Dr. John. This morning he came and gave Mother a complete going over. We have known John and his family ever since we have been coming to Crosswicks; it was John who delivered Bion. He affirmed that Mother is, indeed, doing a good bit of play acting. She can't help it; she's playing games with all of us. He assured us that we are doing all we can, that we must continue to keep her moving, and to take her for a short walk in the afternoon to keep at least a little circulation going. I trust John, and I know that Mother can go on this way indefinitely. Nevertheless, I still see her as in the act of dying.

Alan says that one of the hardest things for all of us is the fear that one day we will be like this. Because I am already a grandmother, this fear is acute in me. It will be a long time before I am able to forget my mother as she is this summer, and remember her as she used to be.

I struggle for *ousia,* for that which does not change with the change and decay in all around I see. Small joys give me glimpses of reality, and keep me going. "Cammy me, Madden," says Charlotte, holding up her little arms. "You not going *anywhere,* Ganmadlen," says Léna, reaching out for security in an insecure world.

I learn from them; I learn from their great-grandmother's *terror anticus;* perhaps the forcible awareness of insecurity is one reason why I respond so deeply to the fugue. I should think that by now Hugh—and the rest of the family—would be sick and tired of Bach's C minor Toccata and Fugue, but it has pulled me through many bad moments, and helped express the joy of happy ones. If I leave Mother after a non-conversation which has me churning and out of proportion, the minutes of working through that particular fugue, which I am in the midst of memorizing, will bring me back into enough perspective so that I can return to Mother with love, instead of indulging in my own reactions. If I want an answer to my questions about all-right-ness, all I need to do is play the C minor Fugue. The family knows how much the piano puts me into perspective. When I am overtly upset or angry, Bion will say, as to a child, "Why don't you go play the piano, Mother?"

It has been a long time since the great-grandmother played the piano, and I learned, in early adolescence, that when she played Bach for several hours, or when she played game after game of solitaire, she was unhappy; I was old enough to understand the fact of the unhappiness but not the reasons, and so got caught up in unhappiness too. Anyhow, I mustn't play the C minor too often this summer, and preferably only when the girls take Mother for her afternoon walk and she can't hear the powerful, austere interweaving of theme, and be reminded of unhappiness.

It is frightening to be in such a position of power over another human being that I must question even what I play on the piano. We are all in positions of power over the great-grandmother, and I know that I can trust this Crosswicks household not to abuse it. Vicki and Janet are unfailingly patient over soiled sheets. Clara will never pinch or hurt while the bath is being given, or be rough when she is brushing Mother's hair and keeping it fresh and clean. Daily I learn lessons in patience and forbearance. Margie questions me about forcing Grandmother to take the walk in the afternoon when she doesn't want to go. I explain that Dr. John has told us it is the only way to keep any blood circulating in the clogging arteries; it hurts me, too, to make my mother walk against her wishes. It would be easier to give in, and let her turn completely into a vegetable. "And that wouldn't be loving my mother, Margie." Slowly Margie nods. "Okay, Madeleine. I understand now."

I do not want power over my mother. I am her child; I *want* to be her child. Instead, I have to be the mother.

12

Meals become a nightmare. Finally, after discussion and support from the family, I decide that we will no longer try to make Mother eat. If her body really wants food, its want will be heard and she will take a few bites of baked potato. But we will stop this farce of urging her to eat, and I will not allow anybody to feed her as though she were a baby.

Do I have a right to make this decision? Perhaps not, but I make it because it is the decision I would want my children to make if I were in my mother's place. There is no dignity to this kind of death at best; but forcing food down her when she is not hungry is simply an added indignity.

The babies and the animals affirm the great-grandmother's reality in a way that I cannot, because they are able to take her for granted exactly as she is. This morning I watched Léna sitting in her small rocking chair at her great-grandmother's feet, sitting with a book of nursery rhymes held upside down, rocking and singing to her great-grandmother. Titus, the yellow kitten, curled up in the old woman's lap, yawned with luxurious contentment. For a brief moment I too could accept, and my heart was warm and freed from the numbness which has enclosed it most of the time during these weeks.

I read somewhere that the subconscious mind cannot understand or accept its own extinction. But I don't think that the conscious mind gets very close to understanding or acceptance either. It is a fact that all men must die; but because my underwater, subconscious mind, the largest part of me, does not believe it, my intellectual acceptance doesn't mean very much.

First of all, I don't know what death means:

Death first intruded upon me when I was three years old, and my paternal grandmother came to visit us in New York and died of pneumonia, in my bed, in my room. My memory of this death is two small fragments; I remember sitting on the floor beside the bed, playing with a pack of cards; it must have been before anybody realized that she was gravely ill. And I remember driving at night to her home, near Princeton, New Jersey; we passed road construction, and I remember the red lanterns hanging from the barriers blocking our way and the unknown dark ahead. After this, memory betrays me chronologically. Although I know we were driving to New Jersey for the funeral, my tricky memory projects me into the comfortable living room of my grandmother's house, and I am sitting in her ample lap, being rocked by her, and we are flooded with golden light from a Tiffany lampshade.

ॐ

I was in early adolescence when my other grandmother, my maternal grandmother, died at the beach cottage in North Florida.

We had to drive from the beach up to town, and

I remember my sense of shock as we drove through the hot and crowded streets; the familiar city was new to me; it was as though I had never passed through these streets before. The entire world was different, and nobody we passed knew it; nobody knew that my grandmother had died; and this seemed to me outrageous.

It was more than a selfish, childish, reaction. Perhaps we are supposed to walk more often through the streets of that different world, where all our awareness is more acute, not our awareness of ourselves but an awareness that we *are* part of each other, that we are all as intricately and irrevocably connected as the strands of a fugue.

This is the world I walk in this summer.

ॐ

This world is crystal-clear, and yet it is not bathed in the white light of intellectual certainty. It has more to do with the underwater world, the world in which I meet the characters and people of my stories, the world in which I understand the language of the C minor Fugue.

I first came across this fugue while I was in college during a time of confusion and unhappiness. I still had not come to terms with my father's death, which occurred during my last year in boarding school. It was a premature death, caused by mustard gas during the First World War; Father would not take his men anywhere he would not go himself, and his action saved most of his men from gassing. If my memory of Mother begins with smell and sound, so does my memory of Father: smell of clean linen, after-shave lotion, whiskey; sound of coughing.

And I was afraid of death, all death, afraid for

my mother, for myself. The C minor Fugue spoke to me in a language even more positive than that of John Donne's beautiful sonnet, "Death be not proud."

What do I believe, this summer, about death and the human being? I'm not sure. But I know that it is in the language of the fugue, not the language of intellectual certainty. And I know that I could not survive this summer if I could not hope for meaning, meaning to my mother's life, to Hugh's and mine, to our children's, to all the larger family, to everybody, to all things, including the rock at the brook and the small frog. What that ultimate meaning may be I do not know, because I am finite, and the meaning I hope for is not. But God, if he is God, if he is worth believing in, is a loving God who will not abandon or forget the smallest atom of his creation. And that includes my mother. And everybody, everybody without exception.

I cannot believe in meaning by myself, alone, but it is often the small things which sustain me. Someone will say, after a particularly difficult, tiring day, "Madeleine, dinner tonight was just great." Or I will sit, in the twilight, in the old rocker with one of the babies and sing, and take strength from the small and perfect body drooping into sleep in my arms. At least once a week Alan, or Tallis, will celebrate Communion, and from this I receive the same kind of strength which, in a different way, comes to me in the C minor Fugue, and I am able to return to the routine of these difficult days with a lighter touch.

Would I be able to go on, one day at a time, this way, if we lived in a small pre-fab house in Levittown, or a cramped apartment in the City? It would take a great deal more strength and courage than is being called from me here in Crosswicks, and there are days even here, even with the help of the household and the quiet minutes at the brook, when I am so exhausted by nighttime that I barely have the strength to climb the stairs to the Tower and fall into bed.

Somehow, despite the fact that I feel that my mother's slow dying and birth are opposites, I still turn to the analogy of birth. When I walk down the lane at night and pray for Mother's death, I must know what I am praying for, and I am praying not just for her release from the prison her body has been turned into, but for birth. Alan was with Josephine during Charlotte's birth, and was amazed not only by the violence with which the mother works to expel the baby but by the violence with which the baby struggles to be born. Charlotte—typically—did not need to be spanked into life; she emerged shouting. Only a few hours earlier she had been safely inside her mother's womb, swimming comfortably in the amniotic fluid. Everything was done for her; she was sustained and nourished in the dark warmth. And suddenly the calm waters started churning, and she was shoved through a dark tunnel into blinding light, air knifed into her unused lungs, and she greeted the trauma of birth with a bellow of rage.

It's a good analogy for me, birth, and certainly has nothing to do with pie in the sky by and by. Perhaps the great-grandmother is as much afraid of the violence of a new birth as she is of the act of dying.

Do I believe all this? Not with my intellect. But my intuition keeps insisting that there are more things on heaven and earth, Horatio, than your philosophies can tell.

I'll leave it there for now. The only thing to do is to get up in the morning and move through the day, trying to do what has to be done, as it comes. When Mother's face crumples pitifully and she says, "I'm scared, I'm scared," I put my arms around her and say, "It's all right, Mother," and I do this well aware of the enormity of the promise. There is a chill and empty feeling within me; nevertheless, there is something which impels me to put my arms around the Madeleine who is ninety and the Madeleine who has just turned three, and say, "Don't be afraid. It's all right."

II

The Mother I Knew

1

I was a much longed-for baby. It wasn't for want of trying that my parents were childless for so long. But Mother could not hold a baby past three months. "All I needed to get pregnant," she once remarked, "was for your father to hang his pajamas over the bedpost." She had miscarriages all over the world— Paris, Berlin, Cairo, and—I think—one in China. Sometime toward the end of "the war," my parents' war, World War I, Father came home on leave from Plattsburg, and I was conceived. Because Father was sent immediately overseas, Mother was able to spend most of the nine months in bed. Even so, I am a witness to her determination. The first doctor she went to told her that she could not possibly carry a baby to term, and that if she did not have a thera-peutic abortion, both she and the baby would die. Then she went to a Roman Catholic doctor: that was in 1918. So I am here to tell the story.

My Southern grandmother, Dearma, came north to take care of her daughter. Mother carried me the full nine months, and started labor late on a bliz-zardy Thanksgiving night. Dearma went out onto Park Avenue to try to call a taxi to take Mother to the hospital, but the storm was so fierce that no taxis came by. There the elderly lady stood in the snow, wind blowing her clothes about her, whipping her white hair free of its pins, and finally two young men in a long touring car stopped and asked if she needed help. So my mother was driven to the hospital by two friendly strangers.

Father didn't see me until I was several months old, because he was kept overseas after the Armistice. I wish that we had not wiped out Armistice Day in favor of Veterans Day. It strikes me as part of our reluctance to accept the horrid reality of death. We are afraid of that dark silence when for a minute everybody in the nation was supposed to pause and think of the dead. And I remember the ancient verses,

> *The gude Sir Hew of Eglintoun,*
> *And eik Heriot, and Wintoun,*
> *He has tane out of this cuntre;*
> Timor mortis conturbat me.

And I add,

> *Remember Charles of Crosswicks town*
> *And those beside him who went down.*
> *The flesche is brukle, the Fiend is sle;*
> Timor mortis conturbat me.

I share in the primordial terror.

Otherwise I could not sit by my mother at night and hold her dry and burning hand in my still quick one. Her hand is as dry and fragile as a leaf in November.

She told me that once she and Father had had their long-awaited baby, I became a bone of contention between them. They disagreed completely on how I ought to be brought up. Father wanted a strict English childhood for me, and this is more or less what I got—nanny, governesses, supper on a tray in the nursery, dancing lessons, music lessons, skating lessons, art lessons . . .

Mother had the idea that she wanted me trained by a circus performer, that it would give me grace and coordination and self-assurance, but Father was horrified. I wish Mother had had her way. However, I did have Mrs. O.

Mrs. O. Nanny: odd, obsolete, un-American idea. But Mrs. O is worth a book in herself, as are so many of the other people in this tale. She's English, a Liverpudlian, and her family for generations had belonged to the highest order of English servants—and there is nothing more rigid or more snobbish than the English-servant class system. It started to break down during World War I, and vanished during World War II. There are a few nannies left, but not many. Mine is ninety-one this summer, still completely *compos mentis*, and passionately concerned with all the doings of my family. She has clucked with me many times about Mother's decline, and somehow she always manages to phone me on a day when things have been particularly difficult, and by the end of the conversation we are both laughing.

She was born Mary McKenna and came to the New World when she was fifteen, to spend a summer on Prince Edward Island taking care of four small children. At summer's end she went to visit one of her aunts, who was housekeeper for a wealthy family on Park Avenue; the enormous house is still in existence, now a club. There were four in the family, and forty on the staff, which included gardeners, coachmen, and outdoor laborers. The staff

79

ate dinner at noon, around a long table below stairs, having a "joint" each day, bowls of potatoes, vegetables, salad. They were well fed, if hard-worked. The family dined at night. One of the daughters of the family, Miss Amy, fourteen, was blind as a result of scarlet fever. She was spoiled and demanding. Young Mary McKenna's aunt suggested that Mary take Miss Amy for a walk. When Miss Amy began to be difficult, not wanting to walk, whining, wanting to go home, Mary said, "My aunt said that you are supposed to walk for an hour, doctor's orders."

Miss Amy said, "I won't."

Mary said, "You will."

Miss Amy said, "I'll lie down in the street."

Mary said, "Go ahead, for all the good it will do you." It was the first time anybody had crossed Miss Amy since her blindness.

They walked for a full hour, and when they got home Miss Amy said to her mother, "I want Mary."

So Mary McKenna, barely older than blind Miss Amy, became a lady's maid. The next day the family left for a trip abroad, and Mary sat at the captain's table with Miss Amy, to help her. When the family went to Paris they arrived earlier than expected, and the floor of the hotel which was usually reserved for their use had not yet been emptied, so the servants were sent, just for one night, up to the top of the hotel, under the eaves.

Mary McKenna announced to one of the others, "I've never slept in a place like this before, and I'm not going to begin now." So she went looking for some way to summon help and express her displeasure. At one end of the attic she saw a series of brass bells, took a broomstick and began whacking away at them, making a considerable din. It was not until firemen came rushing upstairs with hoses and hatchets that she knew which bells she had rung.

However, she had made her point. She did not sleep in the attic.

With Miss Amy she traveled all over Europe, went to formal dinner parties, to the opera, to the theatre; because of Miss Amy's blindness she saw far more of the above-stairs world than would most lady's maids.

Then she met and married John O'Connell, whose brother is still remembered in Ireland as one of the great fighters of the Irish revolution. They had three daughters, and then the O'Connell family fell on hard times, and in order to help feed and clothe the children she went back to work, and the only work she could get was as a charwoman—the lowest rung of the English-servant caste system. It was a humiliation to her that few could understand.

She worked on Wall Street cleaning offices at night. My godfather often worked late and got to talking with this rather unusual cleaning woman, and once when his wife was having a large party and needed extra help, he asked Mrs. O'Connell if she could come to their house and help out. My parents were at that party, and later Mother phoned to find out who the splendid extra helper had been, and if she would come help at a party Mother and Father were giving.

When she arrived at our apartment, Mother smiled and said, "I don't even know your name."

"My name is Mrs. O'Connell, but I expect you will want to call me Mary."

"I'd be delighted to call you Mrs. O'Connell," Mother said, and that was the beginning of a friendship between the two women, and my nanny's entrance into my life. I was only a baby, and when I began to talk I called her "O," and a little later Mrs. O, and Mrs. O she has remained, and there are many people who don't know her by any other name. Wherever she is, she brings laughter, and a sense of fun, although her life, after she left Miss Amy, was full of pain and tragedy.

Until arthritis prevented travel, she spent several weeks with us three or four times a year, and I treasure a small snapshot of Mother and Mrs. O sitting on the sofa, side by side, nattering away. They share many of the same memories—of operas all over Europe, of singers; Mrs. O refers casually to Madam Melba, Jean de Reszke, Chaliapin. If Mother knew the people above-stairs, so did Mrs. O, and from the point of view of below-stairs, so she was able to tell Mother all kinds of little titbits she'd never have heard otherwise. She also enjoyed telling stories on herself, such as the time she was sent out to buy pâté de foie gras; when she reached the grocer she couldn't remember the French words, "but it sounds like Paddy Fogarty." The closest she has ever come to being vulgar is when she says, "Ah, well, I must go and shed a tear for Ireland," and heads for the bathroom.

She thought my father a prince, and treated him accordingly. She loves to tell of one summer when Mother and I were out of the city and Father was preparing to sail to Europe on an assignment. He couldn't find some things he needed, and knew that Mrs. O would know where they were. She didn't have a phone, so he sent her a telegram: COME AT ONCE.

She came, and there he was, she said, sitting

alone at the dining table, eating scrambled eggs by candlelight.

She also liked to tell of the times she met him on the street, when he would stand leaning on his cane and passing the time of day, "as though he didn't have anything better to do."

She was deeply religious, in a quiet way, and sometimes when she had a special concern on her mind, she would take me to church with her. She also thought—quite rightly—that I was overprotected, and took me on my first subway rides. She didn't like the fact that Mother would allow no sugar in my breakfast oatmeal; Mother always tasted the oatmeal to make sure no softhearted member of the household had sugared it; Mrs. O got around that by putting the sugar in the bottom of the porringer, and the oatmeal on top of it, and stirring it in after the porridge had been tasted, and Mother never knew, until we told her a few years ago, why I would always eat my oatmeal for Mrs. O. For I never told of the subway rides, or the visits to church, or the sugar in the cereal, or the little packets of butterscotch in the park; all I knew then and all I know now is that Mrs. O never taught me anything but good.

I used to say to her, "Will you help me take care of my children when I grow up?" And she would remind me of this on her visits to us.

When *A Night to Remember,* about the sinking of the *Titanic,* was on television, she sat and watched and rocked and clucked; she knew most of the guests from Miss Amy's family; the captain had been to the house many a time for dinner, and the young Mary would go to the ship bearing the invitation;

some of the crew she knew this way, and some from family and acquaintances in Liverpool; the movie seemed to have been filmed especially for her, and all of us watching it with her were far more moved by it than if we had not been seeing it through her eyes.

She was probably the most normal part of my childhood, and I will always be grateful for her. I think I realized that I was a subject of disagreement between my parents, and yet I managed to think that both of them were always right, and I'm sure Mrs. O had something to do with this. When I was asked by playmates which of my parents I loved best, I answered truthfully that I loved them both best. Maybe it was because I saw far less of them than the average American child sees of his parents; certainly a great deal less than my children saw of me. Mother was never very strong, and after she lost a little boy, at seven months—he lived a few days—it took her a long time to get her strength back. There were many times when she was in bed for weeks, with a white-uniformed nurse bossing the household.

The beginning of my life coincided with an end to my father's old way of life. Before the war he had been a foreign correspondent, traveling all over the world, often taking Mother with him. The dose of mustard gas in the trenches so damaged his lungs that it was necessary for him to live a quieter life than he had been used to. During my childhood he wrote mostly short stories, detective fiction, movies, plays. He had an office in the Flatiron Building, and he slept late and wrote late. Until his lungs took us abroad, to the Alps, when I was twelve, I don't think I ever ate at the table with my parents except on Sunday, and then, Mother said, "You didn't know what to say to us." I preferred eating alone off a tray, with a book propped on my lap. This may explain why the entire family eating together, around the table, is so important to me.

2

———————

DURING THE EARLY YEARS of my parents' marriage, Father was music and theatre critic for the old New York *Evening Sun,* and he knew and loved opera; he belonged to the Opera Club, which meant that he was free to use the club box at the Metropolitan Opera House whenever he felt like it, and often, toward the end of a meal, he would say to Mother, "I think I'll just go down to the Met and catch the last act of *Boris.*"

I must have been around eight when Father decided that it was time for me to go to the opera. On one Saturday a month the men of the Opera Club were free to bring a lady, so I was taken to a matinee of *Madame Butterfly.* I listened and watched in fascination, absorbed by the music and the exotic story, but I was totally unprepared for this fairy tale not to have a happy ending. I went back to the apartment in a state of shock. When Father asked me if I had enjoyed the opera I replied that I had, and I told neither of my parents my pain at being drawn into the Butterfly's anguish.

Thinking that the first opera had been successful, Father next took me to *Pagliacci.* As soon as we had settled ourselves in our seats I turned to him: "Fa-

ther, does this opera have an unhappy ending, too?"
He told me that it did, and I began to cry, long
before time for the curtain to go up. I cried and
cried about the fate of Madame Butterfly, about the
fate of Pagliacci, about all the unhappy endings I
had been forced to realize were being played out all
over the world; I cried until Father got up and took
me home before the opera ever began.

It was a long time before he took me again.

Mother went with him to the Saturday matinees,
and often in the evenings, too. I'm sure they were
home more frequently than I remember, but I
wasn't lonely. As a child, I enjoyed my solitary meals,
my solitude in general, which, as I grew older, was
interrupted by all the various lessons. Piano lessons I
will be eternally grateful for. Dancing lessons were a
horror; I was gauche on the ballroom floor as a
child, and gauche I have remained. School was
mostly something to be endured; I don't think I
learned nearly as much from my formal education as
from the books I read instead of doing homework,
the daydreams which took me on exciting adventures in which I was intrepid and fearless, and graceful, the stories Mother told me, and the stories I
wrote. It was in my solitudes that I had a hand in the
making of the present Madeleine.

ॐ

When I was a little girl—and older—I used to
urge Mother to "tell me a story."

"A story about what?"

"About when you were a little girl."

The world of Mother's childhood, filled with
playmates, most of them cousins, is a world I have
never known. My children, spending their early

years here in Crosswicks, came closer to the kind of childhood Mother had than I did. For the last decade or so, Mother has included reminiscences in her letters, so that I will have them to share with my children and grandchildren. A few years ago she dictated some accounts of the events of her childhood to a friend, but those typewritten pages lack the charm of her letters and conversations. She has not been able to write a letter for a long time. I will always miss the familiar blue paper with her beautiful handwriting.

The mother of my childhood and adolescence and very young womanhood existed for me solely as *mother,* and I suppose it is inescapable that for a long time we know our parents only as parents, that their separate identity as full persons in their own right unfolds only gradually, if at all.

I get a glimpse of what Mother was like as a very young woman when I think of her telling me about her first trip to Athens, before she was married. "I spent the first night on my knees by the window, worshipping the Parthenon."

It is not difficult for me to imagine that scene (and even easier, now that I have been to Athens myself), because it is completely in character.

My first actual memory of her is one of those complete, isolated visual glimpses, and is set in Cornish, New Hampshire, where my parents often spent the summer as part of the Saint-Gaudens Artists Colony. Homer Saint-Gaudens was one of my father's friends from the war, and he found the quiet and companionship a nourishing climate for his writing.

I was standing in a room surrounded by green—the house was aptly named Tree Tops—and Mother was showing me a small, white, embroidered dress, a dress for me, embroidered all around the hem with small red roosters, I thought it was beautiful. That dress, Mother told me later, was given to me by Madam Saint-Gaudens when I was two years old. What a strange, feminine first memory, especially for someone who has never had much of a flair for fashion! I have a feeling that there's more to it than that, that this gentle memory followed something hurtful—but I'll never know.

Although a writer of stories works constantly to train an observant and accurate memory, remembering is not necessarily a conscious act; it is often something which happens to me, rather than something I do. If I am ever tempted to take personal credit for remembering, all I need do is to think of the summer when I was eight or nine years old and Mother had cause to drag me with her around France. I must have driven her distracted, and she was convinced that I saw nothing.

However, my creative unconscious was storing up all that I saw, heard, smelled, tasted. Right now I have a completely sensory recollection of being sent on picnics in Brittany with three small boys, to get us out of the grownups' hair. For lunch we were given sour bread with sweet butter and bitter chocolate, and I still remember the marvelous combination of taste and texture. While we were eating we were surrounded with the sound and smell of ocean and wind, and our eyes were half closed against the brilliance of sky and sun, a blue and gold shimmer which comes only from sunlight on sea water.

Mother remembers a skinny, awkward, sulky little girl who saw nothing as she was dragged through châteaux and museums. Years later I amazed Mother as I described places and people of that sum-

mer in my first serious stories. What does—did—
Mother remember of that summer; what was it like
for her? I don't even know why we were there, without Father, and it is too late to ask her. I can only
remember the summer as it was for me, not as it was
for her.

When I needed memory of that summer for a
story, my subconscious mind, with a porpoise-like
flick, flipped it up out of the water for me. And I'm
still young enough, active enough, that an enormous underwater treasure trove is available to me;
I can swim for hours beneath the surface; or I
can bring a shell, a piece of coral, up into the sunlight. Mother is like a sunken ship held at the bottom
of the sea, with no choice as to the fishes who swim
in and out of the interstices, the eels and turtles who
make their homes in the remains.

When I remember the years in the apartment on
Eighty-second Street, it is mostly the good things
that I remember at home, and the bad at school.
When I look at the apartment in my mind's eye, it is
likely to be Christmas. This was the time when Father lifted from the physical pain in which he constantly lived, and the equally acute pain of knowing
that his postwar work was not as successful as his
earlier work. I did not understand my father's pain,
but I knew that at Christmastime the apartment, instead of being heavy and dark, became sparkling
and light as champagne, with Father sneaking home
with an armload of presents, and writing stocking
poems, and believing (I think) for a few weeks in a
future in which there was hope.

On Twelfth Night he walked out of the house,

leaving Mother and Mrs. O to strip the tree, remove the holly from around the house, the sprig of mistletoe from the double doors to the dining room. And it was over for another year.

There was laughter at other times, too. One of Mother's favorite stories—and I know it only from her telling of it—was of an evening when Father went to the opera, and Mother, who wasn't feeling well, went to bed. After the opera was over, Father returned with a friend—my godfather—who went bounding into Mother's room, climbed into bed with her, and put his furled umbrella between them, announcing, "It's all right, Madeleine, this is Siegfried's sword."

I want to remember everything I can. Whenever Mother has a moment of clearness she is apt to reminisce, but these moments are becoming more and more rare. For most of it I must go deep-sea diving on my own.

3

I AM ONLY BEGINNING to realize how fragmented and uncoordinated I am. My left hand does not know what my right hand is doing. My heart tells me to go in one direction, and my mind another, and I do not know which to obey. I am furious with Mother for not being my mother, and I am filled with an aching tenderness I have never known before. There are rough waters below the surface of my consciousness, and strange, submarine winds. The submerged me is more aware of wild tides and undertows than the surface. One deep calls another, because of the noise of the water floods; all the waves and the storms are gone over me. And above the surface the brazen sun shines, heat shimmers on the hills, and the long fronds of the golden willow Mother planted ten or more years ago droop in the stillness.

I first became aware of the dichotomy between the daily world and the "real" world the year I was twelve. During my first years in New York as a solitary child, the world of my imagination and the world of daily life were not in conflict, because I had not grown up enough to see any difference between them. My real life was not in school but in my stories and my dreams. The people I lived with in books were far more real to me than my classmates. The Madeleine I wrote about in my stories was far more my real self than the self I took to school.

During that winter my father had one of his many bouts of pneumonia. If I was left to my own devices more than many children, it was because Mother's attention was focused on Father's injured lungs. He nearly died of that attack of pneumonia, and when he began, slowly, to recover, it was apparent that he could no longer live in the cities he loved—New York, London, Paris. He would have to be some place where the air is purer than in the city. During those Depression years it was less expensive for my parents to live abroad than in this country; Father's work went with him, with his small portable typewriter (it's still here, in the Tower) which had gone around the world with him on many assignments. But he was able to write little that winter of pneumonia and its aftermath. Money was short and for a few weeks Mother did the cooking—but only for a few weeks.

Fortunately, Mother had inherited her father's flair for business (even though she could not cook), so what investments she had been able to make before the Depression were not wiped out. Her first indication of financial talent came during the early years of her marriage. She had been downtown shopping and was returning home on the Fifth Avenue bus. Two men in dark business suits, bowler hats, and attaché cases sat in front of her, and she overheard them talking of a certain stock which could be bought for "practically nothing" and which was shortly going to increase immensely in value.

That evening she and Father went to a dinner

party in a large town house. After dinner a string quartet provided entertainment. Mother was seated behind a large potted palm, and by a man who was a stranger to her. "I was terribly shy, I felt completely out of place in all that elegance, and just to make conversation I mentioned the stock I had heard about that afternoon. He gave me a very funny look, and changed the conversation, and I thought I'd made some awful gaffe. But the next morning he telephoned me and said that I had startled him the night before, but he felt he ought to tell me that he was putting everything he owned into that stock. He offered to buy some for me, so I bought a hundred shares, which took what was a lot of money for us in those days. When I told your father, he was furious, so when my stock had doubled in price I sold fifty shares and paid him back. It more than doubled."

Mother seldom looked smug, and she did not when telling this story. The closest I have ever seen her come to looking smug was much later, when she told Hugh and me about going against all advice in buying some stock, and hitting the jackpot again. "I had the reputation of being able to put my hand down in the mud and come up with a piece of gold."

I, alas, have inherited none of this financial flair, and I certainly do not have what it takes to be a gambler. Once when my parents and I were in Avignon, Father gave me twenty-five centimes to put in one of the hotel gambling machines. I couldn't lose. Money kept pouring out. When I realized that the machine was broken, I took my ill-gotten gains to another machine and lost everything—except the original twenty-five centimes, which I kept.

Mother wasn't a coward about money, and it was

her financial acumen which kept things going during many lean periods.

The spring after Father's bout of pneumonia, Mother broke up the apartment where she and Father had lived for nearly twenty years, put some of their more treasured things in storage, and off we went into an indefinite future of searching for places where Father could breathe more easily.

We spent the first summer in the French Alps, above Lake Geneva. With my godfather and his family, which included the three boys I had picnicked with in Brittany, my parents rented an old château in Publier, a tiny village off the beaten track. It was found by accident: the real-estate agent had been showing us hideous modern villas which he considered more appropriate, and happened to mention the untenanted Château de Publier, and my parents had to argue him into taking them to see it.

There must have been a hundred rooms, most of which were left with sheets draped over the furniture. The kitchen had not changed since the Middle Ages, but the village girls who came to work for us had never cooked in any other way and would have disapproved of a modern kitchen. In the vast living room was a fireplace large enough to roast an ox, and a small, usable harmonium, which was my delight. Off the duchess's bedroom, in which my parents slept, was a small, octagonal chapel, with old, stained-glass windows, and a carved mahogany *prie-dieu* with a red velvet kneeler. The château actually had a bathroom, put in during the early days of plumbing. Under the tub was a firebox in which a fire had to be built in order to heat the water in the tub. I don't remember having a bath in it, and I probably never did. In all the bedrooms were large china pitchers and bowls, and most of our washing was done there in the old-fashioned way.

I was happy that summer because I lived completely in the world of the imagination—the only way I could escape being drawn into my parents' unhappiness. I wandered through the centuries, being the daughter of the château, Madeleine in the twelfth century, the fifteenth, the eighteenth. I wrote stories and poems, and I lived an interior life which protected me from the teasing of the three boys as well as from the world of the grownups.

It was during that summer that I was punished by my mother for the first time unjustly—at least, I felt it to be unjust. We had driven down to Lake Geneva to go swimming, and I had been allowed to go out by myself in a small sort of kayak, quite safe, since it was flat-bottomed. I paddled well out into the lake, lost, as usual, in reverie. It must have been a long dream, because when I turned my kayak around and paddled back to shore, everybody was furious with me, and I was punished because I had not come when I was called.

"I didn't hear anybody call," I told my mother. Nobody believed me, and it was probably not distance which kept me from hearing, but the depth of my concentration on my dream. My punishment was that I was not to read or write for twenty-four hours, which was the most terrible punishment possible to me, and I felt unjustly treated. At twelve I still stubbornly insisted on seeing my parents as Olympian, above earthly pain or problem. I'm not sure whether I did not realize what an unhappy summer it was for them, or whether I refused to realize. Father was having to face that never again could he live in the cities where he had the intellectual companionship he needed, the sharpening of wit against wit. Friends he had expected to stand by him were turning their backs, now that he was ill, now that his writing was not as successful as it had once been. Mother shared in both the suffering and the exile. The parents of the three boys were often away, and she had the responsibility for them, something she was not accustomed to. As I look back on it now, the fact that Mother and Father managed to keep the summer happy for me speaks of considerable nobility.

The medieval inconveniences of the château which were a delight to me must have been a daily irritation to my mother. It was an unusually hot summer, and there was no refrigeration. Friday was a special day because the fishman came through the village with his horse-drawn, high-smelling wagon, and the fish were kept passably fresh with ice. Mother bought not only fish for the evening meal but a small amount of ice—very small, just enough so that on Friday nights the grownups could have martinis before dinner. After dinner my special treat was to take a lump of sugar and dip it in Mother's or Father's demitasse, and then slowly let the warm, coffee-saturated lump dissolve in my mouth.

The substance of my days was as subterranean as the deepest of the cellars where the vegetables and eggs and milk were stored. This dream world ended abruptly on the day my parents took me away from the château and to boarding school. In my naïveté I hoped that the school would be a continuation of the dream. My first inkling that school was not going to be like a story came during the very first hour, when the matron, in crisp white uniform and even crisper accent, said, "If you have read boarding-school stories, Madaleen, forget them. School is not like that."

It was not. It was, at first, sheer hell. The term had started three days earlier, and I understand now that the decision to send me had been sudden and arbitrary, and had come after bitter quarreling. Mother wanted to take me with them higher into the Alps—for, even in Publier, Father found breathing difficult—and send me to the village school. Father felt that I would not get a proper education there, and that the French I would learn would be a questionable patois. I think also that he thought he was going to die sooner than he eventually did, and did not want me around, for both our sakes.

4

So i went away to school. Those first three days missed were disastrous. The other new girls had already found friends. I was completely alone, and the only American, to boot. The only other foreigners were Teri and Danusch Zogu, nieces of King Zog of Albania, and I have often wondered if they survived the terrors which came to their country. We bitterly resented the fact that they had a suite with a fireplace; the only other active fireplaces in the unheated building were in the infirmary and the headmistress's apartment.

But most terrible of all was that my imaginary world was ruthlessly wrested from me. Nothing was ever said about daydreams or the weaving of stories; daily life in school was set up so that there was no time and no place for the world of imagination. Our life was completely regimented from the moment we were roused to a bell, to the moment our lights were turned off to another bell. We had fifteen-minute bath "hours" twice a week, and anybody who dared stay in a lukewarm tub sixteen minutes was routed out by Matron. Bathrooms were constantly monitored, and a locked door was knocked on after two

99

or three minutes. "Who is in there? What are you doing?"

Most of us had chilblains during the winter months. We used to sit in bed at night with tears running down our cheeks, rubbing Mentholatum into hands which were chapped raw and bleeding. Our diet would have provoked a riot in a present-day prison. I remember mostly watery potatoes, and suet pudding with one seed of raspberry jam as filling, so heavy we could feel it clonk into a cold lump in the pits of our stomachs as we swallowed.

It did not occur to me that there was any way out of this torture until another new girl wrote home asking her parents to take her away, and suggested to me that this was a perfectly possible way out for me, too. When her parents drove up and she left, I wrote to my mother and father in Chamonix, telling them of my misery, and asking them to come for me.

When Mother wrote saying that she and Father had talked my letter over, long and seriously, and that they were asking me to stay and to learn from my experiences, I did not realize how difficult it was for her to say no to me, or how right she was to do so. After a few weeks I did considerable adjusting. I was not happy, but neither was I unhappy. I learned to put on protective coloring in order to survive in an atmosphere which was alien; and I learned to concentrate. Because I was never alone, because (except after the lights-out bell) I was always surrounded by noise, I learned to shut out the sound of the school and listen to the story or poem I was writing when I should have been doing schoolwork. The result of this early lesson in concentration is that I can write anywhere, and I wrote my first novel on tour with a play, writing on trains, in dressing rooms, and in hotel bedrooms shared with three other girls.

Sending me away to school may have been an arbitrary decision on my parents' part, an end to their dispute about me and an answer to "What are we to do with her?" But I was irrevocably changed and shaped by the school and by my reaction to it. In the spring, when our chapped hands finally healed and we moved from heavy woolen underwear and scratchy serge gym tunics to Liberty cottons, we were given small garden plots to cultivate. We were assigned partners; I was Number 97 in the school (even then, the process of un-Naming had begun); 97 on my clothes, my desk, my napkin cubbyhole, my shelf in the classroom, my locker in the common room; and my partner was 96. We were allowed to bring the produce of our gardens in for tea, so almost everybody planted tomatoes and lettuce and radishes and cress. 96 and I planted poppies. Nothing but poppies.

It was possible when I was twelve to be considerably more naïve and innocent about drugs than it is today. All we knew was that opium comes from poppies, and we knew this because our illicit reading included Bulldog Drummond and Fu Manchu. From these paperback books, which we kept hidden in our blazer pockets to read when we got sent from the classroom, we learned that opium produces beautiful dreams. So 96 and I ate poppy-seed sandwiches, poppy-flower sandwiches, poppy-leaf sandwiches, and went to bed every night with our dream books and flashlights under our pillows. My dream book has been lost somewhere, but I am still grateful for it. I soon learned that poppy sandwiches weren't needed to induce dreams, but they did serve to give me an awareness that the waking world isn't all there is.

If we had been allowed more time for daytime dreaming, for excursions into the world of the imagination, if we had been allowed time for what George MacDonald calls *holy idleness,* we would not have had to depend on our nighttime dreams. But holy idleness would not have been tolerated in that school, and any attempt to search for it was considered wicked and immoral. "What! Daydreaming again, Madaleen? You'll never get anywhere that way."

Where did Matron want me to go? Our civilization was rushing toward the devastation of the Second World War; the clouds were visible on the horizon, and my parents saw them, even if Matron didn't; and yet in school we were being taught to live in a climate where it was assumed that man is in control of the universe, and that he is capable of understanding and solving all problems by his own effort and virtue.

What 96 and I were doing with our dream books was instinctively rejecting this false illusion, refusing to think that our whole self is limited to that very small fragment of self which we can know, control, and manipulate; that very small fragment of self over which we have power.

At that time the two worlds lay side by side for me; the imaginary world in which I had been moving was just behind me; I was still fending off the limited, finite world of school with stolen moments of dreaming and writing. I had yet to learn that the two worlds should not be separated. Growing up is a journey into integration. Separation is disaster.

Look at my mother this summer. She is lost

somewhere in the subterranean self; she cannot come up into the light of the day. She is no longer the integrated person I have loved and admired, but a dark shard broken and splintered.

彡❧

Bedtime has always been a time for me when the above-water world of the mind and the undersea world of the imagination, the world of the intellect and the world of intuition, have come close. In boarding-school days I treasured bedtime not only because it was my only time of privacy but because it was daydreaming time, and I was angry if I became sleepy too soon. In my Swiss school the dormitory windows opened out toward Lake Geneva, facing the always snow-crested mountains of France on the other side. When I was fortunate enough to have my bed by the window I could lie and look at one of the most spectacular views in the world; the view itself was a consciousness expander, and disciplined my daydreams.

Long before the language of Freud and Jung became part of our everyday vocabulary, Emerson wrote, "I catch myself philosophising more abstractly in the night or morning. I make the truest observations and distinctions then, when the will is yet wholly asleep and the mind works like a machine without friction. I am conscious of having, in my sleep, transcended the limits of the individual, and made observations and carried on conversations which in my waking hours I can neither recall nor appreciate. As if in sleep our individual fell into the infinite mind, and at the moment of awakening we found ourselves on the confines of the latter."

Our dream books were not so foolish.

I still treasure the time before sleep comes, when I move into the shallows before plunging down into deep waters; and the minutes before I surface into daylight and the routine of the day, when I swim slowly up from sleep and dreams, still partly in that strange, underwater world where I know things which my conscious mind is not able to comprehend.

5

THIS IS A STORY with a double helix. I am trying to write about a particular summer, the summer that will always be for me the great-grandmother's. I am trying to take a new look at my mother's life and world, and I find that I can do this only subjectively. I can look objectively at Mother's life only during the years before I was born, before my own remembering begins, when I did not know her; and even then my objectivity is slanted by selectivity, my own, hers, and that of friends and relatives who told me stories which for some reason Mother had omitted from her repertoire. I learned a good deal of family scandal one Crosswicks summer when I overheard Mother talking to my mother-in-law.

But there attempts at objectivity fall apart, and biology makes me subjective, and this is the other strand of the intertwined helix, my very subjective response to this woman who is, for me, always and irrevocably, first, Mother; and second, her own Madeleine.

❧

Change is a basic law of life, and when change stops, death comes. But change is not automatically good; it can be for the worse as well as for the better. If I need any proof that all change is not good, all it takes is five minutes with Mother. She tries to break things, throw things, fights moving anywhere, cries, "No, no, no, no," over and over; often does not know where she is, or who we are; or, if she does know who, then *whether* we are. "Are you real? You aren't made up?" There's something to learn from this strange, senile madness about the nature of reality.

Am I making Mother up as I remember her? Am I overcompensating, as the jargon would have it? No matter. What I remember is a woman who was fully alive, who enjoyed new tastes, sounds, adventures.

That year when I was twelve and she and Father spent the winter in Chamonix, Mother was not happy. The rented villa was as inconvenient as the château, and cold. At night she had to cover the washbasins with quilts so that the pipes would not crack. The ink froze, and had to be thawed in the morning. She told me, when I was grown, that the mountains closed in on her. The winter was snowy and cloudy, the village enclosed in grey. Only rarely would she wake up in the morning to clear skies and Mont Blanc on fire from sunlight.

But what I remember, from the Christmas holidays I spent with my parents, was the coziness of the villa, which she had somehow made into a home, despite hideous wallpaper with designs that looked like spiders, chairs of brilliant green plush and sagging springs.

I remember, too, the new glimpse of my parents which followed our separation. Nothing would ever be the same again; they would never be the same. I went up to their bedroom one afternoon looking for Mother, and saw her flung out on the bed in an abandoned position of grief, and I backed out in horror. I do not think she knew that I had seen her. And I began to notice that Father was drinking more than was good for him, but I did not understand the reason why.

During this summer of the great-grandmother, I am aware again of my father. His portrait is over the mantelpiece, a charming, impressionist piece done long before I was born, painted in an apple orchard in Brittany. The occasion for the portrait was a swashbuckling felt hat and a red tie he'd bought in Cairo. Mother hates the portrait, which I love. The man who looks at us is vital, full of *joie de vivre;* and he belongs to another, more gracious but equally brutal world; this portrait could not have been painted after that world ended, with World War I. I never knew the man in the portrait; I knew only the man whose world had been demolished in that war, and who took eighteen years to die.

Mother would say, "Your father and Gilbert White used to take a pitcher of martinis and go out to the apple orchard while Gilbert painted; you can see the martinis in your father's eyes." I can't. This is hindsight on Mother's part. I see only the handsome, blond young man full of pleasure, not because of martinis but because he'd just completed an exciting assignment; because the apple orchard was beautiful; because he was full of *élan vital* and *amour-propre.* (Odd: when I try to express joy I turn to the French words, and to German for pain: *Angst; Sturm und Drang; Weltschmerz.* It was my parents' wanderings which gave me these words; I gained many valuable things because of their troubles.)

I began to know Father after his death. During

107

his life I never heard him complain, so I did not understand about his pain until later. Nor did I understand that alcohol, which had been a pleasure in an apple orchard in Brittany, became a painkiller, and occasionally an abused painkiller. As I look back now, I am amazed that it was so seldom abused. My own struggles with pain, with defeat, help me to know my father and to love him, not as I had loved him before that winter in Chamonix, as a small child looking up to an impossible god, but with a love which begins to struggle toward *ousia*.

ॐ

That month in Chamonix was an ambiguous one for me. When I could, I reacted as a child, but I was being forced into growing up. I wanted to balance the pain of school with comfort, safety, changelessness, but I found pain, discovery, change. I listened to Mother playing Bach on a barely playable upright piano, and I watched her play solitaire. Because she could not understand Father, neither could I, and I was drawn into her unhappiness.

And yet that Christmas was one of our loveliest. All the decorations on the small tree were homemade. We still hang on our Christmas tree each year a small silver chain made of little beads of tinfoil, rolled from the paper in Father's packages of Sphinx cigarettes. We cut pictures out of the English illustrated magazines to replace the horrors on the wall which came with the rented villa. My presents were the very books I had asked for, plus colored pencils and a fresh box of water colors and a new notebook with a marbleized cover. What we ate for Christmas dinner I don't remember; all we ate that winter, it seemed, was rabbit, which was plentiful and cheap;

and Berthe, the eighteen-year-old girl Mother had brought with her from Publier (for, even that austere winter, she managed to have help), cooked rabbit every conceivable way. And a few inconceivable, Father would add. We also ate hearts of palm; for some reason the village grocer had an overabundance of this delicacy, and needed to unload it. Berthe bargained with him and came home triumphantly with string bags bulging with cans.

On New Year's Eve I was allowed, for the first time, to stay up with my parents until midnight. I remember only one thing about that milestone: while the village clock was striking twelve, Father opened his small new engagement diary for the year, and we all signed our names in it. It was Father's way of saying *yes* to Mother and to me and to the new year, no matter what it might bring. It would have been much easier for him to withdraw from it, as he occasionally withdrew from the pain with whiskey, but he refused to withdraw, and I knew this without understanding it in the least, and was grateful as I added my signature to Mother's and his.

My father's name: Charles Wadsworth Camp. When I wrote my first published stories and had to decide on a writing name, it was with a wrench that I decided to use my baptismal name, Madeleine L'Engle.

Mother said, "It's as though you're rejecting your father."

"I'm not!" And I reminded her that it had taken her a year to decide whether or not she could go through life as Mrs. Camp. Add to this the fact that many publishers at that time were friends and contemporaries of my father, and I wanted to be a writer on my own. And I'm sure that Father would have been the first to agree that Madeleine L'Engle is a more felicitous name for a writer than Madeleine Camp.

When I married Hugh I was all set to switch to Madeleine Franklin, but my publishers said that I had already made a good start under L'Engle, and Hugh agreed.

My first novel was a success, and it was not until we were living in Crosswicks and I began to receive what seemed an interminable stream of rejection slips (for nearly a decade I could sell nothing I wrote) that I began to understand what the failure of his last years must have been like for Father.

Long after his death Mother told me that one day she went into his room to call him in for lunch. It was at the very end of his life, when they were living in my great-grandmother's cottage at the beach. Father's bedroom and office was a corner room overlooking ocean and dunes, with the sound of the surf and the wind in the palms ever present. He was sitting at his desk, and when she came up to him he stopped typing and handed her several pages.

Mother did not know how to be dishonest, and she sometimes infuriated Father by falling asleep in the evening while he read his day's work to her. Now, slowly and carefully, she read what he gave her, and then she said, "Charles, this is *good.*"

His eyes filled. "I can still write, can't I?"

I cannot set this down without tears coming to my own eyes.

My father's name was his, and I will always honor it. A name is an important thing, and I did not decide on mine lightly. Perhaps it was Father's affirming signature on that cold New Year's Eve in France which underlined forever the importance of a name.

110

During those weeks in Chamonix we went everywhere on skis, the simplest method of moving on the snow-packed streets, and I learned more complex skiing on the slopes above the villa. We spent a memorable day on the Mer de Glace, and those hours of walking over a sea of ice were a revelation of a cold and unearthly beauty I had never before seen. My own vision was deepened because I saw the beauty through the eyes of my parents; their wholehearted response took us all beyond the pain and confusion which were ever present in the villa. One night we rode for an hour in a horse-drawn sleigh, snow beneath us, moonlight and starlight above us, the horse's mane streaming coldly in the wind, while we were kept warm under fur robes. Father hardly coughed at all; Mother relaxed and enjoyed the beauty and the speed. I moved back into my dream world during that ride, not as an escape, but as a respite; I did not try to take the fairy tale with me back into the villa.

ੴ

And I remember a summer evening somewhere in France. We went to a tiny, one-ring circus. The ring was enclosed with a fence as insubstantial as chicken wire, and when a shabby lion came roaring out of his cage I grabbed my parents' hands in an ecstasy of terror, fully expecting the old beast to leap over the flimsy barrier. I think that this memory must precede the winter in Chamonix, though I have lost its chronology, because I still felt complete security sitting between Mother and Father. After Chamonix I would have known that there are lions more powerful than my parents.

The lions I feared during my childhood were the

lions of war. I was born after the Armistice, and yet the specter of another war after the War to End Wars was always with me, not only because of Father's coughing, but because of my own terror of war; I am not sure where this terror came from, but it was always with me. Quite often I would anxiously ask one parent or the other, "Is there going to be another war?"

They paid me the honor of not trying to comfort me with false promises—though I doubt if they foresaw the enormity of change to come in the ways of waging war.

Father's war was not like our wars today. In his war the enemy still had a face. When you killed, you killed a man, not a town or village of people you did not know, had never seen, would never see.

Once, a good many years after the war, my parents were eating dinner in a Spanish inn, and suddenly Father got up from the table in great excitement and rushed across the dining room to a man who, in his turn, was hurrying to greet Father. The two men embraced warmly, and Father brought his friend over to the table to meet Mother: the man was a German; he had been an officer in the Kaiser's army; he and Father had fought against each other at the front. It is difficult to understand such an incident today. These two "enemies" were genuinely happy to see each other; they had shared an extraordinary experience; they respected and honored each other. I wonder if that can happen today, even at the higher levels of combat.

I was in boarding school in Charleston, South Carolina, when we heard the news that Mussolini had taken troops into Ethiopia. I will never forget the leap of terror in my stomach, followed by a dull ache of acceptance: this was the beginning of the war about which I had been having nightmares since I was a small child.

It was a worse war than Father's war, yes, and has continued to be so, through the bombings of England, Europe, Korea, Vietnam, the Middle East.

But there is one small note of optimism: the results of mustard gas were considered so terrible by so many people that it was not used during World War II, nor has it been used since—though we have used worse things. English children during the bombings went to school carrying gas masks, but they did not need to put them on.

We have seen the terrible results of the atom bomb. We know how bad it is. Perhaps it, like mustard gas, will never be used again? It may be a faint hope, but it is a hope.

6

H ERE IN CROSSWICKS I listen to Bion and his friends soberly and painfully discussing the involvement of the United States in Vietnam, Laos, Cambodia. For Bion this is not only the summer of the transition between high school and college, the summer of watching his grandmother become daily less human; he must also decide whether or not he can honestly register as a conscientious objector. One of his friends is a Quaker, and his position is absolute. Bion's is more difficult. He totally disapproves of American involvement in Vietnam; but can he say, truthfully, that under no conditions would he ever fight? Given the circumstances of his Grandfather Charles's war, what would he have done? Is there such a thing as a just war? Could the war with Hitler have been avoided? There are no easy answers.

A little less than a year ago, at the end of the summer, the night before he went back to school for his final year, he announced to us, "I'm not playing football this year."

"Why, Bion?"

"It's a blood game, and I don't want to have anything to do with it."

"Well, it's completely between you and the school. If you think you can handle it, go ahead."

Bion is pushing 6'5", weighs two hundred pounds, and was expected to be a useful member of the football team. There was a good deal of pressure put on him to play, but he was adamant. They said, "But you play goalie in ice hockey. That's much more dangerous than football." "I'm not worried about the danger. The way we play hockey, it isn't murder."

I think he expected to be ostracized. Instead, he was given both respect and support. He went with the team to the games, and one Saturday at an away-from-school game, one of the boys on the other team was hurt—not badly it seemed, and nobody was particularly worried.

That evening many of the boys were in their coffee house when the headmaster came in to tell them that the boy on the opposing team had died. "The chapel will be open all night," he said, "for anybody who wants to use it." There wasn't a boy in the school who didn't go into the chapel, just to sit, to think about death, if not to pray.

During this decisive period Bion came home for a weekend and announced to us that he had become a vegetarian. "I may not keep this up, but it's the way I feel now." We respected the fact that it was a response to his thinking about war and peace, and whenever he was home I cooked quantities of extra vegetables.

He finally decided that he could not say that under no circumstances would he fight, ever. His two little nieces may have played a part in that decision. I think there's no question that he would fight to defend them. He also feels deeply about Crosswicks and the land around it; he was born here; here are his roots. If his land were attacked he would fight to defend it; his land: Crosswicks: his country.

ॐ

His is only one of many reactions to the violence that is increasing all over the world. How strangely contradictory we are: we condone slaughter of villages or towns in our various wars, and yet we will do anything to keep a hospitalized body alive, a body whose central nervous system has been destroyed—a kind of reverse euthanasia. I do not want this for my mother. To be a body without *ousia* was what she dreaded most. She is not in physical pain, though everything within me cries out that she is in spiritual pain.

We all in the Crosswicks household, to the limits of our capacity, share the pain. And we are learning daily lessons in interdependence. I lost my unquestioning dependence on my parents that winter in Chamonix. I am still learning to move into interdependence.

Because of the girls who make up the great-grandmother's retinue, because of the understanding and compassion of the entire household, there is still laughter in the rooms. Yet there are times when for no logical reason I feel an almost unbearable sense of isolation. Not only am I divided in myself, my underwater and above-water selves separated, but I feel wrenched away from everybody around me. This is part of being human, this knowing that we are all part of one another, inextricably involved; and at the same time alone, irrevocably alone.

Alone, and yet interdependent. Much of my

training has been against accepting this paradox, my good Anglo-Saxon boarding-school training. Stand on your own feet. Do it yourself. It's your own business. Don't bother anybody else with it. Take in your belt a notch, pull up your boot straps, and go it alone.

Not bad advice in many ways. Who wants a clinging vine? But there's more to it than that. Mother fought dependency as long as she could, but that's a different thing from interdependency. She lived alone during the winters far longer than I thought was safe for her, and yet I would not take away the dignity of risk until she herself was ready—which was not until the intestinal resection, when she was nearly eighty-eight. When I think of the varied climates and conditions in which Mother lived, I marvel at her ability to adapt. Would I too be able to take with equanimity the enormity of change through which she strode?

7

DURING MY last year in school—the school in Charleston, South Carolina—my parents were living at the beach in North Florida in the drafty old cottage built by my great-grandmother. In late October, Father made his annual pilgrimage to New York and Princeton, and my mother took a trip driving around North Carolina with Aunt Dee—one of my godmothers. Mother arrived home a day or so before Father and drove into town to meet Father's train. "When I saw him get off the train," she said, "I knew he was dying."

That night she wrote to me. The next day I was busy with some project and did not even check the mailboxes, until a friend came bustling up, being the bearer of good news, "Hey, Madeleine, there's a letter in your cubbyhole."

It was a brief note in which Mother told me that Father was in the hospital with pneumonia, and asked me to write to him. She ended the letter, "Pray for him, and for me, too."

I had always been a bad letter writer. I managed to get off one cursory note every Sunday, in which I told almost nothing of what was going on without or within. I didn't really know what or how to write to Father, but I copied out three poems I had written that week, and sent them to him, knowing that they would arrive too late. This knowing was not prescience; I had been watching him die for years, and I knew that he could not last through another attack of pneumonia.

The next afternoon the headmistress sent for me and told me that my father was very ill and that I was to take the evening train home. I was not surprised at her summons, although when it came I felt shaky and cold. Two of the teachers drove me to the station and stayed with me until I got on the train. In those days it was a four-hour trip, and I had taken *Jane Eyre* with me to read, but I could not read. Whether or not I believe in God I have always prayed, and I prayed then, though I did not ask God to make my father get well. I prayed to the rhythm of the wheels, "Please, God, do whatever is best. For Father, for Mother. Please do whatever is best, whatever is best, is best. Please, Father. Please, God, do whatever is best for Father."

My two godmothers met me, Aunt Dee and Cousin Mary, my mother's close friends since childhood. I asked how Father was and they evaded answering me, and so I knew the answer. It wasn't until we were nearly at our destination that one of them told me that Father had died that morning, and that we weren't going all the way to the beach, but to the house of a cousin.

I don't know why Father's funeral was in this house, rather than in church. It seems very strange to me now, and I cannot ask Mother to explain. I remember feeling embarrassed as I kissed Mother, and then even more embarrassed when I was told, in the manner of those days, to go in and look at Father.

He was lying in state in the library. I asked to go in alone, and stood in front of the coffin and looked at him. His face was peaceful and alien, and my father was not there. I closed my eyes, and then I was able to see him a little better.

I remember nothing about the funeral, but I remember the trip to the cemetery, and the canvas canopy put up to shield us from the heat of the subtropical sun, still apt to be oppressive in late October, and that I thought the canopy out of place and would have liked to move out from under it. I remember staying that night in Aunt Dee's great, dark house, and that Mother and I talked about trivial things in a completely calm way. For some reason we talked about toothpaste, but we were really talking about Father.

I do not know whether or not the Church was any comfort to Mother at the time of Father's death. It was not to me. The words of the burial service were strengthening, but not the unctuous men at the graveside.

If the churches and synagogues didn't condone the mortuary mentality, funerals would not be the travesties they so often are. One rainy day when I stood at a favorite cousin's graveside, huddled with family and friends under umbrellas while the rain slanted in from the east and trickled down our necks, I was repelled by the phony carpet of green grass thrown over the pile of earth waiting at the open grave. I think we grossly underestimate the capacity for realism in the mourner.

What would I have wanted for Father, what will I want for Mother if she predeceases me? She may not; at the birthday party in the spring a cousin said, "Don't worry about your mother. She's going to bury us all."

Alan's grandmother, my mother's contemporary, as a young woman in an English village was a "layer-outer." And I would want this, to have a human being (so this is what I think of morticians!) prepare my parents' bodies for burial. Alan's grandmother knew each body she touched, as we know each other in our village.

I would have been happier if my father's body had been buried from the house at the beach, his last home. If Mother should die while she is with us in Crosswicks, I would like to have her body prepared at home, and then to have the four traditional candles placed, one at each corner of her bed, and to take turns watching and honoring her earthly frame during the night, and thinking soberly about death, her death, mine, and being free to do some grieving, some weeping over the mortal remains of my birth-giver.

Many professional religion-mongers I have encountered are so terrified of and so disbelieving about the Resurrection that it is no wonder that they condone cozy coffins and fake grass. My own theology is very shaky here, and I find most strength in the writings of the early Byzantine Fathers, men who, like us, were living at a time of radical change. They have far more in common with the world we are living in today than thinkers of a generation ago. The early Fathers were living, as we are, in the breaking apart of a great civilization. The Roman world was shattering like an ice floe in the spring. Nothing was ever going to be the same again. So the *ousia* of things, all that which was true, is true, and will be true, had the same kind of importance for them that it does for us. I turn to these golden-tongued writers (long turned to dust) with a sense of familiarity, of talking with known and well-loved friends. They are our contemporaries, and I understand their language, even if I myself falter when trying to speak it.

They are more aware of the wild freedom of creation than we tend to be. They probe beyond limited sensory evidence in an effort to glimpse *ousia*—the *ousia* of a parent, or a small green frog on a rock—to glimpse it, not with limited human eyesight and comprehension, but with the whole of themselves, that whole which encompasses the unknown worlds beneath the waters and beyond the stars.

I am often afraid of this world. It would be simpler to restrict myself to the things I can hear and see and touch, to the things I can prove, to the things I can control.

My senior year at boarding school I thought I was pretty well in control of my world; I was editor of the literary magazine, played leading roles in the school plays; I was, for the first time, a success with my peers, and this success was heady wine. And then Father's death pushed me right out of the slippery world of human control, and I had no choice but to try to open myself to the darkness and horror in order to search for a hope of finding a possible all-rightness on the other side.

My father was dead. What was all right?

When Gregory of Nyssa's brilliant sister, Macrina, was on her deathbed, she sent for Gregory, and brother and sister talked throughout the night. He held her hand and told her, "The Resurrection will bring about the restoration of our human nature in its original form." This is strong and difficult language. Gregory and Macrina never doubted the Resurrection, but they thought of it neither as a vague continuing in unending time, much as we are in mortal life, nor as an awakening of the dead body from the grave, old bones and flesh reassembling themselves to make the same flawed body that died. Rather, they thought of it as a radical change of all that we have come to think of as ourselves.

I had not encountered a theology as wild and strong as Gregory's when Father died. I had to struggle alone, and all I knew was that Father's death caused me to ask questions for which I could find no answer, and I was living in a world which believed that all questions are answerable. I, too, believe that all questions are answerable, but not in scientific terms, or in the language of provable fact.

Mother sent me back to school almost immediately. And I wanted to go. I understood only dimly what the loss of a husband who had been lover, friend, companion for thirty-odd years would mean to this woman who was my mother.

Back in Charleston I went at the first opportunity out into the grounds and climbed up into the ancient live oak tree which was my favorite writing and reading place, and coldly and calmly recorded the fact of Father's death in my journal. It was a long time before I was able to cry—nearly three years; and it was falling in love for the first time which freed the tears.

That last year at boarding school I was working on a series of boarding-school stories; it was the world I knew best and instinct told me that I should write out of experience. During the spring term I tried to write about Father's death, and I wrote it almost exactly as it had happened—for my protagonist was a tall, clumsy, nearsighted girl—and the story had a certain amount of verisimilitude, but I knew that I had not yet really written it, that I had not got it out where I could face it. Occasionally I would talk to someone about death—not the girls at school, or the one or two teachers I really trusted, but young men.

The only good I could find in Father's death was that my coming-out party was canceled. But a cousin was being launched and Mother insisted that I go to some of the parties. "Your father would have wanted you to. And I want you to."

I don't think she realized quite how agonizing these dances were to me, the stranger in a tightly knit group of young people who had known each other all their lives, and who were fluent in an agreed-upon set of social mores which were completely unfamiliar to me. Dates were arranged for me, and I'm sure the young men whose parents had coerced them into calling for me dreaded the evenings as much as I did. I was as tall as an adolescent as I am now, and most of my dancing partners seemed to be at least a foot shorter, and leaned their heads against my breast as we danced—or as I tripped over their feet. I was hopeless in the social world, and had none of the highly cultivated charm of my Southern cousins.

One cousin, trying to be helpful, drew up a list of ten questions for me to ask my dancing partners. I was always extremely myopic, contact lenses had not yet become general, and pride forbade me to wear my glasses on a date or at a dance. But there was one dance where I had more partners than usual, and spent less time in the ladies' room pretending to put on make-up, desperately thinking up excuses to keep me off the dance floor, and I was feeling quite pleased with myself, and was prepared to tell my cousin how well her questions were working, when my partner said, "Hey, honey, what's your line? You've already asked me these questions three times before."

I couldn't very well tell him that I was so short-sighted that I hadn't recognized him, so I said, "You haven't really answered them properly."

"You really want to know?"

"Of course, or I wouldn't have kept asking."

We became friends after a fashion, and talked about the primitive pubic rites of the coming-out parties, and felt sophisticated and above it all.

And I learned that when a boy talked to me about God, and death, he was likely to give me a good-night kiss, even if I put on my glasses at the movies.

Through my partner at that dance I met a brilliant, unhappy young man who later became a physicist, and I remember one conversation we had, a conversation which I reproduced, almost verbatim, in a different setting, in my first novel, where I struggled to write the *ousia* of Father's death in depicting the death of the protagonist's mother.

The original conversation was held at the beach, at night. Instead of taking me to the movies as planned, Yandell (named, in the Southern manner, after his mother's family name) said, "I feel like talking," and then drove in complete silence the forty-five miles to the beach. We climbed up onto a high dune and listened to the grave rolling of the waves, and the gentle hishing of the tall sea oats, and Yandell told me that he had a heart murmur and probably wouldn't live for more than a few years. He asked, "How old was your father?"

"Fifty-seven."

"That's a lifetime. At least he had a lifetime."

"It's not very old." I come from a long-lived family.

He shrugged, and we lay back on the dune and looked at the stars. "Did you see him after he was dead?"

"Yes."

"I haven't ever seen a dead body. What did he look like?"

"He looked—he didn't look real. He wasn't there."

"Where do you think he was, then?"

Something in his tone of voice made me sit up. "You don't think he's anywhere, do you?"

"I didn't say that."

"But do you? Do you believe that my father *is*, now—himself, somewhere, actively living, *himself*?"

He picked a long sea oat and began slowly stripping it and dropping the little pieces on the sand, sea oat and sand blending together. "What you believe about things like that is just your own personal opinion, isn't it?"

"You don't think he is. You think he's just nothing, don't you?"

"You're grown up enough to see through all this coming-out zug. But if you want to go on with the tribal superstition thinking your father's more than worm fodder, that's up to you."

I was both angry and frightened. I stood up, and sand slid under my feet. "Yandell, I saw him when he was dead. I saw Father, and it just wasn't Father. It's like looking at a photograph; it looks like the

126

person, but the person isn't there. Father wasn't there, not what's really Father. And if he wasn't there, he's got to be somewhere."

The caustic note had gone from Yandell's voice, and he spoke slowly and calmly. "But what's a soul without a body, without senses? Can you imagine existing, being yourself, if you couldn't see? Or hear? Or feel? And after all, we think with our brains. How could you be you without your cerebral cortex?"

I was so angry that I nearly burst into tears, but they wouldn't have been the right kind of tears. "It's idiotic," I said, "it's crazy. If you die and then you're just nothing, there isn't any point to anything. Why do we live at all if we die and stop being? Father wasn't ready to be stopped. Nobody's ready to be stopped. We don't have *time* to be ready to be stopped. It's all crazy."

"Don't think the idea of extinction appeals to me," Yandell drawled.

I had put on my glasses so that I could see the stars. Now I took them off and the sky became nothing but a dark curtain. I waved my glasses at him. "Look at my glasses. I can't even see that there are any stars in the sky without them, but it's not the glasses that are doing the seeing, it's me, Madeleine. I don't think Father's eyes are seeing now, but *he* is. And maybe his brain isn't thinking, but a brain's just something to think through, the way my glasses are something to see through."

"Calm down," Yandell said. "Let's go walk on the beach and go wading."

One cold winter's night in Crosswicks, many years later, while I was putting the children to bed, my daughter Maria turned to me and said,

"Grandma says my mother got all burned up." True: Liz was cremated. But to the seven-year-old child this insensitive sentence from Liz's mother meant the entire loss of Liz. That day I had given away some of Maria's outgrown dresses, and I reminded her of it, and that we had bought her some new clothes. And I said, "You'd outgrown those old clothes, and you don't need them any more. And now you have clothes which fit you better. Well, if a human parent can get new clothes for you when you outgrow your old ones, God can provide us with new bodies when we outgrow the ones we have now."

I can't begin to guess with what kind of body he may have outfitted Liz or my father, or will outfit my mother. However, I have a feeling that it would be completely unrecognizable to our human eyes. At least the analogy I used for the seven-year-old child was one step away from the thinking of the Middle Ages, where there are records of the burial of a Crusader home from the wars with only one leg; at his death a leg was cut off one of his peasants, on the theory that the Crusader would have more need of two legs in heaven than the peasant.

That medieval horror would have pleased Yandell—who outgrew his heart murmur and is alive and flourishing. And I admit that my thinking isn't a great deal less primitive than that of the Middle Ages. The main progress is that I do not attempt to give an answer to an unanswerable question, but I do ask the question. And it does not upset me unduly that Paul's vision of a "spiritual body" is a scientific impossibility, and can be glimpsed only in poetry and paradox.

When I got back to boarding school after the holidays, Yandell's words obviously remained in my underwater mind, and I worked out a scheme of things which still seems valid to me. It was a logical analogy for one who had spent so many years in boarding schools, because it included thinking of our present lives as being something like nursery school, and to complete the growth of our souls we would need to go all the way through school and college and a great deal further.

I sat, during a free weekend afternoon, out in my favorite live oak tree, and thought of the stars over the ocean during my painful conversation with Yandell, and that all of those stars were suns, and that many of these suns had planets, and that surely the planet earth is not the only planet in the universe to have sentient life. And then I thought that perhaps there might be a planet where nobody has eyes; everybody would get on perfectly well; other senses would take over. But nobody on that planet could possibly conceive of what sight could be like, even if they were told about it. Something as important and glorious as sight couldn't be understood at all.

So then I thought that maybe when we die we might go to another planet, and there we might have a new sense, one just as important as sight, or even more important, but which we couldn't conceive of now any more than we could conceive of sight if we didn't know about it. And then when we'd finished on that planet we'd go on to another planet and develop and grow and learn even more, and it might well take millions of planets before we'd have been taught enough to be ready for heaven.

I haven't gone much further than that adolescent analogy, and even then I knew that it was no more than analogy. But I did feel, and passionately, that it wasn't fair of God to give us brains enough to ask the ultimate questions if he didn't intend to teach us the answers.

8

I T WOULD HAVE BEEN EASY, after my father's death,
for Mother's love to become grasping and demanding. The environment in which she lived encouraged
it. But Mother deliberately opened her hands and let
me go. Many of my Southern relatives expected me
to stay home and take care of my delicate mother;
however, during vacation times Mother carefully
pointed out shriveled female cousins who had spent
most of a lifetime caring for an aged parent "while
life passed by, so now that Cousin Isabella has finally
shuffled off her mortal coil, her daughter has been
sucked dry and it's too late for living."

Some of my shriveled female cousins had just
cause to think of "Mother"—or "Father"—as devourer. But I worry about people who assume that
all mothers are bloodsuckers. The womb is a place of
dark, warm protection only for a term; as soon as
the baby is able to bear the light of day the womb
contracts and expels him, loosens him, frees him.

A friend of mine spoke of college freshmen as
people wandering around with the umbilical cord in
one hand, looking for some place to plug it in. Often
the mother has cut the umbilical cord long before
the child is willing to let go, and yet the child blames
the mother.

When I was sent, so abruptly, to boarding school, the umbilical cord got cut, ready or not, and Mother had no intention of reattaching it. Thanks to her clarity of vision, I was able to go to college free of guilt.

We had spent a happy summer in England and France, visiting relatives. We came back to New York just a few days before college, and then off I went on the train, heading north into New England, and Mother returned to the South.

I did not abandon or forget Mother. I did not understand consciously that she was sacrificing something in sending me away, but I think I must have instinctively felt more than I knew, because from the time of Father's death and on, until she could no longer read letters, I wrote her at least a postcard every day. It became a simple part of the day's routine and took only a few minutes.

I had a good four years of college, by which I mean that I did a great deal of growing up, and a lot of this growing was extremely painful. I cut far too many classes, wrote dozens of short stories, and managed to get an excellent education despite myself.

After college I did not even consider yielding to family pressure and returning South to "take care of your mother," but went to New York to live my own life and work in the theatre, which I considered the best possible school for a writer. The daily epistles, and weekly (collect) phone calls continued, but I was free to become my own Madeleine.

My mother was birth-giver, not devourer, and I hope I have learned from her.

What is time like for Léna and Charlotte? It is longer than for the rest of the household. It is so long that it comes close to breaking time and becoming part of eternity. But it is not that way for the very old. Time unravels, rather than knits up. It is as erratic as nightmare.

My mother's senility has drawn her through the keyhole of reality and into the world of nightmare on the other side. Her fears are nightmare fears, like those of one who has just woken out of a bad dream and cannot get back into the "real" world. Her real world is gone. She is trapped in nightmare and all our loving cannot get her out.

The pressures of time can sometimes weigh very heavily, but this weight is bearable. One of the greatest deprivations of senility is the loss of a sense of time. Time is indeed out of joint. An old man or woman in a "home" or hospital may say tearfully to a visitor, "My children haven't been to see me. They've forgotten me. They brought me here and abandoned me. They don't care any more." The children's last visit may have been the day before, but to the old man or woman it was so long ago that it has been forgotten. Times stretches like old, worn-out elastic. What happens if it is stretched till it breaks?

Two years ago when it became clear that reading my daily epistles was burden, rather than pleasure, to Mother, the phone calls increased from once a week to twice a week, and finally to almost every day. Last winter I was frequently rebuked for not having called for so long. "I called day before yesterday, Mother." "You didn't. You haven't called for at least two weeks " Occasionally I would get a call or a letter from a rriend or relative in the South: "Why haven't you called your mother?"

It is thin-skinned of me to be upset. For several years I have known that when Mother returns South after the summer she will tell everybody who will listen that I haven't fed her properly. Sometimes I will have this reported to me with an understanding smile. "She looks absolutely marvelous. The summer did her a world of good." Sometimes her complaints will be accepted at their face value, and I am a cruel daughter.

It's a very American trait, this wanting people to think well of us. It's a young want, and I am ashamed of it in myself. I am *not* always a good daughter, even though my lacks are in areas different from her complaints. Haven't I learned yet that the desire to be perfect is always disastrous and, at the least, loses me in the mire of false guilt?

Perfectionism is imprisoning. As long as I demand it, in myself or anybody else, I am not free, and all my life—fifty-two this summer—I've believed that freedom is important, that, despite all our misuse and abuse of it, freedom is what makes us a little lower than the angels, crowned with glory and honor, according to the psalmist; how like a god, according to Shakespeare; freedom to remember, to share, to dream, to accept irrationality and paradox is what makes us human animals.

Where is my freedom this summer? I can go no farther from the house than I can walk, because chancy vision no longer allows me to drive. The responsibility of my mother, of the large household, of the kitchen stove, would seem to deny me a great deal of freedom, and yet my freedom is still up to me. Because I have entered willingly into this time, I do not feel that my freedom has been taken away.

But there are times in life when human freedom

is denied us, and not only in prisons and concentration camps. I was once in an extremity of pain and knew that I was close to death. I was fighting hard to live, for my husband, our small children, for myself and all that I still wanted to do and be, for all the books I hoped to write. And then I knew that unless the pain was relieved I was not alive, that death was better than the body continuing in this kind of impossible pain which had me in its brutal control. When they took me to the operating room I barely had strength to move my lips, "I love you," to Hugh. As for prayer, I could do no more than say, "Please," over and over, "please," to the doctors, to Hugh, to God . . .

My freedom was entirely out of my hands.

Once I heard a "good" woman ask if the victims of concentration camps did not find consolation in prayer, and I was shocked by the question. It was directed to me, and I answered, fumblingly, that they were probably in that dark realm which is beyond the comfort of conscious prayer, and I likened it to extreme physical pain. There have been times when I have given way to the heart's pain, too, and again have been outside freedom. We *can* be unmade, un-personed, all freedom taken away. That we do this to each other is one of the great shames of our civilization. It is not people, but atherosclerosis, which is taking freedom away from my mother.

But I still have some freedom, even when I go alone in the starlight down the lane to weep, with the dogs pressing anxiously about my legs; not much freedom, but some, that little luminous pearl which is daily misunderstood and misused, but which makes life worth living instead of a dirty cosmic joke.

9

O~NCE WHEN MOTHER~ and I were in New York, during a college vacation, we had lunch together in a pleasant downtown restaurant before going to the theatre, and I remember, with the same clarity with which I remember the little embroidered dress, that I leaned across the table and said, "Oh, Mother, it's such *fun* to be with you!" And it was. We enjoyed things together, the theatre, museums, music, food, conversation.

When I was pregnant with Josephine I told Mother, "All I could possibly hope for with my children is that they love me as much as I love you."

Josephine, when she was five or six years old, lightened my heart one evening when she flung her arms around me and said, "Oh, Mama, you're so *exciting!*" What more glorious compliment could a child give a parent? My parents were exciting to me, but their lives were far more glamorous than mine. When Jo made that lovely, spontaneous remark I felt anything but exciting; I was in the midst of a difficult decade of literary rejection, of struggling with small children and a large house; and that remark of Jo's restored my faith in myself, both as a writer and as a mother. Even though I knew I might never again be published; even though I could not see any end to the physical struggle and perpetual fatigue,

Josephine helped heal doubt. It is a risky business to hope, but my daughter gave me the courage to take the risk.

I wonder if I ever, unknowingly, gave my mother like courage? I am well aware of all the things I have done which have distressed her, but perhaps simply the fact that I have always loved her may sometimes have helped.

∾

A story should be something like the earth, a blazing fire at the core, but cool and green on the outside. And that is not a bad description of my mother. Her exterior was so reserved that it was a long time before I realized that there were flames beneath the surface. She was, in my presence at least, an undemonstrative woman, undemonstrative with me, with my father, with everybody. What Mother and Father were like alone I don't know, especially what they were like in the early years of their marriage, when they were young, when Father's health was unimpaired. I never knew the young couple who traveled all over the world at any and every opportunity in all sorts of conditions; who, when they were in New York, ran with a pack of artists of all kinds, as well as with a small, close-knit group of intimate friends. It is difficult today to understand the deep and abiding friendships among men who had survived the First World War together, but the inner circle of friends was composed of three or four men who had fought side by side with Father, and of their wives.

As I look back to the New York years, there seem to have been countless parties. Mother told me, "Your father could walk cold sober into a dead

137

party, and in five minutes everybody was having a good time. He was like champagne."

I had only glimpses of this effervescent man in my own life; I understand far more of his *ousia* now than I did while he was alive. Sometimes in restaurants he embarrassed Mother—and so me—by being what she thought was rude and overdemanding. The strange thing was that the waiter or headwaiter she thought he had insulted, instead of being insulted, thought Father was marvelous, and though this always happened, Mother could never get accustomed to it. When he went into a fine restaurant he demanded fine food and fine service, and when he did not get them, he let people know, and in no uncertain terms. After one hotel dinner somewhere in France when Father had been his most imperious, and Mother less understanding than she might have been, she apologized by telling me of a time when they had gone to a restaurant in Paris where Father had made what she considered a scene; several years later they returned to the same restaurant; the maître d'hôtel greeted Father by name, as an honored client; and the headwaiter served them exactly the same meal Father had finally managed to get years before. Even during his last years my father had a quality about him that was not easy to forget.

I remember my parents coming, night after night, to kiss me good night and goodbye in their evening clothes, Father often with his top hat, looking like a duke, I thought.

Why do I remember with such pain going to sit in Mother's lap one day when she had someone in for tea, and she pushed me down, gently, and said in her quiet, just slightly Southern voice, "You're too old to sit on my lap now."

How old was I? I don't remember, but not, I think, very old. Perhaps that is why I let my children make their own decisions as to when they were too old for lap-sitting.

I told this to Mother, once, perhaps in defense of my lap-sitting policy. She did not remember the incident, and I think that this is part of the human predicament, that most of us are not aware of the small things we do—or don't do—that cause pain which is never forgotten.

One memory of being pushed away from Mother's lap? That's all? One memory of being punished unjustly?

Oh, we had our clashes, Mother and I, we're both temperamental enough for that. During school or college holidays I wanted to write or read or paint or play the piano when Mother wanted me to be social. I could not be for her the gracious and graceful young woman she dreamed of. Nevertheless, I often heard her say that one belief in which she never faltered was that I had been born for a special purpose, and this belief led her to set up impossible standards for me, and when I failed to live up to them she would scold. It sounds as though her expectations put an intolerable burden on me, but somehow she managed to keep them from doing so, and it has been only in the past years that she has referred to them frequently.

"I know you were born for something special."

This would have been more of a burden to me if it weren't part of my mythology that this is true of

139

every child. The fairy godmother or guardian angel bestows on each infant a unique gift, a gift to which the child will be responsible: a gift of healing; a gift for growing green things; a gift for painting, for cooking, for cleaning; a gift for loving. It is part of the human condition that we do not always recognize our gifts; the clown wants to play Hamlet.

While Mother was still herself, I never wondered overmuch about this. Whether or not my gift is with words, which she hoped it was, I will never know. In any case, writing is something I'm stuck with, and I realized this when I first hurt her with something I had written—hurt Mother, not Father, because I did not begin to probe the past until after he died. Until then my writing was poetry, which wrote me, rather than vice versa, and stories of wish-fulfillment and wild and improbable fantasy. But the year that Father died, writing began to push me.

One has to listen to a talent, and whether the talent is great or small makes no difference. As I fumbled for truth in my stories I was not consciously aware of responsibility to them, I only knew I had to write what was asking to be written. So I wrote story after story of a man and woman and their young daughter wandering across Europe. Many weaknesses which I did not consciously acknowledge as being part of the make-up of my parents were clearly delineated in these stories, although when I was writing I had no idea how coldly accurate they were. I didn't even fully realize that I was writing about my parents. All I knew was that I thought they were good stories, and I showed them to Mother for appreciation.

I was appalled when she cried. My reserved

mother seldom permitted herself the indulgence of showing emotion, and I had made her cry. I had no idea how close the stories had hit home. I did not know that in the stories I knew more than I knew.

I was full of sorrow that I had hurt her. But I continued to write stories and I continued to show them to her, and occasionally made her laugh instead of cry; and even when I hurt her, she could move from her first, instinctive, "I don't see how you could write that!" to, "But it's a good story. It's very good. Keep on."

§∂

Ever since I have been old enough to drink coffee, we have had our morning coffee together whenever she has been in Crosswicks, or whenever I've been with her in the South, and these long kaffee-klatsches have strengthened our friendship. It frightens me this summer that I can no longer talk to her about her fears. When I went to be with her at the time of the intestinal operation, she was still able to put her fears into words, and to receive comfort from my presence, my hand in hers, if not from anything I tried to say.

Several times she reached out to me. "I know that even if I get through this operation I don't have very long to live, and I don't know where I'm going. I feel hypocritical when I go to church, because I can't say the Creed."

"Why not?"

"I don't believe it any more."

"Did you ever?"

"I don't know."

"Mother, you can't understand the Creed like

your Baedecker guide to Athens. It's in the language of poetry. It's trying to talk about things that can't be pinned down by words, and it has to try to break words apart and thrust beyond them."

"But I'm supposed to believe—"

"No, you're not," I say firmly, holding her hand. "It's all right." Dimly I realize that she is caught in the pre-World War I philosophy, that same philosophy 96 and I rebelled against, that world of human perfectibility and control.

She says, "I can't take Communion because I'm not worthy."

"Oh, Mother, if we had to wait till we were worthy, no one could ever take Communion."

I certainly could not. But Mother isn't the only one to talk to me like this, nor is it only her generation. Students have talked to me in the same words. Someone is still teaching theological hogwash. What is this restrictive thing they feel they have to conform to or be hypocritical? If I have to conform to provable literalism I not only rebel, I propose immediate revolution. How do I make more than a fumbling attempt to explain that faith is not legislated, that it is not a small box which works twenty-four hours a day? If I "believe" for two minutes once every month or so, I'm doing well.

The only God worth believing in is neither my pal in the house next door nor an old gentleman shut up cozily in a coffin where he can't hurt me. I can try to be simple with him, but not vulgar. He is the *mysterium tremendens et fascinans;* he is free, and he understands the *ousia* of this frightened old child of his. No wonder I can't believe in him very often!

That morning, sitting with Mother over coffee, I read the Collect for the day and made a beautiful mistake, reading, "Almighty and merciful God, of whose only gift it cometh that thy faithful people do unto thee true and *laughable* service." Surely *laughable* is a more appropriate word than *laudable*, for even with the prodding and companionship of the Holy Spirit the best we can do must provoke much merriment among the angels.

I get glimmers of the bad nineteenth-century teaching which has made Mother remove God from the realm of mystery and beauty and glory, but why do people half my age think that they don't have faith unless their faith is small and comprehensible and like a good old plastic Jesus?

Mother sips her coffee and says, "I know you were born for something special." Ouch. "I'm glad you go to church."

I sigh. On Sunday I had gone to Mother's church, and I was not happy there. I went mostly for her sake, and my mind kept turning off, turning away from the service, worrying about the upcoming operation which I knew might well be fatal; worrying about the family at home; being anything but worshipful and prayerful. But I did have one creative kind of thought which I tried to share with Mother.

"You know what, Mother, lots of people, ages varying from fifteenish to seventyish, talk to me about the books they could write, if only . . . The reason they don't ever get around to writing the books is usually, in the young, that they have to wait for inspiration, and you know perfectly well that if an artist of any kind sits around waiting for inspiration he'll have a very small body of work. Inspiration usually comes during work, rather than before it. With people around my age the excuse is usually that they don't have time, and you know perfectly well that if a writer waited until there was time, nothing would ever get written."

She nods. "Yes, but what does that have to do with the Creed?"

"Wait. I've talked with a lot of people who think that any kind of formal prayer, like that gorgeous Collect we just read, is wrong, that we should wait for inspiration to pray."

"Well?"

"I don't think it works that way. I prayed very badly in church yesterday. I often pray badly when I try to say my prayers at home. But if I stop going to church, no matter how mad church makes me, if I stop praying at home, no matter how futile it sometimes seems, then 'real' prayer is never going to come. It's—well, it's something like playing the piano. You know what happens when I don't have the time to play the piano for a week or so—my technique falls apart."

"It certainly does. It's never very good."

"Okay, but at least the very small amount of technique I have is needed when I try to play the C minor Toccata and Fugue."

She nods. "You're beginning to play it quite nicely."

"Well, then, do you think prayer is any easier than the fugue? If I don't struggle to pray regularly, both privately and corporately, if I insist on waiting for inspiration on the dry days, or making sure I have the time, then prayer will be as impossible to me as the C minor Fugue without work."

"Where on earth do you think of these things?"

"But does it make any sense to you, Mother?"

"I don't know. Maybe. Yes, I think it does, a little. I knew you were born for a reason."

"Writing. And just to be your daughter. More coffee?"

10

THAT IS one of the good memories. It is typical of many of our breakfast conversations; in the early morning over coffee I am apt to pontificate, which is one reason Hugh and I never eat breakfast together except on vacation, and then I try not to talk until he has had two cups of coffee.

The good memories far outweigh the painful ones. In recent years Mother's and my morning talks have often stretched until nearly time for lunch, and we talk about everything under the sun—literature, politics, as well as theology. We have often disagreed, and argued excitedly, but never, on these large subjects, angrily.

Now there is no longer the possibility of disagreement. Our long discussions are over. The girls bring her in to the living room and she sits on the little sofa for the hour before dinner. She is no longer interested in sipping her drink, or eating her "blotters," as she used to call the crackers for hors d'oeuvres. She is humped over; she does not even notice that the stockings are wrinkled on her still shapely legs.

Our conversation wreathes about her like smoke; she notices it only to brush it away. It is only with an effort of will that I can remember the evenings when she joined in all our discussions. Peter is talking about parallel universes, that all possibilities are somewhere, in some galaxy or other, being played out. She does not hear, she who would once have loved to join in the speculation.

In the old days over our morning coffee I enjoyed sharing my science-fiction imaginings; we discussed theories of the creation of the universe, side by side with local politics. We talked about fashions, food, the development of the children. I sounded off, after Grandfather's death, about funeral practices.

"How can those ghouls blackmail people?" I asked vehemently. *"Do you want to buy a coffin that isn't as nice a coffin as so-and-so bought?*—as though the price of a coffin could be a measure of love."

I considered that family pressure had made her spend too much on Grandfather's. "Mother, haven't we lost sight of how to honor people's bodies?"

She put me right on the spot. "How do we?"

"Not with expensive, cozy coffins, as though Grandfather could *feel* the quilted silk and the little pillow. He's dead. He's lifeless clay and he's going to turn to dust." Then, afraid I had hurt her, even though a hundred years had made a travesty of my mother's father, I said, "Anyhow, I'm glad the funeral service is exactly the same for the Queen of England as for an unknown pauper. Otherwise I haven't any answer." I looked across the room at Mother's chest of drawers, on which stood a small mahogany chest with a swinging mirror; it had gone across the United States with Mado and William L'Engle, her grandparents. It had suffered from exposure to inclement weather, and now from the wet wind from the St. Johns River; some of the beautiful veneer was chipped and buckled. She followed my gaze. I said, "Maybe we honor a human body in somewhat the same way you honor Mado's little chest. Oh, Mother, I don't know. I don't know how we honor Grandfather's—or anybody else's—body, except by giving it to God."

She pushed me further. "How do we do that?"

I drank some tepid coffee and chewed a piece of cold bacon and sighed. "Maybe by accepting that God knows more than we do, and that he really does count the hairs of all our heads. That's what I want to believe, but all I can do is fumble. I just think the people who know all the answers are all wrong."

Here my intellect, my above-water self, and my intuitive, below-water self, are in conflict; but I have learned from painful experience that although intuition must not ignore or discard the intellect, it can often take me further; and I am more apt to find the truth of love in the world which 96 and I were searching for with our poppy sandwiches than in the reasonable world of the adults who thought they were in control of it all.

Mother said, "It's almost eleven o'clock. We ought to get dressed."

But too much coffee has the effect of making me talk. "You know what, Mother, one place we've gone wrong is in thinking of death as failure."

"As success, then?" she asked dryly.

I shook my head. "When Liz and Arthur died, in worldly terms they failed Maria, failed her totally, didn't they?" I did not mention Father. Mother didn't answer, so finally I said, "Oh, Mother, if we aren't free to admit failure we aren't free at all. I don't understand it; it's a mystery; but I know that unexpected good things have come to me out of what I thought was failure."

"Like what?"

"Oh—if *A Wrinkle in Time* had been sold right away instead of going from publisher to publisher all that awful long time, it might have been published and just quietly died."

Mother agreed. "That's true. I don't think I understand anything you've been saying, but I think it's true." Then we turned our talk back to Grandfather. We were glad the 101-year-old body had finally given up the ghost, but we knew we would miss the brilliant being he once was.

We got up and dressed.

ॐ❧

"Who is going with me when I die?" Grandfather had asked. Mother can no longer ask anything. She can voice nothing but fear.

I tell a friend that I hope for Mother's death, and he is shocked; he sees it as a failure in my love toward her.

Perhaps it is. I don't know.

When I try to honor her body as it is now, and as it will be when she dies, I can go no further than when I was an adolescent, talking to Yandell, or when I was sounding off to Mother over morning coffee. Intuition holds me in the direction of Gregory of Nyssa's words to Macrina, and this is enough to keep love alive in my heart.

I love my mother, not as a prisoner of atherosclerosis, but as a person; and I must love her enough to accept her as she is, now, for as long as this dwindling may take; and I must love her enough, when the time comes, to let her go into a new birth, a new life of which I can know nothing, and which I cannot prove; a new life which may not be; but of which I have had enough intimations so that I cannot discount its possibility, no matter how difficult such a possibility is for the intellect.

I will try to share one of these occurrences which I call intimations. I cannot call upon them to come; I have no control of them whatsoever; they usually happen during Emerson's vulnerable moments between sleeping and waking, or when I am so tired that my conscious mind lets down its barriers.

This past spring, after Mother's ninetieth-birthday party, I flew back to England with Josephine and Alan and the babies, to spend a week with them in Lincoln, and a few days in London seeing friends. The flight from New York to London seemed unusually long. We were served lunch immediately after departure, and then nothing else at all, not even tea, though we did manage to get some milk for the little ones.

Because of the time gap it was eleven o'clock at night when we arrived in London, and it took us over an hour to pick up the car in which we were to make the five-hour drive to Lincoln. We were very hungry, but all restaurants and coffee shops were closed. Alan said we would try to find an all-night truckers' café on the way.

I sat in the back of the small car, suitcases piled up beside me, Charlotte on my lap. I was very tired, not because of the trip but because the birthday festivities had been exhausting, emotionally and spiritually even more than physically. Josephine and I began to sing to the little girls, trying to lull them into sleep, taking turns in singing the old nursery and folk songs, many of which had come to us from my mother.

Then, suddenly, the world unfolded, and I moved into an indescribable place of many dimensions where colors were more brilliant and more varied than those of the everyday world. The unfolding continued; everything deepened and opened, and I glimpsed relationships in which the truth of love was fully revealed.

It was ineffably glorious, and then it became frightening because I knew that unless I returned to the self which was still singing to the sleeping baby it would be—at the least—madness, and for Josephine and Alan's sake I had to come back from the radiance.

Alan pulled the car into the parking lot of an open café. I was able to get out and carry Charlotte in, to sit down at the table, to nod assent as Alan ordered bacon and eggs and tea, but I was still not back. I talked through cold lips in what must have been a normal fashion, because neither Josephine nor Alan asked if anything was wrong, and I drank cup after cup of strong English tea until gradually the vastness of the deeper world faded away, and I was back within myself again, talking to my children and eating bacon and eggs.

Was this no more than hallucination caused by fatigue and hunger? That may have been part of it, but only part. I offer no explanation for this vision of something far more beautiful and strange than any of the great beauties I have seen on earth. I only know that it happened to me, and I am grateful.

But I do not need frequent visions to be fortified by the truth of love, my mother's love for me, a love which I cannot conceive of as having any end, no

matter how much it is trapped within her this summer.

Her concern is something I have automatically
assumed, as a matter of fact. It was nearly impossible
for me to hide anything from her. When I phoned
her when I wasn't feeling well, or was unhappy
about something and chatted, perfectly naturally (I
thought), she would say, "What's the matter? Something's wrong." Cool, undemonstrative, reserved,
yes, but tender. Gentle and soft but with a core of
steel.

Now, during my adult years, if I wake up in the
night and am frightened, as occasionally happens, I
control my terror by myself. Hugh needs his sleep; I
am grown up now and I do not wake him to hold
and comfort me—although simply his presence, the
rhythmic sound of his breathing, helps push me
through the fear.

But when I was a child and we were living on
Eighty-second Street I could call for my mother
when I woke up and was frightened, and she would
come to me and sit on the side of my bed and stroke
my forehead until I was quiet and ready to go back
to sleep. When I was a little older I would slip out of
bed and across the hall and into her room and get in
bed with her, knowing she would never reject me.
She would put her arms around me and hold me
close and say, "It's all right," and then I could go to
sleep.

I sleep this summer because I am too tired to stay
awake. If I wake up during the night my ears strain
to hear Mother, although out in the Tower I cannot
hear her. Sometimes in the afternoon I go out to
the hammock, which is strung between two ancient

apple trees halfway to the brook, and out of earshot of the house. Sometimes there, swaying gently, and surrounded by green leaf patterns shifting against the sky, I can relax into peace.

III

---

*The Mother
I Did Not Know*

1

"TELL ME A STORY, MOTHER," I used to demand in the very early morning in the days on Eighty-second Street when I climbed into bed with her before breakfast.

Often she would reply,

> *"I'll tell you a story*
> *About Jack a Minory,*
> *And now my story's begun:*
> *I'll tell you another*
> *About Jack and his brother,*
> *And now my story's done."*

"No, no, Mother! A real story!"

"What kind of a story?"

"A story about you when you were a little girl."

She was born in 1881, my mother, just after the end of the Civil War, with the memory of it still fresh, and she said, "with the memory bitter indeed." Carpetbaggers had arrived in full force, and the old Southern families, most of whom had lost fathers and brothers and homes and money, resented what she termed the "Northern interlopers."

She called her paternal grandparents Amma and

Ampa. "They came from the West, and although they came from real Southern stock, they were Western in their speech and mannerisms." She loved them dearly, particularly Ampa, with whom she often used to spend the night, sleeping with him in a great four-poster bed.

All this talk of being in bed with parents and grandparents: it reminds me that while I was in college I wrote a story about a very small girl who woke up on the morning of her birthday and ran joyfully into her parents' room to climb into bed with them and open her presents there in the warmth and safety of their presence. The professor announced to me that the reason the child wanted to get into bed with her mother and father was that she wanted to sleep with them sexually, a sort of combination Oedipus-Electra complex. I dropped the course without credit. But the remark has obviously left its mark in that I think of it each time I write about getting into bed with Mother, or Mother sleeping with Ampa. Such a thing could—and should—be spontaneous and completely innocent of Freudian connotation, and it is a sad commentary on today's climate that I hesitate in the telling.

Amma and Ampa came to the South from Kansas not long after the war, because Amma's migraine headaches were relieved in the more temperate climate. In Kansas they "had lived the life of pioneers and had no time for social graces. But when they came South, the fact that they were of Southern ancestry was in their favor with the Southerners." And my grandfather, Mother's Papa, was an attractive young man, and a skilled athlete. "He met a good many of the young men around town and was soon taken into their crowd."

Because I grew up in another time and another world, all that she told me was as strange as a fairy tale, and I never tired hearing about it. In an apartment in the city of New York, Mother showed me the vast plains of Kansas. On a hot summer city night she told me of the far greater heat of the Kansas plains at a time when few trees had been planted. "Amma used to take a big watering can on hot summer nights and go about the house sprinkling the sheets until the beds were cool enough to lie down on." Suddenly New York seemed cooler.

"Papa grew up on horseback," Mother told me. "He was given a Kickapoo pony when he was a very little boy."

"What's that?"

"It's an Indian pony, and it has the tribal mark of the Kickapoos—each ear split about two inches. His next pony was a Texas cow pony which was his constant companion. Papa went out with him every evening to bring the cows home. Every household kept one or two cows, and they were all turned out together in the morning to feed on the rich prairie grass. Sometimes Papa would find them two or three miles away, and he said that all he had to do was to get his pony to 'start cutting our cows,' and then he could put his reins down and the pony would do the rest." He was a crack shot and provided much of the food for the table.

Grandfather was living in Scotland during our years on Eighty-second Street, but he came to America once a year, and before one visit Mother told me a story about something that happened to him in Kansas when he was nine years old. While he was whittling, his knife slipped and stabbed him in the right leg. At each beat of his heart, blood spurted from the wound. He called for his father, who checked the bleeding temporarily by pressure. The only available doctor did not know the difference between a vein and an artery, and simply bandaged the leg. As the blood continued to ooze through the bandage, he stopped it by putting a piece of wood on the bandage immediately over the puncture.

Grandfather was left in this condition for nearly two weeks, by which time his entire leg below the bandage was swollen and had turned black. Then a Civil War surgeon happened through the little township of Hiawatha, saw the injured boy, and told his father that the only chance to save his life was to amputate the leg next to the body. Ampa asked if there was no possible way by which the leg could be saved. The surgeon said there was one chance in a hundred that if he ligatured the artery it would hold, but he thought the leg was so diseased that he could not advise it. Ampa said, "I will take the chance."

The operation was performed on the kitchen table, and was successful. It was a long time before Grandfather could walk again, but that did not hold him down; he went everywhere on horseback with his closest friend, the son of the chief of the Sauks and Foxes. When he learned to walk again, it was like an Indian, lithe and silent, one foot directly in front of the other, and he walked that way all his life. This rigorous training made him both an athlete and a beautiful dancer. He overcame his lameness so completely that when he went to the University of Kansas he won the track meet.

Years later he was persuaded to return to Kansas

for his sixtieth college reunion. He was at that time an active and virile man who would have been taken for someone in his late fifties. When he stepped off the train, one of his boyhood friends was there to meet him, and hobbled along the platform, leaning on a cane. In an old, squeaky voice he quavered, "Hello, Bion."

Grandfather took one look at this old man, bounded back up the steps of the train, and never turned back.

He had come a long way from the Kansas plains of his boyhood; he was a highly sophisticated and cultivated man; going back was in all ways an impossibility.

I could never write a biographical book about Grandfather. He was a self-made man and a great man, and like all such he had the weaknesses which were the other side of his strength. He hurt people, and the telling of his story would hurt more people. Perhaps he will come to me sometime as a character in a novel, as my parents have already done, more than once. In a fiction the events of his life would have to be toned down, because they are too incredible. In a story, who would believe in a character who not only survived the ligaturing of an artery in a gangrenous leg but who fell off a hay wagon in a freshly plowed field and had the heavy wooden wheel of the wagon roll over his head? If the field had not just been plowed, his skull would undoubtedly have been crushed. As it was, he had a bad headache for a few days.

Who would believe that, not long after the move to Florida, Grandfather stood on the beach, looking out over the ocean, with colleagues on either side of him, and remained standing when a bolt of lightning from a sudden tropical storm felled and killed the other two men?

When Grandfather neared middle age, he got Bright's disease. He knew that it was fatal, and that his life expectancy was limited. His eyes suffered the kind of massive deterioration which is the result of badly diseased kidneys. But Grandfather was by no means prepared to die. He had a pitcher of water by his side at all times, and he drank countless glasses of water—Florida sulphur water. Not only did he recover from Bright's disease, but he went down in medical annals as the first person whose eyes had deteriorated from kidney disease who recovered his full vision. I remember him sitting, when he was in his nineties, in the library after dinner reading *The Wall Street Journal*. His red chair is now in the Tower, and perhaps it has brought with it a measure of his courage—and stubbornness.

In his early sixties, when he was living in Scotland, he was told that his heart was in very bad shape and would not last a year. Grandfather's response was to go mountain climbing. He would climb until he fainted. When he came to, he would pick himself up and climb until he fainted again—a rather unorthodox way of curing a heart condition.

He had passage on the *Lusitania* ("But *not* the *Titanic,* too," Mother would say, lest I get carried away) and canceled it at the last minute to have dinner with an old friend.

Who would believe Grandfather?

ॐ

When he first went South he still had the West in his speech and manners, and he met Caroline

L'Engle, my Dearma, through her two older brothers. She was as immediately attracted to his Western virility as he to her subtle Southern charm. They were married when she was twenty and he was twenty-two.

It was not a happy marriage. Mother said that between the South and the West there was always the barrier of the manner of living, and this must have been exacerbated because the old manner of living in the South had been taken away by the war; all that the old Southerners had left was who they were, and they held on to social amenities, the small and gentle graces. They wore elegant gowns and suits which were completely impractical for the new, impoverished way of life, but which were all they had. Dearma was married in a made-over ball gown of her mother's; the children's clothes were cut out of the salvageable material of their parents' wardrobes.

Social life was topsy-turvy. "Nobody who had money was anybody," said Mother, and the suspicion of "new money" remained with her always. During the day the young men who were most desirable as escorts to the St. Cecilia Ball or the Patriarch Dances might be selling groceries or working in a pharmacy. "A young man in an apron might sell you a slab of bacon, and present himself at your door in rusty dinner clothes in the evening."

Many things worked against my grandparents' marriage from the start. Add to the differences between South and West, and the general poverty and hardship (all the children were undernourished, many of them rickety, and many not strong enough to survive the normal childhood ailments), that both of them were strong-willed and dominant. No wonder there was conflict in Mother's childhood home.

2

Mother's maternal grandmother, the Madeleine L'Engle after whom I am named, was probably the strongest influence in her life, and had led a completely different kind of life from the Kansas grandparents'; they might have been from different planets. I know her as Mado, a French nickname for Madeleine; and I think of her generation and my further forebears by the names Mother used. A Southern family is usually impossible to sort out; after the immediate uncles and aunts and first cousins, little distinction is made between second, third, and far more distant cousins; they are kin, and that is all that matters.

For me, my mother's Papa is Grandfather, and her Mama is Dearma; and if Mother told me fewer stories about Dearma than about her grandparents and great-grandparents, it is partly because I knew Dearma for myself. I did not need stories to make her come alive for me. And it may also have been because Mother often fled the tensions at home to stay with Mado, with Amma and Ampa, with favorite cousins, and she preferred to limit her reminiscences to happy ones.

There might not have been so much storytelling

had I not been an only child, and had we not traveled so much. Mother whiled away the time on trains, in hotels in strange cities, in restaurants, by the remembrance of things past. The stories were a foundation of security which helped her, I'm sure, as much as they helped me during the insecurity of our nomadic life. The precariousness of both my parents' health; the uncertainty of Father's ability to pay bills—for his work was not going well; the confusion of living in a world so caught in the grip of a great Depression that only a terrible war could bring a semblance of prosperity: all this must have been far more difficult for my mother than I could begin to guess. Her stories helped us both.

I do not know Mother's physical genetic pattern, who left the strongest imprint on her DNA; but Amma and Ampa, Mado, and Greatie are the ones who left indelible imprints on her psychic genetic pattern.

Mother's name, like mine, came from her maternal great-grandmother, and I learned that Mother spoke most often of Mado when she was depressed, because Mado, even in recollection, brought the gift of laughter. She was born Madeleine Saunders, in Charleston, South Carolina, and when she was a young girl her father was ambassador to the court of Spain. Mado was his hostess, because her mother was in poor health. Countess Eugénie Montijo, later to become the wife of Napoleon III and Empress of France, was Mado's closest friend. They had clothes made to match (Dearma's wedding dress came from the Spanish court days), rode together, hunted together, daydreamed together. It was a life of countless balls and great dinner parties. Some years ago, Mother gave me the huge silver tray on which after-dinner coffee was served in the Embassy; it is heavy to lift with nothing on it, and after-dinner coffee in Spain included not only coffee but a large silver pitcher full of hot milk.

The golden world of those dinner parties is something out of a fairy tale to me. It was a world in which the rules of etiquette were fixed and unmovable. One of the table services was of gold (it's long gone, but I would love to have had a glance at it), and one evening Mado almost disgraced herself when a golden spoon fell to the floor and she started to bend down to pick it up, then caught the formidable eye of her ambassador father. She sat through the rest of the meal in misery while the beautiful spoon was trampled beyond repair, because it was not etiquette for any of the servants to pick it up, or acknowledge that it had fallen.

I think of the frequent entertaining Hugh and I do, both here at Crosswicks and in New York, where I am hostess and cook—he, host and butler; of the casualness of it, the laughter and warmth and good conversation, and I would not change it—even all those dishes to wash later. But, just as I would have liked a glimpse of that golden spoon, so too would I have liked to sit in on one of those court dinners.

The change in ways of living has come slowly, and has increased with each of the wars. One night last winter I came home from a full day's work and started to get ready for a dinner party. Much of the cooking I had done the night before, but there's always a lot to do on the day itself, and I remarked to Hugh, who was helping me, "When Mother gave a dinner party she lay down all the afternoon before, and someone extra was brought in to help so the cook and maid wouldn't get too tired."

Mado herself was aware that the world was not all feasting and fun; as my parents anticipated change and difficulty, so did Mado; one day she and Eugénie and Eugénie's brothers were talking about the necessity for physical courage and endurance, and to prove their own stamina, each took a knife and plunged it into the flesh of the forearm.

I try to visualize these fairy-tale balls, these essays in bravery on the part of the young grandees and Mado. Mother said that her grandmother had a beautiful singing voice and played the guitar, and "charmed the Spanish grandees with her voice," and with her open, childlike friendliness, warmth of manner, and quick pleasure in all beauty.

And I remember,

> *Fear no more the heat o' the sun,*
> *Nor the furious winter's rages;*
> *Thou thy worldly task hast done,*
> *Home art gone, and ta'en thy wages;*
> *Golden lads and girls all must,*
> *As chimney-sweepers, come to dust.*

It was a long time before Mado herself came to dust, for she lived to be a very old lady; but the fairy-tale days of court ended when she returned to the American South. When I look at her pictures, and the only ones I have are of her as an old woman, I am humbled by the serenity and joy in her face, there is never a trace of bitterness or resentment, and she had much cause for both. I see also quiet strength, silent endurance; she had need of the courage for which she and Eugénie and the young grandees tested themselves.

She married a young army surgeon, William

Johnson L'Engle, whose family was from Charleston, but who was living in North Florida. I have a picture of him which always gives me a poignant stab; it was taken shortly before his untimely death, and this strong, slightly arrogant young man looks so much like Bion that his school friends have remarked, "Hey, Bion, that's a great picture. When did you have it taken?" And yet Bion looks like Hugh, and I find this genetic paradox delightful.

When William L'Engle was commissioned, he wrote that his successful examination has "relieved my mind of a load of anxiety . . . and I have the certainty of a comfortable income as long as I live. I will write you again when I reach Charleston and let you know when to expect me. . . ."

The army commission made William free to marry Mado, and it was a new freedom for him, because his parents were living as pioneer a life in Florida as Amma and Ampa in Kansas. When William was eleven he wrote to his Aunt Leonis L'Engle Johnson, in Charleston, "Father has failed entirely this year; he has made no corn and the caterpillars have made a clear sweep of all his cotton, and everybody else shares the same fate." I am awed at the education which these unschooled children received at home. In the same letter eleven-year-old William writes of his brothers and sisters, "Edward is nine. He will soon be able to write you. Mary is almost six, and is improving fast. She reads well, and sews well; she has just commenced writing and little Johnnie, too, begins to spell. He has just recovered from a fit of ague. My health is feeble, but no fever. . . . Remember me to all my Charleston friends. . . ." Another time, not long after, he wrote, "Father is engaged near Hibernia, cutting timber. As usual, it is a hard life and not a very profitable one."

The cousin to whom William wrote most often was Miller Hallowes, whose plantation was called Bolingbroke—what lovely, otherworldly names the family houses had: Bolingbroke, Palermo, Hibernia, the names of the Old World translated to the new. Miller Hallowes (who was almost a father to William) had, when he was nineteen years old, left his native England and gone to South America to offer his services to Bolivar. Young Hallowes and Bolivar became close friends, and the Englishman "fought in the wars of Independence for eleven years continuously," and at Bolivar's death he was given the last portrait ever painted of the great hero, as a token of friendship and esteem.

He had gone home to England, and came to America only to see to some property his mother had inherited. He expected to stay in America for a few weeks, but he fell in love and married and stayed until his death in 1877. I would guess that the flora and fauna of the Southern territory reminded him of Venezuela, and that he had become accustomed to a warmer climate than England's.

He was a good friend to William, and later to Mado, and Bolingbroke was always open to them.

William, graduating from medical school before he was twenty-one, was ambitious, probably because of the hard conditions of his childhood, but his ambition was more for his family than for himself and he must have had the gift of healing in his hands and heart, for the medical methods of the day, as he describes them in his letters, make one wonder how anyone survived the prescribed treatments.

Mado and William were married on April 3, 1854, and there was a yellow-fever epidemic in Key West in June. William, who was considered an authority on epidemics, was sent for and left, evidently in a rush, for he forgot his glass retorts at Bolingbroke. Mado followed him as soon as she could arrange for his medical supplies and her guitar to be sent by ship from Savannah to Key West.

In the autumn of 1856 William was sent by the U.S. Army to the Department of the Pacific. Many years later, his daughter, my Dearma, wrote, "They crossed the Isthmus of Darien, now the Panama Canal. My father wanted to give my mother some pear-shaped pearls, but my mother declined the gift on account of the expense of the journey—their baggage alone cost fifty dollars to transport over the railroad. He bought her instead a little china basket of fruit, which she treasured always. It was saved from the great fire in 1901." This was the appalling fire which burned the entire city of Jacksonville, and I shall get to it in its proper chronology.

It was while they were stationed out West that their first child, a son, was born. Mado, with the *joie de vivre* which I have come to think of as her dominant trait, was not held down by motherhood. She went with the other officers' wives from post to post, in rough wooden wagons, to dances. The baby was rolled in a shawl and put on a bed among all the wraps, and she would go in and nurse him whenever he was hungry, and then go on dancing till sunrise. She was adaptable, my great-grandmother. These dances at rough army posts must have been very different from the balls at the Spanish court, or the St. Cecilia Ball in Charleston, and yet I doubt very much if she made comparisons. She seems to have had the ability to stand firmly on the rock of her past while living completely and unregretfully in the present. My mother's adaptability came to her both by blood and by example.

Mado's second child was born while she was on a vacation with her parents, and the third, my grandmother, Dearma, in an adobe hut in Camp Mason, Texas.

When it became apparent that a war between the states was inevitable, William resigned his commission in the United States Army and applied for one in the Confederate Army. As far as I can gather, both William and Mado felt that the cause of the South was a just one, and that the real issues had little to do with slavery. It is impossible to understand their feelings from hindsight; we know too much; and we see things from a perspective impossible to them. But Mado never lost her joy, despite all the tragedy which was to come to her, and this may be what makes me know that she and William were never dishonorable or dishonest in their thinking or in their behavior.

3

AT THE BEGINNING of the war William was called to
the house of Senator Mallory in Lake City, Florida,
why, I do not know, because the senator and his wife
were not at home. William was having a bout of the
malaria which almost everybody endured in chronic
form, and sent to the pharmacy for quinine, which,
in those days, was put up as a powder. A mistake was
made—on purpose? by accident? no one ever
knew—and he was sent morphine instead of quinine,
and took a large dose. He realized quickly what had
happened, and called the servants and told them to
walk him up and down, make him drink hot coffee,
and under no conditions to let him go to sleep. All
the time that they were walking him, giving him coffee, the servants said that he kept groaning, "My
God, my wife and children! My God, my wife and
children!"

By morning the servants were exhausted, and he
thought that the danger was over and told them to
go to bed and get some rest. And then he died.

Remember William, dying alone,
Buried under an alien stone.

The flesche is brukle, the Fiend is sle;
Timor mortis conturbat me.

The confusion of war swept over his death; it was not until his sons were grown that they were able to find out where he was buried.

Mado was left penniless at the beginning of the war, with three small children, and everything else taken away from her. For a while she was matron of a military hospital at Lake City, Florida, and, typically, nursed Northern and Southern soldiers with equal tenderness, for in her heart there was no North nor South. "Many Northern boys died in her arms," Mother told me. "One mother and father of a Yankee soldier were so grateful for her care of their son that they sent her a ring with a beautiful black pearl. It burned up in the great fire with so many other of our treasures."

Illness and death were daily companions in her life. She never ceased to grieve for her husband, but it was a quiet, personal grief; what she offered others was loving care and laughter. She wore only black and white for the rest of her life, though she did not carry an aura of mourning with her, but one of complete zest for life. She could have married many times over, but William the golden lad was the love of her life, and when she lay dying at the age of eighty-seven, she kept calling his name. She also asked for a dish of ice cream, which she ate with great appreciation and pleasure, and died shortly thereafter. Living or dying, I don't think Mado feared the heat of the sun.

ઢ

Just after William's death, Mado wrote a long letter to her cousin Caro Hallowes at Bolingbroke, offering her services in nursing eighteen-year-old Katie Hallowes, who was desperately ill. Despite her own grief, she was able to feel intense compassion for Caro's young daughter. And she added, "How often I have wished since Katie's illness that my precious husband could have been spared, if only for a little while longer, to be with you in this trial. He stood so high as a physician and was such a good, patient nurse."

Letters were long in those days, partly because there was no such thing as instant communication. Mado says, "I did not write to you last week as I was anxiously expecting a letter from you to tell us of Katie's welfare. You know how deeply I sympathize with you, dear Cousin, in your distress and anxiety, and I long for tomorrow's mail hoping that it may bring me a letter to say that Katie is better. We cannot get any letters which may come by the St. Johns [river] until Sunday afternoon, and as the steamer for Savannah returns early Monday morning and Father does not often send to town, we have no means of answering our letters by return mail."

She ends this particular letter, written from Palermo on July 6, 1861: "My paper and time are limited. I would not under any other circumstances ask you, dear Cousin, but do you remember the conversation I had with you in regard to the likeness of William which you have? that it was taken by William for me, and in case of anything happening to him was to belong to me. You will not blame me, I am sure, for claiming it now. I want you please to send it to me here, and I will have a copy of it taken for you, which I will send to you."

I'm grateful that Mother has given me copies of some of Mado's letters which have survived, for they show me glimpses of her ability to accept change, and surely her world changed even more radically than our own. Her friendships were forever; she had continued her friendship with Eugénie when the princess became Empress of France. They wrote long letters, which perished in the great fire. She seems to have been surrounded constantly by children, her own, and various nephews, nieces, and cousins. Only once is there a deep figurative sigh as she remarks on the bliss of a day alone.

During the difficult years between 1861 and 1865 Mado remained in Florida. It was so hot in summer that it was difficult to sleep; one of the little boys remarked, "Oh, Mama, my head is as wet as a bowl of water." It was cold in winter, but they were able to keep tolerably warm because of plentiful fat pine wood.

She wrote another cousin and friend: "This farm is like most farms, surrounded outside the yard by cultivated lands with the usual feature in Southern landscapes, dry girdled pines, and would look dreary if there were not a fringe of date palm trees. Near here, about a quarter of a mile or more, but the path leading to it passing the cultivated fields, there is a beautiful little lake surrounded by high banks densely covered with tall magnolia, cypress, hickory, and live oak trees.

"It is too hot a journey to undertake very often as we must return right in the heat of the day, if we stay. Yesterday we took our work and a very pleasant book, *In and Around Stamboul,* by Mrs. Hornby, and Henry read aloud to us, whilst we sat on the bank under the shade of a large magnolia, and sewed, and watched a dozen wild ducks in pairs, chattering and diving for fish in the lake, and every now and then skimming over the surface. Occasionally a large, white crane goes sailing by, much to Lena's [Dearma's] delight, who with the other children are gathered around Minerva at a short distance, watching her string the red berries of a species of running box, which I think quite pretty.

"It is so dark I cannot see the letters I form. I have written this last page in darkness, but now have lit my candle to continue. We do not use many candles here as tallow is scarce and one dollar or more a pound, but instead have brilliant fires of the fattest kind of lightwood. I do not hesitate to read by it as it really gives such a bright light, though I would never attempt to sew. I generally knit or read after tea for an hour or so. A candle is lit during supper and afterwards blown out."

It would be difficult to guess from her letters how near actual starvation the family often came; how much energy was expended on nursing the ill; and how equal love and energy had at all times to be available for Dearma and her brothers; how many hours were spent in transforming old brocade curtains or silk bedspreads into clothes for the children. Some of Dearma's dresses and the boys' suits were made of the beautiful velvets and satins of Mado's gowns from the Spanish court, completely inappropriate for their Spartan way of life, and an ironic comment.

If she cried alone at night she does not say. What she shared was love and laughter, and I am grateful for her.

4

A<small>T THE CLOSE</small> of the War between the States, Mado managed to get back to her parents, who were then living in Raleigh, North Carolina, "where they were quietly starving to death," Mother wrote me once, "because they had lost everything during the war."

And here is a perfect example of the extraordinary interdependence of all things. Years before, while William and Mado were out in Washington Territory with the United States Army, they became close friends of General Custer, through whom they acquired an Irish cook, the wife of one of his soldiers. During the war this soldier became an officer, "and by one of those strange streaks of fortune, became Captain of the Garrison in Raleigh, N.C." One day a United States commissary wagon drove up, and on the seat beside the driver was the captain's lady, Mado's ex-cook. The two women embraced; the cook took one horrified look at Mado and her family, and brought them desperately needed food. Mother added, "When finally some of the ladies of the town brought themselves to call on the Captain's wife, she put on an apron and, answering the door-bell herself, said the lady was not at home."

It makes me wonder what harvest my own most casual actions may reap; surely Mado never thought that her instinctive loving courtesy to all people would one day be a matter of life and death. Her little daughter, my grandmother, might well have died without the food the captain's lady brought, and I would not be here to write about any of this today.

Mado died a year before I was born, and yet I feel that I have always known her, the stories about her are so vivid. I have never heard her name mentioned by anybody in our enormous Southern clan without its evoking a smile. There have been several Montague-Capulet schisms in my mother's family, but I have never heard an unloving word about Mado..

In a day when grandchildren were supposed to revere and be formal with their grandparents, her many grandchildren adored her, and no one remembers being scolded by her. One of my favorite cousins reports that the closest her grandmother ever came to reproving her was once when Tracy referred to President Theodore Roosevelt as "Teddy." Mado said, "My child, I wish to hear you call him Mr. Roosevelt. He may be a Republican, but, after all, he is the President of the United States."

Another time while Tracy was a student at Wellesley and was home for vacation, her grandmother slipped into French, as naturally as though she were speaking English, and Tracy could not understand, and stopped her. She said that Mado "only smiled gently, and with a little twinkle in her eye replied, 'I beg your pardon, since you are going to college I thought you were being educated.'"

Perhaps the fact that I write at all is a result of

Mado's passion for education. She did not think the schooling in North Carolina or Florida adequate for her children; I don't know why she did not go home to Charleston, but went instead to Winchester, Virginia. Possibly she could not afford Charleston, but could eke out a living in Winchester by taking in boarders, or ill people, and nursing them. The boys went through college, and Dearma to the Virginia Episcopal Institute for Young Ladies—how pompous that sounds, but the girls there were given an education which isn't even available to girls today, Episcopal, ladies, or no. Mado herself had been well taught, and was willing to go hungry, to work long hours, stay up with a patient all night, in order to give her children the learning she treasured. And I'm sure she herself taught her children far more than she realized. I know that not only has my mother taught me many things I never learned in school, but also that the summer Josephine turned three, Mother spent patient hours playing with her, and by the end of the summer Jo could read and write the alphabet and spell out simple words, and the whole process was a game for her.

I wonder what I will be able to teach my grandchildren? Not much, this summer, except for a few folk songs and nursery rhymes when I sing them to sleep.

Did Mado ever have the sudden, intemperate rages which sometimes hit me, and which are produced by what seems completely inadequate cause?

She surely had reason for rage and resentment, and yet these are qualities which are never mentioned in regard to her. If they were there, she kept them to herself, and healed them in her own way, with prayer. I have her battered Bible, which Mother had rebound for me. It was much read, much marked, and there are stains which came, I think, through private tears. Perhaps through it she will teach me an alphabet of grace. She had that spontaneous quality of aliveness which illuminates people who have already done a lot of their dying, and I think I am beginning to understand the truth of that.

ૐ

"My grandmother," Mother said of Mado, "was an incurable romantic, reading and rereading her favorite romantic stories and poems until her death." And yet no one could accuse Mado of having had a protected life, or of losing her grip on reality.

I need my own equivalent of the picaresque novels which may have reminded Mado of the lost years of the Spanish court—although it never occurred to her to bemoan them or try to return to them. I have occasional binges of reading English murder mysteries or science fiction, not so much as an escape but as a reminder that there is still honor and fidelity in the world, despite murder and crime; and that the sky above me is full of billions of solar systems and island galaxies, and that nobody has yet been able to put the creation of a galaxy into the language of provable fact.

We are a generation out of touch with reality. The "realistic" novels push me further away from the truth of things, rather than bringing me closer. We cannot make mystery and miracle acceptable by trying to constrict them into the language of the laboratory or the television commercial.

All that, in finite terms, is left of Mado is her

Bible, some yellowed letters, a few pieces of once beautiful furniture, its veneer buckling from age and exposure to salt air. But there is more to her than that, and it is the mystery of her *ousia* which helps me to see a little more clearly through the dimness of human understanding.

ॐ

I do not want to romanticize about Mother's senility. I know that there is no turning back the clogging of the arteries, and that there is nothing to look forward to but further decline. But if I stop here I am blocked in my loving, just as her thinking is blocked by atherosclerosis.

I try to accept the bare factual truth of Mother's condition, as Mado accepted loss and death; and yet I remember Tallis saying once that "we are not interested in the love of truth *as against* the truth of love." This does not mean that we are not interested in the love of truth; his statement is one which I have to try to understand with all of me, not just my conscious mind. The love of truth without the truth of love is usually cold and cruel, I have found. The truth of love can sometimes be irrational, absurd, and yet it is what makes us grow toward maturity, opens us to joy. Mado, holding a dying Yankee soldier in her arms, was witness to the irrationality of the truth of love. This kind of truth is often painful; it must have been so for her, and I am certainly finding it true in this household this summer. But it is all that gets me through each day.

5

"TELL ME A STORY, MOTHER . . ."

"Well, tell me a story about when Greatie was a little girl."

Greatie: my mother's great-grandmother; William L'Engle's mother; Mado's mother-in-law; Susan Philippa Fatio.

How much will Léna and Charlotte remember of their great-grandmother? They have never known my mother as a full human being, but only as an ancient old woman with the strange title of the Great-grandmother, which they cannot yet pronounce, and so they will remember her mostly through the stories their mother and I tell them when they, too, say, "Tell me a story . . . Tell me a story about Gracchi."

Josephine and Maria and Bion have living memories of their great-grandfather; Jo was eleven when he died. I didn't know any of my greats, but I feel close to Greatie because Mother has given her to me.

Greatie and her parents were as much pioneers as Amma and Ampa and yet, in the early days of North Florida settling, there was an aura of cosmopolitanism and courtliness completely missing in the West. Greatie spoke French, Italian, Spanish, German; read Latin and Greek. She had a vast store of folk and fairy tales from all lands which she told and retold her children, grandchildren, and great-grandchildren. "The one I remember best," Mother said, "is the Spanish folk tale of Don Rat Humperez and Cockroachie Martínez."

The Fatios were originally from Sicily, and left home because of political upheaval and religious persecution; some settled in Italy, some in France, Spain, Switzerland. Why Greatie's father, François Philippe Fatio, came from Switzerland to the New World, and to North Florida in particular, I do not know.

Mother's personal memories of Greatie are, of course, of a very old lady living in quiet poverty; but these last years of Susan Philippa Fatio's life, austere though they were, must have seemed strangely uneventful to the old lady. How many homes were burned out from under her? I'm not sure; I've counted up to six.

"Once upon a time when Greatie was a little girl," Mother said, during that winter of inner and outer cold in Chamonix, while we sat huddled in sweaters and drank countless cups of tea to keep warm, "she was living with her parents on their plantation called New Switzerland on the St. Johns River." One day one of the servants came rushing to them through the woods in great excitement and told them that the Indians were preparing to attack and were going to scalp the entire family. François Philippe refused to believe them, because the Indians had always been friendly with the family. But New Switzerland was caught in the middle of a war between the Indians and Andrew Jackson's forces; the Indians had been unfairly attacked, and they were so angry that they were out to scalp all whites in their path, even those who had been their friends. Two faithful servants, Dublin and Scipio, held François Philippe bodily to keep him from going to reason with the Indians, persuaded him that they were beyond reason at that moment, and urged the entire household into a boat which was always kept at the dock. Scipio had been polishing the table knives and carried them into the boat, "and so the knives were the only possession saved from the fire. Greatie told us that shots followed them across the river and splashed into the water, and why nobody was hit she never knew . . ."

Their next home was burned, too, by vindictive arsonists. Greatie and her family were constantly being caught in the middle of someone else's fight. There was the battle for the Floridas, as the large, southernmost territory was then known; the Fatios lived in a section which passed back and forth between the Spanish and the English on paper—which didn't affect them nearly as much as border warfare between the Florida settlers and a group of bandits, called "filibusters" by Greatie, who came in from Georgia. One of the filibusters called himself Dictator of the Republic of Florida, and François Philippe fought with the Spaniards against this premature Hitler.

"Shortly after this battle, in which he was nearly killed," Mother said, "the roof of their house in St. Augustine blew off in a storm; it was taken up bodily by the wind and settled on top of the family as they were trying to escape. Can you imagine rushing out of the house and then being trapped under your own roof?"

"What happened?" Of course I knew, but I was breathless with excitement no matter how many times I heard the story.

"They were rescued by Commodore Campbell of the United States Navy, who came to their assistance with his sailors. The family were all bruised and bleeding, but they were lucky to get away without being drowned, because the tide was rising and the streets were soon flooded."

"Did they lose everything again, everything?"

"Everything. This time they didn't even save the knives."

Everything. Nor was this the last time.

And yet Greatie wrote, after they finally rebuilt their home on the St. Johns River, a home of pine logs and cypress bark: "We were well content to be there once more, leading a life of tranquility and ease. My father, when well-supplied with reading matter and the society of a few friends, seemed never dull or dissatisfied. Chess, cards, and backgammon varied the monotony of the repose of country life; and to look out on the river, flowing majestically by, seemed always to charm him. He was sixty-five years of age when we returned to New Switzerland, but full of vigor of mind and body. He was possessed of a cheerful and vivacious disposition, and was witty and full of anecdote. I never tired of listening to his descriptions of Switzerland. I remember one afternoon, when sitting on the piazza with him, his calling my attention to some grandly beautiful clouds looming up on the horizon, across the river, and saying, 'Look, look, my child, before it changes; you cannot have a more perfect picture of Mont Blanc than that cloud gives you; no painter could represent it as well. Call your mother to see it. O beautiful, beautiful!' and his handsome face beamed with pleasure as he gazed at it."

But a life of "tranquility and ease" never seemed to last long for Greatie. "In the year 1836 the homestead at New Switzerland was again destroyed, being burnt by Seminole Indians . . ."

Six years earlier Greatie had married Lieutenant John L'Engle, "of the 3d U.S. Artillery, a graduate of the Military Academy of West Point." She does not say a great deal about him. I would gather that he was a literate and charming man, but also a dreamer and impractical. After her marriage she continues to speak of New Switzerland as home, and so this final burning affected her deeply. She writes, "My father and brother having died within six months of each other, Colonel Miller Hallowes, fourth son of my Aunt Louisa, came from England to receive her share of my grandfather's property, which my father had been taking care of for her." Miller Hallowes was at New Switzerland when the Indians attacked, and he was wounded by a bullet. Scipio, the same Scipio who had helped in the escape at the time of the first New Switzerland fire, helped him into a boat. The Indians went into the house, "feasted and drank, dancing and yelling, cut up the piano, and finally set fire to and destroyed the houses with their contents. The houses have never been rebuilt."

Greatie, the teller and writer of tales, was wistful that "in all our wanderings there were no schools or other educational opportunities" for the younger Fatio children. Five of the children received formal schooling, but "Leonora and I had no such advantages. Fortunately for us we both loved books and, more fortunately still, our parents were educated persons, lovers of learning and culture, who took pleasure in imparting knowledge to us. To them we were indebted for all we learned."

No wonder her son, William, was able to write letters to Cousin Miller Hallowes and Aunt Leonis when he was only eleven years old.

Greatie had also memorized reams, and could recite, with flourish and pleasure, from her favorite books, ranging from Plato and the Bible to romantic novelists. This huge store of memory stood her in good stead, for she was blind during her last years. But she lost none of her storytelling ability, or her complete recall of all that she had learned.

"Tell me about Greatie and the African princess."

That was probably my favorite story about Greatie. A wealthy planter and slave trader fell in love with an African princess, and married her. She lived in his huge house partly as wife, partly as servant, bore him many children, and nearly died of homesickness. She was ostracized by both whites and blacks, except for Greatie, who once a week was rowed down the river—it must have been a two- or three-hour trip in the grizzling sun—to spend the day with the princess. First Greatie had to have lunch with the slave trader, while the princess served them. Then Greatie and the princess went off together to the princess's rooms, and talked, and drank cold tea together.

If Mado had strong ideas about what was right and what was wrong in human relationships, so did her mother-in-law. Greatie and the princess were close friends in a day when such a friendship was unheard of, and Greatie simply laughed when she was criticized and sometimes slandered because of this relationship. I was delighted when I learned, only recently, that a good friend of mine is a descendant of this long-gone African princess.

"Tell me the story about Greatie and the pirate."

In the old days of our country when there were many small clusters of settlers in tiny villages which are now large cities, it was the custom for the people in the "big house" to take in travelers for the night, or longer.

One winter a charming Frenchman, Monsieur Dupont, came through the township of San Pablo, in which the young Greatie was living. He was grateful for hospitality for "a night or two," and spent the winter. He was a witty conversationalist; his manners were courteously impeccable; he was a fine musician and he and Greatie played duets by the hour. When at last he left, with many declarations of affection all round, he gave her some of his music and books; and it was only when leafing through them that she saw his signature and discovered the real identity of her guest: Jean Laffite, the famous pirate.

6

Tʜᴇʏ ᴀʀᴇ ᴀʟʟ ᴅᴇᴀᴅ, long dead, these golden lads and lasses, so long dead that the taint of corruption no longer clings to their dust. They are all gone, François Philippe, Dublin and Scipio, the African princess and the French pirate. Greatie is remembered only by a few remaining great-grandchildren.

And by me.

The flesche is brukle, the Fiend is sle;
Timor mortis conturbat me.

Mother said once, "What a passion for education my forebears had!" When I think that Greatie was never formally schooled, it makes me wonder about the present-day school system. These "uneducated" women, Greatie, Mado, my mother, were fluent in more languages, had a far greater background in classics and world history, than most college graduates today.

There was a tradition in the L'Engle family, the Fatio family, that every child in the household should be taught to read and write at an early age, and the children of the servants learned their letters

189

side by side with the children of the family. Interesting; in every single family letter I have come across, the Negroes are always referred to as servants, never as slaves; and service, at that time, had not taken on the connotation of drudgery it now has; it was an honorable word; and if the Negroes on the plantations served their L'Engle and Fatio masters, the masters likewise served their servants.

Maybe there were Simon Legrees in my family but they made little impression on my mother. And I do not believe that she has given me an overidealized picture of Greatie or of Mado; they are very alive for me, rounded, full, erudite women with all kinds of human flaws (which have come down to me): quick tempers, impetuousness, opinionatedness. But they are real. I respect them and love them. I try not to let them down, but I know that when I do, they would understand and expect me to pick myself up, shake off the dust, and start right over.

I'm grateful that Mado and Greatie are part of my roots. I'm unusually fortunate in Mother's repertoire of stories, as wide as Greatie's. My Oklahoman husband knows little of his roots, which is a loss.

Pride of family: is there a difference between pride of family and respect for a family tradition and responsibility to it? I think so, although I have seen people whose pride in ancestry is sheer snobbery and seems to provide only an excuse for laziness and ungenerosity of spirit.

Mado had the most generous of hearts; if I am mean of heart I am letting her down, as well as myself. Greatie had compassion and true friendship for a black woman at a time when such a thing was unheard of. Dearma visited those in jail and fought for prison reform long before it became a *cause célèbre*.

The first hospital in the Deep South with beds for blacks came into being because of the vision of one of Mado's grandsons. These are very small drops in the bucket, but they came at times when the bucket was nearly empty, and they give me a tradition of compassion and generosity to live up to. This is Mother's family, because this is Mother's book, but there are examples of courage and nobility in Father's family, too. And, on both sides, there are examples of meanness and selfishness and greed. A vast, closely knit family such as Mother's had its full share of scandals and skeletons in the closet. Most of these I did not learn from her, and since they were sometimes told me with intent to hurt, they have little place in this book.

If I continue my journey through the past, beyond Mother, Dearma, Mado, Greatie, I come to forebears who settled in Charleston, South Carolina, well before the American Revolution. They were a conglomeration of French Huguenots fleeing religious persecution, and Frenchmen who had come to Ireland at the time of the Norman conquest, who had been given huge grants of land, and later had to flee Ireland when these same grants were taken away from them by Henry VIII's Cromwell, a kind of rude justice.

The name, the unpronounceable name of L'Engle, was originally de l'Angle, which is considerably easier. One spring when we were driving through château country, Mother told me that Dearma had gone looking for the de l'Angle château, and found it. Dearma stood outside the rusty wrought-iron gates and looked across the overgrown gardens to the château. An old woman in black was cutting roses, and hobbled up to the gates to ask Dearma if she could help her. "Mama told her who she was and why she had come, and the old woman said, 'Oh, you're one of the American cousins,' and asked her in to tea."

"But how did the name get from de l'Angle to L'Engle?"

"The story goes that during the rough years of the Reformation, two de l'Angle brothers quarreled over their religious convictions. The French Huguenot brother not only fled France to save his life, he was so angry with his brother that he changed his name." L'Engle: my Southern kin pronounce it Langul; my Northern kin pronounce it Longle. I find it simplest to say it the way it looks: Lengel.

I asked Mother, "When he changed his name, where did he go?"

"He fled with his family to Santo Domingo, and became a planter. But the pattern of building a home and a way of life and then having to leave everything and flee is constant in our family. There was a bloody and violent uprising, and once again he had to take his wife and children and flee for his life. He set sail for the United States, and outside Charleston his ship was caught in a violent storm and wrecked. Only two lives were saved, two of the L'Engle children, a boy and a girl."

The two orphans were taken into the household of Judge William Johnson, and brought up with his children. Both, I think, married Johnsons, but here my genealogy is confused. Greatie's husband, John L'Engle, was an adopted son of William Johnson's. Mado is the one who is a direct descendant of the old judge; he was her grandfather; her mother was Anna Hayes Johnson; so she and William were cousins, but not by blood. Mother knew how it all worked out, and I should have written it down long ago, but somehow it never occurred to me that there might be a time like this, when she cannot tell me.

I'm proud of that distant ancestor, William Johnson; he was Jefferson's first appointee to the Supreme Court, the youngest justice to sit on the bench, and the first dissenting justice. Like most of my family, he was opinionated, articulate, and cared passionately about justice. While I was writing a novel set in the Deep South, *The Other Side of the Sun,* I had to do a good bit of research; my English school taught me more about the Wars of the Roses than about the American Revolution. I was delighted to come across William Johnson's name as a man who stood up for the rights of the black man, both slave and free.

After a slave uprising in Charleston, many restrictions were put on all Negroes, and a law was passed that no slave might be taught to read or write. Judge Johnson was infuriated at this gross injustice, and announced to the Supreme Court that he considered it unconstitutional.

It is a present responsibility to be his descendant. He has left his mark on my genetic pattern, whether I like it or not. Because he came to me, not as a personage out of history, but as a living character in Mother's stories, he has also left his mark on my memory, and so has given me the strength on occasion to speak out and take unpopular stands.

Mother's most treasured possession is a huge portrait of Judge Johnson's grandchildren, my great-great-grandmother and my great-great-great-aunt, one playing the flute, the other the harp; the harp was one of the losses of the war. The portrait was painted by S. F. B. Morse, the man who invented

Morse code but who was first known as a portrait painter. The two young women it portrays are part of me, as are the old judge, Greatie, Mado. Without them I would be someone else; I would not be me. My forebears have bequeathed to me the basic structure of my own particular pattern, both in my cells and in the underwater areas of my imagination.

ᘓ

I look at Mother huddled in her chair by the window and think once more about Mado and Greatie. In a day of what we would consider primitive medical knowledge, and no nursing or convalescent homes, no hospitals as we understand hospitals today, they both lived to a ripe old age, with their wits about them. Up until Grandfather, there is no record of senility in the family, although there were a few "holy fools," like the twins, Willy and Harry, in *The Other Side of the Sun.*

Obviously, nursing homes have not caused senility in the elderly; but when grandmother or great-grandmother continued to live with the larger family, to be given meaning because she could at least stir the soup or rock the baby, the climate for growing old and dying was more healthy than it is today. I cannot reproduce that climate for Mother. Surgery kept her alive at eighty-seven; antibiotics pulled her through pneumonia at eighty-eight.

For what? For this?

But we cannot turn our backs on scientific progress. I did not want her operated on at eighty-seven until Pat assured me that the tumor in the caecum would cause her great discomfort unless it was removed. I could not tell the doctor not to give her antibiotics for pneumonia.

All I can do is to try not to isolate her; is to hold her when she is afraid; is to accept her as she is, as part of this family, without whom we would be less complete.

7

THE PORTRAITS in my mother's family did not lead a static life, and it is a wonder that as many of them survived as did. During the war, when the Northern conquering troops took over and burned some of my forebears' homes, the portraits—when there was time—were taken away and hidden, and some were never found again.

Mother has hanging in her front hall a not very distinguished oil painting which has always fascinated me, because on the back is painted a crude chess or checkers board, which was used by the occupying soldiers. Many portraits and other paintings were wantonly slashed by sword or knife.

So the family portraits mean a great deal to me, not as an aid to ancestor worship, but as beacons to guide me. I have many more portraits from Mother's family than from Father's, largely because Mother was the eldest of four, and the only girl, and Father was the youngest of ten, and the only surviving male. I have a pastel drawing of Mado as an old woman, done by one of her grandsons, my Uncle Bion. Her face is gentle and tolerant and wise, but I know that behind the compassion in the eyes there is judgment; she did not tolerate dishonor or despair.

My mother learned much from her. I will try to learn, too.

෫෨

Tell me a story. My granddaughters are already starting the familiar refrain: "Tell a story about when Gracchi was little."

Gracchi's world is gone, as far gone as is my present mother from her *ousia*. As with all worlds, it was good, and it was evil. It had vision, and it was blind. It was rich, and incredibly poor. How can I tell my granddaughters about a world of which I have had no firsthand experience?

If it is impossible for me, it is doubly difficult for my children and trebly for my grandchildren to conceive of a United States in which the entire population was less than that of three of our major cities today.

Jacksonville, now a major city, is bursting at its seams; yet when Mother was a little girl, it was a small town where everybody knew each other, and almost everybody was kin. Family towns are something few people today have known. We're used to living among strangers and near-strangers, with the biological family dispersed north, south, east, west. But when Mother was a little girl, she could walk across the street to Mado's house; it was only a few blocks to Amma and Ampa's.

Shortly after Hugh and I were married we visited Mother, and when she took us to church with her it was definitely not only to go to church, but also to be looked over, and Hugh was appalled that more than half the congregation was kin. Not so today.

Jacksonville, Mother said, was never a typical Southern town. Even before the war, many Northern families had come to Florida, most of them in search of health, but there was little mingling between North and South. After the war, the chasm was even greater.

Mother was born in Amma and Ampa's house, just a year after her parents' marriage. There was at that time no such thing as a hospital or a trained nurse in Jacksonville, and when Dearma became very ill shortly after Mother's birth, nursing her was not easy. In those days it was thought unhealthy to have kitchen or bathroom in the house; the kitchen was a separate building behind the house. Mado and friends and relatives did the nursing, and there were plenty of relatives.

William L'Engle had been the second of twelve children, all educated by Greatie, and Mother's childhood was spent near a great number of aunts and uncles and cousins. Because of the vast age spans, generations were mixed up—one twelve-year-old boy bragged about dandling his great-uncle on his knee.

Mother wrote, "When I was a little girl, I loved Louisa May Alcott's books: *Little Women, Little Men, Eight Cousins.* As I look back now I can see the similarity in my life and *Eight Cousins.*" There were always plenty of children to play with, aunts and uncles to run to for comfort. Life more or less revolved around St. John's Church, and at the four corners of the church lived four great-uncles and their large, multigeneration families.

Play was simple. The girls had large collections of paper dolls, with enormous wardrobes which they painted by hand, and swapped around. For money they used bent pins. Because life at home was often tense and oppressive, Mother spent a great deal of time playing in the homes of varied cousins. She wrote, "The Daniel family life centered around the big student lamp on the dining table. There the family congregated in the evenings, reading aloud, playing games, studying lessons. I spent many happy hours in that magic circle. It was a warm, loving, family life. Tiny Aunt Emmy, with her little black shawl around her shoulders, her hair parted in the middle and coiled in a big knot at the back of her head, could still play the guitar and sing the old songs of the War between the States and the period before.

"Cold winter nights we cousins used to roast potatoes in a little brick oven out in the yard. No potatoes have ever tasted so good. In the evening after our early suppers, we played hare and hounds. The hare had a bag filled with tiny pieces of paper. After a good head start, the hare began to drop the pieces of paper, with the hounds behind him in hot pursuit, following the scent."

There were many picnics on the banks of the St. Johns River. The great river which François Philippe had so loved is tidal, and salty, and, said Mother, is "the only navigable river that flows in the same direction as the Nile." The trees near their favorite picnic place had enormous wild grapevines hanging on them which made wonderful swings.

Sometimes the cousins, sitting on the floor of a big dray pulled by a mule, would be driven out near Palermo to a sugar-cane plantation, for the sugar-boiling. "I can remember how the hot thick syrup would burn our fingers when we pulled the taffy. We usually pulled in couples. It was hard to get

199

started with our great wad of red-hot syrup, but once we got it going, it was great fun to watch the candy in the making. We would get farther and farther away from each other, while the candy got whiter all the time. The experts could braid it, but we children were usually content with a long rope."

Another activity which qualified as play for the children was taking flowers to the cemetery. In those days of large families and high mortality, my mother and her cousins were well acquainted with death. A scarlet-fever epidemic wiped out four first cousins in one week; malaria weakened resistance; yellow fever was a constant threat. The children who had survived whooping cough and measles and the various lethal fevers went regularly to the cemetery with lilies and amaryllis and cape jessamine, and decorated the graves. "So," Mother said, "I have never had any fear of cemeteries but find them a peaceful place."

When the children were a little older most of them had learned to play the piano or the guitar, the flute or the harp, and sang, and one of their games (which Mother and I used to play, too) was tapping out the rhythm of a song or the theme of a symphony, and seeing who could guess first what the melody was.

Mother's Papa had a fine library, through which she was free to browse, and he was also a superb storyteller to his children. By the time I came along, he had lost the ability or the desire to tell stories. But when Mother and her brothers were little, he told imaginative and fantastic tales every night, in front of the fire on chilly winter evenings, sitting on the steps at the foot of the ramp to the beach in sum-

mer. Mother, and later on, her brothers, would sit by
him, leaning against his knee and keeping one eye
on his cigar, because the stories lasted only as long as
the cigar lasted.

8

She thought of herself as uneducated and almost illiterate, my mother, because delicate health kept her from completing school. When she was feeling unwell she spent days at a time at Ampa's, curled up in a big leather chair in his library, where there was a set of historical novels by Miss Mulbach—*Empress Josephine, Queen Hortense;* and by Charlotte M. Yonge, *The Dove in the Eagle's Nest* (one of my childhood favorites), *The Heir of Redclyffe;* and she devoured these and many other historical novels ravenously. Ampa also had bound sets of *Harper's* and *Scribner's,* in which *Henry Esmond* and *The Virginian* had come out in monthly installments. With her cousins she read aloud by the hour, around a table in the winter, under the trees by the river bank in the warm weather. This habit of reading aloud, or being read to, remained with Mother all her life. Not only did she read to me when I was little, but she and Father read to each other every night of their lives, Dumas, Dickens, Dostoevsky. This is the first summer she has not enjoyed having our friend Gillian read to her in her clear and pleasant English voice.

Does Mother remember, somewhere deep inside her, any of these years of treasure? She is far better read than I am, the great-grandmother who thinks of herself as being ignorant.

And an ugly duckling who never turned into a swan. Dearma was considered a beauty, and Mother far too often heard people say, "This is Lena's little girl. Isn't it a pity she doesn't look like her mother?" Another remark she never forgot was, "I do hope Lena's little girl hasn't inherited Cousin Edwina's blue lips."

I always thought that my mother was beautiful, but she went through life with the conviction that she was the ugly daughter of a Southern beauty.

෨෮

Perhaps ideals of beauty then were as different as everything else. Mother said, and she was right: "It just isn't possible for you and the children to understand the social barriers which existed after the war. We were terribly poor, and we bitterly resented the people from the North with money, particularly the carpetbaggers who had made their money getting fat on our defeat. The old Southerners stuck together, and the people from the North and West, who had come after the war, founded their own social group. They could afford more luxuries. They had more freedom."

Freedom from hunger; freedom to buy new clothes in new fashions; freedom from the strict rules of courtesy which were all that was left of the pre-war way of life; and freedom from the rigid religious observances of the old Southerners. Mother never forgot that the Northerners went to theatre and to concerts during Lent, while she had to go to church every day. There was always morning prayer at home for the entire household. Sundays were spent largely at church, and the only game allowed the children was the Bible game, which they all loved, since it was highly competitive, and dealt with the more colorful stories. The Bible was well known by the children, and Mother laughed as she told us that it was their "dirty book." They used to hide in the closet and read the passages the grownups had not read aloud during family prayer.

Not all that they read was understood. One day in Sunday school Mother innocently asked the teacher (a cousin, of course) what a foreskin was, and could not understand why she was disgraced.

She learned her numbers when she was very small, playing cribbage with Ampa and casino with Amma. Up until this summer she has been able to play cribbage and solitaire; last summer she played bridge, although her game was no longer sharp and swift. I've never been any good at cards, but both Hugh and Josephine noticed when her playing began to slip.

∂❧

Jacksonville when Mother was a little girl had roads mostly of deep sand. Bay Street was paved with round cypress blocks, and a few streets had a kind of shredded palmetto, brown in color, which looked like moss. On some of the larger streets were crushed oyster shells. Even when I was a little girl there were still some shell streets, and the street in front of Dearma's house was made of cypress blocks. That's all changed, now. The swing vines are gone because the great trees they hung from are gone. The wild river banks are lined with houses. But it does not do to look back on that world with too much nostalgia. There was great bitterness and resentment. Mado was one of the few whose spirit was never warped.

ॐ

A large part of Mother's childhood and young girlhood was spent at the beach. When Mado built the beach cottage there was no way to reach it except by boat, but in the 1890's a narrow-gauge railroad was built from South Jacksonville to San Pablo. Mado's cottage was built piecemeal, with rooms added on as extra grandchildren and a little money were acquired. Mother wrote, "We were in Mado's little cottage at the beach at the time of the Charleston earthquake. I was three years old. Aunt Caro Hallowes was visiting us, and Papa was on one of the Clyde ships on his way home from a business trip in the North.

"The earthquake was so terrible in Charleston that we even felt it at the beach. I was sleeping in a trundle bed, pulled out from under Mado's bed. In her fright, Mama rushed in after me and I remember being picked up in her arms, and she ran with me down the causeway to the beach. It was the worst possible thing she could have done, but thank God there was no tidal wave. Papa said they felt the earthquake on the ship far out at sea. The earthquake wasn't as bad in Savannah as it was in Charleston, but Papa said that when the ship put in at Savannah, people were camping out in the streets, afraid to stay in their houses."

The only road at the beach was the beach itself. The cottage fronted the ocean; from the back veranda one could see a sandy track which barely passed for a road, and then there was a long, wild view across the scrub to the marshes and an occasional oasis of royal palms.

"The train made two trips a day, going to town in the morning and back in the afternoon. The great event of the day was to meet the afternoon train. The tracks were level with the platform, and by crouching down and putting your ear on the rail, you could hear throbbing many minutes before the train came in sight. We children used to take two pins, cross them and lay them on the rails, and after the train had come by and flattened them into a cross, we would retrieve them and put them among our treasures.

"There was a big, covered pavilion at the end of the line, right on the ocean front, with an artesian well and a sort of fountain spouting fresh sulphur water." Anybody who hasn't grown up on sulphur water is apt to find it distasteful; perhaps it does smell like rotten eggs, but to me it is good and healthy, redolent of sun and wind and sea.

My childhood visits to Dearma were much like Mother's to Mado. We got up early and bathed in the ocean. When we wanted crabs, we waded in front of the cottage with a crab net. The people who lived in the scrub brought in vegetables and eggs, and there were plenty of fish, which, with hominy and corn bread, was our main diet.

And there was donax soup. Donax are a tiny, multicolored shellfish which, when boiled, make a broth more delicious than oyster or clam. At low tide they bubbled up out of the sand and were easy to scoop up. There were still plenty of donax when I was a little girl, but when automobiles began to drive on the beach the delicate shells were crushed, and now they are very rare.

When Mother was a little girl, the dunes were higher than those I knew, and she wrote, "The cows made well-defined paths under the tall growth which I could follow for miles. I never remember seeing or hearing a rattlesnake, though I was constantly roaming around under the bushes barefooted. From the moment we arrived at the beach until we left, I don't think I ever had a shoe or stocking on, and my big toes were usually tied up in a rag on account of ground itch. We always wore big palm-leaf hats tied under our chins with a string.

"During the heat of the day we played under a wonderful natural arbor of wild grapevine which grew on top of the stunted yaupon and scrub oak trees. My mother could stand upright under this canopy of vines, and when the little sour grapes were ripe she made wonderful grape jelly from them."

When Mother was older and Grandfather was doing well, many weeks were spent on an old ark of a houseboat called the *Daisy*. My mother has never been one to exaggerate, so I believe her story that they threw the dinner dishes overboard at high tide, and picked them up, washed, at low tide.

The young people in their strange bathing clothes—how did they manage to swim with all that heavy wet serge dragging about them?—used to dive off the deck of the *Daisy* and then, when they wanted to get aboard again, would call for someone to throw down the rope ladder. It was impossible to get up on deck without it. One day Mother felt the need of solitude and went for a swim alone. When she got back to the *Daisy*, no one was in sight, so she paddled about, waiting for someone to come who would lower the ladder for her. Suddenly she sensed a presence near her, looked, and there was a large shark, his white belly already exposed, preparing to strike.

The next thing Mother knew, she was on the deck of the *Daisy*. It was impossible, but terror had given her body a surge of power which enabled her to leap from the water, climb up the side of the high houseboat, and onto the deck. There are many authenticated accounts of such incidents of supernatural power; sometimes it is physical; sometimes it may be psychic or spiritual, and usually we don't even know that we're using this extraordinary reserve until the emergency is over.

My own reserves of power are barely tapped most of the time, though I've seen them released with a surge in an emergency, just as Mother's must have been that time in Fort George inlet, with the house of the African princess and the coquina walls of the slave quarters showing whitely through the thick green of jungle.

In the hours immediately after Bion was born, when the doctors could not stop me from hemorrhaging, I fought with this supranormal strength to live. I know that hate can unleash vast energies, but so can love. Sometimes when more than the usual feeble human love is called for, there comes a surge of loving power to fill the need.

ॐ

If I frequently use the analogy of the underwater area of our minds, it may be because the ocean is so strong a part of my childhood memories, and of my own personal mythology. If I am away from the ocean for long, I get a visceral longing for it. It was at the ocean that I first went outdoors at night and saw the stars. I must have been very little, but I will never forget being held in someone's arms—Mother's, Father's, Dearma's, someone I loved and trusted enough so that all I remember is being held, and seeing the glory of the night sky over the ocean.

I remember hot summer nights when the necessary mosquito net kept out the breeze; and I remember the light of sun on water moving against ceiling and walls when I woke up in the morning.

Illyria is gone now and, at the time of Father's death, Mado would not have recognized the setting in which her rambling cottage stood. Not only had many of the great dunes eroded, so that the house was perched atop the last of the dune hills, but the vast, empty beach she knew was gone. The house sat in a few acres of cultivated wilderness, fenced in by a wall of lethal Spanish bayonets. Behind it was a road and small cottages and guest houses; on either side was a boardwalk. Illyria was incongruously in the middle of an amusement park, with roller coasters, ferris wheels, bathhouses, cheap hotels, barkers, bingo, honky-tonk. I accepted this without amazement because, since my twelfth year, life had been constant change. I even enjoyed walking along the boardwalk with friends, and I rode the rickety wooden ferris wheel which had been condemned for years. But, as always, the first act of the morning was to walk across the beach into the ocean, facing the sunrise. Then it was possible to forget the boardwalk and the amusement park and be alone with the water. I would check for sharks and undertow and then swim out beyond the breakers and lie on my back in the long, rhythmic swells, water below and around me, sky above—lie there and let my mind, like my body, float free.

Illyria was Father's last home, and I hope that the ocean helped him through those final months. During school holidays we often walked together on the beach, and it was then that I was able to share poetry with him. He was a ruthless critic, but when he was pleased he let me know that, too. He read one poem of mine slowly, several times, then nodded. "That is a poem, a *real* poem."

I told my parents of my moods by playing the piano. The piano at Illyria was an ancient upright; the action was kept workable in the damp air of the beach by means of a light bulb dangling in front of the hammers. There was one finger exercise I had learned in Switzerland called *Storm*, and I used to play it when I was angry, when I could not understand the tension between my parents, or my father's own angers and depressions. I wish Mother had told me then something she told me later: once when Father was at odds with everything, she finally turned to him, "Charles, how can you be this way with me?" He looked at her in complete surprise: "If I can't take my moods out on you, who can I take them out on?"

There is a Schumann sonata which I do not play any more, and hate to hear when it is occasionally played on the radio, because it was such an exorciser of anguish. But there was also Bach. I came home for Christmas having learned a new prelude, and when Father heard me playing it he asked, "Are you using the pedal?" "No, Father." He turned with his delighted smile to my mother. "She's really learning how to play!"

Illyria was not meant for winter use, and my

parents kept it barely warm enough with constant driftwood and fat pine fires, and an inadequate kerosene heater; however, they had come to Illyria from the Alps, and they were used to being cold around the edges all during the winter months.

Sometimes in the winter the house was enclosed in fog, like a pearl in an oyster shell. The amusement park would disappear then, and there was only the rambling old cottage floating like a ship in the vastness of ocean and sky.

I love the hills around Crosswicks, and the tiny, beautiful lake where we swim, but I will always miss Illyria and the beach.

My Oklahoman, land-locked husband, meeting the ocean only recently, on a small Royal Netherlands freighter, responded to it with equal passion, and not a sign of seasickness in very rough waters. At night we would lie out on the tiny deck and watch the stars swing across the sky as the little vessel rolled in wave and wind.

In the ocean is the mysterious country 96 and I sought for with our poppy-flower sandwiches; in the ocean is the undiscovered world I grope for in my stories, and where I am seeking to understand death, especially the death of the mind as we are witnessing it this summer.

9

ONE EVENING last week when it was cool enough
for us to need a fire, Hugh and I sat in front of it
watching the last logs crumble after the rest of the
household had gone to bed, and he remarked that
watching the fire gave him somewhat the same sense
of proportion and peace as watching the ocean. But
it does not do to forget that fire and ocean, out of
control, are killers. The ocean ruthlessly capsized the
ship in which my L'Engle ancestors were escaping
from Santo Domingo. And the great fire of 1901 destroyed the entire city of Jacksonville.

Mother was twenty at the time of the fire. She
had gone to spend the day with some cousins. Another cousin came running in and told them that
there was a big fire downtown, and they went up
onto the Widow's Walk to watch. It was a hot day,
with a high wind. Some men on the outskirts of the
city had been burning Spanish moss, and the dry
moss hanging from the trees caught fire and within
seconds was out of control. When Mother and her
cousins climbed up onto the roof to watch, nobody
realized how totally out of control the flames were.

As they stood gazing at the fire with the aweful
fascination with which one watches something terri-

ble which is not really a personal threat, Mother saw the wind pick up a flaming brand, carry it six blocks, and drop it on the house of an uncle and aunt. Within minutes, the house was in flames.

She said a quick goodbye to her cousins and ran home. Grandfather was there and she told him what she had seen. "Papa, the whole town is going to go."

Grandfather paid her the honor of accepting her words without question. Like most selfmade men he was not gullible, was, in fact, highly skeptical of anything he had not proved for himself. But he immediately started the process of evacuation. Mother and Dearma packed china and crystal in buckets. Grandfather and the boys cut the portraits out of the frames, buried what silver they could, put a few small pieces of furniture on the river bank. A few precious books were saved—including the one with Jefferson's signature, which he had given to William Johnson. But most of Grandfather's and Ampa's libraries went up in flames, as did the libraries of the great-uncles at each corner of St. John's Church, and all the books saved by François Philippe.

Every few minutes Mother ran upstairs and out onto the roof to see how close the raging inferno had come. When the next house but one started to flame, they left. The carriage and wagons were packed with all they could hold. Then Grandfather let the riding horses out, took his crop and sent them running in the opposite direction from the fire. Many other animals, crazed with terror, ran straight into the flames, screaming in agony.

By now the wind was sending great clouds of ash which darkened and burned their faces. The searing heat of the approaching flames was almost unendurable. The carriage horses caught the terror and began to bolt, and Mother could hear the crash and shattering as buckets of china fell to the road behind them.

The streets were full of terrified people, black and white, draped in sheets to meet the end of the world, waving flaming torches and crying, "Jedgment Day! Jedgment Day!"

Somehow Grandfather managed to get horses, carriage, wagons, across the river to where they were safe from the flames, found a house which was half built, and there the family spent the night, lying on the unfinished floors.

And so an entire city burned, burned as effectively as from a whole arsenal of bombs, because of a few men trying to get rid of some Spanish moss.

10

FATHER CAME from a very different background. When he and Mother were married, both had a good deal of adapting to do. They were married in Jacksonville, went to the Ponce de León in St. Augustine for a brief honeymoon, and then on to New York, where Father was a newspaper reporter. They had a small apartment in what they later discovered was a red-light district, and they were happy. Father was doing work he did well, covering plays and operas and concerts. In the evening they would dress in evening clothes, very elegantly, and then proceed to take the horse-drawn trolley to the theatre.

Many of their friends were musicians, and Mother practiced the piano several hours a day. They were nodding acquaintances with a very young couple in the next apartment, whose baby carriage was left out in the hall. One day the baby carriage was not there, and it did not reappear, and that was how they learned that the overquiet baby had died. Mother went to offer help and sympathy, and the sad young mother told her shyly that whenever my parents had musical parties, or Mother played for Father in the evenings, she and her husband would take pillows and lie on the floor with their ears to the wall, listening to the music, and this was both their entertainment and their comfort.

The pre-World War I New York was very different from the megalopolis of today; it isn't easy for me to visualize horse-drawn vehicles instead of our noisy buses and taxis and subways, and I get an inkling of how small the city was when I remember Mother saying, "The little park behind the Forty-second Street library was the reservoir for the entire city."

In summer they went to visit Father's family in the big old house near Princeton, New Jersey. It was a beautiful house, with the kitchen wing built well before the Revolution. There were secret staircases, a secret room with peepholes through the eyes of a portrait in the next room. The grounds were dotted with marble statues, and the marble privy in the form of a small Greek temple had been designed by Thomas Jefferson.

Father was the youngest of a large family. My grandmother had had a baby every year with what finally came to be depressing regularity. After the birth of one of the little girls she prayed, "Dear Lord, please let me go two years without having another baby." Two years to the day, she had twins.

Whenever possible the entire family, Father's many sisters with their husbands and children, gathered together. I'm not sure how many of the sisters were alive when Mother first visited the tribe; I knew the families of Aunties May, Ida, Bess, Gertie, Edna, and Eva. They were all tall, blond, blue-eyed Valkyries. The entire family kissed every morning before breakfast, and every night before retiring, a new experience for Mother; indeed, communal

216

breakfast, everybody seated at the same time around an enormous oval table, was most unusual for her. At home in the South, breakfast was set out, English fashion, in covered silver dishes on the sideboard. It was a quiet, essentially private meal.

Not for Father's family.

"Tell me the story about the breakfast when Aunt Ida . . ."

Aunt Ida was one of my favorite aunts, beautiful, with the family blue eyes shading into purple.

One morning at breakfast Ida and Edna had a quarrel; family quarrels around the table were not at all unusual, but this time the quarrel grew so heated that Ida threw a glass of water across the table at Edna. Edna rose, dripping, stalked into the music room, sat down at the piano and played and sang, loudly and nasally, "*Jesus* loves me, this I know . . ."

This scene delights me so much that I've put versions of it into almost every book I've written, and have had, with reluctance, to delete it.

Another incident from that same summer concerns the mahogany stair rail, which curved superbly down three full stories. Mother eyed it wistfully every day, finally could not resist its lure, and slid from top to bottom. She was wearing, according to the fashion of the time, a long skirt and shirtwaist, belted in tightly; and to her horror she discovered that the belt buckle had left a long, deep, very visible scratch the entire length of the banister. "I never told anybody, and I've always felt guilty about it, because I know one of the children must have been blamed."

After my birth, when Mother and Father wanted to travel, during the times he was well enough, I was sent to one of the aunts or off to a summer camp.

But it was, I think, Father's lungs rather than my advent which stopped their more exciting journeys. I think that Father knew, because of his work as a foreign correspondent, that the illusion of the Western world as too civilized ever to have another war was soon to be shattered, so they enjoyed such things as the spontaneous trip to Castle Conway with the bittersweet pleasure which accompanies the realization that an end to such carefree excursions is imminent.

Many of their adventures were actually dangerous. One time while they were staying in Shepheard's Hotel, an Arab sheik took a fancy to Mother. He was as tall as Father, and he wore pale blue robes with a wide red sash. At mealtimes he would appear and stalk into the dining room ahead of them, and terrify Mother by pushing Father aside in order to pull out her chair, and then would stand behind her throughout the meal. He had a dagger in his belt, and he meant business; happily, my hot-tempered father was amused.

During one of Father's assignments, early in their marriage, Mother and Father used to walk out to the pyramids at night and make love. I'm not sure how it was that they learned (I wish I could ask Mother: did I know once? does my memory, too, flag?) that a group of murderous bandits thought this lovemaking so charming that they watched benevolently, unseen, instead of robbing them and slitting their throats.

Although I have been fortunate in travel, my journeys have been in a more discovered, more restricted, less colorful world. Travel on jet planes is simpler but (unless one is highjacked) less exciting than travel on donkey, camel, ship, train. In Arab countries, where there were long waits for trains, my parents and their associates would spread a steamer rug out on the station platform, sit around it and play halma. Mother learned this game in the South when she was a child, but it is originally an Arab game, and my parents became accustomed to being ringed by Arabs who bet excitedly on the players. Mother was skillful at all such games, and many Arabs went home slightly richer for having bet on her. It was a more innocent pastime than we would expect to find today. Alas.

ह

Father went without Mother, but with another newspaperman with whom he often worked, somewhere deep into South America to do a story on a newly discovered tribe of Indians who had escaped both persecution and influence by the Spanish conquistadors. The two men returned to New York with a number of artifacts, and some jewelry for their wives, including, for the other wife, Mrs. J., some Indian prayer beads, which consisted of a series of silver beads interspersed at regular intervals by red beads, from which hung, on slender silver chains, curved silver moons.

The two men were sent, later, to Cairo to do a story, and took their wives. In the evening they fell into the habit of wandering slowly through the Casbah, to take advantage of the cooler air. Today's youthful world wanderers are no more adventurous than my parents and their friends; the Casbah has never been a particularly safe place for a white non-Moslem.

They found a small coffee house which became their regular stopping place. There they would sit and talk and sip the strong, sweet native coffee. One evening Mrs. J. wore her South American prayer beads, and the proprietor of the coffee shop looked at them in great surprise, and said, "I have some beads just like those."

"That's not possible," Mr. J. said. "These come from deep in the South American jungle, and they are religious beads."

The proprietor went into the darkness of his tiny shop and returned with a sandalwood box. He opened it and gently withdrew from a bed of pale blue cotton a necklace of silver beads interspersed by red beads, from which hung, on slender silver chains, curved silver moons. The only difference between the Arab's necklace and the South American one was that the Arab's necklace had a phallic symbol at the bottom, from which hung silver moons.

My mother wanted it. She wanted it badly. But the shopkeeper was horrified. No, no, it wasn't for sale. It belonged in his family. It, too, was for prayer, to be used with the Koran.

Mother still wanted it and asked to see it every evening. Every evening the proprietor would bring it out and dangle it in front of her, then return it to the bed of pale blue cotton. One evening he let them know that perhaps, after all, he would be willing to sell it, but at an outrageously high price. Father countered with an outrageously low one. Each evening the shopkeeper would come down slightly, and Father would eke up. It soon became apparent that they would have to stay in Cairo indefinitely if the two prices were ever to meet in the middle, and the time of their departure was not far off.

The Arab suggested that they play dice for it.

Father agreed. He won.

Mother gave me the necklace while I was still in college because it is heavy, and it burdened her to wear it. I love it dearly, for all kinds of iconic reasons. That Indians in the South American jungle and highly civilized Arabs should produce an almost identical piece of religious jewelry is a beautiful and exciting thing to me. To use beads with a prayer, Indian or Moslem or Christian, is to enflesh the words, make thought tangible. Unless misused, it is not in the realm of superstition but is an affirmation of creation, of all matter, of *ousia*. I treasure the necklace on all counts. At the moment it is in Tallis's office, waiting to be restrung, and I miss it.

Would Mother remember it, this summer, and the adventure of getting it? I doubt it. How do I reconcile this sedentary old woman with the mother I never knew? someone who rode donkeys across dangerous mountain passes? who could control a balky camel? who watched from a Moslem harem while Father was with the men during a religious ceremony, watched the fervor which set people to walk, unburned, over hot coals, or to lie comfortably on beds of up-pointed nails? A large nail was driven with a hammer completely through a worshipper's skull, but so sophisticated were these religious frenzies that the nail was driven into the head in a way that did not damage the brain. Even knowing that, Mother fainted.

This pre-Madeleine Madeleine is also my mother, and one I have slowly come to know as she has told me about herself.

Her sharing of herself has helped to make me who I am, and yet I have been free to respond to her stories or not to respond; to be fascinated or to be bored. I owe her an enormous debt of gratitude for all the good things she has taught me, for standards to live by, for criteria learned in childhood which are helping me to live through this summer, which is rushing by, no matter how much separate days may sometimes drag.

I do not know what we will do when we reach summer's end.

IV

Summer's End

1

A YEAR OR SO AGO I wrote in my journal, "Only death will give me back my mother."

But I cannot say, "O komm, süsser Tod." Death is not sweet. I want death for my mother, and this is bitter.

But there are sweet and lovely things, too: this is the summer of the great-grandmother, but it is also the summer of two important weddings; the first, Maria and Peter's; tomorrow, Theron and Joan's. Theron, my agent, my little brother: I am full of happiness for and with him. Another happiness is that this is the first wedding ceremony for Alan to perform. He has officiated at several funerals in England, but this is the first wedding.

We've assembled all the retinue possible for Great-grandmother and the babies, so the exodus—for less than twenty-four hours—won't be too hard on them. Bion and the girls reassure us that everything is all right, they can take care of everything, Grandmother and the babies will be fine, everything is under control.

Jo and Alan leave for New York right after lunch; they'll spend some time trying to get their apartment ready for winter; their furniture is to arrive from England imminently. In the evening they are to go to Theron and Joan's for a wedding rehearsal and dinner. Hugh and I are having dinner at Anton's, with Tallis and some other friends.

We leave about three-thirty, taking Cynthia with us. She's going to Rhode Island with her parents in a few days, and we will miss her in the Crosswicks household. On the drive to New York we talk about the future. I have a sense of hollowness in the pit of my stomach. It is obvious that Mother is not physically capable of making the trip back South. All the girls on the retinue will be returning to school or college after Labor Day. Clara, we know, would be willing to help, but she cannot carry the burden alone. Can we get enough other people who will be gentle with Mother? I will have to move back to New York with Hugh in September, when he will no longer be able to spend several days a week in Crosswicks. And the Cathedral Library must be opened. It runs more or less on the academic year, and I am free to be in Crosswicks all summer, but if I am not in the library it is closed, and I cannot leave it untended indefinitely. Can we get enough of a retinue so that Mother can stay in Crosswicks, and come up each weekend ourselves?

We talk, reluctantly, about the possible inevitability of a "home," despite my promise, but we reach no conclusions. It has not yet quite come to that.

We get to New York just in time for me to change quickly to a long dress, and then we go immediately to Anton's. After greeting our friends I say, "I want to call home, please, and see if everything's all right."

"Of course it's all right," Hugh says, a little impatiently. "Relax."

But the feeling that I must call is very strong. Finally he says, "Go ahead, then." I know he thinks I'm foolish not to take a complete break from the Crosswicks household and the summer's burdens, but I go into the bedroom and call, collect. Vicki answers, accepts the call, and instead of chatting, immediately gets Bion.

I say, "Hello, Beau, it's Mum. How's everything?"

He says, "Grandmother died."

"What?"

"Grandmother died, about four this afternoon."

ॐ

Vicki and Margie were taking her for her walk, with Léna encouraging them. As usual, the old woman balked, said, "I can't," and slumped several times, and they let her sit on the grass and rest, with Léna urging, "Come on, Gracchi, get up, you can do it."

Yesterday and the day before, she walked rather better than usual, but this negative behavior has been regular all summer. When the girls got her to the door they said, "You mustn't fall now, Grandmother, or you'll hurt yourself."

She went in through the screen door with them, said, "I can't go any farther," and dropped in their arms. Not really concerned yet, they called for Bion, and he carried her into her bedroom. While she was still in his arms her breathing faded out and stopped. Later he told us, "Grandmother was alive, and then she was dead. I'm not sure how I knew. I just knew." There was none of the pain she had feared.

Bion put her down on the bed. He was sure she was dead, but he listened for heartbeat and pulse and could find neither. He asked one of the girls to get a hand mirror, to test for breath, and there was none: it was King Lear and Cordelia, rather in reverse. They called for Dr. John and the volunteer fire department, which has the ambulance. As always in a tiny village, news travels quickly, and Quinn, the Congregational minister, came over.

It is selfish of me to want to have been there, and the main thing which has taken away that want is the reports of Bion's quiet strength. Margie said, "I was flustered and panicky at first, but Bion was so steady and cool that he calmed me down."

For my sake, I wish I had not been on the highway when my mother died. But if I had been at home, Bion would not have had this chance to make a leap in growth. I am proud of my son, and, indeed, of all of Great-grandmother's retinue.

It seemed somehow right that the phone call should have been made from Anton's. Hugh went into the living room and told everybody what had happened, and when I returned, arms were open for me. I said, from the heart, "I am only grateful."

Tallis probed, "Are you sure?"

"Yes, I am sure. All I feel is gratitude and joy. I'm going to grieve, and I'm going to cry eventually, but it will be right and proper grief."

Then began the phone calls, the first of what seemed to be, during the next forty-eight hours, hundreds of phone calls. We were able to reach Josephine and Alan at Joan's; Alan got on the phone and I told him. He said, "Jo will want to be with you now. I'll bring her right over." I said, "Can she drive me back up to Crosswicks? It will mean that she'll miss the wedding, but we must get back tonight." It didn't make sense for Hugh to drive me up, and turn around in the morning and drive back again; rehearsal in the afternoon, tapes and rehearsal Friday, and then Monday through Friday, his heaviest schedule all summer. Alan, of course, must stay for the wedding.

He brings Josephine uptown to Anton's. I knew from the brief talk with Bion that the girls had all rallied round him. Not only were Vicki and Margie there, but Janet came over immediately, and then Jane drove the thirty miles between the two homes. I knew that he was surrounded by four loving females, our neighbors were there, ready to help, and the right thing to do at the moment was for Josephine and me to stay and have dinner at Anton's, and then leave for Crosswicks.

Tallis had been planning to drive up the next day with a friend for lunch; this of course would have to be canceled, but he said immediately that he'd come up and do some kind of service, "but I don't believe in repeating the funeral service"—which would be in the South.

I asked, "Would you do a Requiem? There won't be one in Mother's church, and it would make me very happy if you'd do one for her and everybody who took care of her."

That seemed to him, too, to be totally right. Anton asked him, "How are you getting up to Crosswicks?"

And I said, "Anton, would you like to drive him up and be with us?"

"Yes, I would."

Anton is one of the best cooks I know, but I have no idea what we had for dinner that night. Tallis

229

called a car to come pick Josephine and me up and take us to the Cathedral Close, where we park our car.

ॐ

When Josephine and I are delivered at the Cathedral, we see lights in the Chase apartment, so we run up to tell the Chases what has happened, and Cynthia immediately decides to drive right back up with us and stay as long as she is needed.

We get home a little after midnight. There had been many neighbors and friends dropping by to offer help. The girls are all spending the night. "We don't want to go home tonight," Vicki says. "We want to stay here." So we light a fire and sit together and talk and try to unwind. Léna, disturbed by all the noise and confusion, wakes up and comes downstairs to us. I go out to the Tower to get my night things, for I will move, this night, back to Hugh's and my four-poster. Léna follows me. She points to the couch under the eaves and says, "You won't be needing this any more."

I am taken aback at this example of the perceptivity of a child, a perceptivity which frequently gets blunted as we grow older. Léna, just a month beyond three years, is still responding with the whole of herself, for that spontaneous remark is quicker than reason.

We go back to the living room. Bion looks white and tired, but his expression is relaxed and calm. The only outward sign of how much this death has affected him is that he wants to have the three dogs up in his attic bedroom at night.

He had said on the phone, when I called from Anton's, "Dr. John was practically ecstatic." A lovely thing about all the kids is that they accept Dr. John's relief at Mother's death. No one has a sense of guilt about anything; they all know that they have taken good care of her; they all feel that it was right and proper that her last days should have been with her family in the house she has always loved; they all feel that it was right and proper that she should have died at home, in Bion's arms, and they all feel a sense of accomplishment at having shared in this kind of death which is becoming increasingly rare in our day. So here again I am glad that I was not there: my involvement would have taken away from theirs.

ક્ર

I spend the next two days, it seems, on the phone. I call Dr. John to thank him for everything. There are many people to thank, and many people to be told of this death, which, when it finally came, was unexpected. The phone rings, too; there are calls from all over the country. One friend says, "She was a very great lady. We won't see her like again." I hear similar comments from many people, and from almost everyone: "I'll miss her." Occasionally I find that it is I who must do the consoling. I say to one Southern cousin who loved her, and who used to telephone her every day when she was in Jacksonville, "It's all right, Eddie. It's all right."

I phone one of Mrs. O's daughters, and she immediately says that she will call her mother and have her call me, which is a wise decision. When Mrs. O gets on the phone she is in charge, and telling me what to do, just as she has done all my life.

Right after lunch Bion drives Josephine and me down to the funeral home. While we are gone, the rented hospital bed is taken away, and this is the one thing which really upsets the little girls, who cry, "That's Gracchi's bed! You can't take Gracchi's bed!"

The time in the funeral home is the sour note, and the "home" we go to is one of the best, one of the least smarmy. I do not mind giving all the necessary information for the forms, or making arrangements for flying Mother's body down South; the bad thing is choosing a coffin. I know that I will have to choose a "nice" one, because this is what the family expects, pall or no. But even if I were free to choose a plain, unlined pine box, the undertakers' lobby has managed to have them outlawed, in this state, at least.

The coffins are all expensive and horrible, lined with cozy quilted satins and silks in various pastel colors as though the dead body were going to *feel* the pillow and the padding. We very quickly choose the simplest.

It is all very different from what I would have wanted if I could have had my wishes. It is not my mother, this dead shell, but it housed her for ninety years, and I would honor and weep for it before turning it back to the earth. I have not yet been able to cry, and I know that the tears need to come.

ॐ

The next day Tallis comes up with Anton for the Requiem. I make an arbitrary decision to limit it just to the people who have helped take care of the great-grandmother, for many cousins, dearly loved cousins, want to come up to Crosswicks if there is going to be a service, because they can't go all the way down South. I make this decision in the state of non-feeling in which I am moving these days, so I'm not sure if it's the right thing, but probably my instinctive no is correct. Tallis would not want it to be a big affair and the immediate Crosswicks group is all that the living room will hold.

Maria and Peter come right up from Philadelphia, and with the girls and the neighbors who have done so much for us and for Grandmother this summer, we are about twenty. That's enough for a house mass in the living room that Mother loved.

ह⬝

This time out of time in the absolute familiarity of the living room is healing and redemptive for me. Tallis uses a chalice which he designed, setting it with stones which had belonged to his mother; this is the first time he has used it. He has us all sit around the living room as we usually do for our home services when there are too many of us for the Tower. And there in the living room is, for me, the Church, an eclectic group, Congregational, Roman Catholic, Jewish, agnostic, Anglican, atheist. The dogs and the babies wander around. Jo and I sit on the little sofa which Mother bought, and where she always sat. The only additions to the Prayer Book service are from the Orthodox liturgy: stark; terrible; glorious.

The most moving moment is when everybody receives the bread and wine, each person spontaneously holding out hands. This is the Church which I affirm, and the mystery by which I live.

Clara has prepared a sumptuous lunch, and she and Mary, our neighbor across the road, have been bringing in meals for the entire household. They have been doing acts of kindness for us for many years. I never thought I would be too tired to cook, but I have been very grateful to have this chore taken care of.

Maria and Peter will stay with the children while Jo and Alan and Bion and I go South for the funeral; Hugh is tied to New York by his television job. I know that I can count on Clara and Mary; Margie and Cynthia and Vicki and Janet and Jane will all be there when needed. I can go South without any sense of being pulled back to Crosswicks. This is the last journey I will make with my mother, and it is a strange one.

ॐ

When we reach Jacksonville and drive from the airport into town, there is the familiar smell of salt air from the ocean, with a tinge of sulphur from the paper mill. The great wings of the palms droop rustily.

Mother's rooms are full of her presence; and yet they are somehow empty.

It is fearfully hot.

ॐ

The psalmist cries out his anguish: My sight faileth for very trouble; Lord, I have called daily upon thee, I have stretched forth my hands unto thee. Dost thou show wonders among the dead? or shall the dead rise up again, and praise thee? Shall thy loving-kindness be showed in the grave? or thy faithfulness in destruction? Shall thy wondrous works be known in the dark? and thy righteousness in the land where all things are forgotten?

O God. O God.

To the ancient Hebrew the ultimate hell consisted in being forgotten, erased from the memory of family and tribe, from the memory of God. If God forgets you, it is as though you have never existed. You have no meaning in the ultimate scheme of things. Your life, your being, your *ousia,* is of no value whatsoever. You are a tale told by an idiot; forgotten; annihilated.

I will never forget my mother. I do not think that my children will forget their grandmother. Perhaps the little girls will not remember their great-grandmother with "the vivid image and the very scene" but they are not likely to forget that they knew her, and shared in her last summer. They may absorb some of the things we have told them about Gracchi, so that these stories become part of their *ousia.* But their children? And their children's children?

And what of Greatie? And Mado?

How many people have been born, lived rich, loving lives, laughed and wept, been part of creation, and are now forgotten, unremembered by anybody walking the earth today?

Our memories are, at best, so limited, so finite, that it is impossible for us to envisage an unlimited, infinite memory, the memory of God. It is something I want to believe in: that no atom of creation is ever forgotten by him; always is; cared for; developing; loved.

My memory of Mother, which is the fullest memory of anybody living, is only fragmentary. I would like to believe that the creator I call God still remembers all of my mother, knows and cares for the *ousia* of her, and is still teaching her, and helping her to grow into the self he created her to be, her integrated, whole, redeemed self.

ह**❧**

One of the canons of St. John's in Jacksonville comes to the house to talk about arrangements for the funeral, which the dean is very kindly permitting Alan to conduct. The dean is on vacation and offered to return, but he is tired and I do not want to interrupt his rest, and I want Alan to say the final words over the mortal body of my mother.

The young clergyman says that at his cathedral they "like to emphasize the joyful, Resurrection aspect of a funeral," and I find myself saying, probably too passionately, that this is fine as long as the Crucifixion comes first, that we can't have a Resurrection without the Crucifixion. Alan says that the Resurrection is more terrible than the Crucifixion, and this is probably why it is so difficult for us to accept. Certainly neither one is bearable without the other. Right now I am caught between the two.

The young man says that we must use the funeral service in the new, trial liturgy. At least half the people in the church on Monday will be over seventy, brought up in the tradition of Cranmer, on the strong language of the Prayer Book. I do not see why it should be taken away from them at this moment, but the young canon does not understand, so I dutifully look through the new service.

I do not want to hear the usual overfamiliar psalms suggested. From the few permissible ones I choose *Out of the deep have I called unto thee*. The young man then tells me that "we like to sing Easter hymns at our funerals." I tell him that I do not want Easter hymns at my mother's funeral. It is too soon. I am not ready for Easter yet. I have not even had time to weep. He gives me a small list of allowable hymns, and I choose *A mighty fortress is our God*. Strength is what I am looking for, and the courage

236

to hope. I feel frustrated by what seems to me to be, if not the mortuary mentality, at least sentimentality in this attitude toward death.

Then I remember the Requiem in the living room of Crosswicks. The Church was there. And it was in the dining room afterward, when we all shared the food prepared by our neighbors. No sentimentality there. Only the fortifying truth of love.

ॐ

The funeral is to be Monday. We are all very tired. I am so tired that I am confused. I feel the way an actor does after too many consecutive performances of the same play: telling everybody (and the phone and doorbell have rung constantly) the same things over and over again, until I begin to forget lines, stumble over words. I miss my husband.

Bion is having a rough time with a really wicked headache. He stretches out on the couch in the living room and plays Mother's records, until never again will I hear Rachmaninoff's Second Piano Concerto without remembering this time. We go to Pat's for dinner, and she gives him a going over, and says that the combination of a very red throat, plus heat, plus tension, is enough to give him a clobbering headache. Nevertheless, he keeps going.

In a sense, getting Mother back now is going to be the hardest part of letting her go. We go to the funeral home to make final arrangements.

Again I feel trapped; I am plunged into the same atmosphere of unreality and evasion and sentimentality that I felt in the funeral home in Connecticut. Here in this house of death it is impossible to think about the enormity and magnitude of death and the mystery of my mother's empty body. One of the funeral-home managers takes me into the small parlor where my mother's body is coffined; he bows solemnly and leaves me alone.

I stand and look at the casket. I try to say goodbye, in somewhat the same way that I would put a sentence at the end of a sonnet; but this sonnet was completed a long time ago, and so were my goodbyes. What I am bidding farewell to now is not this remnant of decaying flesh, but the *ousia* of my mother, an *ousia* beyond my comprehension. And I am also saying goodbye to all the bad things of the last years and particularly the last weeks. They, too, are part of the mystery.

When we leave the air-conditioned chill of the funeral home and step out into the brilliant, burning, tropical sunlight, it is like moving out of falsehood into reality.

ॐ

On Sunday we go downtown to St. John's for the eleven o'clock service. There, where it is not possible for me to cry, I come near to flooding. This is the church where Mother was baptized, confirmed; from where, after the long Lenten services, she went to visit the families of the great-uncles who lived one at each corner; their homes are gone now, were gone when I was baptized here. So is the original church, which burned in the great fire. I know almost nobody in the pews.

I trickle tears during a good deal of the service, but they are quiet, controlled tears.

I do not know how to say goodbye. All I can say, within my heart, is, "I love you, Mother."

ॐ

Monday. The funeral. I have moved again into that strange, cold, anesthetized place where feelings are frozen. The tears which were brimming on Sunday are no longer there.

The best part of belonging to my enormous Southern family has been their response to Mother's death. I am moved beyond words by the gift of a jar of freshly made donax soup. This delicacy, which was part of all my childhood visits, has become a rarity; there are few donax left; it is a real gift of love.

Many of our closest friends and relatives are away, during the fiercest heat of summer, but there are nevertheless several hundred people in the church, people of all kinds, colors, ages. I feel their love for my mother, and I share in it because I am her child.

It cannot be easy for Alan to take this funeral, but his voice is strong and clear. I listen to the powerful words. Bion is on one side of me; Josephine on the other. Bion takes my hand in his large one and holds it firmly. When we come to *A mighty fortress,* his young baritone is strong and never falters.

We go out to the cemetery. I am moving through a strange, cold place where I do what has to be done, say what has to be said. There are people to be spoken to, thanked. I repeat how grateful I am that Mother died when she did, and that the problem of the old people's home never really had to come up.

This Southern cemetery is familiar to me, not as familiar as to Mother, but still familiar. My grandmother is buried here; my father; my grandfather, in that order. I have been here for the burials of many friends and relatives. When I first came with Mother to bring flowers, to tend flowers, to take away wilted flowers, I was struck by the poignant sight in the family plots of many tiny stones, marking the burial places of infants and small children. I see again the four small stones with dates all within one week—those children dead of an epidemic, nearly all of a family wiped out.

The heat of the sun beats down on us.

The words of the burial service are familiar to me, are part of my roots. One of the undertaker's men gives Alan what seems to be a synthetic clod of dirt to throw on the coffin, and suddenly the master of ceremonies—I don't know what else to call him—comes to me and takes my arm to move me away from the open grave.

None of us expected this. I start to pull away from his unwelcome, uncomforting hand. But Mother, that courteous Southern gentlewoman, would certainly not be pleased if I make a scene here at the cemetery, refuse to leave her grave until the coffin is lowered into the ground and covered with earth. There is symbolic meaning to being with a person you love all the way through to the end; there is validity in waiting while the coffin is let down into the open grave, in honoring someone's mortal frame all the way. This is what I want to do, what I had expected to do, and cannot now, for Mother's sake, do. I go meekly and helplessly with the professional mourner who would take me away; I do not jerk away from his unctuous hand, but let him lead me to the black graveyard car.

ஃ

I've written three poems to help push me through all this. The words which come out help to assure me that there may be God, after all. Perhaps whenever we have felt his presence for a while he must remove it, and by his absence force us to take the next step.

2

It is another summer, and much has happened. There has been the strange experience of assimilating Mother's things into our household, into Josephine and Alan's. The portrait Mother loved is in the place of honor in my study, the Morse portrait of my forebears, the two young women in Charleston, one playing the flute, the other the harp.

And yet—when we went for a flying visit down South to see Pat, and drove by the street which led to the river and Mother's home for thirty-seven years, I felt that if we drove down the street and went in, it would all be the same, the portrait in the living room, with the marble coffee table under it, and Mother sitting out on the little porch, watching the clouds over the St. Johns River.

I have not yet cried properly, and perhaps I never will; there has never been the right time or the right place. When I have felt like tears, I have had to hold them back; when it has been possible for me to let go, the tears would not come.

A portrait of Mother, painted when she was four, is now hanging in Crosswicks, and looks amazingly like Charlotte, who looks amazingly like Alan: intermixture and interdependence.

Léna looks at it and says to me, "You don't have a mother now. But you're my mother's mother. Where is your mother?"

ॐ

The pattern has shifted; we have changed places in the dance. I am no longer anybody's child. I have become the Grandmother. It is going to take a while to get used to this unfamiliar role. It is not so much with my actual grandchildren, Léna and Charlotte, that I feel the difference, but one generation down, with Alan and Josephine; Peter and Maria; Bion. While they called my mother Grandmother, she held the position. Now it has suddenly become mine, and I don't want it, but I will have to accept it, not as matriarchy—our men are all far too dominant for any of us on the distaff side to assume the matriarchal role—but as a change of pattern, the steps of the dance shifting.

The rhythm of the fugue alters; the themes cross and recross. The melody seems unfamiliar to me, but I will learn it.

ॐ

The children grow in all ways. Their vocabulary advances in leaps and bounds. I am no longer Madden or Gan-mad-len. When they are formal with me, I am Grandmadeleine. Mostly it is Gran. Occasionally Charlotte rushes up to me and flings her arms around me. "Granny, Granny, Granny."

One night I put them to bed, and after all the songs and stories they beg for two last songs. *"Long ones."*

So I start the *Ballad of Barbara Allen.* I have sung only a couple of verses when Charlotte says, her

243

voice quivering slightly, "Gran, you *know* that's a bad one."

"What, Charlotte?"

"You *know* that's a bad one."

Both Barbara Allen and her young man are dead and buried at the end of the ballad; I ask, "Why, Charlotte? Because it's sad?"

"No! Because she didn't love *anybody*."

Charlotte knows what it is all about. The refusal to love is the only unbearable thing.

કે•

Another time, when Josephine and Alan are away, I tell the rest of the family that I'll put the little girls to bed and go to bed early myself and finish reading a manuscript. We've had a very happy evening; the little girls—no longer babies—and I had a long bath hour before dinner; we had a lovely meal, with the menu chosen by the children: chicken salad and peas. I added potato salad and a big green salad. It's warm this evening, so the mostly cold meal was just right.

After dinner the children and I sing songs and tell stories while I get them into their nightgowns, and all is comfortable and familiar and safe and loving. We go into the bathroom to brush teeth and wash faces, and suddenly Léna looks at me and asks, "Grandmadeleine, is it all right?"

Slightly taken aback, in much the same way I was in the Tower when she pointed to the couch and said, "You won't be needing that any more," I answer, "Yes, Léna, it's all right."

"But, Gran, is everything really all right? Really?" It is completely cosmic questioning, coming from a small girl in a white nightgown with a toothbrush in her hand, sensing the unfamiliar surrounding the familiar. It is warm and light in the house, but the greater the radius of light, the wider the perimeter of darkness.

"Yes, Léna," I answer again. I think of Greatie fleeing a burning house as shots spattered the water about the little boat, and years later being rowed down that same river to visit the African princess. I think of Mado, holding a dying Yankee boy in her arms, her love and compassion concentrated wholly on his need, despite her own bereavement. I think of my mother watching her husband cough his lungs out in the cold light of the Alps, and of my father setting his name down on the empty page of the diary for the new year. It was not a tranquil world for my grandchildren's forebears, and it is in the lives of these long-gone men and women that I find the answer to Léna's question. I must answer it for her, looking down at her serious, upturned face, and I can answer truthfully only if I have my feet planted very firmly on rock.

I think of the warmth of the rock at the brook, and that I will never know more than a glimpse of the *ousia* of the small green frog—or of my mother—or of the two little girls—

and this is all right, too.

"Is it *really* all right?" Léna persists.

"Yes, Léna, it is all right."

And the two little girls and I climb into the four-poster bed to sing songs and tell stories.

The Irrational Season

Also by Madeleine L'Engle

A Circle of Quiet
The Summer of the Great-grandmother
Ladder of Angels
The Sphinx at Dawn

THE CROSSWICKS JOURNAL · BOOK 3

The Irrational Season

MADELEINE L'ENGLE

HarperSanFrancisco

A Division of HarperCollins*Publishers*

LC 76-46944
ISBN 0-86683-946-1

92 93 MPC 16 15 14 13

For Carmen Gomezplata

Acknowledgements

NONE OF THIS would have been written had not Reid Isaac, then with The Seabury Press, come to me and asked, "Don't you want to write a book for us?" My immediate and vocal response was, "No." But then this book tapped me on the shoulder and said, "Here I am. Write me," and when this happens I have little choice.

Several names have been changed and a few incidents "translated" in order to protect privacy. Nevertheless this book is as "true" as I can make it.

The last third was completed while I was a Visiting Fellow at the Episcopal Seminary of the Southwest in Austin, Texas. My debt to my friends there is incalculable. Not only was I given time to write, and an opportunity to share in the life and worship of the seminary, but I was also fed, chauffeured, and consistently ministered to.

Contents

1... The Night Is Far Spent

NEW YORK.

Two o'clock in the morning. A thin, chill November rain is falling. I stand at the dining-room window, holding a comforting mug of hot bouillon, and look out at the never-wholly-asleep city. A taxi moves slowly along West End Avenue. A young woman walks down the middle of 105th Street with a very large Great Dane. My Irish setter is asleep in the bedroom; he knows that it is much too early to get up.

I enjoy these occasional spells of nocturnal wakefulness, and I am never awake alone. Across West End Avenue there is an apartment building where the eleventh-floor windows are always lit, no matter what time it is. This night, in another building, someone is studying by a single light bulb suspended from the ceiling. The Hudson River is visible through television aerials and between two tall apartment buildings on Riverside Drive. Ours is a restricted view, but it is a view, nevertheless, and I love it. There is a small ship, a freighter, I think, moving slowly along the dark water, its lights both warmly greeting and mysterious. What looks like a star grows brighter and reveals itself to be a plane coming in to land at La Guardia; but there is a star left behind in the wake of the plane, a pale city star.

I sip hot bouillon and feel relaxed and at peace at this beginning of a new year—a new year for me. I have had another birthday, and this is always like opening a brand-new journal to the first page, or putting a clean sheet of paper into the typewriter as I start a new book; it is all ahead of me, clear and bright, the first smudges and mistakes not yet made. I know that they will come, and soon—I don't think

I've ever typed a full page without making at least one error; however, beginnings are always exciting and full of hope.

The beginning of my personal new year comes as the Christian Church's new year, Advent, begins, the four weeks before Christmas. The Jewish New Year is over; it is not yet time for the secular New Year or the Buddhist New Year; the academic year is already well started. Has there ever been a culture or a religion where there has not been a special day to mark the beginning of a new year? I still function more in terms of the academic year than any other, and probably will continue to do so even when we no longer have children in school or college.

A new year can begin only because the old year ends. In northern climates this is especially apparent. As rain turns to snow, puddles to ice, the sun rises later and sets earlier; and each day it climbs less high in the sky. One time when I went with my children to the planetarium I was fascinated to hear the lecturer say that the primitive people used to watch the sun drop lower on the horizon in great terror, because they were afraid that one day it was going to go so low that it would never rise again; they would be left in unremitting night. There would be weeping and wailing and gnashing of teeth, and a terror of great darkness would fall upon them. And then, just as it seemed that there would never be another dawn, the sun would start to come back; each day it would rise higher, set later.

Somewhere in the depths of our unconsciousness we share that primordial fear, and when there is the first indication that the days are going to lengthen, our hearts, too, lift with relief. The end has not come: joy! and so a new year makes its birth known.

In the Christian Church these weeks leading up to Christmas, this dark beginning of our new year, is also traditionally the time of thinking of the last things, of the 'eschaton,' the end.

The night is far spent. The day is at hand.

That day when all nights will be spent, when time will end: we all know it's coming. Scientists know it, and tell us the various ways that it could happen, but as of now they aren't predicting when. Various religious groups have predicted the end of the world off and on for hundreds of years. Whenever one of these groups tells us that Doomsday is going to come at midnight on a certain day, I always feel a little queasy. Maybe this time they're right. It has to happen sometime.

It was a long time before I could begin to think of this ending of all known things, all matter, the stars in their courses, music, laughter, sunrise, daisies and dynasties, starfish and stars, suns and chrysanthemums, as being in any way something to look forward to with joy and hope. It was a long time before I could turn my thoughts to the eschaton without terror. Long before I'd heard about the atom bomb or the hydrogen bomb, or fission or fusion, I feared the end of the world in much the same way that I fear a nuclear holocaust. And the description of the last day in the New Testament sounds very much like atomic devastation: "The present sky and earth are reserved for fire. . . . The Day of the Lord will come like a thief, and then with a roar the sky will vanish, the elements will catch fire and fall apart, and the earth and all that it contains will be burned up."

A nuclear holocaust would probably mean the end of human life on planet earth, but not the rest of the solar system, or the galaxy, or any of the hundreds of billions of other galaxies in the universe. And nuclear warfare would be man's pride and folly rather than God's anger.

The end of the world in the eschatological sense has nothing to do with pride or anger and it is not just the end of this one planet, but of all planets, all solar systems, all galaxies.

And what then? Is that it? Annihilation?

No. Annihilation might follow an intergalactic nuclear battle, but annihilation is the opposite of what the eschaton is about. It is not nearly so much a going as a coming, an ending as a beginning. It is the redemption, not the destruction, of Creation. We've heard the phrases so often and from so many denominations that they've become distorted until the meaning is nearly bled from them:

The Second Coming. The Coming of the Kingdom.

What does that mean?

My son-in-law Alan was asked once by a pious woman if our feet would be wafted from the earth, at the time of the Second Coming, before Jesus's feet touched ground. Ouch. That kind of literalism is not what it's about.

For the simple fact is that we are not capable of knowing what it's about. The Coming of the Kingdom is creation coming to be what it was meant to be, the joy and glory of all creation working together with the Creator. In literal language none of it makes much sense, and

I can only go once again to my adolescent analogy of the planet on which all sentient life was sightless. If nobody could see, other senses would take over, and everybody would get along perfectly well. But if you tried to explain the joy of sight to anybody on that planet you couldn't do it. Nobody could understand something so glorious and so totally out of an eyeless frame of reference. Multiply that gap between a blind planet and a seeing one a billion times and we'll still be far from understanding the difference between creation, now, and creation in the fullness of the kingdom. But I am slowly learning that it is something to be awaited with joy and not terror.

When I try to grasp the nature of the universe with my conscious mind, my humanly limited intellectual powers, I grope blindly. I come closer to understanding with the language of the heart, sipping hot bouillon and relaxing, standing by the dining-room window where I can no longer sit on the window sill because of our accumulation of plants—coleus and Swedish Ivy and ferns and alligator pears and philodendron and anything else we can coax to grow in the polluted air of the city—than when I think with mind alone.

The night is far spent. The day is at hand.

Yes. It's nearly three o'clock in the morning. But I'm not ready to go back to bed yet. I'll be sorry when the alarm goes off in the morning. Meanwhile, I want to stay here a little longer.

Before I can contemplate the end I have to think about the beginning, and no one is very certain about the beginning, that moment when God created the universe out of sheer *joie de vivre.* There are three conflicting theories of the creation of the universe. First, there's the big-bang theory. Once upon a time all matter was One, an incredibly compact mass of unmeasurable compression. And suddenly—and the cosmologists don't know why—it burst asunder and particles of it flew out wildly and eventually became galaxies, and within the galaxies suns, and planets, and planetary satellites like our moon. And all these fragments of the original Oneness are still flying out, out, out into—what? farther and farther away from each other (how lonely outer space must be), so that the distances between galaxies are becoming greater and greater . . .

Then there's the theory of continuous creation. In the vast hydrogen clouds all over the universe, stars are constantly being born, as stars are constantly dying. It's an attractive theory, but where did those hydrogen clouds come from in the first place?

And then there's the flux theory: once upon a time all matter was One. And suddenly there was an explosion and particles of this original Oneness went flying out in every direction, stars and galaxies growing farther and farther apart—and then the direction reverses and there is an implosion and everything moves inward, together, eventually becoming the original One, and then there's another big bang and the Unity explodes and particles go flying out in all directions, and this explosion/implosion continues to repeat itself . . .

Forever?

And none of these theories answers the question of why there's anything at all. Why isn't there just nothing?

My children asked me these things and I was hard put to answer their questions, which are still my own questions.

Why is there anything?

Well, God made something out of nothing.

Why? Didn't he like nothing?

Well, God is love, and it is the nature of love to create.

Could he have created anything he wanted to?

Of course. He's God.

Do you like what he created?

Yes. Yes, I do.

Battlefields and slums and insane asylums?

Well, he didn't create those.

Who did?

We did.

Who's we? I didn't create them.

Mankind did. And you're part of mankind and so am I.

But God created mankind?

Yes.

Why did he create mankind if mankind was going to create battlefields and slums and insane asylums?

I don't suppose that's what he created man *for*.

What did he create him for, then?

Well, it's the nature of love to create . . .

So.

What does that do to all Love? It is the nature of love to create, and what do the children of this Love do? We make battlefields and slums and insane asylums.

Out of all this original nothingness wouldn't you think he could have done better?

Maybe he did. I don't know why we have the conceit to think we're the flower of his Creation. Maybe not all life went wrong—and even with all our wrongness there's the Bach *St. Matthew Passion* and Shakespeare's plays and Rembrandt's paintings and . . .

The morning star is low on the horizon. There are three more stars pulsing faintly in the city sky. But even if I can't see a skyful of stars they are there above me nevertheless; the Milky Way, our own galaxy, swings somewhere in the vast dark above the city lights.

All those stars. Suns. More suns than can be imagined. Great flaming brilliant atomic furnaces, the bursting of their atoms providing life instead of death. Providing life for their planets. Perhaps most of the inhabited planets are different from ours, with no battlefields or slums or insane asylums. Perhaps there are planets where that which was created by love returns love, and there is joy and worship and praise and man sings with the angels—not pink and blue and cute, not angels with weak faces and weaker wings—but

> O sing unto God
> and sing praises unto his Name
> magnify him that rideth upon the heavens
> praise him in his name
> JAH!
> shout it
> cry it aloud upon the wind
> take the tail of his steed
> and fling across the sky
> in his wild wake
> JAH!
> he cannot be caught
> he cannot be fled
> nor his knowledge escaped
> the light of his Name
> blinds the brilliance of stars
> JAH!
> catch the falling dragon
> ride between his flailing wings

leap between the jaws of the lion
grasp the horn of the unicorn
calling with mighty voice
JAH!
caught in star flame
whipped by comet lash
rejoice before him
cry above the voices of the cherubim
shout alongside the seraphim
JAH!
bellowing joy behind kings
scattered by the quaking of his hills
fleeing before his fire
rush like snow through his thunderous flame
crying with gladness
adoration of his Name
He is Lord
*JAH!**

I'm going to be thinking about man, and his part in the world, fairly frequently in these pages, and I want to make it quite clear, right away, that I, Madeleine, sex: f, wife and mother, am just as much *man* as is Hugh, sex: m, husband and father, and that I'm not about to abdicate my full share in mankind. One of the most pusillanimous things we of the female sex have done throughout the centuries is to have allowed the male sex to assume that mankind is masculine.

It is not. It takes both male and female to make the image of God. The proper understanding of mankind is that it is only a poor, broken thing if either male or female is excluded. The result of such exclusion is that in terms of human sexuality the English language is presently inadequate. The word *man* has been so taken over by the male sex that I'm not sure it's redeemable. In the old days the familiar word for male was *wer*—as in werwolf; and the familiar word for female was *wif*—and not just as in housewif; the Amazons were wifs, too.

But if I try to use *wer* and *wif,* or if I make up new words which would be useful, these unusual words would stick out and the meaning of the sentence might easily be lost. So I'll stick with our present mutilated generic vocabulary.

I realize how fortunate I was to have grown up in a household

*From L'Engle, *Lines Scribbled on an Envelope,* copyright © 1969. Reprinted with permission of Farrar, Straus & Giroux.

where I never encountered sexism, where it never occurred to me that female was in any way less than male; different, yes; but equal. In my work, both in the theatre and in writing, I have been in worlds which are not sexist. The reason the mothers in my children's books are usually professional women, respected in their chosen fields, is that this is the kind of woman I've always known best. In my marriage, sexism has never been a barrier. So I realize that it's easy for me to be casual about the words for gender. If I had grown up in an atmosphere where the female was put down, where my sex was relegated to an inferior place, I would not be able to be so casual.

I will have to struggle along with the old, tattered words, trying never to forget that *man* is as much a feminine as a masculine word, and if I abandon my share in it, *that* would be to kowtow to the 'm.c.p.,' who would like to hog the whole human gender for himself, and is aided and abetted by the more thoughtless members of the female sex who do not realize that they are not more free by insisting on falling down personholes, but are blindly relinquishing their true identity. And so the male is given his usual opportunity to say, "It was the woman's fault. She made me eat of the fruit of the tree"— a sniveling and cowardly alibi which immediately broke the proper joyful and creative relationship between male and female.

The Church with blithe disregard of the folly of sexism calls itself the Body of Christ (masculine), and affirms itself also to be the Bride of Christ (feminine), and just as it takes male and female to make the image of God, so it takes male and female to make the Church.

Because I am a female and my sexuality is fulfilled by the male of the species, it is easy for me to respond joyfully to the maleness of the Godhead, but that does not make me see it as exclusively masculine; that would be just as much of a dead end as not acknowledging the essential male genes in myself, or the female genes in my husband, Hugh, which are an important part of our full sexuality.

If, when we were married, Hugh and I became a new entity, he as much as I, then, when Mary conceived by the power of the Holy Spirit, that mighty action affirmed forever the sexual wholeness of Creation. I do not mean that a young and very human girl became one of the persons of the Trinity, but surely the most holy Birth-giver should make us understand that the Trinity embraces all sexuality in a complete and unfragmented manner.

We make complicated what is simple, and the powers of darkness rejoice. But because I, too, am woman and mother, it is my joy and privilege to identify with this young girl who contained within her womb the Power of the universe.

> O thou who bears the pain of the whole earth,
>   I bore thee.
> O thou whose tears give human tears their worth,
>   I laughed with thee.
> Thou who, when thy hem is touched, give power,
>   I nourished thee.
> Who turns the day to night in this dark hour,
>   Dayspring for me.
> O thou who held the world in thy embrace,
>   I dandled thee,
> Whose arms encircle all men with thy grace,
>   I once held thee.
> O thou who laughed and ate and walked the shore,
>   I played with thee.
> And I, who with all others, thou died for,
>   I now hold thee.
>
> May I be faithful to this final test:
> For the last time I hold my child, my son,
> Thy body close enfolded to my breast,
> The holder held, the bearer borne.
> Mourning to joy: darkness to morn.
> Open, my arms; the work is done.

The original relationship between male and female was meant to be one of mutual fulfillment and joy, but that relationship was broken, to our grief, and turned into one of suspicion and warfare, misunderstanding and exclusion, and will not be fully restored until the end of time. Nevertheless, we are given enough glimpses of the original relationship so that we should be able to rejoice in our participation in mankind.

Rejoice I do, and I'm not willing to relinquish one iota of my share!

Mankind: male and female created he them,

and in his image.

Whose image? God's. And *God* is a word as abused and battered as the gender words.

Martin Buber defends the word *God* passionately; soiled though it is, it is the word we have by which to call the One who is so glorious that no one knows his real name. Year by year the word becomes more abused, and still it is the one I cry out in despair or anguish or joy. So it pains me when people try to narrow down the One to whom I cry as no more than a sexist symbol. Certainly domineering males have tried to take God over and make him in their own image, but I do not understand why we accept that image. Juliana of Norwich, with casual casting aside of the sexism of her day (far worse than ours), calls Christ her mother—mother, father, brother, sister, it doesn't matter. The Power behind the universe is all in all. Jesus called the Father *Abba,* a name so personal it might almost be translated daddy—except for what we've done to the word daddy.

The thought of the Original Oneness which preceded the big bang keeps returning to me, the Original Oneness which preceded galaxies and stars and planets and Adam and Eve and you and me. Was that the primordial fall? Are the stars in their courses singing the Lord's song in a strange land?

There was war in heaven: Michael and his angels fought against the dragon; and the dragon fought, and his angels, and prevailed not; neither was their place found any more in heaven. And the great dragon was cast out, that old serpent called the Devil, and Satan, who deceives the whole world; he was cast out into the earth, and his angels with him . . .

So goes the old song, and what does it mean?

The dragon and his angels did not want to be One; they wanted independence and individuation and autonomy, and they broke wholeness into fragments . . .

When will we once again be one?

Perhaps galaxy by galaxy, solar system by solar system, planet by planet, all creation must be redeemed.

Where were we when the morning stars sang together, and all the sons of God shouted for joy?

During my journey through life I have moved in and out of agnosticism and even atheism, as I become bewildered by what mankind has done to God; and so, too often, I see God in man's image, rather than the other way around. But I cannot live for long in this dead-end world, but return to the more open places of my child's intuitive love of God, where I know that all creatures are the concern of the God who created the galaxies, and who nevertheless notes the fall of each sparrow. And from the darkness I cry out: God!

And it is enough.

> *Come, Lord Jesus! Do I dare*
> *Cry: Lord Jesus, quickly come!*
> *Flash the lightning in the air,*
> *Crash the thunder on my home!*
> *Should I speak this aweful prayer?*
> *Come, Lord Jesus, help me dare.*
>
> *Come, Lord Jesus! You I call*
> *To come, come soon, are not the child*
> *Who lay once in the manger stall,*
> *Are not the infant meek and mild.*
> *You come in judgment on our fall.*
> *Help me to know on whom I call.*
>
> *Come, Lord Jesus! Come this night*
> *With your judgment and your power,*
> *For the earth is dark with blight*
> *And in sin we run and cower*
> *Before the splendid raging sight*
> *Of the breaking of the night.*
>
> *Come, my Lord! Our darkness end!*
> *Break the bonds of time and space.*
> *All the powers of evil rend*
> *By the radiance of your face.*
> *The laughing stars with joy attend.*
> *Come, Lord Jesus, be my end!*

When I think of the incredible, incomprehensible sweep of creation above me, I have the strange reaction of feeling fully alive. Rather than feeling lost and unimportant and meaningless, set against galaxies which go beyond the reach of the furthest telescopes, I feel that my life has meaning. Perhaps I should feel insignificant, but instead I feel a soaring in my heart that the God who could create all this— and out of nothing—can still count the hairs of my head.

Our tininess has nothing to do with it. The peculiar idea that bigger is better has been around for at least as long as I have, and it's always bothered me. There is within it the implication that is more difficult for God to care about a gnat than about a galaxy. Creation is just as visible in a grain of sand as in a skyful of stars.

The church is not immune from the bigger-is-better heresy. One woman told of going to a meeting where only a handful of people turned out, and these faithful few were scolded by the visiting preacher for the sparseness of the congregation. And she said indignantly, "Our Lord said *feed* my sheep, not count them!" I often feel that I'm being counted, rather than fed, and so I am hungry.

The glory of the incarnate world is briefly visible for me as I look through the sleeping plants to the planets, to the quiet of streets which will soon be waking; this glory is too often obscured in the city because of what we human beings have done to it. Hugh and I live in a melting pot of a neighborhood which was once solid, respectable, moneyed; Jewish on West End and Riverside Avenues, Irish on Amsterdam; and which is now white, black, yellow, tan; where one hears English in a multitude of accents, as well as Spanish, German, Creole, Taiwanese, Chinese, Japanese, Korean, Hindustani, Yiddish, Hebrew, French—and probably other languages I don't recognize. It is a far more realistic world than the world of New England farmland where we lived for a near decade when our children were little, and now know only in the summer.

The old ethnic stamp of the Bloomingdale section of Manhattan Island, the Upper West Side between the old academic elegance of Morningside Heights and the new cultural elegance of Lincoln Center, is still reflected in the observance of holidays. Markets are open on Sundays, even Easter Sunday, but are closed for the Jewish Holy Days. One Puerto Rican *bodega* placed a sign in the window which read: CLOSED FOR YOM KIPPER. What a delicious red herring!

Sometimes I think in wonder of our years in a New England village, a village still small enough so that everybody was known by name. It was not easy to get lost in our village; it wasn't exactly like living in a goldfish bowl, but there wasn't much that people didn't know about their neighbors. This has its disadvantages, but it's more human than the anonymity of the city where an old man or woman, living alone, can fall and break a hip and not be discovered for weeks. If anybody in our village had an accident, everybody knew about it; a lot of people prayed about it; almost everybody cared, wanted to help. But if I pass an accident in the city while I'm riding a bus or walking along the street, I, like everybody else around me, will stare in horrified curiosity as we pass by; it may be a *momento mori,* but we'll never know who was in that buckled car, who lay on the street after having been hit by that bus; it happens so often that we won't even read about it in the paper. We are forced to be as passive as though we were viewing it on television, and this frightens me. Our cities get more crowded daily; we build bigger and better housing developments where neighbors are strangers and anonymity is a disease and not a privilege. It was predicted that we would feel the radical changes of overpopulation by the end of the century, but overpopulation in the cities has already plunged us into a new dark age. There are rats in the streets, fat and sleek and sinister as sharks.

I think of my children asking me why God created mankind if mankind was going to make battlefields and slums and insane asylums. The city around our pleasant apartment building is not an easy place in which to see the hand of God. Mankind has imposed its imprint of ugly buildings and dirty streets and desperate people. But if I cannot see God's love here on the Upper West Side of New York where we seem to have done everything possible to destroy the beauty of creation, it is going to do me little good to rejoice in beauty in the uncluttered world of the country.

My breath steams the window but I see a young man walking along the street, his head bowed against the wind. It is cold, but for the moment the city is quiet. No sirens shrieking, no grinding of brakes. A light goes on in a window across the street.

It is the nature of love to create, and no matter what we do to creation, that love is still there, creating; in the young man who is holding his jacket closed across his chest; in you; in me.

The last of the bouillon is lukewarm in the bottom of the mug. It's time for bed.

Time: why are we so timebound?

Why should I go to bed?

You'll be tired in the morning if you don't.

Yes. But maybe it's worth it. I don't want to get imprisoned by the clock, that arbitrary, man-made definer of the hours.

Let us view with joy and mirth
All the clocks upon the earth
Holding time with busy tocking
Ticking booming clanging clocking
Anxiously unraveling
Time's traveling
Through the stars and winds and tides.
Who can tell where time abides?

Foolish clocks, all time was broken
When that first great Word was spoken.
Cease we now this silly fleeing
From earth's time, for time's a being
And adoring
Bows before him
Who upon the throne is seated.
Time, defeated, wins, is greeted.

Clocks know not time's loving wonder
Day above as night swings under,
Turning always to the son,
Time's begun, is done, does run
Singing warning
Of the morning
Time, mass, space, a mystery
Of eternal trinity.

Time needs make no poor apology
For bursting forth from man's chronology
Laughs in glee as human hours
Dance before the heavenly powers.
Time's undone
Because the Son
Swiftly calls the coming light
That will end the far-spent night.

Advent.
Waiting for the end. The eschaton.
The night is far spent.
And now I'm sleepy and ready for bed.

In the dark bedroom Timothy, our Irish setter, sighs deeply in his sleep. I can hear my husband's peaceful breathing. I crawl into bed beside him, reaching out as always to touch, very lightly, the reassuring warmth of his flesh, flesh I have known intimately for over three decades.

Who is he, this man I have slept beside for lo these many years?

> *You are still new, my love. I do not know you,*
> *Stranger beside me in the dark of bed,*
> *Dreaming dreams I cannot ever enter,*
> *Eyes closed in that unknown, familiar head.*
> *Who are you? who have thrust and entered*
> *My very being, penetrated so that now*
> *I can never again be wholly separate,*
> *Bound by shared living to this unknown thou.*
> *I do not know you, nor do you know me,*
> *And yet we know each other in the way*
> *Of our primordial forebears in the garden.*
> *Adam knew Eve. As we do, so did they.*
> *They; we; forever strangers: austere, but true.*
> *And yet I would not change it. You are still new.*

Good night.

2... Sometimes I Forget to Tell You How Much I Love You

THE NATIVITY IS a time to take courage. How brave am I? Can I bear, without breaking apart, this extraordinary birth?

The end is the beginning. We have come to the shortest day, the longest night of the year. Christmas is coming, the goose is getting fat. I can turn from contemplation of the eschaton and Christ's return to *anamnesis*, the living memory, the memory in untimebound *kairos* of what has already been.

I've never been to seminary nor taken any religion courses; in college I was through with the religious establishment; so my interpretation of theological words is not always correct. Anamnesis is important to me, but my understanding of it is largely literary.

Anamnesis: against amnesia. This kind of memory is one of the most important of the storyteller's tools. If I am to write about young people in my novels, as well as those my own age, it is essential that I remember exactly what it was like to be young. I have sometimes been asked if my young protagonists are based on my children; no, of course they are not; I would not presume to write out of my children. My protagonists, male and female, are me. And so I must be able to recall exactly what it was like to be five years old, and twelve, and sixteen, and twenty-two, and. . . . For, after all, I am not an isolated fifty-seven years old; I am every other age I have been, one, two, three, four, five, six, seven . . . all the way up to and occasionally beyond my present chronology.

When I am writing in a novel about a fourteen-year-old girl, I must remember what I was like at fourteen, but this anamnesis is not a looking back, from my present chronological age, at Madeleine, aged fourteen. If there is all this distance of years between us, my memory is only from the outside. When I am writing about a fourteen-year-old girl I will not succeed unless I am, during the time of writing, Madeleine: fourteen. The strange wonder of it is that I am also Madeleine: fifty-seven, with all the experience I have gained in the intervening years. But I am not, in the ordinary sense, remembering what it was like to be fourteen; it is not something in the past; it is present; I am fourteen.

I was talking to a psychiatrist friend about the importance of memory, and he said that many of his patients are afraid to remember, because they are afraid to learn who they really are.

I don't know what has kept me from being afraid, because the minute he spoke I understood the fear. Perhaps there's no getting around the fact that if I am to be a storyteller I must have a trained memory. No memory, no story. And so the joy of memory has remained mine.

As I understand anamnesis in my writing, so I understand it in the Holy Mysteries. When we are truly remembering, when we know anamnesis, suddenly the mighty acts of God are present.

And then we are in *kairos*. Kairos. God's time, which isn't really time at all in the sense that we know man's time, *chronos*. It is impossible, while we are living in time, to define *kairos;* it is to be understood by intuition, rather than intellect, and recognized only afterwards, by anamnesis when we are back in time again, for in *kairos* we are completely unselfconscious. Whenever I have loved most truly and most spontaneously, time has vanished and I have been in *kairos*.

The second Christmas of our marriage, and the first with our six-month-old baby, the beautiful flesh of our child made the whole miracle of incarnation new for me, and that newness touched on *kairos*.

Now, all these years later, I plunge into the delightful business of painting Christmas ornaments with my grandchildren; I hear the hammer as Bion puts together a dolls' house which looks remarkably like Crosswicks, our house in the country; the New York kitchen smells fragrant with Christmas cookies: this, for me, is incarnation.

The enfleshing of the Word which spoke the galaxies made the death of that Word inevitable. All flesh is mortal, and the flesh assumed by the Word was no exception in mortal terms. So the birth of the Creator in human flesh and human time was an event as shattering and terrible as the eschaton. If I accept this birth I must accept God's love, and this is pain as well as joy because God's love, as I am coming to understand it, is not like man's love.

What one of us can understand a love so great that we would willingly limit our unlimitedness, put the flesh of mortality over our immortality, accept all the pain and grief of humanity, submit to betrayal by that humanity, be killed by it, and die a total failure (in human terms) on a common cross between two thieves?

What kind of flawed, failed love is this? Why should we rejoice on Christmas Day? This is where the problem lies, not in secular bacchanalias, not in Santa Clauses with cotton beards, loudspeakers blatting out Christmas carols the day after Thanksgiving, not in shops full of people pushing and shouting and swearing at each other as they struggle to buy overpriced Christmas presents.

No, it's not the secular world which presents me with problems about Christmas, it's God.

Cribb'd, cabined, and confined within the contours of a human infant. The infinite defined by the finite? The Creator of all life thirsty and abandoned? Why would he do such a thing? Aren't there easier and better ways for God to redeem his fallen creatures?

And what good did it all do? The heart of man is still evil. Wars grow more terrible with each generation. The earth daily becomes more depleted by human greed. God came to save us and we thank him by producing bigger and better battlefields and slums and insane asylums.

And yet Christmas is still for me a time of hope, of hope for the courage to love and accept love, a time when I can forget that my Christology is extremely shaky and can rejoice in God's love through love of family and friends.

Christology: I'm all right through the first verses of John's Gospel, verses which are in the language of poetry which breaks through reason and strengthens my courage. My heart lifts at that first great cry which brought creation into being; Christ, the second person of the Trinity making all those galaxies burning with incredible brightness, those brilliant flaming suns which themselves are not the light which made them: I rejoice. It's the Word, the Light coming to us as Jesus of Nazareth, which confounds my imagination.

Most of the time the fact that this fact is impossible doesn't bother me. I live by the impossible. Like the White Queen, I find it a good discipline to practice believing as many as seven impossible things every morning before breakfast. How dull the world would be if we limited ourselves to the possible.

The only God who seems to me to be worth believing in is impossible for mortal man to understand, and therefore he teaches us through this impossible.

But we rebel against the impossible. I sense a wish in some professional religion-mongers to make God possible, to make him comprehensible to the naked intellect, domesticate him so that he's easy to believe in. Every century the Church makes a fresh attempt to make Christianity acceptable. But an acceptable Christianity is not Christian; a comprehensible God is no more than an idol.

I don't want that kind of God.

What kind of God, then?

One time, when I was little more than a baby, I was taken to visit my grandmother, who was living in a cottage on a nearly uninhabited stretch of beach in northern Florida. All I remember of this visit is being picked up from my crib in what seemed the middle of the night and carried from my bedroom and out of doors, where I had my first look at the stars.

It must have been an unusually clear and beautiful night for someone to have said, "Let's wake the baby and show her the stars." The night sky, the constant rolling of breakers against the shore, the stupendous light of the stars, all made an indelible impression on me. I was intuitively aware not only of a beauty I had never seen before but also that the world was far greater than the protected limits of the small child's world which was all that I had known thus far. I had a total, if not very conscious, moment of revelation; I saw creation bursting the bounds of daily restriction, and stretching out from dimension to dimension, beyond any human comprehension.

I had been taught to say my prayers at night: Our Father, and a long string of God-blesses, and it was that first showing of the galaxies which gave me an awareness that the God I spoke to at bedtime was extraordinary and not just a bigger and better combination of the grownup powers of my mother and father.

This early experience was freeing, rather than daunting, and since it was the first, it has been the foundation for all other such glimpses of glory. And it is probably why the sound of the ocean and the sight of the stars give me more healing, more whole-ing, than anything else.

We are meant to be whole creatures, we human beings, but mostly we are no more than fragments of what we ought to be. One of the great evils of twentieth-century civilization is the rift which has come between our conscious and our intuitive minds, a rift which has been slowly widening for thousands of years, so that now it seems as unbridgeable as the chasm which separated Dives, suffering the torments of hell, from Lazarus, resting on Abraham's bosom.

And this gap, separating intellect from intuition, mind from heart, is so frightening to some people that they won't admit that it exists. I heard an otherwise intelligent man announce belligerently that there was no gap whatsoever between his conscious and below-conscious mind; his conscious mind was in complete control of his unconscious mind, thank you very much.

We haven't learned much since Paul of Tarsus admitted quite openly that his conscious mind was not successful in dictating to his below-the-surface self. If anything, the gap between consciousness and super- sub- or un-consciousness is even wider now than it was then. How can we possibly bridge the chasm? How can we become free?

I turn again to the night sky, this time to a planet, one of the planets in our own solar system, the planet Mercury. Mercury revolves around our mutual parent sun in such a way that one face is always turned toward the sun and is brilliantly lit and burningly hot; and the other side is always turned toward the cold dark of interstellar space. But Mercury oscillates slightly on its axis, and thereby sunside and nightside are integrated by a temperate zone which knows both heat and cold, light and dark. So the two disparate sides of Mercury are not separated by a chasm; the temperate zone mediates.

Where, in ourselves, can we find this temperate zone which will integrate and free us? The words *freedom* and *liberation* have been used frequently during the last decade, and this would certainly seem to imply that we are less free, less liberated, than we want to admit.

People who are already free don't need to talk about liberation. It is a great mistake to equate freedom with anarchy, liberation with chaos. It has been my experience that freedom comes as the temperate zone integrates sunside and nightside, thereby making wholeness instead of brokenness.

Art is for me the great integrater, and I understand Christianity as I understand art. I understand Christmas as I understand Bach's *Sleepers Awake* or *Jesu, Joy of Man's Desiring;* as I understand Braque's clowns, Blake's poetry. And I understand it when I am able to pray with the mind in the heart, as Theophan the Recluse advised. When we pray with the mind in the heart, sunside and nightside are integrated, we begin to heal, and we come close to the kind of understanding which can accept an unacceptable Christianity. When I am able to pray with the mind in the heart, I am joyfully able to affirm the irrationality of Christmas.

> *As I grow older*
> *I get surer*
> *Man's heart is colder,*
> *His life no purer.*
> *As I grow steadily*
> *More austere*
> *I come less readily*
> *To Christmas each year.*
> *I can't keep taking*
> *Without a thought*
> *Forced merrymaking*
> *And presents bought*
> *In crowds and jostling.*
> *Alas, there's naught*
> *In empty wassailing*
> *Where oblivion's sought.*
> *Oh, I'd be waiting*
> *With quiet fasting*
> *Anticipating*
> *A joy more lasting.*
> *And so I rhyme*
> *With no apology*
> *During this time*
> *Of eschatology:*
> *Judgment and warning*
> *Come like thunder.*

> *But now is the hour*
> *When I remember*
> *An infant's power*
> *On a cold December.*
> *Midnight is dawning*
> *And the birth of wonder.*

But what is that wonder? The marvel of Christianity is its particularity, and if I am to say anything about Christmas it must be through the particular, so let me tell the story of one particular Christmas.

The Thanksgiving before, we were expecting our usual mob for dinner. I dressed the turkey and put it in the oven, and lay down for a brief nap. But I couldn't rest and after a while I wandered back out to the kitchen to baste the turkey. I opened the oven door and was met with a fading glow of dying heat. The oven had gone off with the turkey not half cooked. We took the oven apart, but the gas pilot light would not relight. We called the 'super,' apologetically, explaining that it really was an emergency, and he left his own Thanksgiving dinner and came up. But it was quickly apparent that the problem with the oven was not a minor one, and we were not going to be able to finish cooking our turkey in the oven that day.

"But we have twenty people coming for dinner!" I cried in horror.

There was nothing the 'super' could do except go downstairs to his own dinner, explaining that his oven wasn't large enough for our turkey.

So we began calling friends in our apartment building. Some were away—we got no answer; others still had their own turkeys in the oven. Finally we got friends who had just started to carve their turkey and immediately offered to let us finish cooking ours in their oven.

On one of our various trips up and down the back stairs between apartments, I remarked to our son, Bion, home from college for vacation, "Oh, well, it's just another typical Thanksgiving at the Franklins'."

So if I say that the Christmas I am about to describe was 'typical,' it was not that the events themselves were typical, but that this Christmas evoked in me that response which makes me continue to struggle to understand, with the mind in the heart, the love of God for his creation, a love which expressed itself in the Incarnation. That tiny, helpless baby whose birth we honor contained the Power behind the universe, helpless, at the mercy of its own creation.

We had our usual full house of family and friends. Bion was again home from college. Our second daughter and son-in-law, Maria and Peter, were home from England, where Peter has a research job in theoretical chemistry at the University of Warwick. Our elder daughter and son-in-law, Josephine and Alan, had recently moved into a large and comfortable apartment at the General Theological Seminary, where Alan is associate professor of ascetical theology, and there was a good deal of going back and forth between the two households.

Maria and Peter had not expected to come home for Christmas; it seemed an unwarranted expense. But when Peter's mother, Dorothy, had a heart attack they came immediately. We all visited Dorothy in the hospital, Peter and his sisters daily, and she expected to be home shortly after Christmas, though she told all of us firmly that when she did die she wanted to be buried alongside her parents in an Orthodox Jewish Cemetery. But the present anxiety seemed to be over, so the weekend before Christmas Peter went to Poughkeepsie to visit cousins.

Saturday night the rest of our household went to bed rather late, after a lovely long evening of conversation. We were deep in sleep when the phone rang; it was one of Peter's sisters. One of the hospital nurses had gone to check on Dorothy and found her dead in her sleep.

Maria and Bion stayed up to wait for Peter while he drove from Poughkeepsie. Hugh and I felt that we would be more useful the next day if we got some sleep, so we turned out the light with heavy hearts.

In the morning I was awake before Hugh, so I slipped out quietly. Maria's and Peter's door was open and their lights on, so I knocked and went in. Peter was lying in bed, looking drawn and dry-eyed, although Bion and Maria told me later that he had done a lot of crying the night before, which relieved me, and I knew that he would need to do more crying later.

I sat beside him and took his hand.

"Madeleine, are you going to church this morning?"

"No, Peter, I want to stay here with you."

Peter, as head of the family, was in charge of his mother's funeral. Immediately he said that he wanted Alan to do as much as possible, but since Dorothy would be buried in a Jewish cemetery, the service would have to be led by a rabbi, so Peter asked me to call one of the rabbis from the temple where I recently had been the lay Christian on a panel about Christians and Jews. I did so, and everything was arranged for the following morning, Christmas Eve.

Peter was very torn within himself about his mother's funeral, and Christmas the next day. The loss of a mother is always a grief, but Dorothy had lived her life, and had died as she would have wished to die, with none of the pain and terror she had dreaded. So I put my arms about Peter and said, "On Christmas Day I think it's all right for you to relax and enjoy being with so many people you love, and to help us all make it a happy day for Léna and Charlotte." Peter is very fond of his two little Anglican nieces, and his misconceptions of Christianity had by and large disappeared. He agreed willingly.

Was that advice to a bereaved son all right? Is it proper to grieve and rejoice simultaneously?

If the love I define in my own heart as Christian love means anything at all; yes. If the birth of Christ as Jesus of Nazareth means anything at all; yes.

I don't think any of us will ever forget that Christmas Eve. We sat around the apartment in the morning drinking coffee and waiting for time to go to the funeral parlor.

I have an inordinate dread of funeral parlors. A horror of great darkness falls on me, and I feel further from home than did Abraham; I no longer even know where home is. In a funeral-parlor service I feel dragged into an ultimate pit of darkness. This is an irrational reaction, but I am convinced that the undertakers' lobby is personally led by Satan, who has as chief helpers a group of priests, rabbis, and ministers.

I didn't mention my dread. Instead, I dressed in my most elegant black, and wore high-heeled black pumps in order to please Peter and Maria. Then it was time to go to the funeral parlor with Alan and Josephine. Alan had got out of a sickbed and looked pale and half ill; he had a bad sore throat and he was to preach the midnight Christmas Eve service at St. Paul's Chapel.

Peter's family, sisters, aunts, uncles, cousins, started arriving. The rabbi spent half an hour with Peter and his sisters before the service, while the rest of us chatted in the desultory and fragmentary way of such places.

I felt cold and isolated from reality during the service, which the rabbi conducted with as much dignity as possible, given the setting. Then we got into funeral cars to drive to the cemetery in New Jersey. The rabbi couldn't come, but the cantor did, and Alan was to say the prayers for the dead at the graveside.

The traffic was heavy and we crawled slowly through a chill grey day. When we finally reached the cemetery I was appalled to see a carpet of fake green grass carefully covering the good earth which had been dug to make Dorothy's grave. This isn't a Jewish custom; the phony green is seen in Christian cemeteries, too, trying to conceal the reality of dust to dust. It is a travesty of truth and only makes death more brutal. What it is covering is earth, clean earth, real earth, which is going to cover the coffin. Grass will grow out of it again, and it will be real grass, not plastic.

If the Word coming to dwell in human flesh means anything, it means that Dorothy's flesh is real flesh, that it will now decay; it must be buried, as the seed is buried, before the flower, the plant, the tree, the true flesh, can be born.

We stood in a small circle around the grave while the cantor and Alan recited the service. When it came to the Kaddish—the beautiful Hebrew prayer for the dead—Alan was able to read and recite it in Hebrew. These rich, extraordinarily beautiful syllables moved me to the heart and were, for me, the reality of this other mother's funeral.

When we got back to the city it was time for me to dash down to the seminary, pick up my little grandaughters, and bring them all the way back uptown for the blessing of the crib at the convent of the Sisters of the Community of the Holy Spirit, who run the school where they were in kindergarten, and from which their mother was graduated.

The chapel is small, and in this smallness, holding Charlotte in my arms, with Léna leaning against me, I began to move into Christmas. The Sisters sang Solemn Vespers for Christmas Eve, and their high, clear voices, moving antiphonally back and forth across the chapel, contained for me the same reality I felt in the strong words of the

Kaddish. Then we all gathered round the crèche, the children on tiptoe to see the shepherds, the animals, Mary and Joseph and the infant in the crib, the helpless thing containing the brilliance of the galaxies and the shadow of the cross.

It was impossible, but for the moment I was the White Queen, and the loving and beautiful bodies of my grandaughters made it possible for me to believe: they have not been created to be discarded like dross; the baby lying between the ox and ass affirms the ultimate value of all life.

After the blessing of the crib there was a party: hot cider and cookies and homemade lemon bread. I had to hurry the little girls into their snowsuits and away from this warmth of love and laughter, and then we almost ran home so that I could cook dinner quickly, and once again it was all the way back downtown to the seminary, where Hugh baby-sat so that the rest of us could go to St. Paul's. Peter spent the evening with his sisters, but Maria came with us to church.

And there, in the peace and quiet, Christmas came into even clearer focus for me. We were very early because of Alan, and it was a strangely solemn joy for me to sit there in silence in the beautiful gold and white church where George Washington came to pray after his Inauguration.

The service began with a concert of chamber music, played on ancient instruments. I closed my eyes as the music wove gently about me. My thoughts wove along with the loveliness of sound. I was sitting between my two daughters in an extraordinary clarity of love, having buried so short a time ago the mortal remains of another mother who had beheld with joy her first-born babe. And the memory was vivid that two thousand years ago a young girl bore a child as helpless as any child, a child who would show us that the greatest power is in weakness, the greatest majesty in meekness, a child whose growing up was then, and always will be, out of tune with the tenor of the times.

The birth of my own babies (every woman's Christmas) shows me that the power which staggers with its splendor is a power of love, particular love. Surely it takes no more creative concentration to make a galaxy than a baby. And surely the greatest strength of all is this loving willingness to be weak, to share, to give utterly.

Oh, yes, according to Scripture the Lord throws a few thunderbolts when he is angry, but by now we must have angered him so much that it's a wonder he hasn't wiped us out entirely, at least on this recalcitrant planet. We are surely one of his failures. He loved us enough to come to us, and we didn't want him, and this incredible visit ended in total failure, and this failure gives me cause to question all failure, and all success.

And even after failure he continues to be concerned for us. We can, if we will, recognize him as he is manifested in love, total, giving love. And I believe that in one way or another we are all meant to receive him as Mary did.

The church is quiet. There is no room for sentimentality here after Dorothy's funeral in the sterile atmosphere of the mortuary. It would be easy now for me to close off, to say no, no, to the pain. But the name of the pain is love, love so great that it was willing to share and redeem our living and dying. It was a very small gift that God gave us for Christmas two thousand years ago: only a baby: only himself.

In the funeral parlor that morning I had been alienated from myself in cold and darkness; now I was thrown into myself in a loveliness of light.

When Alan got up into the white and gold pulpit to preach, his voice was hoarse—it was the beginning of an abcess on his tonsils—but his words were clear and part of the light; and the meaning of the Word made flesh was itself the light.

As we got back to the seminary we sat down to relax and have a drink together, and Hugh said that when he had been putting the children to bed Léna had turned to him and said, "You know, Gum, sometimes I forget to tell you how much I love you, but I do."

And that, too, was Christmas.

> *This is the irrational season*
> *When love blooms bright and wild.*
> *Had Mary been filled with reason*
> *There'd have been no room for the child.*

3... Rachel Weeping

THE DAYS BETWEEN Christmas and Epiphany slide by too quickly. We eat turkey sandwiches and cold stuffing—almost the best part of the turkey. The living room is full of the fragrance of the tree.

Every day is a festival. The twenty-sixth is St. Stephen's Day (I find it impossible to think of Stephen as someone who wasn't quite bright enough to go on beyond the diaconate and make it to the priesthood). The twenty-seventh is the feast of St. John, John who speaks most closely to my understanding, who helps put the mind in the heart to bring wholeness.

And on the twenty-eighth of December, Holy Innocents' Day. Holy Innocents' Day is a stumbling block for me. This is a festival? this remembering the slaughter of all those babies under two years of age whose only wrong was to have been born at a time when three Wise Men came out of the East to worship a great King; and Herod, in panic lest his earthly power be taken away from him by this unknown infant potentate, ordered the execution of all the children who might grow up to dethrone him.

Jesus grew up to heal and preach at the expense of all those little ones, and I have sometimes wondered if his loving gentleness with small children may not have had something to do with this incredible price. And it causes me to ask painful questions about the love of God.

St. Catherine of Siena said, "Nails were not enough to hold God-and-man nailed and fastened on the cross, had not love kept him there."

What kind of love was that? More like folly. All the disciples except John had abandoned him. His mother was there and a few women as usual, and a gaping mob, also as usual, and some jeering soldiers. That's all. The cross represented the failure of his earthly mission. God came to the world and the world didn't want him and threw him out by crucifying him like a common criminal. God—God the Father —loved the world he had created so much that he sent his only son —that spoken Word who called forth something from nothing, galaxies from chaos—he sent him to dwell in human flesh, to accept all earthly limitations, to confine himself in mortal time; and when this beloved son begged in agony that he might be spared the cross, what did the Father do? No thunderbolts, no lightning flash. Silence was the answer to the prayer. NO was the answer. And Jesus of Nazareth died in agony on the cross; the love of God echoing back into the silence of God.

That is love? How can we understand it? Do we even want it?

I sometimes get very angry at God, and I do not feel guilty about it, because the anger is an affirmation of faith. You cannot get angry at someone who is not there. So the raging is for me a necessary step toward accepting that God's way of loving is more real than man's, that this irrational, seemingly unsuccessful love is what it's all about, is what created the galaxies, is what keeps the stars in their courses, is what gives all life value and meaning.

But what kind of meaning? It's not a meaning that makes any sense in a world geared to success and self-fulfillment.

Remember the children in the school bus hit by a train? Remember the Vietnamese orphans dying in a flaming plane? What about all the holy innocents throughout time? It was this extraordinary God of love who personally killed all the first-born of the Egyptians in order to belabor a point which surely should have been obvious long before.

First God changed the waters of the Egyptians' river into blood; then he sent a plague of frogs which weakened Pharaoh's nerve considerably so that he almost let Moses and the Israelites go; then God sent mosquitoes against the Egyptians, and then gadflies, and then he killed all the Egyptians' livestock, but spared the beasts of the children of Israel. Then God sent boils to torment the Egyptians, and Pharaoh said, "Go ahead, leave in safety," and God, mind you, God, hardened Pharaoh's heart so that he changed his mind and would not let the people go.

The boils were followed by hail, and Pharaoh begged Moses to stop the thunder and hail and he would let them go, and God stopped the storm and then he hardened Pharaoh's heart again. And this kept right on. Next God sent locusts, and next he blotted out the light of the sun and sent darkness over the Egyptians, and whenever Pharaoh was ready to let the children of Israel go, God hardened his heart again, so that God could send one more horrible plague, and the worst of these was the death of the first-born children of the Egyptians, and these children were no more sinful or guilty than the children in the school bus or in the huge plane or the children under two years of age slaughtered by Herod.

Only a story? But there is no better way to search for the truth of history than to look in poetry and story.

This story really bothers me. I struggle with it.

Sometimes in this groping dark of knowing my not-knowing
I am exhausted with the struggle to believe in you, O God.
Your ways are not our ways. You sent evil angels to the Egyptians
and killed countless babies in order that Pharaoh—
whose heart was hardened by you (that worries me, Lord)
might be slow to let the Hebrew children go.
You turned back the waters of the Red Sea
and your Chosen People went through on dry land
and the Egyptians were drowned, men with wives and children,
young men with mothers and fathers (your ways are not our ways),
and there was much rejoicing, and the angels laughed and sang
and you stopped them, saying, "How can you laugh
when my children are drowning?"

When your people reached Mount Sinai you warned Moses
not to let any of them near you lest you break forth and kill them.
You are love—if you are God—and you command us to love,
and yet you yourself turn men to evil, and you wipe out nations
with one sweep of the hand—the Amorites and the Hittites and the
Perizzites—
gone, gone, all gone. Sometimes it seems that any means will do.
And yet—all these things are but stories told about you by fallen man,
and they are part of the story—for your ways are not our ways—
but they are not the whole story. You are our author,
and we try to listen and set down what you say, but we all suffer
from faulty hearing and we get the words wrong.

One small enormous thing: you came to us as one of us
and lived with us and died for us and descended into hell for us

and burst out into life for us—:
and now do you hold Pharaoh in your arms?

The love of God reveals itself in extraordinary ways. What kind of love kept him nailed to the cross? What kind of a Father did Jesus of Nazareth have?

Are we too intellectual and too reasonable to understand? Jesus said, "I bless you, Father, Lord of Heaven and earth, for hiding these things from the learned and the clever and revealing them to mere children."

We're a learned and clever generation, we of the late twentieth century. Those of us with the heritage of the Anglican Communion are a learned and clever group of people. Did those first-born of the Egyptians, those Holy Innocents in Bethlehem, those Vietnamese orphans in the flaming plane know something that God is deliberately hiding from us? Why would a God of love do such things, permit such things? What does all this teach us about how we are to love one another?

For some time my husband played the father in *The Diary of Anne Frank*, the father who was the only one of the group of people hiding from the Nazis in an attic in Amsterdam who survived concentration camp. One evening while they were still in hiding, they heard a terrible crash downstairs, and they thought the Nazis had found them, and they held their breaths in terror. Nothing. Silence.

So the father goes downstairs to investigate, and they all know that he may never come back. While they are in an agony of waiting, the mother drops to her knees and says the 121st Psalm: *I will lift up mine eyes unto the hills. . . .* She says it all, all those comforting words: *The Lord shall preserve thy going out, and thy coming in, from this time forth and even forevermore.* But the Lord didn't preserve them. He let the Nazis find them and send them to concentration camp and they all died there except the father, a whole group of innocent people guilty of nothing except being chosen of God. The mother who had cried for help died. Anne, the innocent child, died. God, the God they trusted, let it happen. In human terms it would seem evident that the love and faith of the mother who cried out for help was far greater than the love of God.

Do I want this kind of God? Until I saw my husband in *The Diary of Anne Frank*—and I saw it several times—the 121st Psalm used to be strong and comforting to me. Now I say it daily with a kind of terror. Hugh's performance in that play brought about a crisis in my understanding of the love of God, and the saying of the Psalm is a cry in the dark that I still affirm that God's love is more real than mine.

For men make the cozy and comfy promises; not God.

Yes, but how can a God of love stand by and let Anne Frank die, and all the holy innocents in the children's leukemia wards and in rat-infested tenements? Why doesn't he stop the slaughter? If he's God, he can do anything. What kind of love is this?

Okay, Madeleine, but if God interferes every time we do wrong, where's our free will?

But Anne Frank didn't do wrong.

But the Nazis did. When they built concentration camps that was a very big wrong and a lot of innocent people suffered. But it was man who did the wrong, not God.

But he could have stopped it.

And if he did? Do I want to adore a God who allows me no free will, and therefore no potential for either evil or good? Do I want a cosmic dictator, ruling a closed, finished cosmos?

Sometimes when I think of our battlefields and slums and insane asylums, I'm not sure, and I ask: why does God treat in such a peculiar way the creatures he loves so much that he sent his own Son to them?

And what about that son whose love kept him on the cross?

Deep in our hearts most of us really wish that Jesus hadn't resisted the temptations; if he had only been a reasonable son of man and turned those stones into bread, then all the poor of the earth could be fed and we wouldn't have inner cities or ghettos in this country, or children with bloated bellies dying of starvation in India or Cambodia or Venezuela. If he had only come down from the cross in a blaze of power, then we wouldn't have any trouble understanding the Resurrection—why did he have to be so *quiet* about it?—and we wouldn't be afraid of death. If he had only worshipped the prince of this world, he could have ruled and ordered the earth, and legislated our lives so that we needn't make decisions, and he could have taken away all pain (there is no coming to life without pain) and organized our old age so that we could be senior citizens in some happy home, going on happy buses for happy excursions. . . . Our churches and government agencies think that this kind of manipulation is a good thing, and so they're trying to do it themselves, since Jesus failed to take the opportunity offered him.

Why, why did he turn it down?

All those innocent little children . . .

All the hungry . . .

All the old men and women struggling to live alone and being mugged as they bring in their inadequate groceries (we see it on television every night), little girls raped and murdered, little boys mutilated . . .

cancer and blindness and senility . . .

battlefields and slums and insane asylums . . .

He could have stopped it all if only he'd listened to Satan in the wilderness. What kind of love is he teaching us? And who are we in the Church listening to? The tempter, or the one who put the temptations behind him? Oh, he healed a few blind people and lepers, but certainly not all, and he drove out a few unclean spirits, but not all, and he announced that the poor will be always with us.

No wonder the Church often thinks that he was wrong and turns, with ardent social activism, to the promises of Satan. But why hasn't the social activism worked? It ought to have worked. But the social activism of the sixties has, after all, produced the seventies, which are galloping to their anguished end. Have we, then, failed—because we've fed only a few starving children, rescued only a few war orphans, taken care, like Mother Thersa of Calcutta, of only a few indigent dying people?

And who is this Church I keep referring to? It is not limited to my own denomination, or even the Anglican Communion. When I talk of the Church I mean all of us—Episcopalians, Presbyterians, Lutherans, Baptists, Methodists, all, all of the denominations and all of the sects, all who in any organized way call themselves Christians.

St. Paul said, "I was given a thorn in the flesh, an angel of Satan to beat me and stop me from getting too proud. About this thing, I have pleaded with the Lord three times for it to leave me, but he has said, 'My grace is enough for you: my power is at its best in weakness.'"

And there, for me, is a clue, another tiny piece in the incomprehensible puzzle. Man's pride and God's weakness. And if this is to make any sense to me at all, it must be in terms of my own experience, not what I read about, see on television, but what touches me personally.

Of course, that's what this book is about. It may be a small and inadequate response of experience, but it's my own. My profession is writing—stories, novels, fantasy, poetry, thoughts. Writing is not just my job, but a vocation, a total commitment. I started to write when I was five, and as I look back on fifty years of this work, I am forced to accept that my best work has been born from pain; I am forced to see that my own continuing development involves pain. It is pain and weakness and constant failures which keep me from pride and help me to grow. The power of God *is* to be found in weakness, but it is God's power.

He has a strange way of loving; it is not man's way, but I find evidence in my own experience that it is better than man's way, and that it leads to fuller life, and to extraordinary joy.

Nails were not enough to hold God-and-man nailed to the cross had not love kept him there.

Because I am a writer I live by symbol, and because I was born in the Western World my symbolism is largely Judaeo-Christian, and I find it valid, and the symbol which gives me most strength is that of bread and wine. Through the darkness of my uncomprehending, through my pain and weakness, only thus may I try to become open to God's love as I move to the altar to receive the body and blood, and accept with friend and neighbor, foe and stranger, the tangible assurance that this love is real.

It is real, but it is not like our love.

I keep thinking about those Holy Innocents, all those little ones who died that Jesus might live.

And one night I woke up thinking about the nobleman from Capernaum whose son Jesus saved from death, and I wondered if perhaps this man's first-born son might not have been one of the slaughtered little ones, and the memory of that death would stay with him as long as he lived, even if he became a very old man. . . .

. . . And The Old Man Became As a Little Child . . .

He could not sleep.
The tomb was dark, and the stone heavy that sealed it.
He could not sleep for all the innocent blood he had seen shed.
He was an old man. Too old for tears.
Not yet young enough for sleep. He waited and watched.

Thrice he had spoken to him whose body had been sealed
within the tomb, thrice had the old man spoken,
he who was a disciple, but not one of the twelve,
older, gentler in all ways,
and tired, worn with time and experience and the shedding of blood.
He came from Capernaum
and after that his son
who touched the edge of death
was drawn back from the pit
and made whole,
the old man returned to Jesus and said,
"O thou, who hast today been the consolation of my household,
wast also its desolation.
Because of you my first-born died
in that great shedding of innocent blood.
Nevertheless, I believe
though I know not what
or how or why
for it has not been revealed to me.
I only know that one manchild was slain
and one made to live."

And a second time he spoke
when the Lord kept the children beside him
and suffered them not to be taken away:
"These are the ones that are left us,
but where, Lord, is the Kingdom of Heaven?
Where, Lord, are the others?
What of them? What of them?"
And he wept.

And a third time he spoke
when the Lord turned to Jerusalem
and laughter turned to steel
and he moved gravely
towards the hour that was prepared
and the bitterness of the cup:
then the old man said,
"All your years you have lived

under the burden of their blood.
Their life was the price of yours.
Have you borne the knowledge and the cost?
During those times
when you have gone silent in the midst of laughter
have you remembered all the innocence
slaughtered that you might be with us now?
When you have gone up into the mountain apart to pray,
have you remembered that their lives were cut down
for your life, and so ours?
Rachel's screams still shatter the silence
and I cannot sleep at night for remembering.
Do you ever forget your children that sleep?
When will you bring them out of the sides of the earth
and show mercy unto them?
Who will embrace them until you come?
I cannot sleep.
But because I have already tasted of the cup
I cannot turn from you now.
I, who live, praise you.
Can those who have gone before you into the pit
celebrate you or hope for your truth?
Tell me, tell me, for I am an old man
and lost in the dark cloud of my ignorance.
Nevertheless, blessed is he
whom thou hast chosen and taken, O Lord."

He did not speak again.

But he was there when the rocks were rent
the veil of the temple torn in twain
the sun blackened by clouds
the earth quaked with darkness

the sky was white and utterly empty.
The city gaped with loss.

Then, out of the silence,
the Lord went
bearing the marks of nails and spear
moving swiftly through the darkness
into the yawning night of the pit.
There he sought first
not as one might have supposed
for Moses or Elias
but for the children
who had been waiting for him.

So, seeking, he was met
by the three Holy Children
the Young Men
burning bright
transforming the fire into dew as they cried:
"Blessed art thou, O Lord God, forevermore."

And all the children came running
and offering to him their blood
and singing: "With sevenfold heat
did the Chaldean tyrant in his rage
cause the furnace to be heated
for the Godly Ones
who wiped our blood like tears
when we were thrust here
lost and unknowing.
The Holy Three
waited here to receive us
and to teach us to sing your coming
forasmuch as thou art pitiful
and lovest mankind."
So they held his hand
and gave him their kisses and their blood
and, laughing, led him by the dragon
who could not bear their innocence
and thrashed with his tail
so that the pit trembled with his rage.
But even his roaring could not drown their song:
"For unto Thee are due all glory, honor, and worship,
with the Father and the Holy Spirit, now, and ever,
and unto ages of ages, Amen."

And the holy children were round about him,
the Holy Innocents and the Holy Three.
They walked through the darkness of the fiery furnace
and the dragon could see their brightness,
yea, he saw four walkers loose
walking in the midst of the fire and having no hurt
and the form of the fourth was like the Son of God.

And he saw the Son of God move through hell
and he heard the Holy Children sing:
"Meet is it that we should magnify thee,
the life-giver
who has stretched out thy hands upon the cross
and hast shattered the dominion of the enemy.
Blessed art thou, O Lord God, forevermore.

> *O Jesus, God and Saviour,*
> *who didst take upon thee Adam's sin*
> *and didst taste of death*
> *(the cup was bitter),*
> *thou hast come again to Adam*
> *O compassionate One*
> *for thou only art good*
> *and lovest mankind,*
> *Blessed art thou, O Lord God, forevermore."*
>
> *So hell was shriven*
> *while the holy children, singing,*
> *transformed the flames to dew,*
> *and the gates of Heaven opened.*
>
> *Then, by the empty tomb,*
> *the old man slept.*

If the dark prophets who infuriated the people of the Establishment in their own day have anything to say to me today, it is through their constant emphasizing that God is so free of his own creation that he can transform us in our pain into a community of people who are able to be free of the very establishments which are formed in his name. For these establishments inevitably begin to institutionalize God's love and then he teaches us (put my tears in your bottle) what love really is—not our love, not what we want God's love to be, but God's love.

4... To a Long-Loved Love

WHEN I WAS a little girl in France I put out my shoes on the Eve of Epiphany. They were only ordinary shoes, not proper sabots, so I wasn't sure that they would be noticed by the three Wise Men; but in the morning one shoe held a new drawing pad, and the other a box of colored pencils. I like the idea of presents and feasting on Twelfth Night, so that Christmas can follow quietly on Advent. Christmas doesn't start until Christmas Eve, and then it can go on and on and the tree shines as brightly on Epiphany as on Christmas Day.

And there's more time to make things, which is one of the joys of Christmas. Our favorite presents are the homemade ones. Several years ago we decided that we were not going to be bullied by the post office or the Greeting Card Establishment into mailing our cards well before Christmas. We make our own cards, and I may not get an idea for one well before Christmas, for one thing. And there are a goodly number of people we write to only once a year, tucking the letter in with the card. So for the past several years we've taken our time, and as long as the last Christmas letter gets mailed before Lent, that's all I worry about, and Epiphany is a season of joy instead of exhaustion.

EPIPHANY

Unclench your fists
Hold our your hands.
Take mine.
Let us hold each other.
Thus is his Glory
Manifest.

Epiphany is a special time to me in another and extra-special way, because Hugh and I were married during the Epiphany season, thirty years ago, and my wedding anniversary is part of my personal calendar of the Church year. My attitude toward the promises Hugh and I made is a fundamental part of my theology of failure, and the freedom and laughter and joy which this brings.

During Advent, when I contemplate the four last things, I think not only of the end of all time and matter, but of my own end, Hugh's end. A friend of mine said that when two people truly love each other, each one has to be willing to let the other die first. I try to be willing, but it's not easy.

And it's not part of the American atmosphere where the amoeba, rather than the human being, would be the logical symbol of success. Amoebas never betray each other by dying. Nor is there any sexism in the amoeba's culture—though this may be because there isn't any sex. The amoeba produces by dividing and subdividing, which doesn't sound like much fun.

However, fun or no fun, the amoeba is a success—and when I consider the world's definition of success, I doubt if there's ever much fun involved. But the amoeba is way ahead of the human being, because it is immortal. It has no normal life span. Unless killed by some unforeseen accident, the amoeba lives forever.

Radio and television commercials seem directed more to the amoeba than to the human being, especially those for life insurance, where the announcer says, ". . . but in case something should happen to you . . ."

It strikes me forcefully as I listen to those unctuous words that something is indeed going to happen to me, and to that announcer, and to everybody who buys or does not buy insurance. We are going to die. We have a life span, and sooner or later, by accident or disease or attrition, we are going to come to the end of our mortal lives.

Why do we have a life span instead of being like the amoeba? Because of sex. It wasn't until it took two members of a species to produce offspring that a life span came into the evolutionary system. Sex and death came into the world simultaneously. All creatures with a complicated cellular system have a life span: it may be a few days, a few years, or threescore years and ten.

Obviously we are all failures, we human beings. We may have fun, but we're flops. But maybe I'm happy because I *am* a failure, a human failure who enjoys sex, has a limited life span, and who made marriage vows which have added both to the fun and the failure. I wish the American marriage service had not deleted the words of the English service, where the man says to the woman, "With my body I thee worship," because I think the basic difference between Christian and secular marriage is that Christian marriage affirms the pleasures of the body, of creation. Too many people would like to forget that Jesus's first miracle was turning water into wine at a marriage feast, in a glorious affirmation of human love, human joy, human pain. Wine is a word which has meaning upon meaning for the Christian: water into wine; the baptism of water and blood; and it is only when I think of the wedding at Cana that I come close to understanding the words of the ancient prayer: *Blood of Christ inebriate me.* At the Eucharist I pray that our souls may be washed in this precious blood, and that it will preserve our souls and bodies into everlasting life. These are terrible prayers, and it is small wonder that so many of us are afraid to say them, and that many of the new translations try to water them down.

I was taken aback to have a well-known liberal theologian say that he wished that people would not think of sex in terms of morals, and I replied that I had never thought of sex and morals in conjunction, and he said, "You're very lucky. Most people still think that sex is not very nice." What a strange, revealing remark, and what a totally un-Christian point of view. And yet I think that it is often a factor in the breakup of a marriage.

A year ago on our anniversary I had occasion to take a taxi, and the driver and I got to talking, and we talked about marriage, and I said that it was pretty much of a record for a writer and an actor to have been married for twenty-nine years. He turned completely around, disregarding the traffic and the snowy streets, and said, "Lady, that's not a record. That's a miracle."

He's probably right. It's an extraordinary thing to me that Hugh and I have been married for this long. It is also, I believe, a good marriage, although much of it would not seem to be so in terms of the kind of success commercials would hold out to us. However, our own expectations of marriage were false to start out with. Neither of us knew the person we had promised to live with for the rest of our lives. The first bitter lessons of marriage consisted in learning to love the person we had actually married, instead of the image we wanted to have married.

I was twenty-seven. I had been living in Greenwich Village and working in the theatre. I had made a lot of mistakes and failures in love already, and had learned that structure and discipline were essential in my life if I wanted the freedom to write. Shortly before I met Hugh, I had painfully but totally cut loose from an undisciplined group of friends, and I assumed that the kind of pattern needed in my single writing life would also be essential to my married writing life. I was too involved in the ecstasy of love to think much about the inevitable conflicts ahead, and I don't think it would have made any difference if I had been aware of them. I don't ever remember living without conflict of one kind or another, and I'm not at all convinced that life without conflict is desirable. There's not much conflict in the grave, but while we're alive the only creative choice is choice of conflict.

I realize how fortunate I was in the terms with which I started my marriage; I had had one novel published; the second was already in galleys; I had made a good start as a professional writer. When Hugh asked me to marry him, and talked about children, I said that I, too, wanted children, but that he had to understand that I could not stop writing, that he was marrying me as a writer, marrying all of me, not just the part of me which would bear his children. And I rather naïvely told him that writing takes a lot of time, and that I would be glad to do the cooking but he'd have to do the dishes.

The division hasn't been that straight down the line, but we've always shared household chores, and we have also shared the nurture of our babies. Hugh showed a generosity and understanding as rare then as it is now when he accepted me on these terms, and never expected me to be only an appendage, an *et ux.* I have never had to struggle against my husband to be me. This doesn't mean that we haven't had struggles and conflicts in our marriage—we have—but they have been in different areas.

It is the nature of love to create, and Hugh and I did want to make babies together. In my conception of love, something always has to be created during the act of intercourse, but this something may be simply a strengthening of love, a love which is participation, not possession. Daniel Day Williams, in *The Spirit and the Forms of Love,* was the one to bring to my attention the idea of love which is participatory, and not long after I had read this book I was able to talk with him about it, and was taught even more. Just as our friendship was a'birthing he died, and I look forward to learning more from him in heaven.

Too often, love is seen in terms of possession, and this destroys marriage. Until Hugh and I started our first baby, our love-making was a discovery of each other, was creating this strange new creature, a marriage.

I'm glad that I'm a human mother, and not a sea horse; the sea horse might well be a symbol for the more extreme branches of women's lib, because the female sea horse lays her eggs in the male's pouch, and then he has to carry the eggs to term, go through labor pains, and bear the babies.

I don't understand why some women consider childbearing a humiliation; it's an extraordinary act of creativity, and men suffer a great deprivation in being barred by their very nature from this most creative of all experiences. But there's a price on it, as with all good things, especially for a woman who feels called to do something as well as being wife and mother.

I actively enjoyed the whole magnificent process of having children, the amazing months of pregnancy when suddenly one becomes aware that one is carrying life, that a new human being is being created. While I was carrying Josephine, our first-born, I felt quickening while I was in an eye-and-ear hospital with a recurring eye problem; a young nurse happened to come into my room as I felt the first small flutterings, and I cried, "I think I feel the baby!" She ran to the bed and put her hand on my belly, and her joy in feeling the new life was almost as great as my own. From then on, there was a lovely procession of nurses and doctors coming to feel the baby; the quickening of new life is something which doesn't often happen in an eye-and-ear hospital.

I find the birthing of babies even more fantastic. And here I feel profoundly that the husband should be given the privilege of being with his wife during the birth, that he should not be excluded. This didn't happen with Hugh and me until our son, Bion, was born in a small New England village, and delivered by an old-fashioned general practitioner. Hugh was with me to rub my back during pains, to hold my hand, suddenly to see the crowning of his son. Our first baby was born in a big New York hospital, delivered by an eminent obstetrician, and I spent hours left alone and in pain and afraid. It's enough to make the whole process seem degrading.

And nursing: I loved nursing my babies, but when Josephine was born, nursing was not yet popular again in New York City; it's more trouble for the nurses, and I had to fight for the right to nurse my baby: "But nobody nurses babies nowadays." "I do."

My husband's theatre hours are definitely not nine to five. I had seen other young wives up at six with the baby, and unable to manage to be awake and ready to listen and talk when their husbands got home from the theatre, and I was determined that this was not going to happen with us. Our baby was a strong, healthy specimen, so, while I was still in the hospital, the head nurse told me that they had decided that the baby didn't need the 2 A.M. feeding and they were going to cut it out. "But my husband's an actor and we're up at 2 A.M. Let's cut the 6 A.M. feeding." This wasn't hospital procedure at all, and I had my first hospital fight to be a human being and not a cog in routine. I was told in no uncertain terms that it was the 2 A.M. feeding which would be cut. I replied in equally certain terms that if my baby was brought to me at 6 A.M. I would turn my breasts to the wall. I won.

I had made a choice, a free yet structured choice. Why should a man come home at all if his wife isn't awake and available? I had seen other actors go to the local bar instead of coming home to a dark apartment. This choosing the structure of our day was not being an unliberated woman. I chose it for my own pleasure, too; I enjoyed this time with my husband; it was no sacrifice. And I profoundly disbelieve in the child-centered household. What happens to the parents when it is time for the children to leave the nest if all of life has been focused on the fledglings?

We had such fun with Josephine that we wanted more children, and this was when Hugh decided to leave the theatre—it didn't seem fair to our children to have two parents in precarious professions. But I don't think that either of us realized what this complete uprooting was going to involve. I know that I had a glamorous and completely unrealistic vision of life in the country, based on romantic English poetry, and my illusions were shattered in short order.

In refusing to nurse my baby at 6 A.M. I was already moving toward what is now called 'choosing an alternative life style.' And when Hugh and I left New York and the theatre to continue raising our growing family, and went to live in a small village in New England, and ran a general store, we did what was later to be called 'downgrading'—though we certainly didn't think of it as such. Nor was it.

When the children were little I was often on edge with sheer frustration. I was trying to run a big two-hundred-year-old house with no help; for three hours a day I helped my husband in the store—my shift was from noon to three in the afternoon, so that he could go home for lunch and a nap. Two of our best-sellers were teat dilators and bag balm—these are for cows; over half our customers were farmers, many of whom are still our good friends.

Writing was not easy during those years. I struggled to write under the worst possible conditions, after the children were in bed, often falling asleep at my desk. During the early school years Hugh got up with the children in the morning, so that I could sleep a little later in order to be able to write at night, and without that understanding help I don't think I could have managed. Even so, it was not easy, particularly when I ventured into new ways of writing. So I was prickly and defensive, because during the near-decade we lived year-round in the country, almost nothing I wrote sold, and rejection slips for work you believe in are bitter indeed.

I know that I'm a better writer now because of the conflict and frustration of those years, and some of that conflict was in our marriage, and I don't minimize any of the pain.

During the years of Hugh's leaving the theatre forever—thank God forever lasted only nine years—our time together, alone, was the hour before dinner, when we sat in front of the fire and had a quiet drink and talked. At dinnertime we were the whole family, gathered around the table, but the hour before dinner was our quiet hour, our grownup hour, and I do not think that the children felt rejected because of it. But it was a choice, a deliberate choice, and it was part of the structure of the day.

Even if we had had money for servants, I don't think I would have wanted anybody else to have brought up our children; I was an only child and for many reasons I did not see a great deal of my parents when I was very young, and this may explain my feelings. But children and store meant that if I were to hope to write, something had to go—lots of things, in fact. I eliminated all kinds of housewifely virtues. Our house was tidy—I cannot write in a filthy nest—but I will never win an award as Housekeeper of the Year. I did not scrub the kitchen floor daily; commercials for various floor waxes, furniture polishes, and window-cleaning sprays go right over my head; they are not within my frame of reference or the seasons of my heart. It is more important that I have at least an hour a day to read and study; that I walk at least a couple of miles a day with the dog—this is thinking and praying time; that I have an hour a day at the piano. Practicing the piano, rather than just playing at it, got eliminated with the advent of our third child; I'm only now properly getting back to it, and playing the piano is one of the best consciousness and memory expanders there is.

I'm asked with increasing frequency, "But why marry?" a question to be taken seriously, especially when it comes from young people who have seen their parents' marriages end in divorce, or in constant bickering and hostility, which is almost worse. The desire to make sure that there is integrity in love, that neither partner wants to use or manipulate the other, is a healthy one. But ultimately there comes a moment when a decision must be made. Ultimately two people who love each other must ask themselves how much they hope for as their love grows and deepens, and how much risk they are willing to take.

I'm glad that I was twenty-seven when Hugh and I married. As I look back on the men I might have married, I shudder. I needed the time not only to wait to meet the man who was to become my husband, but to do enough growing up so that I was a mature enough human being to enter into the depths of a lifelong partnership. I matured slowly, and I know that I was not adult enough before I met Hugh—and hardly, then.

After all these years I am just beginning to understand the freedom that making a solemn vow before God, making a lifelong commitment to one person, gives each of us. Thirty years ago on a cold morning in January—very cold, it was 18° below zero—when Hugh and I made those vows, we were deliberately, if not very consciously, leaving youth and taking the risk of adulthood and a permanent partnership. It is indeed a fearful gamble. When I looked into the future I knew that there would be more than glorious nights, longed-for babies, someone to come home to. I knew that an actor and a writer are a poor risk. But we had committed ourselves, before a God neither of us was at all sure about, that we wouldn't quit when the going got rough. If I was not fulfilled by my relationship with this particular man, I couldn't look around for another. And vice versa. No matter how rough the going got, neither of us was going to opt out.

Because it is the nature of love to create, a marriage itself is something which has to be created, so that, together, we become a new creature. There are many glorious ways of intercourse besides the sex act, but the emphasis of this country's culture today is focused on the physical, genital act of sex, rather than love, whole love, and so we've lost a lot of these other ways of completion. The intercourse of that quiet hour in front of the fire with my husband; or walking, as we love to do, on the beach, hand touching hand, can be as electrifying as the more obvious forms of love.

To marry is the biggest risk in human relations that a person can take. All the rather pompous sociological jargon about the advisability of trial marriages or short-term relationships as part of the new freedom is in actuality a result of our rejection of freedom and our fear of risk—I had learned this through experience in the Greenwich Village years before I was twenty-seven.

There isn't much risk in a one-night stand except venereal disease, and penicillin will cope with that. The pill has almost eliminated the risk of unexpected babies, and liberal abortion laws will take care of the few surprises. In trial or short-term commitment we don't have to risk all of ourselves; we can hold back.

If we commit ourselves to one person for life this is not, as many people think, a rejection of freedom; rather, it demands the courage to move into all the risks of freedom, and the risk of love which is permanent; into that love which is not possession but participation.

And there is the risk of failure. It doesn't always work. There are marriages which for one reason or another simply do not become marriages. There are times when two people who have taken the risk have to accept the brutal fact of failure, and separation, and divorce. But, far too often, people quit simply because the going is rough, and this is almost more sad than the marriage manque.

It takes a lifetime to learn another person. After all these years I still do not understand Hugh; and he certainly does not understand me. We're still in the risky process of offering ourselves to each other, and there continue to be times when this is not easy, when the timing isn't right, when we hurt each other. It takes a lifetime to learn all the varied ways of love, including intercourse. Love-making is like a Bach fugue; you can't go to the piano and play a fugue the first time you hold your hands out over the keys.

When love is not possession, but participation, then it is part of that co-creation which is our human calling, and which implies such risk that it is often rejected.

John of Kronstadt, a Russian priest of the nineteenth century, counseled his penitents to take their sins of omission and commission, when they get too heavy, and hang them on the cross. I find this extremely helpful, and particularly during the summer when the larger family gathers together and I often cook for a minimum of twelve. We had four summers when we were four generations under one roof—something unusual in this day of small, nuclear families, and something which calls for enormous acceptance and humor from everybody. Sometimes when I hang on the cross something which is too heavy for me, I think of it as being rather like the laundry lines under our apple trees, when I have changed all the sheets in the house. The wind blows through them, the sun shines on them, and when I fold them and bring them in in the evening they smell clean and pure.

If I could not hang my sins on the cross I might tend to withdraw, to refuse responsibility because I might fail. If I could not hang my sins on the cross, Hugh and I probably wouldn't still be married. And I would certainly never write a book.

When Hugh criticizes my writing, no matter how just the criticism, I fight him. He has learned that if he makes a criticism and I say calmly, "Thank you, I see what you mean," then I have no intention of doing anything about it. But when—as usually happens—I defend the work hotly, when I lose my temper, when I accuse him of wanting to "just cut it all," he knows that I have taken what he has said seriously, and that I will do something about it, even if it means six more months of hard work.

I withdraw from him completely at first, feeling abused and misunderstood. I take the dog and go for a long, furious walk. And then my subconscious creative mind—the dark side of Mercury—gets to work, and when I return I am ready to go back to the typewriter—if not to my husband. By the time I have written a few pages the knowledge that all this unwanted work is going to make for a much better book has me so excited that by dinnertime I'm ready to cook a good dinner and give Hugh a grateful kiss.

I've learned something else about family and failure and promises: when a promise is broken, the promise still remains. In one way or another, we are all unfaithful to each other, and physical unfaithfulness is not the worst kind there is. We do break our most solemn promises, and sometimes we break them when we don't even realize it. If a marriage has to be the pearly-pink perfection suggested by commercials for coffee or canned spaghetti sauce or laundry detergents, it is never going to work. A young woman asked me in amazement, "You mean it's all right to quarrel after you're married?" I can look at the long years of my marriage with gratitude, and hope for many more, only when I accept our failures.

If our love for each other really is participatory, then all other human relationships nourish it; it is inclusive, never exclusive. If a friendship makes me love Hugh more, then I can trust that friendship. If it thrusts itself between us, then it should be cut out, and quickly. I've had that happen several times, so I know whereof I speak. Sometimes I have realized myself that a friendship was a destructive one. Sometimes Hugh has said, "I don't think so and so is good for you," and I've resented it, defensively, refused to do anything, and ultimately realized that he was right. It works, of course, both ways.

On the other hand, we both have rich, deep, abiding friendships which have nourished our marriage and helped it grow. Friendship has become more and more a lost art in a society which feels that in order for a relationship to be fulfilled it must end in bed. A true friendship is always amoureuse; it is part of my human sexuality; each encounter with a friend is a time of creation. I see this most clearly in my professional life. My relationship with my editor has got to be amorous. This doesn't mean sexual indulgence, though I don't think that either editor or writer can find the other physically repugnant. It does mean something happening on that non-empirical level, in the mediating band between nightside and sunside. Two editors, reading a manuscript of mine, may make exactly the same comments or suggestions, but with one of them no response whatsoever is evoked in me, whereas with the other, something happens which sets all my little writing wheels and cogs turning. It is not a matter of intellect alone, of an editor knowing what should be done to make a book better; many editors are qualified to do that. But with only a few is the spark set off in me, so that I know what must be done to make a manuscript come alive.

Not long ago the editor with whom I had done eleven books retired, and I started to work with a new one, and this was not unlike the beginning of a love affair for which I had great expectations, and in which I am rejoicing as they are fulfilled; but it is not in any way an act of unfaithfulness in my marriage, any more than is my husband's relations with the women he works with on stage and on television —not that such relations cannot be destructive; I've seen them be so —but in my definition of marriage they should be nourishing rather than devouring.

LOVERS APART

In what, love, does fidelity consist?
I will be true to you, of course.
My body's needs I can resist,
Come back to you without remorse;

And you, behind the footlight's lure,
Kissing an actress on the stage,
Will leave her presence there, I'm sure,
As I my people on the page.

And yet—I love you, darling, yet
I sat with someone at a table
And gloried in our minds that met
As sometimes strangers' minds are able

To leap the bounds of time and space
And find, in sharing wine and bread
And light in one another's face
And in the words that each has said,

An intercourse so intimate
It shook me deeply to the core.
I said good night, for it was late;
We parted at my hotel door

And I went in, turned down the bed
And took my bath and thought of you

Leaving the theatre with light tread
And going off, as you should do,

To rest, relax, and eat and talk—
And I lie there and wonder who
Will wander with you as you walk
And what you both will say and do. . . .

We may not love in emptiness;
We married in a peopled place;
The vows we made enrich and bless
The smile on every stranger's face,

And all the years that we have spent
Give me the joy that makes me able
To love and laugh with sacrament
Across a strange and distant table.

No matter where I am, you are,
We two are one and bread is broken
And laughter shared both near and far
Deepens the promises once spoken

And strengthens our fidelity
Although I cannot tell you how,
But I rejoice in mystery
And rest upon our marriage vow.

There's not as much risk of failure with an editor as in a marriage, but risk there is. A couple of times I've plunged into the risk, and the amoureuse-ness has been abortive rather than creative, and the book has never come properly to term. But the risk must be taken if the book is to be born at all. There are writers who do not need editorial help; I am not one of them. I seldom show more than the beginnings of a book before I have a complete rough draft, but then I need help. And to ask for help involves risk, and the danger of failure.

When I look back on the first years of Hugh's and my enormous risk of marriage, I marvel that we lasted. Certainly in my ignorance I did everything wrong. I drenched Hugh with my love, gave him all of me in great, overwhelming waves. I, in my turn, had a few things to put up with. However, in our naïveté we unknowingly did one thing which was right, and which I recently found superbly expressed by Rilke: "It is a question in marriage not of creating a quick community of spirit by tearing down and destroying all boundaries, but rather a good marriage is that in which each appoints the other guardian of his solitude, and shows him this confidence, the greatest in his power to bestow. A togetherness between two people is an impossibility, and where it seems . . . to exist it is a narrowing . . . which robs either one . . . or both of his fullest freedom or development."

Somehow or other, Hugh and I have managed to be guardians of each other's spaces—most of the time—and because of this the spaces between us are not chasms, but creative solitudes. When we blunder, then the spaces are horrendous and solitude turns into the most painful kind of loneliness; but then a willing acceptance can turn the loneliness back into solitude.

Marriage as defined by Madison Avenue, Hollywood, and TV, would seem to include permanance, whereas, paradoxically, Christian marriage is built on impermanence. Like everything else on this earth it will come to an end; one of us will die, and in our society we think of death as failure, as the ultimate failure. And in worldly terms it is. No wonder we tend to extol the amoeba. Live forever, amoeba. Mortal, you will die. That's cold, stark fact, and there's nothing romantic about it. Death is the enemy, the last enemy to be defeated, and it is not I—or any scientist—who will defeat it. The defeat of death was prefigured in the Resurrection, and what that means not one of us will know in terms of provable fact while we are in this life. But until we stop thinking of death as failure, we will never have either a theology of death or an understanding of Christian marriage.

Sometimes it seems that the Church has forgotten this in its rush to conform to the world. Everything is being made easy for us. Everything is permissible. Divorce and remarriage are almost as unimportant as they are in the secular world, where marriage is a legal contract made before a justice of the peace and not a covenant made before God. I understand casual divorce where the mighty and terrible promises have not been made in the sight of God. And I also understand that sometimes even when the promises are made in good faith, the marriage which follows is not marriage, never has been, or no longer is, and I am glad that the Church is looking on such marriages with more compassion than it used to in the legalistic days. But compassion is not the same thing as permissiveness, and the pendulum, as usual, has swung too far, and no one seems to notice that the sexual permissiveness in the Church hasn't made a happier people of God. Where little is demanded of the people, the pews become emptier each year. All of us, like our children, want standards upheld for us. If I am not expected to grow and deepen in faithful and chaste love, I'm less likely to be able to stand firm when the tempter comes and tells me it's really all right to go out to dinner and probably to bed with the attractive man who sits next to me on the plane; it really won't do anything to my marriage.

In a sense Hugh and I have an 'open marriage,' but it has never involved playing around and making light of our promises. I am free to leave him for a week or more to lecture at universities, to teach at writers' conferences, conduct retreats, just as he is free to go away from me for weeks at a time with a play or to make a movie. We have a theory that one reason our marriage has lasted so long is that we never eat breakfast together. Hugh likes to emerge slowly in the morning, breakfast, newspaper, crossword puzzle, shave, shower; whereas I, once I have managed the heavy athletic feat of getting my feet out of bed and onto the floor, am ready to talk. So I roll into my clothes, fill my thermos with coffee, call Timothy, and set off for the Cathedral library.

A decade ago I wasn't getting enough writing done at my bedroom desk, what with children still at home and a husband apt to be around the house during the day, so I asked Canon Tallis if it was all right if I wrote in the then almost unused library at the Cathedral. My first few weeks there were marvelously productive, and just as I came to the point where I needed to get my penned pages onto the typewriter, the young librarian got called on jury duty, and was quite upset about abandoning his post. I looked longingly at his electric typewriter and told him I'd be glad to keep the place open for him as long as I could use the typewriter. I had a blissful two weeks, and when he came back it was only briefly, and I became librarian by default. I have no training whatsoever as a librarian, but I am very happy in the beautiful paneled room which is used far more now than it was, so that I need an assistant to do the library work while I get on with my writing. I've been prolific during my years there, and have made an extraordinary number of friends.

My dog is welcome to come with me, and he stays dutifully under the desk, only his black nose showing. I have a little radio set for a classical music station, WNCN, and after the eleven o'clock news I call Hugh, briefly, just to check in. When I come home in the late afternoon I check in again, go over the mail, and then head for the piano for an hour and a half. After that we are together, and really together, for the evening, talking and having a drink while I get dinner. It is a free relationship, but it is built on promises. Like every other couple we break our promises one way or another, but we take the breaking of the promises seriously; the fact that the promise has been broken does not make us permissive about breaking it again; instead, we try to mend. We have used an extraordinary amount of glue.

Written words about marriage inevitably come from the mind, from the sunside of Mercury; whereas I know, with nightside, with heart informing mind, that the largest part of marriage and love abides in the mediating zone, in the non-empirical area of our identities. With my conscious mind and with my body I can think about the freedom a promise brings, the joy an explosion of passion. But there's more to it than that.

> Because you're not what I would have you be
> I blind myself to who, in truth, you are.
> Seeking mirage where desert blooms, I mar
> Your you. Love, I would like to see
> Past all delusion to reality.
> Then would I see God's image in your face,
> His hand in yours, and in your eyes his grace.
> Because I'm not what I would have me be
> I idolize two Ones who are not any place,
> Not you, not me, and so they never touch.
> Reality would burn. I do not like it much.
> And yet in you, in me, I find a trace
> Of love which struggles to break through
> The hidden lovely truth of me, of you.

My love for my husband and his for me is in that unknown, underwater area of ourselves where our separations become something new and strange, merge and penetrate like the drops of water in the sea. But we do not lose our solitudes, or our particularity, and we become more than we could alone. This is mystery. I cannot explain it. But I have learned that it makes up for our clashes, our differences in temperament, our angers, our withdrawals, our failures to understand.

No long-term marriage is made easily, and there have been times when I've been so angry or so hurt that I thought my love would never recover. And then, in the midst of near despair, something has happened beneath the surface. A bright little flashing fish of hope has flicked silver fins and the water is bright and suddenly I am returned to a state of love again—till next time. I've learned that there will always be a next time, and that I will submerge in darkness and misery, but that I won't stay submerged. And each time something has been learned under the waters; something has been gained; and a new kind of love has grown. The best I can ask for is that this love, which has been built on countless failures, will continue to grow. I can say no more than that this is mystery, and gift, and that somehow or other, through grace, our failures can be redeemed and blessed.

ON VALENTINE'S DAY, FOR A SAINT MOST MISUNDERSTOOD

> *He was a strange old man*
> *given to solitude on the forest,*
> *eating acorns and locusts.*
> *When he saw a young virgin*
> *he ceased baying at the moon,*
> *lay down, and put his head in her lap.*
>
> *He helped the sun rise every morning*
> *and pulled the ocean high on the shore*
> *at each full moon. He knew that love*
> *is like a sword. He felt its pain.*
> *His blood fell on the snow and turned to roses*
> *and so he was, of all saints, most misunderstood.*
>
> *His eyes are flame, and their look sears.*
> *We pretend he's someone else to avoid burning.*
> *I would go into the forest, silent and alone.*
> *If I find him, will he dry my tears?*

5... Lion and Lamb

LENT. Strange bleak season in the Church year; strange bleak season in the part of the world in which I live. February—how right the Romans were to make it the shortest month of the year. And March. In March I am ready for spring, and spring is not here. When I went to Smith College from Charleston, South Carolina, I could not understand why March was still winter; in Charleston, spring was at its height. In Northampton the sky was clamped whitely over a frozen earth. Ice crackled in the puddles along the paths; snow piled greyly in shady corners.

I am too eager for spring. Around Crosswicks the sere fields need their blanket of snow to prepare the ground for growing. In my heart I am too eager for Easter. But, like the winter fields, my heart needs the snows of Lent. I used to make up lists as Lent approached, lists of small things to give up. But then it occurred to me that if what I was giving up was something bad, it should be given up once and for all, and not just for forty days and forty nights. There is a value to giving up something which is in itself good, as an offering of love. But now I feel that I want to do something positive, rather than something negative, for these wintry weeks. The horror of starvation all over the world makes a moderate diet obligatory at all seasons of the year.

Perhaps what I am supposed to do about Lent is to think about some things I have put off thinking about. The Beatitudes, for instance. They have seemed to make demands on me that I'm not sure I want made. But I have a hunch that if I stop being afraid of the Beatitudes and consider them seriously, I may discover a way of life which will not only be simpler than life usually is in New York City in the late nineteen-seventies, but which will also be more free than life normally is for a middle-class American.

As I glance superficially at these extraordinary directions they seem absurd when set against the United States of America at the end of the twentieth century. Perhaps they were more possible in the smaller and simpler world of two thousand years ago.

But were Nineveh and Tyre that much different from Manhattan and Dallas? Or Sodom and Gomorrah from Chicago and Kansas City?

The days grow longer, the cold grows stronger. According to the new liturgical year in my Church we no longer have the three weeks of preparation for Lent dividing the joy of the Epiphany season from the journey into the darkness of Lent, and I miss them because it appears out of step with the needs of the world, which seem to cry out for a return to the austere observance of Lent. It's not that I want us to go in for breast beating and navel gazing, but I do find the lack of penitence in both the Roman Catholic and the Anglican proposed liturgies extraordinary. Here the world's in the worst mess we've been in for generations, and we no longer get down on our knees and say, I'm sorry. Help!

It's not that I want us to get stuck in that position or to grovel. My mother used to want to say the General Confession from the Book of Common Prayer, and that was fine, but I didn't want her to stop there. After the Confession I wanted her to go on to the Thanksgiving. But I agree with her that the Confession must come before we can rejoice.

Rejoice and be happy—what does it mean? Each one of the Beatitudes begins with *Blessed,* and translated from the Greek, *blessed* means *happy.* In my French Bible blessed is *heureux.* (*Creed* is *symbole* and I find this helpful too.) Sometimes I think that we have forgotten how to be truly happy, we are so conditioned to look for instant gratification. Thus we confuse happiness with transitory pleasures, with self-indulgence. How, in fact, can we live happily when we are surrounded on all sides by so much pain and misery? War and alarums of war, earthquake, flood, drought. Crime is rising; anger and frustration burst into violence, and violence itself becomes a perverse form of gratification. What is this blessedness, this promised happiness? What, if we follow the directions given us in the Beatitudes, is expected of us?—not a general 'us,' but each one of us in all our particularity.

If it is worth being expected of, then something unique, something different, is asked of each of us.

Jesus wanted the rich young man as a disciple; he probably wanted him as one of the twelve. He loved him, and so he asked everything of him. And the rich young man—as so often happens with the very rich—could not respond to the demand.

With Zaccheus it was different. Zaccheus was a small man, so small that he couldn't even see Jesus through the crowd until he climbed up into a tree. What Jesus asked of Zaccheus was what Zaccheus was capable of giving. Maybe it's easier for those who have less, to give what they have, than for those who have much.

Most of us, I suspect, fall somewhere between the rich young man and Zaccheus, and we have to find out for ourselves where we are.

We live in a day of false expectations, false expectations of ourselves, of others. People I know who are professed non-Christians are horrified because their Christian friends behave in what they consider a non-Christian way. It strikes me as rather ironic coming from people who usually affirm their atheism, and who assert that man does not need God in this enlightened age of technocracy; man is perfectable of his own effort; give us enough education, enough technique, and we can cope with everything on our own; virtue and moral judgment are acquirable characteristics. So I am not quite sure what it is they are looking for in Christians, although they are right that most of us, most of the time, behave in a non-Christian way, in that our light too often burns dim and we are not recognized by our love for each other.

I remember one night at the dinner table when two college students asked, rather condescendingly, if I really needed God in order to be happy (blessed). And I said, "Yes. I do. I cannot do it on my own." Simply acknowledging my lack of ability to be in control of the vast technological complex in which my life is set helps free me from its steel net.

Okay, they agreed. So we know we can't control traffic jams and sanitation-department strikes and flu epidemics, but certainly you can't believe in heaven, can you? All that pie-in-the-sky stuff?

Certainly not pie-in-the-sky. Whoever dreamed that one up didn't have much imagination. But the Beatitudes tell me that *Blessed are the poor in spirit: for theirs is the kingdom of heaven.* That's the very first one. I may hold off on heaven till the last of the Beatitudes because it's going to take a steady look at all of them to get me ready. All I know for now is that wherever God is, heaven is, and if I don't have glimpses of it here and now, I'm not going to know it anywhere else.

But of course I have heaven dreams:

> *Perhaps*
>   *after death*
> *the strange timelessness, matterlessness,*
>   *absolute differentness*
>   *of eternity*
> *will be shot through*
> *like a starry night*
> *with islands of familiar and beautiful*
> *joys.*
>
> *For I should like*
> *to spend a star*
> *sitting beside Grandpa Bach*
> *at the organ, learning, at last, to play*
>   *the C minor fugue as he, essentially,*
>   *heard it burst into creation;*
>
> *and another star*
>   *of moor and mist, and through the shadows*
>   *the cold muzzle of the dog against my hand,*
>   *and walk with Emily. We would not need*
>   *to talk, nor ever go back to the damp*
>   *of Haworth parsonage for tea;*
>
> *I should like to eat a golden meal*
>   *with my brothers Gregory and Basil*
>   *and my sister Macrina. We would raise*
>   *our voices and laugh and be a little drunk*
>   *with love and joy;*
>
> *I should like a theatre star*
>   *and Will yelling, "No! No! That's not*
>   *how I wrote it! But perhaps 'tis better*
>   *that way, 'To be or not to be.' All right,*
>   *then, let it stand!"*

> *And I should like*
> *another table*
> *—yes, Plato, please come, and you, too,*
> *Socrates, for this is the essential table*
> *of which all other tables are only*
> *flickering shadows on the wall.*
> *This is the heavenly banquet*
>   *(Oh, come)*
> *the eternal convivium*
>
> *the sky blazes with stars*
>
> *And you, my friends? Will you come, too?*
> *We cannot go alone,*
>
> *Perhaps, then, star-dazzled,*
> *we will understand that we have seen him*
> *and all the stars will burst with glory*
> *and we, too, in this ultimate explosion*
> *of matter*
> *and time*
> *will know what it is*
>
> *to be*
>
> *perhaps*

Relying on that glorious cloud of witnesses to attend to heaven, I want to concentrate on blessing, and on being poor in spirit. I'm coming to a wider understanding of blessing than the old one which implied that if you were virtuous and good, God would bless you by giving you an abundance of material things. Even in the Book of Job this attitude prevails, for Job ends up with more wives and more sons and more cattle than he had before.

But the happiness offered us by the Beatitudes is not material; it is more spiritual than physical, internal than external; and there is an implication which I find very exciting that the circle of blessing is completed only when man blesses God, that God's blessing does not return to him empty. This completing of the circle is difficult for adults to comprehend, but is understood intuitively by children. Our youngest child, when he was a little boy, used to have intimate, leisurely, and long conversations with God. Bedtime was my most special and privileged time with my children; we read aloud; we sang; and then we had prayers, and although I knew that the prayers were often extended to inordinate lengths in order to prolong bedtime, that was all right, too. It's not a bad thing to extend conversation with God, no matter what the reason.

This little boy's conversations with God were spontaneous, loving, and sometimes dictatorial. Many of them I recorded in my journal, so that I would not forget them—such as the prayer one rainy autumn evening when he paused in his God-blesses and said, "O God, I love to listen to the rain; I love to listen to you talk." Another evening he paused again and said severely, "And God: remember to be the Lord." This was during one of the many times when the adults had huddled by the radio during a world crisis; but it took a four-year-old to remind me in my own praying that God is the Lord who is in charge of the universe no matter what we do to mess it up.

And one night this little boy, when he had asked God to bless family and friends and animals, said, "And God! God bless you, too."

But we outgrow this spontaneity and forget the completeness of the circle of blessing. Once again we have come to think of happiness as material prosperity, as affluence. This is the consumer mentality, and is how Madison Avenue would have us think. When we have been turned into consumers we are lowered from being men and women, thinking human beings. Far too often we fall for the not-very-subtle temptation: the more we consume, the happier (more blessed) we will be: more cornflakes, Tang, Preparation-H, automobiles, washing machines, aspirin, Exedrin, Drano, Tide, Bufferin—but it gives us headaches, not happiness. Happiness comes to the poor in spirit.

Who do I know who is poor in spirit? Have I ever, myself, been poor in spirit? What do I have that I can give up, in order to become poor in spirit?

I once talked at length to a Roman Catholic nun about her vows, and the things these vows made her renounce, that she might be poor in spirit. She could understand, she said, her vow of poverty, giving up the material things of the world. She could even understand her vow of obedience, giving up her own will. But, she said, "if sex is good, why should we give it up? We used to be taught that sex is bad, and now we're taught that sex is good, so why should we give it up?"

She, an Irish Roman Catholic, was completely hung up on all our distortions of the Puritan ethic. In my marriage I am certainly not required to be celibate, but I am required to be chaste. Chaste love is participatory and knows, I am convinced, far greater physical joy than possessive, or unchaste love, where either or both partners are using the other.

Chastity for a monastic does include celibacy, and my first understanding of celibacy as a positive, rather than a negative, quality came during the Second World War.

It's easy to be smug about what is going on in another country from the safe distance of one's own, and, like everybody else, I found myself violently condemning the behavior of the Germans to the Jews. But even in the act of condemning I would stop short and ask myself, What would I do if I were an ordinary citizen living in Berlin instead of New York? How strong would my moral convictions be? How far would my courage carry me? If I knew everything that Hitler and his cohorts were doing to exterminate all Jews from the face of the earth, Would I have the poverty of spirit to continue being friendly with the Jewish professor in the next apartment?—knowing that this would probably send me to a concentration camp?

At that time I was unmarried. So, yes, I would be free to act according to my belief in what was right, and probably die for it— *if* I had the courage, the poverty of spirit.

But if I were married and had children? Would I have the same freedom? Would I have the right to endanger their lives for what I believed was right? I didn't know the answer then and I don't know it now; I only know that there is no easy, unequivocal answer. I did learn that celibacy gives a freedom to take mortal risk which is not as easily open to those with families.

I haven't often been tested on poverty of spirit. It was easier to be poor in spirit in the early days of the years of our Lord when all Christians were daily tested in their beliefs. Once Christianity became acceptable, and even mandatory, it lost the early poverty of spirit which sustained it when any group gathered together for bread and wine in his Name had to have one ear open for the knock on the door.

But don't we ever have opportunities for poverty of spirit, we middle-class, comfortable Americans?

We do, though what is asked of us is not as spectacular or as dangerous as what was asked of the first Christians. But it is our response to the small things which conditions our response to the large. If I am unable to be poor in spirit in the small tests, I will be equally unable in the great.

There's one time I'm sure about, though I didn't know it while it was going on. It was while our children were little and we were living year round in Crosswicks, and earning our bread and butter—and not much else—running the General Store in the center of the village.

Hugh's parents' golden wedding anniversary came in late August, and the year of this great occasion we left our butcher and the post-mistress in charge of the store, and flew to Tulsa, Oklahoma, for a week of family gathering and festivities. We were to stay with Hugh's parents, and the big old house was going to be stretched to the limits with our family; with Hugh's sister and brother-in-law, with their two children; and his brother and sister-in-law.

I knew to my rue that I would not have been my mother-in-law's choice of a wife for her beloved baby boy. Hugh had, without consultation, chosen to marry a young woman living alone in Greenwich Village in New York, a 'bachelor girl' who had already had two books published and was working in the theatre. Added to which, we had been married quietly, without what was in those days considered a proper wedding, and although we were married in church it was in an Episcopal church with the oddly un-Protestant name of St. Chrysostom's, and this was probably the worst blow of all to my devout Baptist mother-in-law.

It is easier for daughters-in-law to get on with fathers-in-law. I adored my distinguished father-in-law, known to many who admired him as "Old Judge Franklin," or "Uncle Ben." He had white hair and fine-boned features and it was apparent that Hugh was going to look very much like him as he grew older. I had no trouble in loving and being loved by this gentle man.

But with my mother-in-law I felt inadequate. She already knew that I could not iron a man's shirt so that it would be fit to wear. I was clumsy and inept as a housekeeper. I knew that I could not begin to come up to her requirements for a wife for her baby, and most of the qualities which had drawn Hugh to me were the very ones she approved of least. And so I tended to be awkward and defensive.

When we set off for Tulsa I had decided within myself that I was going to do everything possible to make this a happy time for my parents-in-law, both of them. After all, a golden anniversary is a special occasion. So, from the moment we arrived, I really knocked myself out to be pleasant and helpful. I enjoyed my sister-in-law, and we drank countless cups of coffee over breakfast as we planned the rest of the meals for the day. I may not be able to iron a man's shirt, but I'm a good cook, and cooking is the one part of housekeeping I actively enjoy.

Our children were having a marvelous time playing with the numerous children on the block. We hardly had to think about them, whereas at home playmates had to be fetched and carried, and this freedom to run out to find someone to play with, without pre-planning, was delightful and new. The older children took care of our three-year-old son, so I was free to cook and do dishes and make beds and kaffee-klatsch.

It was an eminently successful week. The great day came and went and I was deeply moved by the joy of these two old people who had lived together for fifty years, and whose love for each other was the brightest gift of that golden day.

When we were on the plane on the way home I suddenly realized that I had been intensely happy all week. Somehow or other I had been given the grace to get out of my own way; all my activities had been unselfconscious; and so, all during that week, I had been given the gift of poverty of spirit without even realizing it.

And there in Tulsa, in a world in which I felt myself to be inadequate and inept, I was given a glimpse of the Kingdom of Heaven.

I am slow to understand the obvious. I have been saying the Lord's Prayer for lo these many years, and only recently did the words *thy Kingdom come on earth as it is in Heaven* click in my mind so that I understood that whenever, somehow or other, we manage to do God's will, there is the Kingdom of Heaven, right here and now.

So I am taught by the first of the Beatitudes and move on to the second: *Blessed are they that mourn: for they shall be comforted.*

Everything in the secular world tries to keep us from the essential comfort of mourning. Even *comfort* has been diluted to mean coziness, rather than comfort, with strength.

My English boarding school trained me to feel that any show of emotion is bad form; no matter what has happened, we must keep a stiff upper lip. Tears, from either the male or the female of the species, are to be repressed.

When my father died, my last year in boarding school, I was true to this training. After all, I was president of my class and president of Student Council. I had a position to uphold, and uphold it I did. I was much too brave to shed tears.

It was a long time before I could write the following lines, on the anniversary of my father's death:

Boarding school: someone cried jubilantly,
"There's a letter for you! Didn't you see it?"

The letter was from my mother. My father
was in the hospital with pneumonia.
This was the autumn before the miracle drugs were discovered.
In any case, his lungs were already half eaten away from mustard gas.

I did not tell anyone. I tried to pray. Perhaps I knew how better then
*   than now.*
I only whispered God's name; then, Father; then, God.

In the evenings we did our lessons in a basement room with many desks,
and windows looking out on the Charleston street.
Little black boys with wildly painted faces and bobbing jack-o'lanterns
peered in on us and shrieked, and their laughter
is all I remember of Hallowe'en.

I sent Father a poem, knowing it would not reach him in time.

The next afternoon the headmistress sent for me; my father was very ill.
I was to take the train right after the evening meal.
It was the night when the Head Girl was to say grace. How odd
that I should remember it, and that all that seemed important
was that my voice be steady.

One of the teachers took me to the train.
I tried to read Jane Eyre.

When my parents had put me on the train for school
my last words as I climbed up the high step onto the train were to
my father:
"Be good." I remember: the last words, and my father standing
on the station platform in a rain-darkened trench coat, and the rain
beating on the dirty glass of the station roof
so that we saw each other only darkly.

I tried to read Jane Eyre *and to pray to the rhythm of the wheels:*
Please, God, do whatever is best for Father. Please, God, do whatever
is best
please
God

My two Godmothers met me. I asked, "How is Father?"
It took the whole drive home before they told me.
I was taken to see my father in the manner of the times.
I did not know him.
I closed my eyes and stood there
seeing him better, then.

My mother and I talked quite calmly
about things like toothpaste.
I remember that. I did not cry.
It was thought that I did not care.

I was a human being and a young one.
We cannot always cry at the right time
and who is to say which time is right?

I did not cry till three years later
when I first fell, most inappropriately,
in love.
But I began, after the tears,
to know my father.

When we are grown up enough
compassed about with so great a cloud of witnesses
that we are not afraid of tears
then at last
we can say
Father
I love you
Father.

It would have been better for both Mother and me if we had been
able to break down, to hold each other and weep out our grief.
Perhaps Mother was able to cry when she sent me back to school—
I was home only a few days, and I was uncomfortably grateful to
escape back to the familiar structure of boarding-school life where I
was expected to be controlled and brave and could thus repress the
grief with which eventually I had to come to terms. Because of this
escape into repression, I went through a very dark period which might

have been avoided had my training allowed me to grieve at the appropriate time.

Odd: my training was nominally Christian; my boarding schools were Anglican, and in the English school there was daily Morning and Evening Prayer from the Book of Common Prayer. So why was I discouraged from natural grief? My grief was for myself, for my mother, not for my father. Father had been ill and in pain for a long time. Father, I somehow knew, was all right. But Mother's life, and mine, had been totally disrupted. Mother no longer had the delightful companion with whom she had traveled all over the world for nearly thirty years. I no longer had the father whose intellect and honor I totally trusted.

So perhaps it was not strange, when I went to college the following autumn, that I was through with the organized religious establishment. It really hadn't given me any help in time of crisis.

Freshman year at college was all right. Everything was new. I enjoyed my studies and the intellectual stimulation with which I was surrounded. I made casual friends. But I do not think that I felt anything. Mother and I spent the summer following freshman year at a rented cottage on the beach, for the old beach house which was so important to me had had to be sold after Father's death. It was a good summer. I worked on a novel, and walked for hours on the beach at night with the companion who is still my friend of the right hand, or canoed with her in the dark lagoons, rejoicing in her knowledge of the flora and fauna of the subtropics. It was a happy summer but there was a seed of unease under the happiness.

Sophomore year came and I was doing well at college, though I had warnings which I did not understand and so could not heed. But I remember one or two of them. As a newly elected class officer I had to make a long list of phone calls, and as I stood there by the phone in the dorm hall, I thought to myself, —I am calling all these people, and that means that I am real.

An even stronger warning came during my daily hour in one of the piano practice rooms. I was working on a Mozart sonata and it became a compulsion with me that I play it through without striking a false note. I had to play it through without making a mistake or I would die.

I must have been in a deep depression for some time before I realized what was happening. My panic fear of death alternated with a state of deadly despair when I would sit and stare into nothing and think nothing and feel nothing. On the surface I was functional, and nobody noticed anything.

I knew nothing about psychiatrists, despite the fact that I was taking a psychology course, and it never occurred to me to go anywhere to ask for help. After all, my Establishment training had taught me to Be Brave, and Do It Myself. I had not yet come across Dean Inge's marvelous saying: God promised to make you free. He never promised to make you independent.

I'm not sure what got me out of the dark pit. Writing helped. I moved, that year, into a new vein in my work, writing more out of my own experience than I ever had before, and becoming conscious of style and structure. And I fell most inappropriately in love, and loving and being loved freed me to weep. At last I was able to shed the tears which I had been repressing for so long. By springtime when I went to my practice room in Sage Hall I no longer felt the bony hand of death at my throat if I made a mistake in the Mozart sonata, and I had emerged from that black, killing depression I can never forget. And I was no longer ashamed of legitimate tears—never tears used as blackmail, or tears of self-pity, but tears when it is proper for a human being to cry.

I'm a little better about mourning, now, though not enough. There never seems to be a right time to cry, and then emotion builds up, and suddenly something inappropriate will cause it to overflow, and there I am with tears uncontrollably welling up at the wrong time and in the wrong place.

I pray for courage to mourn so that I may be strengthened. There is much to mourn, for we feel grief not only for the physical death of one we love or admire. I mourn for the loss of dreams and the presence of nightmare. On a small freighter, passing the Statue of Liberty ('with her crown of thorns,' a friend of mine commented), I mourned the loss of the dream which was responsible for the presence of that great lady. When I was a little girl I loved hearing of all the French children saving their pennies; the Statue of Liberty was dreamed of and paid for by children who were enthralled by the idea of a country which welcomed all the poor of the world and gave them opportunities which could not be found anywhere else.

Until I can mourn the loss of a dream I cannot be comforted enough to have vision for a fresh one. I have not often mourned well, and here again my children teach me. Hugh says that when I have finished a book I can no longer separate what is imaginary in it and what is fact, and he's largely right. There is a brief sequence in *Meet the Austins* which came from experience, but for a few years we had a statistically horrendous number of deaths to mourn, and I'm not sure whose this was—but Rob's prayer is exactly as it was in real life.

The voice is Vicky's, and I am Vicky, far more than Mrs. Austin, who is a much better mother than I could ever hope to be.

"When Mother closed the book, we turned out the lights and said prayers. We have a couple of family prayers and Our Father and then we each say our own God Bless. Rob is very personal about his God Bless. He puts in anything he feels like, and Mother and Daddy had to scold Suzy to stop her from teasing him about it. Last Christmas, for instance, in the middle of his God Bless, he said, 'Oh, God bless Santa Claus, and bless you, too, God.' " (See what I mean?) "So I guess that night we were all waiting for him to say something about Uncle Hal. I was afraid maybe he wouldn't, and I wanted him to, badly.

" 'God bless Mother and Daddy and John and Vicky and Suzy,' he said, 'and Mr. Rochester and Colette and Grandfather and all the cats and Uncle Douglas and Aunt Elena and Uncle Hal and . . .' and then he stopped and said, 'and all the cats and Uncle Douglas and Aunt Elena and Uncle Hal,' and then he stopped again and said, 'and especially Uncle Hal, God, and make his plane have taken him to another planet to live so he's all right because you can do that, God, John says you can, and we all want him to be all right because we love him, and God bless me and make me a good boy.' "

At the age of four he had gone through the acceptance of grief; it was not easy for him to keep Uncle Hal in his prayers that night, with sudden death having taken Uncle Hal out of his grasp; it would have been easier to have left him out of the prayer entirely, and I was afraid he was going to. But he had the courage to mourn and be comforted, and so I was comforted, too.

The following conversation also is a literal reproduction of an actual one.

"Rob slowly got out of my bed. He stood up on the foot of it and said to Mother, 'Do you ever cry?'

" 'Of course, Rob,' Mother said. 'I cry just like anybody else.'

" 'But I never see you cry,' Rob said.

" 'Mothers have to try not to cry,' Mother said. 'Now run along to your own room.' "

I suppose Mothers do have to try not to cry. But never to say that they don't cry. Would it have been better or worse for the children if I had cried in front of them at this death? I don't know. They did know that it mattered to me, though. I didn't try to hide that. And as always whenever anything big happened to us, good or bad, I piled everybody and the dogs into the car and drove up to the top of Mohawk Mountain, four miles away, to watch the stars come out and talk. I hope that it helped the children. I know that it helped me.

Blessed are the meek: for they shall inherit the earth.

The meek? Meekness is not a quality we value much nowadays. People of my generation think of Mr. Milquetoast, and I just checked with a high-school senior and she laughed and said yes, that's her idea of meekness. It goes along with being a coward, and if you turn the other cheek it's because you don't dare fight back, not because you're strong enough to have the courage to turn and let someone hit you again.

Is this what the Beatitudes are talking about? I looked up *meek* in a theological dictionary, and all it had was *meek vs pride,* but I found that in itself helpful.

It was pride which caused the fall of man, that *hubris* which was the tragic flaw in all the heroes in Greek drama. And in Elizabethan and Jacobean drama, too. Faust in Western literature has become the prototype of the prideful man, and fascinated Goethe as much as he did Marlowe or Boito or. . . . Shakespeare understood *hubris* with the mind in the heart. Macbeth, Mark Antony, Prince Hal—all are potentially warrior saints who are felled by pride.

So if *pride,* usurping the prerogatives of the gods, is the opposite of *meek,* that begins to give me a better idea of what meekness is.

One with no pride would therefore be meek, and I can only think of one man who rejected all the temptations of pride, and that is Jesus of Nazareth. So he was meek, then.

My theology about Jesus of Nazareth and Jesus the risen Christ is always wobbly, but I discover that I have no problem at all with Jesus and meekness. He was just as meek when he took a whip and drove the money changers out of the temple as when he turned the other cheek. And certainly his ultimate turning of the other cheek was his acceptance of the cross.

I keep turning back in my mind to Satan and the temptations, because each temptation implied more than it actually said. It wasn't only because Jesus himself was hungry that Satan tempted him to turn the stones into bread. There's also the implication, 'Come along, turn these stones into bread and you can feed all the poor of the earth. ... Nonsense, when you come right down to it, man does live by bread alone. Feed 'em and you've got 'em.' True, as the Grand Inquisitor made clear. But Jesus said the poor are always with us. We may not like it, but that's what he said. Not that the poor are to be ignored, nor did he ignore them, but he wasn't out to win them by magic tricks.

So Satan tried again, innuendoes subtle under the words. "Well, then, just throw yourself down from this great height. You know the angels will hold you up lest you hurt your foot against a stone—one of those stones you so foolishly refused to turn into bread. But just jump! What a spectacle that will be for the mob! They'll adore it—and you."

But that kind of adulation had long since been rejected by Jesus. It was Simon the Magus who fell for it—and from it. And a few others who have been more impressed by the magician than by the priest.

"Oh, well, then, just worship me," Satan cajoles, "and I will give you all the glories of the world, right now, without any waiting, without any suffering, without any cross."

And Jesus still said, No.

Worshipping Satan is more like worshipping ourselves than anything else, and Jesus never confused himself with the Father. It was always, 'Not I, but the Father.' There was no *hubris* in Jesus, and if we want to know what meekness is, we must look to him.

And to his mother. I wish we weren't so afraid to love the most holy birth-giver, as the Orthodox call her. It takes great courage to be truly meek, and the best description of meekness I know is the first four lines of the Magnificat.

My soul doth magnify the Lord, and my spirit hath rejoiced in God my Saviour.
For he hath regarded the lowliness of his handmaiden.
For behold, from henceforth all generations shall call me blessed.
For he that is mighty hath magnified me; and holy is his Name.

It's not nearly as meek and mighty in the new translations. I don't want my meekness watered down.

And how am I, myself, to be meek? Meekness is something else which is not a do-it-yourself activity. Meekness is so wild that most of us don't have the courage for it and certainly would not ask for it willingly.

> *Who shoved me out into the night?*
> *What wind blew out the quavering light?*
> *Is it my breath, undone with fright?*
> *This is the Kingdom of the Beast.*
> *For which will I provide the feast?*
>
> *Who once was daft, with fear am dafter.*
> *Who went before? Who will come after?*
> *Who in this darkness sends me laughter?*
> *I cannot pray, but I am prayed,*
> *The prey prepared, bedecked, arrayed.*
>
> *The dark is sound against my ear,*
> *Is loud with clatter of my fear.*
> *I hear soft footsteps padding near.*
> *I, who have fed, will be the eaten,*
> *Whose dinner will I sour or sweeten?*
>
> *This is not hell, nor say I damn.*
> *I know not who nor why I am*
> *But I am walking with a lamb*
> *And all the tears that ever were*
> *Are gently dried on his soft fur,*
>
> *And tears that never could be shed*
> *Are held within that tender head.*
> *Tears quicken now that once were dead.*
> *O little lamb, how you do weep*
> *For all the strayed and stricken sheep.*
>
> *Your living fur against my hand*
> *You guide me in this unseen land,*
> *And still I do not understand.*

The darkness deepens more and more
Till it is shattered by a roar.

Lamb, stop! Don't leave me here alone
For this wild beast to call his own,
To kill, to shatter, flesh and bone.
    Against the dark I whine and cower.
    I fear the lion. I dread his hour.

Here is the slap of unsheathed paws.
I feel the tearing of his claws,
Am shaken in his mighty jaws.
    This dark is like a falcon's hood
    Where is my flesh and where my blood?

The lamb has turned to lion, wild,
With nothing tender, gentle, mild,
Yet once again I am a child,
    A babe newborn, a fresh creation,
    Flooded with joy, swept by elation.

Those powerful jaws have snapped the tether,
Have freed me to the wind and weather.
O Lion, let us run together,
    Free, willing now to be untame,
    Lion, you are light: joy is in flame.

It is only when the lion has me in his jaws that I am shaken into the courage to be meek.

I knew meekness when John, friend and doctor, dropped my newborn son between my breasts and said, "Madeleine, here is your son," and this after nearly forty-eight hours of work. I knew meekness half an hour later when the placenta wouldn't come and I began to hemorrhage and spent the next hours fighting for my life. I remember thinking, "Hugh will have to marry Gloria to take care of the children," and immediately I thought meekly, "No! I am going to take care of my own children! I am going to be Hugh's wife! I have more books to write!" And then all thoughts had to stop and all concentration had to go into breathing, simply breathing, because I knew that as long as I could breathe I was still alive. The foot of the bed was raised into shock position yet I knew exactly what was going on. I tried to concentrate on nothing but keeping one breath following the one before as the doctors struggled to get a needle for a transfusion into veins which kept collapsing on them. And I kept on meekly breathing. A fresh doctor was called in, one who wasn't exhausted with the struggle of holding, by hand, the uterus closed in order to stanch the flow of blood. The needle found a vein which would hold it, and life-giving blood began to move in my veins, and I meekly kept on breathing, for my babies, for my husband, for my work, and the breathing itself was prayer, please God, please God, please God . . .

And the pain was bad, bad, and I kept on breathing and saying Please God . . .

And after several hours I was all right, and my son was brought to me and put in my arms and my soul magnified the Lord . . .

It strikes me how each Beatitude leads into the next. Poverty of spirit gives us the humble courage to mourn, which in turn frees us to be meek.

But what's this about inheriting the earth? Would we even want it? When God in his strangeness has allowed us to make such an incredible mess of it?

But an inheritance is nothing we ask for or earn or deserve. It is something we are given by the testator, and we can either accept or betray the responsibility.

> We need not wait for God
> The animals do judge
> Of air and sea and grass
> Accusing with their eyes
> Waiting here en masse
> They cry out with their blood
> The whale caught in surprise
> By oil slick's killing sludge
> The cow with poisoned milk
> The elephant's muted roar
> At radioactive food
> The tiger's mangy hide
> The silkworm's broken silk
> (The animals do judge)
> The dead gulls on the shore
> Mists of insecticide
> Killing all spore and sperm
> Eagle and owl have died
> Caterpillar and worm
> The snakes drag in the mud

> *Fallen the lion's pride*
> *Butterfly wings are bruised*
> *They cry out with their blood*
> *Cain! Killer! We are blamed*
> *By beast and bird condemned*
> *By fish and fowl accused*
> *We need not wait for God*
> *The animals do judge*

Adam and Eve stopped being responsible stewards of the earth when they were tempted by Satan to eat of the fruit of the tree of the knowledge of good and evil, 'and ye shall be as gods.'

Our mythic ancestors crashed on the tragic flaw of *hubris* and so they were no longer meek.

We are very blessed that it is the meek who are to inherit the earth, for they can be trusted with it.

Blessed are they which do hunger and thirst after righteousness: for they shall be filled.

The planet earth is filled with starving people.

What are we hungry for?

What are we thirsty for?

When I was in boarding school, one of the very youngest girls stole a watch. She was eight years old. Her parents were divorced. Her father was trying to forget this not very mute reminder of his broken marriage. Her mother flitted from pleasure spot to pleasure spot. There was no room in her frenetic life for a child.

So the little girl stole a watch she didn't want or need, because she was so hungry for love that she had to reach out, blindly, for something, anything, to assuage her hunger.

We're all hungry for something. Uncontrolled overeating usually masks an unacknowledged hunger. We have to know what we are hungry for before we can hunger and thirst after righteousness. Man does not live by bread alone, but bread does matter; it is not easy to hunger and thirst after righteousness with a belly bloated from starvation and bones bent with rickets.

What is *righteousness,* anyhow? Like *meek,* it is a word which has lost most of its original power. I'm afraid it gives rise in me to pictures of gaunt women with thin, repressed lips, who know absolutely what is right and what is wrong, and certainly anything which is fun is wrong.

But that's self-righteousness, and no one ever said, 'Happy are the self-righteous.'

Since it helped me to understand meekness when I looked to Jesus, I look to him again to try to avoid all our distortions of righteousness. What do I see?

I see a man compassionate and gentle with women in a day when this was extraordinary. I remember that the first miracle was turning water into wine at an Oriental wedding feast, and this kind of wild party would definitely be disapproved of by our self-righteous friend. His power is so great that more than once he brings the dead back to life, and yet he feels the power drain from him when the hem of his garment is grasped by the woman with the issue of blood. He has a robust sense of humor, and small children love him.

Righteousness begins to reveal itself as that strength which is so secure that it can show itself as gentleness, and the only people who have this kind of righteousness are those who are integrated and do not suppress the dark side of themselves.

After the baptism there was no question in Jesus's mind as to who he was, and it was this self-knowledge which enabled him to see through the snares and delusions of the temptations. Most of us don't have that certainty, and so we are hungry and thirsty for the wrong things.

It is only when I know myself as a child of God by adoption and grace, a child of a God so loving that he notes the fall of every sparrow, calls all of the stars in all of the galaxies by name, and counts the very hairs on every head, that I am free to accept all of myself, the dark and the bright, and so become free to hunger and thirst after righteousness—and righteousness, ultimately, is a person.

And in this person, righteousness includes the strength of forgiveness—a righteous person has a forgiving heart. The ancient Hebrew understood the word *righteousness* to include judgment, not the cold judgment of blind justice, but a judgment which must be tempered with mercy if it is to be righteous. Heaven knows, the best of us, in looking toward our own judgment, pray that justice will include clemency and compassion. I cannot think of any instance where I could throw the first stone.

'Forgive us our trespasses (or debts or sins or whatever) as we forgive those who trespass against us' means exactly what it says. As we forgive, so shall we be forgiven.

If I am to hope to hunger and thirst after righteousness, then my heart as well as my will must know forgiveness. There are still things I cannot remember without an upsurge of pain, which means that I have not yet completely forgiven, no matter what my intellectual self has said. Deep wounds must heal from the inside out, and this may take a long time, but I must be very careful to do nothing to slow or hinder the healing. Until the memory of a hurt no longer pains me, I have not forgiven the hurter.

When I am angry with husband, children, friend, it is impossible to hunger and thirst after righteousness. This doesn't mean that we are never to get angry—Jesus got very angry on occasion; we mustn't stay locked in anger, but must move on out to forgiveness and reconciliation—and suddenly we'll find that we have been filled.

Righteousness leads directly into *Blessed are the merciful: for they shall obtain mercy.*

But mercy goes further than that forgiveness taught us in the Lord's Prayer. The human being is given the ability to forgive, but that capacity of mercy which not only forgives but also removes the sin is more than human.

The English language, despite what we have done to it with all our jargons, is still extraordinarily rich and powerful in quality, though not in quantity, of words. Both the Greeks and the Hebrews used many words where we have been satisfied with one. As there are many words for our one *love,* so with *mercy.* The Hebrew *chesed* is seen over and over again in the Psalms, and Coverdale frequently translates it as *loving kindness,* that continued forbearance shown by God even when his chosen people are slow to keep his commandments and swift to turn to foreign gods.

Another Hebrew word for mercy is *rachamim,* which has to do with tender compassion, the care of the shepherd for the stray lamb, the pity shown to the weak and helpless. And there is *chaninah,* a joyful, generous mercy, loving and kind.

So mercy, as all the other Beatitudes, is a Christ-like word, and I must look for understanding of it in the small and daily events of my own living, because if I do not recognize it in little things I will not see it in the great.

Again my children teach me. One time, shortly after we had moved back to the city and our children were still young—seven, ten, and twelve—we spanked our son for something the younger of his sisters had done. I don't remember what it was; he was spanked because his father thought he was lying, rather than for any misdeed, and that is not the point of this memory, which is a happy one, so happy that it was easy to find the place where I had recorded it in my journal:

Bion was spanked this afternoon for something Maria had done. And when Maria heard about it when she came home from Scouts she was upset, truly upset that Bion had been punished for something he hadn't done. So we ran to the subway to go down to judo class where Bion was with Hugh, to clear everything up. Hugh had been terribly upset when he spanked Bion, as he thought Bion was lying to him. And I was so proud of Maria for owning up, and for being concerned. And the wonderful thing was how happy and loving *both* Maria and Bion were all evening. We had a hilarious dinner, playing buzz (the math game), which we had such a wonderful time with last night, and laughing almost as hard over it tonight. Funny how something like that can serve to clear the air.

It was the laughter and joy of that evening which is proof of the mercy which mediated between sunside and nightside. I can conceive of forgiveness without this hilarity, but not mercy, which is the step beyond and leads to joy.

O HILARITAS

According to Newton
the intrinsic property of matter on which weight depends is
mass.
But mass and weight vary according to gravity
(It is not a laughing matter).
On earth a mass of 6 kilograms has a weight of 6 kilograms.
On the moon a mass of 6 kilograms has a weight of 1 kilogram.
An object's inertia (the force required to accelerate it)
depends entirely on its mass.
And so with me.
I depend entirely on a crumb of bread
a sip of wine;

> *it is the mass that matters*
> *that makes matter.*
> *In free fall, like the earth around the sun,*
> *I am weightless*
> *and so move only if I have mass.*
> *Thanks be to the creator*
> *who has given himself*
> *that we may be.*

If I look at the Beatitudes not only as though each were a description of Jesus, but also as a definition, they shine in a powerful and brilliant light, so that light and darkness are suddenly alike. He is poor in spirit as we are seldom able to be, because we are seldom that spontaneous. He mourns with them that mourn and dances with them that rejoice and is criticized for both. He is meek, that lamb who is also lion. He hungers and thirsts, as we do, and offers himself to assuage our hunger and thirst, and so we are filled. He is merciful, with a compassion and joy beyond forgiving. There is the power of life and death in his mercy, and it is good to remember this each time we receive the power of his mercy in the bread and wine.

It is only this extraordinary unstrained quality of mercy which helps me to make any sense out of *Blessed are the pure in heart: for they shall see God.*

This is a rough one. We all know that no one can see God and live, it's all through the Bible. And it isn't only a Judaeo-Christian idea— it's in Greek and Roman mythology: in fact, it's a basic presupposition of humankind.

When Semele insisted on seeing Zeus in all his glory she was immediately incinerated. The human being is charred to ash by the glory of the living God. So who has seen God and lived? Who was that pure in heart?

Well, here I come another cropper. The first person who comes to my mind is Jacob, and Jacob does not fit any normal definition of the pure in heart. Jacob was really pretty much of a stinker, cheating his brother Esau, tricking his blind and dying father to get a blessing which did not belong to him.

But he recognized God when he wrestled with him, and he limped forever after. And that limp is important, for the point the Old Testament writer is making by emphasizing Jacob's thigh is that anyone who has seen the living God and survived is marked by this experience and is recognized forever after by the mark.

The early Christians were recognized by the rest of the world, for they bore the mark of the wound of love, and the sign of this love is light, by which they were recognized and for which they lay down their lives. There's a chorus of a song which goes, "You can tell we are Christians by our love."

Can we? Are we wounded enough to be recognized as Christians?

In a church in New Jersey I saw this poster made by the teenagers: *If you were arrested as a Christian would there be enough evidence against you to convict you?*

That arrow really shot me right through the heart.

But I was severely questioned by a young man, a song writer, on this very subject. Oh, sure, he said bitterly, you can recognize Christians by their love for one another because they don't love anybody else.

There's a good deal of truth in this accusation, but of course that kind of self-love isn't love at all, and it isn't Christian, either. But if I am to love others, and not only my own kind as he pointed out, then I must first accept that I am loved; this is the necessary prelude for my acceptance of myself. Then am I able to love those close to me, parents, husband, children, friends. Only then am I free to move out and love those less lovable to me, to love my enemy.

When this young man was a boy he had read *A Wrinkle in Time,* which he said he still rereads occasionally. So I said, "Okay, remember when Meg has to go back to Camazotz to rescue Charles Wallace from the power of It, the naked brain, she knows that if she could love It, her love would defeat It. And she can't do it, so she turns to Charles Wallace because she *can* love her little brother, and that love is strong enough to defeat the cold intellectual power if It. I came to this ending from my own experience, because there was someone I knew I ought to love, and with every effort of will I tried to love and I couldn't do it. But I found that if I turned away completely, and thought about those I could love, my husband, my three children, then I could *get back into love,* and then I could turn with love to the person I had such difficulties with."

And later I said, "But in *A Wind in the Door* Meg has to make the next step into mature love; she has to learn to love Mr. Jenkins, and Mr. Jenkins is not an easy person to love."

We love wherever we can love, and the power of that love spreads until the circumference of the circle of love grows wider and wider. At least that has been my own experience, even though I know to my rue that the circumference of my love is still much too small.

It's too small for all of us; I'm not just breast beating. The circle grows slowly and painfully even with the saints, and so does purity of heart. Who can possibly be pure of heart in this impure world?

Peter. Peter recognized Jesus as the Messiah, the Christ. And Jesus said, "Flesh and blood has not told you this." So purity of heart is not a virtue, it is a gift, and Peter, bumbling, noisy Peter, was given the gift of purity, the ability to see God. And after this he betrayed the God he had seen, he ran from him, he denied him, he was not there when they crucified his Lord. But he believed in the Resurrection, and his confession of Jesus as Messiah was the rock on which the Church was founded, and in the end he lay down his life for what he had seen and known.

The fact that Peter could see God, and thus be pure in heart despite all his faults and flaws, is a great comfort, because it tells me that this purity, like every single one of the Beatitudes, is available to each of us, as sheer gift of grace, if we are willing to be vulnerable.

But Peter saw God two thousand years ago, when the second person of the Trinity came to his Creation as a man, when his footsteps were left in the dust, when the light of his smile lit the sky with the brilliance of the sun. What about now, two thousand years later, when his presence among us has been gone for so long? Who can be pure in heart and see God now?

It is one of the burdens of living in a fallen world that each generation has its war. For Hugh and me it is World War II, and in one of the stories coming from this war I find my image of that purity of heart which allows a human being to see God and live.

This story concerns a Lutheran pastor in Germany who could not reconcile his religion with the Third Reich, which pretended to protect the religious establishment as long as those who belonged to it were pure Aryan (forget that Jesus was a Jew) and were willing to *heil Hitler*. This pastor had met with Hitler, who liked him, and wanted to give him preferment. But the choice was as cut and dried for the pastor as it was for those first Christians when they were asked to burn a pinch of incense to the divinity of the emperor. And he did not have celibacy to make his choice easier. He had a wife and children and he loved his family and he did not take lightly his responsibility to them.

But he could not betray everything he believed, everything that he stood for in his ministry; he could not burn that pinch of incense.

He and his wife and children were sent to a concentration camp, and the wife and children died there. Like Anne Frank's father, he was the only one left.

When it was all over, when Hitler's megalomaniac kingdom had fallen, and the world was trying to put itself back together and return to everyday living, it was remembered that he had seen Hitler. Someone asked him curiously, "What did Hitler look like?"

He replied quietly, "Like Jesus Christ."

And that is what it is like to be pure in heart and to see God.

I'm not anywhere nearly there. I don't know if I'll ever get there, where I can see through my own sin and sham to the image of God in the lowest of his creatures. Like Meg, I do have to start where I *can* love. But that is at least a start.

Blessed are the peacemakers: for they shall be called the children of God.

Never have we needed peacemakers more. There is a peculiar horror in turning on radio or TV for the news and hearing about Christians fighting Moslems, or Catholics fighting Protestants, or Jews fighting Arabs.

If I continue to struggle to think of the Beatitudes as a description of Jesus, it is bound to affect my understanding of peace, because Jesus, the peacemaker, the Son of God, said that he came not to bring peace, but a sword. And the Hebrew word *shalom*—peace—is not a passive word like the Greek *eirēnē*, a primarily negative word denoting the absence of war, but a positive word, *shalom,* the peace which comes after the last battle.

Do we have to think about war before we can think about being peacemakers? A teenager wrote to me about one of my books and then added, "We've been studying the Crusades in school. *Can* there be such a thing as a Holy War? Can a Christian kill?"

It was not an easy letter to answer, nor did I answer it to my satisfaction. Offensive war, never. That's easy. But defensive? Could we, in conscience, Christian conscience, have refused to enter World War II? Could we have stood by and let Hitler take over our friends and neighbors and accomplish his mission of exterminating all Jews? We couldn't, my generation, or at least so it seemed to us. And we had to take on our American selves some of the responsibility for all that caused Hitler and his rise to power. We felt deep in our hearts that the only way to be peacemakers was to fight the Nazis and then cry, Shalom!

Several young men who were close to me were killed in that war, and if we had learned enough to know that there is no such thing as a war to end war, at least they died believing their cause was just, and something in me will not let me say that they died in vain.

But I have to look directly at the fact that the Hitler Jugend believed in the justness of their cause, too. They were saving the world. It's confusing, this trying to think about war, and it makes me understand with deep pain that, despite the bite of that apple, a great deal of the time we do not know what is good and what is evil. We cannot tell our left hand from our right.

I was sorting these thoughts out one morning, and began outlining them to my friend Tallis.

He looked down his nose at me. "Don't be so cosmic."

"Am I being cosmic?"

"Yes. Don't be."

When I tend to go cosmic it is often because it is easier to be cosmic than to be particular. The small, overlooked particulars which are symbols of such things as being peacemakers are usually to be found in our everyday lives. Of course we'd rather have something more dramatic and spectacular, so we tend not to see the peacemakers in our own path, or the opportunities for peacemaking which are presented us each day.

When I need to think particularly rather than cosmically, I turn as always to my family, this time once again to the little boy whose sister hurried to the judo studio the day he had been punished for something she had done.

The judo lessons came about not because of the dangers of living on the Upper West Side of Manhattan, but because of the school bus in our small New England village. When Bion was in first grade the school bus stopped at the bottom of the hill, nearly a mile from our house. The two other boys who got off at the same stop were both older and bigger, and when there was nothing better to do, they jumped on the little first-grader and roughed him up.

Hugh asked, "Why don't you fight them back?"

Bion answered reasonably, "There are two of them, Daddy, and they're bigger than I am."

So when we moved to New York in the middle of the next school year, he had judo lessons. He enjoyed judo, and he was good at it.

One Saturday he took the bus down Broadway to spend the day with a friend. As he was walking the long block between Broadway and West End Avenue, three boys came up to him and demanded his money. All he had was his bus fare, which he handed over. He then went on to his friend's, and in the late afternoon borrowed the bus fare to come home.

He told us about it at dinner, and Hugh said, "Why didn't you use your judo on them?"

"For fifteen cents, Daddy? I might have hurt them."

He was, and is, a peacemaker.

So are many of the people I pass each day on the rough streets of the Upper West Side. I remember one time when we were setting off for Crosswicks for the first weekend in the spring, and Hugh went to the liquor store to see if he could have a carton in which to pack some things. But the cartons had just been picked up, so the proprietor of the liquor store went next door to the pharmacy to see if there was a box there. There wasn't, but the pharmacist went to the laundromat to see if there was one there. . . .

Peacemaking. Peacemaking on Upper Broadway, illumined by this quick generosity of all the shopkeepers on the block knocking themselves out to find an empty carton.

It's there for me to see, as long as I recognize it. And I must recognize, too, the opportunities for being a peacemaker which are daily offered me. Nothing dramatic or spectacular, but lots of little things, and the smallness does not make them less opportunities.

Just on the walk between our apartment and the Cathedral library, for instance; it's a crowded time of day, when I take off in the morning a little after eight o'clock, with mobs of people going to work, sleepy, unready for the damp cold in winter, the humid heat in summer. Each morning I walk past a large supermarket. Across the sidewalk is a metal slide, sloping from a huge delivery truck to a side entrance of the market. There is a small gap in the slide, just large enough to let one person pass through at a time. A man in the truck sends heavy cartons down the slide, and they are lifted over the gap by another man who stands trying to do his job of getting the truck unloaded while people coming from both directions are trying to get through the gap. My dog and I are among them. The man struggles to get the cartons across the gap and onto the lower section of the slide under conditions which are, to put it mildly, frustrating.

One winter the man with this thankless job was large and strong-looking, but older than a man ought to be who has to lift heavy cartons. His skin, which had once been coffee-with-cream, was tinged with grey. His expression was dour, and who can blame him? Most people, hurrying to jobs which are no more than drudgery, thought only of getting through the bottleneck which was impeding their way, a reaction which is no more than natural. But my job is real work, and real work is play, not drudgery. I walk through the dirty and crowded streets to a place of trees and grass and beauty, and within this place to a gracious, book-filled room where I am free to write, and this is joy.

So, one morning as the dog and I slid through the bottleneck, I smiled and said, "Good morning."

I got no response. Naturally. The sour look did not soften. Why should it? It was stubbornness which made me persist in saying "Good morning," or "Thank you," day after day.

One day he smiled back.

One day he smiled first.

Not much in the way of peacemaking, is it? But it is what is offered me each morning. And, as my grandmother was fond of reminding me, little drops of water and little grains of sand make the mighty ocean and the pleasant land.

The way of peacemaking given us may be something so small that it seems hardly worth doing, but it is these small offerings which build our reflexes for the larger ones. The ways of peacemaking given middle-class Americans like me are far less spectacular than—for instance—those given the group of Protestant and Roman Catholic women in Northern Ireland who daily risk their lives to cross the battle lines and pray with each other, but the grace to brave such danger has been built on the foundation of the small responses—even things as small as not wanting to hurt the boys who took your bus fare, or everybody on the block trying to find a carton, or smiling at the dour man who now smiles, too—it may not seem like much; it is not much; but it is what is given at the present moment, and it is what ultimately provides the grace for the greater tests.

When we are given the grace to be peacemakers even in these little, unimpressive ways, then we are children of God, children by adoption and grace, but children nevertheless, who are bold to call him Father, Abba. So we children are helped to become peacemakers, and one day we will truly be able to cry, Shalom!

6... The Noes of God

LENT HAS GONE BY too quickly. Holy Week is here and I have to start thinking about Good Friday; God's Friday; and there is the last Beatitude waiting for my attention, and so I feel that it is somehow appropriate to work it into my Holy Week thinking: *Blessed are they which are persecuted for righteousness sake: for theirs is the Kingdom of Heaven.*

Tallis tells me that the Eastern Orthodox Church emphasizes Easter, whereas the Western Church emphasizes Good Friday, but I have never been able to think of one without the other. As it takes both male and female to make mankind, so it takes both Good Friday and Easter to make Christianity.

On Palm Sunday in the Cathedral the congregation participates in acting out the Gospel, and we are the mob, and I choke as I shout out, *His blood be on us, and on our children. Crucify him! Crucify him!* I choke not because it is something I would never under any circumstances say, but because just as I do not know what I would have done had I been an ordinary German under Hitler's regime, neither do I know what I would have done had I been caught up in that mob. I might well have cried, *Crucify him!* and been convinced that this was the right thing to do.

An even more deeply moving service is on Maundy Thursday when, after the bread and wine has been given and received, one by one the candles are snuffed out. Then everything is taken away. The altar is stripped down and the naked marble has wine poured into the five "wounds" and washed with water. Finally the seven great hanging lamps are, with difficulty, lowered by the sacristan who pulls them down by a long pole with a hook on the end. As he gets each one down he blows it out.

Darkness. Emptiness. There is nothing left.

That is how it must have been for the disciples. For his friends. Dark. Empty.

He was dead. All their hopes were shattered. No one knew there was going to be a resurrection. Their hearts were heavy and without hope. He was just a minor political agitator after all, instead of what he said he was. On Good Friday no one thought about Easter, because Easter hadn't happened yet, and no one could dream of such an impossible possibility.

Perhaps, we call Good Friday good because it was what made Easter possible. But why wasn't there any other way? Does it always take failure in man's terms to make success in God's?

One of my young married students has suffered all her life because she was taught in her Church that she was born so sinful that the only way the wrath of God the Father could be appeased enough for him to forgive all her horrible sinfulness was for God the Son to die in agony on the cross. Without his suffering, the Father would remain angry forever with all his Creation.

Many of us have had at least part of that horror thrust on us at one time or other in our childhood. For many reasons I never went to Sunday School, so I was spared having a lot of peculiar teaching to unlearn. It's only lately that I've discovered that it was no less a person than St. Anselm who saw the atonement in terms of appeasement of an angry God, from which follows immediately the heresy that Jesus came to save us from God the Father.

The quality which has always amazed and rejoiced me about God is his constant loving concern for his Creation. Even when we are most disobediant to the laws of love he still cares; he is slow to anger and quick to forgive—far quicker to forgive than his human creatures, such as Jonah, who is intensely irritated by the Father's compassion. This loving concern is apparent all through the Old Testament, preparing us for the ultimate concern shown in the New where he actually comes to us as one of us.

If he is truly one of us, wholly man as well as wholly God, then his death is inevitable. All men must die. All created matter ultimately comes to an end.

But Jesus as wholly man at the same time that he is wholly God is as impossible as St. Paul's conception of a spiritual body. But on these two absolute contradictions I build my faith.

We still want corroboration of scientific proof behind what we believe. But if something can be proved, then we don't need faith in order to believe in it. I don't need faith to believe in any of the lab experiments we did in high-school chemistry; they are in the realm of provable fact. And when we depend too much on provable fact we blunt and diminish the human talent for faith.

Little worth believing in is scientifically provable. In literal terms, God can neither be proved nor disproved. That the result of living according to the Beatitudes is happiness does not lie in the realm of provable fact; yet when I look at the people I know whose faces are alight with joy, no matter how terrible their outward circumstances, I can see in them poverty of spirit, the comfort of mourning, purity of heart—all those characteristics which, put together, are a description of Jesus of Nazareth:

who died on a cross, publicly, between two thieves, on Good Friday. A failure. In worldly terms, a complete washout, the original non-achiever.

That, too, is part of the blessing we are offered if we call him Lord. Death.

I doubt if it is given to the human being to understand completely the blessed passion and precious death, the mighty resurrection and glorious ascension of our Lord Jesus Christ. I know that I do not understand. But I also know that it has nothing to do with the angry, unforgiving God who so upset my young friend. If the basic definition of sin is lack of love (that love without which all men are dead in the sight of God, as Cranmer wrote in one of his collects), then an inability to forgive is lack of love, and if God is unable to forgive us then he is lacking in love, and so he is not God. At least, he is not the God who makes glad my heart.

So why the crucifixion, then, if it was not to appease the anger of God?

When Christ, the second person of the Trinity, became, in Jesus, wholly man, he had to experience death for us, just as he had to experience being born, and breathing, and eating, and eliminating, and sleeping, just like all mankind. But why on the cross? Why despised and rejected by the majority of the Jews, his people, forsaken by most of his friends? Why a total failure?

And here again I bump headlong into God's failure vs. man's success, and man's success is worth nothing, in comparison with the glorious failure of God.

Experience is painfully teaching me that what seems a NO to man from man's point of view, is often the essential prelude to a far greater YES. The Noes which have been said to me may be as small and inconsequential as the opportunities given me for peacemaking, but they are mine. During the two years when *A Wrinkle in Time* was consistently being rejected by publisher after publisher, I often went out alone at night and walked down the dirt road on which Cross-wicks faces, and shouted at God; 'Why don't you let it get accepted? Why are you letting me have all these rejection slips? You know it's a good book! I wrote it for you! So why doesn't anybody see it?'

But when *Wrinkle* was finally published, it was exactly the right moment for it, and if it had been published two years earlier it might well have dropped into a black pit of oblivion.

Another No which was the prelude to a Yes came way back when I was working in the theatre. I knew early that I was to be general understudy and have a couple of walk-on roles in Eva LeGallienne's and Margaret Webster's production of Chekhov's *The Cherry Orchard*. A young actor in whom I was intensely interested, and who had already made a name for himself, was being considered for the role of Petya Trofimov, the student who is Chekhov's mouthpiece, and I was certain that my friend was going to get the job and my love life was going to be assured. When I went to the first rehearsal he was not there. Instead, I saw a tall thin young man with black hair and great blue eyes who was introduced to me as Hugh Franklin, and I was not pleased.

I think it was after the second rehearsal that Hugh asked me out for a bite to eat; this was at three in the afternoon. It was three in the morning when I unlocked the door to my apartment in the Village. I cannot imagine what the past thirty-plus years, the greater part of my life, would have been, had Hugh not played Petya.

But of course the real example which makes all our little stories pale is seen in the life of Jesus of Nazareth. He begged in agony that he might be spared the cross, and his father said No to him, and this No was the essential prelude to the Yes of the Resurrection. This No was necessary for the defeat of death. In dying, as a mortal, Jesus defeated the power of death. Death is often brutal, but death does not win. The sting has been removed. The victory of the grave is turned to defeat.

So Good Friday is good because it is the defeat of death.

In a Good Friday sermon Alan talked about the human desire to play God. We all have it. The trouble is that we want to play at God rather than be like God. We forget that playing God, if we take it seriously, involves a love so great that it accepts the cross.

It is difficult for us to hear, and even when we hear, it is difficult for us to understand.

The disciples heard, but they didn't understand, otherwise they might not all—all except John—except the women—have run away from the horror of Good Friday.

Blessed are they which are persecuted for righteousness' sake: for theirs is the kingdom of Heaven.

We aren't persecuted very much nowadays, we Christians, at least not overtly. But in point of fact there is a good bit of sub-rosa persecution, ridiculing if not reviling. In children's books death and sex used to be taboo. Now death and sex are 'in,' and Christianity is the new taboo; other religions are appreciated, Buddhism, Hinduism, the pre-Christian Druidism; Christianity is not tolerated. And not only in children's literature. It has been made taboo by those who do not understand it and who are terrified by its wider and wilder implications, and so take refuge in sarcasm and supercilious arrogance: of course we intelligent people don't need God and we certainly aren't interested in the cross. Only those poor creatures who aren't strong enough to manage on their own go in for the false promises of religion.

On the other hand, self-sufficient intellectuals who can't stand Christianity are far too often given a vicious travesty of what Christianity is about by the various Christian establishments. If I want to find a Christian, I look not to the ecclesiastical success as much as to the lame, the halt, the blind, who come to church, because only for us do the promises have any meaning.

One time in London, after I had come from the Holy Mysteries, I wrote:

How very odd it seems, dear Lord,
That when I go to seek your Word
In varied towns at home, abroad,
I'm in the company of the absurd.

The others who come, as I do,
Starving for need of sacrament,
Who sit beside me in the pew,
Are both in mind and body bent.

I kneel beside the old, unfit,
The young, the lonely stumbling few,
And I myself, with little wit,
Hunger and thirst, my God, for you.

I share communion with the halt,
The lame, the blind, oppressed, depressed.
We have, it seems, a common fault
In coming to you to be blessed.

And my fit friends, intelligent,
Heap on my shoulders a strange guilt.
Are only fools and sinners meant
To come unto you to be filled?

Among the witless and absurd
I flee to find you and to share
With eyes and ears and lips your Word.
I pray, my God. God, hear my prayer.

From city streets and lanes we come.
I slip unto you like a thief
To be with you, at peace, at home,
Lord, I believe. Oh, help my unbelief.

Perhaps we must accept our brokenness and not try to repress it before we can affirm the goodness of Good Friday, and all that it promises. We are all broken, we human creatures, and to pretend we're not is to inhibit healing. It is people who consider themselves whole who tell me that the Christian promises are false, but as I look at these 'whole' people I see that they are in fact less 'whole' than some who admit their brokenness.

Are these promises by which I live false ones? If so, I want to discard them immediately. But I don't think that they are. Perhaps they are called false by the people who, underneath, are afraid they are only too true: Good Friday. The Cross. Death. Judgment.

I'm afraid, too. I think we all are. But we are given the grace to move beyond the fear because this is not all of the promise.

Those who look down condescendingly on us struggling Christians call the rest of this promise pie-in-the-sky and hope to demolish it by ridicule. The blessedness of being persecuted does indeed promise us heaven, and we're not very good about heaven. The problem with all that is promised the Christian, and it's all spelled out very clearly in the Beatitudes, is that it's too good to be believed. It has nothing whatsoever to do with the world of provable fact and technology-turned-into-technocracy. And much of the time the Christian establishment is no help to us hungry sheep. I've been shocked at the number of clergymen of all denominations who either ignore the Resurrection or deny it—thereby relegating Jesus Christ to the status of merely a good rabbi—in which case he was wrong about himself, the disciples were wrong about him, Paul was wrong about him, and we've been worshipping a false god for nearly two thousand years.

Often we have indeed been worshipping false gods. The Christian establishment does not always remain true to its Lord. Like the stiff-necked Hebrews we, too, turn aside to our own equivalent of the altars of Baal. I was utterly appalled by a book endorsed officially by the Episcopal Church for use in high-school age Sunday School classes which equated belief in the Resurrection and our own everlasting life as 'no better than superstitious belief in ghosts.'

I stand with Paul here. When we deny the Resurrection, we are denying Christianity. We are no longer the Church; no wonder the secular world is horrified by us.

It is not easy to have the courage to stand up and publicly be counted as Christians, when we know that our Christianity is going to be misunderstood and reviled. It is not easy to stand firm in our faith in heaven, our faith that Good Friday is good because it was not the end of the story, but was followed by the glory of Easter.

Christians are often accused by the secular world of being so hooked on heaven that we consider what is happening in this world unimportant, that we couldn't care less about battlefields and slums and insane asylums; we ignore the poor; we turn our backs on racial injustice; we do not even consider the plight of the lame, the halt, the blind. Throughout the past two thousand years there has far too often been more than a modicum of truth in this accusation, because a great deal of the time Christians are simply not Christian at all.

But if we look at the record of concern for poverty and weakness and suffering, that of the atheist is by and large worse than that of the believer, because if you take seriously the glorious promise that God created all of us to live forever, then what we do here and now matters far more than if this life were all, and at the end of our mortal span we're snuffed out like a candle—so why not eat, drink, and be merry, for tomorrow we die.

If we look back throughout history, the record shows quite clearly that societies where man is god have far less concern for human life than those which believe in God's loving concern for every iota of his creation. Alexander the Great, Tiberius, Hitler/Mussolini were big on causes and small on people. I could list some Americans in my lifetime, but because they are in my lifetime, more water needs to flow under the bridge before I can see with any objectivity.

The Church that went along with Hitler was not the Church. The Church was in the concentration camps. To a Christian, no human being is expendable, and we cannot justify trampling on people now by promising them pie-in-the-sky by-and-by. When this is tried, it is simply not Christian. Our record is horribly smudged, and not for a minute would I pretend that it isn't.

If at death we are to be judged on this life, then what we do here and now matters enormously. It may be of ultimate import whether or not we give a thirsty child a cup of cool water, whether or not we feed the hungry stranger who comes to our door. St. John of the Cross said, "In the evening of life we shall be judged on love." So if, when we die, Christ locks on us with love in his eyes, and we are able to respond with love, then we know heaven. But if he looks at us with love and we respond with fear or hate or indifference, then we know hell. If I have denied bread to one hungry stranger I could have fed, that slice of pie is going to taste bitter indeed.

We can't consider heaven as a result of the cross without considering the other possibility, hell, and we're as bad about hell as we are about heaven.

In the Western Church, we jump directly from Good Friday to Easter Day, with Saturday a vague blank in between. But in the Eastern Church, Great and Holy Saturday is one of the most important days in the year.

Where was Jesus on that extraordinary day between the darkness of Good Friday and the brilliance of Easter Sunday? He was down in hell. And what was he doing there? He was harrowing hell, or to put it in simpler words, he was ministering to the damned.

Christian graphic art has often tended to make my affirmation of Jesus Christ as Lord almost impossible, for far too often he is depicted as a tubercular goy, effeminate and self-pitying. The first 'religious' picture I saw which excited me and stretched and enlarged my faith was a small black and white photograph of the fresco over the altar of the Church of the Chora in Istanbul; a few years ago it was my privilege to visit Istanbul and see this fresco for myself.

The Church of the Chora is now a museum, but when we went there on a chill morning with the smell of the first snow in the air, it was empty. As we stepped over the threshold we came face to face with a slightly more than life-size mosaic of the head of Christ, looking at us with a gaze of indescribable power. It was a fierce face, nothing weak about it, and I knew that if this man had turned such a look on me and told me to take up my bed and walk, I would not have dared not to obey. And whatever he told me to do, I would have been able to do.

The mosaic was preparation for the fresco over the altar. I stood there, trembling with joy, as I looked at this magnificent painting of the harrowing of hell. In the center is the figure of Jesus striding through hell, a figure of immense virility and power. With one strong hand he is grasping Adam, with the other, Eve, and wresting them out of the power of hell. The gates to hell, which he has trampled down and destroyed forever, are in cross-form, the same cross on which he died.

GREAT AND HOLY SATURDAY

Death and damnation began with my body still my own,
began when I was ousted from my place,
and many creatures still were left unnamed.
Gone are some, now, extinct, and nameless,
as though they had never been.
In hell I feel their anxious breath, see their accusing eyes.
My guilt is heavier than was the weight of flesh.

I bear the waste of time spent in recriminations
("You should not have. . . ." "But you told me. . . ." "Nay, it was you
who. . . .").
And yet I knew my wife, and this was good.
But all good turned to guilt. Our first-born
killed his brother. Only Seth gave us no grief.
I grew old, and was afraid; afraid to die, even knowing
that death had come, and been endured, when we
were forced to leave our home, the one and only home a human man
has ever known. The rest is exile.
Death, when it came, was no more than a dim
continuation of the exile. I was hardly less a shadow
than I had been on earth, and centuries
passed no more slowly than a single day.

I was not prepared to be enfleshed again,
reconciled, if not contented, with my shadow self.
I had seen the birth of children with all its blood and pain
and had no wish ever to be born again.

The sound, when it came, was louder than thunder,
louder than the falling of a mountain,
louder than the tidal wave crashing down the city walls,
stone splitting, falling, smashing.
The light was brutal against my shaded eyes,
blinding me with brilliance. I was thousands
of years unaccustomed to the glory.
Then came the wrench of bone where bone had long been dust.
The shocking rise of dry bones, the burning fleshing,
the surge of blood through artery and vein
was pain as I had never known that pain could be.
My anguished scream was silenced as my hand was held
in a grip of such authority I could not even try to pull away.
The crossed gates were trampled by his powerful feet
and I was wrenched through the chasm
as through the eye of the hurricane.
And then—O God—he crushed me
in his fierce embrace. Flesh entered flesh;
bone, bone. Thus did I die, at last.
Thus was I born.
Two Adams became one.
And in the glory Adam was.
Nay, Adam is.

My young friend who was taught that she was so sinful the only
way an angry God could be persuaded to forgive her was by Jesus

dying for her, was also taught that part of the joy of the blessed in heaven is watching the torture of the damned in hell. A strange idea of joy. But it is a belief limited not only to the more rigid sects. I know a number of highly sensitive and intelligent people in my own communion who consider as a heresy my faith that God's loving concern for his creation will outlast all our willfulness and pride. No matter how many eons it takes, he will not rest until all of creation, including Satan, is reconciled to him, until there is no creature who cannot return his look of love with a joyful response of love.

Origen held this belief and was ultimately pronounced a heretic. Gregory of Nyssa, affirming the same loving God, was made a saint. Some people feel it to be heresy because it appears to deny man his freedom to refuse to love God. But this, it seems to me, denies God his freedom to go on loving us beyond all our willfulness and pride. If the Word of God is the light of the world, and this light cannot be put out, ultimately it will brighten all the dark corners of our hearts and we will be able to see, and seeing, will be given the grace to respond with love—and of our own free will.

The Church has always taught that we must pay for our sins, that we shall be judged and punished according to our sinfulness. But I cannot believe that God wants punishment to go on interminably any more than does a loving parent. The entire purpose of loving punishment is to teach, and it lasts only as long as is needed for the lesson. And the lesson is always love.

It may take more years than we can count before Nero—for instance—has learned enough love to be able to look with joy into the loving eyes of a Christ who enfleshed himself for a time on earth as a Jew, but Nero's punishments, no matter how terrible they may be, are lessons in love, and that love is greater than all his sick hate.

We will be quicker to respond with love, under judgment, if we have learned to respond with love, now. Every response of love gives us a glimpse on earth of the Kingdom of Heaven, that brilliant Easter which is born from the dark womb of Good Friday. We cannot repress or deny the darkness, the sinister and mysterious side of love. Without it, Easter, too, is only a fragment of a whole.

On every occasion when we are enabled to do the Lord's will, now, here on earth, we know the Kingdom. I knew it, for instance, during the week of my parents-in-law's golden anniversary. I know it when

I am smiled at by the dour man unloading groceries on Broadway. I know it whan I cook dinner for family and friends, and we are gathered around the table, extraordinary unity in diversity, and are given a foretaste of the Heavenly Banquet, and glimpse the meaning of the cross which leads to life. Then we understand the total failure of God which showed itself by a love so deep that he does indeed die with us and for us and our sins. This dying for us is part of what my young friend was taught, but the next step is left out by her teachers: this dying is something we all must experience; we all die for each other, for if we are children of God, nothing can be left out. When the gates of hell are trampled down, they suddenly become the welcoming door to heaven.

What a good day is this Friday. There is no coming to birth without pain, and out of the pain of this day are we born into the new life of Easter.

7... The Icon Tree

EASTER: that day which follows the harrowing of hell of Great and Holy Saturday; Easter, which turns a terrible Friday into Good Friday. It is almost too brilliant for me to contemplate; it is like looking directly into the sun; I am burned and blinded by life.

Easter completes the circle of blessing, and the joy of the completion remains, despite all the attempts of the powers of darkness to turn it into cursing.

A graduate student wrote to ask if my Christianity affects my novels, and I replied that it is the other way around. My writing affects my Christianity. In a way one might say that my stories keep converting me back to Christianity, from which I am constantly tempted to stray because the circle of blessing seems frayed and close to breaking, and my faith is so frail and flawed that I fall away over and over again from my God. There are times when I feel that he has withdrawn from me, and I have often given him cause; but Easter is always the answer to *My God, my God, why hast thou forsaken me!*

Easter is the most brilliant of all blessings, and all through the Bible, in both Old and New Testaments, comes the message of blessing, and that it is the vocation of the People of God to bless as well as be blessed, and to turn away wrath with a soft answer—a softness which is not flabby, but which has the power of meekness.

That is the point which is most important to me in the story of Balaam and his ass, and perhaps because I loved this story as a child, I responded to it with particular affection when I returned to it as an adult.

One of the best pieces of advice I had from Mary Ellen Chase, that superb teacher I was privileged to study with in college, was that anybody who was seriously considering writing as a profession must be completely familiar with the King James translation of the Bible, because the power of this great translation is the rock on which the English language stands.

So, as a young woman, I turned to the Bible for purely literary reasons. But I discovered that the Bible is a great deal more alive than the Church establishment seemed to be. It is a repository of joy and piety and history and humor and storytelling and great characters, and my writer's mind was nourished. I stayed with the Book all through the years when I kept my back turned on the Establishment.

One of the first messages that struck me is that the Bible is not a moral tract. It may contain all that is necessary for salvation, but the glory of Easter is not a result of self-righteousness. Not long ago I gave a talk to a group of students studying for advanced degrees in education. During the question and answer period one of them asked me about the moral precepts in my stories, and the question alarmed me, because a novel should not be a moral tract, it should be a story. Moralism and moral values are by no means the same thing, but with the slurring of language the two have come pretty close. So I said, somewhat dubiously, because this was a secular lecture to a general audience and I was afraid of being misunderstood, that my point of view about life was going to show under the story, because that's inevitable, but I never consciously write about moral precepts, and I do not like moralism, which is another form of do-it-yourself-ism. And I tried to explain that people who think themselves capable of setting up rigid moral standards are playing dictator, like the occasional prideful people who attempt to get *Winnie-the-Pooh* taken out of the library because they thinks it's immoral.

Other questions came in then, but I went on thinking about it, afraid that some of the students thought that I was advocating immorality. Finally I ventured to mention the Bible. The Bible is not a moral tract and it is not about moral people. Look at them! ordinary human beings, full of flaws, sins, humanness, but found by God. God called Abraham, an old man past his productive years, to be the father of a nation. Jacob, whose behavior was shabby, to say the least, wrestled with an angel. And Rahab was a harlot and Jesus was gentle with a woman taken in adultery.

If a calling committee today were looking for someone to take over an important parish, they'd pass over such people as being completely unqualified. And Paul of Tarsus would certainly never have made it, with his particular list of credentials, such as helping at the stoning of Stephen. But God always calls unqualified people. In cold reality, no one is qualified; but God, whose ways are not our ways, seems to choose those least qualified, people who well may have come from slums and battlefields and insane asylums. If he had chosen great kings, successful and wealthy merchants, wise men with their knowledge of the stars, it would be easy to think that these people, of their own virtue and understanding, accomplished on their own the blessing which God asked them to complete.

And Jesus chose his disciples with the same recklessness as his father; he chose them not in the Sanhedrin, not in the high places of the wealthy; he found them as they were fishing, collecting taxes, going about the ordinary business of life.

The men and women called by God to do his work would never have passed a test in moral virtues. David's getting Bathsheba by conniving to have her husband killed in battle was a totally immoral act. Nathan the Prophet made this quite clear to his king, and David repented. Everything that happened to the shepherd boy who became a king was a lesson, loud and clear, that the blessing is always God's. And what happened after David repented? He sang.

> *Your altar smelled of the slaughterhouse.*
> *The innocent eyes of men and beasts*
> *Lost in confusion of laws and vows*
> *Was the high price paid to you for feasts.*
> *They had to be men of iron, your priests.*
>
> *And so did I, born but to sing,*
> *To tend the lambs and not to kill.*
> *Why, my Lord, did you have to bring*
> *Me down from the safety of my hill*
> *Into the danger of your will?*
>
> *I learned to fight, I learned to sin;*
> *I battled heathen, fought with lust;*
> *When you were on my side I'd win.*
> *My appetites I could not trust.*
> *I only knew your wrath was just.*

What I desired I went and stole.
I had to fight against my son.
You bound my wounds and made me whole
Despite the wrong that I had done.
I turned from you and tried to run.

You took me, also, by the hair
And brought me back before your altar.
You terrified me with your care.
Against your rage I could but falter.
You changed me, but refused to alter.

So I grew old, but there remained
Within me still the singing boy.
I stripped and sang. My wife complained,
Yet all my ill did I destroy
Dancing before you in our joy.

O God, my God, is it not meet
That I should sing and shout and roar,
Leap to your ark with loving feet?
I praise thee, hallow, and adore
And play before thee evermore.

And so would I, my Lord.

But at that lecture one of the students, still hung up on moralism, said, "But you're looking for something in your books, you can't deny that." "Of course I'm looking for something. But I'm not looking for morals, I'm looking for truth." Probably in searching for the truth of love I'll discover something about morals, though I'm not sure. The older I get and the more I learn, the less qualified I become to make correct moral judgments; that may not stop me from having to make them—an event must be assessed before it can be blessed—but I have learned with hindsight that with all the good will in the world I may be wrong, and it is only by offering my judgments to God that they can be redeemed and blessed.

Slow am I as always to recognize what is right in front of me. Of course: all I'm fumbling on about moralism has already been said for me by Paul. Moralism belongs to the old law and the old covenant. Jesus Christ in his life, death, and resurrection oveturned the laws of moralism. *Christ hath redeemed us from the curse of the law, being made a curse for us.* That's not very acceptable language, but it does help to put my fragments together.

It is difficult to bless and not to curse when one's control of a situation is taken away. I witness daily the cursing which is the result of impotence. My threshold of anger is much lower than it used to be. Small annoyances provoke much too strong a reaction of irritation. I may not curse, but blessings do not come to my lips as often as I would like.

The doors of many of the neighborhood shops around our apartment are no longer open to welcome the customer. One has to be buzzed in, because there have been so many shopkeepers shot or stabbed that it has become necessary to live in this sadly realistic climate of suspicion, which increases my own feelings of impotence. When Hugh is late coming home from theatre or television studio I pace about nervously, fearful that he may have been mugged. And the very muggers themselves are reacting irrationally to an impotence and frustration far greater than mine, so it is no wonder that they respond with a curse.

But our television commercials, our political speeches, our 'how-to' and 'do-it-yourself' books would seem to offer us a world in which, if we only eat a low carbohydrate and low cholesterol diet, or buy a new combination washing machine and outdoor barbecue, we will be in charge of our lives.

We aren't, and most of us know we aren't, and that isn't easy to accept.

If we have so little control over the world in which we live, can our lives, and the lives of those we love, have any meaning?

Easter affirms meaning, even though it's not possible for finite brokenness to define the meaning of infinite wholeness. The acceptance of this not-knowing is nothing new; rather, technocracy has refused to accept what the anonymous author of *The Cloud of Unknowing* understood and expressed for us so beautifully.

It is only when I am not afraid to recognize my own brokenness, to say, "Turn us again, Lord God of hosts, cause thy face to shine and we shall be whole"—that the broken bones may begin to heal, and to rejoice. Without this *phos hilaron,* this joyous light, we fight against our impotence, in our spiritual lives, our intellectual lives, a large portion of our physical lives.

But in the small events of daily living we are given the grace to condition our responses to frustrations. It's something like driving a car. If you're driving along a highway and a car comes at you from a side road, and you have to think what you ought to do, you're not likely to avoid an accident. In an emergency you don't have time to stop and think. You act before thought, on your conditioned reflexes.

So it is with all of life. If our usual response to an annoying situation is a curse, we're likely to meet emergencies with a curse. In the little events of daily living we have the opportunity to condition our reflexes, which are built up out of ordinary things. And we learn to bless first of all by being blessed. My reflexes of blessing have been conditioned by my parents, my husband, my children, my friends.

Blessing is an attitude toward all of life, transcending and moving beyond words. When family and friends gather around the table to break bread together, this is a blessing. When we harden our hearts against anyone, this is a cursing. Sometimes a person, or a group of people, do or say something so terrible that we can neither bless nor curse. They are anathema. We put them outside the city walls, not out of revenge, not out of hate, but because they have gone beyond anything we fragile human beings can cope with. So we say, Here, God, I'm sorry. This is more than I can handle. Please take care of it. Your ways are not our ways. You know what to do. Please.

But sometimes I am confronted with a situation which demands a response of either blessing or cursing, and from me. I cannot refuse to meet the emergency by turning aside. And I have cause to remember Balaam, who was ordered by King Balak to go and curse the children of Israel. Rather reluctantly he saddled his ass and went to do the king's bidding, and his ass stopped in the middle of the road, because she saw something Balaam didn't see; she saw the angel of the Lord standing in the path, and she refused to allow Balaam to go on. And in the end Balaam heeded the ass, and he blessed the children of Israel, blessed instead of cursed.

Blessing is no easier for me than it was for Balaam, and there was a Friday after Easter, two years ago, when I was put to the test.

When we open our house in the country in the spring we know that it will still be winter on our hill; Crosswicks is a good three weeks behind New York, where the Cathedral Close is bursting with blossom, and the cement islands which run down the middle of Broadway are astonishing with the glory of magnolia blooms. At Crosswicks the forsythia will show no bud, though if I bring it indoors it will take only a day or so before it bursts into gold. The house, even with the furnace running, will not be quite warm enough, and we'll huddle around the fire and rush upstairs to bed to plunge beneath the covers. Things which were part of the burden when we lived in Crosswicks year round are fun when it's only on a weekend basis.

I look forward with intense anticipation to the first weekend in the country. Each year the city gets more difficult. Each year the world seems in a worse mess than it was the year before. Our own country is still in trouble, and this trouble is reflected in the city and on the Cathedral Close. I need to get away and find perspective.

On that particular Friday after Easter it had been a bad week in the world, a bad week in the country, a bad week on the Close. I looked forward to the peace and quiet of the first weekend the way, as a small child, I had anticipated Christmas. When we got up to Crosswicks it was still light, one of those rare blue-and-gold afternoons when the sky shimmers with radiance. Hugh said to me, "I bet you're going right to the brook."

"Would you mind?"

"Go ahead, but don't stay too long."

So I called Timothy from sniffing the rock garden and set off across the big field and over the stone wall. Easter was late that year, and the trees were beginning to put forth tiny gold shoots which in another couple of weeks would be green leaves. Some of the budding maples were pale pink, and the beech trees were almost lavender. I could feel myself unwinding from the tensions of the past weeks. I felt surrounded by blessing.

I have several favorite places where I like to sit and think. Probably the most favorite is a large rock above the brook. Directly in front of the rock is an old maple tree. When the trees are fully leafed it is always shaded, and on the hottest day it is cool there. I knew that now the brook would be rushing, filled with clear, icy water from melting snow.

The summer before, I had gone with Josephine and Alan and the two little girls to a fair at Regina Laudis Monastery in Bethlehem, Conn. I have a good friend among the Sisters there, and that afternoon she gave me a small, laminated icon of a medieval Mother and Child, and a little cross. I had put these on the trunk of the big maple, and in the late afternoon it was my habit to go to my thinking rock and say my prayers and then, with the icon tree as my focus, to try to move beyond the words of prayer to the prayer of the heart.

So that spring afternoon I headed straight for the rock and the icon tree. But as I started down the tiny path through the trees which leads to the rock, I felt that something was wrong. I quickened my steps and when I had climbed up on the rock I saw. Someone had shot the icon at close range. It was split in four parts. There was a bullet hole through the face of the holy child. The cross had been pulled from its ring; only the broken ring still clung to the nail.

I felt an incredible wave of hate flood over me. I was literally nauseated. What had been done had been done deliberately; it was not an accident; it was a purposeful blasphemy, an act of cursing.

I was beyond any response of either blessing or cursing. But I knew that I couldn't go home until I had been washed clean of the hate. The very trees around the rock seemed to draw back in horror and apology because they had not been able to stop the intruder.

Feeling sick and cold I called Timothy and walked and walked.

Seeking perspective in a hate-torn world,
Leaving, for respite brief, the choking city,
I turn to trees, new leaves not quite unfurled,
A windswept blue-pure sky for pity.
Across a pasture, over a stone wall,
Past berry brambles and an unused field,
Listening for leaf sound and the brook's clear call,
Turning down path by bush and tree concealed,
Forgetting human sin and nature's fall
I seek perfection in the cool green still.
Small trees with new spring growth are tall.
Here is no sign of human hate or ill.
   Unexpecting any pain or shock
   I turn to climb upon my thinking rock.

The rock stands high above the snow-full brook.
Behind the rock an old tree breaks the sky,
And on the tree where bird and beast may look
An icon and a cross are hanging high.
So strong are they, placed lovingly together,
I need have little fear for their protection
Through wind and snow and bitter wintry weather.
They speak to me of joy and Resurrection
And here my self-will stills, my heart beats slow.

God's presence in his world is bright and strong.
Upon the rock I climb, and then—No! No!
The sky is dark and here is hate and wrong.
   O God! Make it not be! Oh, make it not!
   The icon: target for a rifle's shot.

A wave of dark blasts cold across my face.
My stomach heaves with nausea at the dirt
Of hate in this pure green and loving place.
The trees pull back and cower in their hurt.
Rooted, they could not stop the vicious gun
Fired straight at God's birth-giver and her child.
There's only death in this. It's no one's fun
To blaspheme love. A shot has made a wild
Distortion of the young and ancient face.
I give the broken fragments to the brook
And let the water lap them with its grace.
And then I sit upon the rock and look
   At the great gouge in the tree's wood.
   Evil obscures all peace and love and good.

My dog knew that something had upset me. He kept close as we walked, instead of tearing off in great loops. We kept walking until I had come to the point where I could simply turn over to God whoever had shot the icon and the cross. This person was beyond my puny human ability to understand. I could not add to the curse by cursing. But I did not know how to bless. I went back to the house and told Hugh what had happened. The next day I carried tools and took the remains of the icon off the tree and gave them to the brook. I took away the small nail with the broken loop. Then I sat on the rock and looked at the gouge in the tree's wood. What I describe in the next sonnet did not happen that day, but it did happen, and redeemed the act of hate, and made the tree far more of an icon for me than it was before.

As I sit looking at the shot-at tree
The rough wound opens and grows strange and deep
Within the wood, till suddenly I see
A galaxy aswirl with flame. I do not sleep
And yet I see a trillion stars speed light
In ever-singing dance within the hole
Surrounded by the tree. Each leaf's alight
With flame. And then a burning living coal

> *Drops hissing in the brook, and all the suns*
> *Burst outward in their joy, and the shot child,*
> *Like the great and flaming tree, runs*
> *With fire and water, and alive and wild*
> > *Gentle and strong, becomes the wounded tree.*
> > *Lord God! The icon's here, alive and free.*

Balak sent Balaam to curse the children of Israel, and the ass saw an angel of God and sat down under Balaam and refused to move, and the curse was turned to a blessing.

I don't understand and I don't need to understand.

Bless the Lord, O my soul, I cry with the psalmist whose songs after all these thousands of years still sing so poignantly for us. O bless his Holy Name, and may he bless each one of us and teach us to bless one another.

Throughout these pages there has been an affirmation, explicit as well as implicit, of my faith in the promise of Easter, of the Resurrection, not only of the Lord Jesus Christ but of us all; the Resurrection not as panacea or placebo for those who cannot cope without medication, or as the soporific of the masses (Simone Weil said that revolution, and not religion, is the soporific of the masses), but as the reality which lights the day.

The experience with the icon tree was a *symbole* of resurrection for me, an affirmation which helps me to respond with a blessing where otherwise I might curse.

There are too many books which affirm resurrection now and can't quite believe in resurrection after death. Resurrection now is indeed important for resurrection then, but resurrection now means little if after death there is nothing but ashes to ashes and dust to dust. The God who redeemed the icon tree for me will not create creatures able to ask questions only to be snuffed out before they can answer them. There is no pragmatic reason why any of my questions should be answered, why this little life should not be all; but the joyful God of love who shouted the galaxies into existence is not going to abandon any iota of his creation. So the icon tree is for me a *symbole* of God's concern, forever and always and unto ages of ages, for all of us, every single one of us, no matter what we think or believe or deny.

So let there be no question: I believe in the resurrection of Jesus of Nazareth as Jesus the Christ, and the resurrection of the body of all

creatures great and small, not the literal resurrection of this tired
body, this broken self, but the body as it was meant to be, the fragmented self made new; so that at the end of time all Creation will be
One. Well: maybe I don't exactly believe it, but I know it, and knowing is what matters.

ALL THAT MATTERS

Nothing.
Out of nothing
out of the void
(what?
where?)
God created.

Out of
nothing
which is
what?
But it is
not a what
or a where
or an opposite
of something
or anything.
Nothing is
nothing
we can know.
Does it matter
that matter's mind
must not mind
not knowing
nothing
doubly negatively
or in any way
positively
not.

O Mind
that alone knows
nothing
O Word
that speaks
to matter
that

> *speaks matter*
> *from the unspoken:*
> *that you mind*
> *is all that matters.*

And this minding makes my lack of faith no matter, for I know; I know resurrection, and that is all that matters.

The strange turning of what seemed to be a horrendous No to a glorious Yes is always the message of Easter. The destroyed icon and the wounded tree are a poignant symbol of the risen Christ. The gouge in the tree is beginning to heal, but I will always know that it is there, and it is living witness that love is stronger than hate. Already things have happened which have put this knowledge to the test, and sometimes I have been where I could not go to the rock and see the tangible assurance of the tree's tall strong trunk. But I can turn in my mind's eye and see it, can image the whole chain of events from the cruel destruction of death to the brilliance of new life.

I need to hold on to that bright promise.

8... The Blue Balloon

THERE IS a theory that Jesus of Nazareth, like many other
extraordinary men who have walked this planet, was in reality a
visitor from the stars, a man of a higher race than we terrans, who
came to help us out of the muddle we were making of our world and
then, his mission accomplished (or failed, depending on your point of
view), got into his space ship and ascended into the heavens and
returned to his own galaxy.

The idea of extraterrestrials coming to visit their lower brethren
does not seem to me particularly farfetched (after all, I both read and
write science fiction), but it doesn't work with my theory of incarnation. It's simply a modern variation of an old heresy, that Jesus wasn't
really man. He came and lived with us and shared our lives with
magnificent compassion and generosity, but he wasn't really one of us.
He went through the motions of death, but being an immortal he
didn't really die, he only seemed to.

Throughout the centuries we have teetered back and forth on this
paradox of Jesus as wholly man and wholly God, and too often for
comfort have found it too difficult to believe. We emphasize either the
divinity or the humanity, to the weakening of the other.

One evening Tallis and I were talking, after teaching a class together. One of the students had been defining God, and everybody
agreed that this is impossible. But I said afterwards to Tallis, "*We*
can't define God, but didn't God define himself for us, in Jesus
Christ?"

He replied, "That's all very well, as long as you remember Kierkegaard's saying that Jesus came to us and looked like us and ate like

us and talked like us, and the disguise was so perfect that we believed that he was just like one of us."

I hesitate to disagree with either Kierkegaard or Tallis, but this bothered me so much that I blundered on. "But Jesus *was* us: isn't that the whole point? Jesus is us; and it's we who aren't us, and haven't been, not since Adam and Eve."

And I still think that's true. The second Adam was what the first Adam was meant to be, what we were *all* meant to be: spontaneous, free, aware, unafraid to love, without *hubris:* whole. Not as we are, fragmented, inhibited, sunside and darkside in collision instead of collaboration, so that we are afraid of all that we might find in the sinister world of the subconscious, are suspicious of intuition, and close our doors to the knocking of the Spirit.

> *Go away. You can't come in. I'm shutting the door.*
> *I'm afraid of you. I'm not sure who you are anymore.*
> *I'm closing the door. I'm staying safe and alone.*
> *Batter against it all you like. This house is built on stone.*
> *You can't come in. I've shuttered the windows tight.*
> *You never say who you are. If it's You, then it's all right,*
> *But you might be the other, the beautiful prince of this world*
> *Who makes my heart leap with his cohorts and banners unfurled.*
> *I could be unfaithful with him without any trouble*
> *If I opened the door. He could easily pass for your double.*
> *I've buried my talents. If I put them to use*
> *I could hurt or be hurt, be abused or abuse.*
> *I wish you'd stop blowing. My whole house is shaken.*
> *I'll hide under the covers. Be gone when I waken.*
>
> *What's that light at the windows, that blast at the door?*
> *The shutters are burning, there's fire on the floor.*
> *Go away. I don't know you. My clothes are aflame,*
> *My tongue is on fire, you are crying my name;*
> *I hear your wild voice through the holocaust's din.*
> *My house is burned up.*
> *What?*
> *Oh, welcome! Come in!*

It's not easy to understand the fire of the spirit which burns and does not consume, to keep our door open so that we are helped to understand a God so loving that he can actually be one of us, and still be God.

The idea of a Jesus who really wasn't one of us after all is easier to believe in than the technical impossibility which I daily struggle to believe, the extraordinary paradox which is all that makes the universe bearable. Jesus of Nazareth was wholly man as well as wholly God. He did die. For our sakes he suffered everything we suffer, even doubt. And then he broke the powers of death and returned briefly to quite a few people—not everybody, but enough so that his presence was noted—though he was never recognized on sight. And then, after a time, he ascended, whatever that means.

What it means in terms of physical, provable fact, I cannot know. Whatever really happened has been lost in the mists of two thousand years. I do know that it has something to do with love, the kind of open, joyful, giving love I fail in daily, and struggle daily to understand.

I know it's not like that sunny Sunday afternoon
when we went to the zoo; evening came too soon
and we were back on the crowded city street
still full of pleasure from the afternoon's treat,
and our little girl clutched in her fingers a blue balloon.

It bobbed above our heads. Suddenly there came a cry,
a howl of absolute loss. We looked on high
and there we saw the balloon, ascending,
turning and twirling, higher and higher, blending
into the smoky blue of the city sky.

We wiped the eyes, blew the little nose, consoled the tears,
did not, of course, offer a new balloon, instead were silly,
*   waggled our ears,*
turned sobs to laughter, accepted loss, and hurried
home for dinner. This day is not like that. And yet they must
*   have tarried,*
looking up into the sky the day he left them, full of loss and fears.

He had come back to them, was with them, and then was lost
again, or so perhaps it seemed, the table left without the host.
The disciples did not understand all that he had said,
that comfort would be sent, there would be wine and bread.
Lost and abandoned (where is my blue balloon?) they did not comprehend
*   until the day of Pentecost.*

Even after he told them, his followers did not hear and see:
"What is this that he saith unto us? A little while and ye

Shall not see me, and again a little while, and ye shall. . . . when?
tomorrow?
We do not understand." Lord, nor do I, and share thus in their
sorrow
at the same time that the Spirit sets my sorrow free
to turn to love, and teaches me through pain to know
that love will dwell in me and I in love only if I let love go.

So the Ascension is freed to move into the realm of myth.

It doesn't bother me when people talk condescendingly about the Christian myth, because it is in myth that sunside and night-side collaborate and give us our glimpses of truth. But when I use the word *myth* I bump headlong into semantic problems, because myth, to many people, is a lie. Despite the fact that during the last decade myth has been rediscovered as a vehicle of truth, there are still those who cannot help thinking of it as something which is false. We give children the Greek and Roman myths, the Norse or Celtic myths, and expect them to be outgrown, as though they are only for children and not to be taken seriously by realistic adults. If I speak of the Christian myth it is assumed not only that I am certainly not a fundamentalist, but that I am an intellectual who does not need God and can speak with proper condescension of the rather silly stories which should be outgrown at puberty. But I am far closer to the fundamentalist than the atheist when I speak of myth as truth.

The rediscovery of myth hasn't helped, because what does his Satanic Majesty do when the sons of Adam stumble upon something which would further the coming of the Kingdom and destroy the Prince of this World? He infiltrates, and so myth becomes part of the jargon, and jargon has no power.

Nonetheless, myth is the closest approximation to truth available to the finite human being. And the truth of myth is not limited by time or place. A myth tells of that which was true, is true, and will be true. If we will allow it, myth will integrate intellect and intuition, night and day; our warring opposites are reconciled, male and female, spirit and flesh, desire and will, pain and joy, life and death.

God became man, was born of a woman, and we would have liked to keep this man-child with us forever; and that kind of possessiveness leads to disaster; as most parents know.

When I wrote the following lines I thought of them as being in Mary's voice, but they might just as well be in mine—or any parent's.

Now we may love the child.
Now he is ours,
this tiny thing,
utterly vulnerable and dependent
on the circle of our love.
Now we may hold him,
feeling with gentle hands
the perfection of his tender skin
from the soft crown of his head
to the sweet soles of his merrily kicking feet.
His fingers softly curl
around one finger of the grownup hand.
Now we may hold.
Now may I feel his hungry sucking at my breast
as I give him my own life.
Now may my husband toss him in the air
and catch him in his sure and steady hands
laughing with laughter as quick and pure
as the baby's own.
Now may I rock him softly to his sleep,
rock and sing,
sing and hold.
This moment of time is here,
has happened, is:
rejoice!

Child,
give me the courage
for the time
when I must open my arms
and let you go.

I looked at my last baby lying in his cradle, knowing that he was the last child I would bear, for I nearly didn't survive his birth; looked, touched, listened, with an incredible awareness I might not have had if I had been able to expect to bear more children. As each change came, I had to let the infant-that-was go, go forever. When he was seven months old I weaned him, as part of that essential letting go, letting him move on to child, little boy, young man. . . . Love, and let go. Love, and let go.

It's always pain, this letting go, and yet it leads to joy, and a kind of lightness which is almost physical.

> *Pride is heavy.*
> *It weighs.*
> *It is a fatness of spirit,*
> *an overindulgence in self.*
> *This gluttony is earthbound,*
> *cannot be lifted up.*
> *Help me to fast,*
> *to lose this weight.*
> *Otherwise, O Light one,*
> *how can I rejoice in your*
> *Ascension?*

We tend to be heavy, we middle Americans, heavy in all ways. More than half the world is starving, and we go on crash diets to try to take off weight. Nor are we jolly fat people. Affluence tends to bring with it a stupor, a flatulence of spirit. It is difficult to laugh freely as long as we are clutching all that we have accumulated and are afraid to lose.

One day in early spring Pat and I drove up to Crosswicks. There was snow on the ground; I made Pat put on boots and a heavy coat and trek with me across the fields to the brook. I strayed from the path several times, fell, laughing, into snowdrifts, from which she had to pull me, but at last we reached the brook, which was rushing noisily, at its fullest from melting snow. And Pat looked at it and then said in a bemused voice, "It's not polluted!"

Pat is a physician who is Chief of Health for a large Southern city. Part of her job is understanding problems of pollution, overconsumption. This was three years before the oil crisis, but she had already seen that it was coming, and told me so. Standing there on the rock bridge over the brook I asked her, "Are we going to be able to save planet earth?"

She replied calmly, "No. Not unless we're willing to make drastic changes in our standard of living. Not unless we're willing to go back to being as cold in winter as our grandparents were, and as hot in summer."

That is even more true now than it was then. But we are loath to let go all the creature comforts which are the result of the distortion of the American dream. The idea of the recovery of the real dream is an exciting one. My family and I do try to live simply, and the simpler our lives, the freer. Not that I enjoy being hot in summer, sitting at the typewriter with the sweat trickling down my back and the inside of my legs. In late afternoon with the sun pouring onto my desk it is often so hot that I cannot stay in my workroom. But there's always a moderately cool place somewhere. The leaf-protected rock at the brook is always cool.

We eat largely out of Hugh's magnificent vegetable garden, and we are indeed blessed in having the space for it. I freeze vegetables all summer long, so that the garden feeds us for much of the winter.

When we lived in the house year round we got used to putting on more clothes when it got cold, as the English do, rather than turning up the heat. But I'd better be careful not to get sentimental about being hot in summer and cold in winter, as our forebears were. The old, the ill, the weak, did not survive the excessive temperatures of either winter or summer. And we have become delicate, with our thermostats set to keep us at a constant temperature of around 70° year round. Pat told me that college football coaches discovered the hard way that they had better warn their athletes not to take a summer job in any kind of air-conditioned office, but to work outdoors in the heat of the sun. When the body becomes accustomed to a constant temperature, our inner thermostats lose the ability to adjust, and so a young man who has spent the summer sitting at a desk in an air-conditioned office drops dead on the playing field on a hot autumn day, because his body's thermostat can't cope.

I console myself when I'm wet with heat in summer, shivering with cold in winter, that I'm helping my body's thermostat to become functional once more.

I would like to travel light on this journey of life, to get rid of the encumbrances I acquire each day. Worse than physical acquisitions are spiritual ones, small grudges, jealousies, hurt feelings. I am helped by the fact that nursing a grudge gives me no pleasure; I cannot bear to go to bed angry; I am compelled by an inner drive to 'make up,' to reconcile, to restore relations. It doesn't always work, of course. It does take two, and there are people who not only cannot make an apology; they cannot accept one. Once when this happened to me, Tallis said, "You've done what you had to do. That's all you have to worry about. Let it go." Letting go, again.

I once had an acquaintance who was a far more regular church-goer than I, rose early to go to Holy Communion each morning before he went to work, and yet hated all Orientals. Whenever an Oriental priest celebrated communion, he refused to receive the bread and wine.

I knelt behind him in a small chapel on a morning when a Japanese priest, one of my friends, was the celebrant, and I knew that this man would not touch the Body and Blood because it was held by yellow hands. And I was outraged.

I am not in love and charity with this man, I thought, and therefore, according to the rubrics, I should not go up to the altar. And yet I knew that my only hope of love and charity was to go forward and receive the elements.

He did not know that he, himself, was acting wholly without love and charity. Something within him obviously justified this abominable reaction, so that at the next Eucharist, if it was presided over by somebody he recognized as priest, as he was unable to recognize the Japanese priest, he would hold out his hands and receive in love and humility.

He does not know what he is doing. He does not know.

Surely within me there is an equal blindness, something that I do not recognize in myself, that I justify without even realizing it.

All right, brother. Let us be forgiven together, then. I will hold out my hands for both of us today, and do you for me tomorrow morning when I will be asleep while you trudge through the dirty streets to church. It is all right for me to be outraged by what you are doing here in the presence of God, as long as it does not set me apart from you.

It was heavy, heavy for a while there. I put on several hundred pounds in a few minutes, and now they are gone, at least for a while. My spiritual scales fluctuate wildly. They are always on the heavy side, but there are days when I am able to travel light, and these days show me the way.

The most difficult thing to let go is my *self*, that self which, coddled and cozened, becomes smaller as it becomes heavier. I don't understand how and why I come to *be* only as I lose myself, but I know from long experience that this is so.

9... Whispers

THE HOLY SPIRIT, the third person of the Trinity, is the easiest of this not-at-all-easy concept for me to understand. Any artist, great or small, knows moments when something more than he takes over, and he moves into a kind of 'overdrive,' where he works as ordinarily he cannot work. When he is through, there is a sense of exhilaration, exhaustion, and joy. All our best work comes in this fashion, and it is humbling and exciting.

After *A Wrinkle in Time* was finally published, it was pointed out to me that the villain, a naked disembodied brain, was called "It," because It stands for Intellectual truth as opposed to a truth which involves the whole of us, heart as well as mind. That acronym had never occurred to me. I chose the name It intuitively, because an IT does not have a heart or soul. And I did not understand consciously at the time of writing that the intellect, when it is not informed by the heart, is evil.

But a further proof that my books know more than I do came later, again with this same book, when my husband's television wife, Ruth Warwick, who plays Phoebe Tyler in *All My Children,* was on the *Today Show* with Ed Mitchell, who was one of the second group of astronauts actually to walk on the moon. His present job is to explain scientific concepts of space to laymen. And, he told Ruth, he finds this very difficult to do; scientific concepts of space are not easy to understand. So he uses a book, a book which he said can get these concepts across far better than he is able to. "It's supposed to be a children's book," he said, "but it really isn't. It's called *A Wrinkle in Time.*" "Oh, yes," said Ruth, "my husband's wife wrote it."

So my book knows more about physics than I do, and I find this very exciting. I did, indeed, study physics while I was writing *Wrinkle,* but I've never taken a course in physics, and surely I could not have learned enough, reading on my own, to make my book useful to an astronaut.

It was not until I was nearly forty that I discovered that higher math is easier than lower math. Lower math lost me way down in the grades when I was informed that three multiplied by zero=zero. Now, I understand that if I have nothing, and I multiply it by three, three somethings are not suddenly going to appear. But if I *have* three apples, and I multiply them by zero, nobody has been able to explain to my satisfaction why they are going to vanish—and yet this is what lower math would have us believe.

It was not until I discovered higher math that I understood $0 \times 3 = 0$. First of all, I had to accept that arithmetic is simply an agreed-upon fiction which makes life easier. Secondly, I realized that $0 \times 3 = 0$ is a philosophical rather than an arithmetical problem, and I worked this out in writing *The Other Side of the Sun.* But I have a hunch I understood it already, with my intuition, while I was working on *Wrinkle;* any kind of hate which would annihilate, any kind of lust for power which makes people expendable, is an example of three multiplied by zero equals zero.

When I talk about my books knowing more than I do, I am not referring to something magic. Nor is it an easy way out which eliminates the hard work of putting together a story. Writing a book is work; it involves discipline, and writing when I don't feel like writing. Robert Louis Stevenson said that writing is ten percent inspiration, and ninety percent perspiration. The inspiration doesn't come before the perspiration; it's usually the other way around. Inspiration comes during work, not before it. The hardest part of the morning is the first half hour or so when I will put off for as long as possible the actual work on whatever book I'm currently writing. I'll sharpen pencils I don't intend to use; I'll check over my black felt pens, with which I write when I'm not near a typewriter; I'll even change the typewriter ribbon; anything to put off the moment of plunging in. But after I've dipped my toes in the cold water for long enough, I hold my breath and jump in. And once I'm in, if it is a day of grace (and it often isn't), then something will happen, and just what that something is remains, for me, a mystery. But it is involved in servanthood, my servanthood, in a day when service is considered degrading.

I am convinced that each work of art, be it a great work of genius or something very small, has its own life, and it will come to the artist, the composer or the writer or the painter, and say, "Here I am: compose me; or write me; or paint me"; and the job of the artist is to serve the work. I have never served a work as I would like to, but I do try, with each book, to serve to the best of my ability, and this attempt at serving is the greatest privilege and the greatest joy that I know.

At its highest, the relationship between the artist and the work shifts, and artist and work collaborate. In my own way I have known such moments—I think all artists know them, because it has nothing to do with the degree of talent. And, just as in my tiny efforts at peacemaking I must not reject the small things which are given me in my daily life, so I must not worry about comparisons between great and small. I used to irritate my children by frequently quoting Marlowe: "Comparisons are odious."

As I understand the gift of the spirit in art, so I understand prayer, and there is very little difference for me between praying and writing. At their best, both become completely unselfconscious activities; the self-conscious, fragmented person is totally thrown away and integrated in work, and for the moments of such work, be it prayer or writing, I know wholeness, and sunside and nightside are no longer divided.

Whence comes this rush of wind?
I stand at the earth's rim
and feel it streaming by
my hair, my eyes, my lips.
I shall be blown clean off.
I cannot stand the cold.

Earth shrinks. The day recedes.
The stars rush in, their fire·
blown wild as they race by.
This wind's strange, harsh embrace
holds me against the earth,
batters me with its power.

My bones are turned to ice.
I am not here   nor there
but caught in this great breath.
Its rhythm cracks my ribs.
Blown out   I am expelled
Breathed in   I am inspired

The wind broods where it will
across the water's face.
The flowing sea of sky
moves to the wind's demand.

The stars stretch fiery tongues
until this mortal frame
is seared to bone, to ash,
and yet, newborn, it lives.

Joy blazes through the night.
Wind, water, fire, are light.

One of the holiest of archbishops, Father Anthony Bloom likens the Holy Spirit to a shy and gentle bird who must be approached quietly and slowly, lest he be frightened and fly away.

Whereas Alan likens the Holy Spirit to a ravening hawk, and while both similes hold truth, when I have been aware of the Spirit at the time (rather than later, by hindsight) my experiences have been more hawklike than dovelike. But considerable violence is needed to pull my fragments together, to join sunside and nightside; it's a rather wildly athletic act to place the mind in the heart, and a lot of muscles get pulled.

And, of course, whenever we become whole, Satan moves in to fragment us again. There's a renewed awareness of the gifts of the Spirit nowadays, but Alan reminded me that not all spirits abroad are the Holy Spirit.

We have forgotten the warning in the Letter to the Ephesians, where the people of the Church at Ephesus are warned that "we wrestle not against flesh and blood, but against principalities, against powers, against the rulers of the darkness of this world, against spiritual wickedness in high places." When we limit ourselves to the rational world of provable fact, a warning like this tends to sound like something out of science fiction rather than the Bible, but as I look at the world around me, in the city, as I listen to the news, the warning seems like anything but fiction, and I read on gratefully as Paul continues, "Wherefore take unto you the whole armour of God, that ye may be able to withstand in the evil day."

In his letter to the People in Rome, Paul talks reassuringly about the help of the Holy Spirit in this battle against the dark spirits, "for we know that the whole creation groaneth and travaileth in pain together until now. And not only they, but ourselves also, which have the firstfruits of the Spirit, even we ourselves groan within ourselves. . . . Likewise the Spirit also helpeth our infirmities: for we know not what we should pray for as we ought: but the Spirit itself maketh intercession for us with groanings which cannot be uttered."

Paul's language is strong, too strong for many of us. We'd like the joys of the Spirit without any of the groaning. But any spirit which promises us easy ecstasy is not the Holy Spirit. Indeed, one of the quickest ways to make sure that the spirit is not the Holy One is to be convinced, at the moment of inspiration, that it *is.*

If I am conscious of writing well as I am writing, those pages usually end in the wastepaper basket. If I am conscious of praying well, I am probably not praying at all. These are gifts which we know only afterwards, with anamnesis.

Trouble always comes whenever we begin to take credit for any of the gifts of the Spirit, be they gifts of prayer, tongues, prophecy, art, science. This can be as fatally true in the secular world as in the religious—but one of the greatest victories of the Enemy has been the separation of sacred and secular, and placing them in opposition. All of creation is sacred, despite everything we have done to abase and abuse it. Healing used to be looked on as a sacred calling, and surely the Hippocratic oath is a prayer. Modern medicine suffers, despite all its advances, because it has almost completely forgotten that healing is a gift as well as a science. I want my doctor to have every possible amount of training, but this training will not make him a great doctor unless he has the gift as well.

We need to recover and reverence vocation in this time of confusion between healing and curing. We have forgotten the Spirit.

I believe in prayer, and I believe in miracle, because I have seen enough evidence, pragmatically and scientifically documented, to satisfy the coldest scientist. But it is not the proof which has convinced

me. It is far greater and more exciting than proof.
As the woman with the issue of blood knew:

> *When I pushed through the crowd,*
> *jostled, bumped, elbowed by the curious*
> *who wanted to see what everyone else*
> *was so excited about,*
> *all I could think of was my pain*
> *and that perhaps if I could touch him,*
> *this man who worked miracles,*
> *cured diseases,*
> *even those as foul as mine,*
> *I might find relief.*
> *I was tired from hurting,*
> *exhausted, revolted by my body,*
> *unfit for any man, and yet not let loose*
> *from desire and need. I wanted to rest,*
> *to sleep without pain or filthiness or torment.*
> *I don't really know why*
> *I thought he could help me*
> *when all the doctors*
> *with all their knowledge*
> *had left me still drained*
> *and bereft of all that makes*
> *a woman's life worth living.*
> *Well: I'd seen him with some children*
> *and his laughter was quick and merry*
> *and reminded me of when I was young and well,*
> *though he looked tired; and he was as old as I am.*
> *Then there was that leper,*
> *but lepers have been cured before—*
>
> *No, it wasn't the leper,*
> *or the man cured of palsy,*
> *or any of the other stories of miracles,*
> *or at any rate that was the least of it;*
> *I had been promised miracles too often.*
> *I saw him ahead of me in the crowd*
> *and there was something in his glance*
> *and in the way his hand rested briefly*
> *on the matted head of a small boy*
> *who was getting in everybody's way,*
> *and I knew that if only I could get to him,*
> *not to bother him, you understand,*
> *not to interrupt, or to ask him for anything,*

not even his attention,
just to get to him and touch him . . .

I didn't think he'd mind, and he needn't even know.
I pushed through the crowd
and it seemed that they were deliberately
trying to keep me from him.
I stumbled and fell and someone stepped
on my hand and I cried out
and nobody heard. I crawled to my feet
and pushed on and at last I was close,
so close I could reach out
and touch with my fingers
the hem of his garment.

Have you ever been near
when lightning struck?
I was, once, when I was very small
and a summer storm came without warning
and lightning split the tree
under which I had been playing
and I was flung right across the courtyard.
That's how it was.
Only this time I was not the child
but the tree
and the lightning filled me.
He asked, "Who touched me?"
and people dragged me away, roughly,
and the men around him were angry at me.

"Who touched me?" he asked.
I said, "I did, Lord,"
So that he might have the lightning back
which I had taken from him when I touched
his garment's hem.
He looked at me and I knew then
that only he and I knew about the lightning.
He was tired and emptied
but he was not angry.
He looked at me
and the lightning returned to him again,
though not from me, and he smiled at me
and I knew that I was healed.
Then the crowd came between us
and he moved on, taking the lightning with him,
perhaps to strike again.

The woman with the issue of blood was both cured and healed, and that is easy to understand, but curing and healing are not always the same thing.

It is always all right to pray for healing. It is also all right to pray for curing as long as we are willing to accept that this may not be God's will, and as long as we are willing to accept God's will rather than our own. Above the lintel of a church in New England are carved these words:

REMEMBER, NO IS AN ANSWER.

But we don't like Noes; and sometimes we like the Noes of God less than any other No. This is a problem prayer groups must face. I believe in the power of prayer to heal, and in the power to cure as well as heal—for curing and healing are like mind and heart when they are separated. One young man told me of being called home from college to see his father in the hospital. His father had been ill for a long time, and he was warned that this was probably the end, and he was rebellious and angry. His father was in his early fifties, an active and brilliant man. It was not time for death. But when my friend got to the hospital and saw his father, his anger ebbed. He told me later, "I find this very difficult to explain, but I knew that my father was healed. I told this to my sister, and she said, 'But Dad's dying, the doctor says so.' And I tried to tell her that that didn't make any difference. I knew that Dad was dying, that death was very close, but I also knew that Dad was healed. And so it was all right."

That was a profound lesson, and few of us learn it so young. I think I learned, in nightside, at any rate, something of this lesson at the time of Father's dying; and when I was asking God, "Do whatever is right, do whatever is right for Father," what I was asking for was healing for this brave man.

I have witnessed the healing which is more profound than curing, several times in my adult life. There was one young girl, a few years ago, who came frequently to the Cathedral, borrowed books from the library, found on the Close the kind of accepting community she was seeking. She was a pretty girl, with soft blue-black hair, and matching blue-black eyes with long, fringed lashes, too pretty for her own good. She wasn't very bright; not retarded, but just not quite up to making any kind of adult decision. She leaned too heavily on a few of us, and we tried, as best we could, to help her be her own self. Until she was stricken with an acute and especially painful form of cancer. The symptoms had been there for over a year, but she had tried to pretend to herself that if she didn't look at them they'd go away, and when she finally told someone, and was taken to the doctor, the disease was so far gone that there was nothing to do but put her in the hospital and hope that the end would be swift.

One time when I went to visit her she clung to me and repeated over and over again, "I'll be all right as long as you don't leave me alone."

I don't think that anyone prayed that Bethie be cured. But we all knew that she had no tolerance whatsoever for pain, and that she was not equipped to bear the pain which we were told was an inevitable part of her form of cancer. So we prayed that she not have more pain than she could endure.

Bethie herself had no faith in her own prayers, and absolute faith in the prayers of half a dozen or so of us.

She was able to leave the hospital. She came back to the Cathedral, where she was given odd jobs. For about six months she worked happily in her adopted family, and took aspirin for what she called her arthritis; the doctors told us that cancer was so deep in her bones by this time that morphine shouldn't have been able to cut the agony. When she went back to the hospital, she was only there a few days before she died, and someone was with her all the time, and the prayers never stopped, and the pain never got too bad to be relieved.

As far as I am concerned, that is miracle, corroborated by the doctors. Bethie wasn't cured. She died. But she was healed.

There's a lot about this kind of healing that I don't understand. The gift of intercessory prayer is not mine, though that does not let me off from praying for others. I know that when I prayed for Bethie, I hurt. I don't think it was physical pain, but it was pain. During her dying I would wake up at night and pray for her, and this praying hurt. I knew that there were others praying for her, too, and that they, too, were probably hurting, and hurting worse than I. In some way all of us together took Bethie's pain. I doubt if one of us could have done it alone; it would have been too much—though sometimes we are required to bear what is too much and we are given the strength to bear it. And what we bear is not, I think, pain by substitution, about which I am wary. I think of the stern face of the Christ in the mosaic in Istanbul, and know that when and if I am required to take such a burden without help, I will be given strength to do it; it will not be my strength, but it will be available for me.

One of my favorite cousins had, at one period, excruciating back pain, and she had an old friend with the gift of healing in her hands who used to come and massage her back. The old woman would knead gently, and then she would take her hands and rub them, hard, against the carved posts of the bed, and Lacy asked her why she kept on doing this.

"Why, Miss Lacy, I take the pain from your back, and I have to put it somewhere, and it's not going to hurt the bedpost, so I put it there."

That explains something to me, but it's still in the realm of mystery and miracle—not magic, definitely not magic, which has to do with man, but with miracle, which has to do with God.

And it helps, when we are praying for others, if we have some understanding of what we are praying about. I can pray better about pain, because I have had severe pain. Whether this is my ill fortune or my good, it does help to enlarge my capacity for compassion for those in pain.

One compassionate and deeply loving Russian Orthodox priest said that he was often baffled when asked to intercede for those who were ill, because their suffering did so much good for their souls. This sounds callous, but it isn't. I'm sure he wouldn't have hesitated to pray for Bethie. I think that it has something to do with my theology of failure, and the Noes of God, and that out of the events in life which seem most negative, positive joys are born.

When I was nine or ten I had my first attack of iritis, a little-known disease which causes an inflammation of the iris. When I had a second attack the following year, the doctor told my mother, in my hearing, that if I had a third attack, I would go blind. So the shadow of blindness has always loomed over me. But it has also caused me to see far more than I might have otherwise. This visual awareness is an extraordinarily positive joy.

Medicine knows more about iritis than it used to. I have had more than a dozen attacks, and although each one sends me into momentary panic, I have come out of it and, again, am more intensely and joyously aware of everything I see than I was before.

A few years ago the effects of iritis caused secondary glaucoma.

This complication was compounded by the fact that the eye drops which are essential for the control of glaucoma irritate iritis, and the medication for iritis increases the high pressure of glaucoma. A vicious circle. A terrifying circle. I was very much afraid. My eyes' reaction to the eye drops was not good. I knew that these were essential if my sight were not to be destroyed by glaucoma, but they gave me a constant headache, and acute photophobia; I, who so much loved the light, could see nothing when facing directly into light.

This threat has been with me for so long that its very familiarity was a help. Like Bethie, I did not pray for myself. It was not so much that I had no faith in my own prayers, as that intuition told me to leave God alone about this, and let others do the praying. I did not hesitate to ask for prayers. I went running to my confessor. I asked him for (at the very least) courage. I told him that I was incapable of being brave for myself, but that I could be brave for those who expected me to be.

Now, five years later, I know that his prayers, the prayers of a number of Sisters, both Anglican and Roman Catholic, of friends, of companions, of all kinds of people with the gift of intercessory prayer, are responsible for the fact that these two incompatible eye diseases have kept at least a kind of truce. I may not see as well as I used to, and I am, as always, myopic, and can't see two feet in front of my nose without my glasses, but I SEE. I see to revise my own manuscripts. I see the faces of those I love. I see sunsets and mountains and babies and rain and daffodils and snow and oceans and storms and daybreaks.

One winter a young English priest came to stay at the Cathedral for a semester of sabbatical leave. He was taking one or two courses, and he did most of his studying in the pleasant Cathedral library. Obviously we did a good bit of talking: about his life in England; about the girl he hoped to marry; about the failures of the established Church on both sides of the ocean; about his studies; about a paper he was writing on intercessory prayer. I told him about Bethie.

One day he pointed at something far across the Close, and when I couldn't see it, he was concerned. I made light of it, but a couple of days later he asked me if I would be willing to accept healing for my vision.

"Ewen, of course I would, but I'm really all right, you know. Lots of people can't see things as far off as you can."

But he said that he was well aware that there was more to it than that. Wouldn't I like to be able to go outdoors without dark glasses? to drive a car again? Wouldn't I like to be able to see as well as I once used to?

Again I told him that of course I would, but that I already knew healing, that the very fact that I saw, that I was still visually functional, was miracle, and miracle enough.

"But could you accept healing?"

"Of course I could. But I can also accept it if this is not what God wants for me. I've learned a lot from having to accept a few limitations on my rugged independence."

I had also been through days of painful rebellion and struggle, and had worked through to at least a kind of acceptance, largely during several days spent alone on retreat at the House of the Redeemer, where the Sisters lovingly protected my silence, fed me, and shared their Offices with me. I did not at that time tell them that I had come to do battle with panic, but they helped me without words, and I worked out my fear and rage in silence and prayer, and when silence and prayer were too much for me, in writing reams of poetry. Perhaps the most useful was one I called

ABRAHAM'S CHILD*

Towards afternoon the train pulled into the station.
The light came grey and cold through the dirty glass panes
* of the terminal roof,*
and the passengers on the platform blew upon their hands and stamped
* their feet,*
and their breath came out like smoke.
In the comfortable compartment I leaned back against the
* red plush of the seat*
and looked out the window. All the signs were in a language
* I could not read.*
I got out my passport and held it, waiting in readiness.
My papers were in order and the train was warm.
The conductor slid open the door to the compartment and said to me,
"This is the last stop on this train. You will have to get out."
I held out my passport. "No, no, my journey's barely half over,"

*From L'Engle, *Lines Scribbled on an Envelope,* copyright © 1969. Reprinted with permission of Farrar, Straus & Giroux.

*and I told him the cities through which the train was going
   to pass.*
*He handed me back my passport and said again, "You will have
   to get out,"*
*and he took me by the arms and led me from the train. His hands
   were so strong*
my arms cried out in pain. On the platform it was cold.
"But I don't know where I am!" I cried, "or where I am going."
"Follow me," he said. "I have been sent to show you."
*Through the glass of the station roof I could see the sun was
   going down*
and a horror of great darkness fell upon me.
"Come," the conductor said. "This is the way you are to go."
And he led me past the passengers waiting on the platform
*and past the foreign signs and a burning lamp in this strange
   land*
*where I was a stranger. He led me to a train with no lights,
   and broken windows,*
and a pale wisp of smoke lifting from a rusty engine, and said,
"Get in. This is your train."
*I fell upon my face and laughed and said, "But this train isn't
   going anywhere."*
*And he said, "Get in," so I got in, and through a hole in the roof
   I saw the stars.*
He said, "You may sit down," and I sat on a wooden bench
*and he put my satchel on the rack over my head. "I must have
   your passport."*
*I gave it to him. "Where are we going?" I asked. The train was
   cold.*
*"The way will be shown," he said, and closed the compartment
   door.*
*I heard a puff of steam. The old engine began to pull the dark
   car*
and we ventured out into the night.

It was not that I did not believe in prayer in general, or in Ewen's
prayers in particular, because I did. Of course I wanted to drive again,
to be able to go out into the bright sunlight without pain. I don't know
why something in me was bothered by Ewen's questions. It's partly
prickly pride if anybody notices any curtailment of my independence.
But it was more than that. Ewen and I had become friends. I really
didn't mind his knowing my visual limitations.

He persisted. "But you wouldn't reject healing?"

"Of course not. I don't have any masochist or martyr complexes. I just want you to understand that the fact that my eyes are still seeing is already the result of prayer. I already know miracle. I expected to be blind long before now, and I am not. My marvelous present eye doctor doesn't cluck gloomily like the last one and give me dour warnings. He just tells me he'll keep me going, and I believe him. I see, Ewen. I see you. God has already said Yes in all kinds of ways."

But his loving heart wanted me to see perfectly. One unusually quiet morning when almost everybody on the Close was tied up with a big conference, we locked the library door and prayed. It was a beautiful and healing experience. We prayed for each other. The sound of tongues was limpid and lovely. I shall never forget that morning. And I was healed.

Not my eyes. For a few days nothing changed. Then, shortly after Ewen's brief sabbatical was up and he had returned to England, I became radically allergic to my eye drops, an allergy which manifested itself by a black headache. I lost the rest of that spring and summer to pain. My doctors tested me for everything, from brain tumors on down, to make sure that the eye problems were not masking another cause for the headache. The pain was so severe that I was unable to write, and usually I can write my way through anything. I managed to stay on my feet, to cook the meals. But I was anything but whole, and it seemed particularly ironic that this should have happened almost immediately after the beautiful morning of prayer with Ewen when I had felt so strongly the presence of the Spirit.

Ewen had said to me, "I don't think God can want anybody not to be whole. Of course he wants your eyes to be perfect." And I thought of the Orthodox priest who found it difficult to pray for his people who were ill and in pain, and I said, "I think God wants us to be whole, too. But maybe sometimes the only way he can make us whole is to teach us things we can learn only by being not whole." And I remembered reading *The Limitations of Science,* by J. W. N. Sullivan, the only book which made sense to me during my dark agnostic period, and the book he wrote on Beethoven, in which he said that Beethoven's deafness was necessary for his full genius. As I think over Beethoven's work chronologically, this seems to be indisputable. How amazing to think that the paean of joy in the great Ninth Symphony was written when Beethoven was totally shut off from any external sound. And Milton wrote *Paradise Lost* after he was blind.

I don't think that my months of pain had anything to do with Ewen's prayers for my eyes. Ewen is truly 'a beautiful person' (I wish that had not become jargon); he lives his faith; he is dearly loved by his parish and he ministers to each of his lambs with a tender and constant gentleness which leaves me in awe. And I don't think either of us was to 'blame.' It wasn't our 'fault.' I do think that there were things I had to learn from those bad months. One of my friends, a wise and compassionate woman, was so distressed by my pain one afternoon when she dropped in to see me that she asked, "If it's going to go on like this, wouldn't you rather be blind?" And my immediate response was, "No!" Anything, anything to be able to keep on seeing those I love, the world around me.

That was one of the times I learned enough about pain to be able to be compassionate about pain in others. I learned more than I had known before about Hugh's loving patience. I learned to stay on my feet even when tears were constantly close to the surface, and too often overflowed—always at the worst possible moment. I learned what real friendship means, and what it is to be let down by those I had expected to hold me up. I undoubtedly learned a lot of things I'm not even aware of yet. I think some of what I learned in this still not quite conscious area has to do with the gifts of the Spirit. Certainly, as St. Paul said, more important than speaking in tongues is interpreting tongues, is understanding each other, as did those early Christians of all races and tongues on that first Pentecost.

If I speak with the tongues of men and angels and have not charity I am hollow, unreal.

Meanwhile, my doctor experimented with eye drops and found some on which I was quite comfortable for about a year. Then, on the night before I was to fly West to teach at a writers conference, my eyes declared a new allergy, and I taught through the conference weeping copiously!

Experiments again, and now a glorious miracle! I am on brand-new eye drops which are hardly properly on the market and to which my eyes are almost completely tolerant. I walk through many days without headache for the first time in over five years. When it is cloudy and there is no glare facing me, I even know once again the joy of driving our car along familiar roads. This may be a miracle of science, but as far as I am concerned it is sheer miracle of grace, and I know that Ewen's continuing prayers are part of it, and the prayers of other friends and companions along the way. Please don't stop!

But somehow we have all, all of us, lost something since the tongues of fire descended on those first Christians. We've fallen headlong into every mistake they made, despite all of Paul's warnings. That outspoken man was loud and clear in his condemnation of anyone who felt special and singled-out by any gift of the Spirit.

Something has been forgotten, forgotten for two thousand years, or maybe it's far, far longer than that; we're not very good about chronology. We've forgotten something of ultimate importance, something I ought to remember, I do remember, no, it's only the faintest of echoes, only the sad susurration of whispers:

It was there once; we could hear the melody; we knew the words; we understood the language:

I listen for the dim whisper, funneled down the ages, of the dark parables of the old prophets telling the people of God that God is One and God is All, and whenever we make any part of his creation into God, or think of any of his people as divine, or think that we can do anything of our own power and virtue rather than his, we sin. But the voices are faint, and we heed them as little now as the ancient Jews did then.

> *The children at the party*
> *sit in a circle playing games,*
> *rhythm games, singing games, clapping games,*
> *and finally the whispering game:*
> *the little girl in the white organdy dress and blue sash*
> *whispers a sentence to the little boy in grey flannel shorts*
> *and he in turn whispers it to the little girl on his right*
> *and so it goes all the way around the circle*
> *round and round*
> *as the earth whirls round the sun*
> *and the sun swings in the great circle of the galaxy*
> > *he is risen*
> > *we thought he was the one who*
> > *we thought it was he*
> > *he is risen*
> > *he is exactly like us but sinless*
> > *not like us then*

> *sinful*
> *he is risen*
> *three in one*
> *and one in three*
> *and the great hawk cracks the sky*
> *he in us*
> *we in him*
> *bread and wine*
> *ashes to ashes*
> *and*
> *dust to dust*
> *he is risen*
> *is he*
>
> *And the sentence returns to the little girl*
> *and she says the nonsense words aloud*
> *and everybody laughs and no one understands.*

The whispers are no more than echoes and we forget there is something to be heard. We forget that there are two sides to Mercury. We sit in the brilliant sunshine of intellect and don't even know that we are not whole.

It is not popular to be willing to admit to sin. The churches are still deleting *miserable offenders* from the General Confession. There appears to be a general misconception that if we admit to sin, then we are wallowing in it, like hippopotamuses in mud. Maybe some people are.

But freedom and lightness follow when I say "I'm sorry" and am forgiven.

It is equally unpopular to say "I can't do it myself." The misconception here is that this means a whining attitude and an unwillingness to try, being a coward under the blows of fate, instead of fighting back. Nor can I blame my favorite scapegoat, Madison Avenue, for this. Again I have to unlearn the 'virtues' I was taught in my Anglican boarding schools. But Jesus of Nazareth always said, 'I don't do this. It is my Father speaking through me.'

Once Alan preached about the necessity for Christian atheism; we must stop worshipping the false gods which have crept into Christianity (all those Anglo-Saxon moral virtues); we must be atheists for Christ's sake. He did not mean, of course, that we are to stop believing in God, God who is One, God who is All, but that we must be certain that it is God we believe in, and not all those false spirits masquerading as the Holy One. We must shun the lovely little idols Satan erects for us, idols much easier to accept than the One God who is so difficult to believe in, whose ways are not our ways, who says No and expects us to understand that this is the prelude to a true Yes, who would make us whole, for whom sunside and nightside are alike, who is willing to be in our hearts and who would ask us to put our minds in our hearts that we may know him there.

But I have trouble with the words *Christian atheism,* which are too likely to recall the God-is-dead-ism of the sixties, an *ism* which was certainly the appropriate response to the activism of those days when man was convinced that man-on-his-own can take care of all the problems of the world, and the help of the Spirit is irrelevant.

I read some of the God-is-dead books, though by no means all, because they dealt with problems which simply did not exist for me, and I disposed of them rather ribaldly by writing: "If God is dead/ And man's the Head/We're in a hocus focus./We've all been spliced/ To an orphaned Christ/And that's a bogus Logos."

It is impossible for us human beings not to keep coming up with anthropomorphic gods. The righteous Lord of the Old Testament is an analogy of human righteousness as it was understood then. The gods we make today are equally anthropomorphic, God in our own image, because it's inevitable with finite human nature. Occasionally we are given the grace to turn away from our own image and toward God's image in us, and we have the model for this image in Jesus. He may have been fully man, but he was most unlike us, or we are most unlike him, in that his Father was not an anthropomorphic God, but a Being entirely new, so new that we still can't understand the glorious Father Jesus showed us in everything he did and said and was.

If I cannot be a Christian atheist because of the confusion which this term arouses, I can shun Christolotry; I can try to live by *symbole* but *sans idole,* though, being human, I will never entirely succeed. But I can keep on trying, and listening for the whispers of the Spirit.

When I am referred to in secular reviews and articles as a 'practicing Christian,' it usually is not meant as a compliment, and on the rare occasions when it is said with approval, it still makes my hackles rise, and this reaction disturbs me. Why should it make me uneasy to be referred to as what I am struggling to be? If I reply by announcing that I am a Christian atheist, or that I am against Christolotry, not many people are going to understand what that means, either.

It annoys me least and amuses me most when my Christianity is referred to with condescension: 'Poor dear, she sometimes writes quite nicely even though she isn't clever enough to know that only fools believe in God.'

D'accord. I am basically intuitive rather than intellectual (which is probably why the the third person of the Trinity is the least difficult for me), although I don't discard or discount my intellect; nightside alone is as incomplete as sunside alone. I stumbled back into Church after years away, not out of intellectual conviction, but intuitive need. I had learned through sorry experience that I cannot do it alone. I am often so irritated in church that I can manage to sit through the service with a reasonably good grace only by writing poetry or memorizing my favorite Psalms. If I go to services with reasonable regularity it is largely because I believe that if I am attempting to understand what it means to be Christian, this cannot be done in lofty isolation.

I may not want to be associated with much that passes today for Christianity; nevertheless I am part of it, even when I rebel because being Christian is becoming more and more a do-it-yourself activity. I rebel when the Church feels that it has to succeed. My theology of failure is incomprehensible to many, intolerable to some. I am saddened when the very air I breathe throughout Christendom is Pelagian: the Church can take care of all the ills of the world as long as we are morally virtuous and politically liberal. Not that I am against either virtue or liberalism! But I watch in horror as a great liberal, passionately interested in the cause of—shall we say—the leper, very carefully avoids speaking to the leper in his path, in order to get on with the cause. And it occurs to me that Jesus couldn't have cared less about the cause of the leper or the rights of the leper. But when there was a leper in his path he did not walk around him, like the priest walking on the opposite side of the road from the man set upon by thieves, on his way to Jerusalem to preach his famous sermon on compassion. Jesus stopped. And healed. And loved. Not causes, but people.

If I see and rebel against activism in others, it is because I have had to see and rebel against it in myself. We can't see a fault or flaw in others unless we have at least the potential for it in ourselves. I don't want us to sit back smugly and serve ourselves, and ignore the suffering around us, but neither do I want us to fall into those temptations which Jesus saw for what they were, and had the meekness to reject. And I remember again that it was the Spirit who led Jesus to be tempted. The Spirit, too, sees through the snare of avoiding pain by taking up causes. It was the Spirit who gave St. Francis the stamina to return day after day to the stench and ugliness of the leper house, to minister to the lepers—not as a group, not as a cause, but one mutilated person at a time. The people who make up causes are often too revolting to be loved easily, but the Spirit will give us the strength to love the unlovable if we ask for help.

An intelligent and thoughtful young woman interviewed me for a course she was taking at Columbia. In answer to one of her questions I talked about doing the small things which are daily put into my path to do, such as smiling at the dour man trying to deliver those boxes of groceries down the metal slide, and she said, "Some people would consider that self-serving." Is it? It may be, but if I cannot see the hungry people I pass each day, if I do not smile at the dour man, if I do not feed the stranger who comes to my door, or give a glass of cool water to the thirsty child, then I cannot see the starvation of people in India or South America. Perhaps if I see pictures on the news or in the papers of victims of earthquake, flood, drought, I will write a small check for the cause of world hunger, and I may even refrain from meat on Wednesdays; but as long as I am responding to a cause it will not affect my entire life, my very breathing. It is only when I see hunger or thirst in one human being, it is only when I see discrimination and injustice in all its horrendous particularity as I walk along Broadway, that my very life can be changed. If it was necessary for God to come to us as one of us, then it is only in such particularity that I can understand incarnation. I am not very good about it. I don't pray, give, give up, nearly as much as I should. But a response to a cause will never change my life, nor open my heart to the promptings of the Spirit.

We may be a global village, but instant communication often isolates us from each other rather than uniting us. When I am bombarded on the evening news with earthquake, flood, fire, it is too much for me. There is a mechanism, a safety valve, which cuts off our response to overexposure to suffering.

But when a high-school student comes to me and cries because the two- and three-year-olds on her block are becoming addicted to hard drugs; when the gentle man who cleans the building in which the Cathedral library is located talks to me about his family in Guatemala, rejoicing because they are alive although their house has been destroyed by earthquake; when a goddaughter of mine in Luxembourg writes me about the hungry children of the immigrant Portuguese family with whom she is living, then in this particularity my heart burns within me, and I am more able to learn what it is that I can and ought to do, even if this seems, and is, inadequate.

But neither was Jesus adequate to the situation. He did not feed all the poor, only a few. He did not heal all the lepers, or give sight to all the blind, or drive out all the unclean spirits. Satan wanted him to do all this, but he didn't.

That helps me. If I felt that I had to conquer all the ills of the world I'd likely sit back and do nothing at all. But if my job is to feed one stranger, then the money I give to world relief will be dug down deeper from my pocket than it would if I felt I had to succeed in feeding the entire world.

Even spirituality and meditation and mysticism have become activities with easy success offered. Do such and such and you will have a mystical experience. You may have an experience, but it won't be a mystical one. Such experience cannot be bought.

Evil doesn't bother to infiltrate that which is already evil. Where there is darkness there is no need to snuff out the light. No wonder Satan rushes to churches filled with the sound of tongues—to any church at all. The Tempter has acquired many hard-working followers within the Christian establishment, and often in the name of the Holy Spirit. What better place for him to work than in the Church which is essentially a place for his redemption. I often feel his breath during a church service, am tempted by his sweet, seductive whispers. He is reasonable, never offends my intellect; whereas my Trinitarian God is frequently unreasonable and intellectually offensive—and yet speaks to the whole of me, mind and heart, intellect and intuition, and speaks most clearly to that element in me which accepts the incomprehensible beauty of love: married love; the loves of friendship; to that element in me which participates in music, poetry, painting. Bach's

Toccata and Fugue in C minor will take me a lot further than any number of books on theology.

After I had given a lecture at a very Protestant university, three postgraduate students, all married and with children, approached me, and the spokesman blurted out, "Does your Church mean less and less to you?" I paused, said "Yes," then "No," then, "What is the Church?"

Not the building in which I stand or sit, often uncomfortably, often irritably. Not any denomination of any kind—and the fact that the Body of Christ is broken by denominations is another cause for Satan's pleasure. Why can't we worship in our differing ways and still be One?

I doubt if Christian unity will ever come through paperwork and red tape. The time has come for us to leap across boundaries. I gave the same series of lectures on myth, fantasy, and fairy tale at a Fundamentalist college and a Roman Catholic monastery, and the responses and questions were the same, and that rejoiced my heart. I am comfortable and at home when I sing hymns with my most Protestant friends. One time I was off to Wheaton College, Illinois, a fundamentalist college with extraordinarily high academic standards, and I said to Josephine that I was going to be met in Chicago by my Baptist priest friend; I used this appellation several times before she said, "Mother, what are you saying?" And only then did it strike me that 'Baptist Priest' is an odd combination. And yet this man *is* my 'Baptist priest friend' and one year I sent him an icon for Christmas.

I have lovingly been offered, and received, communion in the Roman Catholic Church, and while this may be irregular, it is the only response of love possible. Last summer the elder daughter of my beloved nanny, Mrs. O, celebrated her golden anniversary as a Sister of Charity, and I was asked to read one of the lessons at the Festival Mass.

As we drove from Crosswicks to the convent in the Bronx, I wondered what I ought to do about receiving. On the way to the church I whispered to one of the Sisters, "Is it all right if I receive?" And she whispered, "Of course, as long as it's all right with you." "It's fine with me." But even without this unofficial permission the problem would have been quickly resolved. I sat up in the chancel with two of the Sisters; two Sisters who dressed completely in secular clothes; so the priests there that afternoon consistently called me Sister, and there was no question, when it came to the bread and wine, that I was to be with all the others gathered there that day, part of the unbroken body.

It's not quite that easy with the Protestant denominations where the communion service is simply a memorial service, a looking back at Maundy Thursday and Jesus's celebration of the Passover. But I have always felt that God is quite capable of taking care of his own table, and that thousands of nonbelievers are not going to rush up to receive the body and blood without any belief in the Real Presence if we have 'open communion.' And even if some do, isn't God still in control of what is going on? And if we believe in the real and very power of the body and blood, may this power itself not make all the difference?

Tallis used to talk about the academic problem of what a priest ought to do if a pious Turk came up to take communion. And one day he was celebrating Mass and a man whom he knew to be a pious Turk did indeed appear at the altar rail. And was given the body and blood. And was there because he had read the Book of Common Prayer and taken seriously all that it had said. And became a far better Christian than most of us born to it. What might have happened had the letter of the law been obeyed and he turned down?

Perhaps we will once again be One when all the hungry sheep have broken down and leapt over the denominational barriers in order to be nourished together, and ultimately the Hierarchies will recognize that unity is already here, and can throw away all thouse millions of miles of red tape.

When I contemplate the problems of intercommunion, especially Roman Catholic/Anglican/Orthodox vis-à-vis those who do not believe in the Real Presence, it occurs to me that these genuine problems about the Lord's Table are once again problems of our own making. If those who are terrified at the idea of the Real Presence in the bread and wine, those who shudderingly call it cannibalism (but we are all in one way or another cannibals; we do nourish each other; all life lives at the expense of other life), if those who staunchly assert that their communion services are purely memorial services—well, then, if they really remember, in the fullest sense of anamnesis, the problem becomes a semantic one. If the mighty acts of God are truly present, then it is human beings who create divisions among each other. It is our nature to do so, but at least we are coming more to realize how futile and wasteful is a divided Christendom, and how we ourselves, far more than those outside the Church, are willfully slowing down the coming of the Kingdom.

Of course anamnesis doesn't always happen during a service, not in any communion or denomination, just as it does not always happen when I am writing. Tallis told me about an Orthodox attitude which I love; it is also enlightening! During an Orthodox service (and these are longer than those we complain about as being too long) no one worshipper there is able to concentrate on what is going on, to exercise anamnesis, at all times. Our minds do wander. During even the most moving of church services, I constantly have to pull my thoughts back into focus. But the Orthodox feel that this does not matter, because all of the time *some one* is concentrating; there is always someone in the Body who is wholly focused on the Holy Mysteries; there is always someone keeping the strong rope of anamnesis unbroken, and so my belief in interdependence deepens, and my wayward heart is turned toward God, God who is One, who is All, and who must be saddened and perhaps amused by all the theological problems we continually manage to create for ourselves.

My tongue has been informed by Anglican thought; my favorite century of English literature is from the mid-sixteen-hundreds to the mid-seventeen-hundreds, and all the literary masters I look up to speak with Anglican voices. I was born an Anglican, and even if I left the Church forever, just as once Hugh left the theatre forever, that tradition flows in my very bloodstream.

I am grateful for our Crosswicks years in the Congregational Church, when Hugh was a deacon and lay preacher, when I directed choir and taught the high-school discussion group. I learned a lot about the priesthood of all believers which is still important to me. So I go to church, not for any legalistic or moralistic reasons, but because I am a hungry sheep who needs to be fed; and for the same reason that I wear a wedding ring: a public witness of a private commitment.

There was one Pentecost Sunday in our village church which I am not likely to forget. I wrote about it later, for some of the young people involved who are close to me:

It is an old church,
two hundred years old,
and that is old for this gawky country
though perhaps young by other standards.
The congregation today (as in most churches)
is sparse.
In the old New England tradition
we amble into our seats
and only a few outsiders
indulge in the impropriety and popery
of bowing their heads in prayer
(nobody would dare kneel).
So of course nobody remembers that this is
the time of the rushing wind and the tongues of fire.
Today is the Sunday when the Young People's Group,
the Pilgrim Fellowship, is going to lead the worship.
They are dressed in jeans, shirts—
the girls as well as the boys—
and someone puts on a record
and in the chancel they dance to the music
separately
(nobody touches anybody else)
and not very well. But it is Their Own Thing,
their response:
two women get up and leave the church.
Then one of the girls goes to the lectern (she brought me a kitten once)
and tells us that they are not there to shock us
but to tell us what is on their minds.
Another girl talks about the importance of individualism;
what she really means is that she cares
about the fall of the sparrow
and the gloriously unutterable value of persons.
But somebody else walks out.
Then a boy (his mother and I were pregnant
together with our sons; I have seen him
learn to walk and talk)
gets up and says he does not believe in God
or life after death
or anything he's been taught in Sunday School.
If there is a God, he says,
we have to find him where we live,
and he finds church when he walks alone
in the woods.
There is a movement in the back of the church
as someone else leaves.

Then our nearest neighbors' boy,
our son's close friend,
talking too fast in his urgency,
cries out against war
and napalm
and job recruiters for Dow Chemical
and killing killing killing
and more people walk out.
Then the young people (still trying) come to
pass the Peace
and they put on another record and sing to it
and they CARE
And someone else leaves

oh stop
oh stop
STOP

This is Pentecost
the wind is blowing
the flames are bright
the Spirit burns

O stop
listen
all you Parthians, Medes, Elamites,
dwellers in Mesopotamia, Judea, Cappadocia,
in Pontus, and Asia, Phrygia and Pamphylia, in Egypt
and in the parts of Libya around Cyrene,
O stop
strangers of Rome, Jews and proselytes, Cretes and
Arabians, dwellers in New England, New York,
Indiana, India, California, Chile,
China, Russia, Africa.

Stop and listen
to these children who speak in your own tongue
the wonderful works of God.

But the tongue is dulled, the whisper blurred. We do not listen to each other. We are more often known by how we quarrel than by how we love each other. I had a horrendous picture of the face we present to the world when I was asked to be the lay Christian on the panel of Christians and Jews where I met the rabbi who performed Peter's mother's funeral.

But the rabbi and I did not become friends that first night. Fortunately it was an ongoing panel, because the first evening was as full of misunderstanding and refusal to listen as that Pentecost Sunday in the Congregational Church. My job, at that initial meeting, was to respond to a keynote speech by a visiting rabbi who had done some work with the World Council of Churches and who had therefore been brought in to lead the discussion.

He talked more about Christianity than he did about Judaism, but the Christianity he held up to the congregation bore no relationship whatsoever to any kind of Christianity I can believe in. But where, where did he get his picture of Christianity? From Christians, that's where. I listened with growing horror. There was nothing I could respond to. Certain words meant one thing to him, another to me, so that it was as though we spoke foreign languages—and the Holy Spirit did not come that first evening to touch our tongues so that we would understand each other. It was an evening of confusion and, on occasion, hostility toward me and the young priest friend who had got me into this—hostility because we represented to the gathered assembly everything the rabbi was saying about Christians.

At the depressing end of the evening I asked if I might be given ten minutes at the beginning of the next session to say something about what Christianity means to me, and was told that I might. Ten minutes to tell a hostile congregation what the Incarnation means to my life! Impossible, of course. All I could do was to try to speak completely honestly, completely vulnerably. I spent all week trying to choose the few words I could use in ten minutes. I was certainly earnest, and perhaps the very earnestness was what broke the ice, because after that we were able to talk to each other as human beings created by the One same God.

Then we were able to start untangling some of the misconceptions. It's easy enough to respond to "All Christians blame the Jews for killing Jesus, and they're still making us pay for it." We talked about the Palm Sunday service at the Cathedral, and the moment that the 'we' or 'us' becomes 'they' or 'them,' we are no longer Christian.

But there were other, subtler misconceptions, and they have been set up by Western Christianity as it has attempted to conform to this world—not to accept it, to be in it, but to conform to it. The visiting rabbi insisted that Christianity is a religion of superstition, rather than reality, and offers its people the psychological satisfactions of mysticism. Psychological satisfaction? I doubt if any of the great mystics received any more psychological satisfaction than we would if we received a hundred volts of electricity. A mystical experience is not a satisfying one. It is burning. It is a ride on the tail of a comet, freezing, searing—for cold can burn even more than fire. It is not psychologically satisfying to have nightside and sunside meet in a blaze of ice and fire, to understand God as utterly distant and unknowable and yet so close that the comfort of the shadow of his wings can be intimately felt. In this rare, almost unbreathable atmosphere, sunside and nightside are resolved in paradox, and the incomprehensible is yet in some measure comprehended in contradiction.

But the visiting rabbi insisted that Christianity is hung up on such psychological highs, while Judaism accepts this world, enjoying the creation of God, meals together, friendship, the beauties of nature. Jews accept the word; Christianity rejects it. Ouch, again.

This visiting rabbi, whose name I have happily forgotten, did not have a stupid or diabolic version of Christianity. It was prepared for him by the Christians he has encountered. But to deny the world, as he suggests Christians do, is to deny the Incarnation. It is quite possible to have an incarnational view of the universe and not be a Christian; all artists are incarnational and not all artists are Christians, for instance. But it is not possible to be a Christian and not have an incarnational view of the universe. Christianity without incarnation is not Christianity.

The rabbi, given his clue by Christians, told us that Christianity is a pleasant religion. It promises the faithful the joys of heaven to make up for the difficulties of life. And he referred to the Eucharist as 'a magical act,' and said that the Jews, instead of turning to magic, face reality.

Magic? Reality? Who can blame the rabbi? I know that I, too, have misconceptions of Christianity. Sharing my thoughts with the members of the panel and, afterwards, with the congregation, helped me to clarify my own thinking, and by the end of the panel the crackling antagonism was gone and we were moving a good deal closer to understanding and acceptance than we would have thought possible the first night. And the women of the Hadassah asked me to come and share thoughts about being a woman.

During the summer, when we are in the country and there is no

Episcopal church nearby, I very much miss what the rabbi considered a *magical act.* I struggled to work out the difference between miracle and magic in *The Other Side of the Sun.*

> "Honoria," Aunt Olivia asked, "what is a miracle?"
> Aunt Irene said, "Honoria, I'd like some more soldier beans, please."
> Aunt Olivia held up her hand. "Wait. Honoria, what's the difference be-
> tween magic and a miracle? That ought to interest you, Irene."
> Honoria stood, holding the silver dish in a linen napkin. "A human being
> can do magic. God do the miracle. Magic make the person think the power
> be in hisself. A miracle make him know the power belong to God." She went
> out to the kitchen.

But there are many people besides Aunt Irene and the rabbi who would like to toss off the Holy Mysteries as magic, and ineffectual magic at that, and it is Christians who have been responsible for this. The teachers from whom I have learned the most have never tried to make God comprehensible to me by intellect alone. The mind must be flexible enough to bend down to the heart; the mediating band must join nightside and sunside. To receive the bread and wine as the real body and blood of the Lord has indeed in some times and some places degenerated to superstitious magic; this can happen to all ritual, particularly at times when man's power seems so sufficient that God's is not needed.

But all power is God's, and God's power is an expression of his joy, and all earthly ritual is afire with the powerful joy of the Resurrection. I do not fully understand the mystery of the Eucharist, but my lack of human understanding makes no difference; I am nourished and strengthened; this is what I know.

> *Rejoice!*
> *You have just given me the universe,*
> *put it in my hands, held it to my lips,*
> *oh, here on my knees have I been fed*
> *the entire sum of all created matter,*
> *the everything*
> *that came from nothing.*
> *Rejoice!*
> *Who can doubt its power?*
> *Did not this crumb of bread*
> *this sip of wine*

burst into life
that thundered across nothing
and became the cause of all our
celebrations?
Oh, the explosion of nothing into something,
into flaming, raging suns and shouting comets
and drops of dew and spiders' webs
into mountains bursting forth with brilliant volcanoes
valleys falling and rising
laughing with joy
earth's cracking, primordial rains flooding
a snowdrop's star, a baby's cry
oh, rejoice!
rejoice and celebrate
eyes to see and ears to hear
fingers to touch
to touch
the body's living warmth
hand stretched to hand
across nothing
making something
celebrate
lips to smile
to kiss
to take the bread and wine
rejoice
flowers   grass   pavements
gutters   garbage cans
old people remembering
babies laughing
mothers singing
fathers celebrating
rejoice
around the table
hold hands
all round
like a ring circling a finger
placed there as a promise
holding the universe together
nothing into something
into joy and love
rejoice
and celebrate!

So I struggle with my theology of failure and the Noes of God. I cannot totally withdraw from the Establishment again, no matter how sad and angry the Establishment may make me. Of course I find it easier to feel God when I go alone at night to walk Timothy on the upper level of Riverside Park and move quietly through the fog or the falling snow; or in summer when I go out with him at night and walk under the glory of the stars. It is easier to feel and see and touch God thus than it is in church, but this private religion is not enough, is destructive when it is all there is; to find God only in a private mysticism is to break off from the Body, to leave the mainland, and ultimately to worship myself more than my Creator.

On the first Pentecost the Holy Spirit came to the Body gathered together, not to separate individuals. But each one of those individuals was essential to the Body, because the Spirit teaches us that our understanding comes through particulars, never through generalities. Here my long years of writing again inform my groping theology. A story must be about particular people; the protagonist must be someone we recognize, and with whom we can identify.

So should it be strange that this is how it has to be with the Incarnation, too? God shows us his nature through what has been called 'the scandal of particularity.' It *is* a scandal to think of God being fully God in Jesus of Nazareth, but there's no other possible way for us to glimpse his love. Generalities get no further in religion than in fiction.

I am helped to understand the Incarnation because Jesus Christ is the protagonist of Creation. This is the shocking aspect of particularity, that he is the hero, and although all of us want to play leads, we are, in fact, only supporting actors. But, as Stanislavsky, the director of the Moscow Art Theatre, said, "There are no small parts. There are only small actors."

I learn my part only as I am guided by the Spirit. And often I understand this guidance through hindsight, anamnesis, understanding something only after it has happened, as the Disciples could look back and understand Good Friday only after the glory of Easter and the joy of Pentecost.

I know the gifts of the Spirit not only when I hear the rippling of tongues but also in the gift of silence, when understanding and joy come without words, in that mediating circle which is beyond and through the limitations of language, any kind of language at all.

I stood with my friend Gillian at the bedside of a woman who was dying, badly, of a brain tumor, and she asked, "Will I ever again be whole?" And Gillian responded, "More whole than you have ever been before." And we held hands and prayed together and there in the midst of human illness and the shadow of death we were touched with tongues of fire. The Spirit does not only come to us when we rejoice; the Spirit comes when we are most beaten, most in need.

The Spirit broods over the waters before the beginning of man's time; speaks through the Prophets; guides Michelangelo's chisel, Shakespeare's pen, Serkin's fingers. I understand and I do not understand; I know and I do not know.

One evening I was up in Tallis's apartment, leafing through an obsolete icon calendar which he had kept for the beauty of the photographs. One of them struck me with that extraordinary arrow of revelation and recognition which is one of the brightest of human joys. In this icon the prophet Elijah is sitting in the desert, and is telling God that it is better for him to die than to live, in much the same angry way as the prophet Jonah.

In the icon a raven has come, as God promised, to feed the prophet. And in the raven's beak is the round white circle of the communion bread: Chronology once more broken apart by *kairos,* by the truth of love.

> *Silence was the one thing we were not prepared for,*
> *we are never prepared for.*
> *Silence is too much like death.*
> *We do not understand it.*
> *Whenever it comes we make up thunders and lightnings*
> *and we call anxiously for the angels to sing for us.*
> *It is all right for Elijah to kill all those false prophets,*
> *though they were comfortingly noisy;*
> *it is all right for him to bring that poor widow's boy*
> *back to life with his own audible breath;*
> *that is only a miracle. We understand miracles.*
> *But he survived God's silence, and that is more extraordinary*
> *than all the sounds of all of Israel's battles rolled into one.*
> *Why is God silent? Why does he not sound for us?*
> *He came silently to birth. Only the angels,*
> *Taking pity on us, sang to make that silence bearable.*

When he came to dwell among us men on earth
only his mother understood the silence,
and when he died she made no sound of weeping.
Why does silence make us shiver with the fear of death?
There was more sound to comfort our ears
when he was hammered to the cross
and cried out through the strangling bonds
and the temple veil was rent and graves burst wide,
than when he was born. I am not sure
that death is silent. But Easter is.
The angels did not sing for us, heralding the glory.
There was no sound to prepare us, no noise of miracle,
no trumpet announcing the death of death—
or was it what we call life? We did not understand
and we ran from the empty tomb and then
he came to us in silence. He did not explain
and at last I knew that only in silence is the word
even when the word itself is silent.

Thus in silence did that strange dark bird
Bring to Elijah in the desert the whole and holy Word.

If I cannot receive the gifts of the Spirit in silence, I will never be able to receive them in any other way. Often I understand that this strange dark bird has been with me only when I am turned again and look back, with anamnesis, and realize that the No of God, when I felt most deserted, was a Spirit-filled No preparing me for a Yes.

Hugh and Alan and Tallis are my teachers, and better teachers no one could hope for. When I go flying off on a tangent, as I so frequently do, one of them will reach out and pull me back. One time I evidently gave a limiting adjective to God in front of Alan. I don't remember what I said, nor what his rebuke; I only know my response, which was to go off and scribble these lines which, a few minutes later, I put into his hand.

LOVE LETTER ADDRESSED TO:

Your immanent eminence
wholly transcendent
permament, in firmament
holy, resplendent
other and aweful

incomprehensible
legal, unlawful
wild, indefensible
eminent immanence
mysterium tremendum
mysterium fascinans
incarnate, trinitarian
being impassible
infinite wisdom
one indivisible
king of the kingdom
logos, word-speaker
star-namer, narrator
man-maker, man-seeker
ex nihil creator
unbegun, unbeginning
complete but unending
wind-weaving, sun-spinning
ruthless, unbending:

Eternal compassion
helpless before you
I, Lord, in my fashion,
love and adore you.

It is a strange love affair I have with this One who breathed his Spirit into me, baptized me with it all those years ago, willy-nilly, who never betrays me, though I am consistently unfaithful to him, like Hosea's wife. Not only do I listen to the wiles of the dragon, I become the dragon, and then I remember Rilke's words:

How should we be able to forget those ancient myths about dragons that at the last minute turn into princesses who are only waiting to see us once beautiful and brave . . . Perhaps everything terrible is in its deepest being something helpless that wants help from us.

I know that when I am most monstrous, I am most in need of love. When my temper flares out of bounds it is usually set off by something unimportant which is on top of a series of events over which I have no control, which have made me helpless, and thus caused me anguish and frustration. I am not lovable when I am enraged, although it is when I most need love.

One of our children when he was two or three years old used to rush at me when he had been naughty, and beat against me, and what he wanted by this monstrous behavior was an affirmation of love. And I would put my arms around him and hold him very tight until the dragon was gone and the loving small boy had returned.

So God does with me. I strike out at him in pain and fear and he holds me under the shadow of his wings. Sometimes he appears to me to be so unreasonable that I think I cannot live with him, but I know that I cannot live without him. He is my lover, father, mother, sister, brother, friend, paramour, companion, my love, my all.

Until I can say this, I cannot understand my theology of failure, or the Noes of God.

MARCH 25TH: THE ANNUNCIATION

> *To the impossible: Yes!*
> *Enter and penetrate,*
> *O Spirit, come and bless*
> *This hour. The star is late.*
> *Only the absurdity of love*
> *Can break the bonds of hate.*

10... Show Me Your Hindquarters and Let Me Hear You Roar

WHAT'S ALL THIS stuff about a Trinitarian God? We're rugged individualists, we Americans, and all this gabble about three in one and one in three is pluralism and not *E pluribus unum,* whatever that used to mean; we don't have to take Latin in school anymore. This Trinity thing is one way of allowing ourselves polytheism instead of monotheism. And it's tied up somewhere with the family as a unit, but nowadays the validity of the family is being questioned, and even by bishops of the Church.

We've come near to discarding the Trinity season as part of the Church calendar, because 3 in 1 and 1 in 3 makes even less sense than $0 \times 3 = 0$ instead of 3. And if we are becoming free to ignore the Trinity, then we can ignore the breakup of the family as a coherent and creative unit. Most families aren't, so why pretend?

Because of the United States industrial patterns, with many middle-class families consistently being uprooted every few years, thus breaking familial community, we've been forced into rationalizing this breaking up by denying the value of parental and grandparental relationships, and calling them manipulative and abnormal, all full of Freudian nastiness. Few children today grow up with easy coming and going between uncles and aunts and grandparents. This is the way things are, and we tend to justify the way things are as good and right, and so the family as the living image of the Trinitarian God becomes denigrated—otherwise old people couldn't be shuffled off to institutions as so many are. Sometimes there is no choice. The 'nuclear' pattern of family life makes it inevitable. But not always. Sometimes it is simply easier. It's not nice to see someone growing old and incontinent. It's easier to put the sight away. So families fall apart, and divorce is made easy, because this is the way of the world, and put Grandma in a home because it's really horrid for the kids to see her sitting there drooling, and last night she wet her bed. . . . The rector was telling me of a place where they're really very kind to them. . . .

The breaking up of families and the cult of youth has encouraged us to dishonor old age and to ignore the Fourth Commandment as being out of date. It was one thing for those nomadic old Hebrews who didn't have the advantage of Senior Citizens' Villages and Old People's Homes and Nursing Homes and all that technocracy has given us, but it has little bearing on the realities of life in the enlightened United States.

If one thinks of Mother as being devourer and emasculator (some are, but not all; mine wasn't), then it's easy to feel one needn't honor her, or if Father is only the image of the paternalistic male chauvinist pig Old Testament God (some are, but not all; mine wasn't), then one needn't honor him, either. It strikes me as being a weaselly way out of responsible and creative (and therefore painful) relations.

I have been tested about this, and in the fire, too, and I've written about this testing in *The Summer of the Great-grandmother,* and I wouldn't have been able to go on honoring my mother had it not been for the support and compassionate help of the entire family. I may not have thought consciously about the Trinity that summer, but in my intuitive subconscious I learned a lot about it.

We've been trying to understand the Trinity in terms of provable fact instead of poetry, and so we stop saying the Creed at many services. But the Creed is not a blueprint for faith; the Creed is a *symbole.* If I have to say the Creed in terms of scientific proof, I cannot say it all. But the Creed, like the Trinity, is best understood in the open language of poetry, of myth, that language in which we participate when we try to express ultimate things.

Athanasius and his friends, hammering out the *Quicunque Vult* in order to defend the Trinitarian God they adored, struggled to move beyond the literal level of daily words and yet make the point, and sometimes blundered into absurdity (as Dorothy Sayers noted): the Father incomprehensible, the Son incomprehensible, the Spirit incomprehensible—the whole thing incomprehensible. Of course it is. That's partly the point of Athanasius's powerful wielding of words as though he were trying to catch hold of the whirlwind. The Trinity is trapped in neither time nor space. *Before Abraham was, I am,* cries the second person. *I will be what I will be,* shouts the first. And through the brilliant flame of the Spirit I know that the Christ on whose name I call was creating galaxies and snowflakes long before there were living beings naming the animals in the Garden.

Perhaps the morning stars still sing together, only we have forgotten the language, as we have forgotten so much else, limiting Christianity to a mere two thousand years. We've known it by that name for even less, but that is our shortsightedness. When God came to us as one of us he was misunderstood and betrayed and part of that misunderstanding and betrayal is our dimming his brilliance because it's too much for our feeble eyes; our limiting his power because we're afraid of the unsheathed lightning; our binding him with ropes of chronology instead of trying to understand his freedom in *kairos.* Not that we've done any of this to the Lord himself, only to our image of the One we worship, and that's bad enough.

We're so dependent on the literal level that many Christians today have never even heard the Athanasian creed because it's just too much for sane modern man come of age. It was all so long ago, when Christianity was first formulating its *symboles* against the early heresies that it seems irrelevant, and we don't even recognize that we're surrounded by the same old heresies today. Satan doesn't need new weapons to confound us as long as the old ones still work.

In the last couple of decades there has been a new interest in community, so perhaps the idea of a Trinitarian God will once again be valid for us.

Unity in diversity has not always been as difficult for the human mind to understand as it is today. In the Psalms, for instance, we often don't know whether the psalmist is talking of himself, or of the community. And for the psalmist there is very little difference. He is who he is because he belongs to the people chosen by God. Without his community, he has no identity.

The same kind of assurance was known by the early Christians. They knew exactly who they were, through their baptisms, and each one literally held the lives of the others in his hand. That doesn't mean that they were identical, all good little Christians exactly alike, any more than my big toe and my elbow are identical, or my eyebrows and my fingernails. But, with all their radical differences, they had to be one body in order to survive; just as our corporeal bodies must be a unity. If my left foot walks in one direction and my right in another, I'm not going to get anywhere—except flat on my face.

My moments of being most complete, most integrated, have come either in complete solitude or when I am being part of a body made up of many people going in the same direction. A vivid example is a great symphony orchestra, where each instrument is completely necessary for the whole; a violin cannot take the place of a trombone, nor cymbals of the harp; and there are even times when the lowly triangle is the focus of the music.

(I love Chaliapin's definition of heaven: "There will be five thousand sopranos, five thousand altos, ten tenors—I don't much like tenors—a thousand baritones, and I will sing bass.")

Where have I known this unity?

In the Holy Mysteries. Yes.

And years ago when I was in the theatre and was privileged to be a small part of bringing a play to life, I remember one evening during rehearsal lying up on the grid and looking down from this great height to the stage and yet being a complete part of all that was being said and done.

And I knew it when we lived in Crosswicks year round and I directed the choir in the village church, knew it not because I was director, but because I was a part of something which became a whole, and was far more beautiful than the sum of its parts, even in midsummer when all of the tenor and bass section had to be out haying and I sang tenor, or bass an octave high.

And I know it around the family table where all of us different and dominant human beings, with all our diversity, are one.

One night after a small dinner party at a friend's house, I wrote for him:

> *Sitting around your table*
> *as we did, able*
> *to laugh, argue, share*

> *bread and wine and companionship, care*
> *about what someone else was saying, even*
> *if we disagreed passionately: Heaven,*
> *we're told, is not unlike this, the banquet celestial,*
> *eternal convivium. So the praegustum terrestrium*
> *partakes—for me, at least—of sacrament.*
> *(Whereas the devil, ever intent*
> *on competition, invented the cocktail party where*
> *one becomes un-named, un-manned, de-personned.) Dare*
> *we come together, then, vulnerable, open, free?*
> *Yes! Around your table we*
> *knew the Holy Spirit, come to bless*
> *the food, the host, the hour, the willing guest.*

And I knew the beauty of community in the birthing of my babies. We human beings are not meant to give birth to our offspring alone, any more than the dolphin, who delivers her babes with the help of midwife dolphins, in community. The need of the mother for support at this incredible moment has too often been forgotten by science, and it is good that once again the father can be present at the birth of his seed and share in this marvelous communal act.

I wish I knew it more often in church, and that I were a less reluctant Christian. The Church is too grownup for me, too reasonable, too limited. One reason nearly half my books are for children is the glorious fact that the minds of children are still open to the living word; in the child, nightside and sunside are not yet separated; fantasy contains truths which cannot be stated in terms of proof. I find that I agree with many college-age kids who are rejecting the adult world—not those with bad cases of Peter Pantheism, but with those who understand that the most grownup of us is not very grownup at all; that the most mature of us is pretty immature; that we still have a vast amount to learn.

The writers I admire most, who mean most to me, who teach me most, are, by and large, dead. One reason that there are not more great novels or plays or poems written today is that writing, like prayer, has become a do-it-yourself activity. Buy a book, take a course, and you will learn to be in control of your pen, manipulate words, and choose what you want to write, and be a success.

That's not the way it is.

A writer grimly controls his work to his peril, manipulates only in great danger (to be in control of your technique is very different from being in control of the work). Slowly, slowly, I am learning to listen to the book, in the same way I try to listen in prayer. If the book tells me to do something completely unexpected, I heed it; the book is usually right. If a book like this present one, a strange kind of book for a storyteller, pushes me to write it, I have no choice except to pay attention. All I can do, as far as activism is concerned, is to write daily, read as much as possible, and keep my vocabulary alive and changing so that I will have an instrument on which to play the book if it does me the honor of coming to me and asking to be written. I have never yet fully served a book. But it is my greatest joy to try.

It takes courage to open oneself vulnerably to the depths of a book. The moment I set words down on a page I become responsible for those words. Letters from readers have forced me to be aware of this responsibility which I would much rather not know about—but there it is, and I had better accept it. A letter from a teenager ran something like this, "I am thinking about becoming a Christian, but one thing worries me. All my friends who are Christians say that only Christians can be saved. What do you think? I'm writing to you because your stories have made me trust you." That's more responsibility than I want. But we're all of us responsible the moment we get out of bed every morning. I wrote that teenager a long letter (we're still corresponding) and I hope that I gave her a glimpse of God's love which is always greater than our continual misinterpretation of it. But I don't know. And that is frightening.

A woman my age wrote me after reading *A Circle of Quiet:* "I didn't know I was allowed to doubt." And several people, after *The Summer of the Great-grandmother:* "It doesn't worry me any more that I am angry at what is happenning." This is a heavy responsibility, but I blunder into pride if I think that it is all mine, any more than the book is all mine.

A professor and novelist, Dr. Caroline Gordon, from whom I have learned an enormous amount, told our class that we do not judge great art; it judges us. Oh, yes, it does. And the judgment of the work of art is quite apart from the moral virtue, or lack of moral virtue, of the artist. God's ways are not our ways, and quite often the most superbly transcendent work comes from artists who deny God and themselves in their daily living. They may be drunkards, sex-ridden, adulterous, but when they are at work they are wholly thrown out of themselves into collaboration with their work. And a work of art is indeed a work. Serkin does not sit down at the piano and play Beethoven's Appassionata Sonata without doing his finger exercises every single day. I think it was Rubinstein who said that if he did not practice for one day he knew it; if he didn't practice for two days his family knew it; and if he didn't practice for three days his public knew it.

Guernica did not spring in an hour to the canvas. *The Brothers Karamazov* wasn't tossed off in a week; it encourages me to remember that Dostoevsky did version after version of his novels.

To turn closer to home and to a less elevated analogy, one of the girls I lived with in Greenwich Village has gone on to be a concert pianist. No matter what the rest of us were doing, she practiced eight hours a day, finger exercises, one tiny phrase over and over again for what seemed forever. She was working on her first New York concert, and I'll never forget Handel's *Harmonious Blacksmith Variations,* or the Brahms Second Piano Concerto, or the Bach *Chromatic Fantasy and Fugue* as they slowly moved to life as she grew with them. If she diligently practiced her music, it also practiced her.

Montaigne says "the work of its own force and fortune can second the workman and surpass him, beyond his own invention and knowledge." I witnessed the truth of this as I saw the great compositions pushing the young pianist. When a work of art does this, the mediating circle integrating sunside and nightside is widened. Prayer, too, of its own force, can take the one at prayer far beyond the wildest imaginings.

I learned something of the force of the work myself during that same period when I went through my first shattering experience of falling in love and having the love turn to ashes. I not only survived, but did a considerable amount of growing up through the writing of my first full-length novel.

I concentrated on my work because it was what saved me. I had, over this broken affair, left the apartment with the other girls, left my entire group of friends, and moved into a tiny apartment of my own, so the noise and confusion was in my own heart. When I was working on that first novel I was genuinely and painfully unhappy. But during the actual writing I was at play; I was completely thrown out of my subjective misery into the joy of creation, so that what might have been a totally destructive experience became instead a creative one, and a freeing one.

I was freed during the writing as my book wrote me, not as I wrote it. And surely this was an experience of that special kind of unity which makes me understand the Trinity. The pages which built up on my writing table were not me, nor was I typewriter and paper; but we were, nevertheless, one. The same kind of collaboration can come when I read a book; the books which matter to me, to which I turn and return, are those which read me. The music I play, or listen to, is that which actively participates with me in harmony or counterpoint. The same thing is true in graphic art. There has to be an amorous interaction between the work of art and the person who is opening himself to it, and surely the relationship within the persons of the Trinity is one of Love, Love so real we can glimpse it only on rare occasions.

Hugh, or any actor, will tell you that the response of the audience can make or break an evening in the theatre; the audience collaborates, quite literally, with the actor.

As I understand the writing of a book, or a poem, so I understand the Eucharist, so I understand the Creed, the *symboles* by which I live. And in joyful moments I know prayer in the same way that I know great painting, or the Bach B Minor Mass. This is not to say that I think worship and prayer are less real than the daily world of provable fact, but that I think they are more real.

We are a generation out of touch with reality: the 'realistic' novels push me further away from the truth of things, rather than bringing me closer. When once I was asked if I wrote anything other than fantasy, I said that I also write adult novels, and the inquirer grinned, "Nowadays the word *adult* in front of novel means porno."

What about using 'the language of the people' in the translations of the liturgy. What people? We speak English today rather than a form of Norman French because Chaucer wrote in the language of the people, but I doubt if the butcher, the baker, the candlestick maker went around saying, "Whan that Arcite to Thebes comen was/Ful ofte a day he swelte and seyde 'Allas!'/For seen his lady shal he never mo."

Shakespeare, too, wrote in the language of the people, but I doubt if many of his contemporaries talked thus: "We are such stuff/As dreams are made on, and our little life/is rounded with a sleep." The only parts of Shakespeare's plays which seem dated are some of the comedy scenes where he has used the language of the lowest common denominator, and such language is quickly dated and then obsolete.

Nor did Cranmer use the language of the people of the street, but the best language he could possibly offer to God. Using limited vocabulary is to deny us our ability to grow in grace, to move from the limited to the transcendent. I'm glad that those who are working on the new Episcopal liturgies have been aware of this; the most recent draft of the Prayer Book is head and shoulders above the others and gives me hope. As our lives have no future if we have no memory, our language has no future and becomes dead if we forget its roots.

Chaucer and Shakespeare both came along at times when the English language was in need of redemption, and we are at another such time, and perhaps our Chaucer or Shakespeare is yet to be born, or it may be that the English language, like Latin, will dwindle and become obsolete. The Bible becomes more difficult to read with each generation, because the translators for King James weren't threatened by limited vocabulary. This holds true for Shakespeare, too. Recently I reread one of his early plays, written before he had moved into his giant stride, and on a notepad I jotted down all the words which I felt to be valid, useful words which are no longer in our vocabulary. There were over one hundred.

But it is not only the English language which is in danger. It is a fear for languages all over the world. After the Second World War the Japanese lost so many actual written characters that college students today cannot read the great Japanese works of literature, because they no longer know the characters used by the classical writers. This destruction of language is a result of war and is always a curtailment of freedom.

In Russia, where the worship of the Trinitarian God in the full beauty of the liturgy is officially discouraged, it would not be easy for a Russian to read the works of Alexander Solzenitsyn even if these works were not forbidden, because so much vocabulary was lost in Russia after the revolution. In one of Solzenitsyn's books his hero spends long hours reading the great Russian dictionary which came out in the 1890s. Solzenitsyn himself has one volume of this two-volume work, and in his novels he is forging the Russian language back into vitality, taking the words of the people of the streets and the words of the great dictionary and pulling the fullness of language out of the shadows and into the light. This is what Dante did in the writing of *The Divine Comedy*. It is what the English language needs if it is to survive as a great tongue. And surely language and liturgy are intertwined.

When Hugh and I went on a trip to Russia I almost didn't get a visa because our travel agent put down my occupation as *writer*. Writers think. Writers ask questions. Writers are dangerous. She finally persuaded 'them' that I write only for very small children and was not a threat. In any dictatorship, writers are among the first to be imprisoned, and vocabulary is quickly diminished and language deteriorates. Writers, if their vocabulary is not leashed, are quick to see injustice, and rouse the people to do something about it. We need words with which to think; kill words and we won't be able to think and we'll be easier to manipulate.

So I worry about the tyranny of language which is incapable of containing mystery. I worry about the weakening of our theology. For the past few years, for instance, I have missed gifts and *creatures* of bread and wine; this says something theologically important to me: the bread and wine, too, are God's creatures; it is an affirmation of the goodness of creation; when our big vegetable garden is first manured in the spring, the rank, life-giving manure is also a gift and creature, a symbol of incarnation.

If we are children by adoption and grace, how can we drop the *we are bold to say* before the Our Father? We are indeed bold to call the Lord of the Universe by the homely name of Abba, Father, and I don't want this dulled for me, so that in my own eyes the magnificence of the one I worship is dwindled and diminished. I want to cry out to him in all his Trinitarian Glory.

But why only three? If he is indeed the maker of the galaxies, isn't three a small number for his persons? Aren't there probably dozens, if not millions? There well may be, but there is for those of us on planet earth a special quality about the number 3—not magic, though it has been made so—but special. After all, we are the third planet from the sun, so it is bound to be a number of particular significance for us.

CATECHUMEN

A very young star: That, too, is a star?

The wind: Yes, Like you. A sun. But older.

STAR: How old?

WIND: About half way.

STAR: What are those objects circling it?

WIND: They are called planets.

STAR: Will I have them, too?

WIND: It is likely.

STAR: Will this be good?

WIND: It can be very good.

STAR: The ones that travel farthest from their sun—

WIND: Yes?

STAR: There is ice, and flame that is frozen, and much wind that is very unlike you.

WIND: It is part of me.

STAR: And it is good?

WIND: It is very good.

STAR: But I am a blaze of fire and flame—

WIND: And for you I blow, too.

STAR: You blow wherever . . .

WIND: I blow where I will.

STAR: That planet—one, two, three—third from the sun—

WIND: One, two, three: Yes. For it there are numbers, and the number is three.

STAR: Those tiny moving creatures?

WIND: They are men.

STAR: Where the sun shines on their planet they cannot see me; they cannot see stars. How strange. Why is that?

WIND: They could see you if they went down deep, deep, into the bottom of a well.

STAR: Will I, too, have a planet with men?

WIND: It is possible.

STAR: Will this be good?

WIND: Now I must ask a question. What is good?

STAR: Good is—God is—Good is—that it *is.* I cannot answer.

WIND: Then watch these men.

STAR: What is that, which is dark where it should be light?
WIND: It is a hill.
STAR: What is that upon the hill?
WIND: It is a tree.
STAR: What is that upon the tree?
WIND: It is a man
STAR: But I do not understand.
WIND: You need not.
STAR: But I hear this man.
WIND: Yes.
STAR: But I am because he spoke, because he is spoken.
WIND: Yes.
STAR: But he is not like those other men.
WIND: I did not say he was. They are like him.
STAR: I thought that it was dark upon that hill, and now it is so bright that my light is nothing. O Wind, why do I feel pain?
WIND: From the nails.
STAR: It is not my pain.
WIND: Yes, it is yours, because it is his.
STAR: For you, too?
WIND: Creation groans.
STAR: Wind?
WIND: Yes?
STAR: It is over.
WIND: It has begun.

So for us the number is three, and it is enough; it holds the full glory.

"The Church is lowering its standards," I heard someone remark wistfully. In a wakeful period in the wee sma' hours of the night the phrase echoed back to me. What does it mean? And in my mind's eye flashed a vivid picture of a knight on horseback lowering his standard to the dust in defeat.

There are small subtle lowerings as well as the more obvious ones. If we fast now we do it for sociological and ecological reasons; all valid, and important. But we should not forget that fasting is also an aid to the prayer of the heart. It is indeed right and proper to fast in order to give the money thus saved to the starving people of the world, but it is also good to fast as a discipline which opens our hearts to God, and so to our neighbor.

If I am to show my love of God through love of neighbor, through walking a second mile with a stranger, through cutting my cloak in half in order to share it with the coatless, then I am able to show this love of neighbor only because first I must be able to accept my flawed and fragmented self enough to love myself; and I can love myself only when I can accept that God loves me, just as I am, without one plea.

One Lent, lost in the isolation of an attack of atheism, I wrote:

> *This is a strange place*
> *and I would be lost were it not for all the others*
> *who have been here before me.*
> *It is the alien space*
> *of your absence.*
> *It has been called, by some,*
> *the dark night of the soul.*
> *But it is absence of dark as well as light,*
> *an odd emptiness,*
> *the chill of any land without your presence.*
> *And yet, in this Lent of your absence,*
> *I am more certain of your love and comfort*
> *than when it is I who have withdrawn from you.*

I thank God for the characters who come to me in my stories, and who make me realize that the Institution is not the Church; the Church is all of us flawed and fallen people who make up the Body of Christ.

And so we are part of the Trinity, and that is an awesome thought, and the only thing to do is raise our voices and sing!

If I find the Holy Spirit the easiest person of the Trinity to understand, my faith in God the Father is also somewhat easier than my faith in God the Son; but it still involves the calm acceptance of mutually contradictory statements. He is infinite and wholly other and beyond mortal comprehension. And yet I reach out to hold his hand. I shelter under the shadow of his wings and know his nearness. No moral system, no personal rectitude, no code of ethics, is going to get me through this time we live in. I cannot do it alone, or even with the help of everybody around me, though it may be through their help that God is holding my hand.

It is always God the Son I find most difficult: the man Jesus of Nazareth, the dead Jew, is my stumbling block. It is easy to worship the Word who spoke the stars. But that Word made flesh?

There are books attempting to prove that he was an Essene

that he was married

that he was a homosexual

that he was a guerilla fighter, out to free Israel from Rome

that he was not dead when he was taken down from the cross (death by the slow strangulation of crucifixion usually took three days) but that his disciples hid him and produced him, in a horrible hoax, three days later

that he was a demiurge sent to clean up the mess God had made of the world

that he was only pretending to be human and didn't really share in human suffering

that he was a good rabbi with delusions of divinity

that it doesn't matter whether he was God or not

etcetera, ad infinitum, ad nauseam.

All these books mostly tell me what he is *not*. I can only guess at a few things which help show me what he is:

Jesus of Nazareth was a carpenter, which at that time meant that he was of the respectable middle class; he had a carpenter's strength; he had powerful lungs: he stood in a boat and spoke to thousands gathered on the shore (neither Ethel Merman nor Jesus Christ needed a throat mike), and the fact that he could cry out in a loud voice from the cross despite the strangling cords which compressed his rib cage is evidence of enormous physical power.

I don't know what he looked like, but he did *not* have blond curls and blue eyes. He was a Jew of Jews.

Since he did not fall for any of the temptations Satan offered him, he had no *hubris,* and so he is not a tragic hero. With the tragic hero there is always the question of what might have been, how the tragedy could have been averted. If Oedipus had not killed the old man at the crossroads; if Faust had not heeded the temptation of knowledge and youth; if Macbeth had not listened to the witches and lusted for the crown. . . .

With Jesus the might-have-been was answered when the Spirit led him into the desert to be tempted. There is an inevitability to his life, but it is not a tragic inevitability, because his will remained free.

He is hard for the consumer in the United States—or Soviet Russia —to understand, because he couldn't have cared less about the world's standards of success.

And this is the man who housed the second person of the Trinity.

But how? The impossibility bothered me, for a long time, and stopped bothering me only when I could rest with joy in 'the mystery of the word made flesh.'

There are analogies which help me to understand the first lines of John's Gospel. There are times when all of us willingly (and some-times unwillingly) limit ourselves for the sake of others. When my children were little I was hungry for adult conversation, for discussion of abstract ideas and concepts, but until they neared their teens our conversations had to be somewhat limited, even on our excursions up to nearby Mohawk Mountain to thrash out the problems of life and death. So I was only a part of my fuller self, but that part was still me; it was not something other than Madeleine, but it was not the whole Madeleine.

The week of Hugh's parents' golden wedding anniversary I was certainly a different, and perhaps better, Madeleine than the usual one, but the self I brought to Tulsa was still part of the whole me.

Analogies are never completely accurate. The willing limiting of the second person of the Trinity is far greater, and I struggled with it in writing, in Mary's voice, speaking these words from Ephesus when she was old and near time to die.

> *Now that I have spent these years in this strange place*
> *of luminous stone and golden light and dying gods,*
> *now that I have listened to the wild music*
> *of given-son, John, I begin to understand.*
>
> *In the beginning I was confused and dazzled,*
> *a plain girl, unused to talking with angels.*
> *Then there was the hard journey to Bethlehem,*

and the desperate search for a place to stay,
my distended belly ripe and ready for deliverance.
In the dark of the cave, night air sweet with the moist breath
of the domestic beasts, I laughed, despite my pains,
at their concern. Joseph feared that they would frighten me
with their anxious stampings and snortings,
but their fear was only for me, and not because of me.
One old cow, udders permanently drooping,
lowed so with my every contraction
that my own birthing cries could not be heard;
and so my baby came with pain and tears and much hilarity.

Afterwards, swaddled and clean, he was so small and tender
that I could not think beyond my present loving
to all this strange night pointed. The shepherds came,
clumsy and gruff, and knelt and bought their gifts,
and, later on, the Kings; and all I knew was marvel.
His childhood was sheer joy to me. He was merry and loving,
moved swiftly from laughters to long, unchildlike silences.
The years before his death were bitter to taste.
I did not understand, and sometimes thought that it was he
who had lost sight of the promise of his birth.

His death was horrible. But now I understand
that death was not his sacrifice, but birth.
It was not the cross which was his greatest gift;
it was his birth which must have been, for him,
most terrible of all. Think. If I were to be born,
out of compassion, as one of the small wood lice
in the doorsill of our house, limit myself to the comprehension
of those small dark creatures, unable to know sea or sun or song
or John's bright words; to live and die thus utterly restricted,
it would be as nothing, nothing to the radiant Word
coming to dwell, for man, in man's confined and cabined flesh.

This was the sacrifice, this the ultimate gift of love.
I thought once that I loved. My love was hundredfold less
than his, than is the love of the wood lice to mine,
and even here is mystery, for who dares limit love?
And has he not, or will he not, come to the wood lice
as he came to man? Does he not give his own self
to the grazing cattle, the ear of corn, the blazing sun,
the clarion moon, the drop of rain that falls into the sea?
His compassion is infinite, his sacrifice incomprehensible,
breaking through the darkness of our loving-lack.

> *Now I am old and sight and thought grow dim, limbs slow.*
> *Oh, my son, who was and is and will be, my night draws close.*
> *Come, true light which taketh away the sin of the world,*
> *and bring me home. My hour is come. Amen.*

I seek for God that he may find me because I have learned, empirically, that this is how it works. I seek: he finds. The continual seeking is the expression of the hope for a creator great enough to care for every particular atom and sub-atom of his creation, from the greatest galaxy to the smallest farandolae. Because of my particular background I see the coming together of macrocosm and microcosm in the Eucharist, and I call this Creator: God, Father; but no human being has ever called him by his real name, which is great and terrible and unknown, and not to be uttered by mortal man. If inadvertently my lips framed the mighty syllables, entire galaxies might explode.

As I read the Old and New Testaments I am struck by the awareness therein of our lives being connected with cosmic powers, angels and archangels, heavenly principalities and powers, and the groaning of creation. It's too radical, too uncontrolled for many of us, so we build churches which are the safest possible places in which to escape God. We pin him down, far more painfully than he was nailed to the cross, so that he is rational and comprehensible and like us, and even more unreal.

And that won't do. That will not get me through death and danger and pain, nor life and freedom and joy.

There is little evidence for faith in God in the world around me. Centuries ago a man whose name is unknown to me cried out, "If God were one whit less than he is, he dare not put us in a world that carries so many arguments against him."

And, if I take the stories of the Bible seriously, when God's people turn from him for too long, he withdraws. He has not answered my knock for a long time, and this is beginning to make me angry. Why isn't he there when I need him so desperately? So I write him another

LOVE LETTER

I hate you, God.
Love, Madeleine.

I write my message on water
and at bedtime I tiptoe upstairs
and let it flow under your door.

When I am angry with you
I know that you are there
even if you do not answer my knock
even when your butler opens the door an inch
and flaps his thousand wings in annoyance
at such untoward interruption
and says the master is not at home.

I love you, Madeleine,
Hate, God.

(This is how I treat my friends, he said to one great saint.
No wonder you have so few, Lord, she replied.)

I cannot turn the other cheek
it takes all the strength I have
to keep from hitting back

the soldiers bayonet the baby
the little boys trample the old woman
the gutters are filled with groans
while pleasure-seekers knock each other down
to get their tickets stamped first.

I'm turning in my ticket
and my letter of introduction
you're supposed to do the knocking.

How can I write to you
to tell you that I'm angry
when I've been given the wrong address
and I don't even know your right name?

I take hammer and nails
and tack my message on two crossed pieces of wood.

Dear God,
is it too much to ask you
to bother to be?
Just show your hindquarters
and let me hear you roar.

Love,
Madeleine.

I have often been told that when one first turns to God, one is greeted with brilliant Yes answers to prayers. For a long time, that was true for me. But then, when he has you hooked, he starts to say No. This has, indeed, been my experience. But it has been more than a No answer lately; after all, No is an answer. It is the silence, the withdrawal, which is so devastating. The world is difficult enough with God; without him it is a hideous joke.

The Trinity is unity in diversity; the Trinity is our model for Community.

What happened?

I turn again to that time when there was war in heaven, and Michael and his angels fought against the dragon. This is indeed a dark parable, this story of the breaking of the Original Community. Does it go as far back as the Big Bang? Or even further?

Once upon a time, back in *kairos,* so long ago that very likely it was before time, that strangeness where there wasn't even *once upon a time,* long before man was made and Adam was called to name the birds and the beasts, the most beautiful and bright of all the angels rebelled against the love of God, and his rebellion was put down by the Archangel Michael and his angels. But Michael's victory was only partial, at least for us human beings, because the bright angel walks our earth, lording it over us, bringing evil and distortion and hate in his wake, and even managing to make us believe that his power of non-ness doesn't exist.

It does. He does. If I can understand the truth of Love only through the Incarnation, so also I can understand destruction and annihilation only in particular. Satan is reasonable, tolerant, beautiful. If he were unreasonable, implausible, ugly, he would have no attraction for us; he would not be the Tempter, the one we pray that we will not be led to. He is immensely attractive and kind. He wants everybody to be happy, right here, right now. He can alleviate all poverty, cure all disease, and give us all the comforts of technocracy. As for free will, who needs that? Free will is a beastly burden a cruel creator has put on us, a creator whose ways are not our ways. If we have any sense at all we will follow the successful Prince of this Earth and reject the Lord of the Universe.

Free will is indeed a strange gift, fit only for the very mature. Why did he give it to us when we weren't ready for it?

When our three children were little, we had friends with one small boy, handsome, though tending to blubber because he ate nothing but ice cream. In the glow of their adoration for this creature of theirs, his parents gave him free will. He was allowed to decide what he should eat (ice cream), what he should wear, when he should go to bed. When there was a family decision to be made, they turned to this child, when he was three, four, five years old, to make it. As we watched this little boy turning into such a loathsome brat that our children groaned when they were forced to play with him, it seemed to us that his parents were not, in fact, giving him the free will they were talking about; they were making him God. They adored him as only God should be adored. They turned to him for decisions with the kind of expectation one should not have of any human being, and certainly not of a child.

So it became clear to us that this small boy was ending up with no free will at all. Somehow or other, the loving parents had swallowed one of the Tempter's hooks, and the child was given total self-indulgence, which is far from free will.

He still tempts. The ancient, primordial battle to destroy Community, to shatter Trinity, still continues. Creation still groans with the pain of it. Like it or not, we're caught in the middle.

Satan is the great confuser. I'm sure he whispered sweet reasonableness into the ears of the men who decided to build a city, and in the city put a tower that would reach heaven.

But the tower fell and they were divided and broken. Up until the time of the Tower of Babel, the children of Israel lived in close-knit communities. Each person, great or small, had an intrinsic share in the life of the community. When one suffered, everyone suffered. Oh, yes, there was sin and evil and too much wine and conniving and all the bad things which come from fallen man in a fallen world. But the paradoxes of human nature were still accepted. And wherever man went on the face of the known earth he spoke the same language; everybody could understand everybody else. It wasn't like that first Pentecost when everyone in that large group gathered together was suddenly able to understand each other's language as had not been possible since the days before the building of the Tower of Babel.

God broke his people at Babel and I doubt if I will ever understand this. But one of Satan's dirtiest devices is to promise infinite under-standing to finite creatures. And so he has promised us success, and his success is delusion, and the breaking apart of community.

Those early communities of the Hebrew children were not suc-cesses. The people bickered. They turned away from God and wor-shipped a golden calf. They coveted each others' wives. But they knew that they could not get along without each other. They accepted their interdependence. When they turned away from God and built their temples to Baal they knew how to repent and to say *I'm sorry.*

It is far more difficult for us to say *I'm sorry* today than it was for the Hebrew children, because to say *I'm sorry* implies admission of failure, and we live in a culture where failure is not tolerated. In school, for instance, a child is not allowed to repeat a grade more than a certain number of times; then he is automatically moved ahead, ready or not. A black student whose high-school education, to our shame, simply has not been adequate to prepare him for college must be admitted anyhow, and given a diploma, which thereby becomes a worthless piece of paper. Some of my college-age friends are dis-couraged from taking a course outside their field which nevertheless may fascinate them, because they may not get the high grade they need on their record if they're to go on to graduate school, and so they take the less challenging course in order to get the high grade which no longer has any real meaning.

When Hugh and the children and I were living in the country year round, I learned a lot about failure and about community, almost in the way that those old children of Israel learned about community.

I had already begun to understand failure as creative in terms of my marriage, and this understanding was tested with the coming of children. There's an odd law about families; they tend to grow; it may be dogs, or cats, or babies, or birds, or plants, but families need to blossom. Our family grew in all kinds of ways, for Hugh taught me early that a family with closed doors is not a family.

During our Crosswicks years, one of our baby sitters, aged thirteen, came for an evening and stayed two years. And because we lived outside the village, playmates for our children had to be fetched and carried, and we usually had at least three extra for the weekends.

Then there was the community of the church, the white-pillared, tall-spired church which stood directly across from our General Store in the center of the village. When we moved to Crosswicks, neither of us had been in church for a long time. For good reasons, of course. We found more real community in the theatre than we did in city churches. The church seemed to hold up to us a God who had nothing to do with the stars which crackled above us on cold nights, or with the frogs whose deep clunking announced that the iron earth would thaw and pussy willows come and the geese honk high and wild.

But our village church wasn't really like a city church. I'm not even sure that it was like what most of us think of as church. It was the center of the village geographically, and became so in our lives, though it had no relation to a social club, although it was the largest part of our social lives, too. In those days, before I'd ever heard of ecumenism, the Congregational Church in our village was truly ecumenical. The war was not long over; there was not one of us who had not in some way been touched by the war, participated in it, either abroad or at home, lost people we loved in it. Two of the women who were to become my good friends were English war brides. We all knew that mankind, left to its own devices, makes slums and battlefields and insane asylums, and many of us had settled in the little village looking for something else, something which bore little resemblance to the success-oriented cities and suburbs. Our doctor had deliberately chosen, when the war was over and he could leave the army, to be a village general practitioner instead of a big city specialist. Hugh and I, too, had rejected the values of the city, being too young and untutored to understand that city or country has little to do with the *symboles* by which we live.

We soon found ourselves swept into a tight-knit little band of struggling Christians. There were six or eight couples of us, all about the same age, all with small children, who threw our lives into the life of the church, guided by the young minister who, also, with his wife and baby, had left a big city church, and come to this small green and pleasant land. It was within the community of these people who sang in the choir, taught Sunday School, visited the sick, that I first experienced, without realizing it consciously, a truly Christian community. I doubt if I will ever experience it in the same way again, not only because I am now grandmother as well as mother, but because there are few villages in the Eastern United States as small as ours was then; it, too, has grown; we now have five hundred telephones and our phone number has had to be changed and I am finding it hard to remember the new one.

I understand the depth of our commitment better now than I did then. A community, to be truly community, must have a quality of unselfconsciousness about it. We knew that we were struggling to be Christian, and that we often failed, and we knew that we couldn't be community on our own, and so the grace of community was given to us.

Today I must seek community in a different way. Traveling along the fjords of Norway one autumn, Hugh and I passed many villages with no more than a dozen houses, and boathouses instead of garages; and I looked at these little clusters with longing, because such a village cannot exist without being a community. But in life as I must live it today, community must have a new form. I do not know what it will be, and I suspect that I won't know until memory tells me that I am having it right now without knowing it, just as we were unselfconscious about it when we lived year-round in Crosswicks.

I sympathize with experiments in communes, but any time we try to go back to the Garden it can mean being led by a Manson.

So I look back without too much nostalgia on those days when our children were young, but with gratitude for the experience, which helps me look to the future knowing in my blood and bones what Christian Community is about. We really did try to minister to each other, to pray together, moving through self-consciousness and embarrassment to freedom, and at first I was paralyzed with embarrassment. If one of us mothers was having a difficult pregnancy or had grippe, two or three of us would go and clean house (and I hated this job as much then as I do now and I was more often on the receiving than on the giving end, but I did try). We took turns taking the children, bringing in meals. Hugh rode the tractor in the summer to help a farmer friend with his haying and came home sunburned and streaked with honest sweat. In the autumn the women canned and froze vegetables together because we were going to need that food in the winter. We moved from house to house, working together, and surely my friends gave unstintingly in helping this city girl who had never before pulled a carrot from the ground, or plucked an apple from a tree. The land on which Crosswicks stands once gave all that was needed for life. Now we have only the orchard, the berries, and a mammoth vegetable garden. We do not render our own soap or dip our own candles. But the fertile land, the great beams of the house itself, cause me to remember—not just the community, which was essential for survival two hundred-odd years ago, but a glimpse of something unbroken, and of which we are still a part.

We were very loosely organized, our little group centered in the spired church, but we were organized by love.

Several years ago when all the rooms in the house had been wall-papered by us with paper we had carefully chosen, I announced that I was too old ever to hang wallpaper again, and if things got too shabby we'd have to bring in a professional. But a couple of years ago I started on the second round, and as I struggled with shears and wallpaper paste, I realized that I was still part of that community which physically was broken by time and distance long ago.

It is once again the joy of memory, for those days are real, and are mine to dip into. I do one of my rare cleaning out of closets and come across a baby's shoe; a little girl's sweater which I had washed in water too hot for it, so that it shrank so small that it was used for dolls; a small stuffed animal with one torn ear and one lost eye which I had once upon a time thought I was going to fix.

I cannot go to the bookshelves and pull out *The Secret Garden* without remembering a rainy weekend when it was our turn to have everybody at our house and I kept a charm of children quiet and happy by reading aloud until I was hoarse.

Our children all quickly grew used to being in half a dozen houses as freely as their own. When the father of one family was stricken with an acute form of cancer, his three little ones were already used to being in other houses, and during his last days they moved from house to house where they were already at home. Death was no less premature and shocking, but the children were not taken from familiar surroundings and sent to strangers, and I think the loving but calm concern given them did help; it helped us, too. I didn't know much about intercessory prayer then, but I do know that our prayers during that period brought healing for all of us, and it seems somehow appropriate that I was listening to Handel's lilting spring cuckoo concerto on the clear winter morning when the phone rang and someone told me that death had come at last.

There were joyful experiences as well as sad ones. On a night when I woke up early with labor pains, Hugh took our sleeping daughter, drove five miles to neighboring farmer friends, and put her in bed, still sleeping, beside her friend Chucky, and drove off without disturbing anybody, even the cows.

When Josephine woke up in the morning it would be in a familiar room, among people she knew and trusted. And everybody in the household would know that the new baby was on the way. Another friend among our community, who had left nursing not long before to stay home with her baby, simply announced that she was going to the hospital with me to be my special nurse—knowing that babies do not birth easily for me. Over this baby's birth she was on her feet for forty-eight hours straight, and that was as much a part of our church life as the Sunday services or the choir practices.

You can tell they are Christians by their love.

It wasn't until our full-time days at Crosswicks had been behind us for a number of years that as I looked back with the blessing of memory I saw that for nearly a decade I had experienced the kind of love described in the Acts of the Apostles, despite all our human flaws. The early Christians quarreled, and so did we. Once Hank got so mad at me during choir practice that he threw a hymnal at me. One wife came into the store one day at noon looking a bit dazed and said, "I just broke a plate over Stephen's head." But despite it all, we were there for each other.

There, in all our particularity. Just as my concern for the victims of starvation across the planet is awakened by my awareness of the hunger of my neighbor, who has a face and a name, so is my love for all humankind awakened by my love for any one part of it. My Christian God is not the exclusive God of the Christians. He is Lord of the Universe, and he notes the fall of the sparrow in every part of his creation, and he counts the hairs of every head, not just Christian or Jew. I learned something of this wider compassion when I lived with my friends in the country who were, except in our ministry to each other, often so different from me that we did not always understand each other. My rejection slips did not seem very cosmic to anybody but me, and I felt that most people thought that I was simply not quite good enough to be doing what I was doing. The things which were cosmic to them were alien to me.

That decade of community was important to me but it was not idyllic. It was for many reasons one of the most unhappy periods of my life. But I did experience Christian community, and it was this which kept much of what happened from being totally destructive.

There was nothing idyllic about the fact that four of our most intimate friends died within three years of each other, and that by the death of one couple we inherited a seven-year-old daughter, and on the same day that she came to us, we found a seventeen-year-old ex-baby sitter huddled in our garage, pregnant and unmarried and certain that we would not throw her out.

There was, for me, nothing idyllic about struggling to raise our children, trying to keep house in drafty old Crosswicks where the washing machine—once I had graduated from doing the laundry in the bathtub and had a washing machine—froze during the winter months at least twice a week, usually full of diapers; and we were never warm around the edges.

There was nothing idyllic in the violent conflict between Madeleine, wife and mother, and Madeleine, writer. I struggled to write under the worst possible conditions, after the children were in bed—that force field of concentration would have been a dangerous idea while they were awake and active. Like most young mothers I was constantly tired. Added to fatigue was struggling to cope with failure, which looked as though it would have no end. I was trying to develop as a writer, but I received from editors nothing but a long stream of rejection slips, mostly the impersonal printed ones, although I had already had several books published, and with moderate success. Theron, my agent, was worried that too much failure would kill my talent, and perhaps, in the end, it would have. I'm not sure how strong I am, and what would have happened if the chill rejections had never stopped.

The failure to sell my writing was coupled with failures within myself, as wife, mother, human being, faltering Christian. Failures must be accepted now, too, in the very different communities in which I find myself: in the Crosswicks summers, full of comings and goings and occasional days when I am completely alone with the animals and the garden; in our winter community in the city, the community formed by Hugh's work in the theatre and my community at St. John's Cathedral—it's a good combination, the theatre and the church, and an evening of friends from both communities works marvelously, and is full of stimulation and laughter.

The church in our village offered me community and so redeemed my failures as wife, mother, writer, and if our village church is different today, that does not change what it gave to me then, or say that the change is not as good as what was. It is simply normal change. And I, too, am different.

Our communities are joyful and creative for me only when I can accept my own imperfections, when I can rush out with my sins of omission and commission and hang them on the cross as I hang out the laundry.

If I could not hang my sins on the cross I might tend to withdraw, the responsibilities of community are so great. And far too often I have taken on myself a responsibility which is not really mine, because my faith is not strong enough, and I tumble, splat, into the do-it-yourself pit.

It is only when I am able to put the subtle whispers of the tempter behind me and accept failure that I am free to be part of a community, and part of that freedom is to accept that the community itself is going to fail—at the very least it is going to change, and it may die, and this, in worldly terms, in Satan's terms, is failure.

I think of my granddaughters learning to find it difficult to say, "I'm sorry," to accept having done something naughty, and I remember seeing the same thing in my own children, and I still struggle with the same error in myself. We are taught early, very early, to set up false expectations of ourselves, and when we fall away from the pearly-pink perfection we have supposed to be our 'real' self, and are faced with what is in fact our 'real' self, we alibi and rationalize and do everything we can to avoid seeing it. And far too often we succeed, and struggle unsuccessfully to live with a stranger who never was, and then we are like my psychiatrist friend's patients who are afraid to remember, because if their memories are true, then their present lives are false.

Charlotte, our younger granddaughter, used to withdraw completely into herself when she was scolded, even if it was just an "Oh, Charlotte!" as the milk was overturned for the fifth time, retreating as completely as though she had gone into another room. She stayed deep inside herself for however long she needed to accept, to herself, that she had been careless, that she was a child capable of overturning a mug; then, in one spontaneous burst, she returned to the community, flinging her arms around father, mother, grandparent, whoever was nearest, bursting with love.

On one of these occasions one of my children reminded me of something I had forgotten: there was a week when they were little when at least one glass of milk was spilled at every meal, and I finally got so irritated that I said, "Whoever spills the next glass of milk will leave the room." Shortly after which I reached for something and knocked over my glass. I left the room.

Our two little granddaughters have a sense of community which many adults have lost; people have developed less a sense of community than a loneliness which they attempt to assuage by being with other people constantly, and on a superficial level only. In both the literary and theatrical worlds Hugh and I are occasionally required to go to enormous cocktail parties, one of our most unfavorite activities (and I have now been introduced to the ecclesiastical sherry party). The cocktail party says something about affluent America, and reveals tellingly that affluence can blur the sense of joy in interdependence which is behind all true community. The loneliness, the namelessness of cocktail-party relationships surrounds us. We meet, but even when we kiss we do not touch. We avoid the responsibility of community.

But it is always a changing community.

The old four-generation Crosswicks community died with the death of my mother and the purchase of Jo's and Alan's house, aptly called Little Gidding. There is much going and coming between the two dwellings; the doors are open and the wind blows through and sometimes I am bold to think that it is the wind of the spirit. I sit lightly to denominations, but I am Anglican enough to think that our frequent house communions have done much to keep our communities living and loving.

There have been times, especially during the summer, when I have longed for solitude, and it took some hard lessons for me to learn that I needed to be what I had thought was selfish; that I needed to take time to myself to write, to go to the brook, to be. When I was able to accept the imperfect Madeleine who could not function without time to work, time to be alone, the summers became rich and Trinitarian for me.

After one of them I wrote

MRS. NOAH SPEAKING

I suppose under the circumstances
there's really no point in complaining
but really! Noah and I had just got accustomed
to living alone and having some peace and quiet
and fixing up the house the way we wanted it at last.
I brought up three boys, wiped their runny noses, changed their messy diapers,
  washed, sewed, cooked, saw to it that they had the proper advantages,
We got them safely married
  (though if I didn't know it before I know it now:
  their wives leave a great deal to be desired).
We liked having them come to visit us on the proper holidays,
  bringing the babies, taking enough food home to feed them for a week,
  and Noah and I could go to bed in peace.
And now look what has happened!

Sometimes I think it would have been simpler to have drowned
  with everybody else—
at least their troubles are over.
And here we are jammed in this Ark—
why didn't the Lord give Noah enough time to build a big enough ark
  if he wanted him to build one at all?
The animals take up almost all the room
and Noah and I are crowded together with Shem, Ham, and Japheth,
  their slovenly wives and noisy children,
and nowhere to go for a moment's peace.
Noah, of course, has hidden several elephant's skins of wine somewhere,
  and when the rain and noise and confusion get too bad
  he goes down to the dirty hold with the beasts and gets drunk,
  sleeps it off on the dirty straw,
  and then comes up to bed smelling of armadillo dung and platypus piss.

Not that I blame him.
It's my daughters-in-law who get me.
They insist on changing the beds every time I turn around.
They won't use a towel more than once, and they're always getting dressed up
  and throwing their dirty linen at me to wash.

The washing is easy enough—we've plenty of water—
But how do they expect me to get anything dry in all this rain?
I don't mind doing the cooking, but they're always coming out to the
*   kitchen to fix little snacks with the excuse that it will help me:*
*   "You're so good to us, Mother Noah, we'll just do this for you,"*
*   and they never put anything away where it belongs. They've lost*
*   one of my measuring cups and they never clean the stove and they've*
*   broken half of the best china that came down to us from Grandfather*
*   Seth.*
When the babies squall in the night, who gets up with them?
Not my daughters-in-law.
"Oh, Mother Noah'll do it. She loves the babies so."
*   Ham's wife is always stirring up quarrels, playing people off against*
*   each other. Shem's wife, who never does anything for anybody, manages*
*   to make me feel lazy and mean if I ask her to dry one dish. Japheth's*
*   wife is eyeing Shem and Ham; she'll cause trouble; mark my words.*

Today that silly dove Noah is so fond of came back with an olive twig
*   on his beak. Maybe there's hope that we'll get out of this Ark*
*   after all.*

We've landed! At last! Now we can get back to normal and have some
*   peace and quiet and if I put something where it belongs it will stay there*
*   and I can clean up this mess and get some sleep at night and—*

Noah! Noah! I miss the children.

When I think of the phrase *The Coming of the Kingdom* it means to me the restoration of community, the healing of brokenness which will enable us to rejoice once more in being one—not a solitary, isolated one, but whole, body, intellect, spirit at peace; mind, heart, intuition in collaboration.

There are those who do not want this wholeness, who want to continue the process of fragmentation, and this has to be fought, with Michael and his angels by our side. If we care about wholeness, about unity in diversity, we are in battle. But it isn't the same kind of warring which confused our children when they were little: 'But I thought the Germans were our enemy? Why are they our friends now?' 'But I thought Russia was our ally? Why are we frightened of Russia now?' It isn't like the kind of warring which polarized the country over Vietnam. On the news not long ago I heard about firefighters who are spending the Fourth of July weekend in continuing to fight a brush fire in California which has already destroyed several homes and threatens to destroy more. The fight against the Powers of Breaking has more in common with these firefighters than it does with battles over national boundaries. It is a hard fact that since Christendom wars have been far worse than they ever were before, but I don't think we can blame Christendom for the making of bombs and bayonets; it is the Destroyer who is at work here, and he has had to work all the harder since the coming of the second person of the Trinity to share in our lives.

Men and women are often happy and fulfilled when they are at war, when the community of warriors holds the life of each one in its care, but I'd guess that effectively stopping an out-of-control forest fire brings the same kind of community, and evokes as much bravery and far more satisfaction than wiping out a city.

I've always been ambivalent about the Fourth of July, that national holiday which falls early in what used to be the Trinity season. As an American, I need to take it seriously, because our forefathers did have a dream of community, of wholeness.

I miss the symbols of fireworks, and it would seem that the occasional injuries from carelessness with fireworks (not firecrackers and noisemakers, but the works of light and beauty) were minimal compared to the injury to personality caused by sitting in front of a television set, the Great Baby Sitter (yes, I used it too; in a world of the small family unit and no servants it is almost unavoidable), and learning passivity. When our children were little the Fourth of July meant a kind of fairy-land beauty, because even the little ones could hold a sparkler, and in the first dusk we would have a procession of a dozen or more children plus their respective parents, weaving through the apple orchard with the sparklers like a skyfall of stars.

At dinner, always a communal affair, one of the grownups would talk a little about the enormous privileges of freedom still open to Americans, and we would all hold hands to say grace, and we took seriously, in our small community, our American heritage.

But the world has changed. Sparklers are outlawed. We've had Vietnam and assassinations and Watergate. And apart from a Bicentennial year, we barely note the fourth. There is an ambiguity about the holiday which embarrasses us.

But it reminds me, with an unexpected jolt each year, that we are still at war, that creation still groans with the strain of it.

But the growing of the garden is on our side. The plashing of the brook is on our side. The green of grass and the brilliance of flowers and the song of the birds are on our side.

In *Dragons in the Waters* an old gentlewoman from South Carolina is rather unexpectedly in a Quiztano Indian village in Venezuela. In the morning before dawn she arises and walks across the greensward to the lake's edge:

Umar Xanai was there before her, alone, sitting in Charles's favorite position.

The old woman sat down silently, slightly to one side and behind him. Around her she could sense the sleeping village. Someone was moving on the porch of one of the Caring Places. Soon Dragonlake would be awake. All around her she heard bird song. A fish flashed out of the lake and disappeared beneath the dark waters. Above her the stars dimmed and the sky lightened.

When the sun sent its first rays above the mountain, Umar Xanai rose and stretched his arms upward. He began to chant. Miss Leonis could not understand the velvet Quiztano words, but it seemed to her that the old chieftan was encouraging the sun in its rising, urging it, enticing it, giving the sun every psychic aid in his power to lift itself up out of the darkness and into the light. When the great golden disc raised itself clear of the mountain the chanting became a triumphal, joyful song.

At the close of the paean of praise the old man turned to the old woman and bent down to greet her with the three formal kisses.

She asked, "You are here every morning?"

He nodded, smiling. "It is part of my duties as chief of the Quitzanos."

"To help the sun rise?"

"That is my work."

"It would not rise without you?"

"Oh, yes, it would rise. But as we are dependent on the sun for our crops, for our lives, it is our courtesy to give the sun all the help in our power—and our power is considerable."

"I do not doubt that."

"We believe," the old man said quietly, "that everything is dependent on everything else. The sun does not rise in the sky in loneliness; we are with him. The moon would be lost in isolation if we did not greet her with song. The stars dance together, and we dance with them."

Thou also shall light my candle, sings the psalmist. The Lord my God shall make my darkness to be light.

To sing this is already to choose sides.

To look for community instead of cocktail-party relationships is part of choosing sides in this vast, strange battle. To say, "I'm sorry"; to be silent; to say "I love you," "I care." It is these little things that are going to make the difference. For God chooses the foolish things of the world to confound the wise, the weak to overthrow the strong. Out of failure he brings triumph. Out of the grave he births life.

It is difficult for me not to make impossible demands on my communities as I sometimes make them on myself. It is difficult for me to accept that there is still war in heaven, and that I must join the battle lines on one side or the other, because the wars of the world's history have confused me about battle lines. It would be easy to fall into the Manichaean heresy, where good and evil were born simultaneously and have been battling since the beginning. But that takes away the Godness of God, and I can't live without God as one, God as all. There was war in heaven, part of God's creation turned against him, and like it or not, we are caught in it and we have to choose creation or destruction; and I might sometimes teeter on the edge of despair did there not shine for me that light in the darkness which the darkness cannot put out.

It is difficult to accept that all my beloved communities are going to die, and that even while they exist there are incredible spaces between human beings, even the closest. And, despite all my urgings toward community, I will always be, like Abraham, a wanderer, far from home. But the people who are most aware of their own impermanence are the most able to throw wide the doors of heart and hearth to the stranger, to hear his message, receive his blessing.

To make community misunderstood is a powerful weapon of the Destroyer—to promise permanence, to insist on perfection, to strangle freedom, so that instead of having community, we have a concentration camp.

Crosswicks may be noisy and on occasion extremely untidy, but it has never, thank God, remotely resembled a concentration camp. And it has taught me about Trinity, that *unity in diversity* which has been mouthed so often that it is now part of the jargon and has become as empty as *meaningful* and *relevant*, but it's still the kind of oneness I mean. The kind which comes when our wildly diverse family is gathered about the dinner table and Bion and Hugh differ noisily (within this unity) as to whether we'll eat entirely by candlelight or turn on one electric light bulb. The kind which I have known, and

Hugh still knows, in the theatre, where everybody is working together to bring a play to life. The kind I know when Alan and I play piano and violin, respectively and together, even the cacophony of our invented Bartók weaving its Trinitarian joy.

3 = 1.

1 is 3.

And this is good.

And this is God.

II... Setter and Swallow

THE EPIPHANY, the Transfiguration, Pentecost, all speak to me in the same luminous language. They are all lit with the same incredible gold light. And the story of Nathanael is also in a brilliant tongue, the language of the dark parable which cannot be comprehended by sunside alone, and I am not at all surprised that it is found in the first chapter of John's Gospel.

Once upon a time there was a man whose name was Nathanael. Jesus called Philip to follow him, and Philip went to Nathanael, and told him that he had found the one for whom they sought, Jesus of Nazareth. Rational Nathanael replied dubiously, "Can any good come out of Nazareth?" Philip replied, "Come and see!"

Jesus saw Nathanael coming to him and said, "Behold an Israelite indeed, in whom is no guile."

Nathanael said, "How did you know me?"

Jesus answered, "Before Philip called you, while you were sitting under the fig tree, I saw you."

Nathanael, his reason knocked out from under him, replied, "Rabbi, you are the Son of God."

One evening I was talking about this story to Hugh, and he said, "I don't understand it."

"What don't you understand?"

"What was so extraordinary about Jesus seeing Nathanael under the fig tree? Why would that make Nathanael say he was the Son of God?"

"Oh—" I said, and remembered and told Hugh about the fig tree in my grandmother's back yard in North Florida. When I was visiting her when I was a little girl and had had too much of the grownups and of the Florida heat, I would go out in the yard, smeared with lavender oil to keep the insects away, and lie in the cool shade under the fig tree and read until someone came out and called me in. Whoever it was had to call; I couldn't be seen in the deep shade of the fig leaves. "So it *was* extraordinary that Jesus saw Nathanael under the fig tree. He probably was sitting there just because it was private and he couldn't be seen."

"Well, maybe."

Nathanael, in any event, was astonished.

Jesus answered him, "Because I told you that I saw you under the fig tree you believe? You'll see greater things than this. I tell you in truth that you shall see Heaven open, and the angels of God ascending and descending upon the Son of man."

For Nathanael this was a moment of total reality, a moment when reasonable, chronological time was broken open, and he glimpsed real time, *kairos,* and was never the same again.

But that once upon a time two thousand years ago might equally well be today. I suspect that most of us are very like Nathanael, eminently reasonable people. Like Nathanael we see things the way they are—at least we think we do. And it's jolting to discover that our reasonable view of things just isn't the real view. When this happens to me, and it often does, I remember Nathanael, and try once again to be like him, not the reasonable Nathanael safe and hidden under the fig tree, but the astonished Nathanael who was told that he would see heaven open and the angels of God ascending and descending upon the Son of man.

He must have been frightened. How could he, how can any of us visualize angels of God ascending and descending upon the Son of man? When I try I get a mindscape, powerful though not very visual, of Jacob's ladder with the angels of God ascending and descending superimposed on Jacob himself wrestling throughout the night with the angel. And I get a vision of a special kind of brilliance, not golden, but like the light of the moon shining on diamond-coated branches and twigs after an ice storm. But that's not it. That's not even a glimpse of angels ascending and descending upon the Son of man.

And yet Jesus promised Nathanael that he was going to see them. And I ask myself exactly when was it that Nathanael actually came to see this promised vision? If I had to make a guess I'd say that it was probably on Good Friday when the sky darkened and the tree whose seed was buried with the first Adam held the second Adam. The old tradition that the cross on which Jesus was crucified stood on the same place, and grew from the very seed of the tree from which Adam and Eve ate the forbidden fruit, and that Adam's skull *(calvarius)* is still there, under that tree, seems to fit in with the opening of Nathanael's eyes.

How can I see in the same way that Nathanael saw his extraordinary vision, a vision which had in it the promise of resurrection? It isn't easy to accept the fact that such a vision is more real, more true, than something within the realm of provable fact. But I'll never accept it if I stay safely hidden under my fig tree, and I want the courage to move out of the shadows so that I may have my own glimpses of transfiguration.

As always, they may be very small things, so tiny that it seems presumptuous to set them down beside something so grand as angels ascending and descending. But they are moments of revelation for me, when suddenly sunside and nightside know each other. This summer there has been the amazing friendship of Timothy, the red Irish setter, and his swallow.

Timothy was three and a half years old when he came to us, and for those first three and a half years he had been beaten. Dog and child abuse in whatever form are mysterious horrors to me. When we got Tim he was approximately twenty-seven in people years, and we were not at all sure we were going to be able to help this miserable, terrified creature who crawled abjectly on his belly. But within twenty-four hours he began to walk upright, and to come sit on the floor by me and hold up his paw to be held. It took him nearly two weeks to learn that it was safe to walk by Hugh to get to me, because whoever had beaten him was evidently a man, and he was still afraid of all men. There are times when Tim is in so paw-holding a mood that Hugh could wish he still inspired a little awe in the big red creature.

He came to us in the early autumn, and by Thanksgiving he had learned that he was allowed to come without a personal invitation into the kitchen with Hugh and me in the evening, while we had a drink and I cooked dinner. The kitchen is large for a city apartment, large enough for two comfortable, if shabby, chairs, and Timothy quickly took over the larger and shabbier—he gets away with things no other dog of ours has been allowed to do. Bion's first night home for the Thanksgiving holidays, he came out to the kitchen with us and sat comfortably in the old green chair. Tim poked his long red nose around the corner, ambled slowly across the kitchen, took a flying leap and landed, legs sprawling every which way, on Bion's lap. After all, Bion was in his chair.

So we knew that there was hope for him. We've had him nearly four years now and he's come a long way, but he's still a neurotic creature full of fears. Any man with stick or cane makes him cringe with terror. And it isn't a full year since he's come to trust the world enough to wag his tail, and only this summer that he's had the confidence to thump it on the floor.

For this summer Timothy has his swallow.

I think it was Bion who saw it first, but we've all seen it. Timothy will rush out to the big meadow, his once-timid tail waving ecstatically. He looks adoringly up at the sky, wagging, listening, and the swallow comes to him, flying very low, and then Tim will run along with the bird while it flies, back and forth, round and about, in great parabolas, all over the big meadow. Then the swallow will fly off and up, and Tim will stand looking upward, swishing his tail, and waiting for his friend to return.

It has been a great joy to us to watch this amazing friendship. Day after day they play together, and the game never palls. There is nothing of the stalker or hunter in Timothy's actions when he is with the swallow. Occasionally he will accidentally flush a pheasant, and then his tail goes straight out and still, and one forepaw curves up and he points. But with his swallow, his tail never stops waving. The two of them are lion and lamb together for me, a foretaste of Isaiah's vision. When I watch them playing together in the green and blue, it is a moment of transfiguration.

And it seems especially right that it should be shy, frightened, loving old Timothy rather than any of the other family dogs who are around Crosswicks during the summer. By and large they don't even seem aware of what is going on, and have shown only the mildest interest in Tim's atypical ecstatic behavior.

We often have friends visit us during the summer, and one weekend it was a family who live in our apartment building in the city. Their son was away at camp, but they came with their two little girls, the same ages as Léna and Charlotte, and their charming mop of a dog, Esau.

It was, despite showery weather, a lovely weekend. Between showers we went berrying, swimming in Dog Pond, walking down the lane. We ate and talked and were comfortable together. On Sunday afternoon when the sun came out we took the children and the dogs for a walk. It was much too wet to go through the high grasses and dripping bushes and brambles and trees to the brook, but we went down the lane and attacked some of the bittersweet which used to be a rare treasure, but which is now growing rampant and strangling the young trees. When we started back to the house we saw that Tim was already in the big meadow playing with his swallow friend. They were swooping about, Tim's nose heavenward, his tail wagging in a frenzy of joy.

Esau, the little mop, saw it too, and unlike the other dogs wanted in on the game. We human beings were so enchanted with Tim and the swallow that we paid no attention to Esau, until Tim saw him and very definitely did not want any interference in his private game.

We all began to run, but they were halfway across the meadow.

Timothy is a big dog and Esau is a small one. If Tim had wanted to, he could have broken Esau's neck with one shake.

The men with their longer legs reached the two dogs first. Bion, watching from the kitchen windows, said that it had looked to him as though Tim were simply standing over Esau, and evidently what he had been doing was simply keeping Esau away from his swallow. But he had drawn blood; there was a definite nick in Esau's neck.

It was not a tragedy. But suddenly we were in a fallen world again. It was no longer lion and lamb in peace and amity. It was the world of battlefields and slums and insane asylums.

What did I expect?

Until the eschaton our moments of transfiguration are essentially flashes of brief glory. To want Tim and his swallow to live in Eden is like Peter wanting to build tabernacles around Jesus and Abraham and Moses.

But while Peter was speaking, foolishly trying to trap glory in a man-made tabernacle, a bright cloud overshadowed them, and they were afraid, and a voice came out of the cloud saying, "This is my beloved son, in whom I am well pleased; hear ye him." And when they opened their eyes they saw Jesus as they were used to seeing him, Jesus of Nazareth, a man like themselves. And he told them not to tell anybody of the vision until the Son of man be risen from the dead.

> *Suddenly they saw him the way he was,*
> *the way he really was all the time,*
> *although they had never seen it before,*
> *the glory which blinds the everyday eye*
> *and so becomes invisible. This is how*
> *he was, radiant, brilliant, carrying joy*
> *like a flaming sun in his hands.*
> *This is the way he was—is—from the beginning,*
> *and we cannot bear it. So he manned himself,*
> *came manifest to us; and there on the mountain*
> *they saw him, really saw him, saw his light.*
> *We all know that if we really see him we die.*
> *But isn't that what is required of us?*
> *Then, perhaps, we will see each other, too.*

Too often we don't see each other. It takes something like Tim and the swallow, Tim and Esau, to open my eyes for a moment. When I watch Tim and his swallow now they are as beautiful as ever, and yet I watch them with a tinge of sorrow because we are still far from home.

When will we once again be one?

Not long after the episode of Tim and Esau, I was privileged to be given an experience of the kind of oneness seldom experienced. It was a spiritual oneness and helps me understand why the Song of Songs, that unabashedly physical love poem, is also the only language for spiritual love.

I have been blessed all the years of my life by the self-giving love of an English nanny known to us all as Mrs. O—for when I was a baby I could not say Mrs. O'Connell. Despite the name she acquired when she married a handsome Irishman, she never left anyone in doubt that her nationality was English. I was always comfortably certain that she loved me, but it was a typically Anglo-Saxon love which did not indulge in demonstrativeness. She did not, as I remember, kiss me at bedtime when I was a small child. One of our pleasant jokes, after my marriage, was Hugh's attempts to give her a kiss; despite much laughter, she managed to avoid the kisses. Nor was she ever a handholder.

Last spring she was ninety-five, and for the past several years has been in a home for elderly nuns, the Convent of Mary the Queen. Two of her three daughters are nuns, Sister Miriam Ambrose and Sister Anastasia Marie, and it was because of them that she was given her pleasant room and bath. During these years of her old age I have been called three times to her deathbed, and each time she has surprised doctors and nurses by recovering. It isn't that she is clinging to life, like a brown and brittle leaf clinging to the tree; she is very ready to go home. When she has been on the road to recovery she has each time remarked with good-humored resignation, "Well, God doesn't want me and the devil won't have me."

The Sisters call me regularly to report on her condition, and we all try to go see her as often as possible, and to bring the little girls for a state visit once a year. This spring she became very weak, and her mind began to wander, but the Sisters urged me not to come. "If there's a day when she's alert and will recognize you, we'll call."

In August I suddenly have a tremendous urge to go to her, and my friend Gillian says she'd love to take a day off from work and drive to the convent with me. So when Sister Ambrose calls to say that her mother seems a little stronger and might recognize me, we decide to go.

It is a brilliant summer day. There has been a lot of rain, so the leaves are a lush, rich green, not dry and dusty as they sometimes are in August. Gillian and I have shared much during the long years of our friendship, death and pain as well as birth and joy. There's nothing we can't talk about, and we've journeyed far together in our attempts to understand life and death and the increasing hope of a God of loving concern and faithful promise.

When we reach the convent I fall silent. A voice calls upstairs on a loudspeaker to announce our visit. We walk through a long room with two rows of rocking chairs where ancient Sisters sit to watch television. When Hugh comes to the convent with me it is an added glory for Mrs. O, for not only do the Sisters watch his show, but most of the nurses, and many of them come hurrying for autographs or simply to shake hands with 'Dr. Tyler.'

Gillian and I go up on the elevator to the fourth floor. Mrs. O's room is just around the corner where she has been able to watch all the comings and goings on the floor. It is hot in the summer, and we have wanted to give her an air-coonditioner, but she won't have one because she'd have to keep her door closed and thus be isolated from the life bustling around her.

Wherever she is, she has always brought with her the gift of laughter. The nurses on the night shift say, when they are tired or discouraged, "I think I'll go to Mrs. O'Connell's room. She's always good for a laugh." The orderlies and cleaning women love her; whenever there has been a crisis in her condition there have been tears, open and unashamed. Perhaps she is being kept here on earth for so long because her gift of laughter is desperately needed. Ill and difficult patients may well be treated with more tenderness because of Mrs. O.

Never very large, each year she has become smaller and smaller. But there is today a startling change since my last visit. She has eaten nothing solid for three months; a little tea, a little thin soup, the Holy Mysteries; on these she has been kept alive. But there is nothing now between skin and bones. The body on the hospital bed looks like pictures of victims of Belsen, Auschwitz, Ravensbrück.

When I first bend over her she does not know me. I wait while she makes the slow journey from the past to the present. I put my hand on hers and say, "It's Madeleine, Mrs. O. It's Madeleine." Suddenly she is fully with me, and she puts her arms around me as she would never have done in the old days, and says, "Oh, Madeleine, my Madeleine, oh, my Madeleine," and I no longer see the ancient wasted body. I have my arms about her so that I am holding her sitting up, with the fragile body leaning against me like a child's, and yet she is still holding me; we are both child, both mother.

She moves in and out of time. We talk in low voices and she asks me how the children are, does Bion still have his nice girlfriend? how are the little girls? She hasn't seen Gillian for at least fifteen years and yet she is completely aware of her presence and who she is, and asks about her family.

Once she gets lost in chronology and asks me, "Are you downstairs in your carriage?" But the next moment she is back in the present and says, "How's the boss?" (Her pet name for Hugh.) "How could I have forgotten to ask about the boss?"

I stay for an hour, much longer than I had expected, but we are in *kairos,* Mrs. O and I, in God's time, free, for the rest of the hour, from *chronos.* "And the extraordinary thing," I wrote in my journal, "was the electric current of love, powerful and beautiful, flowing back and forth between Mrs. O and me. Gillie had expected to step outside and write letters, but she too felt the lovely light of love which was uniting Mrs. O and me, so she stayed, remarking later what a privilege it had been for her to be present. I cannot set down in words the strength and joy of that river of love; it was something which can happen only in *kairos;* it was a time of Transfiguration—and in the octave of the Transfiguration, too—I just thought about that."

So we are given our glimpses of what it is really like, how things are really meant to be. There in that wasted body I saw at the same time the transfigured body, something visible to the spirit and not to the eyes.

These glimpses of reality are the foundation stones of faith.

12... The Day Is at Hand

THE MICHAELMAS DAISIES are purply blue in the fields; the goldenrod is tall. We come to Crosswicks only for weekends. The long weeks after Pentecost stretch out and it seems odd that schools and colleges have started, the house is emptying, and there are still six weeks till Advent.

Hugh and I are often alone on weekends, and we enjoy our companionable solitude. In the bedroom with the four-poster bed there are three rocking chairs, as well as the ancient chest across the foot of the bed, so that when the household gathers upstairs for a nightcap there will be plenty of places for everybody to sit. But now there are empty seats.

The big chest holds the sheets, the eiderdown for winter. It is often a receptacle for anything I feel like dumping down until I find time to put it away, and in the summer everything is casually swept to the floor if someone wants to sit there.

There was one spring when it was regularly an altar. A bad fall had me off my feet and in bed for six weeks. I was allowed to go, on crutches, to the bathroom, but otherwise I was not to get out of bed. Not easy for anyone as used to being as active as I am. It was late spring, and Alan and Josephine were free to be in the country, and Hugh's schedule was at that time fairly flexible, so that he could be more in Crosswicks than on West End Avenue, so I managed to talk the doctor into letting me be driven up.

The drive was typical. I sat in the back of the car with my leg on pillows and two dogs somehow or other stretched across me—one, a collie (Tim's predecessor); the other, half shepherd, half golden retriever (Jo's and Alan's first dog). They made a lapful. The cat perched on the ledge by the rear window. We stopped for something to eat, made the mistake of giving Thomas, the cat, some chicken, which he threw up, messily, before we'd gone another five miles. Much scrabbling for tissues and paper towels, with Josephine leaning over the seat and trying to help and Thomas crouching into his setting-hen position and feeling sorry for himself.

When we finally reached Crosswicks there was the problem of getting me upstairs. I had been warned that I must not touch my foot to the ground. Trying to go up the narrow front stairs of a New England farmhouse, facing forward, and on crutches, proved to be impossible for me, particularly because we were all laughing so hard at my efforts that it made me weaker than ever. I finally made everybody go away and leave me alone, sat down on the steps, facing downstairs, with my leg stretched out in front of me, and went up, step by step, on my bottom, and finally got into bed, no worse for wear.

Dinner was brought up to my room so that I would not have to eat alone, and at bedtime Alan looked at the top of the chest, which was fortunately clear of debris at that moment, and said thoughtfully, "I think I'll set up for Mass."

That became the pattern during those weeks when the house was frequently full of visitors. Anybody who was up in the early morning felt free to come in while Alan celebrated Communion; anyone who felt like sleeping in was free to sleep. And I was part of the Body, not isolated by being shuffled off in bed, but a full part of the community.

That belonging remains with me as I call the dogs and take my staff (a stripped young maple from a grove in need of thinning), and stride alone across the autumn fields.

Michaelmas. Summer is ending. We sniff the wind at night to see if the tomatoes and other tender plants in the garden need covering from early frost. The dragon which Michael fought brings frost with him, but it is not the natural frost for which the countryside is preparing and for which we sniff. The rich earth needs the long fallow months of winter, and the deep blankets of snow, known locally as poor man's fertilizer, to prepare for the full glory of spring.

A Deeper Cold once clutched this land. Even in the New World, where Crosswicks, nearly two hundred and a quarter years old, is young compared with the dwellings of the Old World, there are hints of a time beyond man's memory. The great glacial rocks I pass on the way to the brook are evidence that ice pushed across this land, inexorably grinding down palm trees and great ferns which stood as high as oaks; elephants fled before the coming of the ice, and other animals we glimpse only as rarities in zoos, or in the glossy pages of the *National Geographic.* Time is old, and our memory is lost down its winding labyrinths.

And so we tend to limit ourselves to the near past. We talk of Christianity as being not quite two thousand years old, and forget that the Second Person of the Trinity was, in his full glory, before time was made.

But we human creatures are in time, acted on by time, changed and dwindled and in our mortal aspect finished by it. The time that we 'tell' is as much an agreed-upon fiction as lower math; serviceable, but not very real.

The dwindling of our language reflects the assults of time. I am sorry that we no longer *tutoyer* in English; my little knowledge of French gives me glimpses of how this enriches relationships. When *you* becomes only *you,* we open the door to sexism; and we are taking *thee* and *thou* away even from our public worship. In some of the contemporary prayers I feel that we are speaking to God in much the same way that people used to call black servants 'Boy' and I don't like it any more with God than I do with his people.

In the beginning of Ibsen's play *Rosmersholm,* Rosmer and Rebecca West are on stage with a third person, and they use the formal *you.* When they are left alone on stage they switch immediately to *thee* and *thou,* and there is no question for the audience as to the depth of their relationship. There is no adequate way of getting this knowledge across in English. To have them call each other *dear* or *darling* does not do it; we are all deared and darlinged at the drop of a hat nowadays.

When we lose the ability to convey intimacy in speech, then it becomes easy for us to turn creatures into things; the English language knows things, unlike the Latin tongues, where there is nothing without gender. Maybe there are some who would prefer thingdom to gender, but I'm not one of them. And even the word *thing* has been changed and distorted, so that it no longer makes sense to speak of 'these Holy Things.' Or perhaps it makes the only and complete sense! (Remember the phrase "that holy thing which shall be born of thee" referred to Jesus.)

The Welsh say, "She is casting rain," rather than it is raining. In French, snow, too, is 'she.' And it has always amused me that in Spanish a woman's dress is masculine. But on the whole the male and femaleness of gender makes considerable sense in these so-called 'Romance' tongues. In the old days when one said "She is casting rain," one was referring to a goddess who had power over the clouds. And this is closer to the truth of love than our "It is raining," where *it* is simply part of a blind force over which we have no control. If we truly thought of the earth as Mother we could not do to her some of the things we have done. And if we think of everything in the created order as good, because God is Creator, then gender in rock and rose, tree and turnip, sea and seed, is a form of thanks and praise.

Alan told me that in Chinese folklore there is a mythical bird who is only half a bird: one eye, one wing, one leg. In order to fly, a left-hand bird must find a right-hand bird. Alone, they are earthbound, flopping clumsily about; together they can soar across the sky.

Interpret this Freudianly if you will, but that's only part of it—though it is a part. But it rejoices me to take it beyond that, into an understanding of a deeper wholeness. There are the two Chinese birds within each of us, seeking each other for completion.

How long ago was it that we were sundered from each other, and sundered from ourselves? so that dark, night, earth, mystery, intuition, all became feminine; and light (it's feminine in French!), day, sky, fact, intellect, became masculine? It's achingly sad for the male of the species that he has been taught to repress his intuitive side, his tears, his gentleness, his ability to grieve. When the ability to grieve is repressed, the ability to love is often repressed along with it—except in the roughest act of rutting which has little to do with love.

In interpreting myth and fairy tale, many psychologists see the mother of the hero as standing for the unconscious. The appropriate behavior for the hero is to outgrow this 'fairy tale' or unreal world, and move from the dark into the light. The longing for what the mother has to offer is a longing for the inertia and lack of consciousness of the fetus.

But this is a partial explanation at best. The unconscious aspect of the personality is anything but inert, and this is why it is so fearsome. The hero must fight tooth and claw for what the psychologists call his ego-consciousness, but this ego-consciousness is only a partial consciousness; full consciousness comes only when the ego can trust the subconscious enough to embrace it instead of doing battle; only when nightside and sunside are mediated instead of separated, and so become a whole.

When we limit ourselves to our ego-consciousness, then we close off that part of us which is capable of true prayer, poetry, painting, music. When we embrace the monster it may indeed devour us, and this is the genuine risk. It may also turn out to be the handsome prince or the beautiful princess for whom we have been waiting all these years.

It is only as we recognize and call by name all that we have relegated to the dark side of Mercury, to the deep black waters of the subconscious mind, that we have any hope of wholeness. All those moral virtues I was taught in my Anglican schools must be unlearned, because most of them were neither moral nor virtuous. And many of the things which I was taught to consider bad and nasty are bad and nasty only because we have made them so. For instance, a 'nice' woman, a 'lady,' was not supposed to enjoy sex; she was to do her duty to her husband, and bear children for him, but she was not supposed to enjoy it. The grandmother and great-aunt of a friend of my mother's were baptized Patience and Submit, which gives one a good idea of the frame of mind of their mother. Only the lower classes were supposed to enjoy the natural acts of love.

Even in this supposedly enlightened day and age, a young friend of mine, going to maternity classes when she was pregnant with her first baby, and planning to bear her little one with her husband beside her, and to nurse their child, reported with shock that more than half the young mothers in the class were not going to nurse their babies. One said, with considerable pride, "My husband is not going to have me going around with my boobs exposed." The language may be today, but the attitude, I had thought, was yesterday. But it isn't. Satan still manages to make us look upon that which is natural and beautiful and good, as perverse and ugly and nasty.

All that God created is good. It is only we who have taken this good, succumbing to the wiles of the Destroyer, and seen it as bad.

All the things which we have shoved down into the darkness of the subconscious were created to be good. The darkness itself is good, but we have distorted so many things within it that the Destroyer has taken it over and made it a power for evil, for the breaking and destruction of God's creatures.

I was mercifully spared some of the distortions I would otherwise have had to struggle to unlearn by the most negative aspects of my childhood. Because I was rejected by my peers, and had to accept to myself that I was unlike them, I found myself within, rather than without. Had I been happy and popular in school I would not have plunged deep into the archetypical world of fairy tale and myth, where the night is as important as the day, the dark as light, where there is acute awareness that male and female, when evil powers intrude, battle and struggle and try to possess, but that fulfillment is only in participation. I would not otherwise have devoured George Macdonald and so absorbed, without realizing it, some of his loving theology. One of my books, long lost, was stories from the Bible, and of these stories one of my favorites was Joseph with his coat of many colors—and his dreams; Joseph, the one the others didn't like, the one who understood the dark part of the personality. I would not otherwise have read the fantasies of E. Nesbit and the science fiction of H. G. Wells, so that the larger world of imagination and intuition was not closed off for me as it was for many of my contemporaries.

Had my teacher not ridiculed my homework I might have done my lessons instead of painting pictures, playing the piano, writing stories, and working out my real self, not in the outward self which was rejected by teacher and classmates, but in the interior self. Undoubtedly I neglected sunside for nightside, but that was taken care of when I was wrested out of the world of imagination and plunged into boarding school where I had to learn about the outer world in order to survive.

It was in boarding school that I learned to make my own solitude in the midst of the mob, to surround myself with a force field of concentration, in which I could dream and write stories and poems. The misery of a total lack of privacy during those years has been more than compensated for by the discipline of concentration I was forced to acquire. I wrote my first novel while I was on tour with a play, wrote in railway stations, in trains, in theatre dressing rooms which I shared, in hotel bedrooms which also I shared. I can write in any amount of sound and fury as long as I am not responsible for that sound and fury—as I discovered when I had children, and learned that I was not free to move into this kind of deep concentration until they were safely asleep in bed.

The difficulties of those early days have proven to be advantages which have helped me to be more integrated than I might have been otherwise.

And so, of course, does my profession, and my husband's. In acting and in writing, the artist has to struggle for wholeness, just as in painting, or making music, or sculpting, or making pottery, or weaving. Sunside and nightside, maleness and femaleness, must collaborate. A priest, too, had better be aware of both the masculine and the feminine qualities of the priesthood, the two working together, participating in one person to make the image of God.

The Reverend Alan W. Jones, in an article in *The Anglican Theological Review* (yes, it's the same Alan I've been talking about in these pages, but now I am quoting him and it is appropriate to be more formal), writes, "One of the ways I understand my priesthood is as a midwife—bringing Christ to birth in others. This is no way determines my specific sexual identity. It does, thank God, creatively affirm the feminine within me."

The image of God, feminine and masculine, is, as image, physical. Sarxy: of the flesh. And the sheer physicalness of the image has not been easy for me. I used to find it difficult to talk about the resurrection of the body because it was lots easier for me to think of the soul as being separate from the body, imprisoned by it, and released from it at death like a bright bird suddenly freed and flying from the bars of the cage.

But although Jesus was never recognized on sight after the Resurrection, he went to great pains to prove to his friends that he was indeed body. He ate fish—something not really possible for a disembodied spirit. He showed Thomas the marks of the nails in his hands, and of the spear in his side.

Perhaps he wasn't recognized on sight because we aren't used to seeing bodies as they ought to be, whole, undistorted, complete.

Complete does not mean finished. I cannot understand theologians who assert that when God created the universe it was not only whole and complete, it was finished. He'd done it, and that's that. No change allowed.

When I looked at and ran my hands over my newborn babies I checked to see that they were whole, complete, all ten fingers and toes, everything all there. And they were, praise God, magnificently complete and beautiful creatures. But not finished! Anything but finished! So why should we attempt to limit God to a finished creation? That assumption implies that God is even more limited than his creatures, whereas the God I reach out to has no limitations, and knows no dichotomy between light and dark.

As long as we are unwilling to admit great areas of ourselves into our lives, to conjoin sunside and nightside, it is difficult for us not to put our trust in that which will rust and decay, where thieves can break in and steal.

Is there anything in this life on which we can really and truly count? Certainly not our possessions. Nothing that money can buy. Not even human love. Even the most dependable is flawed and fallible. Participation is very good with Hugh and me right now, but I can't count on this continuing forever. Death, if nothing else, separates all lovers. It strikes a chill to my bones as I see marriages of thirty, thirty-five, even forty years, breaking up, long after the partners have survived the trauma of the fledgelings leaving the nest. We all betray each other. No human being is totally faithful. Of course God is, but I see God through his creatures. Perhaps I can sometimes see him more clearly on weekends when we come to Crosswicks and I go and sit on the big rock at the brook, because I can count on the rock being there; but even the rock could not keep the rifle from firing at the icon on the tree in front of it; even the rock could break apart if there was an earthquake.

So what can I put my trust in that I can really know, here and now? I used to think that when all else failed I would have my memories. Saint Exupéry said that in our old age we will sit under the sheltering branches of the tree of our memories. But I saw Grandfather's memory being taken away from him, and then Mother's, and that was the worst of all.

The Air Bites Shrewdly

There is almost nothing a child cannot bear
As long as the image of its parent shines clear.
Age is acceptable, normal wear and tear,
But poison cannot fall into the ear.
The image distorts; safety is gone; is where?

Hamlet, after the death of his father,
Found, also, changes in his mother,
And it was this latter, rather,
It would seem to me, than the other
That caused the dark storm clouds to gather.

The person changed is blackly unacceptable
(Primeval fears of presence of a devil);
Soma, not psyche, may be corruptible.
How does the distorted one find grace in this black evil?
Help my mother to bear. God, make her able.

It was death, in the end, which enabled her.

The only thing we can count on completely is death. A friend of mine, a fine writer, said, "I am terrified of annihilation." A senior at Harvard wrote me, "What I am afraid of is not-being." I do not believe people who say they are not afraid of death. I do not believe people who say that they do not mind the thought of annihilation, that eternal nothingness sounds pleasant.

The Michaelmas daisies, the goldenrod, the turning leaves, tell me that this Christian year is drawing to a close, and the Christian is taught that death is *not* annihilation, that death leads us into fuller life, *not* non-being. But the promise remains too glorious, too infinite, for us finite, time-trapped creatures to comprehend.

The more I am enabled to give myself away, the more complete I become. When I can let go that part of me which struggles vainly to believe, then with my whole self I rejoice in knowing. The more I am enabled to abandon myself, the more full of life I am. So: death ought to be the ultimate act of self-abandonment in order that we may become wholly alive. To count on death as the only thing a human being can count on, is an affirmation of life.

I think I like this. But then I wonder: if death is the door to life, why not suicide? Is it that if we refuse what we are given in one life, we are not ready to accept another? The answer to 'why not suicide?'

lies, it has to lie, in the Incarnation, the fully lived life of Jesus of Nazareth as the essential prelude to his death and resurrection. He enjoyed life. Friends, food, drink. He took time to Be: when he was drained from all the demands his friends and neighbors made on him, he simply took off, abandoned them for as long as he needed to be alone with the Father and to be refilled—and often they did not like it. He did ask, in agony, to be spared the cross. But he accepted the No.

To abandon the right to put an end to our lives whenever and however we want to (pills and bullets are easier than cancer or the cross) is part of that self-abandonment which is necessary for full being.

I want to enter consciously into my own death. But hospitals and the 'advances' of medicine often deny this. Dearma and Grandfather in very different ways died in their sleep. Mother said that she would like to die as Grandfather did, just slip off quietly, unknowing, and in the end this prayer was granted her as she slipped out of life in Bion's arms.

I think that I would like to know.

But there are not many quiet and conscious deaths nowadays. Dearma, Grandfather, Mother, all died at home, and that is as it should be. Next best, Grandma Josephine, in the hospital, was allowed to die in a way no longer permissible; she said that the needles with the intravenous feedings bothered her; she asked Hugh and his sister Genevieve to have them taken out; and this was permitted; and she died knowing that she was going to meet her Lord Jesus. My mother-in-law's faith never faltered. She both believed and knew.

Euthanasia, I am convinced, is wrong. It becomes far too easy to get rid of the old or the unwanted; the needle is more painless and less expensive and more final than the Old People's Home. But what I call reverse euthanasia is equally wrong. Keeping a body alive which would under normal circumstances die is a kind of murder.

I did make the difficult decision not to force-feed Mother during her last weeks. When a body is no longer able to eat or, even worse, to breathe without machines, unless there is real hope of real cure, of return to full life, then that body should be allowed to die. Keeping permanent vegetables plugged into machines is, as far as I am concerned, sin. And this struggle to keep a mere lump of flesh 'alive' is a result of technology turned into technocracy. I am all for technology; I see because of technology. But technocracy is a symptom of a world where only man is God and death is the victor. Even during my worst periods of atheism I can't accept that.

Atheism is, for me, a virulent virus, put into the world by the Evil One for our destruction, and I come down with it as on occasion I have come down with flu. When the Michaelmas daisies and the goldenrod were gone this autumn, and the leaves stripped from the trees, I had a horrible attack. It was brought on by a long series of events.

Just before Thanksgiving and my birthday and the first Sunday of Advent, Mrs. O died. She had long been ready; we could only welcome her release into glory, and I am sure that there is more laughter in heaven now that she is there. But those of us who love her were very aware of how much we are going to miss her.

When one of the Sisters had called to tell me that her mother had died, I had thought to myself that if they asked me if there was anything of their mother's I would like to have as a keepsake, I would ask for her rosary; surely those glass beads, so prayed on with her fingers and heart, would contain something of her grace. But they were twined about the dead fingers in the coffin, so I said nothing.

At the last moment, just before the lid was shut down, Sister Anastasia went back to kneel before her mothers's body. When she came back she held out her hand, in which something was clasped. "Madeleine, would you like Mother's rosary?" And she dropped it into my palm. For this intuitive understanding, I will always be grateful.

We left the funeral parlor and went to the church. At first we did not realize why it was we could not go into the nave. Then we saw that another funeral was going on inside. When the mourners had filed out, we went in. Nothing can take away completely the beauty and comfort of the Requiem Mass, but it was given life only by the congregation of people who had loved the ninety-five-year old woman; the priest said words which had been repeated so often that they had become empty.

When I was a child I sometimes took a word or a phrase and said it over and over again until it had lost all meaning. The saying of the words of the Mass reminded me of this childish game. But that was my fault as much as the priest's, or even more. It wouldn't have bothered Mrs. O, because nothing could dim for her the reality of the glory.

When we left the church another hearse was rounding the corner for yet another funeral.

I went back to the Cathedral library and finished the work day, and then walked home with Timothy. There was quite a lot of mail and I sat down on the foot of the bed to read it. An extraordinary and unexpected blessing has been birthday cards and even presents from people who have read my books and become my friends, and I opened several of these, my heart melting within me with love and gratitude.

One card seemed to be full of what I took to be potpourri, a thoughtful gift. But then I noticed that it was a get-well card and not a birthday card, which struck me as strange since, thank God, I had not been ill. Then I sniffed the dried flowers and they had no scent. Then I looked closer.

I called Hugh, "Please come here." He got up from his chair and came at the tight urgency in my voice. "Are these cockroaches?"

They were. Someone had taken the trouble to collect about a cupful of cockroaches and put them in a get-well card, and send them to me. The timing couldn't have been more accurate, although I doubt if whoever it was knew that it was near my birthday, or the day of the funeral of the woman who had been a second mother to me.

For a moment I thought I was going to vomit, so physical was my reaction. Then I got the vacuum cleaner and vacuumed the bedspread, the rug, clean of all trace of the shiny brown deadness of the roaches. I said quite calmly to Hugh, "If life in an old building in New York were not a constant battle against cockroaches, this would be even more horrible."

It was horrible enough. It was a manifestation of a hate even more sick than the hate which had taken a rifle and shot through the icon at the brook. I do not know who it was, and I will probably never know, and this is just as well.

That night we had seats at the ballet, seats ordered months before. I took Mrs. O's rosary with me and held it in my hand all evening, tangibly holding off the powers of darkness. Because those small beads were icons of love, hate could not surround me entirely; the circle of love was stronger than the strangling bonds of hate.

But that day did nothing to help my attack of atheism.

Tallis was off to Australia to preach at the consecration of a mutual friend, otherwise I would have gone running to him. I did find myself telling a young friend, a religious staying briefly in New York en route to join her community, the Little Sisters of Jesus. She thought briefly, then said, "You are very much loved, and where there is great love there is also great hate," and her affirmation of the love made the hate less terrible.

And even in my atheism I could pray for this hate, this horrible sickness, could pray for its healing.

Another help came in a letter from France, from a friend who has often been in positions of authority and power, and who has received several anonymous poison-pen letters. "I was upset and hurt and shocked and angered by them, and I remember praying for the person who sent the ugly picture, for the men who drew it, printed it, and sold it. It doesn't worry me now, because it's all part of the dust anyone kicks up who sticks out his/her neck, takes a stand on anything significant, has any impact. If we had *more* impact, we'd probably be shot, like King and the Kennedys."

That lightened my perspective.

A few days later the phone on my desk in the Cathedral Library rang. Long Distance. The eighteen-year-old daughter of a friend of mine, in a small town in the Midwest, had been kidnapped as she went to her car with a bag of groceries, driven out of town, raped, and murdered. Not in New York. In a small town where everybody was known by name. A lovely child had her life taken away from her, brutally and slowly. And there was nothing I, at this distance, or indeed any of the friends at home, could do to help.

That afternoon a college-age friend of mine dropped in to see me as she usually does whenever she's in town. I was appalled at her appearance. Her skin was tinged with grey; there were deep circles under her eyes. She came to kiss me and she was trembling all over. I plugged the pot in for tea, and she told me that she had left the hospital the day before, after an abortion. There was no question of marriage; she had thought the boy loved her, but he didn't, and she did not want marriage under those conditions. But she did want the baby. Her parents, respectable, affluent, arranged the abortion, took her to the hospital with cold efficiency, and left her there for forty-eight hours. "And I knew, when I woke from the anaesthesia, that I had committed murder. I let them force me into it. I could have stopped them if I'd wanted to badly enough." Tears overflowed.

This was no time for reason. She flung herself into my arms like a small child and wept.

A few nights later the attack of atheism took hold. I could no longer fend it off.

I woke up in the night as I usually do with the words of the Jesus Prayer plashing up into my conscious mind like a little fountain, as they have been doing for years. And I thought bitterly, why on earth am I saying these meaningless and empty words? They mean nothing. Lord Jesus Christ is only an illusion. There is nothing. Nada. Nada. Nada.

I lay in cold isolation on my side of the bed, not even reaching out with hand or foot to touch the warm and sleeping flesh of my husband in my usual instinctive affirmation of incarnation.

Nothing. Nothing.

And then I flung myself onto the words of the prayer like a drowning person clutching at a rope thrown into the dark sea. I held onto it with all my strength and I was slowly pulled from the waters which had been sucking me under, pulled out of the dark and into the light and Lord Jesus Christ did indeed have mercy on me.

For a long time I was convalescent, recuperating slowly from the virulent attack, a little less feverish (as it were) each day. I was called to conduct a retreat and this was the best medicine I could have been given.

I know that I am not immune from further attacks. But I also know that the darkness cannot put out the light.

For an English friend I wrote, one winter when he was in New York and staying at the General Seminary:

> *Come, let us gather round the table.*
> *Light the candles. Steward, pour the wine.*
> *It's dark outside. The streets are noisy*
> *with the scurrying of rats, with shoddy*
> *tarts, shills, thugs, harsh shouting.*

*And what comfort is cold within? We're able
to offer a slim repast. The taste of brine
warm from fresh tears, is in the glass. Choosy
guests will not come here. The bread is body
broken. The wine is dark with blood. I'm doubting*

*if half of those invited will turn up.
Most will prefer to choose a different table,
will go elsewhere with gentler foods to sup.
And yet this is indeed a wedding feast
and we rejoice to share the bitter cup,
the crumbs of bread. For O my Lord, not least
of all that makes us raise the glass, is that we toast
You, who assembled this uncomely group: our one mysterious host.*

Bread. Wine. A dinner table. The firm clasp of hands as we say grace. The warm flame of candles. It is all an affirmation of incarnation, of being, versus non-being. Even the sender of those cockroaches was in a perverse and sick way affirming incarnation, while completely misunderstanding the act.

The Lord Jesus Christ whose very name has the power to pull me from the terror of non-ness came to earth in a vulgar affirmation that all creation is good; we can dirty it, turn it to evil, join the angel who fought against Michael, but creation itself, all matter, is good.

We are afraid of the physicalness of incarnation. Jesus of Nazareth was a total man, with every part and function of a man's body—even the parts which Paul described as "less honorable." The more shattering thing is that he was tempted in all ways, including temptations I've never known, some I've probably never even heard about. I worship a Christ who is fully God because he was incarnate more completely than anyone I have known.

This past week while we were in the city, Bobby came to the north field of Crosswicks and spread its browning clover and grasses with manure. During the weekend Hugh goes to the rotting mulch of the composte heap and spreads it over the garden before ploughing it in. And this is good.

Lift up your heads, O ye gates; and be ye lift up, ye everlasting doors; and the King of glory shall come in.

Who is this King of glory? It is the Lord strong and mighty, even the Lord mighty in battle.

Lift up your heads, O ye gates, and be ye lift up, ye everlasting doors, and the King of glory shall come in.

Who is this King of glory? Even the Lord of hosts, he is the King of glory.

Thus cries the psalmist. Thus I cry after him.

Who is this King of glory? A child born of a woman. A man betrayed by his friends as well as by his enemies. A failure who died ignominiously and who should by all logic have been immediately forgotten. A king of no glory on earth, a king who lost his battle with the Powers of this world, or so it would seem from the surface of the story. He performed a few miracles, but miracles were nothing new; others performed miracles. And he couldn't save himself at the end.

If I am to seek for answers to my questions, or even for the questions to ask in the first place, I must hold to this failure, but it isn't easy, so far have we strayed from the original vision. We don't understand the method in his madness. His coming to us as a human child, in total weakness, was the greatest act of warfare against the powers of hate and chaos that I know. And if I, too, am to fight in this battle, it is from his weakness that I must draw my strength.

The *symboles* by which I live are the answers to my questions, are themselves the questions, are the healers of our brokenness. When we deny our wholeness, when we repress part of ourselves, when we are afraid of our own darkness, then the dark turns against us, turns on us, becomes evil. Just as the intellect when it is not informed by the heart becomes vicious, so the intuition, the subconscious, when it is forcibly held below the surface, becomes wild, and until we look at it and call it by name, our own name, it can devour us.

Am I afraid to look down into the dark and acknowledge myself, and say: Madeleine! and know that this, too, is part of what I am meant to be? Yes, I am afraid sometimes, but I become less afraid as my trust in the pattern of the universe deepens. I, too, have my place, as do we all, with the greatest galaxies, the smallest particles. Perhaps it takes all of this, all of creation, to make the Body of Christ, and the bride.

The days are growing noticeably shorter; the nights are longer, deeper, colder. Today the sun did not rise as high in the sky as it did yesterday. Tomorrow it will be still lower. At the winter solstice the sun will go below the horizon, below the dark. The sun does die. And then, to our amazement, the Son will rise again.

> *Come, Lord Jesus, quickly come*
> *In your fearful innocence.*
> *We fumble in the far-spent night*
> *Far from lovers, friends, and home:*
> *Come in your naked, newborn might.*
> *Come, Lord Jesus, quickly come;*
> *My heart withers in your absence.*
>
> *Come, Lord Jesus, small, enfleshed*
> *Like any human, helpless child.*
> *Come once, come once again, come soon:*
> *The stars in heaven fall, unmeshed;*
> *The sun is dark, blood's on the moon.*
> *Come, word who came to us enfleshed,*
> *Come speak in joy untamed and wild.*
>
> *Come, thou wholly other, come,*
> *Spoken before words began,*
> *Come and judge your uttered world*
> *Where you made our flesh your home.*
> *Come, with bolts of lightning hurled,*
> *Come, thou wholly other, come,*
> *Who came to man by being man.*
>
> *Come, Lord Jesus, at the end,*
> *Time's end, my end, forever's start.*
> *Come in your flaming, burning power.*
> *Time, like the temple veil, now rend;*
> *Come, shatter every human hour.*
> *Come, Lord Jesus, at the end.*
> *Break, then mend the waiting heart.*

We have much to be judged on when he comes, slums and battlefields and insane asylums, but these are the symptoms of our illness, and the result of our failures in love. In the evening of life we shall be judged on love, and not one of us is going to come off very well, and were it not for my absolute faith in the loving forgiveness of my Lord I could not call on him to come.

But his love is greater than all our hate, and he will not rest until Judas has turned to him, until Satan has turned to him, until the dark has turned to him; until we can all, all of us without exception, freely return his look of love with love in our own eyes and hearts. And then, healed, whole, complete but not finished, we will know the joy of being co-creators with the one to whom we call.

Amen. Even so, come Lord Jesus.